SHINE NOT IN REFLECTED GLORY

THE UNTOLD STORY OF GRAND TETON NATIONAL PARK

By

N. Wayne Johnson

Jeanette,

I hope you enjoy this bit of history about the Valley I call home.

Wayne Johnson

Bookstand Publishing

www.bookstandpublishing.com

ALSO BY N. WAYNE JOHNSON

Campfire Thoughts: Essays, Poems, and other Doggeral

SHINE NOT IN REFLECTED GLORY

THE UNTOLD STORY OF GRAND TETON NATIONAL PARK

By

N. Wayne Johnson

Published by
Bookstand Publishing
Morgan Hill, CA 95037
4446_1

Front Cover Photograph: John J. Hebberger, Jr.
Back Cover Photograph: "Sunrise on the Cathedral Group"
John J. Hebberger, Jr.
Author Photograph: William McClintock

ISBN 978-1-63498-384-6

Library of Congress Control Number: 2016948064

Printed in the United States of America

DEDICATION

To the Jackson Hole pioneers who struggled to survive in this valley, and having survived, recognized the special character of the area and knew future generations would appreciate their effort to protect it. Particularly, Clifford P. Hansen and Struthers Burt, whose differing opinions on the controversy of the time did not inhibit their ability to maintain civility while seeking solutions.

Grand Teton National Park will not shine in reflected glory of the older and better known neighbor to the north. Its claim to fame is based upon a grandeur all its own, and peculiar to its own boundary limits.

1929 dedicatory address of Grand Teton National Park by
Erwin Charles Funk
1877-1960

No one has seen Wyoming or has gained any appreciation of its scenic beauties who has not visited Jackson's Hole. There is certainly no spot in our country which compares for natural grandeur with this section of our state. Once the people of the United States become acquainted with it, so many tourists will visit Jackson's Hole every year that it will scarcely be possible to provide adequate accommodations for them all.

Senator John B. Kendrick
1857-1933

CONTENTS

LIST OF MAPS

A note about the maps.

Background maps were obtained from several open source Internet sites including the Wyoming Geological Survey, the Library of Congress, and the National Archives. The author's outline drawings of boundaries and shaded areas are intended to imply the boundaries and areas subject to legislative and citizen inspired initiatives that culminated in the creation of Grand Teton National Park. Metes and bounds may not be precise.

ACKNOWLEDGMENTS

As with any endeavor of this type, there are numerous instances of assistance and support from friends and strangers who willingly encouraged, prodded, and critiqued my efforts to document events and attitudes relating to the establishment of Grand Teton National Park.

One of the pleasures of this project has been the opportunity to discuss the events with people who were involved in the controversies and initiatives described in this book. Sometimes I conducted formal taped interviews. Other times over coffee in the Wort Hotel Coffee Shop, I managed to work the conversation around to a particular event in the Park's history. I wish I could share the many conversations and situations I experienced with the people who lived the events documented in this book. Most of those people are now deceased, but the memories of their laughter, their sincerity, and, on rare occasions, their anger, are still real in my mind. If I have failed to present their viewpoint accurately, it is not because they did not make an effort to enlighten me.

Harold and Josephine Fabian allotted considerable time at their home on the original Geraldine Lucas homestead to answer questions and recall events and personalities involved in this narrative. Harold was the on-site attorney and vice president of the Snake River Land Company, the entity established to purchase land for John D. Rockefeller, Jr. William "Slim" Lawrence was not satisfied to sit and talk. He led me on a walking historical/archaeological tour of the north end of the valley. In the summer of 1970, I rented a cabin from Margaretta Corse at the Bar BC Ranch. On several occasions after I'd completed my scheduled trips on the Snake River, we would relax with a cocktail outside her cabin, or walk around the deteriorating ranch buildings while she painted verbal pictures of the ranch's activities and patrons. From Maggie, as she was known to her friends, I gained insight into the early dude ranching industry of the valley. Cliff and Martha Hansen, their daughter Mary Mead, Cliff's sister Parthenia Stinnett, and long-time ranch hands, Lowell Jacobson, Roy Martin, and Ray Magnum tolerated my marginally competent participation in virtually every aspect of cattle ranching over a period of twelve years. I utilized the time while moving cattle to and from summer pastures and other gatherings (calving, branding, feeding, haying, fencing, shipping, vaccinating) to ask questions and encourage recollections of events and issues relating to the national park and ranching.

Other Wyoming residents who endured my questions and shared their opinions and recollections were Homer Richards, Jack Dornan, Grant "Tiny" Hagen, Howard Ballew, Jack Huyler, Garl and Beulah Riggan, Byron and Jean Jenkins, Paul Imeson, Jim VanNostrand, Frank Craighead, Ed Cheney, Mardy Murie, Alan Simpson, and Mel Annis. Mel Annis was 99 years old when I visited him at the Pioneer Homestead, the valley's first assisted living facility.

Constructive comments, criticisms, and encouragement were received from people who read either portions of the manuscript or the entire document. If friendship can be accurately gauged by a person's willingness to tell you bad news as well as good news, I am truly blessed. While none of the people hereafter identified specifically asked to remain anonymous, I would regret any attachment to them of negative impressions regarding their participation in this project. They attempted to influence the end result in ways that would have made the book shorter, more entertaining, and less verbose. The people who endeavored to make the book more readable are Jan Hackett, Clifford Hansen, Mary Mead, Robert Esperiti, Wallace Ulrich, Joan Anzelmo, Marion Buchenroth, Francine Carraro, Debbie Sibley, Clay James, Cort Conley, Bob Blair, Mary McKinney, Suzy Koch, Jo Maltman, Judy Mackay, and Jan and Judy Buehler, who found, it seemed to me, unnecessary delight in my malapropisms.

I also wish to express my appreciation for assistance from Rodney Ross and Carah Smith at the National Archives in Washington, D.C. If you've never had a reason to utilize the services of the National Archives, I'll venture the opinion that the facility and staff are among the most productive and beneficial expenditures of taxpayer dollars. The Truman Presidential Library is also noteworthy. In keeping with the reputation of the President it honors as a man of the people, the Library's archives are accessible to the public without fee or credentials.

Additional assistance was received from the staff at the Bureau of Reclamation office in Burley, Idaho; Willard Dilley and Linda Olsen at Grand Teton National Park during the early years of research and more recently, Grand Teton National Park Archivist and Museum Curator, Bridgette Guild, and her Intern, Desiree Ramirez; Colleen Curry and Anne Foster at the Yellowstone Heritage and Research Center; and Museum Technician Lauran Finn Hauptman at Mesa Verde National Park. Liz Jacobson, Emily Winters and numerous other staff at the Jackson Hole Historical Society and Museum were both helpful and tolerant over a span of years, as was the staff of the Teton Public Library, and Venice Beske at the Wyoming State Library. At the American Heritage Center at the University of Wyoming, Associate Archivist John Waggener and Photo Assistants Malissa Suek and Hailey Woodall provided research assistance and direction. I also wish to thank Archivist Mary Ann Quinn at the Rockefeller Archive Center in Sleepy Hollow, New York for her assistance and help with Rockefeller Family photographs and issues relating to the Snake River Land Company and the Jackson Hole Preserve, Inc. Gravis Roby, a wildlife biologist for the Wyoming Game and Fish Department, provided insight regarding big game management and other wildlife issues attendant to Jackson Hole. Wyoming State Geologist, Wallace Ulrich, and the Wyoming Geological Survey provided invaluable assistance in locating historic maps. Dr. Daivd Love, a long-time mentor and friend, provided encouragement and insight on issues concerning historical geography and geology.

A majority of the photographs came from the Jackson Hole Historical Society and Museum and various National Park Service sources. Some NPS sources were available online, but additional images were obtained from archival repositories at several national parks including Grand Teton National Park, Yellowstone National Park, Zion National Park, and Mesa Verde National Park. Access to family photographic collections of valley residents and events was also appreciated. They include the Hansen/Mead family, Parthenia Stinnett, Harold and Josephine Fabian, Geri Spicer Stone for access to the Spicer Family Collection, Quita and Herb Pownell for permission to use images from the Harrison Crandall Collection, John Turner for permission to use Triangle X Ranch photographic images, Margaretta Corse, Mary McKinney, W. C. Lawrence, Dr. Robert Smith, and Shirley Poore for access to the Charlie Peterson Family Collection. Liz Lockhart and family graciously allowed the use of photographic images from the Bruce Porter Collection.

To all, my sincere thanks for the encouragement and help and especially the memories.

PREFACE

The natural splendor and majesty of the Teton Mountain Range and the valley that forms its foreground are so impressive it seems almost inconceivable that 52 years of controversy shrouded their inclusion into the National Park System. A half century of congressional investigations, legislative and local initiatives, political careers enhanced and diminished, national, regional, and local controversies stridently proclaimed in the press, executive orders and vetoes, lawsuits, the occasional threat of armed conflict, and, finally, compromise, was the catalyst that drew me to investigate the history of Grand Teton National Park.

In addition to the spectacular geologic features that make Grand Teton National Park special, the compromises required to create this park make it unique because of the activities allowed within its boundaries. Until recently only three of our national parks, Grand Teton, Yosemite, and Olympic, contained dams and reservoirs. The Elwha River Restoration Project has eliminated impounded water from Olympic National Park leaving just two parks with dams and reservoirs. Grand Teton National Park is one of only two parks with a commercial airport. Denali National Park is the other. Grand Teton National Park sanctions hunting, although the Park Service prefers to call the activity a reduction program rather than a hunt. There are privately owned residences and ranches within this park as well as the grazing of domestic livestock. The reasons for these sanctioned structures and activities and the compromises pertaining to these issues are an aspect of the area's history that has rarely been publicly explored and explained.

Three potential books could be written about this turbulent period of history in Jackson Hole. One would be a pro-park narrative that would document the efforts of the federal agencies and individuals to protect the scenic values of the valley. For the most part, this is the version that has been presented to the public to date. Another book might concentrate on a more local perspective describing the insensitivity of the federal bureaucracy and wealthy easterners and their failure to consider the constitutional rights and economic concerns of the settlers whose lives were affected by the proposals to protect the valley. (Basically, an anti-park version of this turbulent period.) Both of those hypothetical books would paint a vastly different narrative and perspective while remaining factually correct because truth only requires facts. Accuracy, however, requires disclosure. Thus, the possible third book, the account that follows, provides both perspectives in what I hope reasonably documents the arguments and concerns of the opposing factions. This requires disclosure of disingenuous manipulations and representations perpetrated by both sides.

When I began this research project in the early 1970s, I harbored a pro-park bias with little tolerance for anti-park positions. However, I also recognized that a controversy that endures for half a century is likely to have some valid arguments for the opposing positions. After a three-decade period of interviewing people who participated in the events, reading documents as diverse as their personal correspondence, their testimonies before Senate and House investigating committees, and the inter-departmental memos of federal agencies preserved in the Library of Congress and the National Archives, I can now state that I still have a bias favoring the park. If forced to decide between having Grand Teton National Park or not, I would choose to have the park even though I view sympathetically many of the concerns and suspicions held by the early anti-park populace of the valley.

The failure of most people to recognize the validity of anti-park sentiment in Jackson Hole probably relates to our distance from the events. Hindsight is not always 20-20, especially when viewed from the distance of decades and disparate life experiences. The adage concerning walking in another man's shoes applies here. In the 1920s, it was not at all obvious that tourism was destined to play such an important role in the economic well-being of the valley and that cattle ranching would decline in influence.

Omitted in most published accounts of the struggle to create this park is an attempt to understand the anti-park sentiments of the local ranchers and other residents. Some narratives place the blame for park opposition with this group. On occasion this was true, but not always, and half truths obfuscate a clear understanding of the issues and events. Virtually absent is the fact that the ranchers often opposed only a boundary line that included their grazing allotments, not the creation of the park. Missing in most narratives is the opposition to the park from outside the valley by conservation groups such as the National Parks Association and the Isaac Walton League. Also, absent is the local opposition to development plans by the Park Service for hotels around the glacial lakes at the base of the mountains and the construction of new roads through the area. Two promising pieces of legislation failed because the Bureau of Budget rejected the tax compensation provisions, not because of strong local opposition. Only a single vote in the Senate kept the Tetons from being annexed into Yellowstone National Park in 1918, and that "nay" vote was cast because a senator from a neighboring state misunderstood the proposed boundaries. Even the Ken Burns documentary about the national parks (*The National Parks: America's Best Idea*) speaks pejoratively of the local opposition while omitting all other considerations of the relevant issues.

Also omitted from most published histories of the park are the demerits rightly earned by the National Park Service regarding its political maneuvering and its occasional disingenuous dealings with the valley's residents and their concerns. Like all bureaucracies, the Park Service had to grow into a mature agency. It did not always perform perfectly. It was arrogant in its youth, demonstrated impatience and ruthlessness in adolescence, and condescension in maturity.

The fact is, over that span of decades, the issues affecting attitudes in support of or opposition to the park changed. The rationale and circumstances encouraging the annexation of the Tetons into Yellowstone Park in 1898 were different from the situation in 1917 when the Park Service tried to accomplish the same goal. By 1929, the situation and attitudes of many of the locals had evolved to acquiescence regarding the creation of the first Grand Teton National Park. Attitudes and circumstances were different in 1934 when a preponderance of opinion favored the extension of the park's boundaries from those of 1938 when another extension to the park's boundaries was considered. The controversy surrounding the 1943 establishment of the Jackson Hole National Monument involved issues and circumstances uncommon to the previous controversies. Any narrative that describes the controversies as uniformly cattlemen against the Park Service sacrifices validity.

As I researched, it became evident that although the essential elements of the history of the creation of Grand Teton National Park were known and available through various publications, there had been no attempt to document this history in a balanced manner. The pro-park advocates were often presented as prescient far-thinking altruistic patriots while the anti-park people were short-sighted, unreasonable greedy capitalists whose concerns for the welfare of the valley were unfounded. The injustice in these portrayals is not just to the people involved in the controversies, but also to the process by which our government operates. Certainly, our government relies heavily on the concept of majority rule, but there are also protections for minority rights. Compromise then becomes an essential element of democracy. As slow, agonizing, and cumbersome as it may be, our representative form of government has its laudable moments and the creation of this park demonstrates how our democracy works— warts, diamonds, and all.

After numerous years of guiding river trips in the Park and accumulating information, I was able to present my river trip guests with a park history narrative that I felt was accurate. Tony Bevenito, who was the Public Information Officer for the Park and who floated with me frequently, asked me to write "my" park history for a pamphlet, which he thought the park's History Association might want to publish. Consideration of a pamphlet quickly diminished with a review of the volume of information I considered necessary to present a balanced view of the struggle to establish Grand Teton National Park.

In some cases, my research led me to different interpretations of events and motivations than had generally been accepted, and I felt I would need to provide references to substantiate my interpretation. I read back issues of the valley's first newspaper, the *Jackson Hole Courier*, beginning with the 1914 issues and worked my way forward. Many hours were spent in the courthouse reading the transfers of property titles from homesteaders to the Snake River Land Company (Rockefeller's purchasing organization). It took very little time to realize there was more information than even a weighty pamphlet could contain– more issues and attitudes that required explanation and consideration. There were allegations and rumors that deserved investigation.

The format of this book is also a result of my attempt to present this narrative in a way that portrays the controversies concurrently with the settlement and development of the valley. The motivations, opinions, and concerns of the opposing factions are more easily understood if the events are considered in the context of the era. Photographs help provide this context, and I have included numerous images to help the reader envision what life was like for the people of the valley during this half century of settlement and development. Some photographic images relate directly to the text on that page while other images were added to illustrate the life and times of the era, and hopefully, help the reader envision the life experiences of the valley's residents. The chapters are arranged chronologically by years to document the evolving environmental ethic of the settlers as various activities and initiatives emerged that proposed to either impact or protect the scenic character of the valley and its economic institutions.

Appendix One is a chronological index which allows the reader to locate a particular event or subject by date and go directly to the chapter that documents the details surrounding the issue. Other published histories of the park often quote from documents such as committee resolutions and personal correspondence that they present as evidence to substantiate a particular position on the controversy. I felt those limited quotations out of context sometimes concealed the broader intent of the writers and signers of these documents. I, too, have quoted and paraphrased some of these same documents, with, I hope, a less pejorative slant, but this might still be perceived as merely my interpretation. Accordingly, I elected to allow the principles to speak for themselves and let the reader decide their intent. The documents I considered worth reading in their entirety are included in Appendix Two.

I was fortunate that some of the people involved in the controversies relating to the history of Grand Teton National Park were alive when I began my research. I have noted their contributions in the Acknowledgments section. Although the interviews and recollections of these people were enlightening, I have not relied heavily on those sources. Memory is an imperfect recorder of history. Their memories were, nevertheless, vital to understanding the attitudes of the era and I am grateful for the time they graciously shared to explain issues and motivations and to direct me to additional sources that I probably would have overlooked. I did rely heavily on sworn testimony of witnesses at U.S. Senate and House investigative hearings and newspapers– especially letters to the editor and opinion pieces. Speeches and debates printed in the Congressional Record provided positions of the Congressional delegations. Other published works were helpful in locating source material and are duly noted in the Bibliography.

As one might expect, some sources are contradictory, and given the passage of time, a source will sometimes contradict himself. Accordingly, I formulated a method, or rather a set of guidelines, to aid in the presentation of this narrative. If the same source gave several different versions of the same event, I presented the version that was published or recorded closest to the occurrence of the event and then introduced the discrepancy as a note. An exception to this approach would be if other more substantive evidence supported a later version. If there was more than one version of an event and equal validity for the sources, I presented both versions. Occasionally there were several strongly held but differing viewpoints on a single event, and when available I have presented substantiating evidence for both sides.

Horace Albright, who was the Park Service representative most involved in the efforts to create Grand Teton National Park, was alive when I began my research. I declined to request an interview with him because he had provided over the course of time three sources for his version of the events, one being an extensive interview by Park Service officials. Those three sources sometimes contradict each other and thus my primary question related to which version was the truth. I elected to use the sources he had already provided and search for collaboration for conflicting accounts.

There are several goals that I hoped to accomplish with this book. First, I wanted to document a fair representation of the events by including the opposition viewpoint to the establishment of the park. Second, most books on the history of the park concentrate on the role of John D. Rockefeller, Jr. and Horace Albright. Before either man entered this valley, some of the original settlers were attempting to effect some form of protection for the scenic attractions that they valued. I wanted to recognize their efforts and their foresight. Last, I wanted to investigate the allegations and rumors of nefarious intent and actions leveled by the opposing sides at each other and determine if any could be substantiated or discounted. I was successful with some but failed with others. For instance, it was often rumored that Rockefeller originally purchased land in Jackson Hole because he suspected oil reservoirs in the valley. Having failed to find oil, he donated the land to the Park Service for the tax deduction. I believe this book corrects this misconception. Likewise, Robert Miller, the local banker and first purchasing agent for the Snake River Land Company, was alleged by Horace Albright to have used Rockefeller's money to divest his bank of mortgages, initiating a rash of foreclosures so he could sell the farms and ranches at inflated prices to Rockefeller, thereby making hundreds of thousands of dollars from his position as purchasing agent. Within the text of this book, Miller's contractual obligations and conduct as purchasing agent have been clarified. Miller was also accused of grazing several hundred head of cattle on Forest Service lands, without paying the appropriate fees, while he was Supervisor of the Teton National Forest. This is a half-truth, and the circumstances are explained in the text of this book. I found most pejorative allegations to be demonstrably false or explainable in the context of the event.

The controversies that smoldered and raged within the valley concerning various park proposals often strained social intercourse and caused long-lasting animosities. In spite of the allegations by each side toward the other, I have determined an over-riding truth— there are no bad guys in this story. I have not found anyone who wanted to see the scenic attractions of the valley despoiled. Each side had a different view of the most desirable future for the valley, and each side was a little naive. Both factions can justly be accused of unseemly actions and blatant self-interest, as well as altruism.

In hindsight, it is easy to find fault with some of the arguments espoused by park opponents, but to be fair, it is advisable to avoid condemning a person or a group of people for failing to envision the future precisely. I do not believe that any of the individuals or groups who were so vocal in the events culminating in the creation of Grand Teton National Park, even in their wildest flights of fancy, could have imagined Jackson Hole as it is today. I suspect both factions would be a little bit sad.

Writing this book ranks as one of the hardest things that I have ever tried to do, but the research was one of the most interesting, entertaining, and rewarding activities of my life. I hope you find it informative.

N. Wayne Johnson

INTRODUCTION

...when the moon had gone down in exaggerated volume behind the glorified spire of the Grand Teton, the stars succeeded with their myriad sparkling lights, and these blazed up the setting on the sharp cut edges of the great serrated wall, like Indian signal fires in successive spectral flashes, rising and dying out by hundreds as the hours passed on.

On the wide continent of North America there is no mountain group to compare in scenic splendor with the Great Tetons.[1]

Lt. Gustavus Cheyney Doane
December 1, 1876

Stephen Leek Photo, American Heritage Center, University of Wyoming ah03138_1173

Early tourists in Jackson Hole

Grand Teton National Park has become one of the most popular, and, therefore, one of the most visited national parks in the United States. Its popularity is well deserved, for it offers not only scenic splendor but also a variety of recreational opportunities. Its early popularity was largely the result of dude ranch clientele, sportsmen, and spin-off visitation from Yellowstone National Park. Today Grand Teton National Park is no longer the "little sister" to Yellowstone. The Tetons now attract more visitors annually than does Yellowstone.

The national park status of this spectacular northwest Wyoming mountain range, and of the valley that provides its foreground, is so obviously appropriate that most visitors to the area are surprised to learn that 52 years of controversy surround the history of the formation of the Park. These controversies were sometimes local in nature, but on occasion, they were national in scope.

Ben Sheffield Photo- Grand Teton National Park (unnumbered)

Dude ranch clientele, fishermen, and hunters were the primary non-agricultural economic contributors in the early years of settlement.

Some of these controversies involved, or resulted from, activities in Yellowstone National Park whose southern boundary is just five miles north of Grand Teton's northern boundary.

As might be expected, the two parks have more in common than geographic proximity. They share a nearly parallel human history, presently dating back 8,000 years, as well as wildlife species and a variety of correlative geologic phenomena. However, the scope of this book is primarily concerned with the history of human efforts to provide legal protection for the region immediately south of Yellowstone National Park. Even so, the history of the creation of Grand Teton National Park would be incomplete if Yellowstone Park were to be ignored. Every national park and national monument might justly claim a common origin with Yellowstone if their genealogies were traced backward far enough. The ideals and human values that led to the creation of Yellowstone as the first national park are essentially the same as those involved in the creation of every park and monument in existence today. The difference is that the other parks' and monuments' association with Yellowstone National Park are ideological while Grand Teton National Park's relationship is much more direct and substantial.

The original effort to protect the Teton area began with the military administrators of Yellowstone Park. The unique valley they sought to protect was called Jackson's Hole by fur trappers in the early 1800s. A "hole" to the trappers was simply a high mountain valley that contained an abundance of game. This particular valley, or hole, was named for the trapper David E. Jackson* in 1829. The name was first noted cartographically on what has been called

*David E. Jackson (c.1790-December 24, 1837) was a trapper in the employ of William Ashley from 1822 until 1826 when he, Jedediah Smith, and William L. Sublette, bought out Ashley. Little is known about the man, but he was rumored to have participated in the Battle of New Orleans in 1815 and the Arikara and Leavenworth fights in 1823. Jackson and his partners sold the business in 1830 and established a freight operation between St. Louis, Missouri and Santa Fe, New Mexico. Comanches killed Smith during the caravan's first trip to Santa Fe, but it arrived in Santa Fe on July 4, 1831. Jackson eventually traveled as far west as San Diego, California where he purchased mules for the freight business. After delivering the mules to New Mexico, he returned to Missouri and is not known to have ventured into the far west again. His health deteriorated, and he died from a fever in Paris, Tennessee.

the Ferris Map of 1836[2]. The United States Board on Geographic Names, established in 1890, initiated a policy discouraging the genitive case for geographic names.* Thus, the connotative, Jackson Hole, became the official designation for the valley, although one still occasionally hears the possessive appellation. The same is true for many of the lakes that dot the edges of the valley. For example, Jenny, Leigh, and Jackson Lakes were once referred to in the possessive.

Grand Teton National Park

Photograph of Mount Moran and Jackson Lake from Signal Mountain by William Henry Jackson. Grand Teton Park Archives indicated this photo was taken in 1872. However, W. H. Jackson historian, Bob Blair, notes that Jackson did not enter the Jackson Hole valley in 1872. This photo probably dates to 1883.

Jackson Hole is roughly 50 miles long and 8 to 12 miles wide. The northern geographic boundary is the Yellowstone Plateau, which is approximately 1,000 feet higher than the Jackson Hole valley floor, and the Absaroka Mountains, which are part of the Continental Divide. To the east are the Mount Leidy Highlands and the Gros Ventre Range. To the south, the valley is marked by the Wyoming and Snake River Ranges. If these mountain ranges could be transplanted to the east, they would be famous for their rugged appearance and elevations in excess of 10,000 feet. In their present location, these ranges are hardly noticed by the millions of tourists who traverse the valley each year and are overshadowed by the mountain range that forms the western boundary of Jackson Hole, the Tetons.

The Tetons rise abruptly approximately 7,000 feet from a nearly flat valley floor to an elevation of 13,770 feet. They have no foothills. They are,

therefore, the focal point for the tourists who enter the valley and are one of the premiere scenic attractions of the world. It is from this mountain range that the Grand Teton National Park takes its name.

It is commonly believed that the original name for the mountain range was a Shoshone Indian word, Teewinot, meaning "many pinnacles." However, a Shoshone Indian told this author, in the summer of 1977, that no such word exists in their language. The Shoshonean phrase for "many mountains" would be "shont to-yap-doi-abi". [4] The Nez Perce tribe supposedly called these mountains the "hoary-headed fathers" because of their height and the fact that snow remains on the peaks year round. Less poetic in his

*President Benjamin Harrison created the United States Board on Geographic Names through an Executive Order on September 4, 1890, to expedite a systematic standardization of geographic nomenclature in the United States. It was the responsibility of the Board to adjudicate any unresolved disputes regarding place names. Theodore Roosevelt extended the Board's authority in 1906 to "... *standardize all geographic names for Federal use, including name changes and new names."* [3] Congress reorganized the Board in 1947 with the passage of Public Law 80-242 (80th Congress, 1st Session). The Board is a non-budgeted committee composed of appointees from the various federal departments and independent agencies concerned with the use of geographic names.

There appears to be no definitive reason for the Board's policy of discouraging the possessive regarding geographic names. Nevertheless, since 1890, there have been only five decisions allowing the genitive apostrophe. They are: Martha's Vineyard (Massachusetts) in 1933, Ike's Point (New Jersey) in 1944, John E's Pond (Rhode Island) in 1963, Carlos Elmer's Joshua View (Arizona) in 1995, and Clark's Point (Oregon) in 2003. The Board's policy does not affect congressionally or presidentially designated place names such as Devil's Tower.

attempt to name the peaks, Wilson Price Hunt, in September 1811, called them the "Pilot Knobs" because they were landmarks visible at great distances to overland travelers.[5] A Hudson's Bay Company map lists them as "The Three Paps."[6] The French-Canadian fur traders called them "Les Trois Tetons," or "the three breasts."[7] Ferdinand Vandeveer Hayden, the scientist-explorer compared the mountains to sharks' teeth.[8] The French description has endured. Its first public appearance was in the Bonneville Map of 1837.[9]

The importance of these early white men in the West was not in the names they ascribed to various landmarks, rather their activities provided the basic geographic information which would later aid scientific expeditions in their travels through the area. Eventually, it was the scientists who convinced Congress to establish Yellowstone National Park.

Yellowstone National Park Archives

The Hayden Survey mapped Yellowstone and Jackson Hole providing scientific documentation for the exceptional characteristics of the region.

Ferdinand Vandeveer Hayden (1829-1877) Hayden encouraged Congress to protect the Yellowstone region in a national park.

Yellowstone National Park Archives

As previously mentioned, it was the early military administrators of Yellowstone National Park who first pushed for protection of the Jackson Hole area. The event that brought the military into Yellowstone National Park was the result of still another controversy. Since its creation, Yellowstone National Park had been a political football that was kicked by whichever party was not in power. It seemed that the civilian administrators could do nothing right. It was true that Yellowstone had its problems, and no doubt, many mistakes were made. However, many of the problems faced by these men were the direct result of a lack of congressional action, support, and direction. Also, it should be remembered that this was the first national park in the world. There were no clearly defined long-range objectives and no precedential experience upon which the administrators could draw.

The 1872 legislation that created Yellowstone National Park was responsible for the majority of problems encountered by the civilian and military administrators of the Park. The legislation was not only ambiguous; it did not provide penalties for violators of the law other than expulsion from the Park. Even if penalties had been outlined, they could not have been enforced because Congress failed to place the Park under the jurisdiction of any of the adjacent territories. Thus, there were no courts possessing jurisdiction to back up the law and no appropriations provided to finance enforcement nor any other operational activities.

Six years after the creation of Yellowstone National Park, Congress authorized $10,000 *"...to protect, preserve, and improve the Park."*[10] During the next 23 years, Congress appropriated only $592,609, or an average annual outlay of less than $25,000.[11] The first and second superintendents, Nathaniel P. Langford and Philetus W. Norris respectively, served without pay. The highest paid salary to any of the early civilian superintendents was $2,000 per year, and military superintendents received no compensation other than their military pay. The problem of meager financial support was intensified when Washington failed to act upon supply requisitions. During one season when fires raged within the Park, one visitor, Mr. Lesvis of Pennsylvania, donated $40 for the purchase of rubber buckets after a request for the buckets had been ignored by the Department of the Interior.[12] Mr. Lesvis' gift may have been the first monetary donation by a citizen to the National Park System.*

In 1886, the 49th Congress became involved in a controversy that threatened to destroy Yellowstone as a park. The controversy grew out of the Interior Department's appropriation request for Yellowstone National Park. The civilian administrators of the Park had recently received intense criticism and were accused of corruption and "monopolistic activities." Because of these charges, most of which apparently were unfounded, some congressmen felt that the park experiment had failed, and its continued existence was a waste of public money. Representative John H. Reagan (D) of Texas felt it inappropriate for the government to enter "show business." [13]

If Yellowstone were to continue as a national park, another problem had to be solved. Should the Park continue under a civilian administration or should the administration be turned over to the military? Senator George G. Vest (D) of Missouri was a primary defender of the Park and its civilian jurisdictional status. He voiced fears that the use of the Army would benefit speculators more than the national interest and would initiate an eventual breakup of the park.[14]

Senator John R. McPherson (D) of New Jersey supported the use of the military. It was this direction that prevailed, although more from necessity than by specific congressional action. Congress did not act directly to destroy the civilian administration

of the Park, but neither did they appropriate funds for its continued existence. The result was essentially the same. Without funds to pay the civilian park employees, the Secretary of the Interior, L. Q. C. Lamar, was forced to rely on the Act of March 3, 1883, (Sundry Civil Bill of 1883) which provided that:

The Secretary of War, upon the request of the Secretary of the Interior, is hereby authorized and directed to make the necessary details of troops to prevent trespassers

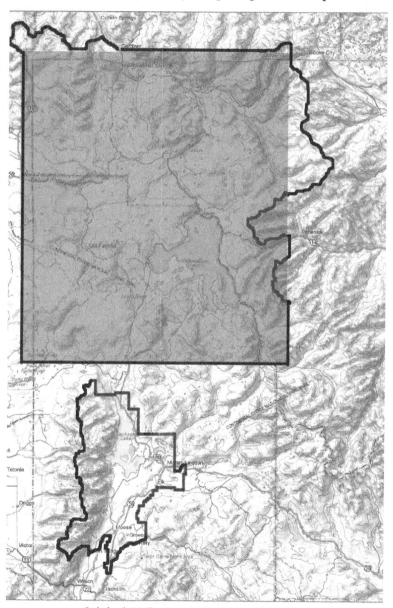

Original Yellowstone National Park boundary (shaded) and current National Park boundaries (solid line) for northwestern Wyoming

*Donations to the National Park System by U.S. citizens are no longer unusual. Much of the Park System, as we know it today, is the result of various philanthropic endeavors by individuals and organizations.

or intruders from entering the park for the purpose of destroying the game or objects of curiosity therein, or for any other purpose prohibited by the law, and to remove such persons from the park if found therein.[15]

Despite the fears voiced by Senator Vest, this move was probably the best course of action at the time because Congress failed to act decisively on issues that could have remedied the administrative problems in Yellowstone. H. Duane Hampton, in his book *How the U.S. Cavalry Saved Our National Parks*, correctly observed that, *"Notwithstanding the earnest efforts of the last civilian superintendent, the military administration of the Yellowstone Park did, in a very real sense, save Yellowstone Park from physical and legislative destruction."* [16] Thus began the military administration of Yellowstone National Park.

The military experiment might have failed but for the high caliber of men assigned to the park. Lesser men might have accepted the assignment as a vacation from the rigors and dangers of Indian fighting. This was not the case. The soldiers accepted the responsibilities of the assignment with exemplary vigor and initiated programs and policies that are now considered standard park policy. For example, the military initiated the policy of designated camping areas. Of even greater significance was the precedent set by Captain F. A. Boutelle, the seventh superintendent of the Park, who attempted to balance the need to develop facilities to provide necessary services for the public and the desire by several businessmen who favored total commercial development of the Park. Captain Boutelle worked to thwart an 1889 proposal by D. B. May of Billings, Montana, to construct an elevator at the Lower Falls of the Grand Canyon of the Yellowstone River.[17] This incident, along with Boutelle's vigilant, watchdog attitude toward the commercial operators within the Park, may have cost him his position as acting superintendent of the Park. Hiram Chittenden wrote that Captain Boutelle was relieved of his position unexpectedly on January 21, 1891, after some *"...political interference and private intriguing ...when Captain Boutelle undertook to enforce the regulations against a prominent employee of the hotel company."* [18]

NPS.gov [Public domain] via Wikimedia Commons
Company M, 1st Cavalry enters Yellowstone in August 1886.

Captain Boutelle was possibly the first to suggest a Yellowstone Park extension southward to include the *"...Jackson's Lake country and the Teton peaks."* [19] General Philip Sheridan, during a tour of the area, had previously suggested a southern extension of Yellowstone Park as far as the 44th parallel. This extension would not have protected the Teton Mountains, glacial lakes, or the valley of Jackson Hole. The 44th parallel would have included only the area north of the upper end of Jackson Lake prior to its impoundment.

~

It is interesting that the reason for the original efforts to protect the Jackson Hole area was to protect the southern Yellowstone elk herd rather than the scenic qualities of the valley. The southern Yellowstone elk herd annually migrated from the high country regions of Yellowstone to the Jackson Hole area where the winter snows and temperatures were generally less severe. Each spring the herd returned to Yellowstone as soon as the melting snows permitted. The military vigorously sought to protect the elk, as well as other animals within park boundaries, from poachers during the summer months. Then, each fall the southern elk herd would abandon their protectors and travel beyond the Army's jurisdiction to areas where poachers had learned they could operate with minimal risk. Some frustration probably haunted the soldiers to the point that elk protection may have taken precedent, at least in their minds, when the issue of park extension surfaced.

∽

There is some evidence that the Jackson Hole region was not totally ignored by Washington during this period of military management. In 1891, Congress passed the Forest Reserve Act (sometimes called the Creative Act) that provided presidential authority to establish, by proclamation, forest reserves. This legislation resulted from recommendations to Congress by the National Forestry Association, who believed it necessary to institute some form of control and protection for large areas of forest lands throughout the nation. Timbering practices and extractive mineral activities had scarred tremendous acreages without a view to future utilization of the land.* President Harrison ultimately set aside some 13,000,000 acres under this designation.[21]

The Yellowstone Park Timber Land Reserve

University of Oregon- Special Collections, Collection Number PH 119, Box 4, 119-055

Captain Frazier Augustus Boutelle (1840-1924) recommended in his 1890 annual report to the Secretary of Interior that Yellowstone Park be expanded to include the Teton Mountains and Jackson Lake.

was the first to be established. President Harrison, on March 30, 1891, signed a Presidential Proclamation establishing the 1,239,040-acre reserve to the east and south of Yellowstone National Park. This reserve contained the area that would later become Grand Teton National Park.[22] On September 10 of the same year, another Presidential Proclamation revised the Yellowstone Park Timber Land Reserve, but it did not appreciably change the acreage. Then, in February 1897, a proclamation issued by President Grover Cleveland created the Teton Forest Reserve by splitting 829,400 acres from the southern portion of the Yellowstone Park Timber Land Reserve. Most of the lands later included in Grand Teton National Park were covered in this new forest reserve.[23] The forest reserves would eventually become national forests.

Yellowstone National Park Archives

Soldiers in Yellowstone National Park with confiscated poached bison heads

∽

* During the late 1800s it was estimated that fire consumed as much as ten times the amount of lumber harvested for human needs.[20]

As needed appropriations finally became available, the U.S. Army Corps of Engineers commenced construction projects within Yellowstone Park. The roads and bridges they built opened Yellowstone to wagons and stagecoaches and thus increased visitation as well as accessibility to the scenic and geologic wonders of the Park. An important by-product of the increased visitation and accessibility was that an increasing number of people began to notice a distant mountain range unlike any they had seen within the Park. These extremely rugged, snow-capped peaks, the Grand Tetons, began to tease the tourists with their beauty and inaccessibility. This, of course, served to increase the interest in preservation of the valley south of Yellowstone National Park. Hiram M. Chittenden was a Captain with the U.S. Army Corps of Engineers in Yellowstone and was one of the first to recommend protection for the Tetons. In his book, *The Yellowstone National Park*, Chittenden states:

Just as the road (the old Norris road) commences to descend from the high plateau between the Gibbon and the Firehole, a glimpse is had of the Teton Mountains. They are among the most striking in the entire Rocky Mountain Region. For half a century after the overland journey of the Astorians, they were the chief landmarks in that trackless wilderness, and long bore the name of the Pilot Knobs. They are distinctly visible from every important peak in the Park, although they are themselves outside its limits. As seen from the point, at which we have arrived, they are fifty miles away. They rise precipitously from the west shore of Jackson Lake (also outside of the Park) and with it form a scene of grandeur which ought to be included in the reservation.[24]

Thus began the long and sometimes arduous history of the efforts to protect the Tetons and Jackson Hole– born amid the military frustration with fighting poachers and the curiosity of Yellowstone National Park visitors.

NPS.gov via Wikimedia Commons

Captain Hiram Martin Chittenden (1858-1917) of the U.S. Army Corps of Engineers recommended in his 1895 book, *The Yellowstone National Park*, the inclusion of the Teton Mountains into Yellowstone.

CHAPTER ONE

1897-1902

The movement to retain and preserve what is possible of wildlife in America along with the enlargement of the national park territory was not inaugurated a moment too soon, or cannot be carried an inch too far. Selfish interest [sic], some of them very powerful, are at work constantly to thwart this movement, but thus far they have not met with decisive success.

We hope they never do, without wishing any bad luck to the ranchers of Jackson's Hole.

Jackson Hole Courier
March 2, 1922

Jackson Hole Historical Society and Museum 1994.6021.001

Touring Jackson Hole
The driver of the lead stage was Russ Egbert.

With increased public interest in the Jackson Hole area, the military administration of Yellowstone initiated the first steps for protection. In his 1897 annual report, Colonel S.B.M. Young,* the acting superintendent of Yellowstone National Park, recommended that the boundaries of the Park be extended so as to include the Jackson Hole region. The Secretary of the Interior, C. N. Bliss,† directed Colonel Young to submit a draft of a bill to accomplish the park extension. This bill, along with Colonel Young's letter of explanation, was submitted to Secretary Bliss in January of 1898. Two weeks later, Bliss sent the draft bill to John F. Lacey, the chairman of the House Committee on Public Lands, along with the following letter:

Sir: I transmit herewith a draft of a bill prepared at my instance by Colonel

Cornelius Newton Bliss (R)
(1833-1911)
Twenty-first Secretary of Interior
Photo date 1898

Colonel Samuel Baldwin Marks Young

S. B. M. Young, Acting Superintendent of Yellowstone National Park, to extend the limits of the Yellowstone National Park, and have the honor to commend the same to your favorable consideration, with the view to its introduction and favorable consideration by Congress. I also transmit herewith a copy of a letter from Colonel Young, together with a map showing Yellowstone National Park, with proposed extensions, fully describing the latter, which approximate about 3,254 square miles, and setting forth the desirability of their inclusion in the park reservation.

*Samuel Baldwin Marks Young (1840–1924) was known for his decisiveness and administrative prowess. He joined the army at the beginning of the Civil War as a private, was wounded four times, cited three times for gallant and meritorious service in action, and advanced in rank to a brevet brigadier general by the end of that conflict. He would eventually serve as Chief of Staff of the U.S. Army. During his stellar military career, he served as Acting Superintendent of both Yosemite and Yellowstone Parks and was again appointed Superintendent of Yellowstone Park after his retirement from the Army.[1]

†C. N. Bliss was a wealthy dry goods merchant with stores in several major cities. He served as treasurer of the Republican National Committee and then two years as President McKinley's Secretary of the Interior. In 1900, Bliss declined an offer to run as McKinley's Vice Presidential running mate. McKinley was re-elected and had Bliss accepted the vice presidential position he would have become the 26th President of the United States in 1901 when McKinley was assassinated.[2] One can only speculate as to the course of American history if Bliss, rather than Theodore Roosevelt, had assumed the presidency in 1901.

The changing of the boundaries of the park as herein recommended will, in my judgement, enable the Department to better preserve and more effectively protect the game in the park from depredation by poachers and others.

There is also transmitted herewith, for your information in this connection, a copy of a letter from the Commissioner of the General Land Office regarding the correctness of the boundaries of the proposed additions to the park as described in the bill, and the number of bona fide entries of land within said territory.[3]

This was the first formal action toward the ultimate protection of the Jackson Hole region.

Instead of acting on these recommendations, Congress decided to seek more information about the region south of Yellowstone National Park. With this intention, the Senate passed a resolution on December 6, 1898, which provided:

That the Secretary of the Interior be, and is hereby directed to send to the Senate all information in the possession of his department in relation to the region south of and adjoining the Yellowstone National Park; also what steps should be taken to preserve the game in the Park, and whether the region south of the Park should not be put under the same control as the national park, in order to prevent the extinction of the herds of large game roaming therein.[4]

In December 1898, in compliance with the above resolution, Acting Secretary Thomas Ryan forwarded a number of reports and documents as well as legal opinions on the jurisdictional problems with the state of Wyoming to the president of the Senate. It was Ryan's opinion that such legislation could be legally accomplished because of a reservation of authority contained in the Act of July 10, 1890 (26 Stats. 222), admitting Wyoming into the Union. That act provided:

That nothing in this act contained shall repeal or affect any act of Congress relating to the Yellowstone National Park, or the reservation of the park as now defined, or as may be hereafter defined or extended, or the power of the United States over it; and nothing in this act shall interfere with the right and ownership of the United States in said park and reservation as it is now or may hereafter be defined or extended by law; but exclusive legislation, in all cases whatsoever, shall be exercised by the United States which shall have exclusive control and jurisdiction over the same; but nothing in this proviso contained shall be construed to prevent the service within said park of civil and criminal process lawfully issued by the authority of said State.

In the late 1890s, most, if not all of the land under consideration belonged to the federal government. The question, therefore, was not the ability of the Congress to incorporate most of the Jackson Hole area into Yellowstone. Rather, would such an action accomplish the stated objective of protecting the elk and other large game indigenous to the region. In a number of cases, the U.S. Supreme Court determined that

Tourists in Yellowstone National Park, early 1900s.

S. N. Leek Photo American Heritage Center University of Wyoming ah03138_1025 ownership of wild game within the boundaries of a state was with that state.*

The existing Yellowstone National Park was not affected by these judicial decisions because Wyoming was made a state after the Park was formed. However, any extension of the Park would be subject to the Supreme Court's interpretation. On the other hand, the U.S. Constitution provided Congress with authority to *"...make all needful rules and regulations respecting the territory or other property belonging to the United States...."* [5] With this authority in mind, Ryan believed that *"While Congress may not be able to authorize the capture or killing of game..."* in the subject area, it *"...can prescribe how and when the public lands may be used and can restrict or altogether deny access to or entrance upon the public lands ... for the purpose of pursuing or hunting game."* [6]

Although the Acting Secretary seemed to have personally favored park extension, Ryan nevertheless described an alternate course of action that might have accomplished the same objective. The previously mentioned Constitutional authority combined with the Act of June 4, 1897 (30 Stat., 35), relating to forest reserves, and a ruling by the U.S. Attorney General on November 17, 1898, may have formed a legal basis for regulations prohibiting hunting on public lands in question without changing the legal status of the land. The Act of June 4, 1897, authorized the Secretary of the Interior to regulate the occupancy and use of the public lands so as to *"...preserve the forests therein from destruction."* The ruling of November 17, 1898, stated that violators of the regulations issued by the Secretary of the Interior were liable under U.S. law. The principal problem with this alternative, a prohibition against pursuing or hunting game, rested with whether or not hunting endangered the forest. Since the land, not the animals, belonged to the federal government only the land could be regulated. There was no evidence that hunting was detrimental to the forest, and no precedent had been set to justify such a regulation. Therefore, because of the reservation of authority included in the act admitting the state of Wyoming into the Union, park extension offered the firmest legal foundation for the protection of wildlife in the region. Such was Ryan's recommendation to the Senate pursuant to the resolution passed in December 1898.

Included with Ryan's recommendation was a report on the region located south of Yellowstone by

Current Park boundaries
Original Yellowstone Park
Col. Young's extension

Colonel S. B. M. Young's proposed extension of Yellowstone National Park, 1898 and 1902

*Perhaps the most famous of these cases was *Ward v. Race Horse* (163 U.S., 504).

Charles D. Walcott, Director of the U.S. Geological Survey. This report is important for several reasons. First, it gave a detailed description of the terrain of the Teton Forest Reserve by township and range and provided information on climate, geology, elevation, timber species, undergrowth, agricultural use, roads, ranching, etc. Second, in this report, Walcott was the first to suggest the idea that a separate national park might be appropriate. He proposed, *"The area south of the park, extending as far as Black Tail Butte, or the southern limit of present Teton Reserve, should either be added to the Yellowstone National Park or constituted as a separate park, to be known as Teton National Park."*[7] Third, the report made an impassioned plea for the protection of large game in the Teton Forest Reserve:

The Government is now brought face to face with the question, Shall it protect the winter range of the game which it has, at large annual expense, protected in its summer range in Yellowstone Park? It owns and controls most of the lands of the winter range. Will it continue in this control, or will it give the lands up to the pasturage of cattle and sheep and thus exterminate the game? In September and October of the present year (1898) parties were camped on nearly every creek in the large region south of the park, waiting to shoot down game, which they can freely do under the game laws of Wyoming, which license the hunting of large game three months each fall. Will the Government prevent the shooting of the game within the Yellowstone Timber Reserve and the Teton Forest Reserve? If it does not, the rifle and shotgun will as surely exterminate the game as will the destruction of their winter pasture.[8]

Fourth, Walcott, in addition to being the first to recommend separate park status for the Jackson Hole area, also suggested to Congress that the

scenic qualities of the area were justifications for park status:

I have personally visited most of the points and regions in the United States noted for their scenery, but in my judgement there is nothing that excels in natural beauty the valley of Jackson Lake and the Teton Mountains. The Tetons are unequaled except in the higher, almost inaccessible points of the Sierra and Cascade

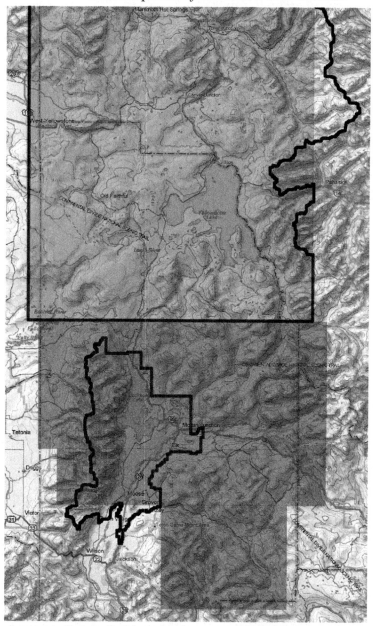

Current Park boundaries
Original Yellowstone Park
Walcott's Teton National Park

U.S. Geological Survey Director Charles D. Walcott's proposed Teton National Park, 1901

13

mountains, and Jackson Lake is a beautiful sheet of water lying directly at their base. It may be more truly called the Switzerland of America than can be any spot known to me. If it were practicable to obtain railroad facilities to the foot of Jackson Lake and thus enable the tourist to see that beautiful region and then go north by stage to the Yellowstone Lake and through the park it would be the grandest trip, for one of limited extent, to be found anywhere in the world. *

...the preservation of the wonderful scenery of this country and the great natural forest areas is a subject of importance to the American people.[9]

Pach Brothers, New York [Public domain] via Wikimedia Commons

Charles Doolittle Walcott (c. 1900)
(1850-1927)
Walcott was perhaps the first person to recommend separate park status for the Jackson Hole Region, and suggested it be called Teton National Park. He was the third director of the U.S. Geological Survey, after Hayden and Powell.

Despite the volume of information presented to the Senate supporting extension of Yellowstone National Park, no action was taken.

Because Congress failed to act positively in this regard, the slaughter of elk in the Yellowstone Park Timber Land Reserve and the Teton Forest Reserve continued. Lieutenant Matt C. Bristol, 13th Cavalry, reported no elk were killed inside the Park during the winter of 1900-1901, attesting to the successful policing activities of the military. Lieutenant Bristol believed that the killing of elk in the Yellowstone Park Timber Land Reserve was accomplished by *"Al Collins, Charles Collins, Henry Maurin, D. W. Spaulding, Herbert Whitman, W. E. Smith, Dave Daugherty, W. Rogers, W. F. King, Frank Tannehill, Joe Staddler, Ed Sheffield, and W. Randolph."* [10] Bristol believed these men lived in the reserve, but had no legal right to be there, and apparently made a living by killing the game.[11] On May 15, 1901, Acting Secretary Ryan authorized Captain John Pitcher, the Acting Superintendent of Yellowstone National Park, to eject trespassers from the reserve using whatever force the circumstances required.[12] In this manner, additional protection was afforded the elk in a portion of their winter range.

As a result of several letters written by J. D. Sargent of Elk, Wyoming, to the Commissioner of the General Land Office concerning the wanton killing of elk in the Teton Forest Reserve, I. A. Macrum, a forest inspector, was sent to investigate the allegations. On July 12, 1901, Mr. Macrum, Lieutenant Bristol, and Peter Holt, an army scout, left Mammoth Hot Springs to investigate Sargent's charges. The inspection tour averaged 30 miles a day traveling in a double-seated buckboard drawn by a team of mules. The investigation obtained little hard evidence, and only a few people were willing to sign statements and testify in a court of law. The reasons for the lack

---

*There is a probable explanation for Walcott stopping his proposed railroad short of Yellowstone's boundary. At that time, the military and Yellowstone's congressional defenders were fighting a strong lobby that wanted permission to construct railroads through the Park. Walcott probably did not wish to make a suggestion that would be counterproductive to existing efforts to maintain the integrity of Yellowstone National Park. At the time, the proposed railroad was considered a negative impact on the pristine nature of the Park. More recently, railroads and monorails have been proposed to ease the environmental impact of tourist travel in the Park, but these construction projects have been deemed too expensive. Had the railroads been constructed in the late 1800s we might have more economically eased the overcrowding and automobile congestion experienced by modern visitors to the Park.

of cooperation on the part of area residents ranged from self-incrimination to fear of reprisals. The prospect of obtaining convictions was not optimistic, and the justice court for the region, being elective, had shown itself to be lenient even when the evidence was obtained. Macrum's investigation moved him to declare, *"From what I saw and heard while there I think this* [the Jackson Hole country] *is the most lawless place I have seen." [13]*

Macrum's report included an evaluation of W. Armor Thompson, the forest supervisor, and the rangers under his command. Macrum was not directly critical of Thompson, but portions of the report revealed administrative shortcomings. Thompson had only two rangers under his command, and he had stationed them on the Idaho side of the reserve. Neither ranger had been informed as to the nature of his responsibilities or authority. Thompson was attempting to supervise the entire Wyoming side of the reserve alone. [14] *

Based on the investigation Macrum made the following recommendation:

> *I would respectfully recommend that steps be taken to remove from the Teton Forest Reserve, Wyo., all persons located thereon who can not show legal right to be there.*
>
> *If it be found impracticable to remove said persons from said Teton Forest Reserve then I would respectfully recommend that the strip of land lying immediately south of Yellowstone National Park, Wyo., being part of the Yellowstone Forest Reserve, about 10 miles in width, and all of said Teton Forest Reserve, Wyo., be added to the Yellowstone National Park and be brought under its management, rules, and regulations. [15]*

After I. A. Macrum's inspection tour of the Teton Forest Reserve, nearly a year lapsed without any congressional action. However, a number of governmental agencies continued to receive letters from concerned citizens with regard to the region south of Yellowstone National Park. William M. Findley of Altoona, Pennsylvania wrote that Yellowstone National Park should be extended 250 miles to the south. [16] A sheepman from St. Anthony, Idaho, F. E. Wyatt, suggested in a November 1901 letter to President Theodore Roosevelt that all of Jackson Hole should be set

Jackson Hole Historical Society and Museum 1958.0950.001P

John Dudley Sargent
1861 – 1913

Sargent was one of the more eccentric settlers in Jackson Hole. The possibly illegitimate child of a prominent New England family, he was one of the few who completed a homestead at the far north end of the valley. Twice accused of murder, but known to be particularly gentle with animals and a lover of music and literature, he was at this time on a crusade to protect elk from illegal hunting. Perhaps the most objective and well-documented account of his life is contained in a booklet, *A Tale of Dough Gods Bear Grease Cantaloupe and Sucker Oil*, by Kenneth and Lenore Diem and William Lawrence.

Sargent homesteaded what is now called the AMK Ranch. His letters to the Commissioner of the General Land Office sparked an investigation into the wanton killing of wildlife in the Jackson Hole region.

---

*Mr. Alva A. Simpson, Assistant Regional Forester, *Journal of Forestry*, **October 1941, pp. 886891, stated that Thompson served only a year or two until the General Superintendent of the forest reserves in Wyoming became dissatisfied with his services and dismissed him. The job was given to R. E. Miller, a Jackson Hole pioneer, and businessman.**

aside as a protected *"...winter ground for the deer and elk, and the settlement set aside and the custom of putting up hay for the elk should be done."* [17] Mr. Wyatt also stated that no sheep should be allowed on a forest reserve, an unusual attitude for a man who made a living selling sheep.

Among all this correspondence was a letter from D. W. Spaulding of Wilson, Wyoming to J. L. Smith, presiding judge of the Kansas City Court of Appeals, charging the forest rangers with poaching elk for their teeth.* Judge Smith passed the letter to E. A. Hitchcock, U.S. Secretary of the Interior.

Spaulding's letter, like all of the other correspondence, expressed a need for additional protection for the elk and placed domestic sheep as the greatest detriment to the wildlife after the poachers.

Apparently, the Secretary doubted the validity of Spaulding's letter because there is no evidence of any action concerning the charges against the rangers. Spaulding was, apparently, an authority on poaching. He was one of the men listed by Lieutenant Bristol as being suspected of poaching on the Yellowstone and Teton Forest Reserves during the winter of 1900-1901. Spaulding was arrested in June 1901, for illegally trapping beaver on the reserve. He pleaded guilty and was fined $20 and costs.[18] E. J. Smith of Elk, Wyoming stated to I. A. Macrum during his inspection tour, *"D. W. Spaulding shipped 22 hides, boxed to his son, to Chamberlain, S. Dak., in June, 1899.*

Jackson Hole Historical Society and Museum 1958.1051.001

Early tourist travel between Jackson Hole and Yellowstone National Park. This is a view of the north end of Jackson Lake before the dam was built and the area was inundated.

They were hauled by Frank Sebastion, of Jackson, Wyo., to Cinnabar, Mont." [19] E. J. Smith and Frank Lovell (also of Elk, Wyoming) signed statements on July 16, 1901 that they would testify in court that Spaulding had shot and killed 8 elk near Gravel Peak in November 1898.[20] Macrum also reported, *"This man Spaulding is an applicant before the Department for a privilege on the reserve to establish a bath house at Mineral Springs on the west side of Jackson Lake. He is a lawless fellow, and I would respectfully recommend that he be denied said privilege."* [21]†

Judge J. L. Smith, to whom Spaulding's letter was addressed, was familiar with the Jackson Hole country and had written a somewhat lengthy article on one of his hunting trips to the area (*The Kansas City Journal,* Sunday, March 4, 1900). This article expounded upon the excellent fishing and hunting opportunities within Jackson Hole. Judge Smith also found evidence of diminished

---

*Many elk were killed simply for their canine teeth, called ivories, which were made into jewelry and sold to members of the Elks Club throughout the United States. Elk have two ivory tusks in their upper jaw in place of the canine teeth of other animals. The only other animal indigenous to North America that has ivory canines is the walrus. In some sections of Jackson Hole, the tusks were sufficiently valuable to be used as money.

†Spaulding, a Civil War veteran having served in the 92nd Illinois Regiment, in later years was remembered as a respected citizen of Jackson Hole. Spaulding died in September of 1924 and was buried on a hill above the JY Ranch as he had requested.[22]

numbers of elk over the 15 years that he had traveled to the area, and he placed the blame for this destruction on the state of Wyoming and the residents of the valley. He apparently believed the Wyoming State Game License to be excessive and wildlife protection to be minimal. The 1899 game license allowed a hunter to take two elk, two deer, three antelope, one mountain sheep, and one mountain goat for a $40 fee.[23]

The increasing public concern for the Jackson Hole area and its wildlife prompted the Interior Department to reintroduce Colonel Young's draft bill through Congressman Lacey on March 18, 1902, along with other evidence indicating the need for expanded protection of the Jackson Hole area. The fact that Representative John F. Lacey, in addition to being the chairman of the House Committee on Public Lands, was also interested in the preservation of wildlife within the forest reserves was not overlooked by officials backing the park extension legislation. Therefore, the Secretary included, with the draft bill, an extract of the December 1901 report by Army scouts Morrison and Holt indicating only 22 bison remained in Yellowstone National Park. This herd comprised *"...8 bulls, 10 cows, and 4 calves."* [24]

Struthers Burt once observed, *"...there is nothing more disheartening than to try to talk straight forwardness to a politician..."* [25], and such was the case with the 57th Congress. Despite the demonstration of the need for wildlife protection in the region south of Yellowstone, no park extension legislation was obtained.

Although the idea of park status for the Jackson Hole region never really died, 16 years would pass before legislation would again be introduced to extend Yellowstone National Park's boundaries to the south.

S. N. Leek Collection, American Heritage Center, University of Wyoming, ah03138_2035

Town of Jackson, 1907, Population - 59

17

Transportation for tourism and survival

During the summer, tourists and mail were delivered by stagecoach that operated between Victor, Idaho and Jackson. The stage operated into the 1930s.

(right) Clay Seaton, Bob Crisp, and Ray Ferrin on the stage, 1924

Donald Hough Photo 1958.0516.001P

(left) Ray H. Osborne, a freighter from St. Anthony, Idaho, hauled supplies to Moran over the Marysville road with a six-horse team pulling a tandem wagon.

Harrison Crandall Photo: 2006.0048.001

1958.0484.001

(right) The Nethercott Ferry near Wilson was the most reliable crossing of the Snake River south of Menor's Ferry.

1993.4996.011

(left) The roadhouse at the top of Teton Pass provided a welcome rest stop for winter travelers.

All Photos: Jackson Hole Historical Society and Museum

CHAPTER TWO

1902-1916

There is not a valuable future asset in the West today, not a lake or a watershed or a forest, the conservation of which is necessary to the health and wealth and security of future generations which is not in danger from forces who do not care a snap of their fingers for future generations so long as they can gut and fell and dam and fill their own pockets. [1]

Struthers Burt 1924

National Archives 6a150604u

Jackson Lake and the Teton Range from near the lake's outlet- 1890. (Prior to the construction of the Jackson Lake Dam.)

Although no legislation was introduced during the period of 1903 through 1917 to obtain park status for the Jackson Hole region, events occurred that affected future efforts to protect the area. Some of these events were detrimental to the scenic beauty of the valley, and they are significant for two reasons. One, they would provide vivid evidence that additional protection was absolutely necessary to protect the area's scenic values, and two, some areas were so horribly impacted as to exclude them, temporarily, from consideration for park status.

∽

Jackson Hole Historical Society and Museum 1958.0386.001p
Deloney's first store in Jackson and Walter Spicer's garage behind. Walt's garage is now the Jackson Hole Playhouse.

William Charles "Pap" and Clara "Burton" Deloney

Deloney was the first supervisor of the Teton Forest Reserve, and he also opened the first mercantile store in Jackson. Deloney, a Civil War veteran who served in Company B, Twenty-ninth Michigan Infantry, moved to Wyoming in 1887. The family moved to Jackson Hole when he was appointed supervisor of the reserve. He resigned the position because of injuries sustained fighting a forest fire.[3]

On May 22, 1902, President Theodore Roosevelt signed a proclamation changing the name of the Yellowstone Park Timber Land Reserve to the Yellowstone Forest Reserve. The proclamation added lands to both the Teton and Yellowstone reserves and transferred some land from the Yellowstone Forest Reserve to the Teton Forest Reserve. This Executive Order resulted in a total of 1,809,280 acres in the Yellowstone Forest Reserve and 4,127,360 acres in the Teton Forest Reserve. At that time, the Teton Forest Reserve was the largest forest reserve in Wyoming.[2]

In January of 1903, Theodore Roosevelt signed another proclamation combining the Absaroka and Teton Forest Reserves with the Yellowstone Forest Reserve under the latter name. The Yellowstone Forest Reserve now contained 8,329,200 acres. This was the largest forest reserve in the United States surrounding Yellowstone National Park on all sides and covering about 9,500 square miles in Idaho, Montana, and Wyoming. In addition to being the largest forest reserve, it also *"...provided the inspiration and basic plan for the development of all our national forest reserves."* [4]

A. A. Anderson, an artist-rancher, was given charge of the enlarged Yellowstone Forest Reserve, and he created four divisions: Shoshone, Absaroka, Teton and Wind River with a ranger responsible for each division.* Each ranger reported to Anderson, who, in turn, reported to the General Land Office, Department of the Interior.

*The Teton Division would later become Teton National Forest. When Grand Teton National Park was eventually established, it included portions of this national forest.

Since June of 1897, the Department of the Interior had operated a Division of Forestry that was part of the General Land Office and administered the Department's responsibilities concerning the reserves in the Jackson Hole-Yellowstone region. The Division of Forestry was a duplication of a similar agency within the Department of Agriculture.* The American Forest Congress, an organization composed of state and federal land management personnel, conservationists, and commercial interests, believed this arrangement to be inefficient. In January 1905, they sponsored a bill to combine the two forestry agencies. The unified support from such a broad spectrum interest group convinced Congress in February 1905 to pass what was commonly called the Transfer Act of 1905 (33 Stat. 628). This act created the National Forest Service under the Department of Agriculture.[6] Thus, control of the Forest Reserves was transferred from the Interior Department to the Department of Agriculture. The areas previously called Forest Reserves were renamed National Forests. As an example, President Roosevelt signed Executive Order 872 on July 1, 1908, abolishing the Yellowstone Forest Reserve and in its place created the Teton, Absaroka, Shoshone, and Targhee National Forests.[7] Northwestern Wyoming has the distinction of being the birthplace of both the National Park Service and the National Forest Service.[8] The Teton Division would later become Teton National Forest. When Grand Teton National Park was eventually established, it included portions of this national forest.

At the time of the transfer of the forest lands from the Department of the Interior to the Department of Agriculture, Robert E. Miller was the superintendent of the Teton Division of the enlarged Yellowstone Forest Reserve. He received his appointment as the third superintendent of the Teton Forest Reserve on August 20, 1902,† and retained the position when the area was transferred to the Agriculture Department and became a national forest.

Under Miller's supervision, some public lands within Jackson Hole were scarred by timbering operations, but the greatest visual destruction resulted from the damming of lakes and streams. Although the congressional mandate of the Forest Service provided for a multiple use concept, with an emphasis on utilization, the blame for the destruction of the scenic values of the lakes and

American Heritage Center, University of Wyoming ah11728_34

Robert Miller- c. 1893.

Miller first visited Jackson Hole as a trapper in 1882. He returned to make a home in 1885, buying a one-room cabin from Teton Jackson, a self-acclaimed outlaw. He seemed to have been a successful trapper as he and W. F. Arneon took 160 furs from the Ditch Creek drainage in 12 days in 1886. By 1904, he was grazing several hundred head of cattle on the forest reserve. He was the first in the valley to file an entry request under the "desert claim" provision of the Homestead Act, and he established the first bank (Jackson State Bank) in the town of Jackson in 1914. As a banker, he earned the nickname "Twelve Percent Miller," as that was the interest rate he charged for loans. Miller would in later years assume a strong anti-park extension position in Jackson Hole, but during his years as superintendent, he was busy building his empire in the valley. His land is now part of the National Elk Refuge and his home is preserved as a historical monument by the Teton County Historical Society. Miller served as superintendent for 16 years, resigning on June 30, 1918[9]

---

*The Department of Agriculture's Division of Forestry was established in 1881 with an appropriation of $2000. Although this division was responsible for investigating timbering practices, the actual control of all public forest lands was with the Department of the Interior.[5]

†The first superintendent of the Teton Forest Reserve was Charles "Pap" Deloney and the second was W. Armor Thompson.

streams in Jackson Hole rested with the Department of the Interior. There were two circumstances most responsible for the visual impact of scenic areas in the valley. Both of these were beyond the control of the Forest Service. In fact, the consumptive practices allowed under the utilization ethic of the Forest Service were almost insignificant by comparison.

~

Prior to the establishment of the National Forest Service, the Reclamation Service (which was then a part of the U.S. Geological Survey, which was an agency of the Department of the Interior) began to look at Jackson Lake with the view of a future dam. The Reclamation Service managed an irrigation facility in southern Idaho called the Minidoka Project. Officials of this facility realized the operational capacity of the Minidoka Dam would soon be reached because of the increased development of irrigation in Idaho and the soon to be constructed Twin Falls North Side (irrigation) Project. It was, therefore, evident that additional storage facilities would be needed, and Jackson Lake was the first to be selected.

By the fall of 1905, the initial surveys had been completed, and the outlet of the lake had been selected as the dam site. The construction plans for the dam were completed early in 1906. The plan called for the erection of a temporary timber dam that would raise the level of the lake 10 feet providing a storage capacity of 350,000-acre-feet of water.[10] This would presumably supply the expanded irrigation needs for four or five years at which time a permanent and larger dam would be constructed, most probably downstream.[11]*

Floyd Bous Photo: Jackson Hole Historical Society and Museum, p19580795001

Survey crew maps Jackson Lake for the Temporary Jackson Lake Dam- 1903.

According to the U.S. Reclamation Service 1903 annual report, 47,671,616 acres of Wyoming's 62,448,000 total acres were unappropriated and unsurveyed. Uinta County, which at the time encompassed what would eventually be split to accommodate the creation of Lincoln and Teton Counties, being a narrow strip of territory along the entire length of Wyoming's western boundary (including Yellowstone National Park), contained nearly 9,000,000 acres. Approximately 2,000,000 acres were already appropriated for Yellowstone Park. Of the remaining 7,000,000 acres, 5,233,536 acres were unsurveyed and unappropriated.

National Archives. Neg. No. 95-G-152701

Hauling supplies from Ashton, Idaho on the Marysville road

---

*In recent years, new residents to the valley frequently question why Wyoming allowed Idaho to appropriate control of the waters of the Snake River drainage. As with many issues in this narrative, it is necessary to step back in time to grasp a fair understanding of the logic and motivations of people who made decisions as much as a century ago. From the point of view of 1903, the congressional representatives of neither state could envision that there would ever be an appreciable settlement in Jackson Hole. Tourism and recreation had not yet manifested themselves as an economic force in the valley. Nor was there a conspicuous rush of settlers to this remote valley with its harsh climate, poor agricultural soils and short growing season. It seemed obvious that Wyoming could not use the water and Wyoming acquiesced to Idaho's request for a storage facility on Jackson Lake.

In June of 1906, the Union Pacific Railroad extended its lines to Ashton, Idaho, allowing freight for the dam construction to be brought to Moran, Wyoming (a community near the outlet of Jackson Lake), over the Ashton road north of Jackson Lake.* The terrain of this road was easier for horse-drawn wagons than the mountain pass, 30 miles south of Jackson Lake's natural outlet. Don Taylor, Ray Shinkle, and W. C. Shinkle hauled nails, steel, cement, hay and grain from Ashton while the lumber for this dam came from Jackson Hole.[12] According to John Markham, the lumber was sawed by *"....J. W. (Bill) Woodward in a water powered saw mill owned by Coffman and Barker in Phillips Canyon, just north of Wilson, Wyoming."*[12] He described the freight wagons as *"...Studebaker wagons with a length of 14 feet; width of 3 feet 8 inches, and having side boards from 3 feet to 3 feet 6 inches high so wagons had a cubic measure of nearly 180 cubic feet. The wagons could haul up to 9 tons, but loads greater were hauled in two or more wagons in tandem or trailing behind the lead wagon."*[13]

Construction of the dam began in July 1906 under the direction of D. W. Ross, the supervising engineer. The plans called for:

...a rock filled crib base 185 feet long faced upstream with a double row of sheet piling and surmounted by a framed super-structure 15 feet high, supporting 25 gate openings. The timber abutments were to be flanked at either end by low earthen embankments, 1500 feet long and 0 to 13 feet high at the north end, their crests being 19 feet above low water level of the lake.[14]

In order for such a dam to be constructed, the outflow of the lake had to be controlled. Therefore, a cofferdam of shrubs, small trees, and gravel was constructed upstream to divert the water. This diversion dam was 230 feet long and 20 feet wide at the top. After the cofferdam had been constructed, a delay of several months resulted because of right-of-way negotiations for the area to be flooded.[17] Upon settlement of the right-of-way problem, construction began on the crib section. The center section, built first, was floated to the desired position, and sunk by filling it with rocks. During the remaining construction season, the *"... entire crib foundation ... was ... placed and partially filled with rock, a double row of sheet piles was driven along the upstream face, the superstructure on the gate section was*

Minidoka Project Archives, Bureau of Reclamation, Burley, Idaho
The Jackson Lake log crib dam completed in 1908

Adjusted for inflation, the cost of constructing the temporary Jackson Lake Dam would be equivalent to approximately $700,000 in 2010 dollars.

*Today the road is called the Ashton road or the Grassy Lake road. At the time of the dam construction, it was called the Marysville road.

completed, and 500 feet of the south embankment was partly finished...." [18] When work on the dam was abandoned for the winter on December 24, the cofferdam was cut to allow lake waters to flow normally during the winter.

Work was scheduled to begin again in May, but the crews were unable to close the cofferdam. They were not successful until mid-September. Despite this setback, an enlarged workforce enabled considerable progress to be made on the dam that summer. When work was abandoned in November for the winter, only one month's labor was required in the following summer of 1908 to complete the dam. On July 2, 1908, the gates were lowered, and sufficient water was stored to provide for additional irrigation in August. The cost of the temporary Jackson Lake Dam was distributed as follows:

Buildings and quarters	$ 361.91
Crib dam and embankment	5,770.73
General expense-engineering	715.79
Right-of-way	3,056.69
Road building	297.91
	$30,203.03[17]

The effects of the Jackson Lake storage facility were advantageous to the irrigation companies in Idaho but provided little benefit to the Jackson Hole area. The storage capacity of the temporary dam was greater than needed for the Minidoka Project. The excess, 155,000-acre-feet, was sold to the Twin Falls North Side Land and Water Company and the American Falls Canal and Power Company.[18] The elevated lake waters flooded a historically significant area at the north end of the lake. Traditional Indian campsites, as well as the historical trail used by trappers and Indians to gain access to Conant Pass, were inundated. The greatest visual impact, however, resulted from the failure of the engineers to remove the trees and other vegetation from the area to be flooded. What had once been a view of pristine beauty was reduced to a vision of dead and rotting trees and the smell of decaying vegetation. Never again would the valley of Jackson Hole be free of the influence and impact of the Idaho irrigation interests.

The shoreline of Jackson Lake, marred by the rising water behind the dam, was considered an eye-sore that complicated and delayed the lake's inclusion in a national park.

Grand Teton National Park GRTE-00430_250

J.E. Stimson Photo: 1931 Jackson Hole Historical Society and Museum P1958.1466.001

Jackson Hole Historical Society and Museum p1958.1465.001

Jackson Hole Historical Society & Museum 1958.1464.001

One year after the completion of the Jackson Lake Dam, it was discovered that considerable damage had occurred to the crib foundation of the dam. The dam was supposedly repaired that fall by dumping 3300 cubic yards of rock at the toe of the structure.[19] On July 5, 1910, ten days before the stored water would be needed in Idaho, the center portion of the cribwork failed, releasing a flood of 194,000-acre-feet of stored water, flowing at 10,000 cubic feet per second. One Reclamation Service official stated that *"A small amount of damage resulted to several local bridges and a ferry, 40 miles below the dam."* [20] This official evidently failed to appreciate that the bridges and the ferries offered the only safe and reliable links between the eastern and western portions of the valley. Therefore, any adverse impact on the residents' ability to cross the Snake River was of greater than just passing significance. The damage to crops in Idaho by the failure of the dam was minimized by carefully manipulating the water in the equalizing reservoir at the Minidoka diversion dam.[21]

Jackson Hole Historical Society and Museum 1958.0995.001

Town of Moran with Frank Lovell's toll bridge prior to the construction of the Jackson Lake Dam, c. 1904.

An inspection of the broken dam revealed the timbers had rotted, and reconstruction of the missing section would provide, at best, an unsafe structure. It was decided at that time to initiate the construction of a permanent dam. Although three potential sites for a permanent dam were determined at the time of the original survey of the lake, the final selection had been postponed. Site one was at Moran near the outlet of the lake, essentially the site of the temporary dam. Site two was several miles downstream and was called the Conrad Dam Site.* The third was at the confluence of Pacific Creek and the Snake River. If the temporary dam had not failed, the Conrad and Pacific Creek Dam Sites might have received more consideration during the selection process in 1910. Both provided a narrower span of the river and better geology for anchoring the dam. The Pacific Creek site would have captured runoff from that drainage and provided considerably more area for storage. Because the Reclamation Service felt a need to have a storage

Minidoka Project Archives, Bureau of Reclamation, Burley, Idaho

Center section failure of the Jackson Lake Dam-1910

*According to historian John Daugherty, the Conrad site was the location of an early ferry constructed and operated by James Conrad to facilitate the transportation of supplies across the Snake River to the Whetstone Mine. The ferry operated for only a short time in 1897, but Conrad homesteaded 157 acres at the site. He received title to the land in 1902.

Demolition of the remaining log crib dam in preparation for construction of the 1910 dam

facility for the 1911 irrigation season, the Moran Site was selected as being the most expedient. Also, the failure of the temporary dam forced the engineers to make another construction decision based on the required early completion date. This decision concerned the height of the new dam.

According to the original survey, a dam could be built at any of the three sites which could raise the level of the lake as much as 72 feet storing nearly 1,500,000-acre-feet of water. The decision, based on time and available appropriations, was to build a dam that would raise the level of the lake a total of 18 feet, storing 380,000-acre-feet of water.[22] By the fall of 1910, construction crews were working on the new dam. The Ashton road was again used to transport supplies, equipment and men to the dam site while the purchase of supplies and services from the Ashton merchants created an economic boom for that Mormon community.

Because the plans called for construction to continue through the winter, large quantities of supplies had to be transported to Moran before the winter snows closed the road. The Reclamation Service realized that the construction crews would be completely isolated once the road was closed, and they had a telephone line installed from Ashton to Moran. A four-man crew cleared the right-of-way and strung the 70-mile line as they went, attaching the line to trees in heavily timbered areas. Due to strong winds or heavy snow loads, the line rarely worked that fall and did not work at all during the winter.[23]

During the winter of 1910-1911, work on the dam was continuous with day and night shifts. Gradually the tons of supplies which had been hauled from Ashton and stored in government buildings at Moran merged into a new and permanent dam. Despite the severe and undesirable working conditions, the Reclamation Service encountered relatively few labor problems. Once the crews were snowed in, it was impossible for them to leave and work was the only activity available. Therefore, the only loss of personnel resulted from illness, injury and death except for two men, the cook and his helper, who were fired for homosexual activity.[24]

In general, the dam and the work crews were not well liked by the residents of Moran, which combined with the lack of communication with the outside world and infrequent mail service, added to the isolation. Such isolation was advantageous to the early completion of the structure. Before spring arrived, the dam was complete. All

Jackson Hole Historical Society and Museum p19581641001
First permanent Dam, 1910-1911

Its $453,300 construction costs would equal approximately $10,472,425 in 2010 dollars.

Jackson Lake Dam
Enlargement Project

This view is looking
northeast. The tent camp
for the workers can be
seen in the background.

that remained was excavation work on the channel between the dam and the lake plus some fill work on the dikes.[25] It was during this last phase of construction that the first mail of the winter arrived at Moran. It was delivered by Absalom Nace who had snowshoed from St. Anthony, Idaho, over Teton Pass to Jackson and then to Moran.[26] Elliot Paul,* in his book *Desperate Scenery*, described Nace on this occasion.

> *If he had been dumber, he could not have made that perilous first trip into The Hole that Spring, and if he had been smarter he would have refused to undertake it. His cheekbones were frozen and discolored and his lips were running sores, having been split, frostbitten, thawed and resplit a score or more of times.*[27]

Included in that first mail delivery was a telegram from Director Newell of the Reclamation Service to Frank Crowe, the head engineer, requesting cost estimates for raising the dam ten additional feet, thus increasing the storage capacity of the lake to an estimated one million acre feet.[28] In August of 1910, Norman Torrance, the assistant engineer and designer of the dam that had just been completed, and Frank Crowe† had attempted to persuade Reclamation officials to approve

a structure similar to the one Newell asked about in his telegram. Because their earlier recommendation had been refused,‡ the approved structure completed, and because everyone was anxious to leave the valley, Director Newell's telegram was not happily received.

The total cost of the 1910-1911 construction was $453,300.[29] Torrance and Crowe knew the proposed enlargement project would be more expensive than the original construction because it would require the demolition of portions of the newly completed dam. They estimated a cost of $850,000 to enlarge the dam.[30]

Minidoka Project Archives, Bureau of Reclamation, Burley, Idaho
A Henry I gasoline dinkey powered by a Ford engine hauled gravel.

---

*Elliot Paul (1891-1958) became a celebrated writer of books and screenplays. Among his better-known works are *The Last Time I Saw Paris*, *The Black Gardenia: A Hollywood Murder Mystery*, and *That Crazy American Music*.
†Frank Crowe would later gain acclaim as the head engineer for the Boulder (Hoover) Dam construction project.
‡The larger structure was refused in August 1910 because the Reclamation Fund was low. Prospects for more money seemed doubtful due to opposition by some eastern congressmen to the large sums of money then being spent to develop arid lands in the West. Newell sent his telegram after additional funds had been obtained.

The Reclamation Service was obviously aware of the previous efforts to include the Jackson Hole area into Yellowstone National Park, and that park status would prohibit the Jackson Lake Enlargement Project. Elliot Paul implied in his book that the Reclamation Service actively sought to discourage any efforts to extend the Yellowstone Nation-

Minidoka Project Archives, Bureau of Reclamation

A general view of the dam and camp from the quarry- 1916

al Park boundaries by convincing the community of Ashton that their economic boom would continue if the enlargement project was approved. It was suggested that the leaders of that Mormon community could, through the leaders of their church in Salt Lake City, convince the Utah Congressional delegation to join the Idaho Congressional Delegation in opposing any park extension plans which would affect the enlargement project.[31]

During the summer of 1911, water was stored behind the Jackson Lake Dam, but the Reclamation Service elected not to fill the lake completely. The reasons for not filling the lake to capacity are not clear, but the decision may have been made in anticipation of the start of the enlargement project. However, construction did not begin in 1911. The construction season of 1912 also passed without the initiation of the enlargement project. The reason for the delay was not due to the lack of authority as Congress had provided for such activities in the Reclamation Act of 1902 (32 Stat., 388). The motives of the Reclamation Service concerning the Jackson Lake Storage Facility are again unclear, but the Warren Act, passed in February of 1911 (36 Stat., 925), may have influenced their decision to delay the project. That Act allowed the United States to enter into contracts whereby private investors would finance such projects as the Jackson Lake Enlargement Project. It was, therefore, possible, if the investors could be found, for the Reclamation Service to enlarge the Jackson Lake Dam without depleting the Reclamation Fund.[32]

American Heritage Center, University of Wyoming. Neg. No. 24130

Left to right: Margaret, Ben Jr., Morrow, and Ben Sheffield, Sr., 1918

Ben moved from Oregon to Montana Territory trailing a herd of sheep. He guided his first hunting expedition into Jackson Hole in 1890. Eventually, he established an outfitting business at Moran that expanded to rental cabins and a hotel. His hunting guide service attracted wealthy European noblemen and American sportsmen.

In February 1913, the Reclamation Service entered into such a contract with the Kuhn Irrigation and Canal Company and the Twin Falls Canal Company.[33] The investors agreed to contribute to the project in the proportions of 61/80ths by the Kuhn Irrigation and Canal Company and 19/80ths by the Twin Falls Canal Company.[34] The stored water was to be shared in the same proportions. It was decided to begin construction on the project early in the summer of 1913.

Permits were filed with the Wyoming State Engineer for the additional storage of water, and a sawmill was erected near the dam site. The trees for the mill were cut on the Moose Creek drainage and with the use of Mundy single drum reversible steam hoist mounted on a logging scow 44 feet by 20 feet by 4 feet, the logs were towed across the lake.[35]

Construction was halted when, on July 8, 1913, word was received to stop work on the project. The Kuhn Irrigation and Canal Company had

Minidoka Project Archives, Bureau of Reclamation

The *Titanic*, a side-wheeler logging scow, towed logs across Jackson Lake.

experienced financial problems and was unable to pay its share of the construction costs.[36] An additional complication developed in August when the Wyoming State Engineer notified the Reclamation Service that action on the storage permit was being withheld because residents of Jackson Hole had petitioned him to reject the permit. They wanted the Reclamation Service to make suitable provisions for bridges across the Snake River before the permits were approved. The concern of the residents resulted from the discharge practice of the Jackson Lake Dam officials. Typically, large volumes of water were released sporadically to reduce the opportunity for intermediate irrigators to divert water to which they were not entitled. The released water was then stored at the Minidoka Dam for use by the project's participatory irrigators. The sporadic discharges caused damage to the existing bridges and ferries and made fording the river dangerous.

The Reclamation Service was aware of this problem and had taken steps to rectify the situation by supporting a bill (S. 3947) that was

Jackson Hole Historical Society and Museum p1993.4376.015

Digging the Flat Creek irrigation ditch
While the Federal Government built the Jackson Lake Dam in Wyoming to aid Idaho farmers, the local homesteaders, without federal assistance, had to dig irrigation ditches to provide water from sources other than Jackson Lake and the Snake River.

The completed Jackson Lake Dam

approved by Congress in March of 1913. S. 3947 provided for the construction of the Jackson Hole Highway Bridge. The bill provided that three-fourths of the cost of the bridge should be supplied from the Reclamation Fund and one-fourth by Lincoln County.* Evidently some of the residents of the valley wanted the Reclamation Service to pay the total cost of the bridge.

When the construction season closed for the winter, the staff at the dam was reduced to three people, S. R. Wilson, R. W. Miller, and F. E. Menaugh. The end of the season left the Reclamation Service facing three problems: the rejected water storage permit from the state engineer, the deficient financial support for the enlargement project, and the refusal of Ben Sheffield, a Moran resident, to allow work crews to cross his land which stopped all work on the south side of the dam.[37]

In January 1914, the Wyoming State Engineer gave the Reclamation Service 30 days to show cause why the permits, which provided for the enlargement of the Jackson Lake Reservoir, should not be rejected. The Reclamation Service failed to respond, and the permits were denied in February. The Reclamation Service then filed an appeal from the State Engineer's actions. In June,

the private companies interested in the construction project agreed to pay Lincoln County's share of the bridge construction, and the State Engineer approved the construction permit for the dam.[38]

In spring, when the financial problems that had delayed work during the previous season had been resolved, the Reclamation Service resumed negotiations with Ben Sheffield for the portion of his land which was needed to construct a bridge across the Snake River immediately downstream from the dam. Because of the construction process, it was impossible to transport equipment and men to the south side across the top of the dam. It was likewise impossible to ford the river below the dam during the discharge of stored water. A bridge was the only option to provide consistent and safe access to both sides of the dam. Sheffield was offered $10,000 for two lots containing 63.02 acres upon which his buildings were located, and a tract of 1.15 acres that was needed for a road. This offer allowed Sheffield one year to remove his buildings.[39] He refused the offer and the Reclamation Service advised him of the possibility of condemnation proceedings. In the early morning hours on May 31, the Reclamation Service sawmill was destroyed by a mysterious fire. The cause of the fire was never determined, but it

---

*Teton County had not yet been established. Jackson Hole was part of Lincoln County.

Dedication of the Jackson Hole Highway Bridge (Wilson Bridge) constructed by the Bureau of Reclamation, 1915

appeared that the fire started at the farthest point from the boilers. The Reclamation Service never openly accused any of the Moran residents of arson, but from that time, the Service employed two watchmen to guard the construction site. The total damage resulting from the fire was estimated to be $4,700.[40]

After Sheffield's refusal of the offer, a suit, *United States v. B.D. Sheffield* was filed in the Federal Court at Cheyenne, Wyoming to condemn only the land necessary (22.15 acres) for the continued construction of the enlargement project. Less than a month after the fire, the court gave the United States immediate possession on the condition that $1,107.50 be deposited with the clerk of the court to cover any damage to the

defendant.[41] The eventual settlement received by Sheffield for the loss of his property involved the right of entry and use of other federal lands adjacent to his remaining property.[42]

By the end of the 1914 construction season, considerable progress had been made on the enlargement project. The Reclamation Service had hired 480 men during the peak season and had established a coal mine on Lava Creek which fired the boilers for the steam driven equipment.[43]

During the 1915 construction season, the work crews advanced the enlargement project considerably, and the Jackson Hole Highway Bridge was completed. Also, the Reclamation Service began purchasing supplies from Jackson Hole residents instead of Ashton merchants. This, along with the

Safer, more reliable, and providing year-round ability to cross the Snake River, the Jackson Hole Highway Bridge near Wilson was a significant improvement for valley residents.

new bridge quieted much of the local animosity toward the enlargement project.

On November 18, 1915, the appeal that had been filed a year and a half previously concerning the rejection of permits 84/356 and 94/117 was argued before the Wyoming Board of Control. The state engineer had approved a permit (No. 2659 Res.) allowing the continued construction of the dam when the bridge problem was settled, but the original permits were needed to allow for the increase in storage capacity of the reservoir, and to allow the flooding of additional land.[44] The Wyoming Board of Control reversed the action of the state engineer and restored the original permits to good standing.

The Jackson Lake Enlargement Project was completed in 1916. The enlarged dam raised the level of the lake a total of 35 feet, storing 790,000-acre-feet of water. In the 1920s, the dam was raised four more feet. The additional four feet, combined with a dredging project in 1917, provided a storage capacity of 847,000-acre-feet. As with the previous construction projects on Jackson Lake, the Reclamation Service failed to clear the flooded area of vegetation causing a tremendous scar on a beautiful valley. Owen Wister (author of *The Virginian*) would later remark:

> *...that disgusting dam. There is more beauty in Jackson's Hole than even such a beastly thing could kill; but it has destroyed the august serenity of the lake's outlet forever; and has defaced and degraded the shores of the lake where once the pines grew green and dark. They stand now white skeletons drowned by the rising level of the water.*[45]

The other significant impact inflicted on the land that would later become a part of Grand Teton National Park was predestined in 1894 when Congress passed the Carey Act. The Carey Act was introduced by Wyoming Senator Joseph M. Carey.* The act withheld from public entry, for the purpose of homesteading, about one million acres of arid and semi-arid land, much of it in the Jackson Hole country. It granted to private companies, where the government did not wish

to act, the right to provide water for the withheld land if it was too difficult for an individual or group of individuals to provide for their own irrigation. Such projects usually required a great deal of capital investment by the companies that operated under the act. Once the irrigation ditches and canals had been constructed, the land was opened for homesteading. The homesteaders had to pay an annual rental for the water they received, plus the cost of land improvement, their initial investment for supplies and equipment. The source of the water was, of course, the lakes and streams of that particular area. In Jackson Hole, this meant impounding the waters of the streams and scenic

wyoarchives.state.wy.us via Wikimedia Commons

Joseph Maull Carey(R)(P)
(1845-1924)

Carey was born in Milton, Delaware, and earned a law degree from the University of Pennsylvania at Philadelphia. After being admitted to the bar in 1864, he moved west and became the first United States Attorney for the Territory of Wyoming. He served in that capacity from 1869 to 1871. From 1871 to 1876, he was an Associate Justice of the Supreme Court of the Territory of Wyoming. After retiring from the bench in 1876, he became a rancher and later entered politics. He was elected mayor of Cheyenne (1881 to 1885) and then served in the U.S. House of Representatives representing the Territory of Wyoming from 1885 to 1890. When Wyoming became a state, he was elected to the Senate (1890 to 1895). He re-entered politics in 1911 and successfully ran for Governor. He later served as Vice President of the Federal Land Bank and as a member of the Board of Trustees of the University of Wyoming. He died in Cheyenne at the age of 79.

---

*Joseph M. Carey was the only registered Republican elected as Governor of Wyoming on a Democratic ticket.

lakes that had previously added to the unique charm of the valley.

Although the bill was passed with the best of intentions, Secretary of the Interior Lane would later find that *"...99 percent of all private irrigation schemes had to be taken over by the government because they were either fraudulent or inefficient."* [46] The author of the bill, along with seven other Wyoming men, established the Wyoming Development Company, which became the third Carey Act project in the state of Wyoming. As if to verify the findings of Secretary Lane, by 1951, the Wyoming Development Company, lost $1,622,687, although the community it served, Wheatland, Wyoming prospered.[47]

In accordance with the Carey Act, and with the blessings of the state of Wyoming, a Cheyenne company obtained damming privileges in Jackson Hole on the Buffalo Fork River and Spread Creek in 1909 and on the Gros Ventre River in 1912. This irrigation company was supposed to provide water for homesteads on the northeastern side of the valley, but, like all other Carey Act irrigation projects in

Grand Teton National Park GRTE 430 01 50-042A
The dam on Spread Creek authorized by the Carey Act.

Grand Teton National Park GRTE-00430_52-52A

The dam on Two Ocean Lake

S. N. Leek Collection American Heritage Center, University of Wyoming ah03139_1050

The east end of the Jackson Hole Highway Bridge washed out in the high runoff of 1916. Cross-valley transportation was divided by the river for a time with the exception of a cable car from the end of the bridge to the shore.

the area seemed more interested in selling water to the irrigation interests in Idaho.[48] The irrigation needs of homesteaders in Jackson Hole were sometimes cited, but the underlying motives primarily focused on Idaho irrigation needs. It was anticipated that due to the soil condition, the climate, and the altitude, many of the homesteads would fail, thus providing greater portions of the stored water for sale to Idaho. Some evidence exists to indicate that at least one of the irrigation companies anticipated selling the water twice.[49]

The Osgood Land and Livestock Company of Idaho and the Utah-Idaho Sugar Company did not try to hide the fact that their projects were designed to supply Idaho with additional water. These companies, acting within the Carey Act, obtained permission from the Wyoming State Engineer to impound Emma Matilda and Two Ocean Lakes. Eventually, the residents of the valley began to apply pressure on state officials to curb the activities of the irrigation projects, and the state finally revoked the damming privileges in the 1930s. The dams on Emma Matilda and Two Ocean Lakes were not removed until that area was included in Grand Teton National Park in 1950.[50]

In his book, *Diary of a Dude-Wrangler,* Struthers Burt devoted many pages to the disfiguring impact by the irrigation companies on the scenic lakes in Jackson Hole. As a resident of the valley, he offered the following observation:

The great and beautiful lake [Jackson Lake] twenty miles north of our upper ranch is the best example I know ... an example so good that it is constantly being used as an object-lesson by enemies of stupid spoliation. Here is one of the most beautiful lakes in the world, eighteen miles long, snow-capped mountains to the west of it, a lake that in a few years, possibly a generation, would have been as famous and profitable as the Italian lakes, and yet it has been ruined forever unless the dam that holds it is broken down or forced to keep its contents at an even level. All around its shores, gaunt trees, millions of feet of them, stand up like skeletons. After a while, of course, these trees will disappear, but twenty feet or so of evil-smelling mud that marks the recession of the waters will never disappear.

The Swiss, the Canadians, the Norwegians, all wise nations who know the value of scenery, would laugh at us for the fools that we are.[51]

Jackson Hole Historical Society and Museum hs0603

"A liver pill sign on the Statue of Liberty could not be as terrible a desecration as this."
Senator John Kendrick, 1922

CHAPTER THREE
1915-1919

...here was one of America's greatest scenic areas and as it was the policy of Congress to protect the supreme natural features of our country in national parks it seemed inevitable that this region must become a park.

Horace M. Albright[1]

One of God's chosen spots where Nature revealed herself in all her glory, and with a view of Rocky Mountain peaks that would inspire a man to be a hero, if he was born a rogue.

Edith Sargent
New York Times, 1913

Jackson Hole Historical Society and Museum 1958.0943.001p

Edith Sargent playing the violin at the Sargent homestead on Jackson Lake.

As early as 1907, the military superintendents of Yellowstone suggested the introduction of a civilian force to operate the Park.[2] The military believed the attitudes of the residents around the Park and the visitors within the Park had changed since 1886, and the Army was no longer fighting poaching to the degree necessitating military involvement. By 1915, the troops were checking cars, registering tourists, working on roads, stocking streams with fish and, in general, performing duties outside the "protective" scope of the Act of March 3, 1883, that had introduced them into Yellowstone.[3] In fact, it was sometimes argued that their presence within the Park was largely illegal.

After a great deal of controversy, Congress passed, and President Woodrow Wilson signed, an act establishing the National Park Service on August 25, 1916 (39 Stat. 535). Stephen T. Mather* was appointed Director of the Park Service by Secretary Franklin K. Lane, and Yellowstone National Park was officially transferred from the War Department to the National Park Service in October.

The news of the transfer was not received well by a number of Montana communities located near the Park. They had become accustomed to a certain amount of revenue associated with

Stephen T. Mather touring Yellowstone National Park

Yellowstone National Park Archives

the military, and although their Senators, Thomas J. Walsh and H. L. Meyers protested the transfer loudly, their protests were too late to stop the exit of troops from Yellowstone.

In the next session of Congress, the Montana delegation used their influence to attach a provision to the sundry civil bill for the fiscal year 1918 prohibiting the use of the Yellowstone Park appropriation for the civilian protection of the Park. It provided for park protection to be accomplished only by the military. The Department of the Interior and the War Department protested this provision because the war with Germany required every soldier. Despite the logic of their argument, the bill, with its illogical provision, was passed.[4]

The Secretary of the Interior was faced with a decision to either close Yellowstone National Park completely or request troops. The troops were requested and upon the arrival of a squadron of the Seventh Cavalry in June 1917, the civilian ranger force† was dismissed. The civilian superintendent remained in Yellowstone to handle administrative details, but the joint occupancy of the Park was not successful.[5]

This time the soldiers, unhappy with their assignment, failed to impress the public with

www.fs.fed.us via Wikimedia Commons

Bob Marshall 1901-1939
Marshall was originally asked to lead the Park Service, but he declined. A forester by training, he is credited with founding the Wilderness Society.

---

*Stephen Mather was a special assistant to Interior Secretary Lane with responsibilities for establishing a separate bureau for national parks. Mather originally appointed Bob Marshall to head the agency, but Marshall resigned rather quickly, and Mather was persuaded to take the position himself.

†The ranger force included 21 soldiers who, by prior arrangement between the Department of the Interior and the War Department, had elected to remain in the Park as civilians.

Ben Sheffield's dining lodge at Moran as it looked in 1912. It burned in 1916.

their abilities, and the public began to question the propriety of troops in Yellowstone while their relatives were fighting a war. Also, a sergeant stationed in Yellowstone wrote a letter to the *New York Times* claiming that 450 combat trained men were performing peaceful duties which could be accomplished by 40 civilians.[6] Congress eventually recognized its folly and in 1918 withdrew the senseless provision from the appropriations act, allowing the civilian ranger force to be reintroduced.

~

In late 1914, when the military was trying to convince Congress to establish a civilian park agency, the Secretary of the Interior asked Stephen T. Mather to assume the job of Assistant to the Secretary of the Interior. Mather accepted the position and in January 1915 he was given the assignment of establishing a Bureau of National Parks.[7] This required an inventory of the existing national parks. That summer Mather and his assistant, Horace M. Albright, began a tour of the western parks.

Also that summer, Mather approved opening a portion of Yellowstone National Park to automobiles, as an experiment, and in September he and Albright made their first visit to Yellowstone. They drove as far south as Moran and immediately recognized the desirability of including the Tetons in the National Park System.

In July 1916, an official inspection tour of the Yellowstone region had been arranged and the dignitaries* gathered at Thermopolis, Wyoming. Automobiles were uncommon in many parts of Wyoming in 1916, so Albright arranged for cars to be brought from Denver for the tour. The original itinerary, in addition to a tour of Yellowstone

Because of the 1916 fire, Sheffield served meals in a tent.

---

*In addition to Albright and Mather, the official party included Huston Thompson, Assistant Attorney General; Alexander T. Vogelsang, First Assistant Secretary of the Interior; and George Purdy of Illinois, as well as their wives.[8]

National Park, included traveling south through the Jackson Hole region and exiting the valley through Hoback Canyon. Because of the unsafe road conditions in Hoback Canyon, the party did not travel farther south than Moran. The trip by automobile to Moran was difficult because the Reclamation Service had flooded the road when they built the Jackson Lake Dam. The party had to make their way through the timber from Lizard Creek to Moran.[9]*

The group stayed overnight at Moran with Ben Sheffield.[10] Sheffield operated a big game hunting camp and was the Moran postmaster. In the spring of 1916, a fire had destroyed his log dining room and post office, so the official guests dined in a large tent.[11] Albright recalled that:

> *The party was entranced by the Teton Range. After lunch we went out in a boat with Ben, and during the evening after dinner we sat and watched the twilight come over the mountains and finally the night shut out all details, but the sharp outline of the peaks still presented a magnificent horizon where mountains met sky.*[12]†

The official inspection party found time to meet with many state, county, and community representatives (none of whom represented Jackson Hole) who stressed the need and desire for improved roads and increased tourism. These meetings led the officials to believe that everyone in Wyoming wanted more roads. This assumption on the part of the National Park officials would later alienate some Jackson Hole residents and delay any cooperative effort to protect the Tetons.

During the winter of 1916-1917 several meetings were conducted between the National Park Service and the Wyoming Congressional Delegation. Senator Clark, Senator Warren and Representative Mondell agreed with the Park Service that recreation would be the most appropriate

utilization of the Jackson Hole region and agreed to support the appropriate legislation if a provision could be made for the *"...continuance of hunting under state authority...."*[13]

The agreed upon Yellowstone Park extension bill was initially delayed for a number of reasons. First, Stephen Mather suffered a nervous breakdown that winter and was hospitalized in a sanitarium near Philadelphia.[14] Secretary Lane then assigned the responsibility for all national parks to Horace Albright, who had been working on the Yellowstone Park extension. Second, the United States entered World War I on April 6, 1917, and appropriations for "nonessential" agencies were not of primary concern. A small

U.S. House of Representatives [Public domain] via Wikimedia Commons
Franklin Wheeler Mondell (R)
1860-1939

Wyoming Representative Frank Mondell introduced legislation to extend the boundaries of Yellowstone National Park to include the Teton Mountain Range and the smaller lakes at their base. He served as Wyoming's Representative in Congress from 1895-1897 and again from 1899-1923. He was majority leader in the 66th and 67th Congresses and chairman of the Republican National Convention in 1924.

---

*Upon returning to Washington, Mr. Mather met with Secretary Lane and Director Davis of the Reclamation Service concerning the road from Yellowstone to Moran. The Secretary ordered the Reclamation Service to allocate $10,000 to build a new road from Lizard Creek to the dam.

†Albright later maintained in an interview that the group did not stay overnight at Moran, but returned to Yellowstone that afternoon. The account presented above was recorded closer, chronologically, to the event, and Albright's description of viewing the Tetons at night could not have occurred if they had returned to Yellowstone earlier in the day. It seems equally unlikely the group would have attempted to drive back to Yellowstone after dark considering the hazardous road conditions described by Albright between Moran and Yellowstone during this tour.

deficiency appropriation was obtained in April 1917, but there was no money for expanded operations.[15]

A year later, Representative Mondell introduced H.R. 11661 in the 65th Congress, 2nd Session to extend the boundaries of Yellowstone National Park. The bill was then referred to the House Committee on Public Lands. In July Executive Order No. 2905 was issued withdrawing the public lands described in the bill from settlement

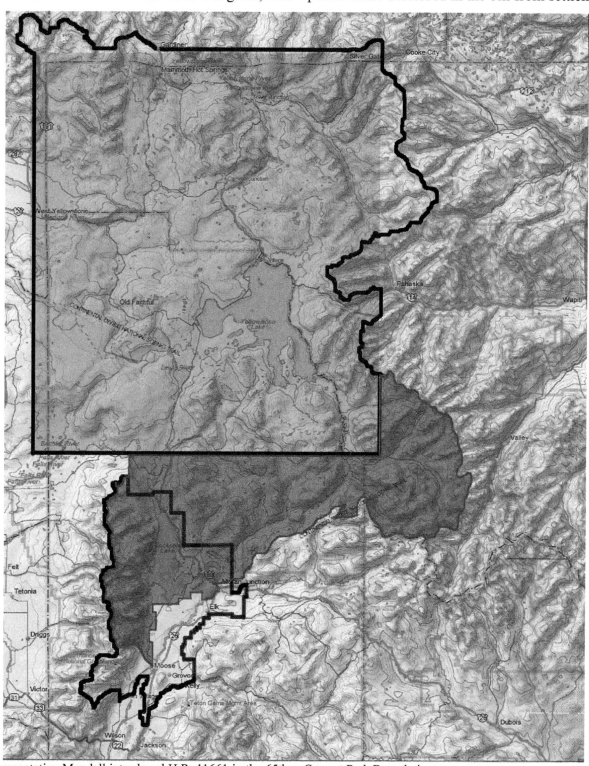

Representative Mondell introduced H.R. 11661 in the 65th Congress, 2nd Session, but the bill was held in committee at the request of the Secretary of Interior Franklin K. Lane pending a review of the boundary extension.

Current Park Boundaries
Original Yellowstone Park
Yellowstone Park Extension suggested in H.R. 11661

pending legislative action. Before the House could consider the bill, Representative Mondell received a letter from Secretary Lane that stated in part:

> *Since our preliminary report on H.R. 11661, 'A Bill to add certain lands to the Yellowstone National Park,' was submitted to the House Committee on Public Lands, a further study of this park extension project has developed the fact that certain modifications should be made in the boundaries as prescribed in the pending legislation.*[16]

biography.congress.gov/ [Public domain] via Wikimedia Commons

John Nugent (D)
1868-1931

Idaho Senator John Nugent killed H.R. 13350, to extend the boundaries of Yellowstone National Park, in 1918. Nugent worked in mines in Idaho and Australia, studied law, and was admitted to the bar in 1898. He was appointed by Idaho Governor Moses Alexander in 1918 to succeed deceased Senator James H. Brady. Nugent won the special election to complete Brady's term but lost his re-election bid. In 1921, he accepted an appointment to the Federal Trade Commission in the Wilson administration. He would eventually develop a private law practice in Washington, D.C. where he lived until his death in 1931.

H.R. 11661 received no action pending a study of the appropriate boundaries.

In 1918 Mather was back at his office, and although not capable of assuming all his responsibilities, Albright was able to make a trip to Jackson Hole in July and became acquainted with Richard Winger, owner of the *Jackson Hole Courier*, the local newspaper. Arthur Demaray,* Mrs. Demaray and their daughter accompanied Albright on this trip.

Also during the summer of 1918, Colonel Henry S. Graves, Chief Forester for the U.S. Forest Service, visited the Jackson Hole area at the request of Representative Mondell for the purpose of determining which areas should be included into Yellowstone National Park. After he returned to Washington, Mather, Graves and Mondell agreed that the Park should include the headwaters of the Yellowstone River, (locally called the Thorofare area), the Teton Range, and the region north of the Buffalo Fork. Accordingly, in December 1918, Mondell introduced H.R. 13350 in the 65th Congress, 3rd Session.

Both the Department of the Interior and the Department of Agriculture submitted favorable reports concerning H.R. 13350 to the House Committee on Public Lands. The House passed the bill unanimously on January 17, 1919, and it was forwarded to the Senate.[17]

Park Service officials were feeling confident at this point because they expected no trouble with the Senate. However, the bill met opposition in the form of Senator Nugent of Idaho. Senator Nugent and the Fremont Wool Growers Association misunderstood the boundaries of the proposed extension. They thought the western boundary would be the Wyoming-Idaho State line, thus eliminating their sheep grazing rights on the western slope of the Teton Mountains. Actually, the proposed western boundary was drawn along the crest of the mountain peaks and would not have affected any part of the grazing permits.

One account of the bill's fate in the Senate stated that a legislative jam occurred as the session neared its end. There seemed to be no chance of a vote on the bill unless it could be advanced

---

*Arthur Demaray (1887-1958) would later serve as the fifth Director of the National Park Service retiring in 1951.

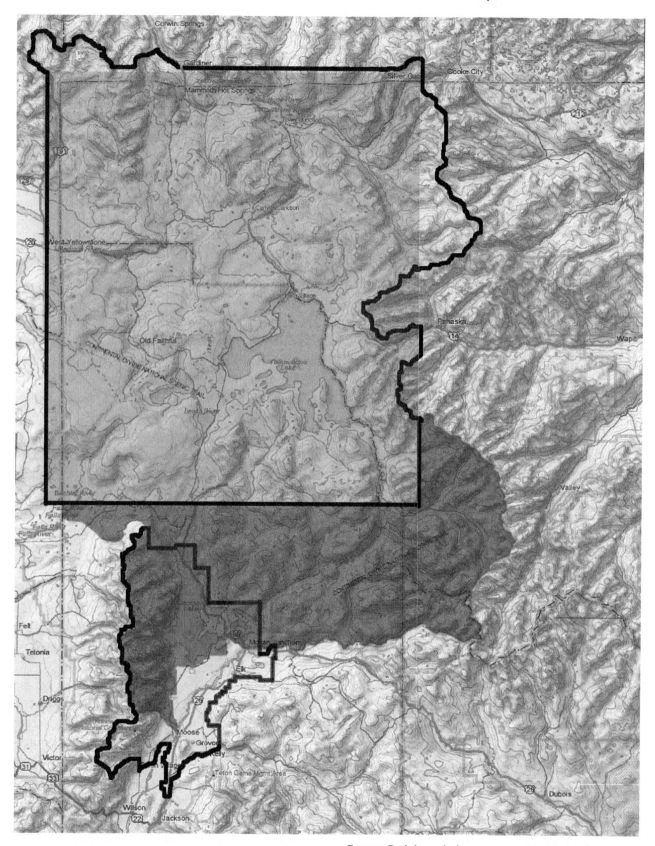

The proposed extended Yellowstone Park boundaries described in H.R. 13350 (65th Congress, 3rd Session) were the same as those proposed in H.R. 1412 (66th Congress, 1st Session).

Current Park boundaries
Original Yellowstone Park
Yellowstone Park Extension proposed in H.R. 13350 and H.R. 1412

on the calendar. The procedure for advancement required a unanimous vote by the Senators and Senator Nugent cast the only dissenting vote, thus killing the bill.[18]

Horace Albright recounted a different set of circumstances. In this version, the Park Service, with some difficulty, was eventually successful in convincing Senator Nugent that the park extension would not affect his constituents. Nugent agreed to support the bill, but a filibuster ensued on another issue and no legislation was considered during the remainder of the session.[19]

Supporting evidence for the former account of the actions in the Senate concerning H.R. 13350 is found in a letter from Senator Nugent to the Fremont Wool Growers Association. The Association determined that their interests were not endangered by the proposed park extension, and had withdrawn their objections to a similar bill (H.R. 1412) that was introduced in the following session. Senator Nugent wrote to the Association in September 1919, stating in part, *"I of course, shall follow your advice in the matter as I did when **I killed** said bill during the last session of Congress."*[20] (author's emphasis)

Also, in testimony given by Horace Albright before the House Committee on Public Lands in 1943, in which he recounted the history of the proposed park extension, he contradicted his previous statement regarding the boundary misunderstanding. He stated, *"...it was not possible in the closing days of the session of 1919 to get this impression straightened out, and the bill died."*[21] The National Park Service and Representative Mondell, although disappointed with the fate of H.R. 13350, had great hopes for the next session of Congress. In May 1919, Representative Mondell introduced H.R. 1412 to extend Yellowstone National Park in the 66th Congress, 1st Session. It was about this time that local opposition to the park extension became strong enough to be heard.

The opposition that developed surprised everyone who had supported the park extension. One reason for the surprise was that until that time every indication by residents of Wyoming had pointed to a desire for better and more roads and the increased tourism that those roads would bring. Also, the National Park Service thought

they had overcome any opposition in Jackson Hole. Local newspaper articles supported this view. One article entitled "Many Outsiders Interested in park extension" stated:

> *When extension was first talked of some bitter opposition was manifest in this valley, but this has gradually given way until many who were bitterly opposed are now heartily in favor of such a move....*
>
> *Numerous businessmen, ranchers, and guides have already written our Congressmen to the effect that they favor this action and the Courier will henceforth lend its voice to urging the extension of Yellowstone Park.*[22]

Another reason was that when Albright visited Jackson in 1918, he told Richard Winger, then owner of the local paper, that he had met very little opposition to the park expansion, but a wide difference of opinion as to where the boundary lines should be drawn.[23]

The first real evidence of opposition occurred in May 1918 when a few cattlemen, led by Peter C. Hansen, decided the inclusion of certain lands north of the Buffalo Fork River would be detrimental to their grazing rights. This group was not large, and other members of the Jackson Hole Cattle and Horse Association expressed regret that these few ranchers had taken such a stand.[24] These ranchers were not formally objecting to the extension of Yellowstone National Park to include the Tetons and the scenic lakes at their base, but rather to the inclusion of other lands they deemed important for their industry.

By July 1918, the opposition faction of the Association had gathered a little strength, and P. C. Hansen, the president of the Association, wrote Representative Mondell requesting a boundary change in the bill to extend the Park.[25] This boundary change would have deleted the area north of the Buffalo Fork River and much of the Pacific Creek drainage.

Mondell replied that such a deletion would create significant problems in protecting the Park boundary since the Buffalo Fork was a natural feature and the ranchers proposed an invisible survey line. To convince the ranchers that their rights and privileges would be protected, Mondell sent a copy of the bill, which provided:

That nothing herein contained shall affect any valid existing claim, location, or entry under the land laws of the United States, whether for homestead, mineral, right of way, or any other purpose whatsoever, or shall affect the rights of any such claimant, locator or entryman to the full use and enjoyment of his land: Provided. That under rules and regulations to be prescribed by the National Park Service, all bona fide claimants or entrymen shall have the right

Jackson Hole Historical Society and Museum p1958.0020.001

Peter C. Hansen, president of the Jackson Hole Cattle and Horse Association, was not opposed to protection of the Tetons but objected to the inclusion of prime grazing lands important to the cattlemen.

Mead Family Collection

Peter C. and Sylvia Hansen

to graze, ... such number of livestock as they have been accustomed to so graze in the past, or as may be reasonably necessary to the use and utilization of their lands.... That the National Park Service shall have authority ... to grant grazing permits... on lands hereby added to the Yellowstone National Park: to the extent that livestock have heretofore grazed upon these lands under permits issued by the Forest Service, and at fees not to exceed those charged by the Forest Service on adjacent areas.[26]

Mondell was convinced that a full understanding of the bill would end any opposition within the valley. He also believed everyone wanted more roads, so he sent a map showing a proposed road from Cody along the eastern side of Yellowstone Lake, over Two Ocean Pass and down Pacific Creek to Moran.[27]

The opposition might have remained a minor voice in the valley had Representative Mondell not mentioned the proposed road. As the news spread that the Park Service planned a new and better road from the north, the favorable attitudes of the residents toward park expansion began to change. At that time, Jackson Hole was perhaps the only place in the west that did not want more roads. Horace Albright would later declare that *"...this road project never even had tentative approval of the National Park Service."*[28] Albright's declaration that the proposed road was unofficial is contradicted by the fact that it had been placed on a National Park Service map. In addition, the Secretary of the Interior, in his favorable report to Congress concerning H.R. 13350, stated that this road *"... must be built..."* to complete *"... the automobile road system of the park."*[29] The Secretary also stated that the *"Extension of the hotel and permanent camping systems of the park into this region is also highly desirable."*[30] It was, perhaps, this last statement which united the cattlemen, the dude ranchers, and other local businessmen into a strong anti-park extension group.

On April 26, 1919, the Jackson Hole Cattle and Horse Association unanimously passed a resolution opposing the park extension.[31] This resolution explained the cattlemen's concerns.

First, the cattlemen felt that too much grazing land would be placed under park jurisdiction. Although certain guarantees were included in the proposed legislation, the bill did not provide for expansion of herd size or the leasing of lands which had not been grazed previously. This would, of course, limit their ability to improve the size of their herds and, therefore, limit the future growth of their industry.

Second, the cattlemen feared that the extension of the park would *"...create a larger territory for the breeding of predatory animals..."* causing *"...it to become absolutely non-productive of revenue...."* [32]

Third, the cattlemen believed the park extension to be sponsored by the railroad, hotel and transportation companies who would profit at the expense of the very livelihood of the residents of the valley.

Fourth, the cattlemen had a satisfactory working relationship with the Forest Service and they felt this agency could protect the lands in question as well, if not better, than the Park Service.

The third objection was perhaps the least expected by the supporters of the legislation. The Park Service and Representative Mondell had not guessed that the people of Jackson Hole did not want a large and sudden influx of tourists or that they wanted their roads kept in their present condition. Many of the dude ranchers believed their business depended on the continued inaccessibility of the valley. The difficulty in getting to Jackson Hole was considered to enhance the charm of the place.

What the supporters of the bill failed to understand was that in the minds of many of the valley

Struthers Burt, 1915
1882-1954

Struthers Burt- homesteader, dude rancher, author, and poet- was the articulate spokesperson for the group of early settlers who believed the valley needed to be protected from unsightly developments and commercialism. He opposed the Park Service attempts to include Jackson Hole into Yellowstone because of that agency's proposed development of roads and hotels within the valley, and their tendency to issue "monopolistic" concessionaire contracts and leases for services within the national parks

residents, park status meant the opposite of preservation. The residents wanted, as much as possible, the valley protected. Not maintenance of status quo but a natural economic growth along a naturally evolving trend that had been developing since the first settlers had arrived in the valley.

Most tourists who came to Jackson Hole stayed a month or more and spent their money for goods and services within the valley. At that time a trip to see the Jackson Hole area generally required several days. Even a tourist from Yellowstone might stay at least several nights in the valley, during

The Bar B C Ranch truck used to transport guests and luggage between the ranch and the train depot in Victor, Idaho.

which they would purchase camping supplies or rent rooms from local businessmen.

The cattlemen predominately utilized that portion of the valley on the eastern side of the Snake River whereas tourist related businesses predominately utilized the western side of the Snake River. The town of Jackson supplied the two industries while providing additional tourist services. Each economic interest had an opportunity to make a profit while the scenic resources were hardly touched.

Because Representative Mondell publicly favored the proposed road over Two Ocean Pass, and because Secretary Lane favored the expan-

National Archives, Neg. No. 95-G-152680

The improved Teton Pass road in 1920

sion of the hotel and campground system into the Jackson Hole area, the residents were convinced that the real forces behind the park extension movement had to be the existing commercial interest within Yellowstone National Park. The residents of Jackson Hole could envision large hotels scattered throughout the western side of the valley and the transportation companies rushing the tourists from Victor, Idaho, through the town of Jackson and north to the new hotels. Therefore, very little, if any, revenue would be realized by the inhabitants of the valley. At the same time, it was feared that this rapid commercialization would destroy the rustic charm of the valley and the clientele who had previously supported the tourist-oriented businesses would no longer wish to visit the area.

Struthers Burt, in a letter to Representative Mondell, expressed this negative attitude which many residents held toward the "commercialized" Yellowstone National Park:

> *You propose to render this country similar to Yellowstone Park: In other words you propose to make it a dust heap, pyramid it with carefully collected tin cans, put signs all over it, and herd whoever visits it around as livestock is herded. You propose to utterly ruin a country that Mr. Roosevelt, three months before his death, told me was in his opinion 'the most beautiful country in America.'* [33]

At least part of this animosity toward the Yellowstone Park concessionaires was a result of the personal experiences of the valley residents who visited the Park. They also heard stories of disappointing experiences from tourists who returned from the Park. [34] The residents of the valley generally believed that the commercial interest in Yellowstone dictated park policy to the National Park Service. Thus, they were sure the guarantees, which were included in all three pieces of legislation, would be subverted by the concessionaires. It was feared that the vaguely worded guarantees which contained phrases like, *"... or as may be reasonably necessary to the use and utilization of their lands..."* [35] could and would be interpreted for the benefit of the commercial interest and to the detriment of the cattlemen.

It was impossible to convince the opposition group in Jackson that the park extension plan was not an effort on the part of the Yellowstone concessionaires to extend their authority and their profits. The Jackson Hole Cattle and Horse Association gained the support of the Wyoming Stock Growers Association and finally the support of the Wyoming State Legislature in opposing the legislation.[36]

Due to this opposition, neither the National Park Service nor the Wyoming delegation pushed H.R. 1412, and it was not reported from the House Committee on Public Lands.

Gill Huff Photo, Jackson Hole Historical Society and Museum

Harry Scott and family ran the roadhouse at the top of Teton Pass. Harry also hauled freight and mail and according to Slim Lawrence, "…swore a lot and shoveled an awful lot of snow."

CHAPTER FOUR
1919 - 1922

Yes, the park extension idea has been temporarily abandoned, but not forgotten by its promoters. We are told that Mr. Albright has 'lieutenants' at Cody, Gardiner [sic], Yellowstone, Moran, Wilson, Victor and other points, who are serving him well. Of late we have obtained positive evidence of their activities.

Consequently it behooves the people of this valley, who are most directly concerned, and who will be affected most, to be constantly on guard, and ready to protest said extension. 'Eternal vigilance' should be our Motto.[1]

Jackson Hole Courier

August 5, 1920

Jackson Hole Historical Society and Museum p1958.0564.001p

Town of Jackson looking north on Center Street on the east side of the town square. c. 1920s

After the failure of H.R. 13350, Horace Albright intended to resign from the Park Service, but he was offered the superintendency of Yellowstone National Park. Albright was attracted by the challenge of being what he considered the first civilian superintendent of Yellowstone since the military was introduced in 1886.* He accepted the position at the beginning of the 1919 season.

During his trip west to assume his responsibilities, Albright stopped in Cheyenne, Wyoming, to meet with Governor Robert D. Carey. Albright found the governor to be very courteous and accepted an invitation to dine that evening at the executive mansion. During the meal, the predominant topic of discussion was *"...the tourist business as it related to Wyoming."* [2] Albright discovered that the governor had little patience for the dude ranching industry or what he called the "ten-gallon hat philosophy." Carey felt the destiny of the state belonged to agricultural and industrial development, and that dude ranching was a passing fancy that was not in line with the state's destiny of progress.† Upon Albright's departure, Governor Carey promised to visit Yellowstone National Park as soon as possible.

In August of that year, the governor and his wife visited Yellowstone and the Jackson Hole country. It appeared that the primary reason for the visit to Jackson Hole was to attend a meeting in which the Yellowstone Park extension plan would be discussed. Mr. Albright's involvement in the events leading up to this meeting is unclear.‡ He maintained in correspondence in 1933 and under oath before a congressional committee in 1943 that he was unaware of the meeting until Governor Carey, during his visit to Yellowstone, invited him to attend the meeting. In 1967, Albright claimed he arranged for the meeting through Dick

Yellowstone National Park Archives

Horace Albright as Superintendent of Yellowstone National Park in 1919.

*Albright apparently liked the designation of "first civilian superintendent" because he bestowed that appellative upon himself on several occasions. Technically, he was not the first civilian superintendent since the introduction of the military in 1886. S. B. M. Young was appointed superintendent after his retirement from the Army. He served as superintendent from June 2, 1907, until November 28, 1908. Between the departure of the U.S. Army and Albright's arrival Chester Lindsley performed the duties of superintendent. Albright relegated Lindsley to the position of "Chief Clerk" in his 1967 interview, but other official Park Service histories list Lindsley as Yellowstone Superintendent.

†Carey had been elected Governor of Wyoming on a Progressive ticket. At the time of his election, the only paved roads in the state were in the cities of Cheyenne and Casper. It was largely due to Governor Carey's efforts regarding road construction that the present system of roads in Wyoming was accomplished.

‡The primary documentation of Mr. Albright's role concerning this meeting are his own recollections of the event. Over the years he has provided three basic sources: A letter to Wilford Neilson, the editor of the *Jackson Hole Courier*, in 1933; his testimony in 1943 before the House Committee on Public Lands regarding a bill to abolish the Jackson Hole National Monument; and an interview conducted by Grand Teton National Park's Assistant Superintendent Haraden and Chief Park Naturalist Dilley in 1967. The differences in the three sources most often, but not always, pertain to Albright's personal role in the initiatives, rather than the factual aspects of the events. The first two accounts are less divergent, although there are some contradictions while the most recent source frequently differs in the details. In the third source, Albright assumes a more contributory role in the events concerning the creation of Grand Teton National Park. Despite the discrepancies in Mr. Albright's representations, his recollection of the results and importance of the events are generally consistent in all three sources.

Horace Albright with black bears.
The Park Service promoted close proximity to tourist-acclimated black bears to attract visitors to Yellowstone National Park.

Winger. He also recalled in that interview that he had traveled to Jackson Hole *"...a day or so ahead of time to look around the country...,"* [3] and that he was staying at Moran when he learned that the governor intended to attend the meeting.

Whatever the sequence of events, Governor Carey and Horace Albright attended the meeting. Albright also brought Clay Tallman, the Commissioner of the General Land Office, Mrs. Tallman, and a Mr. Hey, the president of a hotel company in Yellowstone National Park. Two rooms had been reserved at a hotel in Jackson. One for Mr. and Mrs. Tallman, and one for Mr. Albright and Mr. Hey. When the governor and his wife arrived in Jackson, Albright discovered that Wyoming's Chief Executive had not made reservations, and no rooms were available. Therefore, Albright and Hey gave their room to the Careys.

Neither Albright nor Carey was prepared for the reception they received at the meeting. The locals who attended the meeting were hostile. Albright recalled, *"I just took a beating that night. Every time I made a move I was talked down, sometimes shouted at and the men that made the most telling arguments against me were these dude ranchers, among them Struthers Burt and Horace Carncross who sat right in the front*

row. *Nobody would support me...."* [4] One local was run off the road by a Yellowstone Park concessionaire's bus, and he evidently held the Park Service responsible. The dude ranchers were enraged about the new road that had been proposed over Two Ocean Pass. Albright related, *"They accused the Park Service of wanting to civilize the regions. They said we were ruining the country. They claimed the bringing in of tourists would ruin the country and anything we did down here would ruin the dude ranch business. They did not want tourist development!"* [5] Fourteen years after this meeting, Albright remarked concerning the Park Service map showing the proposed road, *"How many times later we wished that map had never seen the light of day!"* [6]

The meeting ended about 11:00 p.m. and only two people approached Albright after the meeting.* Struthers Burt informed the Superintendent that his treatment during the meeting should not be perceived personally and invited Albright to lunch the next day at his ranch. The other man, Frank L. Petersen, offered Mr. Albright and Mr.

The Clubhouse (left of the Jackson Mercantile store), 1907. Albright's 1919 meeting with Jackson Hole residents was held at the Clubhouse. The Clubhouse was one of the first buildings constructed around the area that would become the town square. In addition to commercial space, it provided facilities for social gatherings such as dances and public meetings.

*Albright stated before the House Committee on Public Lands in 1943 that everyone came up and shook his hand.

Hey a place to sleep for the night and breakfast the next morning with plenty of eggs. According to Albright, eggs were a rarity in Yellowstone

Jackson Hole Historical Society and Museum 1958.3380.001
Roy Van Vleck's hardware store

Charlie Petersen, Sr. Collection
Billy Owen, John Shive, and Frank L. Petersen on the first "documented" ascent of the Grand Teton- 1898.

National Park in 1919. As Petersen got into Albright's car, he remarked, *"I feel like I'm taking Jess Willard home."* [7] Jack Dempsey had just defeated Willard for the 1919 heavyweight boxing title.*

The next morning Mr. Albright and Mr. Hey drove into town to pick up the Tallmans. Mrs. Tallman had been in Roy Van Vleck's hardware store that morning and overheard several men talking about hanging all the government men in the valley. The men had evidently recognized Mrs. Tallman when she entered the store and decided to have some fun with her. They discussed the various qualities of the different ropes displayed on the spools in the store, trying to decide which would make the best hanging rope. Mrs. Tallman believed the men were serious, and although Albright tried to convince her otherwise, she could not be calmed until they left town.

Albright recorded his assessment of the importance of that meeting in his letter to Wilford Neilson.

That was a momentous night in the history of the Grand Teton Park project, because Governor Carey apparently became convinced then that public opinion in the Hole would always be against any park plan. As for myself, when the smoke cleared away, I found that I was at heart in agreement with the Jackson Hole people. They wanted to preserve their country intact, and this was what I wanted to do. They wanted no new roads. Neither did I; but it was a new thing for me to find a whole community against the march of

---

*As previously stated, there are three sources for the accounts of this particular event, all by Horace Albright. In 1933, Albright referred to Petersen as *"... my old friend Frank L. Petersen...."* In 1943, he called him *"... an old farmer named Petersen...."* In 1967, he remembered him only as *"...a man named Petersen...."*

Frank L. Petersen, William O. Owen, Franklin S. Spalding, and John Shive reached the top of the Grand Teton on August 11, 1898. Nathaniel P. Langford (the first superintendent of Yellowstone National Park) and James Stevenson claimed to have made the ascent on July 29, 1872. The 1898 party could not find Langford's summit record, and since his description of the summit differed from their observations, the Owen Party, as it is now called, claimed the first ascent of the peak. This resulted in what has been considered one of the major controversies in the history of American Mountaineering. After 30 years of controversy, the Owen Party was given official credit for the first ascent of the Grand Teton. Twenty-five years passed before the summit was again visited. However, more recent research into the issue is supportive of the Langford/Stevenson ascent in 1872. Orrin and Lorraine Bonney's *The Grand Controversy* is currently the definitive examination of the evidence for claims of first ascent status for the Grand Teton.

progress as expressed in highways, especially in Wyoming where people were exceptionally determined to have a modern road system. It must have been a shock to Governor Carey who was so doubtful about the potency of the "ten gallon hat" spirit.[8]

Albright had the advantage of being able to view the problem in a broader sense, and, possibly, with a more realistic view of human nature. He realized that as long as the locals maintained their present attitude, the unique qualities of the valley would be protected. However, the sense of values of the residents could change at any time. Degenerative impacts to the scenic values of the valley could occur as easily from the actions of an individual landowner as it could from a group of landowners. Albright knew that as time passed the number of landowners would increase, and that would increase the problems of protection in the future. His early legal status with the Interior Department must have convinced him that the only sure method of assuring the future protection of the valley was to obtain park status for at least a portion of the Jackson Hole area.

The meeting had placed Albright and his movement for a Yellowstone Park extension at a disadvantage. Everyone in Jackson knew he had met defeat at the hands of the local dude ranchers, and everyone was now familiar with the arguments against the park extension. Albright believed that he had inadvertently omitted a crucial step in attempting to deal with the park extension issue in Jackson Hole. He failed to consult the man he thought of as "king" of the valley before approaching the populace. According to Albright, Robert E. Miller was the undisputed monarch of Jackson Hole. He was, supposedly, the richest man in Jackson. Since he owned the only bank in the valley, he was one of Jackson Hole's most influential men. Albright always felt that had he recognized this fact and played the game accordingly, much of the future opposition that would plague efforts to obtain park status for the Tetons might never have appeared. It is impossible to know if Horace Albright was correct, or if Miller's opposition resulted wholly from Albright's

Jackson Hole Historical Society and Museum p1958.0179.001
Dick Turpin and Frank L. Petersen
Petersen would later serve as a County Commissioner at the time of the creation of the first Grand Teton National Park.

failure to consult him at the beginning, or if in fact, he controlled the hearts and minds of the valley's residents, but Miller, from that time forward, seemed opposed to anything of which Albright was a part. On the other hand, Albright claimed to have been defeated at this meeting by the dude ranchers, not by the banker.

Albright, having failed at his first attempt to gain local support for the park extension, attacked the problem from a different angle. He approached the residents on an individual basis, creating friendships and feelings of mutual respect. He also guided many influential Yellowstone Park visitors down to the Tetons in an effort to gain outside support for the project. Albright rarely missed an opportunity to show off the Tetons. Among those whom Albright entertained in Jackson Hole during 1919 and 1920 were George Horace Lorimer, editor of The *Saturday Evening Post*, and some of his writers: Elizabeth Fraser, Emerson Hough and Hal G. Evarts; Herbert Corey, a writer for *Colliers*; L. W. Hill, President of the Great Northern Railway; U.S. Senators C. B. Henderson of Nevada and T. J. Walsh of Montana; Secretary of the Navy Josephus Daniels and his wife; and Secretary of the Interior John Barton Payne.[9] Albright hoped that at the appropriate time these people would be able to rally national support for another Yellowstone Park extension movement.

Albright recalled the route of the tours he conducted in 1919 and 1920:

> *...I had to take my parties east to the old crossing on the Buffalo Fork, going thence to 'Cy' [sic] Ferrin's place and on to Menor's Ferry. This trip gave us the magnificent panorama of the whole Teton Range which can only be gotten from the east side of the river. We could get back to Moran by dropping down the steep hill to the dam, but it took a four horse team to drag a car up that hill. Occasionally Ben Sheffield would let me have a team to pull my car up the hill, and thus avoid the long hard drive around Menor's Ferry.[10]*

The road between Moran and Jenny Lake was not built until 1921 when the Forest Service obtained the necessary appropriations. Until that time, Albright's trips between those sites were strictly cross-country and must have been rough for the car and the passengers.

Albright's informal contacts with the residents of Jackson Hole began to bear fruit late in 1920. While returning to Yellowstone National Park from Jackson, Albright stopped at Bill Crawford's place for lunch. Crawford talked about the difficulties the ranchers and farmers were having making a living in the valley. He complained of the cold climate and the barren soil, and stated that *"...people were destroying the lives of themselves and their families by trying to ranch in this country."[11]* Because so many of the ranchers were heavily in debt, Crawford felt many locals would support a park plan if the government or private parties would agree to purchase their lands.

The economic problems that plagued the Jackson Hole ranchers were reflected throughout most of the nation. This era of farm and livestock depression began, on a national scope, in 1921, but in Jackson Hole, it began two years earlier. Nineteen-nineteen was a drought year in the Tetons and Yellowstone National Park. During that tourist season, the rangers fought forest fires almost continuously. This critical economic period was especially hard on Jackson Hole ranchers and farmers because many were marginal operations even in the best years. This may have been due to climate and soil conditions as much as an individual lack of initiative and desire. Once the Depression was in full effect, farmers in other parts of the nation would form protective associations to save their farms from foreclosure, driving away the sheriffs at times. Although no such associations were formed in Jackson Hole, the concerns of the residents were equally real. In addition to the economic concerns of the locals, they began to see for the first time that the valley and the scenery they loved so much could be ravaged. Their options gradually became apparent. If they held onto their land, they might lose everything. If they sold their land to speculators, the possibility of despoliation was great. The only compromise was to sell the land to the federal government or individuals who would protect the land. This seemed to be a way they could get out of debt and

Jackson Hole Historical Society and Museum p1958.0569.001
Cowboys and gas pumps marked the transition of an era.

gain a reasonable assurance of protection for the valley.

Nineteen-nineteen, the drought year was followed by a severe winter, and many elk died of starvation. The late melting snows hid the grasses and created a short growing season in the high country and a shorter than normal tourist season. Although the Yellowstone Park snow plows began working on May 20 of that year to open the Park roads, the complete road system was not usable until the first of July. In an attempt to save the elk herds that wintered in northern Yellowstone, the Park purchased hay until its money ran out. The price of hay reached $60 a ton when it could be found. After the funds had been depleted, the Park sought donations from the public and wildlife organizations to buy hay and cottonseed cake. Thus, the nucleus of the northern elk herd was saved.[12] The heavy winter of 1920 added to the problems of many of the human inhabitants of the area and financial destruction seemed even closer than it had during the drought. Rather than leave the valley they cherished, some landowners went heavily into debt in hopes that future years would be better.

The same year Bill Crawford and Horace Albright talked about the economic problems of the land owners, Albright received another indication of the willingness of some of the landowners to deal with the government regarding the protection of the valley. While in Washington, D.C., Albright met with Struthers Burt and discussed the need for future protection of the valley by the U.S. Government. Albright recalled that Burt indicated a reassessment of his anti-park position and stated

he no longer thought the individual residents of the valley could maintain the protection of the valley without some outside assistance. Burt now seemed willing to support Park Service protection for at least a portion of the valley.[13]

It was about this time that a division in attitudes of the valley populace became apparent. Although the dude ranchers and many smaller

Bruce Porter Collection, Courtesy Liz Lockhart Jackson Hole Historical Society and Museum bc.0117

Elk in their historic wintering grounds south of the town of Jackson- approximately on what is now the Rafter J subdivision.

S. N. Leek Collection, American Heritage Center, University of Wyoming ah0318_0741

As homesteaders settled on critical elk winter range, the problem for the elk became more intense. When the herd population increased beyond the winter food supply, many elk starved. Local initiatives supported by conservation groups such as the Izaak Walton League prompted the establishment of the National Elk Refuge in 1912.

landowners maintained their preservationist positions concerning the northern end of the valley, merchants within the town of Jackson began to realize the possible economic advantages of increased tourism. Most cattlemen probably did not care about tourism one way or the other, but they disliked the federal government. The government controlled the majority of grazing land and, thus, regulated the cattlemen's use of that land. The cattlemen associations and the woolgrowers associations fought all efforts of the government to extend its authority in the West. The dude ranchers and small land owners saw government involvement as the only practical means of protecting the Tetons from the irrigationists and the tourists. Since the merchants wanted more tourism and development, the lines were drawn with the Park Service, dude ranchers, some small landowners, and a few north valley ranchers on one side and the south valley cattlemen and the merchants on the other. The stockmen, being the most powerful political entity in the state, had the local press on their side.

After Albright's disastrous meeting with the valley residents in 1919, when it seemed there was unanimous opposition to development in the valley, particularly in the form of roads, he worried about the possibility of a change in attitudes in the

Jackson Hole Historical Society and Museum bc0301
"Traffic" over Teton Pass during the summer, 1920.

future. He later wrote, *"The thing that puzzled me most was how we could preserve the country in its primitive condition, and at the same time keep the local people from changing their minds."* [14] Albright's fear that locals might change their minds was soon realized. In less than a year's time, the *Jackson Hole Courier* was pushing for new, better and more roads to the valley. On April 15, 1920, the *Jackson Hole Courier* published an article entitled "More Roads: More Tourist [sic]." The article reported that an organization of communities south of Jackson had petitioned the Wyoming State Highway Department for more roads to Jackson and Yellowstone. The editor remarked, *"The best we can wish them is a certain and speedy success. The more roads that are built toward and into Jackson's Hole the better we will like it. Like Rome, we would that all roads might lead this way."* [15]

On April 29, 1920, the *Jackson Hole Courier* reported that Wyoming's road construction projects were well under way. Forty-four states were behind Wyoming in the amount of road work projects in progress, and only the state of Washington had more work planned than Wyoming.[16] On June 22, the valley participated in the state's Good Roads Day, where each county encouraged its populace to improve its local roads. Throughout the state, citizens gathered with picks and shovels to repair their community's roads.

Jackson Hole Historical Society and Museum bc.0042
Automobile camping was common for visitors to the Jackson Hole valley. A lack of services and accommodations required tourists be self-sufficient, c. 1920s.

Because of heavy snows, the tourist season had a late beginning in 1920, but the *Jackson Hole Courier* reported that tourism was greater than the previous year. The editor observed that five to 15 cars were traveling through Jackson each day.[17] By today's standards, 15 cars a day would not be considered tourism, but in 1920, it indicated prosperity to those who desired tourist development in the valley.

Also in 1920, Albright gained additional respect from those locals who wished to see the valley protected when he opposed four irrigation projects within Jackson Hole and several major projects in Yellowstone National Park. Two of these projects would have impounded two of the most beautiful lakes in the valley. An irrigation company had proposed a dam 20 feet high on Jenny Lake and, in an associated project, a dam 15 feet high on Leigh Lake. The other projects would have enlarged the dams on Emma Matilda and Two Ocean Lakes. Albright prepared a report on these projects that convinced the Secretary of the Interior, John Barton Payne, to cancel the Carey Act applications that would have permitted the impoundments to be accomplished.[18]

The irrigation projects in Yellowstone National Park were not easily defeated. Several years of casework and testimony were required to maintain the Park in its natural state. Montana wanted to obtain irrigation water by damming Yellowstone Lake while Idaho wanted to dam the same lake, drill a tunnel through the Continental Divide and drain the Yellowstone Lake water into Heart Lake, and thus into the Snake River. Idaho also wanted to dam the Bechler Basin drainage.[19] Albright's constant battle with the irrigationists over Yellowstone National Park and Jackson Hole placed him in direct conflict with Wyoming State Engineer, Frank C. Emerson.* Emerson had jurisdiction over all Wyoming's water and was a staunch supporter of irrigation projects. Albright's firm hand

in affairs which affected Yellowstone National Park and Jackson Hole was viewed by the cattlemen of the west as more government intervention and stimulated bad press for all federal agencies as well as for Albright personally. The use of the press to condemn the federal government was illustrated in an article published in the *Jackson Hole Courier*. The article was reprinted under the heading "Yellowstone Park Extension Propaganda." [20] It was a criticism of the U.S. Biological Survey and did not relate to Jackson Hole or mention park extension. Evidently, since most federal agencies seemed to be equally distrusted, a criticism of one agency could be used to condemn any other agency by simply changing the title.

Mary McKinney Collection c.1915
The Victor, Idaho railroad station was the primary destination hub for dude ranch guests traveling to Jackson Hole. It remained a transportation portal into the early 1970s.

Despite, or perhaps because of, Albright's problems with irrigation interest, Wyoming State officials, and the press, he was winning the confidence of the preservationists in Jackson Hole. The Park Service position on the future of Jackson Hole had become more acceptable to the dude ranchers because Albright had expressed a willingness to try to prevent development within the valley. Dude ranchers began to realize that a more restrictive federal land status might be the most practical method of obtaining long-term protection for the valley.

*Frank C. Emerson would become governor of Wyoming in 1927. His strong support for the Ditch Creek irrigation project in Jackson Hole would later complicate John D. Rockefeller, Jr.'s land acquisition project.

In 1920, an incident occurred that would have lasting effects on future efforts to protect the valley as a national park. The Park Service, through Yellowstone's appropriations, maintained a portion of the road south from Yellowstone National Park, but the actual jurisdiction of the land was with the Forest Service. Supposedly, the Forest Service prohibited grazing of domestic livestock immediately south of the Park, a policy designed to ensure the integrity of the Park's southern boundary. When Albright brought Interior Secretary Payne and Navy Secretary Daniels down to the Jackson Hole area, it was clear that the Forest Service had neglected to enforce the policy.

The Hatchet Ranch, in the northeast corner of Jackson Hole, was owned by a wealthy and influential man named D. E. Skinner. He had

Bain News Service [Public domain] via Wikimedia Commons
John Barton Payne (D)
1855-1935
27th Secretary of the Interior

Payne was born in West Virginia and was admitted to the bar in West Virginia, but moved to Chicago in 1883 where he practiced law and became involved in politics. Nationally, he was probably better known for his work with the American Red Cross than for his political career during the Wilson administration. His donation of art and money led to the founding of the Virginia Museum of Fine Arts in Richmond. The World War II Liberty ship *SS John Barton Payne* was named in his honor.

been a ship builder during the First World War and was a "Henry Kaiser" of his time. Skinner purchased cattle in Idaho and had them trailed into the valley over the old Ashton road (originally called the Marysville road) north of Jackson Lake. Apparently the drive ended there, 30 miles short of the ranch. The cattle roamed at will over the "protected" area and caused considerable road damage. This resulted in constant road repair work and expense for Yellowstone National Park.

When Secretary Payne visited the valley, the road from the Park's south entrance to Moran was nearly impassable. At times the uncooperative beasts blocked the road and at many places rocks, some of them quite large, had been loosened by cattle grazing the nearby slopes and rolled down to block the road. These obstacles had to be physically removed by the men before their journey could continue. The Secretary seemed more upset with the cattle than the desolate shoreline he viewed at Jackson Lake. Although he was appalled at the scar created by the Reclamation Service when they built the dam, his wrath was directed at the cattle and the Forest Service.

He instructed Albright to use park rangers to drive the cattle off the road and out of the protected area. Albright, fearing such an action might result in a ranger war between the Park Service and the Forest Service, reminded the Secretary that the land belonged to the Forest Service and suggested the Secretary of Agriculture be contacted first. When the group returned to Yellowstone, Secretary Payne sent a telegram to the Secretary of Agriculture requesting the cattle be removed within one week. The telegram also informed the Secretary that if the cattle were not removed within a week, Albright would be directed to accomplish the task with his park rangers. The Secretary wired back that he would do his best to comply with Payne's wishes. When no action had been taken at the end of a week's time, Albright, with half his ranger force, moved the cattle out of the area and up the Buffalo Fork River where they belonged. Albright recalled, *"...that didn't help us any, Rangers coming out of the Park and removing cattle from the Forest land. It didn't help us with the community and it didn't help us with the Forest Service...."* [21]

Two problems resulted from this incident. First, the relationship between the Forest Service and the Park Service, which had not been healthy, became even more tense. Throughout the West, the Park Service had been actively seeking special areas for inclusion in the National Park System. Many of these desired areas were found to be wholly or partially administered by the Forest Service, and this agency had become defensive concerning its territory. This activity by the Park rangers in the Forest Service domain only made the agency more possessive and less cooperative when the park expansion issue resurfaced.

The second problem was an outgrowth of the first. The interagency conflict fed the fires of the anti-federal government sentiment causing more bad press for all federal agencies in the West. Politicians made the most mileage possible from the issue, blaming a variety of problems, such as slow progress, on the agency conflict rather than on depressed farm and cattle market prices. Along this line, Wyoming's Governor Carey, during a visit to Jackson, claimed the conflict between the agencies was responsible for the valley's lack of progress. The Governor evidently chose to ignore the drought of 1919 and the severe winter of 1920 claiming the agencies created *"...a problem called 'federalitis."* [22]

American Heritage Center, University of Wyoming ah03138_0908
Crossing the Snake River at Menor's Ferry by cable car.

In October 1920, Yellowstone National Park released its travel figures for the season through September 18. Despite the delayed opening (due to heavy snows) total Park visitation increased by 27 percent over the previous year. Private motor vehicles increased by 26 percent, and travel via the south Park entrance increased by 33 percent. Another figure illustrates the relative remoteness of this northwestern Wyoming area. As of September 18, 1920, the total visitation to Yellowstone National Park since its establishment in 1872 was only 679,225 people. [23]

By his patient efforts, Albright had developed some support for his Yellowstone expansion project within the valley of Jackson Hole in 1920. In support of this effort, Secretary of Interior Payne requested and received Executive Order No. 3394 that withdrew additional lands in Jackson Hole from settlement. However, Albright soon began to feel pressures from outside the valley that would strain his relationship with the valley's preservationists. The increased tourism of 1920 stimulated various Wyoming communities to push for a Yellowstone Park access

Jackson Hole Historical Society and Museum p1958.0731.001
The ferries adapted from horses and wagons to automobiles as transportation modes evolved.

through their towns. The Commercial Clubs of Lander, Dubois, Riverton and Shoshoni wrote letters to Representative Mondell and Superintendent Albright encouraging an extension of Yellowstone National Park.[24] Surficially, this seemed to be additional support for Albright's plan, but the real motive behind the movement was the desire for a new road connecting these communities with the south entrance to Yellowstone National Park.

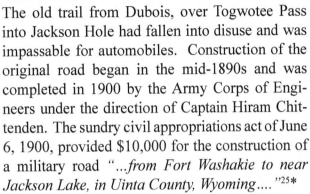

Jackson Hole Historical Society and Museum bc.0041
Automobiles parked in front of Teton Lodge at Moran

The old trail from Dubois, over Togwotee Pass into Jackson Hole had fallen into disuse and was impassable for automobiles. Construction of the original road began in the mid-1890s and was completed in 1900 by the Army Corps of Engineers under the direction of Captain Hiram Chittenden. The sundry civil appropriations act of June 6, 1900, provided $10,000 for the construction of a military road *"...from Fort Washakie to near Jackson Lake, in Uinta County, Wyoming...."*[25]*

Governor Carey, although not supportive of a park extension, was quick to support a new road, especially one built with federal money. Representative Mondell and Senator John B. Kendrick were also quick to apply pressure for the new road. The town of Jackson opposed the road for obvious reasons. The new road would allow tourists to enter and leave Yellowstone National Park via the Park's south entrance, bypassing Jackson and denying them the privilege of depositing some of their money with the local merchants. The dude ranchers opposed the road because it signaled increased commercial development in the valley, and Albright suddenly found himself in another uncomfortable situation. He realized that his active affiliation with the proposed road could jeopardize his relationship with the dude ranchers.

By the beginning of the 1921 tourist season, the proposed road was no longer a debatable subject. The Secretary of the Interior directed Albright to make the necessary repairs on the road over Togwotee Pass.[26] This directive created two more problems for the superintendent. To comply with the Secretary's directive, Albright once again had to take his rangers out of the Park and into the Forest Service domain. The other problem was financial. Although Albright was given the authority to work on the road, he was not given the money to accomplish the repairs. Yellowstone National Park's appropriation for road maintenance in those years was $7,500 per year.[27] This amount was primarily intended for use on the road between the Park's south entrance and Moran, but Albright was ordered to make that sum stretch to Dubois, Wyoming, on the east side of Togwotee Pass. To accomplish the construction of the new road, he was forced to abandon all the repair work for which the funds had been originally intended. In addition to repairing the Togwotee road, culverts and bridges had to be repaired, and the Park Service built a new, temporary bridge across the Buffalo Fork River at Turpin Meadow. When the construction crews reached Dubois, a sufficient amount of money remained in the road maintenance fund to continue the road repairs as far as the Wind River Indian Reservation.

After the road had been completed, a celebration was held. Superintendent Albright remembered, *"There were over 160 cars in Togwotee Pass, and the celebration was a great success*

---

*During the time span of this chapter the Jackson Hole area was part of Lincoln County, with the County Seat in Kemmerer. Prior to the creation of Lincoln County the entire area was contained in Uinta County, with the County Seat in Evanston.

from the standpoint of the cities east of the mountains, but the beginning of a different kind of an era for Jackson Hole." [28]

Businessmen from Casper, Lander, Riverton and other communities attended the celebration, as well as Wyoming's Senator Kendrick and Governor Carey. Newspapers from Colorado and Wyoming were represented, including the publisher of the *Wyoming State Tribune*, William C. Deming. Deming would later become the head of the U.S. Civil Service Commission. Accompanying Horace Albright to the celebration was Emerson Hough, a writer for the *Saturday Evening Post*, who was at that time writing *The Covered Wagon*. Dr. Henry Van Dyke also attended the function with Albright. Van Dyke was a friend of Struthers Burt and had been spending part of his time in Yellowstone National Park and part at Burt's ranch in Jackson Hole.

After the celebration, Senator Kendrick joined Albright and his guests for the trip back to Jackson Hole. This was the Senator's first trip to the north end of the valley, and Kendrick's presence during the trip back from Togwotee was significant for Hough. During the trip, the Senator reminisced about his youth on the plains and the cattle drives between Texas and Wyoming. The stories he told during that drive to Jackson Hole formed the basis for Hough's novel *North of '36*.[29]*

When the group reached Moran, Senator Kendrick received his first view of Jackson Lake. Kendrick, like others before him, found the scarred lake shore a horrible sight. The dead and downed timber extended out from the shore a couple of hundred yards in some places and the Senator was shocked at the scene. On this occasion, he is reported to have stated to Albright, *"A liver pill sign on the Statue of Liberty could not be as terrible a desecration as this."* [30]

The fears of the valley dude ranchers regarding the new road over Togwotee Pass were quickly realized. Tourists use of the south entrance to

Jackson Hole Historical Society and Museum 1958.3035.001

Togwotee Pass road dedication celebration, 1922.

The military built the original Togwotee Pass road between Fort Washakie and Yellowstone Park. By the 1920s, the road had deteriorated and was impassable for automobiles. Although the road was entirely within the National Forest domain, Congressional pressure resulted in the Secretary of the Interior directing Yellowstone Park Superintendent Albright to use Yellowstone's appropriations to improve the deteriorated road in 1922. Park rangers working on improvements in the National Forest increased tensions between the two agencies and stiffened opposition to future compromises relating to the expansion of Park Service authority in Jackson Hole. Today the highway over Togwotee Pass into Jackson Hole is designated U.S. 287.

---

*The silent film, *North of 36* was based on this novel and distributed by Paramount Pictures in 1924. It starred Jack Holt and Lois Wilson. The film was preserved and restored by the Library of Congress. Hough's early writings on conservation issues encouraged Congress to pass a law making the poaching of animals in National Parks a punishable offense in 1894. He advocated the establishment of the National Park Service and was a co-founder of the Izaak Walton League.

Yellowstone National Park increased dramatically in 1923. In 1922, the south entrance of Yellowstone National Park recorded 5,724 people. In 1923 travel via the south entrance increased to 14,774.[31] Total visitations for the Park reached 138,352.[32]

Prior to the opening of the new road, commercial development in the north end of the valley was minimal. Most tourist-oriented developments were established at the southern end; in the town of Jackson, near the Teton Pass road, and near the Hoback Canyon road. The increased tourism at the north end caused an almost immediate response by those who recognized the economic opportunities. The year after the Togwotee road was opened, Herbert Barber of Lander and Jim Gratiot of Casper built the Amoretti Inn not far from the Jackson Lake Dam.[33] As tourism increased so did road signs and commercial establishments.

The Jackson merchants pushed for and obtained improvements on the Teton Pass and Hoback Canyon roads to lessen the detrimental economic effects of the Togwotee Pass road. With these improvements, tourist travel increased throughout the valley, closely followed by gas stations, road signs, gift shops and other nondescript structures. By 1923, it appeared that Jackson Hole, with its pristine scenery and rustic charm, would soon be just a memory to those who found value in such qualities.

The "Petticoat Government"
Jackson Town Council

Wyoming (the Equality State) was the first state to ratify the 19th Amendment (Women's Suffrage). In 1920, Jackson residents elected an all-female town council, and Jackson became the first incorporated town in the nation to have an all-female government. Less commonly known is that Wyoming women had been voting since 1869 although federal law prohibited their participation in federal elections.

(L to R) Mae Deloney, Rose Crabtree, Grace Miller (Mayor), Faustina Haight, Genevieve Van Vleck. (Rose Crabtree defeated her husband 50 votes to 31.) Other women in the local government were Pearl Williams, town marshal; Edna Huff, health officer; Marta Winger, town clerk; and Viola Lumbeck, treasurer.

Jackson Hole Historical Society and Museum 1958.0090.001

Mayor Miller stated, *"We are not campaigning for the office because we felt the need of pressing reforms. The voters of Jackson believe that women are not only entitled to equal suffrage, but they are also entitled to equality in the management of governmental affairs."*

Jackson Hole Historical Society and Museum 1998.0027.001

Jackson Town Marshall Pearl Williams

Jackson Hole Historical Society and Museum 1991.4034.037

Faustina Haight (right) was a single woman homesteader and school teacher. She was elected to a four-year term on the Town Council and retained the seat in the next election. c.1906

CHAPTER FIVE
1922-1923

*...if the country could develop as it is now developing I would be at present oppos-
ing the extension. But it won't develop that way and the change will come quickly. We
have the choice between seeing it go into entirely irresponsible private hands, or seeing
a small part of it, but enough to balk these selfish interests, controlled intelligently and
for the use of the whole public by a government that I for one have been convinced is
trying to do its job as fairly as it knows how. We're up against it; we can't let things
slide anymore; we have to make a choice.*

Struthers Burt[1]
January 19, 1923

Jackson Hole Historical Society and Museum 1958.0509.001

Valley residents were quick to embrace new technologies, but transportation for the next three decades would remain a
mixture of horse and automobile, 1922.

As the dude ranchers watched the clouds of gaudy commercialism gather around them, they were even more convinced that federal intervention and regulation was the only course of action that could save the still pristine scenic assets of the valley. Although not yet convinced that a national park was the appropriate status for the valley, they were sure that protective action of some type was needed quickly. Since the failure of Mondell's bill to extend the boundaries of Yellowstone National Park in 1919, very few pro-park attitudes had been expressed publicly in Jackson Hole. Anti-extension publicity and some of the events of 1922 may have coaxed the dude ranchers into public action.

~

During 1922, the *Jackson Hole Courier* had published numerous articles opposing the park extension while encouraging new and better roads into and within the valley. In one article the *Courier* stated that what Yellowstone needed was more roads, not extended boundaries.[2] Local community organizations "resolved" and "whereased" quite liberally to make their protests appear more official.

The opening of the Togwotee Pass road provided additional access to Jackson Hole, but it was perceived by locals as detrimental to the local economy because it allowed tourist traffic to by-pass the town of Jackson. To counteract the anticipated lost revenue from the newly opened Togwotee Pass road, local merchants, with the vigorous support of communities in southwestern Wyoming, pushed for improvements to the Hoback Canyon road. Communities like Rock Springs, Pinedale, and Kemmerer hoped to benefit from tourists traveling to and from Yellowstone Park by a southerly route. Roads that directed tourist travel through the town of Jackson were considered desirable by locals who profited from tourist traffic while roads that bypassed the community were deemed inappropriate. The improvements to the Hoback Canyon road were completed in July.

Since the communities east of the valley had sponsored a celebration for the opening of the Togwotee road, Jackson and the communities to the south could do no less. Of course, their celebration had to be bigger and better. This celebration lasted a week beginning with two days of festivities in Kemmerer, Wyoming, followed by two more days of entertainment in Pinedale including a rodeo, two bands, and an orchestra. Then on to Hoback Canyon where two steers were barbecued, and 3,000 fish were cooked for an anticipated crowd of three thousand people.* Since a large number of state

Courtesy Liz Lockhart, Bruce Porter Collection Jackson Hole Historical Society and Museum, bc0118

The crew that built the improvements to the Hoback Canyon road in 1923.

---

*In addition to food, music, rodeos and speeches a movie film company was present for the Hoback event. The film company was not particularly interested in the dedication of the new road, but rather in obtaining footage of a crowd scene for the movie they were filming in the valley. This film company, The Mary Miles Minter Company, was the second to use the scenery of Jackson Hole in a movie. This particular movie, *The Cowboy and the Lady*, starred Tom Moore and, of course, Mary Miles Minter. The director, Charles Maigne, was the favorite with the locals. He was almost considered a resident because his father, Colonel Gregory Maigne, had accompanied General Sheridan through the valley in 1889.

and local officials attended the Hoback function, quite naturally, some speeches had to be endured. The next day the people were entertained in Jackson, and then moved on to Yellowstone National Park where another celebration was held.[3]

Pressure on the dude ranchers increased in 1922. During this election year, Representative Mondell decided to run against John B. Kendrick for the latter's Senate seat. Mondell had completed 12 consecutive terms in the House and had been Jackson Hole's favorite politician until he introduced his park extension bill.

Within the valley, the dominant campaign issues included park extension (past and future) and government intervention in the lives of the residents. Mondell had favored a new and unpopular road from Yellowstone to Jackson Hole; he had introduced bills to extend the boundaries of Yellowstone National Park south so as to include prime grazing lands necessary to the cattlemen's prosperity, and he was known to have friendly attitudes toward woolgrowers. Thus, his campaign did not have a strong footing when he came to Jackson, and his popularity was rapidly declining.[4]

Mondell opened his unsuccessful campaign with an explanation of his stand on the park extension issue. He explained that during a trip through the area, he received a suggestion to include the Tetons in the Park and later received a petition requesting such an action. This petition was signed by 300 people from Jackson and Cody, Wyoming. When the proposal was published, only one letter opposing the plan was received and that objection was based on the loss of grazing rights. Since the bill protected the grazing rights, Mondell introduced the bill. He later stated, *"My efforts were put forth in good faith. When the opposition was shown, the bill was dropped as far as I was concerned and if I am in Congress for the next hundred years I will not advocate park extension, unless the people change their minds and want it."* [5]

Senator Kendrick also campaigned in Jackson. The *Jackson Hole Courier*, on September 21, 1922, reported, *"Richard Winger, in introducing Senator Kendrick, called attention to the Teton Pass road and the proposed Snake River Canyon road and then explained to us that he had*

the 'inside dope' on the Park extension question and unhesitatingly gave Mr. Kendrick the credit for standing pat against the bill and through his effort, defeating it in the Senate."

There is some confusion here as to Richard Winger's stand on the park extension issue. Winger testified before a Senate subcommittee that he opposed park extension during the 1917-1919 legislative controversies. He stated he sold his newspaper, the *Jackson Hole Courier*, in 1919 to work full time on behalf of the ranchers of Jackson Hole gathering information to support opposition to the park extension.[6] Yet during his ownership

Paramount Pictures Jackson Hole Historical Society and Museum 1958.3349.001

A scene from *The Cowboy and the Lady*- the first full-length movie filmed in Jackson Hole.

film Studies Library [Public domain] via Wikimedia CommonsF

Mary Miles Minter
1902-1984
Minter, born Juliet Reilly, starred in 54 silent era movies
from 1912 to 1923.

of the *Courier,* some pro-park extension editorials and articles were published in his paper; some of which were quoted in Chapter Three. Also, Horace Albright in 1967, stated, *"Dick Winger had always been with us from 1918 on."* [7] In the remaining history of the events which culminated in the establishment of Grand Teton National Park, he was an outspoken advocate of the park, testifying at public hearings, gathering data for Rockefeller's land acquisition plan and was even employed by Rockefeller for a time as a purchasing agent for land in Jackson Hole.

The dude ranchers were also affected by the establishment of Teton County as a legal entity. Prior to this event, Jackson Hole had been a part of Lincoln County with the county seat in Kemmerer, Wyoming. Before Teton County was established, the desires of the residents of the valley were compromised by the desires of the remainder of the county. The major political force in Jackson Hole was the cattlemen; whereas, the major political force in the rest of the county was the sheepmen.

The sheep provided perhaps the only issue with which a clear majority of the Jackson Hole residents could find accord. Sheep were almost universally hated. One particularly brutal article appeared in the *Jackson Hole Courier* in 1922 exemplifying the cattlemen's attitudes towards sheep and the men who raised them. The wooly animals were described as *"...crawling bands of range maggotts* [sic].*"* The author of this article, J. R. Jones, spoke of the woolgrowers as *"...men whose blood held the taint of sheep scab, but for the years ... dared not reveal the distress of their condition."* Jones also warned of the consequences if sheep were allowed in Jackson Hole:

Our wonderful mountain streams will be contaminated, the waving grass of our

hill sides will vanish and the stench of their presence shall cling in our nostrils. The din of their bah-bah will ring in our ears and the dust of their trails shall bake in our throats. The inheritance which we gained by the foresight and valor of those who preceded us will cease to be, and we shall pass on to future generations a foully polluted region. [8]*

With such basic differences in attitudes and industries, it is not difficult to understand the desire of many Jackson Hole residents for a separate county government. With the creation of the new county came a new feeling of self-determination. The people now had, appropriately, a greater voice in the destiny of their valley.†

Seth Hawley Photo Jackson Hole Historical Society and Museum
2007.0011.009

Marta and Richard Winger

Dick Winger homesteaded in the valley in 1912 and bought the local newspaper in 1913, which he ran for six years. After selling the *Jackson Hole Courier,* he was hired by local ranchers to represent them in opposing the efforts of the Park Service to extend the boundaries of Yellowstone National Park southward into Jackson Hole. He also worked as a contractor for road work and as a real estate agent. Ultimately he became a strong and vocal supporter of the protection movement and aided the Rockefeller project in Jackson Hole.

---

*An interesting example of the independent nature of valley residents is demonstrated by the actions of two local ranchers when the Cattle and Horse Association passed a resolution barring sheep from Teton County. Peter C. Hansen, the former president of the association, and J. G. Imeson promptly purchased a small number of sheep that they then ran on their respective ranches for several years. These men may not have approved of sheep on the local range, but they would not be told which animals they could raise.

† Since the original efforts to protect the valley of Jackson Hole were based on the need to protect its wildlife, it seemed appropriate that the first case tried in the new county was for the wanton destruction of game animals. William Sherill and Bill Gardner were convicted and fined $500 and $300 respectively for illegally killing and abandoning three moose.

Struthers Burt and the other dude ranchers, having endured a year of adverse publicity, increased tourism, and an election year in which no one would claim to support a movement to protect the Tetons and its lakes, may have felt that the general optimism associated with the creation of the new county offered an opportune time to state their case.

In January 1923, the dude ranchers revealed another initiative to protect the scenic values of the valley when the *Jackson Hole Courier* published a letter written by Struthers Burt. Burt did not attack the cattlemen or the merchants directly,

Jackson Hole Historical Society and Museum 2008.0038.067

Maxwell Struthers Burt

Struthers Burt (1882-1954) was perhaps the most articulate spokesperson for the protection of the Tetons and Jackson Hole. Educated at Princeton and Oxford, he worked as a reporter for the *Philadelphia Times* and taught English at Princeton. He homesteaded the Bar BC Ranch in 1912 establishing one of the premier dude ranches in the West. He gained respect outside the valley as an author of books, articles, screenplays, and poetry. In the West he is probably best known for *Diary of A Dude-Wrangler,* and *Powder River; Let 'er Buck.* His wife, Katherine Newlin, was also a noted author and screenwriter.

but he was less than gentle with the irrigation interests that were once again trying to dam Jenny, Leigh, and other lakes. This approach to the park question was shrewd as it allowed Burt to encourage park extension from a position that the opposing parties could understand. He pointed out that no matter how many times the irrigationists were defeated, they would continue trying to dam the lakes until they were successful or the lakes were provided legal protection. The merchants were aware of the economic benefits of the lakes as scenic and recreational tourist attractions.

The cattlemen also were opposed to more homesteads that would decrease the amount of public land on which they could graze their cattle. The availability of irrigation water would likely stimulate more homesteading in the valley. In support of Burt's point, twice in 1922, the U.S. Government had withdrawn land from the Teton National Forest and opened the areas to settlement. The first withdrawal occurred in February 1922, and it concerned tracts of land south of the Buffalo Fork River and north of Spread Creek.[9] The second withdrawal, in March, opened 19,000 acres around Jenny and Leigh Lakes.[10]

The Idaho irrigation schemes could, Burt reasoned, be defeated if the valley residents joined to support a park extension along what he called the "Van Dyke Line." The "Van Dyke Line" was a compromise boundary suggested by Dr. Henry Van Dyke. As mentioned in the previous chapter, Dr. Van Dyke was a friend of Struthers Burt and had attended the Togwotee Pass road celebration as a guest of Horace Albright. In 1919, the cattlemen opposed the inclusion of the area around the Buffalo Fork River because they considered it prime and necessary grazing land. The "Van Dyke Line" eliminated this area from the proposed park extension by drawing a line down the Pacific Creek Divide, then around the shore of Jackson Lake, excluding that lake; then south to Taggart Lake; then west to the crest of the Teton Peaks; then north along the crest of the peaks to the southern boundary of Yellowstone National Park.[11] This proposal eliminated the most controversial areas but protected most of the scenic lakes at the base of the Teton Mountains. The Reclamation Service had already ravaged the scenic values of Jackson Lake and, therefore, it did not qualify for national park status. Burt then told the readers of the *Courier,* *"...there is all the difference in the world between developing a country sensibly, taking into account its natural assets, and being played for suckers by selfish interest."*[12]

Horace Albright had predicted the dude ranchers' stand, but this may not have been coincidental. In December 1922, he stated to a *Wyoming State Tribune* reporter that a renewal of the park extension effort would be forthcoming. The article was reprinted in the *Jackson Hole Courier* on December 21, 1922, less than a month before Struthers Burt's letter was printed. Albright, in explaining the new boundary proposal did not refer to the "Van Dyke Line," but it is clear from his description that his and Burt's proposals were identical. He stated, *"Under this plan ... the lakes and the territory surrounding the Tetons will be preserved for the generations of all time, the efforts of Idaho and other interests to ruin the landscape through irrigation schemes would be defeated, and Wyoming stockmen would in no wise be harmed."* [13]

Albright, also at this time, disclaimed any intention of actively pushing for the extension, and stated that *"If the park is to be extended ... it will have to be done on the initiative of Wyoming people, inasmuch as whatever the National Park Service officials did might be misconstrued."*[14] The article reported that Albright was of the opinion *"...that the people of Lander, the Jackson's Hole and other communities will get busy early next year and attempt to put the revised project across."* [15]

Judging from the timing and the content of Horace Albright's statements for the *Tribune* reporter and Struthers Burt's letter to the *Courier,* one might conclude that the 1923 initiative was planned. However, one other possibility existed. It may be that Albright no longer wished to stand alone in the controversy, and felt it was time for the locals who supported federal protection for the Tetons to become publicly involved in the extension effort. If this was the case, he effectively put the dude ranchers on notice through his statements to the *Wyoming State Tribune,* that no official effort to protect the valley would be forthcoming until local support was demonstrated.

In either case, Burt's letter in January 1923 began a new era of conservation activity in Jackson Hole. From this time forward, there would almost always be at least two publicly supported sides to the park controversies within the valley.

Struthers Burt's letter, of course, did not go unanswered. The first to respond was Ben Sheffield. He agreed that the lakes should be protected from the irrigationists, but thought private home sites, as well as a few large hotels, should be allowed along the shores of the lakes. He also stated, *"As to the Park extension, I have always been in favor of it from the beginning, and am yet, providing that the boundary lines are practical, and that the same conditions will exist in regard to grazing cattle that are in force now."* [16]

The following week, the *Courier* reprinted an article from the *Rock Springs Miner.* The editor of this southwestern Wyoming paper read Burt's letter and reprinted it for his readers along with his summation of the situation, which suggested Burt's viewpoint. Eventually, he stated, *"Let us*

Dr. Henry Van Dyke
1852-1933

Dr. Henry Van Dyke was a noted Presbyterian clergyman, author, and educator. He taught English literature at Princeton and was U.S. Minister to the Netherlands from 1913 to 1916. Among his more famous inspirational books are *The Other Wise Man, Little Rivers,* and *Fisherman's Luck.*

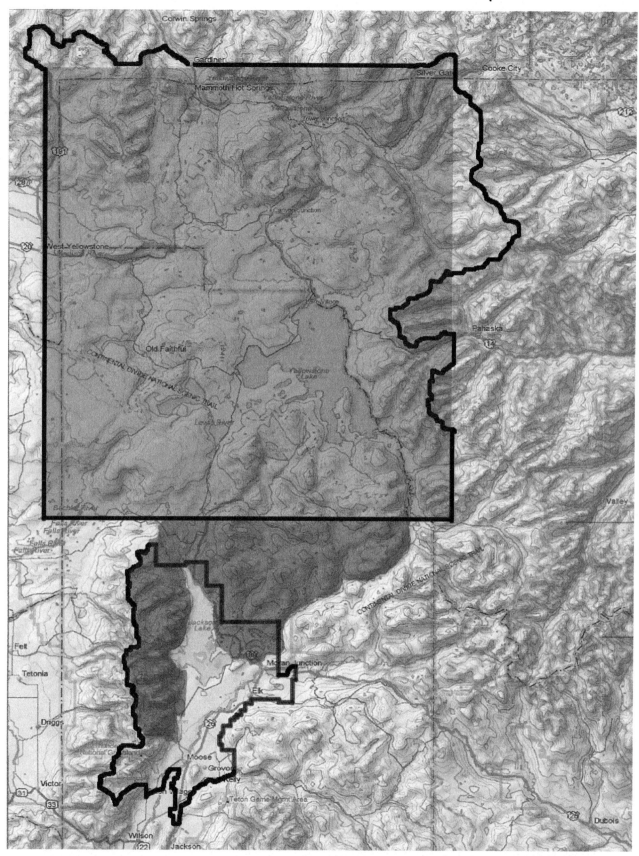

Yellowstone Park extension suggested by Dr. Henry Van Dyke in 1922

Current Park boundaries
Original Yellowstone Park
The Van Dyke proposed
Yellowstone Park Extension

all do everything in our power to preserve this little corner of Wyoming as a pleasure ground for the people of the whole world." [17] Immediately beneath that article, the *Courier* printed a two-paragraph note informing the public that the state's Federal Relations Committee had introduced House Joint Memorial No. 4, which objected to any enlargement of Yellowstone National Park.[18]

A week later, the *Courier* printed a letter from M. R. Grimmesey opposing the park extension. Grimmesey, like Sheffield, favored private home sites around the lake shores if there were some *"..regulations as to the type of buildings constructed, as unsightly old shacks would not help the country any."* He simply could not see *"...what benefit Park Extension would be to the people of Jackson's Hole or to the many tourists who come in here every year."* [19]

Finally, E. H. Johnson of Salt Lake City, Utah wrote to object to the park extension. He felt the cattlemen would be put out of business if the Park was extended, and he accused Burt of advocating a proposal which would benefit the dude ranchers to the detriment of all other residents of the valley. He concluded, *"What is the matter with the present deal, the world is large and big enough for all, so why not let good enough alone?"* [20]

Struthers Burt, being a man of letters and sure of his cause, made his reply in a lengthy letter to the editor of the *Courier*. He began by saying:

May I protest vigorously, but of course in the most friendly spirit, against some of the arguments used against my letter favoring Park extension. They have nothing what-soever to do with what I said and tilt at windmills that don't exist. Like 'the last word' anywhere, however, they leave a false impression on the mind of the reader and so I feel called upon to do my best to answer them. [21]

Burt devoted a large portion of his letter to answering E. H. Johnson's accusations of selfishness and harmful intent to his neighbors. He also defended Stephen Mather and Horace Albright as honest and honorable men, stating that although some might disagree with them *"...no fair man knowing the facts could impute to them any sinister motive."* [22] The most important part of his letter dealt with the two biggest questions of the controversy as they existed at that time. The first

Jackson Hole Historical Society and Museum p1958.1002.001

The Moran Hotel, owned by Capt. Smith, was built to accommodate the increased tourist traffic in the north end of the valley.

question being, why was it necessary to give park status to the mountains and lakes? Why couldn't the Forest Service continue to manage the area? Or, as E. H. Johnson asked, "why not let good enough alone?" The answer to this rested with the issue of protection for the lakes at the base of the mountains. As long as the lakes remained in the domain of the Forest Service, the agency doctrine of multiple use would apply. Because of this doctrine the door would always be open for the irrigationists to continue in their attempts to dam the lakes. The state of Wyoming had little jurisdiction over the lakes within the federal domain, and, therefore, could not provide lasting protection.* Burt explained:

> *...recently certain interests seeking to destroy our lakes have gained power, and I am therefore strongly in favor of Park extension as the only means of preserving those lakes for what I think are their intelligent uses. That these lakes should be preserved I believe is practically the unanimous opinion of Jackson's Hole. They are too obviously an enormous future business asset to give away. But how are you going to preserve them except by Park extension? Anyone who can answer that question will be discovering something new. Local action won't save them, even state action won't save them; only federal action- and action at that not subject to change with changing administrations will save them. The Wyoming Legislature can pass any number of resolutions and no one knows better than the Wyoming Legislator that these will not save the lakes.[23]*

The other major question in this controversy dealt with the types of development that should be allowed along the shores of the lakes. The letters by Sheffield, Grimmesey and Johnson suggested that some, if not a majority of the people, favored opening the lake shore areas for private summer homes. The reason for this attitude was financial. Grimmesey and Sheffield felt private home development would be a stimulus to the economy of Jackson Hole. The materials and supplies for building and equipping these homes would probably be purchased from Jackson Hole merchants while the labor required to construct the buildings would provide employment for Jackson Hole residents.

Burt, on the other hand, viewed the lakes as great scenic attractions that would, in the future, attract even more people who would spend their money in the valley. The type of utilization he envisioned was more aesthetic in nature so that tourists in July would not be visually aware that there had been tourists in the same spot in June. A few carefully supervised campgrounds would

Grand Teton National Park GRTE (unnumbered)
Scenic turnout for tourists at Jenny Lake

*It is true that the Wyoming State Engineer could disapprove storage and construction permits, as in the case of the Jackson Lake Dam (discussed in Chapter Two). However, there was no legal method available to the state of Wyoming that could guarantee that future state engineers or state administrations would continue to deny the permits. Therefore, the state of Wyoming could not provide any assurance of future protection for the lakes in Jackson Hole. The National Park Service was the only federal agency with the congressional mandate to legally provide enduring protection for the lakes in question.

be allowed near the lakes, but litter would not be tolerated. The people who favored development were evidently unconcerned that all the space around the lakes would eventually be taken for private homes, and thus eliminate public access and use of the lakes by the general public. Therefore, the lakes would, after a time, become the exclusive playground for relatively few people who might spend only a few weeks per year in the valley.

Burt felt that development around the lakes would discourage the growth of the tourist industry in the valley.* Sheffield's and Grimmesey's proposals would provide a short-run economic benefit to the valley while destroying the long-run economic potential of Jackson Hole. Without general access to the scenic lakes of the valley, the recreation potential south of Yellowstone National Park would decrease. Tourists would be less motivated to spend their time, even less their money, in Jackson Hole. Eventually, the tourists would simply pass through the valley when traveling to or from Yellowstone National Park. Burt stated, *"...we won't be able to camp on a single one of our lakes unless we camp on some other fellow's place; in the end we won't want to."* [24]

Despite Burt's logic, there was not sufficient support within the valley to convince any of Wyoming's Congressional delegation to introduce a bill to accomplish the park extension.

~

That summer, a group of Jackson Hole residents, most of them dude ranchers, invited Superintendent Albright to meet with them at the home of Maud Noble, near Menor's Ferry. This meeting marked the beginning of the dude ranchers'

second and most ambitious attempt to save the valley and their way of life. Not all of the locals who wished to see the valley protected were in attendance at this meeting, but it was Albright's impression that each of those attending represented small groups of their neighbors.[25] When Albright arrived, he found a gathering that included J. R. Jones, Richard Winger, Jack Eynon, Horace Carncross, Struthers Burt, and Si Ferrin.[26] During this meeting, those in attendance arrived at the conclusion that what they wanted for the valley was a federal status along the lines of a national recreation area rather than a national park. The appeal of a national recreation area, as opposed to a national park, rested with the ability of the former designation to protect the valley from unsightly development with a less restrictive policy regarding the public's ability to enjoy the area.

National Archives 17456pu

Maud Noble's Cabin

Maud Noble came to Jackson Hole from Philadelphia, Pennsylvania in 1915 as a guest at the Bar BC Ranch. She hired Harold Clissold to build the cabin on the east side of Cottonwood Creek in 1916. She had Clissold disassemble the cabin and move it to its present location at Menor's Ferry in 1918 when she purchased the Ferry and associated property from Bill Menor. Miss Noble stopped operating the ferry when the bridge was constructed across the Snake River in 1927. She eventually sold the property to the Snake River Land Company in 1929.

*Apparently Struthers Burt had by this time reversed, accepted, or at least moderated, his previous position adamantly opposing increased tourism within the valley.

Albright, of course, wanted an extension of Yellowstone National Park to the south, but he kept quiet and agreed to support the recreation area plan. In 1967 Albright explained why he did not push for the park extension at that time, *"...my thought was, 'I'm happy to get anything we can get; if we can get support from the local people.' If they want a recreation area that's part way; someday it will all be a National Park because that would be about the only way you could administer it. So it was up to me to participate and go along and agree to do what I could to help although a Park wasn't mentioned."*[27]

Richard Winger's recollection of the meeting contradicts Albright's version on some of the issues. For instance, Albright maintained that the park idea was not mentioned at the meeting. Winger, on the other hand, recalled that the park issue was discussed and a compromise reached.

According to Winger, the plan agreed upon at Maud Noble's cabin was originated by himself, Jack Eynon and J. R. Jones. The plan was presented to a few residents, mostly dude ranchers, including Struthers Burt, who was very enthusiastic about the idea. Burt suggested the plan be presented to Albright, but Winger did not trust Albright's motives. He thought Albright would try to convert the plan to a park extension project rather than a national recreation area proposal. Burt, by this time, had developed a friendship based on respect for Albright and assured Winger that he did not have to worry about Albright's motives.

The meeting at Maud Noble's cabin was arranged by Struthers Burt to accomplish two objectives: first to present the plan to Albright in hopes of gaining his approval and support and second, to eliminate any distrust and animosity by local supporters of the plan toward Horace Albright. Winger stated that because he was unsure of Albright, he was careful to state his opposition to any park extension plan, but he pointed out that his proposal was an even bigger project than Albright had supported in 1919. According to Winger, Albright found one flaw with the plan. Everyone agreed that 10 or more years might be required to complete the plan, and Albright pointed out that during that time, the irrigation interests could destroy the scenic lakes in the valley, and a great deal of commercialism could occur. Albright suggested that they separate the mountains and the lakes at their base from the recreation area plan and seek national park status for the mountains and lakes. He convinced the people at

Jackson Hole Historical Society and Museum bc0047

New cars were brought over Teton Pass during the winter on horse-drawn sleighs.

this meeting that the most pressing need was to provide protection for the lakes as quickly as possible while they worked to complete the recreation area idea. He agreed not to agitate for a larger park if the locals would support park status for the western portion of the valley.[28] Winger recalled, *"Mr. Albright argued that if we didn't do something with that particular area, in the course of years it would be impossible to put across our larger plan, and we agreed that was probably true, and we agreed to withdraw our objection to the creation of the park for the protection of that particular section of the country."* [29]

Winger required a promise of Albright. He asked specifically:

...that no attempts be made by him to create any sentiment favoring the inclusion of this larger area in a national park, for the simple reason that as soon as he did it would start an interdepartmental quarrel between himself and the Forest Service, which would wreck the project, at least until we had found out whether it was possible to get the money to do this and whether it was possible to put this thing across, and until then that no attempt should be made to determine who was

going to handle it. He agreed to that, and, so far as I know, he has never done anything out of line with his agreement.[30]

In addition to the discrepancy regarding the discussion of a national park, there was a contradiction relating to the scope of the proposal. Albright stated that the group was primarily interested in the property north of the town of Jackson while Winger maintained the plan encompassed the entire valley including the town of Jackson.[31] Of course, anyone who wished to sell his land could, but no one would be forced to sell. Dude ranchers would be encouraged to remain, providing services and accommodations to the traveling public.

Despite the contradictions, the group did seem to agree on their vision of the completed project. They envisioned the reintroduction of various species of indigenous wildlife which had disappeared. They hoped that the bison and antelope would once again be a common sight and the sage grouse would be protected. They decided that:

Jackson would become again a frontier town. It was hoped that all houses would be of log, and that the streets would never be paved. Each year there would be a celebration when

Jackson Hole Historical Society and Museum

The Amoretti Inn, later renamed Jackson Lake Lodge.

scenes of the fur trade and mining excitements of the early West would be re-enacted. There would be a huge rodeo. The celebration would last for days, and everybody would be encouraged to dress in the costumes of the pioneer days.[32]

Struthers Burt thought it *"...an opportunity, if taken in time, to construct the greatest natural history museum on the hoof in the world ...."*[33]

According to the dude ranchers' plan, the cattle ranches south of town *"...would continue to operate illustrating another great and important phase of the development of the West."* They foresaw *"...native wildlife, cattle, humans, all living again for a brief time each summer the life of the early West with as much of its glamour, romance and charm as could be re-established."*[34] Hunting would be continued in the mountains to the east of the valley and cattlemen would continue to drift their herds to and from the summer ranges across the valley floor. Likewise, dude ranches would be allowed to remain in all parts of Jackson Hole.

Although no one would be forced to sell his land, an estimated one million dollars would have to be raised to buy out the ranchers who wanted to sell. Indicative of the times, or perhaps the independent nature of the plan's supporters, there is no evidence to suggest that the possibility of government acquisition of these lands was ever discussed at this meeting. This group did not expect

federal, state, or county funding for their project, nor did they envision the passage of regulatory restrictions forcing their neighbors' compliance with the group's ideal. A number of wealthy eastern families, such as the Vanderbilts and the Morgans, had been entertained at some of the local dude ranches. It was decided to seek financial support for the project from the wealthy dude ranch clientele.[35] They believed if most of the privately owned land could be purchased from willing sellers the threat of unsightly development would be thwarted, and the federally owned lands, along with the acquired private property, could then be given national recreation area status.

Albright felt it would be difficult to find financing for such a project, but agreed, along with Struthers Burt, to try to raise enough money to send a couple of people back east to talk to their wealthy customers. In 1933, Horace Albright wrote, *"Mr. Burt and I, with the aid of friends, raised $2,000 which we turned over to Jack Eynon and Dick Winger. They went East and tried hard to interest wealthy men in the project. Men could*

Jackson Hole Historical Society and Museum p1958.2994.001

Bruce Porter Collection, Courtesy Liz Lockhart Jackson Hole Historical Society & Museum bc0116

Horace Albright sometimes complained about the road conditions in the north end of the valley, but during this period, Jackson Hole residents were more concerned with accessibility from Idaho over Teton Pass and southward through Hoback Canyon. Teton Pass was the lifeline for the valley, particularly during the winter. Above left, horse-drawn wagons and stages were more reliable than automobiles during the winter and when the pass road was muddy. Above right, a gas truck attempts to deliver gas to Jackson.

Teton Pass Road

Modern travelers over Teton Pass may be impressed by the sharp turns and steep grades, but the original road had seven tight switchbacks that added to the challenge, especially during the winter. Buick became a favored automobile for winter travel because its automatic Dynaflow transmission (1948-1963) provided a smooth transition between gears reducing tire spin during acceleration thus maintaining better traction on snow or ice.

not have worked harder nor more conscientiously than did Eynon and Winger, but they were not successful. " [36]

Among the contributors of the $2,000 were Albright, Stephen Mather, the Audubon Society and the American Game Protective Association.[37] With the failure to obtain financial support, the project conceived at Maud Noble's cabin was doomed and Albright was thus released from his promise not to attempt another Yellowstone Park extension in Jackson Hole. He recalled in 1967, *"...I had reason to feel that our Yellowstone extension plan had been enlarged to cover lands north of Jackson."* [38] Although the project conceived at Maud Noble's cabin had failed, the idea behind it didn't die. Those who attended the meeting at Maud Noble's cabin would be among the first to join future initiatives to protect and preserve the valley of Jackson Hole.

CHAPTER SIX
1924 - 1925

There aren't over a half-dozen residents of the valley that are for extension, and those few are for it only for mercenary reasons. It has been my observation that those who would turn our beautiful valley over to the monopolies are invariably lacking in local civic interest, and never figure in anything that is done to promote the best interest of the valley.

Wilford Neilson
Jackson Hole Courier
December 3, 1925

A petition signed by over one hundred land owners of Jackson's Hole state that they believe that the entire Jackson's Hole should be set aside as a recreational area.
Jackson Hole Courier
December 10, 1925

Jackson Hole Historical Society and Museum 2009.0057.010

The town of Jackson looking north from the corner of Cache and Broadway. The town square is the fenced area on the right.

Nineteen twenty-four was a slow year for an-ti-park extension publicity if judged by the local press. This lack of attention by the *Jackson Hole Courier* was perhaps due to a change in ed-itors more than a change in attitudes by the local opposition group. The former editor, Warren G. Bunn, like the editor before him, T. H. Baxter, op-posed the Yellowstone Park extension. In October 1923, Mr. Bunn died when he fell off a cliff while hunting sheep. Richard Winger, a former editor and now a supporter of the protection movement, took over the paper until July 10, 1924, when two brothers, Kenneth and Walter Perry of Pinedale, Wyoming bought the *Courier*.

There was little to report on the issue as no initiatives were made that year. However, two events did occur outside the valley that would eventually have profound effects on the issue of protection for Jackson Hole. One of these events was a tour of several western national parks by John D. Rockefeller, Jr. and three of his sons, John D. III, Laurance, and Nelson. The trip was simply a vacation for Mr. Rockefeller and provided an opportunity for his sons to see some of the West.*

Horace Albright received word that the par-ty would arrive for their stay in Yellowstone by train and would be traveling under the name of Davidson, Rockefeller's middle name. In 1967, Albright recalled his instructions concerning the Rockefellers.

I was to make arrangements for two sev-en-passenger private automobiles from the transportation company and two drivers. I was to outline a trip for them for a certain number of days but under no circumstances was I to propose any kind of a program that would involve any expenditures; ... he was having a vacation with his boys and the idea was not to trouble him with any proposals for grants. [1]

When the superintendent met the train, he was surprised to find that the Rockefellers had trav-eled in a public car rather than a private coach. Albright was directed to the appropriate Pullman

Rockefeller Archive Center, 812998_me

Three of the four Rockefeller sons on a western tour of na-tional parks. Left to right: Nelson, John D., III, Laurance and John D. Rockefeller, Jr.

The photo above was taken in 1920. That trip was cut short because Nelson contracted measles in Colorado and a pe-riod of quarantine caused them to abort the rest of the trip. The photo below is from the 1924 trip on which they visited Grand Canyon, Mesa Verde, Glacier and Yellowstone Na-tional Parks. Rockefeller Archivist Mary Ann Quinn con-firmed that they traveled down to view the Tetons and ate lunch at the Amoretti Inn before returning to Yellowstone.

Rockefeller Archive Center, 812999_me

Nelson, John D., III, and Laurance, 1924

---

*Peter Collier and David Horowitz included Mrs. Rockefeller on this trip in their book, *The Rockefellers: An American Dynasty.*

by the railroad's chief detective. The detective was on the train to watch after the Rockefellers although Mr. Rockefeller supposedly was unaware of his presence.

Mr. Rockefeller put his sons to work helping the porters unload baggage and left the boys to catch the bus to the hotel. He rode with Albright to the Park headquarters at Mammoth Hot Springs where Albright reviewed the tour he had planned.[3]* The Rockefeller party then toured Yellowstone National Park on their own and although Albright did not mention the Jackson Hole project, he included a trip down to Moran on the tour so the Rockefellers could see the Teton Mountains.

1900 Report of the War Dept., Army Corps of Engineers, Vol.2, Part 8
Yellowstone Park road near the south entrance of the Park, 1889.

When clearing ground for a road, the Army Engineers typically left trees and other debris beside the roads. Rockefeller eventually donated some $30,000 to have approximately 50 miles of roads cleared of stumps and cut trees. (Around $388,000 in 2010 dollars.)

It may have been this tour of the scenic areas of the West which stimulated Rockefeller's interest in protection of the national parks and scenic areas in general. He later wrote to Superintendent Albright expressing his pleasure with the tour and complimenting the park rangers, but identifying one troubling aspect of the Park. Rockefeller wrote, *"There is just one thing in the Park which marred my enjoyment of that wonderful region, and I have wondered if I might be helpful to the Park administration in improving that situation. I refer to the vast quantities of down timber and stumps which line the roadsides so frequently throughout the Park."* [4]

Since 1878, when road construction began in Yellowstone National Park, the cut trees had been piled beside the new roads and had never been removed. Also, two sets of telephone lines paralleled the roads. One was a Park Service line, constructed by the military, and the other belonged to the hotel company. Albright informed Rockefeller that the Park Service had repeatedly requested money from Congress to clean up the roads, but the appropriations were never approved. Rockefeller suggested that Albright conduct a cleanup of a few miles of road to determine an approximate cost, promising to underwrite the expense of the experiment up to $2,000. Subsequently, over a span of several years, Rockefeller paid $30,000 to have 50 miles of roadside cleared of unsightly debris. The Park Service moved its telephone lines out of view of the road and the hotel company cooperated by doing the same with its lines.[5]

The other significant event originated with the President of the United States. President Coolidge, recognizing the economic and spiritual benefits of recreation in this country, established the President's Committee on National Outdoor Recreation.† Coolidge hoped this committee could

---

*This was from an Albright interview, but Collier and Horowitz again presented a slightly different situation. They maintain that Rockefeller had already arranged for a chauffeured limousine and already had his timetable prepared. They identified their source for this information as Horace Albright.[2] Substantiating the first (Albright interview) version presented above was a letter from Rockefeller to Albright dated August 15, 1924, thanking Albright for the arrangements he (Albright) made for the Yellowstone tour.

†The committee was composed of War Secretary Weeks, who was in charge of the national military parks and who was the author of the Weeks Act which made possible the purchase, for conservation, of extensive forest lands in the White Mountains and the Appalachians; Interior Secretary Work who controlled the national parks and the general land office; Agriculture Secretary Wallace, who administered the national forests and the biological survey; and Secretary Hoover who controlled the bureau of fisheries and was the president of the National Park Association. The fifth and last member was Colonel Theodore Roosevelt, the Assistant Secretary of the Navy. A nature lover by inheritance, Roosevelt served as chairman of the committee.

formulate a national policy concerning the appropriate utilization of the nation's vast outdoor resources with relation to recreation. This move perpetuated a tradition of protection of the public domain by Presidents Wilson and Harding. Wilson had backed a popular movement which forced through Congress in his administration *"...the act exempting the existing national parks from the jurisdiction of the new water power commission,*

Rockefeller Archives Center, Series 1005, Box P105, 813001_me

Rockefeller Archives Center, Series 1005, Box P105, 813000_me

Before and after pictures of the Yellowstone National Park road cleanup project financed by John D. Rockefeller, Jr.

thus heading off immediate danger of commercial invasion." [6] It was President Harding who announced upon the 50th anniversary of Yellowstone National Park a policy which promised to protect all parks from commercial invasion.[7]

The committee operated under the philosophy that:

> *... outdoor recreation furnishes opportunity to gain abounding health, strength, wholesome enjoyment, understanding and love of nature, good-fellowship and keen sportsmanship and, above all, has a direct beneficial influence on the formation of sturdy character by developing those qualities of self-control, endurance under hardship, reliance on self, and co-operation with others in team work which are so necessary to good citizenship.* [8]

The President's Committee recognized that the enduring feud between the Park Service and the Forest Service was an impediment to the accomplishment of its goals. Several bills to establish new national parks had received no action in Congress because the two agencies could not agree on the boundaries. A coordinating commission was appointed to arbitrate the various boundary disputes between the agencies. The members of this commission were Henry W. Temple, Congressman from Pennsylvania, who served as chairman; Charles Sheldon of the Boone and Crockett Club (later to be Chairman of the Jackson Hole Elk Commission); Major William A. Welch, Manager of the Palisades Interstate Park; Stephen T. Mather, Director of the National Park Service; and W. B. Greeley, Chief Forester of the National Forest Service.[9]

In July 1925, this commission visited the Yellowstone and Jackson Hole country. Charles Sheldon was unable to make this trip, so Barrington Moore* of New York substituted for him.[10] Yellowstone National Park's original boundaries had been arbitrary survey lines. The Park Service

---

*Barrington Moore was among the first generation of scientifically trained foresters and published numerous articles in the *Journal of Forestry*. His research resulted in articles pertaining to the reproduction of several forest species and osmotic pressure as an index of habitat. Prior to serving on this committee, he was president of the Ecological Society of America (1919-1920). He would subsequently serve for 12 years as editor-in-chief of *Ecology* magazine.

had been attempting to readjust the borders along geographic features. The commission crossed Yellowstone Lake by boat and then traveled by horse into the southeast section of the Park. It was unanimously agreed that the Thorofare area, the headwaters of the Yellowstone River, should be included in the Park. As the men stood on top of the Two Ocean Plateau viewing that vast wilderness, Greeley, of the Forest Service, turned to Mather, of the Park Service, and said, *"I yield it to you, Mather, and God have mercy on your soul if you ever build a road up here."* [11]* They then came down the Buffalo Fork into Jackson Hole.

The commission was successful in the peaceful arbitration of Yellowstone's northern and eastern boundary adjustments, but when the subject of the southern boundary was approached, the Forest Service refused to compromise. The Park Service, of course, wanted the southern boundary extended to include the Tetons, but the Forest Service wanted a portion of southern Yellowstone National Park excluded from the existing Park so the timber could be cut. Specifically, they thought the southern boundary of the Park should be where the Snake River flows west from Heart Lake. This would allow timber from Wolverine, Rodent, Coulter and other creeks to be floated down the Snake to Jackson Lake where sawmills would be established to cut the trees into lumber. The Forest Service also wanted sawmills located on Pacific, Arizona, Lizard and Mink Creeks. The Park Service replied that such operations would harm the scenic value of the area and that the watersheds should be left natural. They also contended the timber was primarily useful for railroad ties, and these could be obtained from other areas in Wyoming and Idaho.

The Forest Service then described the mineral wealth of the Jackson Hole country stating that the coal and phosphate beds were important to the nation. They also cited one asbestos claim at the north end of the Teton Range. The Park Service countered that deposits of these minerals existed in greater volumes in other locations in the state and that these alternate locations offered more economical mining and marketing of the minerals than the Jackson Hole area.

The Forest Service stated that the area was a great cattle country, and the industry needed the land to thrive. They advocated the development of summer homes along the lakes at the base of the Tetons. The Park Service countered that their proposal to extend Yellowstone's boundaries would not take in any of the land necessary to the cattlemen, and if summer home development

www.foresthistory.org via Wikimedia Commons
William Buckhout Greeley
1879-1955

Greeley was a graduate of the University of California and the Yale Forest School. In 1904, he joined the Bureau of Forestry and by 1918 had advanced to Assistant Chief in charge of Silviculture. In World War I he served overseas with the 20th Engineers (Forestry) and returned to the U.S. as a lieutenant colonel, and thereafter preferred to be addressed by his military title. After the war, he resumed his position with the Forest Service as Assistant Chief to Henry S. Graves. When Graves retired, Greeley became the 3rd Chief of the Forest Service. Greeley wrote that nothing *"... illustrates the democracy of the American forest policy or the decentralization in administering national forests than the conscientious effort of the Forest Service to weight the importance of different uses on each unit and to give every use its merited place in a bewildering regimen of administrative detail."*

www.foresthistory.org/ASPNET/People/G

---

* It may be presumed Greeley was aware this was the area where the National Park Service had intended to build a road in 1918. Mather's response, if any, was not recorded.

were desired it should, more properly, occur on the eastern side of the valley near the Gros Ventre Mountains, or in the southern part of the valley.[12]

The commission held a public hearing in Jackson on this issue. The hearing was reminiscent of the meeting which Albright and Governor Carey attended in 1919. Albright wrote:

We lost our fight the second day in Jackson. A local stampede meeting, such as I faced in 1919, occurred the night before the commission's final meeting. It was not so one-sided as the meeting six years earlier.

Jackson Hole Historical Society and Museum p1958.1039.001
Bill Hutton and his dog at his talc mine near Berry Creek. Albright claimed the northern portion of the Teton Range was eliminated from national park consideration because of an "unproven" mining claim. However, John Graul's asbestos mine up Owl Creek and Bill Hutton's talc mine up Berry Creek were valid mining claims. Although both mineral deposits ultimately proved to be of minor extent and importance, the miners had legitimate claims that deserved fair consideration by the President's park boundary coordinating committee.

Jackson Hole Historical Society and Museum p1991.3560.001
John Graul's cabin on Owl Creek near his asbestos mine. The Park Service eventually burned the cabin.

I had plenty of champions this time, but the eloquent Will Deloney was then against us, and his brilliant oration was a powerful aid for our opponents.[13]

In 1967, Albright again recalled Deloney as an eloquent orator. Albright stated that Deloney, *"...could make the rafters ring with his oratory. He took me over the coals backwards and forwards. Winger, on the other hand, jumped to his feet and took after him. Winger wasn't much of an orator, but he had all the courage in the world."*[14] Winger was apparently in the minority as most of the locals who attended this meeting were against any southern extension of Yellowstone's boundaries.

The next day, behind closed doors, the commission held its last meeting. The result was a three to two vote for including the Tetons and the Thorofare area into Yellowstone National Park, as well as extending the Park boundary to include the watersheds of Wolverine, Coulter and other streams and half of Big Game Ridge. However, the commission preferred that all their recommendations be the result of a unanimous decision, so they met once again. A compromise was necessary to achieve a unanimous vote; Albright recalled the outcome of the compromise, *"...in addition to the Thorofare country only a part of the Teton Range was approved for park status, the northern third of the range being omitted because of one unproven asbestos claim!"*[15] Both the Park Service and the Forest Service were unhappy with the decision and the animosities between the two agencies continued.

Some residents had hoped that this commission would settle the park extension issue permanently. Walter D. Perry, the editor of the *Jackson Hole Courier*, expressed this view in an open letter to the members of the commission. He stated, *"Our future has rested under a cloud of doubt."*[16] He reviewed the reasons for the opposition to park extension and then concluded:

We recognize the sincerity of National Park Officials in pushing for the Extension of the Yellowstone Park. We do not condemn them in their activities and beliefs. But we do believe that in this case

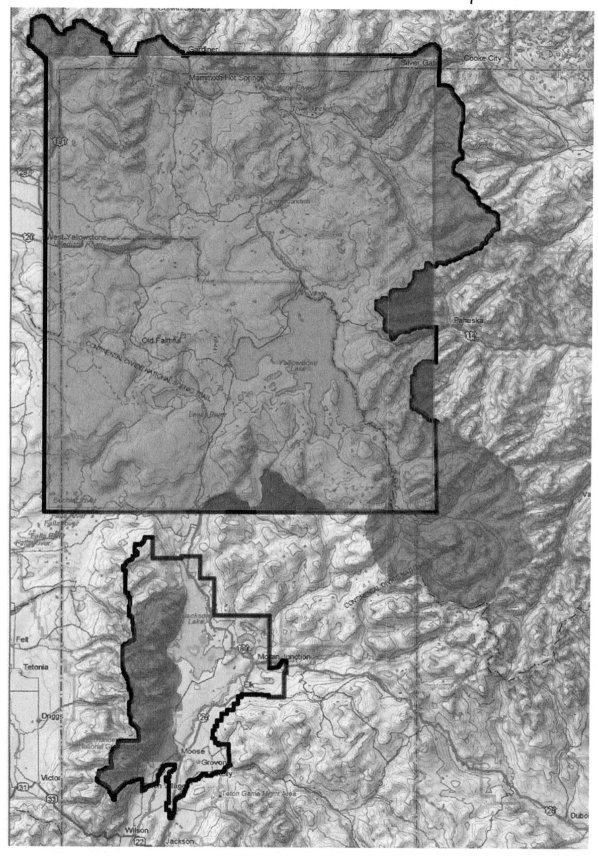

The boundary compromise developed by the President's
Commission on National Outdoor Recreation. 1925.

Current Park boundaries
Original Yellowstone Park
Extensions to Yellowstone Park
Deletions from Yellowstone Park

Park Extension is fundamentally unsound, and that it will not solve the problems with which we are face to face. Gentlemen, you are the jury. The case is now in your hands. Make your decision in the shortest possible time. We of Jackson Hole have been held in suspense too long.[17]

Judging from the adverse publicity that followed the commission's report, the press misunderstood either the report's recommendations or allowed emotion to influence their reporting. The criticisms directed by the press toward the commission bear little resemblance to its conclusions. First, the commission's recommendation for park status for the Tetons did not include any private or state lands. The Forest Service managed entirely the area designated for park status. The commission would simply have changed the managing agency. Therefore, the federal government would not have extended its authority within the state. Also, the proposed Teton section of Yellowstone Park would not have been connected to the original Yellowstone Park. That portion of the Tetons with park status would be a separate area but managed by the Yellowstone Park administrators. No ranches would have been affected, and no grazing rights would have been endangered.

Once the commission's decision was known, the emotional level of the anti-park extension faction was raised to a level which surpassed that of 1919. Newspapers throughout western Wyoming, and, at least, one in southeastern Idaho, attacked the extension plan and the coordinating commission. The primary emphasis of the attacks centered on the "certain" despoilation of the Tetons and Jackson Hole by the Park Service through its concessionaires. In most of the printed articles, the term "concessionaire" was not used. The writers preferred to call them monopolies. Although this term was appropriate, it also carried a negative connotation to the people of Wyoming. Wyomingites have always been avid states righters, but they are even more adamant about individual rights making monopolies particularly unpopular with the people. Like the bell that caused Pavlov's dogs to salivate, the word "monopoly" could elicit a predictable negative emotion.

The first adverse publicity to come from the commission's recommendations was another open letter written by Walter D. Perry. Among other things, he could not understand why Jackson Hole should be the recipient of the commission's impositions while supremely beautiful areas like the Green River country should be ignored. He stated, *"...the Green River country*

Charlie Petersen, Sr. Collection

The milk man collected milk from various farms and ranches and delivered milk to other valley residents. He allowed children to hooky-bob as he made his deliveries.

82

is extremely lucky in one respect - they have no Yellowstone Park at their door stretching out to grab and turn over to monopolies the wonderful attractions of the region."[18] Perry suggested that the Forest Service withdraw the photographs they had published to advertise the recreational opportunities of the Green River area. He warned, *"The President's Commission may somewhere see one of those pictures, and so give the Park Service a chance to give some 'deserving son a dukedom.'"*[19]*

In fairness to Mr. Perry, it should be noted that near the conclusion of his letter, he made one of the very few rational observations to be printed in this period of controversy. It also exemplified the feelings of many Jackson Hole residents more correctly than any of the articles that followed. He wrote:

> *Congressman Winter expressed his desire that the people of this valley back this proposed extension to the utmost, but will he back us in our demands that the Teton Division be forever free from entrance fees, that no monopolies will ever exist thereon.... If he can assure us on these few points then perhaps we can see our way clear to stand not opposed even tho we do not boost for a greater Yellowstone Park.*
>
> *People of Wyoming this is your problem even tho it affects more closely we who border Yellowstone Park. Realize that we of Jackson's Hole are not believers of spoliation. That we love our country and believe in its future. Consider the problems that confront us from all angles, the benefits the Yellowstone Park has conferred upon us, the demerits the Park Service has rightly earned, what is best for the state in which we live, what is best for the people of Jackson's Hole. We will try to be fair. If you believe that Extension is desirable give us the benefit of your protection in preventing the undesirable features connected with Park*

Charles Edwin Winter (R)
1870 - 1948

Winter was born in Iowa, studied law at Wesleyan University in Lincoln, Nebraska, and was admitted to the bar in 1895. He moved to Wyoming in 1902, practiced law, served as a judge of the sixth judicial district of Wyoming (1913-1919), and was elected to Congress in 1923. He failed to unseat Senator Kendrick in 1928. He was attorney general of Puerto Rico in 1932 and 1933 and also served as acting governor of that territory.

Harris and Ewing [Public domain] via Wikimedia Commons

Service being saddled upon the Extension areas. Back us in our few demands. We wish only to protect the inalienable rights handed down to us and to you by generations past.[20]

Other writers were more emotional and were not only frequently incorrect, but some of their accusations were topographically impossible. These articles, nevertheless, demonstrated the residents' fears regarding Yellowstone Park control of even a small portion of their valley. Many people were still unwilling to believe that park status would provide protection rather than desecration for the Tetons and the undeveloped lakes at their base. The Park Service had been unsuccessful in dispelling the belief that they were controlled by the profit interest in Yellowstone National Park.

---

*The reference to a "dukedom" is a direct jab at Horace Albright. Prior to the commission's trip to Wyoming, the *Saturday Evening Post* had published an article about Albright and Yellowstone National Park. Kenneth Roberts, the author, referred to Albright as *"... the Grand Duke of Yellowstone."* Although it was intended to be a laudatory remark, the timing could not have been worse. Albright's "monarchy" was no more welcome in Jackson Hole than Yellowstone's "monopolies."

One of these articles alliterated that the proposed extension was an *"... illadvised, inequitable, indiscreet incursion on the inalienable rights of the people of the state of Wyoming."* [21] The *Idaho Falls Post* declared, *"'They' want to 'hotelize it' and 'campize it' and 'modernize it' until its whole autocratic bureaucratic length is putrefied with the filth of plain travel and they have made it as common as the park."* [22] The *Kemmerer Gazette* contributed, *"...we are unequivocally against turning over the wonderful Jackson's Hole to federal denomination, which means ultimate control by the transportation and hotel*

Jackson Hole Historical Society and Museum 19924351001

Automobile travelers expected to change and repair their own tires.

By the mid-1920s tourism still had not revealed itself as an economic force in the valley. The highways were not crowded with automobiles and the sometimes long stretches of lonely roads with few amenities required an adventurous and self-reliant spirit for the western traveler. Just getting to Jackson Hole could be an adventure. The photo below shows the first automobile to enter the valley over Teton Pass under its own power.

Jackson Hole Historical Society and Museum 20050043002

monopolies. At present there is no monopoly, and the wonderful scenery, undefiled by commercialism, is available to all, with no fee." [23]* And this one from the *Wyoming Eagle*, *"The action of the investigating committee is just about what one could expect. A group of officials from the east, making a superficial examination of the situation, listens to a vigorous protest from the private citizens whose interests would be most affected, and then makes recommendations directly counter to the wishes of the permanent settlers."* [24]

The preoccupation so many people had with the evils of the concessionaires in Yellowstone was not as farfetched as it might seem. The commercial operators in Yellowstone National Park had exclusive commercial rights within the Park's boundaries. Many locals feared that when the legal name, Yellowstone National Park, was placed on the Tetons, the operations in Yellowstone would have an automatic and exclusive right to control commercial activities in the extended area. This issue of extended commercial rights was not addressed by either the Park Service or the Commission. Local dude ranchers and outfitters depended upon access to various scenic sections for their livelihood. Local businessmen profited by selling supplies to tourists. The question, therefore, was not if commercial activity would occur, but who, if anyone, would control it. At that time in the history of Jackson Hole, the residents were not inclined to impose their personal values upon each other regarding commercial activity as long as a proposed business did not impose an adverse impact on other businesses. The rights attendant to private property and opportunity were considered inalienable. Thus, the perceived threat of extended commercial monopoly from Yellowstone concessionaires was an important issue.

Many residents were sure these Yellowstone operations wanted the Tetons, and that they were responsible for the various efforts to extend Yellowstone's boundaries to the south. The Park Service had maintained all along that these companies had nothing to do with the movement.

---

*The *Kemmerer Gazette* either elected to ignore or was not aware of the rapid commercialization taking place along the roads and scenic areas of Jackson Hole. Since the opening of the Togwotee Pass and Hoback Canyon highways, the roads throughout the valley had become littered with signs, hotdog stands, gas stations and gift shops. Commercialism had arrived.

Indeed, there is no evidence that these companies ever pushed, encouraged or forced the Park Service to make any initiatives for the extension, but it would be erroneous to conclude that they were not interested in the Jackson Hole country. D.B. Sheffield stated that a group of men including Henry Child* the son of the president of the hotel and transportation company; Jack Haynes, a photographer; Emerson Hough, the writer; Horace Albright; an architect and others visited his place in the summer of 1918. Sheffield said Mr. Child offered him $50,000 for his lodge. He also stated, *"...the Yellowstone Transportation and Hotel Co. were paying more in current rental than any other company in any other national park in the United States, and ... what led them to try to get a greater Yellowstone was to get a greater haul, because the Glacier Park ... and the Great Northern [Railroad] was cutting in on their business."* [25] Sheffield said they wanted to build a road on the west side of Jackson Lake, up Pacific Creek, and back into Yellowstone.[26] In other words, the transportation company wanted to extend their lines to the south to make up for losses incurred at the northern entrance of Yellowstone National Park.

~

While newspapers in western Wyoming continued to voice indignation with their literary emotionalism, another Wyoming paper found much of the state's population to be apathetic on the issue. The *Casper Herald* sponsored a discussion on the park extension issue devoting two columns a day to the subject. One column was for pro-extension opinions while the other column accommodated anti-extension articles. It appears that very few people elected to express their views. Horace Albright recalled that Tom Cooper of Casper wrote a few articles in opposition while Edward Gillette of Sheridan wrote a few articles as a proponent. When the discussion period was over, the *Herald* called for a vote on the issue. Sixty-seven people voted "no" while 59 voted "yes."[27] Park extension, evidently, was not a burning issue in other parts of Wyoming.

The *Jackson Hole Courier* reported that, in an attempt to gain statewide support for the anti-extension movement, five local men had presented a petition to the state Chamber of Commerce Convention in Casper. This anti-extension petition was supposedly signed by a majority of Jackson Hole residents. The *Courier's* article was incorrect on at least two counts. First, the paper listed the five men as *"...Deloney, Lovejoy, Leek, Cunningham and Ferrin."* [28] Although J. P. Cunningham and J. D. Ferrin did attend the meeting in Casper, they did not present an anti-extension petition. They carried a petition signed by 97 residents requesting that all of Jackson Hole be

Jackson Hole Historical Society and Museum p1958.12017.001

Ben Sheffield's Teton Lodge at Moran in winter

*Sheffield may have misremembered Child's given name. He may have been referring to Huntley Child, who was the son of Harry Child, the president of the Yellowstone Hotel and Transportation Company.**

set aside as a recreation area. In this petition, they also agreed to sell their lands, at what they considered to be a fair price, to further that end. The second error in the article was, according to Ferrin, that no anti-extension petition was presented by anyone.[29]

Ferrin told of the origin of "his" petition during his testimony before the Senate Investigating Committee in 1933. Ferrin recalled that he heard about the anti-extension petition through friends outside the valley. He maintained, to the committee, that he was never able to find anyone in Jackson Hole who had even seen the document. His friends in Casper had told him that the petition gave the impression that everyone in Jackson Hole was satisfied with the existing situation and that the people would not sell their land for any price. The misrepresentation of the situation upset Ferrin, and he conferred with J. L. Eynon and J. P. Cunningham. Ferrin stated, *"...to offset that, we talked it over and met down here and got a fellow by the name of Huff, I believe it was, to fix up this petition, and then we circulated it. We were*

only out a couple of days, but every rancher up in the country signed that petition that we talked to about it." [30]

This petition received little publicity at the time, but portions of it have frequently been quoted in books and articles about the recent history of Jackson Hole. The quotes out of context do not do justice to the people who signed it. The excerpts were usually used to indicate support for the park extension movement, or for Albright personally. In truth, the entire document, while allowing that the proposed, limited extension was proper, did not recommend park status for the entire valley. It is not likely that many, if any, of the people who signed the petition, would have approved a greater extension than that proposed by the coordinating commission. The petition was not an endorsement of the National Park Service or Yellowstone National Park. Neither was it a condemnation of the Forest Service nor the Biological Survey. It did not disparage the appropriateness of the valley for cattle raising or indicate that it was unprofitable. It was simply a statement

American Heritage Center, University of Wyoming, JHHS&M bc.0382

Town of Jackson, 1924. Population - 307

of the signer's belief that the destiny and most appropriate utilization of the valley rested in recreational values. It mattered not which agency administered the land as long as the administration followed guidelines that enhanced the recreational opportunities appropriate to Jackson Hole.[31] [See Appendix Two-A to read the petition.]

Although the recommendations of the coordinating commission formed the basis for future congressional action, legislative initiatives were

not attempted in 1925. The commission had tried to soothe the tensions in Jackson Hole, but it created more controversy and stirred more emotion than had previously existed in the valley. However, the petition signed by a significant number of residents indicated the continued interest in some form of protection for the scenic features of Jackson Hole.

Mining in Jackson was usually viewed as a minor and probably misspent effort by wealthy easterners and securely employed people such as Horace Albright. They considered these mining claims insignificant compared to their larger and altruistic goal of national park status for the northern portion of the valley. The miners, however, undeterred by hard work and long hours, were able, in many cases, to make a living from their labors. These mining claims offered them an opportunity for survival in an era of hard times and the absence of federal or state welfare programs.

Horace Albright Photo, Jackson Hole Historical Society and Museum
1958.1514.001

Above: Galena mine in Death Canyon.

Jackson Hole Historical Society and Museum 2004.0109.218
Above: Bill Rodenbuck with his rock crusher.

American Heritage Center, University of Wyoming, ah03138_0843
Gold mining on the Snake River.

Jackson Hole Historical Society and Museum p1958.0198.001
Above: Frank Coffin, Dan Graham, and Jim Webb working their gold mine claim on Pilgrim Creek.

CHAPTER SEVEN
1926 - 1927

An increased territory means not so much necessary additional land for useful and desirable purposes as it means extension of federal bureaucratic control and further dictation to and ordering of the people by petty officials ... more don'ts and musts to be observed by the people of Wyoming and the others from elsewhere, who visit the park.

Casper Daily Tribune
January 1926

S. N. Leek Collection ah03138_1365, American Heritage Center University of Wyoming

A well-mannered horse could replace the need for waders.

Although anti-park extension oratory and petitions continued to receive newspaper publicity around the state, the furor gradually began to decrease. There was a brief injection of energy when, in March of 1926, Representative Sinnott of Oregon and Senator Nye of North Dakota introduced Yellowstone Park extension legislation in the first session of the 69th Congress.[1] The purpose of their respective bills was to accomplish the boundary adjustments recommended by the Coordinating Commission on National Parks and Forests. This created renewed interest in the controversy in Wyoming, but the *Salt Lake Tribune* observed, *"Wyoming formerly was overwhelmingly opposed to adding more lands to the park, but sentiment there is now divided, and since the proposed additions have been cut down to include practically no lands now used for grazing livestock, the opposition is not particularly rampant."* [2]

In April, Wyoming Congressman Winter expressed his support for the House version of the extension bill. The *Courier* quoted him as stating before the House Committee on Public Lands, *"...rather than side step the issue for political reasons, sentiment being divided, this question should be settled now and for all time, thus ending the longstanding withdrawal pending legislation status of huge areas which has retarded settlement and development."* [3] Winter, however, suggested an amendment to the bill. His amendment provided Wyoming the right to tax private property within Yellowstone National Park or for the Park to provide an annuity of $5,000 each to Park and Teton Counties from Yellowstone Park receipts. He cited a resolution signed by 44 ranchers from Jackson Hole, who were formerly opposed to the extension, now favoring the amendment. His amendment was received well by the committee.[4]

The news that Congressman Winter was backing the park extension bill did not generate the expected volume of emotional publicity in the local press. Instead, the issue was dealt with in a rather calm manner. State Senator William Deloney of Teton County, expressed his concern by writing the Congressman to determine his exact position on the bill. Winter wired back:

> *Did not state to Public Lands Committee or to anyone that the opposition of Jackson or Jackson's Hole removed. I introduced every resolution sent me in opposition. Will send you a copy of hearings as soon as printed. Passage of bill inevitable regardless of my attitude. My concern is to get taxation amendment for benefit of our state and your county. Firmly believe great financial benefit to Jackson and Jackson's Hole.*[5]

The reasons for the reduction in anti-park extension publicity were unclear. Perhaps the people were simply tired of the controversy and were satisfied to have the question resolved at long last. The bill protected the extended Park areas from encroachment from the Yellowstone monopolies by providing, *"That no new roads shall be constructed on the lands hereby added to the park and no hotels or permanent camps*

Jackson Hole Historical Society and Museum 2003.0054.007
Horace Albright provided a tour of Yellowstone and Jackson Hole for Wyoming Governor Nellie Tayloe Ross in 1926.

shall be authorized or permitted to be maintained on such lands at points not now accessible by roads without specific authority from Congress."[6] This would certainly have decreased some of the opposition. Another factor may have been that attention was at least partially diverted to other local issues. One such issue was the initiation of attempts to arbitrate water rights to the Snake River with the state of Idaho. The dispute over the amount of water available to Wyoming for irrigation purposes from the Snake River had long been a sore spot in western Wyoming, and the birth of what would later become the Snake River Compact was just beginning.

Also, a long ensuing court battle was moving toward completion. Before Teton County had been established, Lincoln County had attempted to tax the physical improvements built by the private irrigation companies from Idaho on Jackson Lake. The county reasoned that since the dam on Jackson Lake was primarily constructed with private funds from private companies for profit, the dam, or a portion of it, and the value of the stored water should be taxable by the county. The county viewed the dam as a taxable asset just like private summer homes or other improvements built on leased federal land within the boundaries of the county. The irrigation companies felt they held a unique position because of the nature of their contract with the Reclamation Service. They felt that taxing them was the same as taxing a government contract, and that was the same as taxing the government, which was illegal. The irrigation companies refused to pay the tax and the county sued. The county won the first court battle, but the irrigation companies won the appeal. The county appealed to a higher court and so the battle gradually moved through the courts by way of the appeals process. When Teton County was established, it joined the suit with Lincoln County. In 1926, the suit was, of course, a matter of interest to the residents of Jackson Hole. The court would eventually decide in Idaho's favor.

Another issue that attracted the attention of the valley residents in 1926 was a renewed controversy concerning the Jackson Hole elk herd. Several national publications printed articles critical of the management policies of the Biological

American Heritage Center, University of Wyoming ah00948_004444

Nellie Tayloe Ross (D)
1876-1977

Nellie Tayloe Ross was the first woman elected to the governorship of any state in the union. She was a staunch supporter of Al Smith in the 1928 presidential election and at the Democratic National Convention received 31 votes from 10 states for the vice-presidential position on the first ballot. In 1933, Franklin Roosevelt appointed her the first female director of the U.S. Mint. She lived to the age of 101.

Survey, the Wyoming Game and Fish Commission, and, in some cases, the actions and attitudes of the valley residents. The elk herd was often a subject of local pride, and the *Jackson Hole Courier* was predictably critical of these nationally circulated articles.

Whatever the reason for the noticeable lack of anti-park extension publicity, Congressman Sinnott's bill passed the House of Representatives with ease. It is not likely that the bill would have failed to pass the House even if an aggressive anti-park extension campaign had existed in Jackson Hole. The House was acting on the recommendations of a group of prestigious men who visited the area and considered the issue from a variety of viewpoints. This particular bill, therefore, seemed reasonable to the congressmen. President Coolidge, in support of this pending legislation, signed Executive Order No.4486 on July 29, 1926, withdrawing more of the public lands in Jackson Hole from settlement.

The Park Service, once again, was feeling confident that at last they had added the Tetons to their domain. Little, if any, controversy was perceived to exist within the Senate over the proposed boundaries. However, Senator Frank R. Gooding of Idaho attached an amendment to transfer the southwest corner of Yellowstone National Park to the Forest Service to Senator Nye's version of the bill (S. 3427). The Idaho irrigation interests selected this time and this bill to renew their attempts to dam the Bechler River Basin. By transferring this area to the Forest Service, with its multiple-use mandate, and away from the preservation ethic of the Park Service, their cause would be greatly advanced. Senator Gooding introduced a resolution (S. Res. 237.) in the Senate, which was approved on July 2, 1926, providing for investigative hearings to be conducted in St. Anthony, Idaho.[7]*

The testimony presented at this hearing dealt with the Bechler River Basin of Yellowstone National Park and did not contribute substantially to the proposed Yellowstone extension controversy. However, the hearings were significant for several reasons. First, the transcript of the hearing indicated an apparent, though brief, change in attitude of Wyoming's Senator Kendrick toward the national parks. In 1922, he defeated Mondell in Jackson Hole largely because of his stand against national parks in Wyoming. His comments during this hearing placed him in a position of protector of the Park for the people of America. Senator Kendrick quietly listened to a great deal of testimony favoring the proposed reservoir before stating:

It is clear that the situation is serious and an effort should be made to provide water. And water should be provided, but it ought not to be overlooked that this territory was dedicated over 50 years ago to all the people, and, therefore, it behooves us to proceed very cautiously and not interfere with that plan of dedication.... I have heard it said that this area had no scenic value. Personally, I never saw the place until yesterday, but I am impressed with the simple fact that it is the most beautiful meadow I have ever seen; it is a most beautiful place to camp and fish.

...we from your neighboring State of Wyoming are concerned as much in your welfare as if your farmers were men of our own state. And yet, we are tremendously fearful of the fact that when the initial step is taken in this sort of interference with the

bioguide.congress.gov [Public domain] via Wikimedia Commons

Frank Robert Gooding (R)
1859 – 1928

Born in Devonshire, England, Gooding immigrated to the United States in 1867. After residing in Michigan and California, he settled in Idaho Territory in 1881. His immigrant spirit took him from working as a mail carrier in Ketchum to becoming one of Idaho's largest sheep ranchers. After Idaho statehood, he served in the state legislature and was elected the seventh Governor in 1904 before becoming a United States citizen. Gooding was elected to the U.S. Senate in 1920 and represented Idaho in that body until his death in 1928. The Idaho city of Gooding and Gooding County were named for him.

---

*The Senate Subcommittee that was appointed to investigate the amendment was composed of Robert N. Stanfield, Oregon, Chairman; Peter Norbeck, South Dakota; Ralph H. Cameron, Arizona; John B. Kendrick, Wyoming; and Henry F. Ashurst of Arizona. Also attending the investigation was Congressman Winter of Wyoming and Congressman Smith of Idaho. The feelings of the residents of southeastern Idaho were quite strong on the need for the dam and a good many farmers and irrigation company representatives attended the hearings.

Grand Teton National Park- Bound hearing transcription S. Res 237, 1926.
1926 Senate investigating committee Subcommittee of the Committee on Public Lands and Surveys, United States Senate, crossing the Bechler River, Yellowstone National Park. In 1926 horses and wagons were often more practical transportation than automobiles.

territory dedicated to the use of the people that there is extreme danger ... because of what it means in future years. This park was dedicated many years ago and used by very few people, but now there is an ever increasing number of people using it every day. We should proceed very carefully in the determination of this important problem....[8]

Later in the hearing, Mr. W. G. Swendsen, the Commissioner of Irrigation for the state of Idaho, was questioned concerning the operation of the proposed reservoir in the event it should become a reality. Mr. Swendsen was asked if the proposed reservoir could be operated so as to avoid the unsightly shoreline created at Jackson Lake by the Jackson Lake Dam. He responded by stating that no one needed to worry about Idaho's respect for beauty. Whereupon Senator Kendrick, perhaps recalling his first view of Jackson Lake, entered the discussion affirming his requirement that the scenic values of the Bechler Basin be maintained. It was obvious from the subsequent discussion that some of the people believed the reclamation of profitable fertile lands superseded scenic values while others tried to assure Kendrick the proposed reservoir would not adversely affect the area. It was eventually suggested that

if the bill that was the subject of the hearing became law, and the Bechler Basin was transferred from the Park Service to the Forest Service, a different jurisdictional issue would arise. Wyoming had jurisdiction of all water within its boundaries and outside of Yellowstone National Park. If the Bechler area was removed from Yellowstone, the water Idaho irrigation interests wanted to impound would automatically revert to Wyoming jurisdiction. Thus, the state of Wyoming could impose construction and operational requirements to avoid the unsightly consequences that occurred as a result of the damming of Jackson Lake. When asked if it was not likely that Wyoming would insist on such requirements, Kendrick responded, *"It is to be hoped that my State will not be lacking in diligence again."*[9]

The second reason the Idaho hearings are important is that during an exchange of opinions between Senator Kendrick and Congressman Winter, it was revealed that Kendrick had ambitions for the Tetons that did not allow for their inclusion into Yellowstone National Park. Kendrick suggested that if the Bechler River Basin was excluded from the Park, it might be necessary *"...to add other lands to the park in lieu of it...."* Whereupon Congressman Winter stated, *"The people of Wyoming have contributed 300,000 acres to the park now."* Kendrick retorted, *"I might say, Mr. Winter, that we are not contributing that as a part of Yellowstone Park. If that becomes a national park, it is going to be called the Grand Teton National Park."*[10] Not only had the Senator implied his opposition to the extension bill, but more importantly, he became the first man to suggest a separate national park status for the Tetons since Charles D. Walcott's report to Congress in 1898.

The third important aspect of the hearings was the testimony of Fred T. Dubois, a former Senator from the state of Idaho relating to the Jackson Lake Dam, to the reservoir in question, and to the future of all national parks. Concerning Jackson Lake, he recalled that in 1902 he visited Jackson Lake on horseback with the head of the Forest Service, the head of the Reclamation Service, Congressman Mondell, and a group of engineers. He further testified:

It was a very beautiful lake, nestling there at the foot of the Tetons. While we were camped there at the lake, Congressman Mondell said to me: 'Unfortunately

Fred Thomas Dubois (R)/(D)
1851-1930

Dubois was of French-Canadian heritage whose grandfather, Toussaint Dubois, immigrated to the U.S. and fought at the Battle of Tippecanoe. His father was involved in Illinois Republican Party politics and was a close friend of Abraham Lincoln. After studying at Yale, he entered business but moved to Idaho Territory in 1880 where he was appointed United States Marshall for that territory in 1882. At that time, he was probably best known for his successful effort to disenfranchise Mormon voters in Idaho Territory because of their practice of polygamy.

In 1886, he was elected as a Republican Territorial Delegate and held the position until statehood in 1890. He was elected to the U.S. Senate in 1891 but returned to his ranch in Blackfoot, Idaho after he was defeated in his re-election attempt in 1896. Dubois changed political parties and returned to the Senate in 1900. He was the only person from Idaho to serve in the U.S. Senate as both a Republican and a Democrat. He is best known for his strong opposition to Mormonism and Chinese immigration, but, he also broke with other Democrats by supporting Theodore Roosevelt's agenda of environmental conservatism. His environmental concerns regarding the proposed Bechler Meadows reservoir were evident in his testimony before the Senate Committee in 1926.

Wyoming can not use these waters, and I am sure that the people of Wyoming will be glad to turn them over to you; that is, to the people of Idaho.' So you can see that I had something to do with that project.

I returned to the project some 20 years after it was completed, and when I saw that blackened waste, that ghastly, muddy bank ... I said: 'Will the Good Lord ever forgive me for what I had to do with that?' ...after seeing Jackson Lake as it is now, I resolved that I would never have anything to do with a matter of this kind again.[11]

Concerning the proposed reservoir the former Senator stated:

Imagine, if you can, that road built up the Bechler River; you are traveling over it, there are those beautiful meadows, and the beautiful falls. What would you see after this reservoir had been in operation? You would see blackened and dead trees, and the black mud bank the same as you see in Jackson Lake. Do you think you are going to cut all those trees out? You are not; that is only a dream, they will be there as they are in every reservoir which has ever been built. They would tax you people to death if you do all you promise to do to get this water.[12]

Concerning Yellowstone National Park and the future of all national parks the Senator warned:

I have been aiding irrigation in Idaho all my life, but I will never consent, neither will the people of Idaho consent, to the despoiling and desecrating of the national park at the expense of all the people in order to benefit a favored few.

If you built the reservoir, that is the end of anyone ever seeing the beauties above the reservoir site ...and the most beautiful section of the national park will be denied to the people of the United States, to whom it belongs and was dedicated. In my judgement, Congress will never do it, if they do, it is the end of our park. If our Senators are strong enough to be allowed to use the most beautiful portion of the park for commercial purposes, then every Senator will want to assert his rights by reason of the precedent established, and I do not want Idaho to be responsible for that precedent.[13]

The result of the Subcommittee's investigation was that a sufficient number of committee members were impressed with the water needs of eastern Idaho to include the Gooding Amendment with Senator Nye's bill. The Park Service was then faced with the situation of either gaining the Tetons and the Thorofare area while losing the Bechler River Basin or gaining nothing. They chose the latter and refused to support S. 3427. Enough senators also feared the precedent proposed by the amendment that the bill failed to pass the Senate.*

Early in 1927, the Wyoming State Legislature made a move to block any future attempt to annex the Tetons into Yellowstone Park. Senator Lundy introduced a State Park Memorial, which opposed the Yellowstone National Park extension and provided that the same lands which would have comprised the Teton Division of Yellowstone Park in S. 3427 be ceded to the state of Wyoming for state park purposes. The memorial seemed to have little effect on the U.S. Congress as a whole, but it did have implications for Wyoming's Congressional delegation. If any member of the delegation voted for a park extension bill, he would be acting in opposition to his own state's wishes as expressed by the state Legislature. This, according to Teton County's Representative, William Deloney, was one of the desired effects.[14]

$\sim$

While the hearing on the Nye Bill was in progress in Idaho, John D. Rockefeller, Jr. was again visiting Yellowstone National Park. This time, he was accompanied by Mrs. Rockefeller and their three youngest boys, Laurance, Winthrop, and David. At the request of Mr. Rockefeller, Albright again made all the arrangements for the party. In 1967, Albright recalled an important difference in the situation, *"Nobody put any restrictions on me*

that time. So I just declared myself into the party and went with them." [15] Albright, of course, brought the family down to see the Tetons and the Jackson Hole country. They spent their first night in the valley at Jackson Lake Lodge and continued to the Bar BC and JY ranches the next day. While traveling on the Forest Service road between the Jackson Lake Dam and Jenny Lake, the Rockefellers were able to view the unsightly commercial developments that had converged on the valley. In addition to the commercial structures, there were abandoned shacks of unsuccessful homesteaders and a telephone line that the Forest Service had constructed between the road and the mountains. The telephone line was built in spite of Albright's protest. Albright recalled, *"I had recommended that the line not be built between the road and the Tetons, but the Forest Service had done*

K. Greenwood NPS.gov [Public domain] via Wikimedia Commons

Union Falls (250 feet) in the Bechler area is Yellowstone's second highest straight falls, as opposed to cascading falls.

*The Bechler Basin continues to be one of the least visited areas of Yellowstone National Park because of the limited road system. For the few who have made the effort to visit the area on foot or horseback, the basin is considered to be the most spectacular portion of the Park. The mountain meadows, alpine streams, and numerous spectacular waterfalls remain "undiscovered" and unappreciated by the majority of Park visitors.

Rockefeller Archive Center Series 1005, Box 43C

Mr. and Mrs. John D. Rockefeller, Jr. and unnamed park ranger at a picnic in Jackson Hole.

it anyway. It would have been better if I hadn't recommended because they probably would have built it right if I hadn't said anything. My advice was what they wanted to go against." [16] When the party arrived at the JY Ranch for lunch, a tall, thin man, who was supposedly the son of the Earl of Exeter, opened Mr. Rockefeller's car door and stated, *"Mr. Rockefeller, my name is Hope. They call me Slim Hope. I don't think you have had the pleasure of meeting me."* [17] This pleased Mr. Rockefeller greatly and apparently contributed to the harmonious atmosphere during their lunch.

After lunch, Albright took the party back to the Jackson Lake Lodge along a road which paralleled the river. At a high point along this road, the party stopped to view the valley and the mountains. It was at this point that Albright told the group about the meeting at Maud Noble's cabin. He explained the recreation area idea that many of the residents favored stating that it was a dream that had faded. He also stated his own dream that the area would one day be a national park. During a discussion about the unsightly structures and commercial properties which they had seen on the drive to Jenny Lake, Rockefeller requested that Albright bring him a map showing these properties, a general layout of the valley and an estimate of the value of the private lands

in question. The party spent that night at Jackson Lake Lodge and then returned to Yellowstone for the rest of their visit.

This trip to Jackson Hole marks the beginning of Mr. Rockefeller's interest in conservation in the Jackson Hole area. His perseverance, backed with sufficient financial resources, sustained what would eventually become one of the longest and most contentious conservation struggles in American history.

There were two versions of the events culminating in Rockefeller's decision to initiate his Jackson Hole project. Albright recalled that he arranged for Richard Winger to draw up the map and make the estimates for the land on the west side of the Snake River from Jackson Lake as far south as Menor's Ferry. He said he thought going as far south as Menor's Ferry might be pushing for too much land and he was not sure if Rockefeller would be interested in such a large area. However, he did not want to forfeit any land simply because he had failed to include it on the map. Winger's estimate of the value of all the private lands in this area was $280,000. Albright claimed that during the winter of 1926-27, he took his map and estimates to New York to present to Rockefeller. Rockefeller, having looked at the map, told Albright that the area depicted on the map was not what he had expected. While Albright thought Rockefeller was interested in purchasing and cleaning up just the unsightly section through which they had driven that morning, Rockefeller was thinking of all the land he had viewed from the high point near the river. Albright recalled Rockefeller explaining:

You took me up on a high point where we could see the whole valley and the mountains behind us and you could see across the valley and the great plains there and way up to the north; you called it a dream. Now, Mr. Albright, I am only interested in ideal projects; that appealed to me as an ideal project, that's what I expected you to bring me.

Albright answered, *"Mr. Rockefeller, that will cost you from a million to a million and a half dollars and maybe more."* To which Rockefeller replied, *"That isn't the point, the point is that is an ideal project, and I'm interested in it and I would like to know more about it."* [18] Albright was then sent to talk over the proposed project with Colonel Arthur Woods, Rockefeller's chief administrative officer. Albright wrote Winger for a new map and new estimates that arrived within a month.

The above recollections by Albright regarding the details of Rockefeller's decision to embark on the Jackson Hole project is the most often printed and repeated narrative. However, it does not completely agree with details contained in correspondence between the two men. Thus, the second version of Rockefeller's initiating steps in his project to aid in the protection of the northern portion of Jackson Hole.

In a letter dated September 29, 1926, Albright wrote:

> *Referring to our day in the Jackson Hole and to our discussion of the desirability of protecting the approach to the Tetons from dance halls, lunch stands and other objectionable structures, I have at last secured the information you asked me to obtain. I have been amazed to find that there was vastly more settlement in the area between the Teton Mountains and the Snake River than I had supposed there was. I have had two Jackson Hole business men, who are close friends of mine and who have been working hand in hand with us in the park for years, make a study of the settlement in this area and land values.* [19]

Elsewhere in this letter, Albright indicated his regret that he had been unsuccessful in his attempts during the previous ten years to convince Congress and the Interior Department to

Jackson Hole Historical Society and Museum 1992.0030.001
The new bridge at Menor's Ferry

Horace Albright remembered suggesting Menor's Ferry as the southern extent of the land purchases he proposed for the Rockefeller project.

Bill Menor homesteaded on the west bank of the Snake River in 1892 and built the ferry that provided the only reliable crossing 30 miles south of the toll bridge at Moran and 15 miles north of the Nethercott Ferry near the present site of the Wilson Bridge. His brother, Holiday, joined him in 1905 and built a cabin on the east side of the river. Ferry rates ranged from $.25 to $2 for a horse and rider up to a four-horse team and wagon. Foot passengers could cross free if they waited for a paying customer. The ferry did not run in very high or very low water or if the brothers did not feel like operating the ferry. Ice was sometimes a problem in the winter, so a small platform was attached to the cable for people to cross. Bill sold the ferry to Maud Noble in 1918 and retired to California. The bridge negated the usefulness of the ferry and thus its commercial opportunity. Highway 26 originally bisected the Dornan property at Moose where a new bridge replaced Menor's Ferry in 1927.

Jackson Hole Historical Society and Museum 1958.0132.001P

Bill Menor

prohibit homesteading in the Jackson Hole area.* Also in this letter, Albright informed Rockefeller that Richard Winger submitted the requested report that indicated the initial investigation was not restricted on the south by Menor's Ferry, but rather an east-west line one mile north of the community of Wilson, Wyoming, an additional 12 miles to the south. Winger's report identified 14,170 acres of privately owned land between the south end of Jackson Lake on the north, the Snake River on the east, and the line one mile north of Wilson to the south. He suggested the property ranged in value from $10 to $100 per acre, averaging about $28 per acre. He estmated a probable total purchase price of $397,000. Winger's map and estimates did not include acreage and prices for the Geraldine Lucas, the Bar BC, or the JY ranches. He did not think Geraldine would sell at any price, and it would not be necessary to purchase the other two ranches because *"...they are owned by the right kind of conservationists."* Winger also noted, *"Using the last two years as an indication, the price of land in this neighborhood will increase each year. If it were only possible to start operations during the winter season while the natives are undergoing their annual attack of cabin fever it would be splendid."* [20]

Rockefeller responded to Albright's letter on November 9, 1926. The letter revealed that Rockefeller may not have had as clear a vision of the Jackson Hole project as attributed by Albright in later years. Rockefeller wrote, *"The boundaries that we talked of last summer are no longer fresh in my mind. A simple map showing them clearly would be helpful."* [21]

Although Albright remembered presenting a map he maintained was prepared by Richard Winger to Rockefeller, his (Albright's) response on November 27, 1926 stated, *"Referring to your letter of November 9 in regard to the Jackson Hole lands, I am having a special map made up in the Washington office which will go to you in a few days."* [22]

On February 16, 1927, Albright wrote Rockefeller that the heavier than normal snow fall in

Wyoming had, reportedly, a depressing effect on Jackson Hole settlers residing on the east side of the Snake River, but the record tourist travel during the previous summer had kept west side residents optimistic. The implication was that land values on the east side of the valley might

Library of Congress HABS WYO.20-MOOS.V.7-3

Geraldine Lucas filed her homestead in 1913 after retiring from her teaching career in New York in 1912. She received title to the land in 1922 and expanded her holdings to 428 acres. She opposed the Rockefeller purchases in the valley and refused to sell to the Snake River Land Company. Her land was purchased by J. D. Kimmel after her death and was eventually obtained by the Rockefeller organization in 1944. Harold and Josephine Fabian were given a life tenure on the ranch by Rockefeller for loyal service to the purchasing project.

Jackson Hole Historical Society and Museum 1958.0391.001

In 1924, at the age of 58, Geraldine Lucas was the second woman to make a successful ascent of the Grand Teton. Her guide was 16-year-old Paul Petzoldt (on right) who made his first ascent earlier that year.

---

*While Albright certainly had the right to suggest to Congress any action he deemed appropriate, his admission in this letter that he actively sought to deny United States citizens the opportunity to homestead in the Jackson Hole area substantiates the general suspicion and distrust with which he was viewed by many valley residents.

remain steady or decrease, but west side land values were likely to remain strong or increase.

In that same letter, Albright presented a definite proposal for action in Jackson Hole. He wrote:

My judgment is that we have two distinct projects, one of which includes the other:

1. The west side of the Snake region is involved only in what we may call 'The West Side Plan.' It is naturally a part of the Teton National Park project. Should these west side lands be acquired, they would round out and complete the Teton Park, preserve the foreground of the mountains, and put into the park an interesting glaciated region of great recreation and scientific value. Standing alone, this plan is a tremendously worthy one, and could be consummated without reference to the larger project.

2. The proposal to turn the entire Jackson Hole back to Nature as the greatest scenic and wild life preserve (including, of course, the Yellowstone Park), on the face of the earth. This project, we might call 'The Jackson Hole plan.' It is immensely bigger, and includes 'The West Side Plan', but most of the lands involved are far less valuable.[23]

Albright's description of the larger plan mirrored the proposal agreed upon at Maud Noble's cabin in 1923 (see Chapter Five), with the exception that Burt, Ferrin, Winger, and others at the 1923 meeting supported a willing buyer/willing seller position regarding private property in the valley. They assumed cattle ranching would continue as part of the economic base of the community. In this letter, Albright foresaw eliminating all private property except for a few dude ranches. However, he allowed it might be appropriate to maintain one cattle ranch at the south end of the valley to dramatize that aspect of the historic West. This proposal, when combined with Yellowstone National Park, would produce *"... about 10,000 square miles of wild territory, with native animals, birds, flowers and forest, a region useless for any other purpose, and therefore destined for perpetual preservation as a wilderness*

country." [24] If the larger plan could be attained, he noted only one blemish would mar the grand picture— the shoreline of Jackson Lake, but even that, he suggested, *"...could ultimately be cleaned up under pressure of public opinion."* [25] He then outlined a plan by which he felt the Jackson Hole project could be accomplished.

It was important that Rockefeller's name not be associated with the purchases lest the land prices become too exorbitant. Albright suggested that a land or cattle company be formed to make the purchases. He also thought that some lands might be acquired by dude ranchers who supported the program to obfuscate further the initiative. Albright would later explain that *"...dude ranches would not be purchased, because it was part of the plan that they should remain as a part of the unique institutions of the project."* [26] The initial purchasing program would concentrate on properties west of the Snake River and expand

National Park Service digital image archives

Horace Marden Albright
1890-1987
2nd Director of the National Park Service.

A graduate of the University of California, Berkeley, he attended night school at Georgetown University to obtain a law degree while working as the confidential secretary to Secretary of the Interior, Franklin Lane. He was acting director of the Park Service during Stephen Mather's illness (1917-1919), superintendent of Yellowstone National Park (1919-1929), director of the National Park Service (1929-1933), and vice president and then president of United States Potash Corporation (1933-1956).

to the rest of the valley after the foreground of the Tetons had been secured. He suggested that it might be a good idea to have a lawyer from the area represent the project and suggested Harold P. Fabian of the Salt Lake City firm of Fabian and Clendenin.*

Albright stated he would have the Park Service and the General Land Office produce a map of all the private land holdings in Jackson Hole, and noted that as of December 1923, there were 402 landowners in the valley controlling nearly 100,000 acres. He suggested the value of all the private property would be at least, and possibly slightly more than, $1,000,000.[28]

There is some confusion regarding the stated scope of the proposal and the estimated financial expenditure. It is possible that both Rockefeller and Albright, not being natives or residents of the valley, considered "Jackson Hole" to be essentially that portion of the valley north of the town of Jackson. However, the approximate acreage of privately owned land north of the town of Jackson would have been closer to 51,000 acres. The 100,000-acre estimate was a fair approximation of the privately held property in all of Teton County in 1927. (Total acreage for Teton County was 1,788,800.) The conflict arises from the fact that $1,000,000 would have been woefully insufficient to purchase all the private property in Teton County, including the towns of Jackson, Wilson, Moran, and Kelly with their developed improvements and business values. State valuation of private property in Teton County in 1930 was $2,500,000. Evidence presented in subsequent chapters will show that individuals closely related to the project believed Rockefeller never intended to buy the entire valley. It may be that the grand scope of the project as identified in the correspondence cited in this chapter was simply

downsized because of circumstances and increasing property values.

After proposing the plan, Albright addressed several reasons why such an action might not be practical. The first potential problem Albright identified was that there was no guarantee Congress would accept the purchased land for inclusion in a national park. However, if the government refused the donation, it would be possible to sell the land and it was unlikely that the land would decrease in value. The second problem was that the land would remain subject to taxation until transferred to the federal government. Albright believed some ranch lands could be operated at a profit to defer expenses, particularly for the raising of hay or for cattle grazing and other properties could be leased for recreation purposes. The third problem was that once the

Jackson Hole Historical Society and Museum
1999.0040.001

Harold Fabian

Fabian, an attorney in the law office of Albright's childhood friend, Beverly C. Clendenin, agreed to provide pro bono legal services for creating the Snake River Land Company. The relationship with the Rockefeller holding company would lead to a life-long friendship with Horace Albright and a full-time position with the Rockefeller project.

---

*Beverly C. Clendenin had been a childhood friend and classmate of Albright's during law school and Albright often stopped to see his friend when passing through Salt Lake City. It was through this old friendship that Albright met Fabian. This new friendship was based on a common interest in the outdoors and Fabian's interest in the Yellowstone and Teton country. It occurred to Albright that Fabian would be an ideal person to handle the Rockefeller interests in western Wyoming. Fabian recalled the first time he heard of the project:

He [Albright] *knew of my general fondness for this section of the country, and he asked me if I would be interested in handling the legal work for whatever group it was that was going to carry on this project in purchasing the privately owned lands. Nothing was said about what it was expected to be, excepting that it was a philanthropic undertaking and that I would have to expect my remuneration to be mostly my own satisfaction in participating in the undertaking, rather than any financial rewards.*[27]

purchasing began, there was the potential for homestead speculation on unappropriated public land increasing the amount of private land to be purchased. Albright thought relatively little public land remained available for homesteading and that it would attract undue attention to the project to try to arrange a sudden prohibition on homesteading in the valley. Albright concluded, *"These objections may impress you as serious obstacles, and I hope you will ask for more details if you regard them as controlling."* [29]

Albright, in several other more public sources, maintained he informed Rockefeller that because of his position with the Park Service, he could not be involved or help with the purchases in Jackson Hole but would be willing to act in an advisory capacity if needed. In this letter, he suggests a less distant association with the operational aspects of the plan. After recommending his friend's law firm as agents for the project he wrote:

I could go to Salt Lake City as soon as possible and put them in possession of all necessary facts and papers. They could deal with my Jackson Hole operators, one of whom I would have meet me in Salt Lake City. They could also coordinate the efforts of 'dude ranchers' like Burt and Stewart. I could be in constant and confidential touch with them, and they could also communicate with your confidential agent in New York. [30]

Finally, Albright wrote:

I have written at length, Mr. Rockefeller, not with any idea of trying to urge favorable action, but just to give you this big park and wild life preserve plan as we have visualized it. I think if it could be consummated, it would go down in history as the greatest conservation project of its kind ever undertaken, and never again could another be undertaken as there would be no place for it to start.

However, I realize it has many angles, and that its present status is not ideal as a foundation on which to build. [31]

Rockefeller made the decision to embrace the Jackson Hole project shortly after receiving Albright's letter. On February 28, 1927, he wrote to Arthur Woods, an associate responsible for the implementation and accomplishment of a number of Rockefeller's special projects, explaining the proposal and authorizing the expenditure of funds. This letter clarifies Rockefeller's original intent and understanding of the scope of the project. He accepted Albright's two-phase proposal of land acquisition and the concept of purchasing all the private land *"...not held by friendly Dude*

Rockefeller Archive Center, Kenneth Chorley Papers, Series 2, Scrapbook, 812995_me

The Jenny Lake Dance Pavilion

John D. Rockefeller, Jr., possibly because of his Baptist upbringing, found the "disreputable" dance halls (and other commercial structures) objectionable during his visit to Jackson Hole. However, the locals and the dudes considered

the Saturday night gatherings the social highlight of the summer season. Many seasonal romances between dudes and cowboys/wranglers began during these weekly events. The term "dude" in the context of early Jackson Hole tourism was neither derogatory nor gender specific. It originally meant "fancy dresser."

Harrison Crandall Photo- Jackson Hole Historical Society and Museum
BC.0355

101

Ranchers..." [32] in Jackson Hole. He expressed his intention to donate eventually the purchased properties to the U.S. Government for management by the Park Service and Forest Service. Although he explained the plan to purchase approximately 100,000 acres for an amount in excess of $1,000,000, he directed Woods to concentrate on the 14,170 acres west of the Snake River. He wrote:

> *Many unsightly and some disreputable places are being built on it to attract the increasing summer visitors. These places are rapidly marring the beauty and attractiveness of the country. To prevent their increasing and to terminate their existence is a matter of first importance. It is believed that this western tract should be bought during the next few months, if at all.* *
>
> *The tract to the east of the Snake River can be considered another year.*
>
> *I desire to place this entire matter in your hands, to plan, organize and carry out. I am turning over to you certain maps and*

George Grantham Bain Collection Library of Congress [Public domain] via Wikimedia Commons

Arthur Woods
1870-1942

Arthur Woods was active in many civic projects and was a former New York City Police Commissioner. He was President and Chairman of the Board of the Rockefeller Center. His office also directed the Colonial Williamsburg project.

letters bearing on the subject. Mr. Albright is ready to see you at once to plan the campaign with you. [33]

Rockefeller issued a formal notification of his decision to the Director of the National Park Service, Stephen Mather, and Superintendent Albright. He listed two motives for the initiative. *"First, in order to restore and preserve the valley landscape which formed the foreground and general setting for the Teton Mountains, and second, to aid in the preservation of wild life through elimination of fences and other barriers impeding natural drift to winter range and to provide additional winter feeding grounds."* [34] With Rockefeller's approval of the plan proposed by Horace Albright, another attempt to protect the Tetons and Jackson Hole was initiated.

The Rockefeller project needed a man in Jackson to act as purchasing agent and Albright suggested Richard Winger because he had provided the estimates and was familiar with the properties to be purchased. Kenneth Chorley and Vanderbilt Webb, Rockefeller's publicly acknowledged representatives for the project, preferred Robert E. Miller, the Jackson banker. Miller was probably the last person Albright would have suggested as he was a long-time opponent of the Park Service and Albright was, evidently, not one of his favorite people. This meant that in addition to keeping Rockefeller's involvement a secret, Fabian would also need to keep secret Albright's relationship to the project. Fabian was cautioned not to reveal Albright's role in the project.

In May 1927, a conference was held in Salt Lake City in which Chorley, Webb, Miller, and Fabian discussed the project and how best to implement the plans. Fabian summarized the results of the conference as follows:

> *(1) Mr. Miller and I were advised that the sum of $1,000,000 would be available for the purchase of lands.*
>
> *(2) Neither Mr. Miller nor I was advised at that time, or for a year or more later, as*

***Mr. Rockefeller evidently believed the "West Side Project" could be accomplished in several months and the larger initiative within a year or two. It is a matter of speculation whether he would have embarked on the purchasing plan at all if he had known it would require 23 years to consummate his plan to convert the valley floor to a national park.**

to the identity of the principal or principals for whom we were acting.

(3) Both Mr. Miller and I, however, were assured that the lands to be purchased would be devoted to the use and enjoyment of the public.

(4) Mr. Miller stated that a substantial number of the people in the valley whose lands were included in the plan of purchase were neighbors and friends of his of long standing, and that many of them were in financial distress, and that he would not care to be a party to any plan for taking advantage of their financial condition, but would expect to make all purchases at fair prices. Mr. Miller and I were both assured that there was no intention or desire to take advantage of the financial distress of any of the property owners and that he would be expected to pay fair values in all cases.

(5) Proposed property schedules were then worked out in detail, showing the individual parcels of property involved and the prices at which Mr. Miller thought they could be purchased on the basis referred to above.

(6) Mr. Miller stated that he would like to have the assistance of Mr. P. W. Spaulding of Evanston, Wyoming, as local counsel, whom he had known for many years and who he felt would be of great help to him in title matters and other legal questions. It was agreed that this would be arranged.

(7) The compensation which Mr. Miller was to receive as purchasing agent was discussed and it was agreed that it should be arranged on the basis of the acreage purchased.

(8) It was agreed that a corporation should be organized under the laws of the State of Utah in which title could be taken to all properties purchased, as such a corporation would give no indication that the purchases were being made on behalf of eastern people.[35]

On June 15, 1927, after Webb and Chorley had returned to New York, Webb wrote a letter to Miller in the form of a proposal which outlined the results of the Salt Lake City conference. It was worded so that if Miller accepted Webb's summation of the conference, the letter could be considered a contract between them. The contract was conditional on three factors. One of these factors was an assurance from the Forest Service regarding its management policies for the Jackson Hole area. The second factor was a withdrawal of the public land in the purchase area that was still open to homesteading and other forms of public entry. Although Albright had recommended against such a move, a withdrawal was deemed necessary to prevent speculators from filing on the public lands once it became clear that a purchasing program was under way. Such actions on the part of speculators would increase the amount of private land that would have to be purchased. The third factor was a determination of the policy of the state of Wyoming concerning two school sections in the purchase area. Webb wanted an assurance that the state would not sell these lands or dispose of them in such a way as to create more private land in the purchase area. Webb said he would take care of the first two from his end and asked Miller to take care of the third or suggest how that situation might otherwise be covered.

On July 2, Miller wrote to Webb expressing his approval of the outlined plan. He also stated he was ready to begin the purchases as soon as Mr. Webb had obtained his assurances of the three conditions of the plan. With regard to the third condition, the position of the state of Wyoming concerning the state land, Mr. Miller believed *"...it might be better to follow the leasing statute and purchase these lands outright with the attendant obligation on the part of the state not to take any action in the future that would operate to the disadvantage of its grantee."*[36] On July 21, Miller was notified that the desired assurances had been obtained on the first two conditions, but *"...a more satisfactory determination should be made of the matter of the Wyoming State lands."*[37] Webb thought Miller should meet personally with Wyoming Governor, Frank Emerson, to discuss the matter. He also suggested that Miller and Fabian meet to consider the appropriate means of dealing with the problem of the third condition.

At Mr. Webb's request, the two men met in August to review the situation. It was Miller's opinion that since the state land in question was of relatively small acreage, the project should not be delayed on its account. He thought the state authorities could be approached after the project was on a better footing. On August 23, Webb agreed to the suggestion and issued a notification for Miller to proceed with the project.

Two days after Webb's notification, the Snake River Land Company was established under the laws of the state of Utah and thereafter qualified to operate in the state of Wyoming. The Snake River Land Company was to act as a holding company for the lands purchased with the funds provided by Rockefeller. Fabian explained the ownership of the company:

> *...all of the stock of the corporation was endorsed in blank and sent to Mr. Webb in New York for Mr. Rockefeller, who is its sole owner, except for the necessary qualifying director's shares. Mr. Webb, Mr. McCann (an associate in Mr. Webb's office) and myself became ... the directors of the company. Mr. Webb is the President of the company, I am its Vice-President, Mr. McCann is its Secretary and Treasurer, and my secretary, Miss Cunningham, is its Assistant Secretary and Assistant Treasurer.*[38]

During Fabian's visit to Jackson in August, he learned that a number of people were already aware that a purchasing project had been undertaken. The reaction of the people was not favorable and the purchasing project became embroiled in its first controversy. The controversy arose out of the solution to the second condition listed in Mr. Webb's letter of June 15. Kenneth Chorley met with the Secretary of the Interior asking that the public land within the proposed purchase area be withdrawn from settlement. The Secretary of the Interior convinced President Coolidge to make the withdrawal order on July 7, 1927 (Executive Order No. 4685). This withdrawal caused the controversy.

The circumstances that allowed the valley residents to learn about the proposed purchasing project almost before it was initiated were

Charles Alexander Sheldon
1867-1928

Sheldon secured financial independence by investing in silver and lead mining operations in New Mexico. He was a devoted big game hunter with a particular interest in mountain sheep. Like many hunters, he developed an intense appreciation for the outdoors and expended considerable effort on conservation issues. He is considered the "Father of Denali National Park." In addition to his position on the Jackson Hole Elk Commission, he served on the board of directors of the Boone and Crockett Club, National Parks Association, American Forestry Association, National Recreation Committee, and the National Geographic Society. One biographer aptly remarked that *"Sheldon was anything but a conservation dilettante."*

as follows: Early in 1927, the President's Committee on National Outdoor Recreation appointed a commission to study and solve the problems of the Jackson Hole elk herd. The Commission on the Conservation of Jackson Hole Elk was composed of Charles Sheldon, Chairman; Arthur Ringland, Secretary; and representatives of the concerned federal agencies and wildlife organizations. Robert E. Miller from Jackson represented the local cattlemen, and W. C. Deloney, the state Senator from Teton County, was Governor Emerson's personal representative on the commission. Feeling it to be an interference in state affairs, the governor was not impressed with the commission. However, since the invitation had been

Arthur Cuming Ringland
1882-1978

Ringland obtained a forestry degree from Yale and began his government employment with the Forest Service in 1900. Although he had a long and distinguished career with that agency, he is best known as the "Father of CARE," the relief organization formed after World War II. He was honored for his international relief work by the United Nations in 1958.

with the ability to withhold the governor's signature from the commission's recommendations. At least once, he threatened to walk out and return to Wyoming.* At other times, a simple recommendation or suggestion was sufficient to make his point. During one of the meetings Horace Albright, representing the Park Service and aware of Rockefeller's plans, suggested that all the unappropriated public lands north of the existing elk refuge be withdrawn from entry to provide a protected driftway for the migrating elk. This would have been extremely convenient for the Rockefeller project as it would have accomplished Webb's second condition without the project's involvement. Deloney recognized the need for a driftway, but he opposed such a large withdrawal. He recommended a smaller withdrawal of 12,000 acres, only the amount necessary to accomplish the objective. Albright, not being at liberty to discuss Rockefeller's project, could not offer a reasonable rebuttal. Deloney's recommendation was accepted.

In accordance with the commission's recommendation, President Coolidge issued the 12,000-acre withdrawal on April 15, 1927 (Executive Order No. 4631). This withdrawal was generally well accepted by everyone including the people of Jackson Hole. However, the withdrawal of

extended to him to have a personal representative on the commission, he appointed William Deloney. Deloney was the perfect man for the job, not because he thought like the governor, but because he cared so much for the elk. He had been particularly supportive of the state Game and Fish Department and had fought to obtain the necessary appropriations from the state to feed the starving elk during severe winters. He had done as much for wildlife in Wyoming as any other man, and never hesitated to criticize Wyoming authorities when they failed in their responsibilities to Wyoming's wildlife.

In February 1927, the commission held its first meeting in Washington, D.C. During this conference, a number of problems and compromises had to be negotiated between the federal and state agencies. Deloney, as the governor's personal representative, held a powerful hand in the negotiations

Jackson Hole Historical Society and Museum 1994.6034.001
Feeding Elk in the winter, 1911.

*Mr. Rachford of the Forest Service tried to place the commission on record as favoring the establishment of a federal game preserve embracing nearly all of the valley north of the town of Jackson. Deloney threatened to walk out unless the proposed resolution was dropped. He then informed the governor of his actions. Governor Emerson wired back succinctly, *"Stand pat."* [39]

an additional 23,617 acres on July 7 (the result of Chorley's efforts) created some very special problems which Sheldon and Ringland of the Elk Commission were quick to recognize. This larger withdrawal had been discussed at the commission meetings but had been rejected because of the opposition of the Wyoming delegates, especially Deloney. Everyone had agreed upon the compromise withdrawal of 12,000 acres. It now appeared to the Wyoming members of the commission that other members acted in bad faith, recommending to the President a larger withdrawal. If the commission's plans for the conservation and protection of the Jackson Hole elk herd were to succeed, the cooperation of the state of Wyoming would be necessary. That cooperation could not exist under the cloud of suspicion that rested over the commission. Since the recommendation of the commission to withdraw 12,000 acres had already been published, this new withdrawal placed the commission in an embarrassing position. Ringland immediately went to work to salvage what he could of the commission's integrity. He later wrote to W. C. Henderson of the Biological Survey, *"It seems that this land was withdrawn at the suggestion of a Mr. Chorley, of New York, representing a group interested in a plan to purchase lands in Jackson Hole and vicinity to conserve the elk."* [40] He explained the ramifications of the July withdrawal and then concluded:

> *The whole affair is inexplicable to me and disturbing. For years an effort has been made to reach an agreement on plans for the conservation of the Jackson Hole herd. When the commission concluded its work and for the first time brought together all interests, there was every reason to believe that a plan for concerted action had been devised. The fact that this committee was at work has been widely advertised. Invitations to participate were broadcast. Now comes an independent movement which might prove not only ineffective itself (for political and biological reasons) but destructive to the one which the Elk Commission has agreed upon as a whole. It may well be that the wide sweeping plan of*

> *purchase now under consideration is better than that proposed by the Elk Commission. That is a matter of opinion. But what should admit of no doubt is the necessity of working together to reach a common objective. It is most unfortunate that there has been an apparent lack of coordination with the body specifically set up to make coordination possible.* [41]

Sheldon and Ringland contacted all the members of the commission to assure them the July withdrawal was not the work of any of the other members of the commission. They also stated they were willing to do everything possible to get the withdrawal canceled. Mr. Deloney also received a copy of Mr. Ringland's letter to Henderson that mentioned the proposed purchase plan. Thus, Jackson Hole residents, through William Deloney, learned of the project even before the Snake River Land Company was created.

~

In addition to Rockefeller's land purchasing project, there were other initiatives in progress that would potentially affect the Jackson Hole area. In late April 1927, Senator Norbeck of South Dakota requested the National Park Service prepare two bills for introduction in the next session of Congress. One bill provided for the boundary changes in Yellowstone National Park as recommended by the coordinating commission, with the exception that the Teton Division should be excluded. Norbeck described the second bill as follows:

> *I would also appreciate it if you would also prepare a bill for the establishment of another national park in Wyoming to include the Teton Peaks.... I doubt that this can be made a part of the [Yellowstone] National Park. It will in all probability have to be made a separate park. I have not yet decided what the name should be. I think in the Bill as I introduce it I will call it the Kendrick National Park. It is possible that the Senator from Wyoming is still of the same mind that he was previously - that it should be called the Grand Teton Nat'l Park of Wyoming. It may be best for you to have the Bill ready, leaving the name blank.* [42]

~

It soon became apparent that the July 7 withdrawal could create sufficient anti-government sentiment to threaten the Teton and Yellowstone Park bills. In September, Wyoming's Congressional delegation voiced its opposition to the withdrawal.[43] The Snake River Land Company finally realized its mistake in not consulting Wyoming state officials, the Congressional delegation, and the Elk Commission before taking independent action. The lack of communication caused a number of important and constructive projects to be threatened with failure. The proposal to protect the Teton Mountain Range and its lakes had gained opposition. The attempt to adjust Yellowstone's boundaries along topographic and more logical lines was in doubt. The long overdue recommendations of the Elk Commission for protection and management of the Jackson Hole elk herd existed under a cloud of mistrust. Even Rockefeller's project was threatened with defeat when a movement was begun to nullify the July withdrawal. If successful, the unappropriated public lands in the purchase area would be open for speculation and Rockefeller's project would then be impractical. The Snake River Land Company moved to rectify the situation before proceeding with the purchases. On October 17, 1927, Webb wired Miller, *"Must ask you to discontinue all operations till further notice."* [44] On October 26, 1927, Miller wrote to Fabian, making the following suggestions to settle the problem:

My suggestion would be to arrive at a boundary of the area desired to purchase, the unappropriated lands within and adjoining to be withdrawn for protection against appropriation under the law, the unappropriated school land desired and to take the matter up with the Wyoming representatives in Congress and the Governor of Wyoming with full information of the object and purpose of the proposed purchase and get their approval of withdrawal, lease or purchase of school land and eliminate the question from the Elk Commission project entirely by making it a conservation and preservation move by private ownership, separate and

apart, to which all good citizens will add praise.

If our people will stand pat on the present withdrawal until they can decide on a boundary of their proposed purchase then amend the withdrawal to include the land within and adjoining the proposed purchases necessary to protect them from further appropriations by individuals under the land laws, we can get it without any political interference.

Harris and Ewing [Public domain] via Wikimedia Commons

Hubert Work (R)
1860-1942

As 29th Secretary of the Interior, Work facilitated the Rockefeller organization's efforts to purchase lands in Jackson Hole by convincing President Coolidge to issue Executive Orders restricting settlement in the valley. Work received a medical degree from the University of Pennsylvania in 1885 and moved to Colorado. He established the Woodcroft Hospital in Pueblo, Colorado in 1896. He served in the U.S. Army Medical Corps in World War I and attained the rank of Lt. Colonel. Work was appointed Postmaster General in the Harding administration and served as Interior Secretary in both the Harding and Coolidge Administrations. As Secretary of the Interior, he rid the agency of anyone associated with the Tea Pot Dome scandal and reorganized the department. This reorganization reportedly reduced the agency's expenditures by $129 million during his first three years as Secretary. He was not fond of "clock watchers" and ordered all clocks removed from the Interior Department offices. Native Americans were granted American citizenship during his tenure.

The Elk Commission cannot back up, but we will all welcome a segregation that will clear the cloud over us by the July 7 withdrawal which as I have said so many times was a serious mistake.

When the object and purpose is made public through our Representatives and Governor, the gladhand will be extended to us.[45]

On November 23, Webb met with Charles Sheldon of the Elk Commission and Congressman Winter in an effort to clear up the confusion and avoid a potentially disastrous controversy. He explained the project and its objectives, but he did not reveal the source of the private funds. Congressman Winter agreed to withdraw his opposition to the Executive Order of July 7 and, in fact, stated he would not oppose additional withdrawals affecting the same area if the Department of the Interior could make certain assurances to him. First, he wanted to be assured that future withdrawals in the area were connected to the project that had been explained to him by Webb. Second, he wanted assurance that the individual or individuals backing the project were financially capable of seeing the program through to its conclusion. Finally, he wanted to be convinced that the backers of the project *"...would not use the land thus acquired for private gain or enjoyment, but would dedicate it to the use and enjoyment of the public after its acquisition."*[46] The Secretary of the Interior supplied the assurances, in writing, to Congressman Winter on November 26, 1927.

Since Governor Emerson was scheduled to be in Washington in December, a conference was arranged with him at that time. Attending the conference, was the governor, Senator Kendrick, Congressman Winter, Charles Sheldon, former Congressman Mondell, Mr. Miller and Mr. Webb. During this conference, Webb and Miller explained the details and objectives of the project as well as the

importance of the July 7 withdrawal. Two days later, on December 4, Governor Emerson requested an additional meeting. The governor wanted to reassure himself that he fully understood the proposed project, and thus, the project was again explained to the state's chief executive.

It was the opinion of Webb and Miller that, as a result of these conferences, there would be no more objections to the project or the withdrawal of July 7. On December 6, 1927, Fabian and Miller were authorized to proceed with the project. At the close of 1927, it appeared that the dude ranchers who met at Maud Noble's cabin in the summer of 1923 would, at last, have their "dream" realized.

Grand Teton National Park GRTE-00430_64-68C
Top: the first wagon road between Jackson Lake Dam and Jenny Lake.
Bottom: Forest Service road built from Jackson Lake Dam to Jenny Lake in 1921.

John Walter Collection, Jackson Hole Historical Society and Museum
2005.0051.048

CHAPTER EIGHT
1928-1929

Another Park Extension bill has been introduced in Congress. Someday such a bill will pass regardless of the opinions of Jackson Hole people concerning the merits or demerits of an enlarged Yellowstone National Park. The creating of a new National Park to include the Grand Tetons and adjacent areas is in our minds only political expediency, a sort of balm to the state. Economy in time will demand that the newly created park be added to Yellowstone National Park, however the political situation will have to be cleared first.

Editorial
Jackson Hole Courier
December 13, 1928

It is public opinion that the beauty which God created in these sublime mountains should not be marred by the commercialism or carelessness of men. Accession to public opinion may be delayed, but it may not be avoided. The time has come for the Tetons to be made a National Park.

Editorial
Cheyenne Tribune
January 1929

Grand Teton National Park GRTE-00430_197B

A stage coach tour near the Oxbow Bend of the Snake River

Early in 1928, the Snake River Land Company proceeded with its purchasing plan while Congressman Winter worked to obtain the passage of a bill (H.R. 478) that he introduced on December 5, 1927. This bill, commonly referred to as the Winter Bill, was introduced to accomplish the acquisition, by the federal government, of certain private lands near the elk refuge as recommended by the Elk Commission. In support of this proposed legislation, President Coolidge signed Executive Order No. 5040 withdrawing from entry additional lands in Jackson Hole. The bill was not controversial, but it had difficulty clearing the Bureau of the Budget. All bills requiring the expenditures of public money had to be approved by the Director of the Bureau of the Budget, in this case, General H. M. Lord. The bill provided for an appropriation of $275,000 to which General Lord objected. He suggested an appropriation of $150,000 with the balance of the money to be obtained from private donations matching the federal money dollar for dollar.*

Rather than mount a campaign for donations, Paul Redington, Chief of the Biological Survey, and Congressman Winter tried to reach an agreement with Director Lord by approaching the problem from a different direction. It was hoped that if General Lord could be made aware of the Snake River Land Company project, and the fact that its purchases for the benefit of game protection would far exceed the dollar for dollar ratio that had been suggested, the director might approve the original appropriation request. In April 1928, Mr. Webb met with Director Lord to explain the Snake River Land Company project. The director was asked to consider the project as a part of the total financial operation in Jackson Hole for the conservation of the elk. Instead of private donations being sought to match a federal appropriation, the government was asked to provide an appropriation to match a private donation up to the amount of $275,000. For a while, it appeared that General Lord might agree, but in the

end, he failed to approve the bill, and it died in committee.

Senator Norbeck's bill to establish the Kendrick National Park also failed to survive the committee. The National Park Service and the Department of the Interior did not object to the bill, but Senator Kendrick did not favor the name.[1] The bill was passed over in favor of a proposed bill which would accomplish the Yellowstone Park extension recommended by the Coordinating Commission and establish Grand Teton National Park. This proposed bill was the subject of a Senate investigation pursuant to Senate Resolution 237 of the 70th Congress, 2nd Session.

In April, prior to the visit by the Senate investigating committee, the editor of the *Jackson*

bioguide.congress.gov {public domain} via Wikimedia Commons

Peter Norbeck (R)
1870-1936

South Dakota Senator Norbeck was born in a dugout on his parent's homestead in Dakota Territory. A well driller by trade, he became the 9th Governor of South Dakota in 1917. He was elected to the United States Senate in 1920. During his career in the Senate, he was a supporter of the tourist industry in his state as well as several parks including Badlands National Park, Custer State Park, and Wind Cave National Park. He introduced legislation that would have created the Kendrick National Park to protect the Tetons.

---

*A number of sources, including Albright, Winter, Fabian and Webb, verified that the Winter Bill was designed to accomplish the recommendations of the Elk Commission. However, William Deloney testified at the Senate hearings in 1933 that the proposed purchases did not conform to the commission's recommendations. Deloney also stated that $275,000 was extremely inadequate to purchase the lands identified by the commission or the Winter Bill. He was sure the Elk Commission had never recommended such a figure.

Hole Courier took notice of the purchase of several of the large ranches in the northern part of the valley. The editor noted that, *"According to the records of the Snake River Land Co., a Utah Corporation has recently bought the land holdings in whole or in part of the following men: J. D. Ferrin, Leonard Ferrin, Bruce Prather, Roy Nipper, H. C. McKinstry, F. Buchenroth, and totals above 7,000 acres to date."*[2] The *Courier* mentioned that no one seemed to know anything about the corporation or its purchases except the local agent, Robert Miller, and he would only say that the purchases would be of great benefit to the valley. This left the editor free to speculate about the company. He wrote, *"The consensus of opinion is to the effect that the game herds are the attraction which interested these unknown people here."*[3] He came even closer to the truth when he noted that these purchases began very soon after the President's withdrawal order of July 7, 1927. He, therefore, reasoned, *"...we are of the opinion that the men instrumental in the withdrawal of July 7 last are interested in the Snake River Land Company. However, time will tell."*[4]

Also in April, Webb inquired of Miller whether an amendment to the withdrawal of July 7 would hinder his purchase plan. The withdrawal was deficient in that it failed to protect certain lands in the purchase area, leaving them open to speculation, while withdrawing some lands south of the town of Jackson, an area in which the Snake River Land Company was not initially interested. Miller favored such an amended withdrawal and sent his recommendation to Webb. A supplemental withdrawal was executed by the President on April 16, 1928 (Executive Order No. 4857).[5]

On July 12, the *Jackson Hole Courier* announced the forthcoming visit by the subcommittee of the Senate Public Lands and Surveys Committee. It stated that W. C. Deloney received a letter from Senator Kendrick informing him that a public hearing would be held on July 22 in the afternoon or early evening, and requested Deloney's assistance in arranging the meeting. Deloney publicly requested *"...all who are interested in any manner in Park Extension be at the meeting to be held in Jackson."*[6] The Committee, on its way to Jackson, stopped in Cody, Wyoming

Jackson Hole Historical Society and Museum 1958.2428.001

Subcommittee of the Senate Public Lands and Surveys Committee at Jackson Lake Lodge. The hearing was held on July 22, 1928.

to allow the people of that community to express themselves on the park extension issues. Most of the people who attended the Cody hearings were surprised to find that the proposed park extension area was considerably smaller than they had expected. Because of the limited extension under consideration, much of the opposition was calmed.

The Jackson hearings promised to be more exciting. Both the supporters and opponents of the bill encouraged their people to attend the meeting. Albright recalled, *"We expected ... a real free-for-all with our opponents."* [7] The meeting began at 3:30 in the hall above Porter's Drug Store with 77 people in the audience. The chairman of the committee, during his opening remarks, requested a show of hands of those in favor of the establishment of Grand Teton National Park (76) and those against its establishment (1). A number of people made statements at this hearing, including William Manning, the one person who voted against the establishment of the park.

> ...[He] *made a brief statement to the committee in which he said that he had spoken to people generally who were opposed to Federal extension and against taking land from the tax rolls that are of value to the State, but when apprised by the chairman of the fact that the area proposed to be placed in the Grand Teton National Park is now national forest land and, therefore, not on the tax rolls of the State, and that the creation of the park would mean merely a change in administration, he withdrew his objections to the proposal.*[8]

After the hearings, the committee went to the JY Ranch where they spent the night. Most of the committee retired after dinner, but a few sat around a fire talking until nine o'clock when a number of men appeared at the ranch requesting a conference with Senator Kendrick. These men were part of the opposition and explained that they expected the hearings to occur later in the day, and they wanted a chance to be heard. Kendrick awakened Senator Nye, the chairman, and arranged for another hearing the next day. On the following day, the committee met with 12

William Manning, 1922.

Manning testified in opposition to the creation of Grand Teton National Park. In 1895, he was the constable who organized the posse to arrest the Bannock hunting party for violating Wyoming game laws. The incident culminated in the Supreme Court ruling affirming state control and ownership of wildlife. A man with a fierce pioneering spirit, he was awarded a contract to haul mail across Teton Pass at the age of 94.

local men in attendance. S. N. Leek stated he opposed the proposed park status because he feared the Park Service would not allow the cutting of beetle infested trees where the Forest Service allowed such a policy. R. C. Lundy claimed the whole issue was a matter of states' rights, and the area should be ceded to the state of Wyoming for a state park. William Deloney, up to this point, had been one of the leaders of the park opposition movement for years but stated he could *"...see the writing on the wall..."* and agreed to support the park if a specific provision could be inserted into the bill prohibiting any new hotels or campgrounds in the park. Struthers Burt, a strong proponent of the new park, was quick to agree with Deloney's suggestion, adding that no new roads should be built in the park. On the spot, Horace Albright drew up the desired provision so the men could approve the proposal. The following amendment was approved and inserted into the bill:

Jackson Hole Historical Society and Museum 2003.0117.415

Provided, That no new roads shall be constructed on the lands hereby included in said park and no hotels or new permanent camps shall be authorized or permitted to be maintained on such lands without specific authority of Congress.*

This amendment was desired for several reasons. It would protect the Tetons from commercialization by the Yellowstone monopolies which were so distrusted by the Jackson Hole residents, and second, it would have the effect of forcing

S. N. Leek Collection, American Heritage Center, University of Wyoming, ah03138_1075

For a while, the Hotel Jackson (above) offered the only commercial accommodations for tourists. As tourism grew, the Reed Hotel (below) expanded the accommodation base and, along with other town merchants, opposed tourist accommodation expansion in other parts of the valley. The Reed Hotel was originally a sanitarium for "consumptives" operated by Dr. Luther T. Palmer.

wyomingtalesandtrails.com

tourists to purchase services from businessmen in the town of Jackson and prohibit competition with tourists services already established in the northern portion of the valley. Deloney foresaw the loss of business that would result from the Snake River Land Company's purchase plan. He correctly predicted that many of the people who sold their land would leave the valley and, therefore, decrease the year round business which had supported the local merchants. The amendment, Deloney thought, would stimulate additional tourist business to compensate the merchants for losses resulting from the Snake River Land Company project.

Although the opponents of the park obtained their desired amendment, they did not leave the meeting satisfied. Deloney, as well as some of the others, would later state that the park had been pushed down their throats. This feeling was the result of statements attributed to Senator Kendrick at the July 23 hearing. The alleged statements were not a part of the record of the hearings but were substantiated by Horace Albright. Deloney related these statements to a different Senate investigating committee in 1933:

I was present when Senator Kendrick told us that the time had come that he had to forget the fact that he was a citizen of Sheridan, and, being a citizen of that city, he could not forget also that he was a citizen of the State of Wyoming, and being a citizen and official of the State of Wyoming he could not blind himself to the fact that he was also a citizen of the Nation at large, and the time had come when the people of the country wanted that park, and we had to submit to the creation of the Teton National park. That is pretty nearly exactly Senator Kendrick's words.[9]

In an effort to be fair to the Senator and the people of the valley who favored the park, Deloney

---

*Nearly identical language had been included in every Yellowstone Park extension bill introduced after 1919. The primary concern of the valley residents was not to prohibit appropriate new roads or development in the area but to remove the authority for development from the Park Service and place it with the people's representatives in Congress. The Park Service was not trusted to protect the Tetons from commercial development.

also stated, *"I do not mean to say to you that the country was unanimous in opposition to that—possibly the country may have been as much as 50-50, or there may have been a preponderance of the people in favor of it. I won't say there was not, but there is a good strong element in opposition to that, and I was leading that element."* [10]

Albright remembered Kendrick's comment as more emotional, strident, antagonistic, and less tactful. Although Albright's version did not sound like a politician speaking to his constituents, the idea behind the statement corresponds. The time had arrived for the inclusion of the Teton Mountains into the National Park System.

⁓

Senator Kendrick's comments to the opponents of the park were not easily forgotten. Nineteen twenty-eight was an election year and the local press and Congressman Winter, who tried to unseat him, used Kendrick's stand on the park issue against him. Winter accused Kendrick of attempting to give away the state of Wyoming to the federal government,[11] evidently forgetting his own pro-park extension stand in 1926. Winter, like Mondell in 1922, was a worthy opponent for the Senator. He had been a lawyer, a judge, a poet (he wrote the words to the state song), a novelist, and a defender of states' rights.[12] Kendrick, on the other hand, received only seven years of formal education before leaving his native state of Texas in 1879 at the age of 21. He traveled to Wyoming on a cattle drive and found a job on a northern Wyoming ranch. Unlike most cowboys of the era, he used his free time to educate himself. He eventually married his boss's daughter and proceeded to build the ranch into a large estate before entering politics.[13] Despite the fact that Wyoming voters favored the Republican presidential candidate, Herbert Hoover, they nevertheless again chose Kendrick, a Democrat, to represent them in the Senate.

⁓

The proposed bill that was the subject of the Senate hearing during the summer of 1928 was not introduced until December 6 of that year. The *Jackson Hole Courier* reported that Senator Gerald P. Nye of North Dakota, the chairman of the Committee on Public Lands and Surveys,

Library of Congress [Public domain] via Wikimedia Commons

Gerald Prentice Nye (R)
1892-1971

Senator Nye (North Dakota) was associated with the more liberal wing of the Republican party but was more isolationist than pacifist. As Chairman of the Public Lands Committee, he actively pushed the investigation into the Tea Pot Dome scandal. Nye visited Jackson Hole several times as part of Senate subcommittees investigating issues related to Yellowstone and Grand Teton Park. He introduced several pieces of legislation that sought to protect portions of Jackson Hole.

sponsored the bill (S. 4674). The *Courier* also commented:

At the time the committee was in the valley a meeting was held in Jackson which was decidedly in favor of the proposed changes.

Park Extension has been agitated here for years and we believe has gradually found favor, especially in the northern end of the valley. Jackson and the southern part of the valley is [sic] still decidedly against such a move.

Judging by newspaper reports the state as a whole is favorable to an enlarged park regardless of legislative resolutions to the contrary. [14]

Senator Nye's bill to establish Grand Teton National Park could not overcome the opposition of Idaho's two senators. These two men were not opposed to the creation of Grand Teton National Park but agreed to block any legislative move to protect the Tetons until they won approval of a bill to remove the Bechler Meadows area from

John Calvin Coolidge (R)
1872-1933
Coolidge became the 30th President at the death of Warren Harding. As one of his last acts as president, he signed the bill creating the first Grand Teton National Park on February 26, 1929.

Yellowstone National Park. (The original initiative to remove the Bechler Meadows from Yellowstone to allow for irrigation projects in Idaho was discussed in the previous chapter.) It became apparent that Idaho's power play could be effective indefinitely. The public lands committee, therefore, agreed to a compromise (Senate Joint Resolution No. 206) which allowed for the creation of the Grand Teton National Park. Senator Kendrick introduced S. 5543 on January 24, 1929, with the knowledge that Idaho's Congressional delegation would not oppose its passage. In return, Idaho's Congressional delegation was assured the passage of their bill (Public Law No. 74, 70th Congress, 2nd Session), which authorized the appointment of a Presidential Commission of five

to study the *"...lands along the south boundary of Yellowstone Park, particularly the southeast and southwest corners, with the view to the elimination of the Bechler Meadows and the addition of a large wild area of the southeast corner."* [15] Kendrick's bill removed the Grand Teton National Park issue from the Yellowstone National Park boundary problem. The boundary proposed in Kendrick's bill was essentially the same as that recommended by the 1925 coordinating committee. It provided for the construction of trails within the park but prohibited the development of new roads and commercial structures, unless authorized by Congress. Kendrick provided that the land within the boundaries described in the bill were *"...hereby reserved and withdrawn from settlement, occupancy, or disposal under the laws of the United States, and dedicated and set apart as a public park or pleasure ground for the benefit and enjoyment of the people of the United States under the name of the Grand Teton National Park of Wyoming...."* [16]

In February, Kendrick's bill passed the House and the Senate and it was sent to the President for his approval. President Coolidge, as one of his last official acts, signed the bill into law on February 26, 1929.* The pen that Coolidge used on this occasion was given to Horace Albright, who, on January 12 was appointed Director of the National Park Service following Stephen Mather's resignation due to illness. Albright worked for the protection of the Tetons and Jackson Hole since his first visit to the area. He endured years of adverse publicity in the western press but never lost hope for his dream. Although that pen must have been priceless to him, Albright knew that Senator Kendrick had hoped the pen would go to the Wyoming State Historical Library, so he sent the pen to Kendrick for its eventual presentation to that institution.[17]

As an interesting sidelight, February 26, the date on which Grand Teton National Park of Wyoming was established, was also an important date for several other national parks. On that same date in 1916, Sieur de Monts, later renamed

---

*At the time, an outgoing President did not relinquish office until the end of February in the year after the election. Congress later moved the date forward to reduce the time a lame duck President held office.

Arcadia National Park, was established. On February 26, 1917, Mount McKinley was included into the park system, and exactly two years later, Grand Canyon joined the growing list of National Parks.[18] Grand Canyon National Park was established after 35 years of controversy while Grand Teton required 31 years of effort. The *Deseret News* (Salt Lake City) noticed this similarity and remarked, *"...a more than thirty year Congressional struggle was required to secure national parkhood for the picturesque area, almost an average of a year per mile for its length. But it was worth the effort."* [19] Also, Glacier Bay National Monument was established on February 26, 1925.[20]

The Idaho senators were not as successful in attaining their goals as was Senator Kendrick. Their bill calling for a presidential commission was, of course, successful, but the commission's findings were not favorable to the irrigationists.* The result of the commission's recommendations was that Idaho lost its proposed Bechler Meadows Reservoir in the southwest corner of Yellowstone; the Forest Service lost its desired acquisition between the southern boundary of Yellowstone and the portion of the Snake River which flows west below Heart Lake; and the Park Service lost the headwaters of the Yellowstone River, or Thorofare area, at the southeastern corner of the Park. In other words, the commission recommended the southeastern, southern, and southwestern boundaries remain the same as was established by the original park legislation in 1872. They did, however, recommend that the Thorofare area be managed as a wilderness area which would provide more restrictive protection than management as a national forest.[21] The "wilderness" recommended by the commission should not be confused with modern wilderness designated wildlands. The Wilderness Act was not passed until 1964. The commission's recommendation was a management directive rather than a legislative mandate.

The appointment of the President's Commission served to separate the southern Yellowstone boundary disputes from the northern and eastern

Harris and Ewing (Library of Congress [Public domain] via Wikimedia Commons

John B. Kendrick
1857-1933
Ninth Governor of Wyoming
Kendrick was elected Governor of Wyoming in the 1914 election. In 1916 while still governor, he ran successfully for the U.S. Senate. He served in the Senate from 1917 until his death in 1933.

boundary disputes allowing Senator Norbeck to introduce S. 3001. President Hoover signed this bill on March 1, 1929, which added 159 square miles of Forest Service land to Yellowstone while giving 81 square miles of Yellowstone Park land to the Forest Service.[22] Thus, it appeared the Yellowstone National Park extension movement had finally reached a conclusion.

The creation of Grand Teton National Park caused a flood of publicity outside the valley that praised the new Park and predicted an economic boom for the Jackson Hole area. The *Jackson Hole Courier,* however, did not seem particularly excited about the new park and was content to report events and developments as they occurred.

---

*The commission was composed of Doctor E. E. Brownell, Chairman; Arthur Ringland, Secretary: Arthur Morgan, President, Antioch College; Doctor T. Gilbert Pearson, President, National Association of Audubon Societies; and C. H. Ramsdell. Although the commission received some criticism for not having a Wyoming resident as a member, it was generally non-controversial in the Jackson community.

Grand Teton National Park GRTE 430-02-59-020
Grand Teton National Park original entrance near Jenny Lake.

In fact, throughout much of the history of Yellowstone National Park, the state of Wyoming never really advertised its three approaches to the Park, while Montana communities had actively sought to attract tourists by promoting the glories of that Park. When the Tetons were made a national park, the situation did not change appreciably. The *Cheyenne Tribune* was one exception to this observation. The *Tribune* stated in a March 1929 editorial entitled "An Idea Crystallizes" that:

> *No man, regardless the range of his vision, can foresee what the future holds, but in the establishment of Grand Teton National Park America has guaranteed insofar as humanly is possible that the beauty of the Tetons and their immediate environment shall be preserved. A generation hence, ten generations, a hundred, shall this nation that long endure, the charm of this region still should exist virtually pristine, to delight the souls of men.*
>
> *For a half-century or more the idea of a Teton national park fermented. Now it has set. Enactment is a fair heritage from this generation to those that are to follow.*[23]

This statement of approval of the federal action was still a long way from actively supporting the two parks and the men who worked to protect them. While the Wyoming press was largely non-committal, the *Missoula Sentinel* (Montana) praised the recreational opportunities of the new Park and reported that the Northern Pacific railway would include the Teton attractions in its advertisements.[24] The *Livingston Enterprise*, the *Helena Independent*, and the *Butte Free Press* also carried similar articles while the *Jackson Hole Courier* simply reported that the President had signed the bill.[25] Despite the fact that most of Yellowstone National Park was within Wyoming's borders, it was spiritually, if not physically, a Montana park.

When the Park Service announced the appointment of Samuel T. Woodring (the chief ranger of Yellowstone Park) to become superintendent of Grand Teton National Park, the Montana press heaped praise on the man and applauded his appointment. The *Livingston Enterprise* stated:

> *It is with more than a general feeling of pride that Park county folks express their gratitude to the officials who had the job of selecting a new park superintendent. Of course we know the selection was a good one, and that there is not a single note of discord. Everyone wishes Sam the best of luck and is happy that the zenith of his career is to find him in command of a park, and one*

that will not remove him far from the picture where his greatest success has warranted this splendid promotion.[26]

While the *Jackson Hole Courier* merely reported the appointment of Woodring to Grand Teton Park, the *Billings Gazette* praised three Park Service administrators:

On June 15 Yellowstone re-opens, and Grand Teton National Park makes its debut as a national playground, and it is a source of much satisfaction for Montanans to note that these attractive institutions are supervised by men who know their work and who know and love the Treasure state and its people. Horace M. Albright, a native of the west and for years superintendent at Yellowstone, is now director of the national park service. Roger W. Toll ... is Mr. Albright's successor at Yellowstone. Samuel T. Woodring, who for 30 years has lived in the Yellowstone and Tetons ... took up his duties as superintendent of the new park. If the people out here were to cast votes to select men for

Grand Teton National Park GRTE-430_1117C
Grand Teton National Park staff, 1929
Fritiof Fryxell, Samuel Woodring, Julia Woodring, Edward Bruce, Phil Smith

these three important posts it's an odds-on bet that the selections would have been Albright, Toll, and Woodring.

Their promotions were merited by years of zealous, intelligent work. Each is known personally by men and women in all parts of this state who have long admired the administrative abilities which have brought reward from the secretary of Interior. We can confidently expect that the tens of thousands

Harrision Crandall Photo: Jackson Hole Historical Society and Museum p2004.0055.007

Dedication of Grand Teton National Park at String Lake, 1929.

who each month travel through this state to the gateways of the parks will be increased through their sound management and enthusiasm for these western playgrounds. [27]

The support which these three Park Service men received in the first year of their respective jobs and the success of Grand Teton National Park in its first season of operation was largely due to publicity generated outside the state of Wyoming.

Sam Woodring, whose appointment as superintendent did not technically become effective until May 15, had very little time to organize himself, his staff and the new Park for the expected tourist onslaught. The park rangers repaired trails, cleaned and prepared the existing campgrounds, and converted the Stewart Ranger Station (formerly a Forest Service facility) into a Park headquarters building and ranger housing. Additionally, the rangers had to prepare for the new park's dedication ceremonies that were scheduled for July 29. All this was accomplished with an appropriation of only $11,750, $7,500 for administration and protection and $4,250 for maintenance. [28] Woodring supervised the park through an almost unbelievably successful first season. During the park's three month season, 51,500 tourists visited the Tetons, two and a half times the number that visited Bryce Canyon National Park in Utah which was established a year earlier. [29]

The dedication of the new park was the major event of the summer in Jackson Hole. The National Editorial Association, which was holding its annual convention in Wyoming, was asked to dedicate the park. The *Jackson Hole Courier* suddenly began to print articles of a positive nature concerning Grand Teton National Park. In a matter of weeks, the *Courier* became an absolute supporter of the park and Sam Woodring. Regarding the dedication ceremony, the *Courier* stated, *"Alright folks pledge your support ... that this affair may go over big. It means much toward the growth and development of the valley. In many ways it is the most important event of the season. Let's get busy."* [30]

During the evening prior to the dedication ceremonies, a campfire program was conducted at Jackson Lake Lodge for the members of the National Editorial Association, interested Jackson Hole residents, and park visitors. Roger W. Toll, the new Yellowstone Park Superintendent, presided over the campfire. Dr. Grace Raymond Hebard, a history professor at the University of Wyoming; William O. Owen, who claimed the first ascent of the Grand Teton; and S. N. Leek, a local naturalist, and photographer (and park opponent) gave talks on the valley.

The following morning, at 9:30 the actual dedication ceremonies began at String Lake. Governor Frank C. Emerson presided over the program. The governor in presenting the Park to Horace Albright expressed the hope that *"...it may always be jealously cherished for the high purposes to which it is now dedicated."* [31] The governor's speech was obviously written with the knowledge that four hundred of the nation's editors would be in attendance. Considering the

Harrision Crandall Photo: Jackson Hole Historical Society and Museum bc.217

Horace Albright at the podium during the dedication of Grand Teton National Park, 1929 history of efforts to establish the park, the governor's speech seemed rather incongruent. The *Salt Lake Tribune* reported that Emerson "... *told of the welcome with which his state greeted the federal legislation setting aside the Teton territory as a national park, and expressed a sincere wish that the entire nation would come to enjoy their profound beauties as Wyomingites and the comparatively few easterners who have enjoyed the peaks.*" [32] On the other hand, the state's chief executive could hardly be expected to denounce the Park while conducting its dedication ceremonies. Also, by this time, the economic benefits that would accrue to the state from an enlarged tourist industry were obvious to nearly everyone.

Albright, responding to the governor's speech, stated:

In accepting this park from Governor Emerson, I come into the realization of a dream I have cherished for many years. No other section of the country is so worthy of becoming a national park. The Tetons are

Erwin Charles Funk
1877-1960
Funk, the past president of National Editorial Association, gave the dedicatory address at the String Lake ceremony.

the most beautiful peaks in America, and with the charming lakes that nestle among them, they offer one the greatest beauty spots we have .... [33]

After Albright's speech Erwin Funk, the past president of the National Editorial Association gave the dedicatory address. Mr. Funk stated that Grand Teton National Park "...*will stand as an everlasting monument to the wisdom of the commonwealth of Wyoming, preserving this great park in all its virgin beauty, and to the generosity of its people in sharing it not only with millions today but with generations to come after us.*" [34] He also stated:

Grand Teton National Park will not shine in reflected glory of the older and better known neighbor to the north. Its claim to fame is based upon a grandeur all its own, and peculiar to its own boundary limits. It is fitting, however, two such wonder spots of nature shall lie side by side that travelers from distance may include them in the same pilgrimage, and find there by the cool waters of Lake Jackson, and in the long morning and evening shadows of the mighty Tetons, quiet that brings a soothing rest to the weary soul, the solitude that inspires, true communion with Mother Nature and knits up again frayed nerves and shattered sense, the keen relief from worries and noises of our towns and cities only to be found in

American Heritage Center, University of Wyoming, F.M. Fryxell Collection, Box 80, File 17

Ranger Phil Smith takes his turn packing the plaque.

chapels of towering mountain peaks and in holy places of timbered hollows.[35]

Immediately following the dedication, Joseph Weppner presided over a ceremony commemorating the first ascent of the Grand Teton. In 1928, the 19th Legislature passed Joint Resolution No. 2 recognizing the Owen Party as the first to gain the summit of that peak. The following year, the 20th Legislature passed Joint Memorial No. 3 authorizing and appointing a commission to arrange for the ceremony and to place a plaque on the top of the Grand Teton honoring the event. Weppner, the chairman of that commission, presented the plaque to the new Park's superintendent. Woodring then commissioned Dr. F. M. Fryxell, a professor of geology at Augustana College and the first naturalist ranger in Grand Teton National Park, along with William Gilman and Phil Smith, both of Jackson, to install the plaque on top of the Grand Teton.[36] The three men began the climb immediately. During this ceremony, three of the members of this original mountain climbing party were introduced. Owen was there, having provided the plaque in his own honor, as was John Shive and Frank L. Petersen, who was at that time

a county commissioner. Petersen died a month and a half later, on September 12, 1929.

With the completion of the ceremonies to dedicate the nation's 21st national park, the editors were entertained at a fish fry at Jenny Lake. Following the fish fry, they left for Yellowstone National Park, leaving behind an impromptu party that lasted the rest of the day.

A year before the dedication, during the summer of 1928, Chorley traveled from New York to review the progress of the purchasing project. He evidently was not pleased. He requested Fabian and Miller to meet with him and Webb in January 1929. During this meeting, which took place in New York, Chorley and Webb expressed their disappointment with the amount of land purchased on the west side of the Snake River. Very little of the approximately 13,419 acres* which Miller

American Heritage Center, University of Wyoming, F.M. Fryxell Collection, Box 80, File 17

Rangers Smith and Fryxell preparing to unveil the plaque.

Fryxell and Smith had been climbing partners since 1925. They are credited with many of the first ascents of peaks in the Teton Range as well as names for topographic features. According to historian John Daugherty, the history of mountaineering in the Tetons was preserved largely as a result of Fryxell's research and initiation of procedures and documentation now considered standard park policy. In 1932, Fryxell authored *The Teton Peaks and Their Ascents*- required reading for those interested in the history of mountaineering in the Tetons.

American Heritage Center, University of Wyoming, F.M. Fryxell Collection, Box 80, File 17

William Gilman in the background. Smith hammering a drill hole to mount the "first ascent" plaque.

---

* Forty-seven deeds were transferred to the Snake River Land Company in 1928. Only the Anna B. Loomis purchase failed to list the acreage. However, the Snake River Land Company schedule of proposed purchases indicated she owned 177 acres.

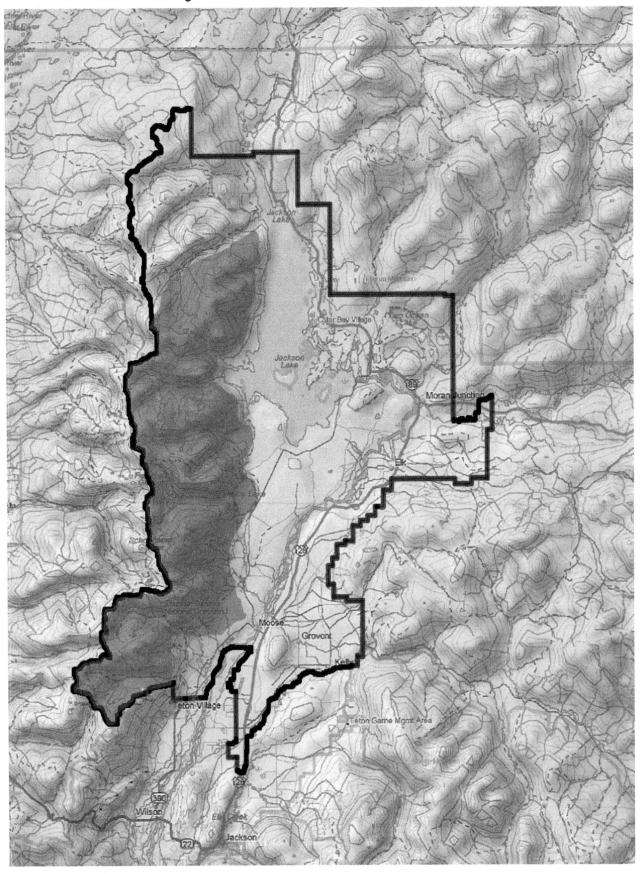

Senator Kendrick's bill, S. 5543, established the 96,000 acre Grand Teton National Park of Wyoming.

Current Teton Park boundary
Grand Teton National Park, 1929

Rockefeller Archive Center 812990_me

Kenneth Chorley
1893-1974

Kenneth Chorley was one of the public principals of the Snake River Land Company, the holding company established to cloak Rockefeller's involvement in purchasing land in Jackson Hole. He also represented John D. Rockefeller, Jr. with other restoration projects including Colonial Williamsburg. He was President of Colonial Williamsburg, Inc. for 23 years (1935-1958), treasurer (1952-1955) and vice-president (1954-1964) of Jackson Hole Preserve, Inc., and president of Grand Teton Lodge Company (1952-1963). Chorley was born in Bournemouth, England but came to the United States at the age of seven. In 1959, he was made an honorary commander of the Most Excellent Order of the British Empire by Queen Elizabeth II for promoting British-American relations. (*Williamsburg Times*, March 22, 1974)

---

purchased during 1928 was situated west of the Snake River.[37] According to the purchase plan, these western lands were of primary importance while purchases east of the river were secondary. Miller's activities appeared to be an unauthorized reversal of priorities. Harold Fabian recalled the banker's justification for his actions, *"Mr. Miller was reluctant to become a party to purchases of land in this area at the prices which were being demanded, and constantly advocated and acted upon a policy of delay."* [38]

At the very beginning of the project, Fabian was warned that Miller might have difficulty purchasing the lands west of the Snake.[39] During a 1927 trip to Jackson Hole, Harold Fabian discussed portions of the project with Henry Stewart, owner of the JY Ranch. Stewart pointed out

that the early settlers in the valley had been interested in agriculture and ranching and had, therefore, settled in the eastern portions of the valley where the soil conditions were more conducive to their enterprises. The soil on the western side of the river was largely composed of loosely consolidated glacial gravel while the eastern side contained alluvial deposits from the older Gros Ventre Mountain Range. The Snake, therefore, divided the northern half of the valley into two economic sections, that is, the east for agriculture and ranching and the west, having generally unproductive soil, for tourism. The economic divisions of the valley, based on the geology of the area, also created a sociological division following the same boundaries.

Tourism, being the more recent of the two industries, was plied by the "newcomers" on the west while the "old timers" lived east of the Snake. Stewart reasoned that since Miller was an old timer residing east of the river, he (Miller) would be more successful in purchasing the eastern properties and less successful in purchasing the western lands. Therefore, Stewart offered to handle the western purchases feeling he knew the people better than Miller. Miller would not agree to such an arrangement stating, *"...he did not want anybody buying in addition to himself because that would create a competitive atmosphere."* [40] At the time, Webb and Fabian thought Miller's point was well made and declined to use Henry Stewart to aid the project on the west side of the Snake River. With the establishment of Grand Teton National Park, the prospect that land prices might decrease dimmed considerably. Miller was again urged to purchase the primary lands west of the Snake, but he still refused to pay the prices asked.

During the summer of 1929, Webb and Fabian visited Jackson Hole to see if anything could be done to improve the progress of the purchasing program. They approached Richard Winger, Albright's initial suggestion for a local purchasing agent, to determine if he would agree to help with the project. According to Fabian, Winger agreed and explained that he had long been interested in the project, having prepared the original estimates upon which the project was based. His agreement to assist in the purchasing of land was predicated

123

on one condition. Winger evidently did not want to work for Miller and agreed to help only if Fabian would stay in the valley as his supervisor.[41] This time, Miller agreed to an additional purchasing agent and the purchasing program picked up a little speed. Because of the rising land prices west of the Snake River and the unanticipated initial purchases made east of the Snake River, it appeared that the original $1,000,000 which Rockefeller had allotted to the Snake River Land Company would be inadequate to complete the project. Therefore, Rockefeller added another $500,000 to the purchasing project.

Richard Winger gave a more detailed and complicated account of how he came to be employed by the Snake River Land Company. In 1926, after the Maud Noble's cabin group had conceded their proposal was dead, Winger's hopes for the valley's protection had been raised again when Albright requested estimates to present to a wealthy easterner. However, when Rockefeller's men selected Miller over Winger as the purchasing agent, Albright informed Winger that the effort had been unsuccessful.[42]

Because the tourist business in the valley was growing, Winger decided to enter the dude ranch business. With that intent, he filed an entry application on slightly more than 137 acres of land at Dead Man's Bar under the Timber and Stone Act (20 Stat., 89). The Evanston Land Office, where the entry was made, rejected the filing on the grounds that that particular area was more valuable for its scenic qualities than for its timber and stone. Winger then wrote to Albright, whom he now considered his friend, and to Senator Kendrick for advice. Albright was not in Washington at the time but stated, perhaps disingenuously, he would have someone look into it. Winger asked Senator Kendrick if he thought he should hire a lawyer in Washington as he wished to appeal the decision to the commissioner of the General Land Office. Kendrick replied that he would take care of it himself and did indeed get the decision reversed. Winger was allowed to file his entry.*

Because of the Executive Orders prohibiting entry on much of the public lands north of Jackson and the activities of the Snake River Land Company, Winger suspected someone might be trying to implement the 1923 plan. While the prospect that the dream might become a reality excited him, he was upset that as an originator of the idea he had not been informed that the project was in progress. When Miller approached Winger about selling his land at Dead Man's Bar to the Snake River Land Company, Winger set an exorbitant price of $25,000. The Snake River Land Company refused to pay that amount, and Winger believed that Miller spread a rumor that he had filed the entry just for speculation purposes.[44]

Later, when Webb and Fabian approached Winger about helping with the purchasing program, Winger was still miffed at being excluded from the project at the start. He agreed to help with the purchasing, but he refused to accept any compensation and refused to lower the price on his land at Dead Man's Bar. After he had worked for the Snake River Land Company for five months without compensation, the company offered to buy him a car, but Winger refused the offer. He did accept $700 which he used, in addition to the trade-in value of his old car, to purchase a new car.

The Snake River Land Company continued to urge Winger to sign an employment contract providing compensation for his services but always tied the employment contract to the sale of his land for a more reasonable amount. Winger still refused to sell his land for less than $25,000. Eventually, in March 1930, Winger consented to an agreement. He recalled the arrangement as follows:

> *I ... insisted I would not sell this land to them for less than $25,000, and they insisted they would not pay it. I first insisted I would work for nothing, but I was going to make them pay $25,000 for the land just because I was piqued, I admit it. It was not even a sensible argument, but they made the contract in such a way that the payments*

---

*Senator Kendrick was one of the most influential politicians Wyoming ever sent to Washington. The above incident is not an unusual example of his power. T. A. Larson, in his book *History of Wyoming*, quoted the *Denver Post* as stating, *"Senator Kendrick has a way of getting things done. Wyoming sends big men to represent her in Congress. We send professional politicians who seem to have no influence."* [43]

they made me per acre applied against this price. They had an option on this land, and, if they bought it, all of the payments they made me applied on the purchase of the land. In other words, if they bought my land for $25,000 I would probably work for 3 or 4 years for nothing.[45]

Originally Winger had been offered $2 per acre purchased by a certain date and $1.25 per acre purchased after that time. He refused that proposal and was then offered $1.25 per acre plus a bonus for the acres purchased below the company's purchase schedule. He also declined that offer. Eventually, Winger and the Snake River Land Company agreed on a compensation of $1.25 for each acre purchased.[46]

～

The editor of the *Courier* was quick to notice the purchases of land on the west side of the Snake. He earlier guessed that the purpose of the Snake River Land Company was to protect the wildlife because a majority of the acquisitions had been in the area of the annual elk migration routes. In August 1929 he reported, *"We have learned upon good authority that The Snake*

Harrision Crandall Photo: Jackson Hole Historical Society and Museum
2002.0055.001

Ray Lyman Wilbur
1875-1949
31st Secretary of the Interior

Wilbur served as Secretary of the Interior from 1929-1933 in the Hoover Administration. He was also President of Stanford University from 1916-1943.

River Land Company is a company of rich eastern sportsmen." But he seemed confused by the purchases on the west side of the river. Although he did not understand the reason for these new purchases, he allowed, *"Certainly any company can buy land wherever it chooses, provided it has the wherewithal or the credit to buy with. The Snake River Land Company seems amply provided with cash to carry its land buying to completion."* After speculating that the land might be used for recreation purposes, the *Courier* remarked, *"...it probably is none of our business as to what disposition the company makes of its land holdings in the future."* However, the editor reasoned, *"That the project is meant for all to enjoy seems assured, else why the signs of governmental cooperation?"* [47]

～

Also, in 1929 the Snake River Land Company was given the opportunity to explain its project "in the field" to the Secretary of the Interior, Ray Lyman Wilbur. Wilbur was touring some of the western parks and Horace Albright arranged the schedule in such a way to allow Harold Fabian and Kenneth Chorley the time to explain the project in detail. *"Secretary Wilbur was very enthusiastic over the project, and pledged his fullest support in carrying it through. He reported to President Hoover on his return to Washington, and the President said he was ready to assist when the time came to advance legislation."* [48] That this meeting was anticipated by the representatives of the Snake River Land Company is evidenced in a letter from Harold Fabian to Horace Albright, dated August 26, 1929. Fabian thought Wilbur's trip would be *"...a good opportunity to explain the entire project to Secretary Wilbur."* He also stated, *"I hope you are making provision for us to have enough time to take him around the valley for the purpose of getting our picture."* [49]

The Snake River Land Company also found opportunities to present their plan to other influential people in 1929. In September, Wyoming Senator Francis E. Warren made what would be his last trip to Jackson Hole. He became interested in the project and two weeks before his death in November visited Horace Albright in Washington. Albright recalled that Senator Warren expressed "*...a very great interest in the Jackson Hole project. He asked me some questions about it, and told me he thought it was a great plan and one that would greatly benefit Wyoming.*" [50] Had Warren lived to lend his support to Rockefeller's project, the eventual extension of Grand Teton National Park might have been accomplished with less controversy. Warren carried much influence in Wyoming and the U.S. Congress. T. A. Larson, in his *History of Wyoming*, classified Senator Warren as one of the three grand old men of Wyoming. Warren was a territorial governor of Wyoming before becoming the first state governor. He then served 37 years and four days in the Senate– a service record unsurpassed until 1964 by Carl Hayden. At the time of his death Senator Warren, then 85 years old, was planning to run for reelection the following year.[51]

Another opportunity to gain support for the project occurred in early December of that year when the Commission on the Conservation of the Elk in Jackson Hole held its second meeting. During this meeting, Webb made a presentation to the commission detailing the Snake River Land Company's goals, activities, and progress. The commission then discussed a proposed resolution which stated in part, *"That upon an offer of donation, for the purposes indicated ... from the Snake River Land Company or other owners, such offer be accepted by the Federal Government as adequate compliance with the Governmental policy in acquiring lands of this character."* [52] No action was taken pending a report by a commission subcommittee established to study the issue as well as the advisability of recommending legislation for the purchase of additional private lands in Jackson Hole. Thus, the second conference of the Elk Commission accomplished little, or as Horace Albright put it, *"...nothing tangible came out of the meeting."* [53]

~

The Snake River Land Company's purchases, with the added enthusiasm of Dick Winger, picked up tremendous speed. During the first six months of 1929, Miller purchased 13 pieces of

Francis Emroy Warren (R)
1844-1929

Warren, a Massachusetts native, moved to Wyoming when it was still part of the Dakota Territory. He was a veteran of the Civil War having served initially as a non-commissioned officer in Company C, 49th Massachusetts Infantry. By the end of that conflict, he held the rank of Captain. At the siege of Port Hudson, Louisiana, Warren, a 19-year old corporal, volunteered to join a pre-general assault charge on an artillery position. Wounded, and the last survivor of his platoon, he captured and disabled the Confederate artillery. For this action, he received the Medal of Honor for battlefield gallantry. He was the last Civil War veteran to serve in the U.S. Senate.

Harrison Crandall Photo: Jackson Hole Historical Society and Museum
2004.0055.002

Albright provided numerous opportunities for the Snake River Land Company to explain their project to dignitaries visiting the national parks. Pictured above left to right: unnamed, Roger W. Toll, Secretary of the Navy Curtis Wilbur, Kenneth Chorley, Harold Fabian, Horace Albright.

property whereas 38 were purchased after Winger was hired.[54] This was probably a factor in the decision not to renew Miller's contract when it expired on December 31, 1929. Fabian recalled:

...in the latter part of the year Mr. Webb wrote Miller that, since his contract was terminating, he assumed it was not going to be renewed, to which Miller agreed. But there was no thought of any ill-feeling between us.... Miller would not pay the prices that were being demanded for the lands on the west side of the river. Our people were willing to pay the prices and get the land bought, feeling that each year they were left the prices would go higher. That was the reason for it.[55]

Miller recalled for a senate committee the circumstances of his departure from the Snake River Land Company with only one notable difference. Under questioning by Senator Nye of that committee, Miller substantiated Fabian's assertions that there were no ill feelings between himself and the Snake River Land Company, but he stated no one had expressed dissatisfaction with his land purchases on the east side of the Snake River. He concluded, *"My contract expired, and I advised them in advance that I did not care to obligate myself to them further. I also stated I would be pleased to help them continue the project in any way that I could, and I have."*[56]

Miller's failure to actively pursue the acquisition of lands west of the Snake was not the only criticism he received from supporters of the Rockefeller project. Horace Albright's criticism extended back to the time Miller was selected as the purchasing agent for the Snake River Land Company. In the 1967 interview, Albright recalled the reason for his opposition to Miller's selection. He explained:

Well, I thought, and I am sure I was right, the first thing he would do would [be to] clear up the mortgages of his bank

and there were many of them. The orders were for him to buy everything west of the Snake River first. He didn't do any such thing! He cleaned up the mortgages of his bank and, of course, he had a commission coming to him on each purchase. I think ... Miller got a couple of hundred thousand dollars out of this whole deal.[57]

Mrs. Josephine Fabian, who was Harold's secretary before and during their marriage and was the Assistant Secretary of the Snake River Land Company, stated during an interview with the author that Miller used his position as the purchasing agent to clear his bank of quite a few mortgages.[58] Others claimed he foreclosed on mortgages and sold the land to the Snake River Land Company at inflated values.

According to Miller's testimony at the 1933 Senate hearings, he made only one purchase that was mortgaged to the Jackson State Bank. However, Miller held personal mortgages on six parcels of land with a total value of roughly $10,000. Most of these he purchased for the company. After he became the purchasing agent, two landowners defaulted on their loans and deeded their land to

wyomingtalesandtrails.com

Jackson State Bank- (undated).
This building had previously been the site of Dr. Bloom's dentist office. Bank clerk Harry Wagner stands at right. Wagner was also the first Mayor of Jackson when it incorporated in 1914. The bank occupied several locations but in 1936 moved from East Broadway to its current location on North Center Street. In 2008, it became part of the Wells Fargo chain of banks.

him to avoid foreclosure. He promptly sold these to the Snake River Land Company, but little, if any, evidence can be amassed to discredit Miller's integrity. Both parcels were adjacent to other lands purchased for the Snake River Land Company and, although they were east of the Snake River, they were well within the total purchase area. Neither did Miller pay himself top dollar for the properties. He sold one of the properties for $20 per acre while adjacent land had sold for $15 to $25 per acre. For the other parcel, he received $30 per acre whereas adjacent lands brought $20 to $40 per acre. The latter transaction provided Miller with a net loss equivalent to one year's interest on the original loan.[59]

Judgement of Miller's purchasing activities and motivations is further complicated by Vanderbilt Webb's written instructions concerning purchases. Webb wrote Miller in December of 1927:

...it is still understood that you have noauthority [sic] to purchase any parcel at more than the maximum price shown on the attached schedules, unless you purchase at the same time one or more additional parcels at less than the prices shown in these schedules, so that the total price of all the parcels which shall have been acquired at any given time will never exceed the total maximum prices of such parcels as shown in the attached schedule.[60]

Thus, Miller may have had to purchase more parcels east of the Snake River, at lower values, in order to purchase fewer parcels west of the Snake River where people were demanding higher prices. The price for each parcel included in the purchasing schedule had been set according to the perceived fair market value of the land in that area. Miller would have been required to pay people east of the river less than fair market value in order to pay the higher prices west of the river. Forcing settlers east of the Snake River to accept less than fair value for their property, especially during the Depression, would constitute taking unfair advantage of those settlers. Miller warned Webb and Fabian that he would not be a party to any scheme to take unfair advantage of his neighbors. His position in this regard, while verbal, was as much a part of the contract as the compensation provision. It also appeared that more of the people east of the river, composed mostly of farmers and ranchers, were willing to accept the amount offered by the Snake River Land Company than were the tourist oriented settlers west of the Snake River.

Nevertheless, Miller may be justly criticized for his reluctance to purchase lands west of the Snake River. He undoubtedly knew the primary focus of the project required a quick acquisition the lands composing the immediate foreground of the Teton Range. Had he followed the purchasing

Bridger-Teton National Forest, Jackson Hole Historical Society and Museum 1991.3574.001

The first airplane to land in Jackson Hole was flown by H. H. Barker from Blackfoot, Idaho.

plan as originally envisioned, two decades of controversy, political maneuvering, and social angst might never have occurred. If the purchasing schedule for properties west of the Snake River was inadequate to accomplish the goal of the project, he should have encouraged his superiors to make the necessary adjustments to the plan. It appears he did not make that suggestion.

Additionally, Albright's estimate of Miller's compensation appears to be exaggerated. Miller's contract provided for a commission of $1 per acre purchased within a certain time limit and $0.50 per acre for all land purchased after that time. If money had been his sole ambition, he would have made more by purchasing land as fast as possible. He was being paid by the acre, not by how much he saved the Snake River Land Company. Fabian maintained Miller was not purchasing land as rapidly as the company wished.

Miller testified that he had earned about $13,000 during his two and a half years as purchasing agent. Undoubtedly, Miller benefitted in other ways from the activities of the Snake River Land Company. Since his was the only bank in the valley, he would obviously receive some advantage from the input of $1,000,000 into the local economy, especially during the Depression. However, the benefits that accrued from the influx of new money into the valley were shared by the total business community, of which the bank was merely a member. It, therefore, appears that despite the accusations leveled at Robert Miller, his conduct, based on available evidence, as well as logic, was guided by his personal ideals of integrity rather than desires for personal monetary gain. If one generously calculates the average per acre value of the six properties Miller admits selling to the Snake River Land Company, it can be surmised that he received approximately $29,000. Combining this estimated amount with the compensation paid for his purchasing agent services cited above, it is possible Miller received a total of about $42,000 in Rockefeller funds. However, that amount should be reduced by the outstanding amount (unknown) that he previously loaned against the properties. Whatever financial gain Miller received from his association with the Rockefeller project appeared to be considerably less than that pejoratively supposed amount suggested by Albright.

Rumors that Miller ran his own cattle on the Teton Forest Reserve without paying the requisite fees while serving as supervisor were largely an attempt by pro-park and pro-Rockefeller advocates to disparage Miller's integrity. Prior to the spring of 1901, cattlemen grazed their herds on public land in Jackson Hole without a permit because permits were not required. Both Miller and his wife Grace obtained grazing permits in 1901. Grazing fees were not instituted until 1906, and complete records of grazing permits were not kept prior to 1906.[61] Thus while the allegation may be true, there is no evidence of unethical behavior by Miller because fees were not required at the time.

While there is no evidence to substantiate Albright's assertion of a financially nefarious motive by Miller while acting as agent for the Snake River Land Company, it can be noted that Albright, also without evidence of moral or ethical malfeasance or intent, benefitted financially from his association with Rockefeller. In a letter dated January 4, 1927, Albright thanked Rockefeller for sending a check that he indicated would be used to provide for the education of his children.[62] In January 1929, Albright acknowledged another financial gift from Rockefeller apparently made in celebration of Albright's promotion to director of the National Park Service. Albright indicated this money would be used to purchase a home in the nation's capital, *"...out on the edge of the city where my children can have opportunities for outdoor life such as they have been accustomed to in winter times."* [63] With no pejorative allegation intended, today's standards (and possibly the Hatch Act) would consider Albright's acceptance of such monetary gifts inappropriate. There is, nevertheless, the appearance of hypocrisy in Albright's criticism of Miller regarding the money the banker earned during the performance of his contractual employment while he (Albright) was accepting cash gifts.

~

Even though 1929 witnessed the beginning of the Depression, the valley of Jackson Hole experienced a successful and eventful year. The

129

creation of Grand Teton National Park provided a greater economic stimulus than even the most optimistic park supporters expected. Travel into Yellowstone National Park by the south entrance increased 30 percent while travel out of Yellowstone through the south entrance increased 100 percent.[64] Thus, the prophecy by J. D. Ferrin, J.P. Cunningham, Struthers Burt, Horace Albright, and others that the future of the valley lay in recreation was given credence in terms of actual tourist dollars. While the rest of the nation suffered from the economic Depression, Jackson Hole began to prepare for an even more prosperous season in 1930.

CHAPTER NINE

1930

A well known Wyoming Editor writes asking the prevailing opinion here concerning all this Snake River Land Company buying activity and Park Extension. Personally, we don't know the prevailing opinion, there doesn't seem to be any. Some say take the entire valley, some say stop where they are now, some say take all east of the highway to Jackson plus all the north country and some say this and some say that.[1]

Jackson Hole Courier

Rockefeller Archive Center Series 1030 SRLC Scrapbook

A lonely homestead on Mormon Row in Jackson Hole, Wyoming.

Nineteen thirty began with renewed fears that the National Park Service would soon create new problems for the residents of Jackson Hole. This concern resulted from speculation that Grand Teton National Park would attempt to extend its boundaries to include privately owned land and, therefore, reduce the county's tax base. Perhaps this speculation was partly based upon a mere association of the recent land purchases west of the Snake River by the Snake River Land Company. The editor of the *Jackson Hole Courier* had correctly guessed in 1928 that the principals behind the Snake River Land Company were interested in perpetuating the elk herd. This was based on the land purchases east of the Snake River. In 1929, the editor again correctly surmised that the company was also interested in recreation based on the purchases west of the Snake River and the obvious federal cooperation in the form of public land withdrawals. However, the strongest basis for this fear may have been a piece of legislation, H.R. 15089, passed during the summer of 1929. This bill provided appropriations to Grand Teton National Park, among others, for the purpose of condemnation of adjacent privately owned land.

It was not likely that officials of Grand Teton National Park pushed for such legislation, the Park having only recently been established. The bill may have been the result of well-meaning congressmen or other government officials who were merely trying to straighten and simplify some of the more irregular boundaries of a few parks. Grand Teton's eastern boundary was extremely erratic because of the compromise required to ease opposition to the Park. Had the boundary been drawn in a straight line so as to include the small lakes at the base of the mountains, certain private lands would have been included within the Park. The associated loss of taxable property to the county would probably have created sufficient opposition to prohibit the establishment of the Park. Conversely, had a straight line been drawn omitting the private land, excluding the lakes, the supporters of the Park would not have been satisfied. The protection of those lakes had been a major argument for the necessity of national park status as opposed to the mandate of any other federal or state agency. The 1929 boundary, as irregular and as complicated as it was, provided the necessary compromise that resulted in the creation of the Park.

Additionally, a number of government officials were aware that Rockefeller was in the process of buying these lands and that the boundary problems would eventually be resolved. In short, there appeared to be no reason for the National

Grand Teton National Park GRTE-430_00191

First Grand Teton National Park Headquarters.

Park Service to enter into the potentially controversial realm of condemnation in Jackson Hole. It is possible that the Department of the Interior did not oppose the legislation because Grand Teton National Park was only one of several parks designated in the bill for condemnation appropriations. The bill provided the money for such activities; it did not require each park to utilize the funds. Since the other parks listed in the bill were in need of boundary adjustments the Interior Department may have decided to refrain from tampering with the bill.

A more cynical view would be that the Park Service allowed Grand Teton National Park to be listed in the bill, or even instigated its inclusion, in order to aid the Snake River Land Company with purchases west of the Snake River. Even if the Park Service never intended to exercise the powers and appropriations allowed by the bill within Jackson Hole, the Snake River Land Company could use the threat of the law as a club to encourage reluctant land-owners to sell their property. In fact, the Park Service official most closely associated with both the Grand Teton Park project and the Rockefeller project, Horace Albright, as Director of the National Park Service, was in a position to do just that. Albright was in a position to either support the bill or recommend the deletion of any of the parks as inappropriate. However, there is no evidence to show that Albright or anyone else acted in an unethical manner concerning this legislation.

Nevertheless, the bill created a potential tax problem for the residents of Teton County and the *Casper Tribune* reported that the county faced a *"...threatened loss of 40% of taxable property. There is good reason, therefore, for the action of Teton County property owners in protesting to Washington against depletion of the tax roles for national park purposes without providing for remaining taxpayers."* [2] If the *Casper Tribune* was correct in its assessment of the situation in Jackson Hole, one could conclude that condemnation

American Heritage Center University of Wyoming Fritioff Fryxell Collection, Box 80, Folder 17

1930 Grand Teton National Park Staff

Left to right: Fryxell, Smith, Bruce, Woodring, Clark, Sherman, Secrest

was not the issue, but that the remaining property owners would be over-burdened because of the decrease in the tax base. The *Tribune* article later stated, *"Not that the people are opposed to park extension and preservation of their unexcelled wonderland in a state of natural beauty. They merely seek protection against heavy tax burdens."* [3] Since condemnation of private land by the federal government had never been a popular action in the West, the *Tribune* probably understated the situation in Jackson Hole.

Regardless of the prevailing attitude toward the government's right of eminent domain, the tax situation was an important concern for the valley residents. Teton County had, since its creation, viewed the private developments in Yellowstone National Park as an additional source of income. However, the concessionaire's physical assets were within a federal reserve that was established before Wyoming became a state. Neither the county nor the state had the authority to impose taxation on the commercial developments in Yellowstone. Therefore, the state and the county, in a rather intelligent move, refrained from attacking the condemnation bill and instead used it to illustrate their critical revenue problems and pushed for legislation permitting the taxation of nonfederal commerce within Yellowstone National Park.

133

Teton County was not the only entity that wanted to tax private developments in Yellowstone. Park County, on the east side of the Park, coveted the potential revenue, as did counties in Montana and Idaho. Accordingly, Montana's Senator Walsh introduced a bill to *"Expressly authorize the assessment, taxation, and collection of taxes upon property in private ownership situated within the boundaries of Yellowstone National Park."* [4] In support of this legislation, the Wyoming Legislature estimated that $15,000,000 in taxable property was escaping taxation. It also claimed that should the Snake River Land Company holdings be transferred to the federal government, Teton County's valuation would be reduced from $2,500,000 to $1,500,000.[5] If Grand Teton National Park condemned private property adjacent to its boundary, this reduction would be greater.

While this legislative effort dealing with the tax issues was in progress, the Snake River Land Company was experiencing complications with its purchasing program from Wyoming's chief executive. In December 1927, Governor Emerson gave his full approval to the purchasing plan, but late in 1929, he developed second thoughts about portions of the purchase area. The governor was concerned with the Snake River Land Company's purchases of what he considered good agricultural land east of the Snake River, particularly the Mormon Row area. Robert Miller evidently did not agree with the governor's assessment of the agricultural potential of those lands, and feeling he could change the governor's mind, invited him to visit the area. The governor visited the valley and was given a tour of the entire project, but his opinion concerning the agricultural potential of certain lands did not change. Emerson believed that with proper irrigation, those lands could become profitable.*

Prior to his election as governor, Emerson had been the State Engineer, which gave him jurisdiction over all the state's water. In that position, he had given his blessings to various irrigation schemes in Jackson Hole, many of which were killed by federal agencies or local opposition. Although he ultimately recognized the value of preserving the lakes at the base of the Tetons, he was, by trade, a reclamation engineer and his new found opposition to Rockefeller's purchases in the Mormon Row area may have resulted from his support for the proposed Ditch Creek Irrigation Project. If Rockefeller bought the land and discontinued its agricultural use, there would be no one to buy the water except Idaho irrigators. At that particular time, many people in Wyoming were alarmed at the volume of resources being exported to other states for processing and use. Emerson's administration would have been criticized if he supported a water project that benefitted only Idaho.

Olie Riniker Photo Jackson Hole Historical Society and Museum
1995.0400.006

Regardless of the season, visitors to Grand Teton National Park find evidence of the homestead past a favorite attraction. The few remaining outbuildings in the Mormon Row area are among the most photographed scenes in the Park.

---

*Governor Emerson's apparent change of heart regarding the purchasing project may not be quite the reversal it appeared to be. The project, as it was explained to him originally, proposed land purchases primarily west of the Snake River with the east side being of secondary importance. Miller's concentrated purchases east of the river probably did not match the governor's initial understanding of the project.

Harold Fabian recalled that after the tour of the Snake River Land Company project, Governor Emerson wrote to the project administrator, Mr. Webb, stating,

> *...while the purposes behind the undertaking were most laudable, and he heartily approved the effort to prevent unwholesome development of the region adjacent to the majestic Tetons, ... he thought the movement was going too far when purchases were extended into the area around the Grovont post office and to the valley of the Gros Ventre lying east of it....* [6]

Webb responded to the governor's letter reminding him that he had already approved that part of the purchase area. The governor, on November 5, 1929, replied that *"...the area around the Grovont post office was for the most part a good quality of soil, well adapted to profitable farming and he would greatly regret seeing this area withdrawn from agricultural development."* [7] Since the Snake River Land Company wanted to maintain the support of the Governor for its activities, Webb wrote the following letter to Governor Emerson on January 2, 1930:

Dear Governor Emerson:

I received in due course your letter of November 5th, for which I wish to thank you. We have given considerable thought to your recommendation that we eliminate from the purchasing program of the Snake River Land Company the land around Mormon Row and extending eastward to the Gros Ventre River. As I understand it, this would include all of the privately owned property in Sections 10-15, 20-29, and 32-35 Township 43-115 West and in Sections 1-12, Township 42-115 West. Since you feel that this land should not be included in our project, we are willing to defer to your wishes in the matter, to leave this property out of our purchasing program at your request, and to make no further purchases in this area at the present time, other than the few parcels we have already acquired and one or two additional parcels which we are under obligation to purchase from the present owners.

Sincerely yours,

V. Webb [8]

Floyd Naegeli photo Jackson Hole Historical Society and Museum hs4269006
Bound grain on Mormon Row

135

Photo courtesy Dr. Robert Smith

Mormon Row looking northeast from the top of Blacktail Butte, 1937

It was, perhaps, this letter that ensured the governor's continued support for the project even though opposition was growing in the public mind concerning the loss of taxable property in Teton County. In late January 1930, the governor was asked how he felt about the problem of Teton County's possible loss of its tax base and the activities of the Snake River Land Company. He stated, *"I feel convinced that friendly cooperation with these folks will lead to satisfactory solutions of the whole problem."* [9]

The Snake River Land Company's compliance with the governor's request eased the situation temporarily but created a new problem for the company within Jackson Hole. Governor Emerson failed to consider that there might be property owners in the area who desperately wished to sell their land. In the spring of that year, 1930, J. D. Ferrin approached Harold Fabian, stating that some of the residents of Mormon Row were upset that their lands had been eliminated from the project. These people sent a petition to the governor asking that he withdraw his objections to the purchase of their lands by the Snake River Land Company. [10]

On August 3, 1930, the governor met with the people of Mormon Row and agreed to withdraw his objections to the inclusion of their lands in the project. Ferrin reported the outcome of this meeting to Fabian who recalled his response as follows:

The only answer I could give Mr. Ferrin was that the Mormon Row lands had been formally withdrawn and were now entirely out of the project; that the money which had been appropriated for their purchase had been diverted to meet the higher prices we had been required to pay for other properties; that Mormon Row could not be reincluded without an additional appropriation of funds; and that the proper procedure for that purpose would be for Governor Emerson to write Mr. Webb requesting that these lands be reincluded. [11]

In September, Governor Emerson returned to Jackson Hole and met with Fabian. He still maintained that the land was too valuable to be withdrawn from production, but since the people wanted to sell, he would write to Webb withdrawing his objection and request the area be reincluded in the project. [12] Mr. Fabian, at the governor's request, met with the property owners of the Mormon Row area. He recalled:

I met with them with Mr. Winger in the meeting house on Mormon Row and again

Photo courtesy Dr. Robert Smith

Agriculturally developed acreage west of Blacktail Butte. This view is from the top of the north end of the Butte looking southwest toward Moose, Wyoming, 1937.

explained the necessity of an additional appropriation if the lands were to be reincluded. I further told them that we would not again undertake the piecemeal purchase of their property and that if they desired to have their lands reincluded it would be necessary for them to agree among themselves on a lump sum to be paid for the entire Mormon Row section, and if that price were fair and reasonable, it would be submitted to our principal with a recommendation that it be accepted. They asked if Mr. Winger could help them in working this out and I replied that so far as I was concerned he could, and he agreed to do so.[13]

By the next spring, all the details for the purchase of the Mormon Row lands had been agreed upon, and the request for an additional appropriation was ready for presentation to Mr. Rockefeller.* However, Senator Robert D. Carey, who had been elected the previous fall, began to complain about the Snake River Land Company and its purchases of land within Jackson Hole. Because of the Senator's opposition to additional purchases,

the appropriation request was never presented to Rockefeller. Fabian later explained this action (or lack of action) in a letter to Wilford Neilson, the editor of the *Jackson Hole Courier*. Fabian stated:

In view of Senator Carey's ... attitude toward the project as a whole since his election, which he had indicated on several occasions, it did not seem advisable to recommend any additional appropriation of this sort, and all further consideration of the purchase of these Mormon Row lands was therefore abandoned.[15]

⁓

While the Snake River Land Company was busy trying to please everyone, another Yellowstone National Park Boundary Commission was at work. The park extension issue, which most people thought was settled, was once again the topic of discussion within the valley. The deep-seated animosities toward Yellowstone were revived and, in some cases, projected onto the Snake River Land Company. This time, the commission suggested the southern boundary of Yellowstone National Park be extended south to the northern

---

*The proposal requested the purchase of 7,319 acres for $314,075 – an average of nearly $43 per acre including improvements. In 1927, Robert Miller had appraised the same acreage at $199,420, a little more than $27 per acre.**

boundary of Grand Teton National Park.[16] One local fear was that if the boundaries of the two parks were contiguous, the smaller park would eventually be absorbed into Yellowstone Park. The Forest Service, not wanting to lose any more ground to the Park Service, opposed the extension. The ranchers who historically moved cattle to the railhead at Ashton, Idaho, along the road just north of Jackson Lake, feared the loss of that route if it should be included in the Park. Hunting, mineral and timber interests also opposed the extension.

Although the Snake River Land Company had nothing to do with the boundary commission, some locals found the company "guilty by association." Governor Emerson, however, did not confuse the two organizations even though one was rarely discussed without the inclusion of the other. In a February interview with the *Wyoming State Tribune* in which the governor opposed the Yellowstone Park extension, he distinguished between the two groups by dealing with them separately. After voicing his opposition to the Yellowstone Park extension, he referred to the Snake River Land Company, stating:

At the present time, there is a serious threat of the withdrawal of taxable assets of Teton County to the extent that would seem unnecessary. The purchases of the Snake River Land Company have presented a problem by reason of the extent to which

Jackson Hole Historical Society and Museum 2003.0117.140

Homesteads in the northern section of the valley were isolated and, in winter, desolate abodes in a harsh climate. However, they had spectacular views of the Teton Mountain Range.

lands will be withdrawn as taxable property. This company has agreed to confine their future purchases within certain limits set out by myself. The motives of this company appear to be commendable.

It has been my conclusion that the company has extended their purchases to cover too much territory. It is upon the question of the extent of their land acquisitions that I hope reasonable agreement can be reached. A large part of the area of Jackson Hole is well fitted for agriculture development and the raising of livestock. These areas should be retained for such valuable purposes.[17]

This controversy over the Yellowstone National Park extension, the possible condemnation of private land by Grand Teton National Park, and the ultimate disposition of the property purchased by the Snake River Land Company had a detrimental effect on another project. During its December 1929 meeting, the Elk Commission agreed to delay a recommendation to Congress that certain lands necessary to the maintenance of the Jackson Hole elk herd be purchased, and that a portion of the Snake River Land Company holdings be accepted by donation for elk preservation purposes. The reason for the delay was to allow a subcommittee to investigate the lands and make recommendations. In March 1930, the subcommittee completed its investigation and its report, authored by Seth N. Gordon, stated in part:

...we have come to the conclusion that because of the unsettled status of the park boundary question, the general state of turmoil in the minds of Wyoming people concerning possible effects of the Boundary Commission's recommendations and purchases made by the Snake River Land Company, also the general legislative situation in Congress at this time, it will be wise to defer introduction of the bills for the purchase of lands or to authorize to take over Snake River Land Company lands until the next session.[18]

All the factors that led to this delay created an atmosphere that hampered the Elk Commission's goal of providing a secure winter refuge for the elk.

~

Nineteen thirty was also the year in which the Snake River Land Company publicly identified its benefactor. The disclosure of the true purpose of the Snake River Land Company and the identity of its principal resulted from the repeated suggestions from a number of supporters of the project. According to Harold Fabian, Governor Emerson recommended on a number of occasions that such a statement be made to inform the Wyoming people of the project. The editor of the *Kemmerer Gazette*, Lester G. Baker, had the entire project explained to him by Fabian in January of 1930. Fabian maintained that Baker *"...expressed his approval, but said that he had always been an opponent of so-called Park Extension, and he did not feel he could take a position which apparently would be reversing himself until we had placed the facts of our project publicly before the people of Wyoming."*[19] Also, C. R. Van Vleck, a local merchant and president of the Jackson Chamber of Commerce, stated to Fabian that *"...he had concluded that the Snake River Land Company project was a worth while undertaking and he too recommended that we give full publicity to our plan."* [20]

Accordingly, on April 6, 1930, the Snake River Land Company made public its benefactor and its intentions. Harold Fabian made the news release in Salt Lake City. It was fairly long and in addition to expounding on the beauty of the area and its abundant wildlife, traced the history of the idea from the 1923 meeting at Maud Noble's cabin. The release stated that roughly 35,000 acres were being purchased for an amount *"...substantially over $1,000,000."* [21] The news release also included a statement by Vanderbilt Webb, the president of the Snake River Land Company, which read in part:

The Jackson Hole country is the last stand of the frontier west and of the big game of North America. To date, it has withstood the inroads of civilization and is much the same magnificent wilderness in which the beaver trappers and hunters held their annual rendezvous in the days of Colter and Jackson. It is our purpose, while yet it can be done, to assist in saving at least a portion of this old west for the future generations of America- its magnificent scenery unspoiled, its timbered mountains and rolling parks crossed only by game trails: its rivers, streams and lakes filled with fish, and its wild life perpetuated by proper refuges and by effectively regulated hunting.

Yesterday an act of Congress could have caught the picture as it was and held it in perpetuity for the nation. Today, before Congress can act effectively, a very substantial expenditure is required, and these funds must come from private sources. Tomorrow the proposed plan will be practically impossible of accomplishment at any cost. The Snake River Land Company has been organized and is functioning solely for the purpose of acquiring as much of the private holdings in this area as possible, in order to turn these lands over to the United States

Parthenia Stinnett Photo Jackson Hole Historical Society and Museum
2005.0023.064

The winter school "bus" picked up children at the various ranches and delivered them to the nearest school and returned them home in the evening.

so that Congress can yet, before the opportunity has gone, establish and perpetuate this historic wilderness area and wild game country.

It is not the purpose of the Snake River Land Company to attempt to impose on the government its views as to the manner in which this area shall be administered. The company's present plans are to turn over to the United States government by the end of this year such lands as it may require and to leave to the government the matter of acquiring any additional lands which may be deemed necessary. The company's work will then have been accomplished, and we shall have done our part to make a reality of the dream of that little group who met in Miss Noble's cabin in 1923. The rest will be entirely a matter for the United States government.[22]

This release also explained that land had been purchased on each side of the highway approaches to the new Park *"...in order that the first view of the Teton peaks will be across a foreground of unmarred natural scenery."* [23] While the Snake River Land Company stated it did not intend to impose its views on the government, it did state that its purchases west of the Snake River might best be utilized by the Park Service for an extension of the present park boundary eastward to the Snake River. It also believed that portions of its purchases east of the river were best suited to the Biological Survey for elk wintering purposes and the raising of hay for the feeding program. It was suggested other lands on the east side of the river could be managed by the Forest Service as special wilderness areas.

While the company's original intent for its purchases east of the river was to provide an *"...unbroken trail (drift) connecting with the winter feeding grounds for the game herds coming down from*

John D. Rockefeller, Jr.

the summer ranges of the Buffalo and the Gros Ventre,"[24] the article explained, Governor Emerson objected to certain lands being withdrawn from agricultural production and the continuity of the project had been broken.*

The response on the part of Jackson Hole residents, as well as other Wyomingites, to the news that Rockefeller was behind the Snake River Land Company, and that his purchases were intended for inclusion within the public domain was predictably divided. Those who opposed Rockefeller's plan cited the hardships his actions would impose on the county due to the loss of taxable land. Although this was a valid argument, at least in the short run, another underlying factor was prevalent in the minds of many of Rockefeller's detractors. It was not (and is not) uncommon for westerners to distrust big eastern money. The *Casper Tribune-Herald* expressed that feeling in

*The position of the Snake River Land Company regarding lands east of the Snake River on occasion appeared contradictory. Documents, correspondence, and testimony before investigating congressional committees stressed the primary importance of purchasing private property west of the river. Dissatisfaction with Miller's purchase of properties east of the river was well documented. However, public statements released by the company often blamed Wyoming political officials for disrupting the purchasing program by opposing purchases they (the company) had maintained were of secondary significance. It seemed even less appropriate for the company to have publicly blamed the governor in this manner after he had defended them to a critical press.

John D. Rockefeller, Sr. and Jr. in their "Robber Baron" attire. Westerners learned to be distrustful of wealthy easterners who seemed willing to influence and control the lives of the less affluent "commoners."

an article on April 13 suggesting that the Snake River Land Company was not an altruistic enterprise but rather a "commercial scheme." [25] This feeling may have been reinforced by the "Robber Baron" reputation of the Rockefeller name. In fact, that reputation would eventually lead to speculation in the national press that the Snake River Land Company used force and intimidation to purchase lands cheaply. And while there may have been a few people who felt they had been deceived– that had they known Rockefeller was actually purchasing their property, they could have held out for more money– it was not presented as a condemnation of the Snake River Land Company in the local press or in subsequent congressional hearings on the matter.

However, Rockefeller and the Snake River Land Company were not without their supporters. One of the most vocal was Struthers Burt, who in June wrote another lengthy letter to the *Jackson Hole Courier* supporting the project. He began by stating *"...Jackson Hole has experienced through the coming of the Snake River Land Company an almost unbelievable stroke of luck."* [26] He maintained that of the 35,000 acres purchased

by Rockefeller *"...at least three fourths ... would not have been worth one cent to its owners, the county, or the state."* [27]

He continued:

While the Snake River Land Company has been at work, I have watched them carefully, and their conduct has been admirable. They have made mistakes, and they will make more of them, for they are engaged in a gigantic undertaking with hundreds of individuals to deal with and a score of separate problems, but their whole intention has been and is to be as fair as it is humanly possible. They will listen to any reasonable suggestion put to them. I repeat, I do not know anywhere a more disinterested or finer lot of men. They are all working on salary, there is not a single one of them who has anything to gain through this project, but, on the other hand, they are all trustees of another man's money and therefore are honor bound to spend it wisely and well.

There is only one question that needs debate, and that is the question of taxation and Teton County, but it seems to me that the question can be solved by Mr. Deloney's suggestion of a gradual withdrawal of land from taxation, or even better, by a little patience. The Grand Teton National Park and– if left alone– The Snake River Land Company will in the future bring so much money into Jackson Hole, and the solidification of land and population in the south end of Jackson Hole will in the future so increase land values and other values, that it will not be many years before Teton County will have more than made up in its valuation what it will temporarily lose in Taxation.

It all depends upon whether you wish to take the long view or the short view, upon whether you are penny wise or dollar wise, upon whether you are a far-sighted business man or a near-sighted one. The man who supports the Snake River Land Company and tries to understand what it is attempting to do, will realize that the Snake River Land Company is attempting to put into effect a magnificent plan never before attempted in the history, not alone of the United States, but of the world. A plan so unique that by it alone Wyoming and Jackson Hole will be famous throughout the world and the country. The possibilities are unpredictable, but one thing is certain, any resident of Jackson Hole who has enough sense to exercise a little patience and enough sense to keep quiet cannot help but profit.

It seems to me that we would be wise to settle our own affairs and did not listen too much to the opinions of other communities who, not unnaturally, may be a trifle jealous of the undoubted miracle that has befallen Jackson Hole.[28]

There was only one public response to Burt's letter. John L. Dodge thought Burt's letter was fair, but he was not as optimistic about the future ability of the ranches in the southern portion of the valley to carry the tax burden. He stated:

My residence here is eight years longer than my friend Burt's yet land remains at about the same value today that it had when I came. There are several reasons for this, an accommodating Supreme Court made us into a new county before we had the legal requirements in population and capitalization. Our principal occupation, the raising of cattle, became unprofitable on account of the increased cost of labor and a fall in the price of beef. Further restriction of the range also discouraged stock raising. I think the best solution of the difficulty is for the Snake River Land Company to buy all the ranches and turn Jackson Hole into a game preserve.[29]

It is impossible to know if John Dodge's suggestion about the game preserve was serious or not. It was not uncommon to hear similar versions of that suggestion throughout the valley at that time. It was a facetious remark meant to indicate the seriousness of the county's tax problem if the Rockefeller lands were removed from the tax base. However, Dodge's personal history would lead one to believe he was probably serious, at least for the time being.

Jackson Hole Historical Society and Museum p1958.3276.001

John Lockwood Dodge
1864-1957

John Lockwood Dodge first homesteaded in Jackson Hole in 1902. He and his family made additional homesteads and gradually he was able to buy the neighboring properties of discouraged homesteaders. At the time of his death in 1957 at the age of 93, he had amassed approximately 700 acres which he called the Wilderness Ranch. Upon his death, the ranch passed to blood relatives who sold the property to Hunter Lockwood Scott, John Dodge's nephew. After flunking out of Princeton in 1927, Hunter Scott was sent west to spend some time with his uncle. Scott maintained he would always keep the ranch as a wildlife refuge and established a corporation for that purpose. However, in recent years, the ranch was sold and subdivided.[31]

Dodge was a "character" in the valley and the recollections by his contemporaries provided a colorful and humorous insight into the man. While these vignettes, as interesting and sometimes outrageous as they are, are not germane to the subject at hand, it should be noted that he was a graduate of Harvard Law School, worked for a prestigious New York law firm, and was employed by Theodore Roosevelt when he was running for governor of the state of New York. His uncle was General Grenville M. Dodge, Chief Engineer for the Union Pacific Railroad during its construction to Promontory Point. When John Dodge decided to drop out of eastern society, his uncle gave him a railroad pass so he could tour the west. Eventually, he settled in Jackson Hole.[30]

〜 While the controversies raged, Grand Teton National Park enjoyed a second successful season. Its appropriations were substantially increased from $11,750 in 1929 to $66,800 in 1930, but only a small portion ($9,300) of this money was spent for administration purposes. The remaining $57,500 was spent as follows: $17,500 for Park roads, $18,600 for new trails, $12,400 for maintenance and $9,000 for construction.[32] During the summer, work crews began construction on three new trails within the Park. One followed the south and west shoreline of Jenny Lake and connected with the Leigh Canyon Trail. Another began at Jenny Lake and extended to the Teton Glacier. The construction of the third, the Skyline Trail, employed two crews working toward each other; one started at the mouth of Death Canyon, and the other began at the mouth of Leigh Canyon.[33]

As part of the construction allocation, comfort stations, water, and sewage systems were installed at the Jenny Lake Campground while other crews worked to widen and improve the approach roads to the Park. The Park Service also invested in fire fighting equipment in anticipation of careless campers during the dry season.[34] Thus, in addition to extensive spending by the Snake River Land Company and an expanding tourist trade, the economy of Jackson Hole received a boost from

Jackson Hole Historical Society and Museum p1958.0124.001
The Jack Fee family were typical homesteaders attracted by the offer of "free" land. They came to Jackson Hole seeking to establish a life raising crops or cattle. If they worked hard and survived the harsh climate, they could hope for a rewarding and self-sustaining life with their children. Such people were not always amenable to the ideas presented by wealthy easterners, whose financial security had been inherited from prior generations. Many settlers had short tolerance for those outsiders who suggested that their homes and hopes for the future should be abrogated to provide an unrestricted view of the Tetons for the general public that might visit the valley. Photo c. 1916.

the federal government due to increased spending and employment by Grand Teton National Park.

Appropriations were not the only area of increase experienced by the new Park. In spite of the Depression, the number of visitors to the new Park also increased. The *Jackson Hole Courier* reported that as of July 19, 1930, *"Travelers from Grand Teton to Yellowstone increased 350 percent over 1929 and those from Yellowstone to Teton increased 271 percent."* [35] The total visitation for the season was 60,000– a 20 percent increase over 1929.[36]

Most important of the above figures, as far as the local economy was concerned, was not the total number of visitors, but the direction they traveled. Prior to 1930, the majority of Jackson Hole tourists visited Yellowstone first, then traveled south to the Tetons. However, in 1930, this trend was reversed, allowing Jackson Hole merchants the first opportunity at the pocketbooks of the travelers. This reversal also illustrated

New Teton Park fire engine, 1929

143

Jackson Hole from Teton Pass in the 1930s.

the need and importance of good highway access to the valley from the south. Local businessmen began to push for improvements to the Hoback Canyon road and for the construction of a new road through the Snake River Canyon.

Jackson was not the only community which recognized the economic advantages of tourist travel. Support was easily obtained for the road improvement and construction projects throughout southwestern Wyoming. Neither were the benefits of tourism ignored by communities in adjacent states. The *Salt Lake Tribune,* on July 24, 1930, stated:

Because Salt Lake is the natural gateway to the region, this city is deriving considerable benefit from the travel, both to and from the park. Salt Lake is sure to receive more benefit when the large tract adjacent the park is set aside for the government as a wilderness and big game section, a permanent resort dedicated to the memory of early western history.[37]

The 1930 tourist season saw the arrival of a number of dignitaries who wished to see the new Park. Among those who were deemed sufficiently important by the local press to be mentioned

were Assistant Secretary of the Interior Judge John H. Edwards; Dr. Louis J. Tint, a physician and surgeon from Chicago who was a member of the Geographic Society of Chicago and was widely known as a photographer and rather famous for his collection of (rare for that time) color photographs; Mrs. Robert E. Schenck, formally Mildred Leo Clemens, the granddaughter of Mark Twain; and Arthur Chapman. *"...famous author, poet, traveler, and lecturer."* [38]

In 1930, John D. Rockefeller, Jr. returned to Jackson Hole to view the progress of the Snake River Land Company. Harold Fabian conducted the tour showing where and how unsightly buildings, garbage dumps and signs had been cleaned up or removed. As part of the tour, Fabian took Mr. and Mrs. Rockefeller to the community of Wilson and up to the top of Teton Pass. Fabian recalled:

...when we got that magnificent view on Teton Pass, they were delighted with it, and I made the remark to Mr. Rockefeller that some day in some future generation somebody would stand where we were and would say, 'How short-sighted those people were that they did not take the whole valley and preserve it for the people of this country while they had the chance.' He [Mr. Rockefeller] turned to Mrs. Rockefeller and asked her if she had heard that, and she said that...she had heard my statement and that she had thought so, too. [39]

Rumors of the above conversation would fuel the fires of opposition among those who opposed the Rockefeller plan. As with most rumors, the context of the conversation changed with the telling until it was widely circulated and believed that Rockefeller had stated he would take the valley from "rim to rim." The *Jackson Hole Courier* reenforced the validity of the rumor, in the minds of the public, when it stated, *"It is reported that John D. Rockefeller, Jr. while in the Hole this past summer made the statement, 'We need the whole valley.'"* [40] The belief in this rumor has persisted to the present even though Harold Fabian recalled that the concept was his and that Mrs. Rockefeller simply agreed with his view of the future. Fabian also stated that he approached his superiors with the concept of expanding the boundaries of the project, but the idea was rejected. The project, as originally conceived, or at least subsequently adjusted, was considered ample to complete the purposes for which the Snake River Land Company was formed.[41]

Adding to the ambiguity of the origin of the term "rim to rim," Richard Winger claimed credit for the concept of preserving the whole valley. According to Winger, the concept of the national recreation area, as endorsed by the group who met at Maud Noble's cabin in 1923, originated during conversations between J. R. Jones, Jack Eynon and himself. Although the term "rim to rim" was not used, the concept of purchasing the entire valley was presented at that time. Winger, who had prepared the original land and cost estimates, maintained the Snake River Land Company never intended to purchase the whole valley. He believed the rumor might have found its origin in the proposal agreed upon at Maud Noble's cabin.[42]

Despite at least two men giving public testimony clearing Rockefeller of the offending remark, the term "rim to rim" remained a catch phrase associated with and attributed to Rockefeller by those who opposed him or who (even today) would discount his altruistic intentions.

In September, the Special Committee on Conservation of Wildlife Resources, established in April 1930 by the U.S. Senate, visited Jackson Hole to view the country and gather information regarding the elk herd. The committee stayed at Moran and held informal meetings with federal agency personnel, state and local officials, interested organizations and concerned citizens.*

On September 25, 1930, at one of these meetings, another locally originated proposal to preserve the valley was unveiled. This proposal, which became known as the Jackson Hole Plan, was essentially a compromise put forth by four men: Richard Winger, Jack Eynon, J. D. Ferrin and William Deloney. The first three men were long time supporters of protecting the natural and scenic values of the valley while Deloney, although not opposed to protecting the valley, was a long time opponent of the national park. [See Appendix Two-Document B to read the proposal.]

Their proposal began by explaining that the future of the valley and the welfare of its residents would be enhanced if a compromise could be reached regarding the ultimate disposition of the land north of the town of Jackson. For years, that area had been the subject of conflict by development interest, conservation interest, interagency squabbling and political maneuvering. The uncertainty of the future of that large portion of the valley needed to be removed in order for the valley to develop economically. They believed that any fair compromise would recognize the right of the cattlemen to continue to utilize lands necessary to their operations, recognize the rights of businesses that

Jackson Hole Historical Society and Museum

The Special Committee on Conservation of Wildlife Resources at Moran, 1930

---

*Among those attending the meetings were: Senator Frederic C. Walcott of Connecticut, chairman; Senators Key Pittman of Nevada and Peter Norbeck of South Dakota; Governor Emerson; former Governor Robert D. Carey, who was at the time running for the U.S. Senate; Wyoming Congressman Vincent Carter; Bruce Nowlin and Jack Scott of the Wyoming Game and Fish Commission; Horace Albright of the National Park Service and Sam Woodring of Grand Teton National Park; R. H. Rutledge and C. E. Rachford of the U.S. Forest Service; A. C. McCain of the Teton National Forest; Paul G. Redington, head of the Biological Survey; Almer Nelson and O. J. Murie, also of the Biological Survey from Jackson; and Harold Fabian of the Snake River Land Company.[43]

had developed to accommodate visitors to the valley, provide protection for the scenic and recreational values of the area, and allow the continued management of the elk and other wildlife by the state of Wyoming. Their compromise proposal included:

(1) That the boundaries of the present Grand Teton National Park be extended.... This will insure the protection of the scenic side of the valley and a game sanctuary for the elk drift as they are driven from the mountains by the winter storms and as they follow the receding snow in the spring- and for their winter range and feeding grounds. This area should never be open to hunting; but kept inviolate as a game sanctuary.

Harold Fabian photo Rockefeller Archive Center Series 1030 SRLC Scrapbook

Harold Fabian photo Rockefeller Archive Center Series 1030 SRLC Scrapbook

The Lee Prather homestead (Pat. # 0028928) before and after the purchase by the Snake River Land Company. The company's "cleanup" activities removed distractive structures from the scene but also reduced the tax revenue to the county because of the eliminated taxable improvements on the land.

(2) That the upper Gros Ventre should be kept open to summer ranging of cattle, without the harassing restrictions now imposed.

(3) That, where and when necessary, suitable crossings and thoroughfares be provided through Park areas for cattle going to and from summer ranges.

(4) That, as a part of the legislation effectuating this plan, Congress appropriate $7,500 a year for five years and $5,000 a year for the next five years to be paid to Teton County to compensate for the withdrawal of its taxable lands.

(5) That there be appropriated the sum of $500,000 to purchase the privately owned lands... outside of and in addition to the area in which the Snake River Land Company is making its purchases.

The predominant thought in our minds is that this region be kept in its primitive state as nearly as possible with no more improved roads than are required to provide trunk highways through the area, and with only such accommodations for the traveling public as are necessary to meet that demand and as are in keeping, in location and design, with the general character of this country.

...we are deeply concerned to have the general legislation passed which will assure the perpetuation of this country as a great outdoor recreation area for the people of America.[44]

This proposal, with an attached map, was discussed in detail by the committee and the people who had gathered for the meeting.

Deloney, who was the self-admitted leader of the park opposition faction in Jackson Hole, later explained why he signed and vigorously supported a proposal that would greatly increase the size of Grand Teton National Park. First, he believed that protection and proper management of the valley's wildlife and other natural assets were

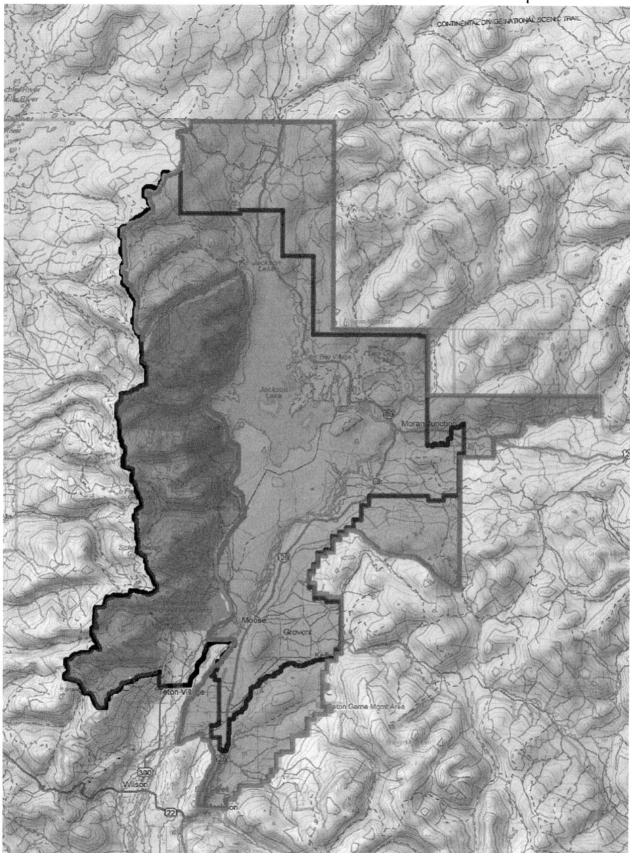

The Jackson Hole Plan suggested by William Deloney, Richard Winger, J. D. Ferrin, and Jack Eynon to compliment the goals of the Rockefeller project and provide protection for the valley from the settler's perspective- 1930.

Current GTNP boundary
Original GTNP (1929)
Jackson Hole Plan Extension of GTNP

147

Town of Jackson in 1930.   Population - 533.

necessary. He never opposed the concept of pre-serving the valley; he simply did not believe the Park Service was the desirable agency to accomplish that objective. Second, although the Forest Service had been Deloney's first choice as a management agency, he had been convinced that because the property in question was not classified as forest lands, it would be impossible for the Forest Service to take over those lands.[45] The Biological Survey was Deloney's second choice, but as he pointed out, *"...the Biological Department is the poorest department in the Federal Government, as far as spending money is concerned; they do not get it. They have never yet been able to get their appropriation to complete this little* [elk refuge] *project up here."* [46] Thus, DeLoney was not optimistic that the Biological Survey could accomplish all the objectives of the proposal. The Park Service was the only agency left who could do the job, so the group suggested Grand Teton National Park be the recipient of the lands. Last, he was, like most other residents, tired of the continuing controversies and wanted to see a permanent solution adopted.

The Jackson Hole Plan created a possible conflict with the legislation that had created Grand Teton National Park. Deloney had succeeded in including a clause in that legislation that prohibited the Park Service from authorizing concessions and other new commercial activities within the Park. The problem resulted from the fact that just outside the Park boundaries, there were commercial activities operating on both private and leased Forest Service lands. If these areas were included in the Park, as the plan suggested, the Park Service would have to recognize and honor those leases. The inclusion of these commercial activities might technically violate Grand Teton National Park's enabling act.

While Deloney and the others expected the conditions of Grand Teton's enabling legislation would also apply to the extended area, they recognized the rights of those people who had businesses in the affected area. It was agreed that those businesses would be allowed to continue operating until their leases expired. At that time it would be left to Congress, not the Park Service, to decide if various concessions would be allowed to continue. This decision would be based on the quality of the operation and the need to provide services to the traveling public.

The committee to which the plan was submitted generally favored the proposal but suggested the plan be circulated around the valley to determine how much support actually existed. After the committee had departed, the plan was presented to the valley residents and the general election of 1930 demonstrated the feelings of the voters toward the proposal. Harold Fabian recalled the event and stated, *"...it* [the Jackson Hole Plan] *was made the issue of the local election on November 4, 1930. Its supporters won by so large a majority as to leave no question that the sentiment of the people of the valley was decidedly in favor of some such plan."* [47] Also, William Deloney, who was a candidate in that election, testified at a Senate hearing that he, a Republican, and Carl Bark, a Democrat, were elected to the state legislature based on their pro-Jackson Hole Plan positions.[48]

∼

While the opponents of the Yellowstone National Park extension, the Grand Teton National Park extension, the transfer of Snake River Land Company properties to the federal government, and the Jackson Hole Plan warned that the loss of taxable property would cause Teton County to

"...cease to exist," [49] the overall economic conditions in the valley continued to improve. The Wyoming Legislature set aside $200,000 for road improvement in Teton County for the following year and building within the valley was up by $220,000.[50] The only negative economic note came from the U.S. Senate. The Senate struck out a house appropriation of $100,000 to be used to clear the dead timber from the Jackson Lake Reservoir.

The Senate committee eliminated the appropriation not only because it had not been recommended by the budget, but because they felt the entire burden should not be assessed against the government; that part of it should be borne by the water users in the Snake River Valley [Idaho]*, in whose interest Jackson Lake was converted into a storage reservoir.* [51]

The *Jackson Hole Courier* summed up the year by stating, *"In spite of the depression that has existed over the whole of the United States during the past year, Jackson Hole has forged steadily ahead. The past year saw a great increase in building and in businesses established throughout the valley."* [52]

In Jackson Hole, even during the Depression, there was reason for optimism.

CHAPTER TEN

1931 - 1932

Seems like in the past when Jackson Hole opposed park extension we got little if any support from the rest of the state or its officials. Now when a measure comes up which might protect this valley through a payment of a stipulated amount to the county and a chance through increased business for the merchants and others the whole state is 'agin it.'

Jackson Hole Courier[1]
January 8, 1931

Jackson Hole Historical Society and Museum 1958.0755.001

A Yellowstone Park Company tour bus and private automobile at Brooks Lake on Togwotee Pass

The Jackson Hole Plan, as conceived and presented by William Deloney, J. D. Ferrin, Jack Eynon and Richard Winger, was perhaps the first locally originated, publicized proposal which merited and attracted a following that was truly representative of the majority of the valley residents. While a majority of the Jackson Hole residents seemed to favor the plan, the rest of the state seemed equally opposed to the idea. Jackson Hole had opponents to the plan, and although their numbers may not have been large, their voices were loud. This opposition group was successful in stirring up an emotional fervor throughout the state and especially in Jackson Hole, which surpassed any previous level witnessed in the valley.

Part of the reason for their success rested in their ability to tie the Yellowstone Boundary Commission to the Jackson Hole Plan in the minds of their uninformed listeners. Since almost everyone opposed any Yellowstone Park extension, the negative feeling was transferred to the Jackson Hole Plan. The tactics used by the opposition resulted in an unprecedented quantity

American Heritage Center University of Wyoming, Fritioff Fryxell Collection, unnumbered

1931 Grand Teton National Park Staff
Front row from left: Secrest, Hayden, Mrs. Woodring, Sam Woodring, Frank Smith, Watson. Back row from left: Ed Smith, Sherman, Fryxell, Phil Smith

of articles and letters to the editor of the *Jackson Hole Courier* by local people supporting the plan. The opposition, however, stimulated a comparable volume of adverse publicity in newspapers throughout the rest of Wyoming.

Another reason the opposition was successful was that much of their publicity was composed of half-truths and in some cases outright lies. The proponents were kept busy answering accusations, defending their members and trying to present the facts of the issue. Rarely, it seemed, were they able to take the offensive in the publicity battle.

The first significant negative response to the Jackson Hole Plan came from Jack T. Scott, president of the Wyoming Game and Fish Commission, in a letter to the editor of the *Dubois Frontier.* The letter demonstrated the confusion resulting from the association of the activities of Snake River Land Company, the Yellowstone Boundary Commission and the provisions of the Jackson Hole Plan. Scott stated:

> *Personally, I have fought this boundary extension ever since its first inception several years ago, and am still unequivocally and unfalteringly opposed to any such expansion idea in our State. The Commission has*

Grand Teton National Park (unnumbered)

Wyoming Senators Kendrick and Carey with Grand Teton Park Superintendent Woodring, 1931

always stood unanimously and uncompromisingly against park extension, and so far as I am informed it still stands opposed to any expansion of our park system in Wyoming.[2]

Scott went on to state that he had just returned from Washington where he discussed this issue with Wyoming's Congressional delegation. According to Scott those men were:

...against the inclusion of ... the Snake River Land Company's lands in the National Parks. This attitude of our congressional delegation was very pleasing to me and it is to be hoped that these lands may be turned over to the Biological Survey to be administered by that department, the State of Wyoming and the Forest Service. This will I believe prove satisfactory to the people of Wyoming and will insure the future of our Wyoming elk herd and its proper management.[3]

Scott's letter indicated more than a position on the issue. It exemplified an underlying theme in past and future park extension controversies—states' rights. It also illustrated an ironic reversal of the role of elk in the park extension issue. Initially, the military had recommended the extension of park status to the south for the protection of the elk herd. Scott's position seemed to advocate protecting the elk by opposing park extension.

The editor of the *Jackson Hole Courier* reprinted Scott's letter and in a separate article discussed several aspects of Scott's position as it related to the current situation of the valley residents and the county. The article stated, *"Teton County is fighting for its life. Its people are fighting for a chance to live and enjoy the land they call home, and this regardless of their attitude on the question of park extension."*[4] The editor noted that some of the people who sold to the Snake River Land Company had moved out of the valley. He commented, *"The losses of those residents has affected the year round business of the merchants of the valley, especially in implements and ranch supplies of various kinds. Yet Jackson has grown; businesses catering to the tourist have grown. Prospects are that both will continue to grow. But business may become more seasonal*

Rockefeller Archive Center Series 1030 SRLC Scrapbook

Rockefeller Archive Center Series 1030 SRLC Scrapbook, 812996_me

American Heritage Center University of Wyoming ah03138_1137
Garbage dumps, collapsing and abandoned buildings, and discarded refuse marred the scenery for John D. Rockefeller, Jr. The Snake River Land Company purchased as many of these properties as they could and restored the properties usually to their natural appearance.

than ever." [5] The editor pointed out that Scott's suggestion that the Rockefeller lands be turned over to the Biological Survey and the Forest Service would solve nothing. The land would still go to a federal agency and be removed from the county's tax rolls. The article commented, *"We can not see in this instance where one bureaucratic agency is any better than another."* [6] In general, the *Courier* felt that Scott's plan did not offer as many benefits to Teton County and its people as the Jackson Hole Plan. The editor stated:

Teton County must have revenue from some source to exist. The plan to enlarge Teton Park contemplates turning to the Park Service approximately 96 miles of road to construct and maintain, a drift area to protect Jackson Hole cattlemen in taking their herds to and from the summer ranges, an annual income to the county from Federal sources in lieu of taxes now received therefrom. Does Mr. Scott's plan include these items? He made no mention of them in his letter ....[7]

The *Courier* also noted that the Jackson Hole Plan, in placing responsibility for the 96 mile stretch of roads with the Park Service, *"...would free the Bureau of Public Roads funds enough to insure the immediate completion of the Hoback Canyon road, needed improvements on the Togwotee Pass road, and early construction of the Snake River Canyon road. All of which mean more tourist* [sic]. *"*[8]

Other newspapers were quick to jump on the opposition bandwagon as were organizations such as the Lions Clubs. This adverse publicity prompted an editorial in the *Courier*, which stated:

Some Federal agency or agencies is going to get a goodly portion of this valley. We're not so particular as to who gets it as we are for the protection of our county and its citizens. Protection means aid from a federal source for the county and business from another source to take the place of that of the people who have sold out and moved to other communities. Before any organizations opposes the present plan let them suggest another that will meet the approval of the people here.[9]

The logic of this editorial was lost on some of the members of the Jackson Lions Club. That organization, which doubled as a chamber of commerce for the community, passed a resolution opposing the Jackson Hole Plan one day after the editorial was published. However, the resolution was more than an opposition statement. Carl Bark, who was a member of the club and

was present at the meeting, called it *"...a masterpiece of misrepresentation."*[10] The resolution made several declarative position statements that usually included inflammatory language that seemed designed to enrage people with opposing views rather than convert public opinion with its logic. [See Appendix Two- Document C to read the complete document.] It began by placing the Lions Club in opposition to the extension of both Grand Teton and Yellowstone National Parks or the creation of any new national parks in northwestern Wyoming. Second, they opposed the purchase of private property by individuals for the purpose of extending the national parks. Third, they opposed the "secret methods" used by the Snake River Land Company to hide its source of "Eastern money" and the proposed donation of acquired property to any Federal agency other than the Forest Service for the expressed purpose of raising livestock or preserving wildlife under the control of the state of Wyoming. Fourth, the resolution declared that the ultimate objective of the Snake River Land Company was to gain control of all the concession rights within the proposed Grand Teton Park extension area. Fifth, they predicted that the park extension would result in federal bureaucratic control of wildlife, leading eventually to its extinction. Sixth, the resolution

American Heritage Center, University of Wyoming, Fritiof Fryxell Papers, Box 80, Folder 5,

Rangers Ed Bruce and Phil Smith (in sidecar) on a Park Service motorcycle. These two rangers were hired as "extras" when portions of the movie *The Big Trail* were filmed in Jackson Hole. The movie starred John Wayne, Marguerite Churchill, Tyrone Power, Sr., and El Brendel.

stated that the efforts to extend the boundaries of Yellowstone and Grand Teton Parks were for the primary purpose of gaining control of Wyoming's wildlife. Seventh, the document declared that the county representative to the state legislature (William Deloney) *"...in no way represents this community in its view point on Park Extension...."* The resolution was passed at the January 9, 1931, meeting by all in attendance except for one abstention and one nay vote.[11]

This resolution was inflammatory to the people of Jackson Hole, not because it represented an opposing viewpoint, but because it alleged to represent a majority of the citizens of the valley. That representation, as well as some of its statements, was false. Many residents were further angered by the arrogance of the Lions Club's suggestion that a land-owner could not sell or donate his or her land to anyone he or she chose. The resolution was not even representative of the Lions Club membership. In fact, the resolution was defeated by the membership at a previous meeting. At the earlier meeting, Carl Bark, feeling that many of the members lacked a complete understanding of the Jackson Hole Plan, suggested that Richard Winger be invited to present the plan to the club. According to Bark, the president of the club objected to the suggestion stating that he *"...wished the matter of park extension had never come up in the club and also expressed the hope that it never would come up again."* [12]

Concerning the meeting on January 9, 1931, at which the resolution was passed, Carl Bark recalled:

> *There were present thirteen active members, of whom eleven voted for the resolution and one against, and one refused to vote. I have heard since this resolution passed that some of those who voted for the resolution have expressed the hope that the plan would go through and that the park would be extended according to the Jackson Hole Plan. Practically every statement contained in the resolution was a misrepresentation.* [13]

In a letter to the *Jackson Hole Courier*, Carl Bark addressed three issues presented in the Lions Club resolution. The first concerned the

Jackson Hole Historical Society and Museum p1958.0114.001

Carl Bark (second from left) denounced the Lions Club resolution and resigned his membership. Bark, a Democrat, and William Deloney, a Republican, were both elected to the state legislature in the previous election. They both had expressed support for the Jackson Hole Plan during their campaigns.

resolution's claims about the "unfair methods" of the Snake River Land Company and its agents. Bark allowed, *"...that people outside the valley might believe the accusations, but no one in Jackson Hole will believe it. Personally I have sold them some land and if I had the cash in the bank today I would not buy it back from the Snake River Land Company at the price they paid me for it."* [14] The second issue was the resolution's statement that W. C. Deloney *"...in no way ... represented the community ... in its view point on Park Extension."* Bark stated, *"Mr. Deloney was elected solely on a platform favoring the Jackson Hole Plan. Everyone knew he stood for the park extension and the results of the election speaks very clearly. It is almost a certainty that most of those who condemned him in the Lions Club voted for him knowing his stand on the question."* [15] The third issue concerned the resolution's position that park extension, in any form, was *"...inimical to the best interests of the people of the State and its future progress."* Bark stated:

> *The fact that towns like Cody, Sheridan, Thermopolis, Lander and other towns*

Courtesy Shoshone-Bannock Tribal Museum Fort Hall, Idaho

Chief John Racehorse

The Supreme Court trial that is the subject of the page note below was actually a habeas corpus filing to free Chief Racehorse from jail, not a game violation procedure. However, all parties realized the constitutional importance of the legal action. Racehorse agreed to surrender himself for prosecution rather than surrender the tribal members involved in the incident, with the purpose and assurance that this would initiate a test case relating to the conflict between treaty rights and state law. Thus, the progression to the Supreme Court. The Treaty of 1868 provided the right for the Indians to hunt on unappropriated public lands. The act admitting Wyoming into the Union as a state bestowed equal standing with all other states. All other states had been granted ownership and control over wildlife within their boundaries, thus, Wyoming, having been assured equality of status, argued it had the right to control hunting of wildlife within its boundaries. Any restriction of this right would place Wyoming in a subordinate status to the other states in the Union in violation of the congressional action transferring the area from Territorial status to Statehood. To read the arguments, majority decision, and minority opinion online, search *Ward v. Race Horse* (163 U.S., 504). (The chief spelled his name as one word rather than two.)

oppose the creation of this great park and recreational area making Jackson one of the most popular entrances to the park, convinces me more than ever that I am for it whole-heartedly. It is only natural for them to hope to stop it if they can. It would be anything but pleasant for them to see thousands of people headed for our country and town and be allowed to forget for a while that there was another park entrance off the beaten trail to these towns.[16]

In this letter, Bark also addressed an article by S. N. Leek that had been printed earlier in the *Courier*. Leek recounted how the early pioneers in the valley sacrificed to save the elk herd and fought off Indians* and sheepmen to protect the valley for the elk and themselves. Leek felt that since the settlers of Jackson Hole had done so much to protect the elk and the valley, it was time some help was given to the people of the valley to protect them from the federal government. He stated there was no need for a park extension.[17] Bark responded:

I have been a resident of Jackson Hole for twenty years and every so often have been given an opportunity to sympathetically bleed with these early pioneers, who saved the elk herd and fought the Indians and ran off the sheep. I can't look sympathetic any more and before I die I want to get this off my chest. I don't believe a word of it. I doubt if the early pioneer gave the elk anything. I think the elk did all the bleeding and furthermore, I think the elk herd saved the pioneer.[18]

Bark's statement was unusual. He was perhaps the only resident who has ever publicly challenged

---

*The only Indian fighting of note by Jackson Hole settlers related to issues attendant to the hunting of big game animals. Prior to the creation of Wyoming as a state, the Bannock Indians, by treaty, were guaranteed the right to continue to hunt on public lands not claimed by settlers. In 1895, the settlers had to obey the state game laws regarding hunting seasons and limits, while Indians hunted whenever they wished. In the name of preserving the elk and maintaining the state's game laws, a group of Jackson Hole men arrested a hunting party composed of 27 Indians, 18 of whom were women and children. Subsequently, one unarmed Indian was killed and another wounded when the Indians escaped. Chief Racehorse chose to fight for the Indian's rights in the courts. The Supreme Court ruled in favor of the state of Wyoming. For a more detailed account of this incident, see David J. Saylor's *Jackson Hole, Wyoming, In The Shadow of The Tetons*, pp. 138-141, or Elizabeth Arnold Stone's *Uinta County: Its Place in History*, pp. 236-238. Stone's book presents a narrative less pejorative to either the white settlers or the Indians but is out of print and harder to find. Brigham D. Madsen's *The Northern Shoshoni*, pp. 136-138, is also pertinent.

the generally accepted role of the settlers in preserving the Jackson Hole elk herd.

However, Carl Bark was not alone in his opposition to the Lions Club resolution. Most of the letters received by the *Courier* expressed similar dissatisfaction with the inequities of the Lions' resolution's statements, and the majority of the published letters were from Lions Club members. George T. Lamb wrote:

I wish to explain publicly that I had nothing whatever to do with the passing of a resolution in the Lions Club Meeting held in Jackson on January 9th, 1931. The resolution is absolutely opposite from my views in the matter of the extension of the Teton National Park. As a member of the Lions Club I do not oppose any purchase of lands by private individuals. As a Lions member I feel that W. C. Deloney is a representative of the people of Teton County.

I further wish to state that until the Lions Club of Jackson sees fit to deal fairly in the matter of the discussion of park extension I wish to sever my connections with the club.[19]

Dr. C. W. Huff, the mayor of Jackson, wrote, *"When I became a member of the Lions Club of Jackson it was with the hope that its activities might be directed along constructive lines. However, I should hesitate to be further associated with an organization which would offer to the public a document as embarrassing as the Resolution of January 9."* [20] Carl Bark, who cast the only dissenting vote at the Lions Club meeting, resigned from the club by stating, *"I would like to state publicly that I am discontinuing my membership in the Lion's [sic] Club and that I do not care to share any of the responsibility for the enactment of the resolution passed on the ninth of January 1931."* [21]

The *Courier* published a considerable number of letters opposing the Lions Club's allegations in subsequent issues. The letters generally took exception to three aspects of the resolution and the number of letters belied the contention of the Lions Club that it represented a majority of the populace of the valley. One category into which some letters could be sorted supported the Snake River Land Company and its objectives. Thirty-four landowners from Kelly, Grovont, and Mormon Row approved a letter addressed to Wyoming's Congressional delegation. The letter stated, in part:

We deplore the attitude of some of our people in the State of Wyoming in their apparent lack of gratitude to the Snake River Land Company for the splendid altruistic work they are trying to carry on here and we especially deplore the circulation of statements by misinformed individuals that our section of the country, as designated by Kelly, Grovont and Mormon Row, is being unfairly dealt with by these people.[22]

Jackson Hole Historical Society and Museum 2012.0007.001

George T. Lamb with one-year-old son Tom on the sled. George homesteaded south of Astoria Hot Springs in 1914 and eventually became a prominent contractor in the valley. With Charlie Fox, he built the Chapel of Transfiguration at Moose. During the winters, George contracted for mail delivery by dog sled to various locations around the valley. He was a supporter of the Jackson Hole Plan as conceived by Deloney, Ferrin, Eynon, and Winger, and resigned from the Lions Club in protest of its inflammatory resolution.

Another category of letters verified that William C. Deloney was elected to the Wyoming Legislature on a platform of park extension as outlined in the Jackson Hole Plan. A second letter from the above-quoted group of property owners stated, *"The majority of the voters stated that they had cast their ballots in the recent election for the return of W. C. Deloney to the State House of Representatives almost solely because he openly sponsored the Jackson Hole Plan for*

Park Extension." [23] N. E. Smith, a resident of Grovont, wrote, *"The statements contained in the Lions Club resolution are false and misleading. I know that our precinct is almost entirely in favor of the plan. I know personally that W. C. Deloney was elected solely on this platform. There was no other issue in the last campaign."* [24]

The third category of letters supported the Jackson Hole Plan and park extension as beneficial to the valley and the people. W. C. Thompson stated, *"I feel that park extension, as laid down in the Jackson Hole Plan, will materially benefit the Town of Jackson, The County of Teton and the State of Wyoming."* [25] E. G. Van Leeuwen, the County Treasurer, wrote:

> *To my mind not only is it a big thing for our State, but it is our only salvation as a County. The same ones who are saying it will hurt the town are at the same time enlarging and expanding their business. Why do they own and control most of the vacant lots suitable for business purposes? (Try to buy one of them). Why are others coming here all the time seeking locations to go into business? Certainly a few selfish interests will not be permitted to control the destiny of this country. The plan will ultimately succeed.* [26]

As the controversy continued to escalate throughout the state, Wyoming's Congressional delegation took a stand opposing any further park extension within the state. The *Salt Lake Tribune* reported the politicians' position stating, *"Because of the divided sentiment and because of the fact that the issue is not pressing, the Wyoming delegation has decided that it would be advisable to defer all legislation on the subject for the time being."* [27]

The issue eventually reached an emotional level at which no compromise seemed possible. At this point, a tragedy for the state of Wyoming and the Jackson Hole Plan occurred. Governor Emerson died.* Had he lived, Emerson might

Harrison and Ewing [Public domain] via Wikimedia Commons

Frank Collins Emerson (R)
1883-1927

Born and educated in Michigan, Emerson earned a B.S. degree from the University of Michigan in 1904. He moved to Cora, Wyoming, and operated a general store and served as postmaster. He held the position of Wyoming State Engineer from 1919 until he was elected Governor in 1926. He was elected to two terms as governor but died one month and two weeks into his second term.

have been able to accomplish a compromise concerning the park extension issue. The governor had been consulted as to the nature of the Snake River Land Company project nearly from its beginning, and the company cooperated with his wishes throughout its history. He believed the Snake River Land Company was attempting to accomplish a truly altruistic objective, and that its representatives were reasonable men and that a limited extension of Grand Teton National Park was an advantageous action. In fact, Governor Emerson advised a member of the Wyoming Congressional Delegation that a small park extension was advisable. Early in December 1930, Senator

---

***Governor Emerson spent much of the previous week at the bedside of his son who was critically ill with influenza. As his son began to recover, the governor contracted the virus which progressed to pneumonia. Emerson died on February 18, 1931.**

Robert Davis Carey (R)
1878-1937

Carey, a Yale graduate, was elected the 11th governor of Wyoming in 1918. In 1930, he was elected to fill the Senate vacancy that occurred when Senator Francis E. Warren died. He was re-elected for a full term in 1931 but failed to retain his Senate seat in the election of 1936. He died two weeks after leaving the Senate.

Carey wired the governor requesting his position on the Jackson Hole problem and stated his own— he opposed any park extension, he opposed the transfer of Snake River Land Company property to the federal government, and he was opposed to any further purchases by the Snake River Land Company.

In a letter dated December 5, 1930, the governor responded that he approved of an extension of Grand Teton National Park to the east for two reasons. First, to provide for a straight boundary line to replace the irregular or zigzag line created when the Park was established. Second, to place the responsibility for the maintenance of a stretch of state highway with the federal government. He also stated he would approve a nominal extension of Yellowstone National Park to the southeast *"...if it would mean a rather permanent adjustment of the general problem which has continued to face the Jackson Hole region."*[28] Noting

the Senator's opposition to the transfer of Rockefeller's lands to the federal government, he stated:

> *In this position, I can concur in a general way, even though I believe we will have to meet the desire and intention of the said company to relieve itself of ownership of most of the land purchased, through transfer to the Government. It would be to the advantage of Wyoming if at least a portion of these lands could be transferred to the State. In this connection, I have specially in mind the lands upon the Buffalo Fork in the vicinity of Elk Post Office, which could profitably be used by the State in raising feed for the elk. In the case of the necessity of meeting the proposition of a transfer to the Federal Government, you will note that I have suggested the Biological Survey or the Forest Service as the agency to accept control.*[29]

Also in conflict with Senator Carey's position, the governor supported a limited continuation of purchases by the Snake River Land Company, particularly in the Mormon Row area.

Senator Carey, therefore, did not receive the wholehearted support he had expected for his position from the state's chief executive. He ignored Emerson's assessment of the Jackson Hole situation and throughout most of his term as Senator, as far as park extension and the Snake River Land Company were concerned, maintained a posture resembling a politician looking for an issue. However, it should be remembered that Carey, when he was governor, attended the meeting in Jackson with Albright in 1919 when there was a very vocal expression of anti-park sentiment. He may not have imagined the reversal of opinion that had occurred after that time. It is also possible he was receiving only the negative reporting of the issue by the Wyoming press and from selected members of the local opposition.

While the governor's logic was lost on Wyoming's Congressional delegation, he might have been able to lend some authority to the claims by a majority of Jackson Hole residents that the Lions Club resolution was a ridiculous document. The whole controversy might have been viewed in a less emotional light had Emerson lived to express his opinion.

Although most newspapers accepted the resolution for what it professed to be, a voice representative of a majority of the valley residents, a few newspapers were not fooled. The *Casper Star* called it "An Embarrassing Document" and stated, *"It is most regrettable that such a resolution should have been made public, let alone passed as a voice of a community so divided upon a thought, which is most embarrassing to the people of that section and to their county representative in the state legislature."* [30]

The resolution also had the effect of prodding the local newspaper to take a position on the issues. Until that time, the *Courier* had seemed content to report both sides of the argument without openly declaring itself. In the April 30, 1931, issue, the *Courier* finally printed its position. The article admitted that while it had printed little about park extension in the past, most of its articles on the issue had favored the extension. The editor stated, *"We've tried to maintain a one-man bandwagon and ride the fence. In so doing the editor got so confounded dizzy that he took a tumble and now finds himself on that side of the fence known as Park Extension. So why get sore, the editor might have fallen on your side."* [31] He listed the following reasons for his decision:

1. The plan will recompense Jackson for loss of upper country ranch trade by additional tourist trade.
2. Recreation is the true business of this valley from every point of view. Ranching for years has been a secondary business.
3. A wilderness area with big game hunting and fishing and other savory outdoor sports will attract enough summer home people to use all desirable locations in the lower valley.
4. It leaves for our ranchmen our best located ranch lands.
5. We have a right to our opinions and to air 'em if we so wish, and we might as well

make some others angry besides the officers of the P.T.A.
6. Progress generally lies in following the trend of the times not in throwing obstacles in its way.
7. and final (for now). We honestly believe it best for ourselves, for you, and for the nation at large, that its advantages amounts to more for the majority than does its disadvantages. [32]

Although this decision cost the paper some advertising revenue at a time when it was in financial trouble, the editor actively supported park extension according to the Jackson Hole Plan. He reprinted opposing articles and editorialized away each anti-extension argument. He often referred to the Lions Club as the "Ly'in Club" and challenged editors around the state to visit the valley and investigate the situation first hand.

In May 1931, a local election again confirmed that a majority of residents favored the Jackson Hole Plan. As in the previous election, the plan and park extension were the main campaign issues. Those who supported that action won by a margin greater than two to one. Dr. C. W. Huff was re-elected to the office of mayor over L. G.

Jackson Hole Historical Society and Museum bc.0345

(Left to Right) J. Chester Simpson, Lee Simpson Vande Water, Huston Simpson, unnamed adult

Simpson owned a hardware store and was one of the first to install a gas pump and sell gasoline for the increasing number of automobiles appearing in the valley. He was a successful pro-Jackson Hole Plan candidate elected in the 1931 election for town councilman.

Gill. For the office of councilman, Bruce Porter and J. C. Simpson, the pro-plan candidates, were opposed by C. R. Van Vleck and Henry H. Francis. According to the *Jackson Hole Courier,* this election drew the largest voter turnout in the county's history. Huff received 211 votes to Gill's 81; Porter and Simpson received 197 and 199 votes respectively while Van Vleck and Francis received 86 and 88 votes respectively.[33] Perhaps the biggest mistake the opposition group made during the campaign was to announce their intention of making the town officially against park extension.

Jackson Hole Historical Society and Museum 2009.0057.008

A horse-drawn snowplow was used to help clear the town streets of snow.

The loss suffered by the opposition group in the local election did not stop their steady flow of inflammatory news releases. The *Casper Tribune-Herald* published an example of the misleading nature of their news articles in July 1931. The article, entitled "Home At Jackson Burned - Indignation Meeting Called," stated in part:

> *The home was alleged to have been burned by interests seeking to have a vast area in this section set aside as a national park. It was construed by a portion of the Jackson townspeople as an unfriendly gesture toward those who oppose the park extension.*
>
> *The house was part of the Pederson estate and was one of the largest and most*

> *valuable in this section. It was located only a short distance from town and recently was acquired by interests favoring establishment of the national park.*
>
> *It is proposed that the park would be kept in a wild and primitive state with no human habitations.*[34]

While it was true that the Snake River Land Company did purchase the property in question and the house was deliberately burned, the circumstances were not at all similar to the implications made in the article. To begin with, the "indignation meeting," which the article said was attended by some prominent Jackson Hole residents, was the annual Lions Club banquet which had been scheduled prior to the incident. The "valuable" house was 20 years old and had been constructed at a cost of $7,000. The original owner was officially the J. P. Ranch Company, which had been defunct for several years before the purchase by the Snake River Land Company. During the years of its abandonment, this house had been vandalized and stripped of anything of value. Since the structure was visible from the highway and because it was considered an eyesore, the Snake River Land Company decided to dispose of the building. The house was offered for sale with the condition that the buyer had to move the building. Lamb and Reed, a local contracting firm, presented the best offer of $50, but the Snake River Land Company rejected the offer. The house was then offered to Henry Crabtree for $100, but he did not feel it was worth that much money because of the associated labor required to move the building. Eventually, Clarence Blain purchased the privilege of stripping the building of all that was left of value for $15. The Snake River Land Company was unable to sell the structure for firewood because the logs of the house were spiked and held together with drift pins. Therefore, the shell of the house was burned as the most economical means of disposing of the building.[35]

These news releases were not confined to misrepresentations of the activities of the Snake River Land Company. Some were blatant attacks on individuals. One such attack was printed in the *Kemmerer Gazette* on August 7, 1931. The *Courier*, under the caption "Kemmerer Gazette Again Embarrasses Wyoming" reprinted the article. During that summer, Utah's Senator Smoot vacationed in Jackson Hole staying with his friend Harold Fabian. The article maintained that Senator Smoot's visit " *revealed the political trickery that is being used in promotion of the so-called Jackson Hole plan, which would disrupt Teton County as a Wyoming unit, destroy its government, its schools and its business institutions.* "[36]

The article continued:

For the benefit of Wyoming people, let it be known that Harold P. Fabian, Utah's biggest mogul in Utah Republican official circles, and linked with Smoot like two peas in a pod, is Rockefeller representative in the Jackson's Hole country, and the grand master of the exchequer in doling out the money for property "in the way" of extending the boundaries of Teton National Park of Wyoming, spreading the money where it will do the most good, without any consideration whatever to the State of Wyoming or its people.[37]

The *Gazette* stated that Senator Smoot and Harold Fabian gathered the cattlemen of the valley for a meeting and told them, *"The Snake River Land Co. ...now owns all the lands over which you have to graze on in going to and from summer and fall ranges; we have let you use it, and will continue to let you use it free of charge, but you must come to the endorsement of the Jackson's Hole Plan, or out you go."*[38] The *Gazette* article stated that some of the cattlemen would fight, and that it was not likely that "*...the Fabian-Smoot compact, with all its power, can bulldoze Wyoming's Congressional delegation and the Wyoming State Legislature, to whom they yet have to present their 'Jackson's Hole Plan.'"*[39]

Neither the Snake River Land Company nor the National Park Service took a public position regarding the Jackson Hole Plan. The Snake River Land Company never officially supported the Plan. Eventually, the Rockefeller organization would present its intentions which incorporated some of the ideas presented in the Plan, but those were not a carbon copy of the local initiative.

The *Courier* responded to the article. In addition to maintaining that the meeting between Fabian, Smoot and the cattlemen never occurred, the *Courier* reprinted a letter that was sent to Senator Smoot from the Jackson Hole Cattle and Horse Association. The cattlemen expressed regret for the attack by the Kemmerer paper and

Grand Teton National Park GRTE-00430_382

Harold Hammond (owner of Whitegrass Ranch), Senator and Mrs. Smoot, Harold and Josephine Fabian.

Reed Owen Smoot (R)
1862-1941

Reed Smoot was an influential Utah politician and Mormon Apostle. He served in the United States Senate from 1903 to 1933. He is most commonly remembered for his co-sponsorship of the 1930 Smoot-Hawley Tariff Act that raised tariffs on 20,000 dutiable items. The Act was often blamed for exacerbating the Great Depression.

stated, *"...those 'reports' did not emanate from any of the honest citizens of this valley."* They also defended Fabian and stated, *"...we wish you to know that from the first inception of the Jackson's Hole Plan the cattlemen have had their place in the picture; were consulted in the drawing of the Plan and gave approval to it, through the association, almost a year ago."* [40]*

In the same issue of the *Jackson Hole Courier*, the editor reflected on the controversy stating:

Jackson's plight today is simply this: A number of her citizens can not see that a bad situation is righting itself, thanks to the Snake River Land Company; that the Jackson Hole Plan will protect the town, the county, the stockman and the town resident.

If we will but work together our future is much brighter than the past has ever been. The Jackson Hole Plan is Jackson's only salvation, any compromise will see its end. [41]

Adding to the controversy, Senator Robert Carey continued his belligerent attitude toward the Snake River Land Company. He demonstrated an almost uncanny ability to jump to false conclusions, to make statements and accusations which he later found embarrassing and which indicated his failure to understand the real situation in Jackson Hole.

After his unsuccessful attempt to obtain the full support of the governor for his stand against park extension and the Snake River Land Company, Senator Carey falsely accused the Snake River Land Company and the Park Service of attempting to block the construction of a telephone line into the valley from Dubois. Carey had been encouraging President Hoover to visit Jackson Hole during his vacation. The major stumbling block in the selection of Jackson Hole for a presidential vacation seemed to be the lack of communication facilities at the north end of the valley. Accordingly, Senator Carey had encouraged the telephone company to construct

the necessary lines to Jackson Lake Lodge. When Mountain States Telephone and Telegraph Company requested a right-of-way across Snake River Land Company property, Mr. Chorley responded that no right-of-way should be allowed *"...which would in any way mar the scenery."* [42] Therefore, the Park Service and the Forest Service laid out a slightly different route for the proposed line that was more secluded yet still acceptable to the phone company. The Snake River Land Company then granted a right-of-way for the line across its property without charge. Senator Carey, however, misunderstood Chorley's requirement for the granting of the right-of-way and instead thought Chorley had refused to grant the right-of-way on the grounds that it would mar the scenery. Senator Carey, on May 16, wrote to Harold Fabian stating, *"...Mr. Chorley, in taking a position of that kind was not only taking an unreasonable stand, but also one that would not help the present relations existing between the citizens of Wyoming and the Snake River Land Company ...."* [43] Fabian then wrote to Carey explaining that the right-of-way had already been granted and that construction was already under way. Senator Carey replied to Fabian's letter on May 22 stating:

I must confess I was somewhat upset about the matter, not so much on your account, but

Courtesy Josephine Fabian

Vanderbilt Webb, Harold Fabian, and Imer Pett

Pett was a member of the Fabian and Clendenin law firm and helped with legal matters relating to the Snake River Land Company operations.

---

*This letter was signed by the following cattlemen: Orin H. Seaton, Jas. Budge, J. D. Ferrin, L. W. Francis, James Boyle, E. H. Martin, A. H. Chambers, R. H. Charter, Jas. A. Francis, Charles Wilson, W. L. Winegar, and Joy Wilson.

due to the fact that it is apparent that the National Park Service was interfering and endeavoring to block the building of this line.

It does seem that things are constantly happening in Jackson's Hole which are being reported to me that make a settlement more difficult. I have in mind, not only this matter, but other things covering the activities of the Snake River Land Company. I hope at an early date we can get together and talk matters over.[44]

Fabian answered Carey's letter asking which activities he found objectionable and offered to travel to Cheyenne to discuss the matter. On June 10, Senator Carey wrote Fabian stating his opposition to the extension of either Yellowstone or Grand Teton National Park but said he hoped a compromise could be reached. To accomplish this, he had invited Senator Walcott, Chorley and Webb to meet with him in Jackson that summer. He stated:

While we had no definite understanding that the Snake River Land Company or the National Park Service would allow things to remain as they were, I took it for granted that nothing would be done until after we made our visit to Jackson's Hole. Now I find that the Snake River Land Company is continuing to purchase land and the Park Service is active in carrying out its plans for park extension.

It seems that those who are interested in park extension are continuing to make the problem more difficult to solve, in fact, to them there is but one solution, namely, to carry out their intention of putting all of this land into the National Parks.

I think you will agree with me that the unfortunate thing about the whole situation is that the Governor of Wyoming and the Wyoming Delegation in Congress were not consulted previous to the purchase of these lands by the Snake River Land Company; neither were they acquainted with the intention of adding this land to the National

Vanderbilt Webb
1891-1956

Webb and Kenneth Chorley were the public personas of the Snake River Land Company prior to the acknowledgment of John D. Rockefeller, Jr.'s involvement. An offspring of the marital merging of the Webb and Vanderbilt dynasties, he was wealthy in his own right and a part of the eastern social elite. Webb's marriage to Aileen Osborn was an additional merging of wealthy eastern families. Aileen's cousin, Fairfield Osborn, will play a role in this narrative in subsequent chapters. Westerners, including many in Jackson Hole, harbored a bias of distrust toward the wealthy eastern socially elite with their "robber baron" names, even though the descendants of the empire builders have provided immense funding for philanthropic endeavors around the world.

Parks. If it is the intention of those interested in park extension to continue to ignore us, there is no use in our wasting our time in trying to work out a compromise.[45]

This letter, and especially its last paragraph, surprised Webb, who had been reviewing the correspondence. On July 1, he wrote the Senator a long letter detailing the Snake River Land Company's involvement in a number of issues with which Carey was misinformed.

Concerning the phone line, Webb explained the Snake River Land Company's concerns and stated:

...our only position was that the proposed line should be located in such a manner as

not to mar the scenery from the Lander road as the road entered Jackson Valley. I am glad that as the result of certain minor changes in the proposed location of the line this result was accomplished to the satisfaction of all concerned. I have never had any intimation that the National Park Service was interfering, and endeavoring to block the building of this line, ... and should be greatly surprised if this were in fact the case.[46]

Concerning any understanding that additional purchases of land would not be made until after the conferences scheduled for the summer, Webb further stated:

...I had never understood that you had made any request that our purchases be suspended or restricted in any way. It was my understanding that the question as to which we hoped that a solution satisfactory to all might be found after our proposed further conferences this summer involved not the acquisition of land within the original area, but the ultimate disposition and administration of such land. If this is not the case, I wish you would let me know.[47]

As if to turn the knife a bit, Webb told Senator Carey that because of his stated objections to further purchasing efforts, the Snake River Land Company would make no purchases in the Mormon Row area even though the governor had requested that the area be re-included in the project. This put the Senator in the position of having killed a project that had the specific approval and support of his governor. It also placed Senator Carey in an unfavorable light with his constituency in the Mormon Row area who wanted to sell their land to the Snake River Land Company. However, Webb did not offer to discontinue purchases in the rest of the project area.*

The major portion of Webb's letter dealt with the Snake River Land Company's efforts to inform

Jackson Hole Historical Society and Museum 1958.0524.001

Creating a winter tourist economy required three elements- accommodations for visitors when they arrived, activities that would attract the tourists, and, primarily, automobile access to the valley. Road access required more than just convincing the state highway department to plow the roads during the winter. All of the approaches to the valley contained severe avalanche hazards that exceeded the capabilities of a normal snowplow. In the photo above, the 30-foot deep avalanche across a road was cut by men with shovels. Photo 1936.

the state's chief executive and the Congressional delegation of its purpose and its actions to cooperate with their wishes. The letter recounted the many meetings that had been held to gain approvals, provide information, and ensure support from the various agencies, congressmen, officials, and commissions. Webb reviewed the Snake River Land Company's efforts to cooperate with Governor Emerson by removing the Mormon Row area from the project and then reinstating the area at the governor's request. He assured the Senator that the Snake River Land Company never made any purchases outside the area approved by the

*Webb's response seemed specifically designed to use the residents of Mormon Row as pawns to embarrass Senator Carey rather than accommodate Carey's concerns. The Snake River Land Company agreed to consider the Mormon Row purchases if the property owners would present a definite amount for the acquisition of the entire area. The residents met that requirement. Webb reneged on the Mormon Row resident's good faith commitment to these conditions and rejected the governor's request for the area's reinstatement in the purchasing plan to cause political embarrassment for Senator Carey.

various conferences with Wyoming officials nor as modified at the request of Governor Emerson. Finally, Mr. Webb stated:

The Elk, Wyoming school "bus" with a wood stove inside..

In view of the above facts which are a matter of record, I am sure you will agree that not only did we consult the Governor of Wyoming and the Wyoming Delegation and laid before them our entire plans before beginning our purchasing program, but we also went out of our way to place the matter before the Department of Agriculture, the Department of the Interior, and the Elk Commission. I am sure you will also agree that we have acceded to every request made by the Governor of Wyoming and the Wyoming Delegation and went out of our way to assist the Wyoming Delegation in endeavoring to secure the approval of the Director of the Budget to the so-called Winter Bill.[48]

Senator Carey responded to this letter by thanking Webb for taking the time to inform him of the early history of the Snake River Land Company in such detail, yet clearly he remained unconvinced. He stated he felt the governor must have reversed his position. Since the governor's previously quoted letter stated a more moderate position than this last statement implies, the Senator evidently read more into the letter than it contained. The Senator also felt that a misunderstanding must have occurred because Senator Kendrick told him that neither he nor any other representative of the state had been consulted or advised as to the plans of the Snake River Land Company.[49]

It would not be within the known character of Senator Kendrick for him to lie to Senator Carey about the conferences with the Snake River Land Company representatives. Neither would it be likely that he would have forgotten them. While the reason for the confusion about this issue may never be fully explained, it is possible, in the light of Senator Carey's general confusion regarding the situation, that he misunderstood Senator Kendrick.

During the conferences in which Rockefeller's representatives explained the purposes and goals of the Snake River Land Company, the National Park Service may not have been explicitly mentioned as the eventual recipient of the purchased lands. However, the Wyoming officials were told that the land was to be acquired for the benefit of the American people which in itself would imply federal administration. In fact, one of the stipulations for which Representative Winter required assurance in 1928 before he agreed to support the Executive Orders withdrawing public land from homesteading was that the land would be used for the good of the public rather than as a recreation area for a few rich sportsmen. This alone would have obligated the Snake River Land Company to offer the land to the federal government.

It is perhaps a more logical speculation to think that Senator Kendrick may have told Senator Carey that he and other Wyoming officials were not advised that the Snake River Land Company would donate the land to the National Park Service. Senator Carey might then have interpreted this to mean that no one had been consulted or advised regarding any of the plans of the company.

During those early conferences with the Wyoming Congressional Delegation and the Governor, it was likely the Rockefeller representatives would have revealed, only in a general way, the ultimate disposition of the land. Also, while Rockefeller in 1930 expressed a desire to donate the land to the Park Service, the land had not been formally offered to the government. This controversy resulted not so much from Rockefeller's offer of land but rather from the suggestion put forth in a local initiative, the Jackson Hole Plan, that at least a portion of Rockefeller's lands be included in Grand Teton National Park.

The conferences which Senator Carey arranged for the summer of 1931 between the Rockefeller's representatives and the Wyoming Congressional Delegation offered the hope of a compromise and an end to the controversy which had strained relations among valley residents. Unfortunately, Senator Carey doomed his conferences to failure before any were held. Two weeks prior to the scheduled conferences, Senator Carey arranged a meeting of the Wyoming Congressional Delegation and selected opponents of the Jackson Hole Plan. Since only opponents to the plan were invited, the meeting became a platform for the delegation to express their own positions on the issue of park extension and the Snake River Land Company project. They expressed themselves as being unalterably opposed to the entire project. The *Jackson Hole Courier* called the meeting *"...a plumb good publicity stunt for anti-extensionists."* [50]

Harold Fabian recalled that Chorley and Webb were surprised at the statements made by Wyoming's Congressional delegation and considered canceling the conferences at that point. However, they eventually decided to travel to Jackson Hole for the conferences thinking the statements were the result of a misunderstanding. Upon arriving in the valley and meeting with Senator Walcott of the Senate's Special Wildlife Committee, the Rockefeller representatives learned that Senator Carey had already worked up a plan which he hoped would be agreed upon at the conferences. This plan required Rockefeller to donate all the land he had purchased to the state of Wyoming for a state park. His plan did not provide funds for the operation and maintenance of the park, nor did it ensure permanency of policy or personnel. Also, it was in conflict with the original purposes for which the land had been purchased- a gift to the American people not just to the residents of Wyoming. Representative Winter received at the

Frederic Collin Walcott (R)
1869-1949
Walcott was a one-term Senator from Connecticut and a member of the Senate's Special Wildlife Committee. A Yale graduate and member of Skull and Bones, he was active in wildlife issues in Connecticut before his election to the U.S. Senate in 1929. He was unable to retain his Senate seat in the 1934 election.

beginning of the project written guarantees that stipulated the general public as the eventual beneficiary of the project. If the land was donated to the state, Teton County would not receive compensation for the loss of its taxable property. Perhaps the most damaging thing Senator Carey did was to give the plan to the newspapers for release on his instructions.

The first meeting was scheduled for the evening of September 2 at which time Carey planned to reveal his proposal. Before the meeting began Chorley, Webb, Fabian and Senator Walcott met with Senator Carey. Fabian recalled, *"...Mr. Chorley ... reminded Senator Carey that he had been invited by the Senator to come to Jackson Hole to discuss the entire problem and see if it was possible to work out a solution which would be in accordance with Mr. Rockefeller's original purpose and agreeable to the Wyoming Congressional Delegation. Mr. Chorley advised Senator Carey that he had learned of the Senator's State Park plan and that it had already been given to the newspapers, and that therefore it seemed un-necessary for him to attend the conference as he could not subscribe to any such plan."* [51]

While there is no record of the resulting conversation between the two men, it must have been interesting as the formal meeting did not start until 10:30 pm. Senator Carey invited members of the Wyoming Game and Fish Commission, representatives of the U.S. Forest Service, several dude ranchers and some residents who opposed the Jackson Hole Plan. With the absence of Rockefeller's representatives, the meeting was anti-climactic. Carey did not present his state park plan, and the discussion was confined to game management problems. The only accomplishment of the meeting was a unanimous vote favoring the purchase of the Winter Bill lands for the elk herd.[52] Although Chorley, Webb and Senators Walcott, Pittman and Carey remained in the valley for the next week and attempted to work out a solution to the question of the disposition of Rockefeller's land, they were unable to arrive at a compromise acceptable to all parties.

On September 10, 1931, the *Cheyenne Tribune* and the *Rocky Mountain News* (Denver)

printed an Associated Press article which quoted Senator Carey stating that Rockefeller's representatives agreed to approve the Senator's state park plan. On September 22, Chorley wrote to Senator Carey concerning the article, stating, *"I am sure there must be some mistake, because, as you know, we did not indicate that a State Park plan would be approved, but on the other hand very clearly and definitely stated that such a plan would not be acceptable."* [52] On October 12, the Senator replied that he knew nothing about the article.

~

Another congressional committee traveled to Jackson Hole in 1931. Congressman Frank Murphy of Ohio, chairman, led this subcommittee of the House Appropriations Committee. While it appeared the committee was impressed with Grand Teton National Park and with the activities and intent of the Rockefeller project, they decided the Park's budget should be cut to provide only essential services until the controversy in Jackson Hole was settled. At the time, Grand Teton's 1931 budget amounted to $230,427 of which $50,000 was allotted for the cleanup of the Jackson Lake

Left to Right: Front Row: Fabian, Cotton, Smith, Murphy, Taylor, French, Walter, Luce, Hastings, Fares. Back Row: Machsen, Bailey, Woodring, Dobbel, Johnson, Durall, Markham, Darlington, Tate, Edwards.

The House Appropriations Committee held hearings in Jackson Hole in 1931 and decided to cut the Grand Teton National Park appropriations for the following fiscal year.

shoreline. A like amount was appropriated to the Bureau of Reclamation for the same purpose.[53] It is impossible to know if the committee's recommendation was entirely influenced by the division of local opinion concerning the park extension issue. The Depression was a strong influence that encouraged Congress to trim the budget of nonessential expenditures. The decision by the Appropriations Committee to cut federal spending in Jackson Hole promised future adverse effects on the valley's economy. The bickering among valley residents over the National Park and the Jackson Hole Plan had the potential to affect adversely economic conditions as well as the social atmosphere within the valley.

During the final months of 1931 and throughout 1932, the majority of action concerning park extension was verbal. Proponents of the Jackson Hole Plan made some gains in that several Wyoming newspapers began to print articles favoring the plan and supporting park extension. In October 1931, the *Sheridan Press* stated:

> *The Park Plan, instead of giving Wyoming away to the tin can tourist, the cheap defacer of forest trees, and Rocky Mountain boulders is taking it back from vandals - protecting it all for posterity from the pressure of commercialism, exploitation and ignorance."* [54]

Meanwhile, the editor of the *Jackson Hole Courier* was continuing his policy of supporting the Park, the Jackson Hole Plan and the protection of the valley. In a November editorial he wrote:

> *Jackson Hole should never become a hot dog vacation land. We should have something different- a place where people can really enjoy a primitive country without every view being ruined by a billboard, gas station or hot dog stand. A country where one may see game in the wild. Where one may fish with some little chance of success or hunt with the chance of taking home a fine trophy.*
>
> *The State of Wyoming will someday know, regardless of the raving and ranting of a few near demagogs* [sic], *that Jackson Hole as a playground, and protected as such by the National Park Service, is a much greater asset to the whole state than Jackson Hole as an unsuccessful farming community.*[55]

Jackson Hole Historical Society and Museum bc.0224

John D. and Abby Rockefeller celebrated their 30th wedding anniversary on Jenny Lake in 1931. The couple also took a horseback ride into the Tetons.

Rockefeller Archive Center Series 1005 (FA449) Box A 43C

Jackson Lake high water line on dead trees, 1932
Funding to clean the shore of Jackson Lake of dead trees, which had been planned for 1932, was ultimately delayed until 1936.

Other newspapers throughout the state used the proposed park extension as an example of federal encroachment– a favorite evil of states' rights advocates. The Jackson editor responded with the argument that those editors were actively supporting their own communities' efforts to obtain federally funded reclamation projects, VA hospitals, and federal funds for roads. He stated, *"Let Uncle Sam know in sentorian* [sic] *voice that we have no use for his gifts and protection. Let us be the hermit state. How long will we last? Otherwise let us be consistent, quit howling federal encroachment from one corner of our mouth and gim'me from the other."* [56]

In December 1931, Senator Carey again voiced his opposition to the Rockefeller project. He stated to a *Wyoming Eagle* reporter:

> *Mr. Rockefeller has refused to consider any suggestion as to a compromise and his action has put the Wyoming Congressional Delegation in a position where we will have to fight Park extension, as we are all opposed to any further encroachment by the Federal Government. Personally, I believe we have gone the limit in trying to compromise this*

> *matter; in fact, I have gone further than I wanted to, but I felt that some settlement of the question was most important to the welfare of the Jackson Hole country.* [57]

To this statement, the *Jackson Hole Courier* responded, *"...any compromise suggested thus far by Senator Carey or any of his colleagues would be anything but beneficial to the welfare of the Jackson Hole people."* [58]

Early in 1932, the local opposition established their own newspaper to voice their views. The paper, *The Grand Teton*, had limited resources and used the presses of the *Kemmerer Gazette* for its printing. It was basically a two-page paper but included two more pages purchased weekly from the Western Newspaper Union in Chicago. These additional pages were called boilerplate and contained articles of general interest. They were edited and printed for use in small weekly newspapers throughout the country. The editor of the Western Newspaper Union, John Dickinson Sherman, was a friend of Horace Albright and articles favoring the extension of Grand Teton National Park occasionally appeared in the publication. This resulted in a number of embarrassing

Jackson Hole Historical Society and Museum p19871593001n

William L. Simpson

Simpson came to Jackson from Cody, Wyoming where he supposedly killed a man in cold blood. The trial resulted in a hung jury and rather than retry him, an arrangement was reached whereby Simpson agreed to leave Cody and never return.[59] Prior to living in Cody, he had shot (but did not kill) a banker in Meeteetse for bouncing one of his checks. He had the nickname of 'Broken Ass Bill' because he walked with a limp due to polio. It appeared that as a resident of Jackson, he was found guilty of little more than opposing park extension and producing poor journalism. It also appeared that his past was never used against him although he became a very visible spokesman for the opposition. His son, Millward, would serve as Wyoming Governor and U.S. Senator. His grandson, Alan, would serve three terms in the U.S. Senate.

---

incidents for the opposition when their cover page blasted the Park, Rockefeller or the Jackson Hole Plan while the inside pages praised the park extension efforts.

Whatever truth was printed by the opposition in *The Grand Teton* was smothered in the lies, slander and misinformation which characterized the publication. The paper lasted 14 months and was edited by William Simpson, one of the sponsors of the Lions Club resolution.

Evidently, not all of the more established newspapers were impressed with the new paper or its articles. The *Idaho Falls Post-Register* remarked, *"The*

mistaken spirits of Jackson, have from all accounts, 'started a newspaper' in order to further and bolster their cause seeming to forget entirely the only real attraction in and of the place is its picturesque setting and surroundings." [60] The *Post-Register* also stated that Rockefeller's action was a contribution

> *...to society and beauty and in that effort he is being opposed and his plans attempted to be blocked by a mistaken few who seem to have the idea that their visitors think more of a gaudy service station, than they do of an opportunity to gaze on the majesty of the Grand Teton and sister mountains or the beauty of Jenny's Lake.*
>
> *The opposition to the preservation of nature's wonders and beauty is based on an idea– that more money is to be made by converting the Jackson country into a sort of a miniature Coney Island– than maintaining the dignity and effect of a mountain town with generations of tradition behind it more valuable than any publicity that can be received today. The man in Jackson who mars the present rustic beauty of the old log buildings or seeks to modernize the town is untrue to those generations of tradition. There are few places left in the world where an effort to improve is a hindrance and in fact the good community of Jackson could well afford to appoint a committee to protect its interests.* [61]

Jackson Hole Historical Society and Museum p1958.2443.001

Gasoline station and store on the Jenny Lake road

Criticisms of *The Grand Teton* were often well founded. As an example, the newspaper ran an article stating that a well liked and perennial visitor to Jackson Hole, Fred Tucker, had died. When Tucker arrived in Jackson alive and well, the *Jackson Hole Courier* remarked, *"Now we are wondering if Hamlet really saw his father's ghost or if we read it in the Grand Teton."* [62]

Other articles reported strong resistance by the Jackson Hole Cattle and Horse Association toward the Snake River Land Company. One such article was entitled "Feudal Laws Now In Force In Jackson Hole: Rockefeller, Jr., Requires Rendition Of Feudal Service Before Giving Grants And Privileges." Rockefeller had allowed free and unrestricted passage across his lands to ranchers who needed to drift their cattle to and from summer ranges. Some abuses occurred resulting in over-grazing of some sections. At a meeting of the Association, the group *"...voted unanimously to employ riders to protect this country during the summer months, and, to secure funds for the expense, voted to assess all cattle and horses benefitting therefrom."* [64]

It was, evidently, this action which *The Grand Teton* considered a "feudal service." The action, however, appeared to be voluntary, and in any case, it would have been a fair request by the owner of the land affected, no matter what his name. The Cattle and Horse Association objected to the article in *The Grand Teton* and, thereafter, advertised its meetings inviting the public to attend.[65]

The constant bickering between *The Grand Teton* and the *Jackson Hole Courier* eventually prompted the editor of the *Inland Oil Index* to remark that *"All is seemingly peace and harmony among Wyoming publishers except at Jackson ...."* He reported, however, that the *"Only bloodshed is from the murder of the King's English ...."* [66]

In June 1932, Senators Kendrick and Carey obtained the approval of Senate Resolution 226

(72nd Congress). This resolution called for an investigation of *"...activities in connection with the proposed enlargement of the Yellowstone and Grand Teton National Parks."* It provided authority for a subcommittee to:

> *...investigate the activities in the Jackson Hole region, Teton County, Wyo., of the National Park Service, Department of the Interior; the Snake River Land Co.; the Teton Investment Co.; the Teton Hotel Co.; the Teton Transportation Co.; and the Jackson Lake Lodge Co., in connection with the proposed enlargement of the Yellowstone National Park and/or the Grand Teton National Park of Wyoming....* [67]

The Senators specifically wanted an investigation into the alleged methods of the Park Service and its personnel to discourage settlement of the area so that the *"...boundaries of Yellowstone and Grand Teton Parks might be conveniently extended...."* The resolution also focused on the activities of the Snake River Land Company and its employees regarding the methods used in acquiring property and *"...otherwise promoting..."* the boundary extension of the two national parks.[68] The resolution authorized subpoena power, provided the necessary appropriations

American Heritage Center University of Wyoming, Fritioff Fryxell Collection, unnumbered

1932 Grand Teton National Park Staff
(No individual names were attached to this photograph.)

for the committee's expenses, and called for the investigative hearings to be conducted by the 73rd Congress. Therefore, an examination of the hearings and the investigation will be covered in the next chapter.

The Senators suspected a conspiracy by the Park Service and John D. Rockefeller, Jr. to discourage settlement and force existing settlers off their land. The purpose of this conspiracy was to accommodate an extension of national park boundaries in the Jackson Hole area.

Opponents of park extension cheered the investigation, but the implied accusation in the language of the resolution resulted in criticism for the two Senators in several Wyoming newspapers. Concerning the investigations into the methods used by the Snake River Land Company, the *Inland Oil Index* stated, *"All they have done so far is purchase a lot of land from private individuals at a price almost anyone in Wyoming would be glad to sell at."* [69] The *Sheridan Press*, however, had a much more interesting editorial.

One group of people in the Hole have at once become inflamed with fury and many accusations of injustice, double dealing and trickery have been laid at the doors of the Rockefeller interests.

It seems a strange thing in America that a man cannot buy whatever land he wants and then give it to a perfectly good concern in fee simple as a gift. Many private individuals have holdings in other parts of the west a good deal bigger than Rockefeller has in Jackson's Hole. They have not told the public what they are going to do with it all, but whatever they do with it is nobody's business. They have bought it and paid for it.

Senators Carey and Kendrick charge that Rockefeller agents and the Park Service are using methods to discourage settlement of Jackson's Hole. Jackson's Hole has been where it is a lot longer than Rockefeller, but to our knowledge in the past, the rush of eager settlers has not been conspicuous. Will someone kindly tell us exactly to what practical purpose that part of Jackson's Hole which Rockefeller has bought could be put?

If a farmer or rancher can live on beauty alone the villainy of anyone's discouraging settling there could not be underestimated. But if he needs bread and beans we can think of better places to settle than Jackson's Hole right here in this state.

Jackson Hole Historical Society and Museum bc.0205

Road construction and maintenance was a high priority for the new Park.

The government to our mind has erred too many times in the opposite direction by urging settlement of stretches of territory on which a man was lucky if he raised one oat and double lucky if a grasshopper didn't beat him to that one oat before the harvest.

We wonder how we, over here, would feel if some guy should come along and put five or six hundred thousand dollars into our citizen's pockets and thence into our local banks. I suppose that someone would try to tell us that he was a robber, that he had better give the land back to us, that he couldn't do what he wanted to do with it when he owned it. I suppose a half million dollars tossed into this community would be given a kick in the teeth and told to go away.

A half million dollars is a half million dollars and that money has gone to the little ranchers throughout Jackson's Hole and it isn't Rockefeller's fault if the moment they cashed their checks they moved out of Jackson to a country more friendly to farming and ranching and heaved a sigh of relief. It isn't Rockefeller's fault either if he didn't pay them three or four times what their land was worth or even if he drove a sharp bargain.

Is Uncle Sam going to tell us how much we can sell our land for or to whom we can sell it? He may be able to tell the free citizens of Jackson's Hole, but if Rockefeller wants to buy something we have to sell, his money is just as good as John Doe's.[70]

In a later issue, the *Sheridan Press* declared that *"...to attempt to prohibit an individual from giving his property to whomever he pleases invades a right even more fundamental than states' rights."* The Sheridan editor also made another jab at Senators Carey and Kendrick by writing:

The property which Mr. Rockefeller owns at present he bought with his own money. He forced no one to sell. He had no power to condemn as the government has.

He has bought it and paid for it. Now we ask you what right under the blue canopy of heaven has any law-maker, any public official, any Senator or even the President to regulate what he does with that property as long as he remains within the proprieties of society and within the law of the land.

We may not want him to give his property to the National Park Service any more than we want our great grandfather to will his gold watch to his fourth wife's children, but we have no right that we have ever heard of to attempt to prohibit him from so doing.[71]

～

November 1932 offered the residents of Teton County another opportunity publicly to express their views on park extension as set forth in the Jackson Hole Plan. A national election was held on November 8 in which the local candidates once again aligned themselves according to the park extension issue more than party lines. However, park extension was not the only issue in this election. This was a presidential election and national issues such as the Depression and Prohibition was also involved in the voter's decisions. For the third time, the proponents of the Jackson Hole Plan were elected to office. Roosevelt found more favor in the county than did Hoover. The residents voted 620 to 150 to repeal the 18th Amendment ending prohibition.[72]

～

During the years of 1931 and 1932, the economy of Jackson Hole remained relatively strong despite the Depression. One of the reasons for

Grand Teton National Park, unnumbered
Road work by the CCC

174

this was a willingness on the part of some local merchants to adjust their inventories and services to accommodate a changing clientele. As ranchers and farmers sold their properties to the Snake River Land Company and left the valley, the businessmen began to cater to the tourists' needs as well as to the traditional agricultural economic activities. Not everyone who sold to Rockefeller left the valley. Some started new businesses and reinvested their money in the valley. Also, the Snake River Land Company, the National Park Service and the Bureau of Reclamation created more jobs within the valley. The Snake River Land Company hired men to clean up most of its purchased properties and to repair, improve and maintain other properties. In 1932, the National Park Service, in addition to purchasing supplies and equipment from local merchants, hired 76 local men during the summer season and paid them $14,446 in wages. They also contracted for pack horses and teams in the amount of $1,146.[73] Additionally, Grand Teton National Park and the Bureau of Reclamation supervised CCC projects that built trails and improved roads in the area. The CCC eventually operated 34 camps in Wyoming and the Jackson camps contributed to the low unemployment conditions in Jackson Hole.[74]

During these two years, almost every citizen acknowledged the value of tourism and recreation to the valley's economic well-being. The community's businessmen began to search for ways to improve the potential of this industry and especially to extend the season. A winter sports committee was formed to create and promote events and activities that would attract visitors to Jackson during the winter. The main obstacle to the establishment of a viable winter economy based on recreation was access to the valley. The highways leading to Jackson were not maintained or plowed during the winter months and the committee began a concentrated effort to

have the Hoback Canyon road maintained year round. In the latter days of 1932, the efforts of this committee had the support and optimistic praise of the community regardless of their park extension philosophies.

~

Any number of inconsistencies between individual action and public pronouncements could be recounted within the scope of this chapter, but one particular event glares most sharply. This event was a dinner to which Mr. and Mrs. Rockefeller were invited while they vacationed in Jackson Hole on their 30th wedding anniversary. The dinner was sponsored by the Evanston, Kemmerer, and Jackson Lions Clubs. With all the anti-Rockefeller rhetoric produced by the Jackson's Lions Club, *The Grand Teton* and the *Kemmerer Gazette,* it seemed paradoxical that the Rockefellers would have been so cordially entertained.

~

While the park extension issue may have assumed a predominant position in the social life of the valley's residents, other issues were not entirely relegated to obscurity. Water issues with Idaho remained a constant concern, and, at least, one Wyoming editor, William Deming, wrote an article that tied the irrigation issue to the park extension issue. The Jackson Lake shore line

Grand Teton National Park unnumbered
CCC crew building the Skyline Trail in Grand Teton National Park.

provided Deming with an example where the protection of scenic values and states' rights (water allocation) were compatible. Deming watched the sun set behind Mount Moran and wrote:

Nowhere else is to be seen a more inspiring spectacle– if you can forget the depressing foreground of the desolate mud flats bordering once beautiful Jackson Lake. The crime against loveliness, which was perpetrated when this sparkling virgin was raped that Wyoming's most essential resource, water, might be alienated to Idaho lands should never be repeated by the Reclamation Service, nor permitted by those responsible for the preservation of Wyoming's waters. [75]

Deming believed that while the controversies may have divided the people on the issues, the populace was filled with state and local pride. He believed the residents cherished the beauty of the mountains, lakes and forests. To substantiate this belief, he quoted a sign he spotted as he checked into a local hotel. It read, *"This is God's country. Don't set it on fire and make it look like hell."*

Deming also thought the arguments against the Park Service to be petty and potentially harmful to the whole state. He felt there *"...should be a strong movement on the part of the State of Wyoming officials and the citizens of Park County and Teton County to iron out their differences with the National Park Service to the end that both Wyoming Gateways may be brought up to the highest point of efficiency."* He also stated, *"...it is not wise to engage in perennial controversy with the National Park Service, especially through the public press over matters I feel sure our able delegation in Congress can adjust from time to time as problems arise."* Deming pointed out the inconsistency of demanding increased federal funds for roads to and through the National Forests and National Parks and then criticizing their management policies. He wrote, *"There is too much inclination to hand Uncle Sam bouquets when we want something and brickbats when we disagree over details or policy."* [76]

Despite the respected editor's praise of the area and his advice to the various factions, 1932

American Heritage Center University of Wyoming (unnumbered)
William Chapin Deming, (1901)
1869-1949

Deming was the editor of the *Wyoming Tribune*, author, and publisher of periodicals. He was a strident advocate of dry farming in Wyoming and served in the State Legislature. He received several minor political appointments in the Theodore Roosevelt, William Howard Taft, and Woodrow Wilson administrations. He was head of the Civil Service Commission under Coolidge and Hoover. He authored numerous books including *The Life of Robert Burns* (1914), *The Making of A Nation* (1926) and *Theodore Roosevelt in the Bunkhouse, and other sketches* (1927).

ended with little, if any, real progress toward a solution to the problems. If anything, the controversy had resulted in an adverse impact on the valley's economy. In 1932, Grand Teton National Park's budget was $85,700. However, because of the divided sentiment of the people of Jackson Hole, the House Appropriations Committee had decided to cut that appropriation to the bare necessities until more support for the Park was demonstrated. The 1933 budget would be only $15,000, and federal expenditures within the valley would be drastically reduced substantiating William C. Deming's belief that Wyoming would *"...lose rather than gain by any unfriendly attitude toward the National Park Service."* [77]

CHAPTER ELEVEN
1933

...while the opportunity is still here, it seems worthwhile to save from the onrushing hordes, this little spot of American soil which has been the cradle of civilization of the mountain west- to preserve it inviolate in its virgin grandeur as an inspiration for the generations of future Americans, where they can see and feel and touch the scenes and traditions of the frontier West, long after the last pioneer shall have gone.[1]

Jackson Hole Courier
April 13, 1933

Jackson Hole Historical Society and Museum 1958_0497

Edward K. "Roan Horse" Smith (left) and Lew Smith (center) had the school sleigh contract for the area west of the Snake River and north of the Gros Ventre River. Lida Gabbey on right.

In January 1933, the Wyoming Congressional Delegation made the Grand Teton National Park extension issue even more complex by revealing a new compromise plan. Their plan was submitted to the Secretary of the Interior, Ray Lyman Wilbur, on December 12, 1932, but it was not made public until the first of the year.[2]

The plan, as submitted, was a surprising stand for the Wyoming politicians in that some of their proposals contradicted their previous positions on the issues. They felt this plan was a major concession on their part and expected it to be an important step toward finding a solution to the controversy. They were wrong. Instead of receiving praise for their attempt at diplomacy, they generated a new wave of criticism upon themselves throughout the state.

Wyoming newspaper editors had discovered some of the realities regarding the issues and the situation in Jackson Hole, and a gradual decrease in the number of anti-park articles and editorials was noticeable. The *Wyoming-Tribune* called the Senators' plan an "ultimatum" rather than a

Jackson Hole Historical Society and Museum p1958.3368.001

The controversy over park extension did not hinder community pride. In 1933, the first trees were planted in the town square. The population of Jackson at this time was about 500. The Jackson Mercantile Co. store in the background of this photo was founded by Frank and Roy Van Vleck. The landscaping project was financed with private donations. The square, with new landscaping, was dedicated on George Washington's birthday, so it was named Washington Square. Photo 1933.

compromise. Julian Snow in an article in the *Wyoming Eagle* stated, "'Ultimatum' is a good word and has gained us widespread publicity. After all, who is the United States government to oppose the Army and Navy of Wyoming? Just one false move, Uncle Sam, and 240,000 men women and children will spring to arms! Wyoming, the worm, has turned."[3]

The plan which the Wyoming delegation presented to the Secretary of the Interior extended the boundaries of Grand Teton National Park from the southern end of Jackson Lake eastward to the Snake River, then southwesterly along the Snake River to the point where the river met the southeastern corner of Grand Teton National Park. The provision contained in the Grand Teton Park legislation prohibiting new roads and hotels would apply to the new area.

The area east of the Snake River, south of the Buffalo Fork River, west of the Teton National Forest boundary, and north of the Gros Ventre River would be set aside for elk refuge purposes. A commission composed of a representative from the Forest Service, a representative from the Biological Survey, two representatives from the state of Wyoming appointed by the governor, and a fifth member selected by the other four to act as an administrative officer would administer the elk refuge section. This commission would be granted the power to issue permits or leases for summer homes, hotels, and other concessions as long these activities and/or structures were compatible with protection of the wildlife and scenic values of the area.

Cattlemen would be permitted to move their livestock through this area each spring to reach their grazing allotments under regulations prescribed by the commission and, of course, return in the fall. The last element of the compromise required that all land previously proposed by the Park Service for inclusion into Grand Teton National Park, but not described in the above compromise, would be restored to the public domain or to the National Forest Service.[4]*

Their plan, no matter how fair it might have seemed to its authors, was doomed from the beginning for several reasons. First, the people of Jackson Hole would not accept the plan because it failed to provide financial reimbursement to Teton County for the loss of taxable property. Second, the plan required the cooperation of the Snake River Land Company, the owner of much of the property in question, to the extent that certain lands would be used for purposes other than those for which they had been purchased. Since it was unlikely that the Snake River Land Company would abandon its objectives, the plan was impractical.[5] Specifically, Rockefeller initiated his purchasing program to clean up the man-made eyesores that detracted from the scenic beauty of the valley and to remove fences and buildings which served as obstructions to the migrating elk herd. The new plan would allow the construction of summer homes, hotels and a variety of unnamed concessions within the area he had just cleared.

The most surprising aspect of the plan was section four. That section, proposing a commission of federal and state bureaucrats to manage the wildlife east of the Snake River, was a direct violation of the states' rights doctrine. The state of Wyoming and its politicians had always maintained the exclusive jurisdiction of the state over wildlife within its borders. While the Congressional delegation felt this was a significant compromise, the real compromise would have been Rockefeller's. According to the plan, he would have to donate much of the land to agencies which could not provide or guarantee permanency of policy regarding the future use of the land.

After considering the plan, the *Jackson Hole Courier* stated:

Jackson Hole Historical Society and Museum 1993.4820.000

Jackson Hole residents quickly accepted the automobile and other internal combustion and steam-driven engine technologies. However, they were slow to abandon their horses, especially during the winter.

Seldom in history has a congressional delegation, spurred by the thought of political future, displayed more contempt for the rights of home loving people.

After assailing bureaus and bureaucrats by word of mouth and through the press to split the ears of groundlings, these men of might come forth with utter disdain to divide the lands among THREE bureaus.[6]

Apparently, each faction of the controversy was so involved in pushing its own plan; everyone overlooked the possibility that Rockefeller might have some views of his own. Until this time, the Snake River Land Company had refrained from joining the verbal battles concerning the disposition of the land it owned. However, the suggestion put forth by Wyoming's Congressional delegation required a reply. Thus, the Snake River Land Company finally took a stand and made it public. The *Jackson Hole Courier*, in its now familiar tongue-in-cheek style, remarked:

After listening to long and divers [sic] plans by both local people and Wyoming

---

*It may be assumed that the lands the Senators required be returned to their former status did not apply to privately owned property. This provision refers to lands that had been withdrawn from public entry by Executive Orders in aid of legislation previously proposed.

members of Congress for the disposition of the Snake River Land Company's holdings in Teton County imagine our dismay when we read in last week's Courier where representatives of this company had a few ideas of their own in this connection!

It must take a lot of courage to intimate what you would do with your own property when so many others are willing to assume the burden.

However, since they do indeed own the land, it might be well to have a bit of regard for the principles by which they would be guided in making ultimate disposition of their property.[7]

Charles Wesley Andrews photo- Jackson Hole Historical Society and Museum 1992.4104.038

The Jackson-Victor winter passenger and mail stage tried to provide access to the valley in support of a year-round winter economy.

The guidelines that the Snake River Land Company felt appropriate for the disposition of its lands were published in a letter from Harold Fabian to Wilford Neilson. The *Courier* published the letter in which Fabian stated,

...the Snake River Land Company is prepared to present these lands to the United States Government, in order that they may be administered under an ownership, control and management best calculated to make them available for the future enjoyment of the public. It has seemed that this purpose can best be accomplished under the guidance of the following general principles:

1. The lands to be donated to the United States Government to be under the jurisdiction of the National Park Service.

2. The United States Government to match the cost of the lands donated up to an amount necessary to purchase all other privately owned land in such area as it may be deemed advisable to include within the jurisdiction of the National Park Service.

3. All unappropriated public domain and all school sections in such area to be turned over to the National Park Service.

4. The United States Government to transfer to the National Park Service the land in such area now administered by the United States Forest Service.

5. Any lands in such area which in the opinion of the National Park Service might more properly and advantageously be administered by the United States Forest Service or the Biological Survey to be so administered.

6. The United States Government to provide for the preservation of the summer range for game in the area surrounding the Jackson Hole Valley under such plan as will insure adequate protection and grazing for the game, and also for the cattle of ranches now operating in the Jackson valley.

7. The State of Wyoming to continue its work in the management, care, and feeding of its game herds in such area in cooperation with the Biological Survey and the other governmental agencies involved.

8. The United States Government to provide for the reimbursement of Teton County for the loss of taxes due to the taxable property being removed from the tax rolls.

9. The United States Government to make provision for cattle to have the right to cross National Park Service lands to and from the ranches in Jackson Hole and the summer ranges.

Horace Albright and Stephen Mather
(Note the prestige license plate on the car.)

The Snake River Land Company was organized for the sole purpose of preserving the extraordinary natural beauties of the Jackson Hole Country and developing its unique game resources for the benefit and enjoyment of the nation as a whole. Six years of time and effort and $1,500,000 have been devoted to the accomplishment of this purpose. From the study and experience of these six years, the foregoing principles have been evolved. The Company feels that a permanent solution of the Jackson Hole project guided by these principles is of such importance to the country at large as to justify whatever further amount of time and effort may be required.[8]

When it became apparent that the Snake River Land Company would not participate in the new plan presented by the Wyoming Senators, it was quickly forgotten by the newspapers as well as by Senator Kendrick. Less than a month after the plan had been presented to the public, Senator Kendrick reversed his position and sent a wire to Dr. R. A. Hocker, Chairman of the Wyoming Game and Fish Commission, stating:

I am opposed to any change in connection with the administration of wildlife in Wyoming that will in any degree tend to relinquish or lessen Wyoming's right to control and protect the game. I believe our state has

more adequately protected and perpetuated wildlife than almost any state in the Union and she should not consider any plan to transfer her authority altogether or even in part.[9]

Senators Kendrick and Carey, their plan having failed, seemed content to await the Senate's investigation of Rockefeller and the National Park Service. However, other state politicians were not willing to wait. The Wyoming House of Representatives passed House Bill 26, the Teton Land Act, with a 33 to 24 vote. The Teton Land Act was a bill designed to oppose park extension in Wyoming and especially in Jackson Hole. It provided that with the exception of land purchases for the purpose of VA hospitals, administrative buildings and national defense *"...the United States or any bureau or department thereof shall not acquire by gift, purchase, condemnation, or otherwise, any land in this state for any other purpose unless authorized by an act of the state legislature."* [10]

Woody Womald and William Deloney (right).

Deloney originally opposed both the extension of Yellowstone National Park into Jackson Hole and the establishment of Grand Teton National Park. He acquiesced to the latter's creation and eventually became an outspoken proponent of the extension of Grand Teton National Park to include much of the northern portion of the valley.

Debate on the bill in the House transcended party lines. Carl Bark (D) of Jackson spoke against the bill stating that a majority of Teton County residents favored park extension. However, Majority Leader Watenpaugh (D) of Sheridan and Minority Leader Goppert (R) of Cody supported the bill and obtained its approval by the House.[11]

One house does not a legislature make. The Wyoming Senate unanimously defeated the bill. The respected William Deloney (R) of Jackson spoke against the bill, but it probably did not require the eloquent oration for which he was famous to demonstrate the impracticality of the Teton Land Act. It would have been a stumbling block to future water and reclamation projects where government cooperation was required. The bill might also have been unconstitutional because it provided for the usurpation of federal authority as provided in the act admitting Wyoming into the Union.[12]

As the tourist season approached, the *Jackson Hole Courier* began to print more articles and editorials that expounded the uniqueness of the scenery of Jackson Hole, the altruism of John D. Rockefeller, Jr. and the necessity of the Jackson Hole Plan. The *Courier's* responses to articles and attacks by *The Grand Teton* became more satirical, facetious, and predictably more humorous. When other Wyoming newspapers, some of which opposed park extension, also began to criticize *The Grand Teton*, the *Courier* seemed to decrease its coverage of that paper.

In May, another local election occurred and once again the supporters of park extension, according to the Jackson Hole Plan, were returned to office. Dr. C. W. Huff was reelected mayor over C. H. Brown with a vote of 236 to 89. For councilmen, Bruce Porter received 220 votes and J. Chester Simpson received 211 votes to Henry Crabtree's 99 and L. G. Gill's 87 votes. The *Courier* took this opportunity to blast *The Grand Teton* stating, *"For the past several months the administration had been under fire from 'The Grand Teton', a newspaper conceived in anger, championed by ignorance, and dedicated to vicious personal attacks. Although the criticism, because of the source, had not been taken seriously, the election was nevertheless considered a vote of confidence."*[13]

As the date neared for the senatorial investigation, the *Courier* increased its articles and editorials critical of the investigation and Senators Carey and Kendrick, who initiated the proceedings. In one article the *Courier* stated, *"True it is. Wyoming's strutting Bob and trusting John may learn something of what is happening in their own state, but with myriads unemployed, with men working for a dollar a day and thousands going hungry, is this any time to be educating United States Senators?"*[14]

Jackson Hole Historical Society and Museum 2005.0043.001
As the automobile enabled tourism expansion in Jackson Hole, people adapted vehicles to accommodate long distance travel. In the photo above a truck has been converted to provide sleeping platforms– a precursor of the modern motorized camper.

The *Courier* reprinted an article from the *Denver Post* in which Senator Carey was interviewed about the forthcoming Senate hearings. In this article, the Senator accused John D. Rockefeller,

Jr., Secretary of Interior Work, and Horace Albright of waging a campaign of terrorism against the settlers in Jackson Hole. Carey stated the hearing *"...holds potentialities of scandal, thrills and surprises which will equal that of Tea Pot Dome."* Senator Carey charged that settlers who refused to sell had fences destroyed, houses burned and schools removed. He stated that the Park Service prevailed upon the General Land Office to make things difficult for homesteaders. Carey said, *"The list of ordeals to which these men and women have been subjected forms a scandal in itself which the nation should denounce. The fight we of Wyoming are waging against the invasion of eastern millionaires, led by national park officials, is a fight for the west."* [15]

The *Courier* challenged Senator Carey to produce his evidence of terrorism and claimed the only comparison with Tea Pot Dome was the *"...extravagant expenditure of funds for a useless investigation."* [17] The next week's edition of the *Courier* printed a letter to the editor from John L. Dodge concerning the Carey interview. Dodge stated in part, *"It strikes me as the utterance of a demagogue. It is cheap politics to attack Mr. Rockefeller for his philanthropic and public spirited interest in this region. I hope he will ignore these insults and go right on buying up the country. A lot of us on the west side of the river recently signed a petition to the Snake River Land Company to come down this side and buy us out."* [17]

As the time approached for the Senate subcommittee to hold its hearings in Jackson, Senator Carey's publicity campaign to build the importance of the Senate hearing attracted the attention of the nation.* The possibility that the hearing would reveal a conspiracy on the part of an agency of the United States Government with one of the nation's richest men to drive American citizens off their land was hard to ignore. Major newspapers, including the *Christian Science Monitor*, the *Denver Post*, and the *Salt Lake Tribune*, sent reporters, as did three news services. Since Carey assured the press an important scandal was about to be revealed; special arrangements were made to facilitate the distribution of news as quickly as possible. Western Union provided special representatives to handle all press messages, but Jackson did not have wire facilities. Therefore, these special key operators were stationed at the nearest Western Union facility, Victor, Idaho, and four motorcycle couriers were hired to speed the news over Teton Pass to the waiting operators. The showdown was at hand.

As far as the residents of Teton County were concerned, the hearing accomplished very little. Forty witnesses testified, and 77 exhibits were introduced into the hearing record. Valley residents were given a chance to speak their mind, but the real accomplishment of the investigation was to clear the air that had been polluted by Senator Carey and *The Grand Teton*. A great many

S. N. Leek Collection, American Heritage Center, University of Wyoming, JHS&M 2007.0011.042

The Victor, Idaho Union Pacific railroad station was the closest telegraph office to Jackson Hole.

---

* The subcommittee was composed of Gerald P. Nye of North Dakota, Chairman; Henry F. Ashurst of Arizona; Alva B. Adams of Colorado; Peter Norbeck of South Dakota, and Robert D. Carey of Wyoming. John C. Pickett served as the subcommittee's counsel. Pickett was the county attorney for Laramie County and received his appointment to serve the subcommittee after a joint recommendation by Senators Kendrick and Carey.[18]

Jackson Hole Historical Society and Museum 1958.2954.001

Jackson High School
This building, valued at $5000, burned in 1914 and classes were held in various buildings in town until a new school could be built. The bonded indebtedness of $35,000 for the new school offered a valid argument to oppose Rockefeller's proposed donation of taxable land and improvements to the federal government. Every taxable asset was needed by Teton County to pay its obligations.

accusations had been leveled at the National Park Service and John D. Rockefeller, Jr. The hearing brought out the facts and quieted much of the speculation, but it did not provide solutions to the underlying controversy.

When Senators Carey and Kendrick called for the hearings, they wanted certain activities in Jackson Hole investigated. They believed the Park Service was attempting to discourage the legal entry and occupation of public lands in the area. These attempts allegedly occurred both in Jackson Hole and in Washington where the Park Service supposedly worked to secure the cooperation of the General Land Office to reject, deny, closely investigate, and harass claimants on these properties. The purpose of these activities, it was alleged, was to allow the boundaries of Grand Teton National Park to be more conveniently extended at a future date.

The other area of activity about which the Senators were concerned focused on the Snake River Land Company and its methods of acquiring land in Jackson Hole. The Snake River Land Company was accused of various types of coercion to force settlers to sell. Among these methods were intimidation, threats, elimination of mail service in areas where settlers refused to sell, and destruction

of property such as fences, houses, and schools. Lacking among all these accusations, with one exception, was the claim that the Snake River Land Company offered less money for the property than it was worth. The one exception was Senator Carey, in his *Denver Post* interview, where he claimed Rockefeller, was using these methods and was a *"...land bargain hunter."*[19]

The Snake River Land Company was also accused of using trickery and deceit to purchase property, of attempting to monopolize the concessions within the area of the proposed park extension, and of working to prohibit the construction of a new road near Moran. It was alleged that the Snake River Land Company had placed Teton County in financial jeopardy by removing all improvements from the purchased properties thereby decreasing the taxes and thus the revenue upon which the county relied.

John C. Pickett, the subcommittee's legal counsel, obviously was aware that his position with the subcommittee was an honor bestowed at the recommendations of Senators Carey and Kendrick. Since both Senators' positions on the issue were well known, Pickett assumed a prosecutorial attitude toward the Park Service, the Snake River Land Company and any witness who supported either of those organizations. He was given subpoena power to obtain the records of the National Park Service and the Snake River Land Company (the Snake River Land Company made all their records available without a subpoena being served). From these records, he tried to make his case. Some members of the subcommittee were not favorably impressed with Pickett. One member, Senator Peter Norbeck, remarked, *"I am tired of innuendo on the part of the committee's counsel. I have never seen the like of it. I don't like it and I am going to make a report to Congress about it. It is unfair to the witness and unfair to the committee."* [20]

Pickett's conduct was only one of the embarrassments suffered by Senator Carey as result of the hearings. The hearings began with a minor disagreement between the committee's chairman, Senator Nye, and Senator Carey. The chairman wanted three letters placed in the hearing record as an appendix. These three letters were written by Horace Albright, Harold Fabian, and J. H. Rayburn to Wilford Neilson, the editor of the *Jackson Hole Courier*. Neilson, while preparing a history of the park movement in Jackson Hole, requested from Albright a letter explaining his activities as well as those of the National Park Service regarding the Teton Park issue. Neilson also asked Fabian for a history of the Snake River Land Company. Both men complied with lengthy letters. Additionally, Fabian asked Rayburn, President of the Teton Investment Company, to write Neilson to explain the history of several companies operating in the north end of the valley. Senators Kendrick and Carey included these companies by name, along with the Park Service and the Snake River Land Company, for investigation in Senate Resolution 226. The Senators believed, and *The Grand Teton* declared, that these companies were controlled by Rockefeller interests and intended to monopolize the concessions within and around an enlarged Grand Teton National Park. Rayburn's letter cleared Rockefeller of that part of the conspiracy charges which provided more embarrassment for Senator Carey.

Since these three letters dealt directly with the issue at hand, Senator Nye felt they should be included in the record. However, Senator Carey objected to this action on the basis that, if the letters were included in the record, they would assume the weight of evidence. He reasoned that this would be inappropriate since neither Horace Albright nor J. H. Rayburn was in attendance at the hearing, so the information contained in the letters could not be cross-examined. Even though Harold Fabian was present at the hearing, the Senator did not want his letter included in the record either. The Senator maintained that any information Fabian might have would best be obtained through questioning by the committee's counsel.

Jackson Hole Historical Society and Museum 2003.0117.135
Jackson High School, 1933.

While Senator Carey's argument may have been logical, there might also have been other reasons for his objection. The letters (which have frequently been quoted in previous chapters) revealed the Senator's gross lack of understanding of the situation in Jackson Hole. He had promised the press a scandal and made serious charges against people, agencies, and private corporations. The letters could only provide more embarrassment for him. He had charged that the various companies operating tourist-oriented businesses out of Moran were controlled by eastern money and that they were attempting to create a monopoly within and around the Park. Rayburn's letter revealed the financial condition and contractual relationships of the companies as well as the stockholders. Since the stockholders turned out to be Wyoming and Utah residents, it became obvious that Senator Carey had accused some of his own constituents of being controlled by eastern millionaires. This was not the type of information the Senator wanted printed in a Senate hearing transcript.

The Albright and Fabian letters were even more embarrassing for the Senator. If these letters were included in the record, the press and the full committee in Washington, D.C. would read of his blundering mistakes in Jackson Hole. These two letters revealed, among other things, Carey's prediction that tourism was a fad and that it would not contribute to Wyoming's economy, his false accusations against the Snake River Land

185

Company and the National Park Service concerning the construction of the telephone line to Jackson Lake Lodge, and his attempt to intimidate the Snake River Land Company (concerning its purchases) which resulted in the abandonment of the compromise Governor Emerson had approved for the purchase of the Mormon Row properties. In short, all three letters cast doubt on his competency.

In any case, the Senator had little reason to complain about the propriety of the evidence. He had used the United States Senate, through the wording of Resolution 226, to slander a good many people. He also used the press to charge those people with terrorism and conspiracy. In neither instance were the accused present to defend themselves nor to cross-examine their accuser. For over a year, those people lived under a cloud of suspicion which, without producing any evidence, Senators Carey and Kendrick had placed upon them. The *Jackson Hole Courier* noticed another impropriety concerning Senator Carey. The paper stated:

> *It is of interest to note the position of Senator Carey in the coming inquiry. He made the charges, he sponsored the resolution, and he sits on the committee of investigation.*
>
> *Seldom in modern civilization will you find a similar instance where the accuser, the prosecutor, sits in judgement over the accused.*
>
> *If justice is blindfold, surely the rag has slipped.*[21]

Senator Nye assured Senator Carey that he did not intend for the letters to be a substitute for the presence of witnesses. He thought the letters were important and might be useful to the members of the committee for reference during the hearing. Senator Nye also reminded Carey that a second hearing was scheduled in Washington, D.C. where Albright would be available for questioning.

Carey refused to withdraw his objection. Senator Nye then agreed to withhold the letters from the record, reserving the right to refer to them during the hearing and possibly to include them in the record later. Although Senator Nye later ordered the letters included, they were never printed in the hearing transcript. However, the three letters were printed in a pamphlet with a forward by Vanderbilt Webb, the President of the Snake River Land Company. The pamphlet also had a rather lengthy title, "Mr. John D. Rockefeller, Jr.'s Proposed Gift of Land for the National Park System in Wyoming: History of the Snake River Land Company and of the Efforts to Preserve the Jackson Hole Country for the Nation."

One observer, Josephine Fabian, recalled the atmosphere in the hearing room as Mr. Pickett called his first witness and began his questioning. She described it as anticipating an impending explosion. Reporters sat on the edge of their seats, pencils in hand, ready to transcribe the abusive workings of the Rockefeller agents. The reporters expected to hear a witness describe the pressures he had endured before he was finally forced to sell his land.[22] However, the first witness, Struthers Burt, was a disappointment. Burt was a successful author and an articulate supporter of Albright, Rockefeller, the Snake River Land Company and the National Park Service. It was not likely he would provide the ammunition for a damaging newsflash. Burt was called primarily to give the

Jackson Hole Historical Society and Museum 1992.4416.001

Josephine (Cunningham) Fabian was Harold Fabian's secretary before and during their marriage. When the Snake River Land Company was established, she served as the assistant secretary and assistant treasurer for the company. She would later (1963) write a historically-based novel about the valley titled *The Jackson's Hole Story*.

background of the park movement in Jackson Hole. It was from Burt's testimony that the committee and its counsel learned of the movements to protect and preserve the valley and its wildlife prior to Albright's arrival. *The Grand Teton* and Senator Carey charged that the whole controversy was started by Albright's desire to control the entire valley through the National Park Service. It was now clear that the "defense of the country,"

Jackson Hole Historical Society and Museum 1996.0005.001
Struthers Burt's Bar BC Guest Ranch

Burt, with partner Dr. Horace Carncross, homesteaded the Bar BC Ranch in 1912. They established what would be considered one of the nation's premiere guest ranches into the 1930s. The ranch was sold to the Snake River Land Company with an additional partner, Irving P. Corse, retaining a lifetime lease. At the time of the sale, Corse signed the lease agreement "Irving P. Corse and wife" to assure that his wife, Angela, could continue living there and operate the ranch after he died. However, Angela preceded Irving, and he eventually remarried. After Irving's death, the Park Service determined that the second wife, Margaretta, was not the intended "wife" on the lease and required that she vacate the property. With the assistance of Raymond C. Lilly, the manager of Rockefeller's Grand Teton Lodge Company, the Park Service was persuaded to allow Margaretta to remain on the ranch for the remainder of her life.[24]

as Struthers Burt phrased it, began with local support before Albright ever saw the Tetons.*

Burt was questioned about his role in the park movement because he had opposed the park idea originally. It was at this point that one of the seldom stated but universal attitudes of Jackson Hole was voiced– Yellowstone was not a Wyoming park. Yellowstone was created before Wyoming became a state and the state had no control in the area. The Park's early administration and powerful concessions had developed a poor reputation with the Jackson Hole residents, and since early park movements involved the annexation of the Jackson Hole country into Yellowstone National Park, many locals, including Struthers Burt, fought the movement. The people felt that fighting the expansion of Yellowstone National Park was indeed "defending the country." Burt maintained there was nothing unusual about his support for the current park movement because, unlike Yellowstone, Grand Teton National Park was a Wyoming park.

After Struthers Burt was questioned about the sale of his ranch, the Bar BC, to the Snake River Land Company, there was no doubt about his loyalty to the cause of "defending the country." Originally, the Rockefeller project was supposed to follow the ideals set forth at the Maud Noble cabin meeting in 1923. Anyone who wanted to sell would have his or her property purchased, but no one "had" to sell. A special attempt would be made to purchase nonresident owned properties as well as those properties whose owners were creating an eyesore and other "nuisance" properties. It was quickly realized that such a policy would not

---

*Years later, in the 1967 interview, Albright gave little credit to the locals who worked to protect the valley either before or after he arrived on the scene. He stated, "... *this great park is the result of National Park Service efforts mainly with very little help of others.... And when you get down to it that if you have to have an individual, I know it sounds like I'm bragging, it's got to be said that I was the ringleader all those years. I was the fellow who was up here on the job and I was the fellow who was bucking them all and I was probably the worst hated man in Wyoming.*"[23]

be effective. In a glaring example, at the beginning of the purchasing program, the Elbo Ranch started its Hollywood Cowboy's Home and placed billboards and flashing lights to attract customers. Any landowner could commercialize his or her property at any time and defeat the efforts of the majority of landowners. Also, because the federal government was reluctant to accept gifts of land if the gift contained scattered pockets of private property, the Snake River Land Company had to attempt to purchase all the land in the project area.

Struthers Burt did not want to sell, and he did not like the price he and his partners were offered. He had recently acquired another partner, and he felt an obligation to protect the young man's $35,000 investment. Burt, who for 25 years had been associated with the movement to protect the valley, also felt a moral obligation to sell the ranch. He placed what he believed to be the best interest of the valley above his own and agreed to sell. He felt the business was the most valuable asset of the ranch and asked $125,000 for the Bar BC, but the Snake River Land Company did not want the business, just the land. An agreement was reached whereby Burt and his partners received $46,000 for 670 acres of land and a lease to operate the business for payment of taxes.[25] For most people, this would have been sufficient evidence of Burt's dedication to the cause, but the story did not end there.

Even before the sale of the Bar BC, Struthers Burt had lost some of his enthusiasm for dude ranching. He had been quietly searching for another piece of property within the valley where he could establish a simple residence. He found the property he wanted at the north end of the valley and completed the purchase soon after the sale of the Bar BC. Burt claimed he was unaware this new property (the Three Rivers Ranch) was within the project area and was surprised when he was again visited by Rockefeller's agents and asked to sell his land. It might have appeared to those unacquainted with Struthers Burt that the man was merely speculating with Rockefeller's money and trying to turn a quick profit. However, no evidence exists to indicate such a motivation. In fact, the evidence indicates the opposite. When informed that his newly purchased property was

Jackson Hole Historical Society and Museum p1958.2010.001

Jack L. Eynon sold his 160 acres to the Snake River Land Company for $12,000 in 1931. His testimony at the Senate hearings helped exonerate Rockefeller's land purchasing agents and their methods.

also within the project area, Burt sold the Three Rivers Ranch (140 acres) to the Snake River Land Company for $2,500 - the same price he paid for the land - plus a 50 year lease which contained a clause prohibiting commercial activity of any kind on the property. According to the lease, he had to pay the taxes on the land and a rental fee.[26] While Burt's testimony gave valuable historical background for the controversy, it did not provide the scandal Senator Carey had promised.

The next person to testify was J. L. Eynon, a long time resident of the valley. He sold his 160-acre ranch on Spread Creek to the Snake River Land Company in 1931 and then moved to Blackfoot, Idaho. Although there were several interesting aspects of Eynon's testimony, none of them supported Senator Carey's charges. Josephine Fabian recalled that one question had the reporters on the edge of their seats, but Eynon's answer was a disappointment to conspiracy seekers. Chairman Nye asked Eynon if he had been taken advantage of or if any pressure had been brought to bear in order to force him to sell his ranch. Eynon answered, *"If there was any pressure I put on the pressure."* Senator Norbeck then asked, *"Would your ranch sell for more or less at this time?"* Eynon answered, *"Less,"* adding, *"I would not give near what I got for it."* [27] (He received $12,000 for his ranch.)

wyomingtalesandtrails.com

The Elbo Ranch- "Home of the Hollywood Cowboy"
The Elbo Ranch became the example of how an individual land owner could affect the scenic values of the valley. Jim Manges sold 115 acres to Chester Goss, who established the ranch and proclaimed it the "Home of the Hollywood Cowboy." Goss, with his partners, built tourists cabins, rodeo grounds, a racetrack with grandstands, refreshment stands, a baseball diamond, and advertised the facility with billboards.

At one point Eynon provided a bit of humor for the committee. At issue was the question of why the upper valley was better for dude ranching than cattle ranching. Eynon pointed out the obvious fact that dudes *"...are easier wintered."* [28]

Another of the important aspects of Jack Eynon's testimony dealt with the motive of those people who for so many years had supported a movement to provide lasting protection for the valley. According to Eynon, the motive was a blend of altruism and self-service. The altruism was a sincere desire to save the beauty, wildlife and way of life for future generations to enjoy. The self-service part was to find a buyer for their land. The fact that many people had been unable to find a buyer for their land until Rockefeller became interested in the valley did not support Carey's charges of terrorism and coercion. Eynon's ranch had been on the market since 1921. Altruism is considerably more believable

when a touch of profit is involved.

After J. L. Eynon's testimony, the reporters calmed down, and the testimony of the witnesses proceeded. Pickett and members of the committee questioned each one, but in the four days of testimony no conspiracy, scandal or terrorism was revealed or documented. Some minor indiscretions were found, but neither the committee nor the reporters thought them significant.

Concerning the charges that a conspiracy had occurred between the Snake River Land Company, the National Park Service, and the General Land Office to harass homesteaders, Pickett was unable to make a case commensurate with Senator Carey's sensational allegations. He introduced a correspondence between Horace Albright, Kenneth Chorley, Arno B. Cammerer of the Park Service, and Ralph S. Kelley of the General Land Office. Pickett apparently believed these documents revealed an attempt to have the General Land Office deny patents to those people who were trying to homestead land in Jackson Hole. To the majority of those present, though, it appeared that Pickett had read more into the letters than actually existed and he had jumped to some inappropriate conclusions.

The letters showed that the purchasing agent for the Snake River Land Company, Robert E.

wyomingtalesandtrails.com
Racetrack and bleachers at the Elbo Ranch.

Miller, believed many of the pending applicants for homestead patents within the project area had not met the legal requirements for those patents. He also believed some of the applicants had filed entry claims solely for the purpose of land speculation, which was illegal. He recommended that the Snake River Land Company protest these applications and request that the General Land Office investigate each applicant to determine if they had, in fact, met the various requirements for a patented homestead.[29]

The motive for the Snake River Land Company's protests was obvious. There were, within the project area, 56 parcels of land which were subject to the General Land Office for various types of application approvals.[30] Some of the applications were for final approval, that is, the applicants claimed to have met all the requirements for a patent and wanted a clear title to the land. Others were for permission to move onto public land in order to meet the requirements for a patent. Miller especially wanted the latter group investigated. If there were any speculators, they would likely be in this group. Those people who were completing their homestead requirements would have started their homesteads before the purchasing program began. If for instance, a man filed for entry on a parcel of land under the Timber and Stone Act, and an investigation revealed no commercial trees or quarry sites existed on that parcel, the application would be denied. Or, if a grazing homestead were filed on land where no water and little grass existed, the application would be denied. If the application was rejected, the land would return to public domain which would place it under one of the Executive Orders withdrawing most of the public land within the valley from entry and obviating the need for the Snake River Land Company to pay the claimant to relinquish the claim or to purchase the land if the claimant eventually obtained a valid title.

A relinquishment was money paid to a person to abandon his uncompleted homestead and allow the land to revert to the federal government. If all the applications on file with the General Land Office were approved, the Snake River Land Company would have had to pay an estimated $235,206 for improvements and relinquishments.[31] Of that amount, over $200,000 would have been for relinquishments. Other testimony revealed that at the time of the hearing in 1933, the Snake River Land Company had paid $83,637 for relinquishments.[32]

None of the 17 letters obtained by Pickett and introduced in the hearing record, as exhibits 28 through 44, indicated a request by either the National Park Service or the Snake River Land Company that applicants meeting the requirements of the various Homestead Acts be denied their patent or entrance to their desired land. They requested only that these applicants be investigated to ensure the requirements of the laws had been met. The fact that the General Land Office agreed to review the designated applications did not, in the minds of the committee members, constitute a conspiracy, especially since some of the letters, introduced by Pickett, documented the approval of patents in the project area after the investigation request was received. At the request of the Park Service, the General Land Office investigated the 56 pending applications in

Jackson Hole Historical Society and Museum 1958.0498.001P
Lester Eynon and his winter mail sleigh.

Jackson Hole. All but nine were approved, and most of the denied applications were determined to be abandoned filings and were rightly disapproved. Only the Albert W. Gabbey application was deemed to have been inappropriately rejected.[33]

Albert Gabbey homesteaded 126 acres near String Lake in 1926. In 1927, he filed an application for an additional 236 contiguous acres under the "stock-raising" specifications of the Homestead Act. His second application was rejected for several reasons that the Senate committee found improper. The adverse report on the second application stated the identified acreage was not suitable for raising stock even though similar adjacent land previously had been approved for that purpose. Although the law allowed for an extension to the original homestead filing, the General Land Office also based their rejection on the fact that Gabbey's primary residence was on his initial filing (as required by law) and not in the area described in the extension filing. The committee members were not impressed by the contradictory and erroneous General Land Office requirement that Gabbey live in two locations at once. In Gabbey's case, the Homestead Act required the applicant live on the land identified in the initial filing until the patent was granted. He was allowed to apply for an extension prior to the granting of the patent

Jackson Hole Historical Society and Museum p1993.4829.001
Lida and Albert Gabbey

Albert W. Gabbey was inappropriately denied a patent to his homestead extension. Gabby and his wife, Lida, established the Square G Dude Ranch.

if the area sought was contiguous to the land upon which the original filing had been made.

Additionally, the Land Office erroneously determined that the extension area was not available for homesteading because of the July 7, 1928, Executive Order withdrawing certain lands in Jackson Hole from entry. They were incorrect in that the Executive Order cited did not include the land described in Gabbey's extension application. A different Executive Order, dated April 15, 1928, did include Gabbey's requested property, but neither the uncited correct order nor the incorrectly cited order were executed prior to Gabbey's application. Executive Orders of this nature typically were issued "subject to all existing valid claims." Gabbey's application, having been filed eight months prior to the appropriate withdrawal order, should have been considered a valid claim unless it was deemed incorrect or deficient in some manner other than for the erroneous reasons cited. Neither can the argument be made that Gabbey was filing for the purpose of speculating on the future opportunity to sell the land to the Snake River Land Company. First, the Rockefeller purchasing program had not yet

Jackson Hole Historical Society and Museum p1958.1340.001
The Elk, Wyoming post office and school were located at the present Moose Head Ranch.

been initiated. Second, Gabbey could have legally filed on as much as 640 acres, but he elected to seek only the land he thought he needed. A land speculator would have been more likely to seek the most property possible under the law.[34]*

Although Pickett tried, he was unable to establish a case supporting Senator Carey's other allegations against the National Park Service. Among the Park Service files, Pickett found correspondence that documented the participation of Sam Woodring, the Superintendent of Grand Teton National Park, in an attempt to have the mail route for the north end of the valley changed to the west side of the Snake River. Pickett introduced these letters into the hearing record as exhibits 63 and 65 believing they showed Woodring's attempt to pressure ranchers on the east side of the river to sell their land. At the time the change of the mail route was being considered, more people were settling on the west side of the Snake than on the east side. Also, the population on the east side was decreasing because settlers were selling to the Snake River Land Company and moving out of the area. The newer residents initiated the request for change of the existing mail route. As a result of questioning by both Carey and Pickett, it became obvious to Chairman Nye that the mail route controversy was merely a local squabble. Eventually, even Pickett had to admit the mail route had no relationship to the park expansion issue.[35]

Perhaps the most damaging piece of evidence Pickett uncovered concerning the Park Service, or its employees was found in the Snake River Land Company's files. This evidence was a letter, dated August 10, 1929, from Harold Fabian to Kenneth Chorley concerning a group of property owners in the Jenny Lake area. These people, evidently, decided to put up a united front against the Snake River Land Company, not for the purpose of retaining ownership of the land, but to obtain the exorbitant prices they were demanding. In the letter, Fabian noted, *"The Harold Brown, Altenreid, Ferry, Gibo and Elbo purchases have*

pretty well shaken the confidence of the standpatters and I am trying hard to keep the ball rolling at least long enough to clean up Jenny Lake." [36]

Fabian also informed Chorley that Homer Richards, who owned parcels 9, F and G, 44-116 on the Snake River Land Company purchasing map, might be the key to breaking the deadlock. At the beginning of the 1929 season, Richards asked $150,000 for his tourists cabins and land. During the summer, he lowered the price to $100,000 and by August was asking $35,000. Fabian, however, was willing to pay $25,000 and allow Richards to keep the buildings if he agreed to move them completely away from the project area. Fabian wrote, *"If I can do this, I think it will disintegrate this 'nest' at Jenny Lake and open the way for us to clean it up."* [37]

However, it was the last paragraph of the letter that Pickett found most revealing. Fabian stated:

> *I suggested to Sam Woodring that a change in the road at Jenny Lake would be very effective. Consequently, yesterday he went over there and tentatively selected a line for a new road which would throw the present collection of cabins and stores off the highway. He dropped just enough*

Jackson Hole Historical Society and Museum 1991.3552.001
Homer Richards at his gas station at Jenny Lake.

*It would seem reasonable that the evidence presented at the 1933 Senate hearing validating Gabbey's claim should have resulted in the prompt issuance of his patent. However, the Gabbeys would have to fight the Interior Department for an additional seven years before the Secretary of the Interior eventually ordered his patent issued in 1940.

The "nest" at Jenny Lake

The photo above shows the area Harold Fabian referred to as a nest of standpatters who were asking for more money than the Snake River Land Company wanted to pay.

information so that it would become public gossip. This, ... and the knowledge of the recent legislation giving the park power of condemnation, should help us get this problem solved.[38]

Thus, the implication was that the superintendent of Grand Teton National Park, Sam Woodring, conspired with Harold Fabian to encourage, in a devious manner, landowners to sell their property at prices lower than they might otherwise have accepted. When Harold Fabian was questioned about the incident, he expressed doubt that Woodring's actions had been of any assistance in the purchase of the property in question. However, he admitted that in hindsight, he did not *"...think it was a smart thing or a very good thing for any of us to do."* [39]

Later, when Sam Woodring was questioned about the incident, he denied any activity as described in Harold Fabian's letter. He said he had considered a new road at Jenny Lake, but the law creating Grand Teton National Park expressly prohibited the construction of new roads within the Park boundary. He also explained that stakes were placed on the west side of Jenny Lake that some people might have believed marked the site of a new road. The stakes, however, were placed by a Geological Survey crew while making a topographic map of the Teton Range.

In this, his most damaging expose of the Park Service during the hearing, Pickett established next to nothing. All he proved was that each man viewed the incident differently. Also, none of the former landowners that testified at the hearing, including Homer Richards, mentioned the proposed road as a reason for selling his property. So, while Sam Woodring, as a National Park Service employee, may have been suspected of acting improperly, there was very little evidence to substantiate the charge.*

Other charges against the Park Service were equally difficult to prove. Pickett appeared to have consistently reached conclusions by seeing only what he wished to see. In most cases he presented what apparently he believed to

---

*Sam Woodring would later resign his position as superintendent under allegations of moral misconduct not associated with the subject of this book. A lesser peak in the Teton Range that bears his name is still referred to as No Name Peak by some long time residents. The details of this incident have intentionally been omitted to avoid any embarrassment to living members of the families involved. The *Jackson Hole Courier* apparently felt that no First Amendment rights would be violated if the victim and the victim's family were spared a public examination of the incident. The *Courier's* position seems worth perpetuating. Additionally, the details of this incident were revealed to the author during a 1981 interview with Mardy Murie on the condition they not be published.

be damaging evidence only to find the committee's interpretation was not the same as his own. In fact, the evidence he presented when viewed more objectively and as a whole tended to exonerate rather than convict the accused.

For example, it was charged that the Snake River Land Company and the Park Service worked to delay the construction of a new road at Moran for the purpose of allowing the Snake River Land Company to purchase certain properties at a reduced price. This was, in reality, half-true.

In the Moran area, the Snake River Land Company was attempting to purchase commercial and developed properties first. This seemed logical since the tourist industry was growing rapidly within the valley and these properties appreciated faster than the undeveloped properties. The longer the Snake River Land Company waited, the more the developed properties would cost. Accordingly, the town of Moran was purchased rather early for $100,000. This gave them control over the majority of commercial activities in that area while they negotiated for the undeveloped property. It was during the negotiation process that the Snake River Land Company learned that a new road was planned for the north end of the valley. This new road would suddenly give some of the undeveloped land highway frontage and

thus it would become prime commercial property. The Snake River Land Company determined it would be worthwhile to try to have the location of the proposed road moved or, at least, have it delayed until they could complete the purchase of the affected land.

To prove the charge, Pickett introduced as evidence a number of letters into the hearing record as exhibits 10, 12, 13 and 14. The first letter showed that the Snake River Land Company's primary concern was with a particular landowner, Charlie Fesler. Kenneth Chorley wrote Harold Fabian stating, *"I quite agree with you that Fessler [sic] promises to be a real menace. ... Fessler [sic] is so well entrenched at the proposed road junction that it would no doubt be very expensive to buy him out. And from what I can see he is just going to operate and establish another Moran."* [40] In this same letter, Chorley suggested Fabian contact Horace Albright and see if he could help solve the problem of the road. Accordingly, Fabian wrote to Horace Albright, who gave the letter to Arno Cammerer, the acting director. Cammerer then wrote to Kenneth Chorley expressing his understanding of the situation, but he noted the proposed road was planned and funded by the Forest Service and existed completely outside the Park. He did not feel he could

Jackson Hole Historical Society and Museum 1993.4830.023-1

Town of Moran
The Snake River Land Company purchased the town of Moran for $100,000.

Jackson Hole Historical Society and Museum p1958.1026.001

Charlie Fesler's store at Moran.

interfere. He suggested they contact the appropriate Forest Service personnel to seek a solution.[41]

With the introduction of this letter, it became clear that the Park Service had declined to take an active role in this particular problem, and the charge of collusion between the Snake River Land Company and the Park Service to halt the construction of a new road near Moran was false. It might even have appeared that Pickett was trying to absolve the Park Service of involvement. However, the manner in which he questioned witnesses, and his phrasing of the questions demonstrated his belief in the damaging nature of the evidence.

Exhibit 14 revealed that the meeting* suggested by Arno Cammerer with the Bureau of Public Roads and the U.S. Forest Service resulted in an agreement to temporarily delay the start of construction of the proposed road.[42] The Senate Committee did not find the conduct of any of the agencies or the Snake River Land Company to be unethical, primarily because the delay was not indefinite but temporary. That is, the Snake River Land Company was given a few more months in which to purchase the land in question. At the end of that time, the bids for the road would be advertised whether or not the land had been acquired.

Jackson Hole Historical Society and Museum p1958.0181.001

The Snake River Land Company may have considered Fesler a "menace," but he was well-liked by most valley residents.

Another accusation against the Park Service and Horace Albright concerned the granting of concessions within Grand Teton National Park and interference with the granting of concessions within the Forest Service domain around the Park. Two charges were commonly cited by the Park's accusers.

One dealt with the granting of a transportation concession to the Teton Transportation Company while the Park Service rejected a permit to a local transportation company owned by Eugene Harris.

*Attending this meeting were Fabian and Chorley, Mr. Bishop, who was chief of the Division of Construction of the Bureau of Public Roads, Associate Forester Sherman of the Forest Service, and Arthur Demaray of the National Park Service.

Pickett quickly dropped the subject when testimony revealed that Harris had refused to accept any permit which provided for anything less than an exclusive right. He was unwilling to operate on a competitive basis. Also, Harris seemed unwilling to meet the minimum service standards required by the Park Service. On the other hand, the Teton Transportation Company had applied for, qualified for, and obtained a nonexclusive short-term permit. The incident received publicity because Harris had contacted most of the western states' congressional delegations, claiming to be a constituent, and requesting relief from the inequities of the Park Service and the Teton Transportation Company.[43]

Concerning charges that Albright, and thus the National Park Service, interfered with the issuance of permits within the Forest Service domain, Pickett produced little evidence. His evidence took the form of two letters that became exhibits 20 and 21, but like his other evidence, the testimony of witnesses explained away the sinister plots he perceived in the letters.

It was a standing policy for the Forest Service to issue short-term (one to two year) special use permits for commercial activities within portions of their domain being considered for eventual inclusion in a national park. This policy provided, in the event an area became a park, for the easy control of commercial activities by the Park Service. If the Park Service took over the jurisdiction of one of these areas, it could easily renew permits for establishments offering a quality service to the public if they were deemed appropriate. Likewise, a poorly operated and/or inappropriate activity could be eliminated in a relatively short time by refusing to renew the permit.

The evidence produced by Pickett dealt with one of these year-to-year permits in the possession of a man named Olie Warner. Warner's special use permit provided for a tourist camp on the

shore of Jackson Lake about a mile and a half south of Moran. Warner found two men, George Stegner and W. L. Payne, who wanted to invest between $10,000 and $15,000 in his business; however, these men felt that such an investment warranted a longer lease. Accordingly, they applied for a 15-year permit promising to make a variety of improvements including a boat dock.

Payne then suggested to Harold Fabian that the Teton Lodge Company contract with Warner to operate the lodge's boat tours because they (Warner and Payne) already had a 15-year lease on a proposed boat docking facility. Payne also pointed out that if they did not get the contract, they would simply go into competition with the Teton Lodge Company. Fabian was considering giving them the contract when he learned that Payne had lied and the long-term lease had not yet been granted. Upon further investigation, Fabian found that the local Forest Service people seemed unaware that the area in question was being considered for park status.

Fabian's letter to Albright (exhibit 20) explained the situation and expressed the opinion that long-term leases would be unwise at that time. He stated:

I think it most inadvisable to have the situation there complicated by any of these

Jackson Hole Historical Society and Museum p1958.2341.001

W. C. Lawrence and his touring bus in front of Jackson Lake Lodge. The National Park Service often contracted with the Yellowstone Transportation Company for vehicles and drivers when Senate or House committees were visiting Jackson Hole.

long-term permits. I think it much preferable to confine them all to year-to-year basis (including our own at Elk Island). If Olie Warner is permitted to go in there for a long term and build substantial improvements, he will then have substantial rights which will have to be recognized. I think you should go into this situation pretty carefully, not only on account of this particular man [Payne], but the forest departments should have an understanding concerning this entire area and not grant any other long-term permits for any purposes.[44]

On June 18, 1930, Horace Albright wrote to Major R. Y. Stuart, Chief Forester of the U.S. Forest Service. In this letter, Albright restated the policy concerning special use permits for land under consideration for future legislative action. He explained his understanding of the situation concerning the Warner permit and asked Stuart to advise him *"...as to the status of this matter and whether or not there has been any change in the policy of the Forest Service in reference to*

S. N. Leek Collection, American Heritage Center, University of Wyoming
ah03138_1145

The first school house at Moran

granting permits in the neighborhood of Jackson Lake." Albright also requested that the *"...status quo ante be maintained..."* and that the policy in reference to lands withdrawn in aid of park legislation be continued.[45]

With the exception of Senator Carey, the committee failed to see any improprieties in either letter. Senator Carey and Mr. Pickett saw interference on the part of the Park Service in the issuance of permits by the Forest Service– interference in the right of a man to make investments and improve his business. In accordance with the charge that the Snake River Land Company was trying to monopolize the concessions in the area, they believed Harold Fabian was motivated by a desire to eliminate competition. The remainder of the committee felt the only issue in both letters was a question of compliance with an existing policy concerning the issuance of short-term or long-term leases. Based on the policy in question, because other permittees had been refused long-term leases, it would have been improper to issue Mr. Warner anything other than a short-term permit.[46]

After the Warner permit issue had been cleared away, Pickett introduced another piece of evidence that resulted in a sharp exchange of words between Senator Norbeck and Senator Carey, followed by an exchange between Senator

Grand Teton National Park GRTE 430 02 00271

Members of the 1933 Senate Public Lands Subcommittee investigating allegations of conspiracy by Rockefeller and the National Park Service view the valley and the Tetons from Hendricks Point.

Norbeck and Mr. Pickett. The evidence was a telegram from Albright to Fabian (exhibit 22) which read as follows:

> *Harold P. Fabian,*
> *Congressional friends of parks without referring matter to me contemplate holding up Casper Alcova reclamation project until satisfactory agreement is obtained from Wyoming delegation regarding Teton project. This for your information and comment.*
> *Albright.*[47]

Bureau of Reclamation via Wikimedia Commons

The Casper-Acova/ Kendrick Project

The Casper-Alcova Project was a reclamation project in Natrona County in which Senator Kendrick had a great deal of interest. He actively pursued the project until his death in 1933, several months after the hearings on Senate Resolution 226. He supposedly supported the project to show his appreciation to Natrona County for their support during the 1928 election. Kendrick carried the county over Congressman Winter, a Natrona County resident, by two votes. The project was ill-fated because there was not enough unappropriated water to operate the project. The attempt by Wyoming to utilize water already appropriated by Nebraska and Colorado resulted in court battles lasting ten years and costing the state more than $135,000. After 1937, it was called the Kendrick Project. The Senator had estimated that one-quarter of Wyoming would benefit from the project, but by 1961, less than 21,000 acres had been irrigated.[48]

The exchange of words began when Senator Carey implied that the above telegram was proof that Horace Albright was trying to coerce the Wyoming delegation into accepting the Teton Park expansion. Carey stated, *"...Mr. Albright has no right to use Casper-Alcova to force us to do anything."* Senator Norbeck pointed out that so far no one had produced any evidence to show that Albright was doing that. The telegram only reported that others might do it. Carey asked, *"Well, then, how does he find out about it?"* Norbeck replied, *"How do you find out about things in Washington? It is gossip all over. You read the stuff in newspapers and you hear it all over. ...why not be fair about it?"* [49] Whereupon Senator Carey was silenced for a while.

Senator Norbeck then turned his attention to Pickett and stated, *"I think this is getting to be no better than a justice of the peace proceeding. These inferences, this innuendo, on the part of the counsel of a committee, I never have seen the like, Mr. Chairman...."* Pickett responded, *"That is about the second time you have referred to that, Senator."* Norbeck replied, *"Yes; and it isn't the last time, either. If this continues, I am going to make a report to Congress on it."* [50] Senator Norbeck's point was understood by the committee and the press. He would not tolerate the continued conviction by inference.

Other data concerning the activities of the Snake River Land Company was also presented

to the committee. As of the summer of 1933, the Snake River Land Company had purchased 32,423 acres for which it paid $1,300,691. It also paid $83,637 for the relinquishment to the United States Government of 2,087 acres. Additionally, the Snake River Land Company agreed to purchase another 799 acres, pending the clearing of titles, for $15,981. The total expenditure amounted to $1,400,310 for 35,310 acres. This computes to an average per acre price of $39.66.[51]

The committee also learned that Wyoming law required, for tax purposes, that real property be assessed at its true value. The land that the Snake River Land Company had purchased and agreed to purchase for $1,316,672 was assessed, in 1932, at $521,037. The Snake River Land Company paid $12,969 in taxes on the property it had purchased that same year.

In 1927, before the Snake River Land Company began its purchases, Teton County received $9,830 from tax collections on the same properties.[52]

Other data showed that of the 138 properties purchased by the Snake River Land Company, 57 parcels comprising 12,576 acres were abandoned prior to 1928 when the Rockefeller purchases began. Some of these properties reportedly had been abandoned for up to 20 years. The taxes on these properties were delinquent when purchased and were paid by the Snake River Land Company. This information contradicted the charge that the Snake River Land Company had placed Teton County in financial jeopardy by decreasing the value of the property and thereby decreasing the tax revenue.[53] It was true that taxable "improvements" had been removed from much of the property purchased by the Snake River Land Company. However, not all of the improvements were destroyed. Some were sold and moved to other parts of the valley and therefore remained on the tax roles. The above figure reflecting the increase in taxes collected over a five-year period is undoubtedly due to the collection of taxes on property that was previously in default. However, the primary tax consideration in this issue was not how much revenue was collected in 1932, but the lack of revenue the County would receive from that property if Rockefeller's lands were removed from the tax roles through donation to the federal government.

~

Other portions of the hearing concentrated on the conduct of the Snake River Land Company during the purchasing program. Senator Carey and Mr. Pickett seemed most interested in whether or not Rockefeller's agents used threats of force or possible condemnation to coerce people to sell. The testimony revealed no threats of force. However, the wording of the threat of

Jackson Hole Historical Society and Museum bc0140
Jackson State Bank, late 1920s
Robert Miller second from left

In March 1933, President Roosevelt was inaugurated in the middle of a bank panic. He declared a "bank holiday" and ordered all of the nation's banks closed. Miller, having maintained a financially healthy bank, defied the President and kept his bank open. There were no "bank runs" or "bank panics" in Jackson Hole.

possible condemnation was important in determining if there was any impropriety in the presentation. For example, it would have been legal for a purchasing agent to inform the settler of the government's right to condemn land, and that it might be exercised in the future. That would be a statement of fact. On the other hand, it would be improper to imply that the Snake River Land Company had the right to condemn the land if the settler refused to sell.

The testimony during this phase of the hearing was presented to demonstrate the methods used by the Snake River Land Company and its agents. The Snake River Land Company was allowed to present its point of view concerning controversial incidents or questionable methods that were revealed during the testimony.

During the hearing, Pickett would sometimes restate a witness's answer so as to give the response more clarity. Frequently, though, this restated version sounded more damaging than did the original response. At those times, Senator

199

Nye, Senator Norbeck, Senator Adams or Senator Ashurst would ask additional questions which clarified the witness's intent.

At other times during the testimony, the Senators would interrupt in order to have various terms defined or phrases explained. One such instance occurred when a witness referred to "winning his bet with Uncle Sam." It was explained that the saying was common among homesteaders. It derived from a book entitled *Starvation Against One Hundred and Sixty Acres*. The contention of the book was that homesteading was a gamble because much of the land upon which the government encouraged settlement was unfit to support life. The government, in effect, bet the homesteader 160 acres that he could not live on the land for three years.*

Another unfamiliar phrase to the Senators was "booking up." This referred, generally, to bookkeeping, but more specifically in this case to the record kept by the homesteader of activities on the land. Not all homesteaders kept a record, but the smart ones did. It was their memory and their proof of compliance with the homestead regulations.

"Dickering" also had to be defined. The term was used in the context of negotiating a price for a piece of land. Senator Ashurst eventually defined it for the record as *"...the preliminary conversations, and offers and rejections of offers and all that leads up to a deal."* Richard Winger agreed with the definition and stated, *"I might say that probably no community on earth is so peculiar in its dickering as this particular community. There was argument and bluffing both, and on both sides, and plenty of it. Every settler that I dickered with, as a rule, had the best place in the valley, and they had the front seat in the amphitheater, or the best view of the Tetons, or something of that kind. I bluffed them and they bluffed me ...."* [54]

As to the actual testimony, the committee could find no evidence to support the charges of unfair methods on the part of the Snake River Land Company. This was not to say that some settlers did not have complaints. The complaints, however, did not deal with deception or illegal methods.

William L. Stilson testified that he sold his 177-acre ranch on Spread Creek for $6,195. He said the reason he sold was that everyone else seemed to be selling and leaving the country and he feared the loss of the school for his children and the loss of mail service. He stated that someone had mentioned the possibility of condemnation by a federal agency in the future. Richard

LaVerne and William "Billy" Stilson

William Stilson

William Stilson sold his 177-acre ranch on Spread Creek to the Snake River Land Company for $6,195.

---

*The first homestead act was passed in 1862. Prior to 1912, homesteaders were required to live on the land for five years, although Civil War veterans of the northern persuasion (after 1872) could deduct their military time from the tenure requirement. In 1912, Congress amended the 1909 Homestead Act reducing the tenure requirement to three years and allowing a five-month annual absence from the land.

Winger had encouraged him to sell quickly because the Snake River Land Company might stop buying property in his area. When he was asked who informed him of the possibility of condemnation, he said he was not sure, and while it might have been Richard Winger he would not swear to it.[55]

Richard Winger, while giving his version of the Stilson purchase, pointed out that everything he told Stilson was true. In fact, the Snake River Land Company did cease its purchases in that area in order to concentrate its efforts on the west side of the Snake River. Winger gave the committee some other reasons why he would not have taken advantage of Stilson. Winger stated first that Stilson was his friend. Second, before Winger went into real estate, he had been the Justice of the Peace. As the Justice of the Peace, he had conducted the Stilson marriage ceremony. Third, Stilson had married the daughter of Jack Eynon, Winger's best friend.[56]

Jesse P. Chambers testified that Richard Winger offered him $25 an acre for his 161 acres in the Spread Creek district. He stated that he refused the offer and that no suggestion of condemnation or threat of any kind had been made to him. Winger simply left him alone. At a later date, Chambers decided to sell and asked Winger to make another offer. According to Chambers, Winger said, *"That is just like you; how many times have I tried to buy you out?"* Chambers replied, *"I don't see that that is any difference, particularly; I am willing to sell now, and if you want to buy now is your chance."* To which Winger said, *"Just consider that offer cut 50 percent."*[57] The implication in Chambers' complaint was that Winger cut his offer for the land in half out of spite, and Chambers refused to sell his land for $12.50 per acre. At the time of the hearing, he still owned the land.

Winger's version was substantially the same as Chambers. The main difference was in the reasons for Winger's 50 percent offer. Winger maintained Chambers, during the "dickering" process, held out for $30 per acre, but the Snake River

Jackson Hole Historical Society and Museum 1992.4401.028

The Chambers family: (L-R) Lel, Jim, Ed, Rene, Jess, Andy, Pearl.

The Chambers family homesteaded on Mormon Row and worked at almost anything that legally aided in their survival in Jackson Hole. They raised grain and cattle and delivered the mail. The extended family holdings composed a fair portion of the Mormon Row area. Andy constructed one of the earliest windmills in the valley to generate electricity for his house.

Land Company payment schedule, which Robert E. Miller set and Winger had to follow, provided $25 per acre for Chambers' land. He also stated that the Snake River Land Company wanted to cut the schedule for the land in question, but he was able to maintain the $25 figure because the negotiations were in progress. When the negotiations ended, the Snake River Land Company felt no obligation to maintain the offer. Winger recalled for the committee, *"I had used my influence for some time to maintain that value at $25, but it was subsequently cut 50 percent. The coincidence of it was that the cut was made the day before I saw Mr. Chambers. We had not talked about the matter for some time, but the day after the cut was made he spoke to me in front of the Community Market, or in my car, and he said: 'I have decided to accept the 25', and I said: 'You would do that'– thinking of the coincidence– and I said: 'Just yesterday, Mr. Chambers, the price on your place was reduced and I am unable to pay you more than 50 percent.'"*[58] The 50 percent cut in the offer for Chamber's land appeared to have been beyond Winger's control.

Fred J. Topping testified that Richard Winger tried to buy his wife's homestead- 120 acres on

Spread Creek- but he (Winger) never offered what the place was worth. He also stated that no threats were made and all of Winger's dealings with him had been fair.[59]

Winger did not contradict Topping's testimony. Instead, he explained to the committee that the Toppings worked so hard on the place that he could not get the payment schedule increased fast enough to stay up with the improvements. As a

Jackson Historical Society and Museum 19580264001p
Eva and Fred Topping

The Topping's land, the Moose Head Ranch, while no longer in their possession, is still privately owned land within Grand Teton National Park. It is operated as a guest ranch and has a reputation for first class service. Eva Sanford came to Jackson Hole in 1924 to take the position of school teacher at Elk, Wyoming. She filed for a homestead on 120 acres just south of Spread Creek in 1927. Later that same year she married Fred Topping and together they worked to make the necessary improvements for obtaining title to the property. However, in 1930, when she applied for the title, the General Land Office, because of Executive Order 4685 withdrawing certain lands in Jackson Hole from entry, and because of the request by the Snake River Land Company that patent claims be carefully examined, delayed issuing the patent pending an investigation. Providing credence to Richard Winger's testimony regarding the Topping's industrious nature, the General Land Office inspector found four completed log cabins and a fifth under construction, a log barn, a cow barn, a garage, three structures he called chicken coops, but were probably part of Eva's mink and fox farm, and fencing in excess of two miles. Additionally, the Toppings had nearly 20 acres under cultivation and had 20 head of livestock. Eva received her Patent (No. 1052322) in 1931.[61]

202

result, he was never able to get together on a price with the Toppings.[60]

Edward Ketchum Smith, also known as Roan Horse Smith, was not as complimentary of Richard Winger or the Snake River Land Company. However, he was perhaps the most colorful character who testified before the committee.

Smith had homesteaded 160 acres near Jenny Lake. After he had received his title, he deeded a half interest in the homestead to a brother who was living with him. Life, evidently, was not too difficult for the Smiths. Pickett asked Smith how they made a living and Smith replied, *"We worked for the Forest Service when we felt like it, fished when we felt like it, and worked on the homestead when we felt like it."* When Smith was asked if he was in need of money when he sold the land, he said, *"We wasn't too flush, but we wasn't wanting for anything. We had horses, cows, chickens, and pigs and dogs, and tobacco money, and that is all we cared for."*[60]

According to Smith, the negotiations for his land spanned two years and were conducted by two people, a Mrs. Harrison, who was a partner in the real estate business with Winger, and then later, with Winger himself. When Smith was asked if the government's right of condemnation had been presented to him, he replied that both Harrison and Winger had talked about it. Smith was

Jackson Hole Historical Society and Museum 1958.2557.001
Eva Topping's fox farm

unhappy with the deal he and his brother eventually made with Winger; they had wanted $25,000 for the land, but the most they could get was $21,600. It was Smith's contention that Winger had bluffed his brother with the talk about condemnation. He maintained he would never have accepted Winger's price had his brother not been afraid of a lower price Winger said the government might give them. While Senator Carey and Mr. Pickett obviously believed there was something inappropriate about the suggestion of possible government condemnation, the majority of the committee seemed more concerned with whether or not Winger had misconstrued the law providing for the power of condemnation, and if the settler had availed himself of legal advice on the issue.

Winger never denied the charges that he mentioned the possibility of condemnation. In fact, he testified that he often carried a copy of the law with him for the settlers to read.* Since the law existed, and since the possibility of condemnation was real, especially for those landowners close to the Park boundary, Winger did not appear to be taking advantage of the settlers. If a settler had been the subject of a condemnation proceeding, the government appraisers would probably have valued the land according to its homestead status; that is, its value as grazing or farming land. Therefore, the government's offer might well have been substantially lower than what the Snake River Land Company offered.

Even Roan Horse Smith testified that the Snake River Land Company's offer was very fair for farmland. He had asked for more because he felt his land was *"...the most valuable piece of property in the park, or anywhere else in this piece of country."* [63]

Winger's version of this purchase was slightly different from that of Ed Smith. Winger stated that the Smith brothers received $21,600 based on a purchase schedule of $135 per acre. He also stated that the Smiths requested and received the privilege of remaining on the property for one year. As a condition for granting the privilege, the Smiths were to pay the property taxes for that year. However, they defaulted on the tax payment and the Snake River Land Company made the payment.

Additionally, Winger produced two letters from the Snake River Land Company files which appeared to contradict Smith's testimony that he did not want to sell and that Winger's talk of condemnation had forced the sale. Both letters were

Jackson Hole Historical Society and Museum p1958.1666.001
Edward K. Smith homestead near Jenny Lake

Jackson Hole Historical Society and Museum 2004.0111.203

Edward K. "Roan Horse" Smith

Edward Smith and his brother, Lew, sold their 160 acres near Jenny Lake to the Snake River Land Company for $21,600. Edward testified that they would not have sold at that price except that Richard Winger had frightened his brother with talk of possible condemnation by the Park Service.

---

*This was the legislation passed in 1930 providing appropriations to Grand Teton National Park, among others, to acquire property for the purpose of simplifying boundaries. (Discussed in Chapter Eight.)**

from Harold Fabian to Richard Winger. Fabian informed Winger that Malin E. Wilson, a close friend and prominent lawyer in Salt Lake City, Utah had approached him. Without fee, Wilson was representing a third Smith brother who had expressed his brothers' desire to sell their Jackson Hole property, but were afraid they would not receive the most money possible. Wilson, because of his friendship to both groups, was attempting to get the parties together for their mutual benefit. He believed the Smiths would sell if he could assure them that the price offered was all they could hope to get from the Snake River Land Company.

In the first letter, dated November 27, 1929, Fabian wrote:

> *I note on your new schedules that you have a maximum figure of $21,600 for the Roan Horse Smith place, on the basis of $135 an acre. Do you think we should fairly offer him that price or can we in fairness make a lower offer? In any event, whatever price I offer Wilson must be the final one and under no circumstances must we thereafter offer any more in case our offer through Wilson is not accepted. Wilson will absolutely rely on my statement that whatever offer we make is the maximum which the Smiths can get and my word to him must be kept.*[64]

In the second letter, dated December 5, 1929, Fabian told Winger that the offer of $135 an acre had been made and that the Smiths had been instructed to contact him (Winger) to complete the deal. Winger testified that within a few days of his receipt of the second letter, the Smiths approached him and said they were ready to sell.[65]

Briefly, Charles W. Huff, D. B. Sheffield, and J. D. Ferrin testified that their experiences with the Snake River Land Company had been good and they were satisfied with the money they had received. Pickett's further questioning of Ferrin, in addition to not being helpful to his cause, also proved to be embarrassing.

As a result of questioning by the committee members and Pickett, Ferrin described the stock raising industry in Jackson Hole. Like the industry elsewhere, there were ups and downs, but Ferrin

Jackson Hole Historical Society and Museum 1958.2187.001
J. D. "Si" Ferrin, 1904

testified that ranching was generally a successful venture in the valley. Pickett had in his possession a copy of the petition Ferrin had circulated in the north end of the valley in 1925 (see Chapter Six) which contained the sentence, *"We have tried stock raising and from our experience have become convinced and firmly believe that this region will find its highest use as a playground, and in that way will eventually become the greatest wealth-producing region in the State."*

Based upon that sentence, Pickett concluded that the petition stated that stock raising was unsuccessful, and he thought he had caught Ferrin in a lie. The petition stated they had tried stock raising; it did not say it was unsuccessful. Instead of asking Ferrin to explain the apparent contradiction, Pickett began asking questions designed to make the contradiction a part of the hearing record and to enable him to introduce the petition as an exhibit to impugn the testimony of a pro-park extension witness. Pickett used this technique of questioning a witness on a subject and then presenting evidence he thought would contradict the testimony throughout the hearing. It was largely this technique which had caused the confrontations between Pickett and Senator Norbeck. Norbeck was the only member of the committee who was not a lawyer. He was a well driller by trade and while such techniques might be commonplace in a court of law, he felt Pickett's methods and "legal tricks" were devious and unbecoming of a Senate hearing.

Pickett used complex sentences and asked compound questions. He asked Ferrin, *"Did you, during the year of 1925, sign a petition and take the same to Casper, a petition asking for the extension of the park down into this country, and stating as a reason that you had tried the cattle raising business and found it unsuccessful?"* Because of the last part of the question, Ferrin could only answer in the negative. He said, *"No, sir; not a petition of that kind. I didn't sign it. I signed a petition and took it to Casper, but not the way you have described it."*[66] Then Pickett, sure of his case, introduced the petition into the record as exhibit 46.

Ferrin tried to explain that the petition did not say that ranching was unsuccessful, only that the land was better for wildlife and recreation. Pickett, evidently, did not grasp the difference because the following conversation ensued:

Senator Adams: *"What has it got to do with this hearing?"*
Pickett: *"As I recall the testimony of this witness he testified that he found the ranching business very successful."*
Senator Adams: *"Yes; that is his testimony."*
Pickett: *"And he is the signer of a petition that he found it very unsuccessful."*
Senator Adams: *"I assume you are challenging his veracity and, of course, he is not on trial."*[67]

At that point, Fabian interrupted the hearing to assure the committee of Ferrin's integrity and asked that someone else be allowed to handle the questioning of the witness. Senator Carey wanted Pickett to continue with the questioning, but Senators Norbeck and Nye took over and Pickett was not given a chance to ask additional questions of the witness. Senator Norbeck focused on the confusing sentence and repeated it for the committee. Ferrin stated, *"He asked me if I didn't take that petition over there, and tell them that the stock raising was a failure."* Nye responded, *"The petition doesn't say that at all."* Ferrin explained, *"No; the petition don't say that, and that's the reason I told him I didn't take no such petition."*[68]

Under careful questioning, Ferrin revealed the origins of the petition. Senator Nye remarked, *"Then this whole program that now is so nearly completed was really started long before, not by the Snake River Land Co., but ..."* Ferrin interrupted, *"Oh, heavens, no."* Senator Nye continued, *"In other words, long before the Snake River Land Co. or Mr. Rockefeller became interested, you folks, including yourself, had conceived this general program."* Ferrin confirmed Senator Nye's observation and remarked, *"The neighbors had been fighting one another over it right along for years."*[69]

Another area of the investigation dealt with the relationship between the Snake River Land Company and the so-called "Teton Companies" listed in Senate Resolution 226. These were the Teton Investment Company, the Teton Hotel Company, the Teton Transportation Company, and the Jackson Lake Lodge Company. It was alleged that Rockefeller controlled the companies and that he was attempting to establish a monopoly to control all the concession rights within and around Grand Teton National Park. The hearing revealed that the origins and histories of these companies were not as nefarious as some park opponents had alleged.

Harrision Crandall:Photo: Jackson Hole Historical Society and Museum BC.0352
The second Teton Lodge, like the first Teton Lodge, was consumed by fire.

When the Snake River Land Company purchased the Teton Lodge and the town of Moran, a decision had to be made whether to tear down the buildings or repair them and allow operations to continue. It was decided to let the lodge remain, for several reasons. One, the lodge had been there for quite a long time, and the traveling public had come to expect accommodations and services in that area. It was true that another hotel, the Jackson Lake Lodge (formerly the Amoretti Inn) existed close by, but it catered to a rather affluent clientele, not the general public. Second, eliminating the services at Moran would not eliminate the need for those services and new establishments would spring up along the highways on previously undeveloped land that had yet to be purchased. This was not desirable because it would create the type of developments the Snake River Land Company was trying to clean up. At least at Moran, the commercial activity was concentrated in one area.

Even though the decision was made to rehabilitate the Teton Lodge, Chorley did not think the Snake River Land Company should be in the hotel business. It was, therefore, determined that Fabian should try to locate someone to lease and operate the facility. Fabian had in mind a respected acquaintance, J. H. Rayburn, who at the time was managing the Newhouse Hotel in Salt Lake City.

Fabian approached Rayburn and convinced him to take a look at the place. Rayburn later recalled:

I went to Moran with Mr. Fabian to look the place over. I was not favorably impressed with it. It was pretty old, pretty well run down, lacked proper sewage facilities and was unfavorably located. It was a short, seasonal operation with high transportation costs for supplies. I concluded it would not justify the time and attention which I would have to give it. I so told Mr. Fabian and returned to Salt Lake.[70]

Later, Fabian approached Rayburn again and advised him that M. F. Daum, the assistant superintendent of Yellowstone National Park was willing to resign his position with the Park Service and manage the Teton Lodge if Rayburn would direct and supervise it. Rayburn expressed his hesitancy as follows, *"Fabian's ideas about it were all right from an idealistic point of view, but the business management of it was going to rest on me, and I knew that whoever became financially interested in it would expect me to make it successful no matter how much they might be interested in a creditable operation and the preservation of a scenic area."*[71]

Jackson Hole Historical Society and Museum P1958.1647.001
The third Teton Lodge
In the 1930s, horses were still as common as automobiles around the community of Moran, at least in the summer. In winter, snowshoes, skis, and dog sleds were more common.

Jackson Hole Historical Society and Museum p1992.4181.001

Teton Lodge Waitresses, 1927

206

Eventually, Rayburn agreed to supervise the project if certain conditions could be met. First, Rayburn wanted Fabian's help, as a lawyer, setting up the organization. Second, the Snake River Land Company would have to advance the money necessary to rehabilitate the lodge. Third, the Snake River Land Company would have to grant a ten-year lease (they had offered a five-year lease). Fourth, Rayburn felt some assurance was necessary from the Park Service, that if Moran were included within Grand Teton National Park, the lodge could continue to operate. Fifth, he wanted some assurance that neither the Union Pacific Railroad Company nor the Yellowstone Park Hotel Company contemplated establishing large resorts in the area.

Fabian agreed to help; the ten-year lease was approved, and Albright stated a willingness to allow the operation a franchise if it complied with park standards and conformed to park regulations. Rayburn satisfied himself there was no danger from the Union Pacific or the Yellowstone Park Hotel Company, and the Snake River Land Company advanced $35,000 to put the lodge in good operating condition.

With the conditions met, Fabian and Rayburn began seeking investors. Fabian and his law partner contributed $3,500 as did Rayburn and eight others. Another man contributed $500 making a total of $35,500 with which to begin the project. They wanted to include men from Wyoming and Idaho, but they were disappointed in the response from those states. Only one Idahoan, G. G. Wright of Idaho Falls, purchased a share of the venture. In Wyoming, P. W. Spaulding of Evanston put up $1,500, Richard Winger of Jackson paid $1,000, Bruce Porter also of Jackson, paid $3,000, and C. R. Van Vleck subscribed to the project in the amount of $3,500 but he never paid the money. Lester G. Baker and John McDermott from Kemmerer, each subscribed for $1,000 worth of stock, but neither man paid his note.[72]

On January 4, 1930, the Teton Investment Company was formed with $47,500 of invested capital and 475 shares of stock, without par value,

were issued. The company held the stock of those individuals who had subscribed but had not paid their money. Since all the money was needed for supplies, equipment, business expenses, and additional repairs not covered by the Snake River Land Company advance, it was decided to pay for the first year's legal expenses with stock. Fabian's firm agreed to perform these services on that basis.*

At the beginning, Harold Fabian was a director and officer of the Teton Investment Company, but after the organization process was completed, he resigned. He continued, of course, to give advice and to use his influence and contacts in aid of the project, but he was not Rockefeller's man in the Teton Companies.

The Teton Investment Company was a Utah company and never applied for permission to conduct business in any other state. It was merely a holding company. The Teton Lodge Company, although a Utah company, had qualified to conduct business in Wyoming. All of its stock was held by the Teton Investment Company. It was soon realized that the hotel would need adequate and reliable transportation for its guests between the railroad at Victor, Idaho and Moran. Fabian's investigation revealed the existing bus service was not acceptable because of the equipment and the reputation of the operator, Eugene Harris. C. R. Van Vleck recommended a friend who had recently sold his transportation company to the Union Pacific Railroad. This man, Howard Hout, agreed to a conference to discuss the proposed service, but Rayburn recalled that Hout *"...on learning that the service we had in mind contemplated first class motor bus equipment to make only one round trip a day between Moran and Victor- twice a day crossing Teton Pass- ... wasted no time in telling us that he was not interested in it."* [73] With no other viable alternatives, it was decided to form the Teton Transportation Company. This company was also formed in the state of Utah and qualified to operate in both Wyoming and Idaho. It received its transportation certificates from the Public Service Commissions

*350 shares were issued to the firm of Fabian and Clendenin. Of that stock, 20 shares each were issued to Imer Pett and John Fitzpatrick for services and time contributed and ten shares were given to Fabian's secretary, Miss Josephine Cunningham, for the same reason.

Harrision Crandall Photo: Jackson Hole Historical Society and Museum 20050023127
Teton Transportation Company's new bus.

of both states and a franchise from the Park Service. It purchased a new bus for $5,651 and, like the Teton Lodge Company, the Teton Investment Company held all its stock.

With the exception of Fabian's involvement with both the Snake River Land Company and the Teton Investment Company, there was little to connect the two companies. There was a lease agreement between the Snake River Land Company and the Teton Lodge Company, but there was nothing unscrupulous about the contract. The lease provided for a ten-year duration and an advance of $35,000. The advance was to be repaid in seven yearly installments of $5,000 each. Also, the Snake River Land Company was to receive 6 percent of Teton Lodge Company's gross receipts from all of its operations. The lease included the right to operate stores and gas stations at Jenny Lake and Menor's Ferry Bridge. The lease did not require the Teton Lodge Company to purchase its gas from Standard Oil or any other company.* Additionally, the lease granted

an option allowing the Teton Lodge Company to purchase, at any time during the term of the lease, the buildings and equipment for $100,000. If the option were exercised, any payments made to the Snake River Land Company according to the above provisions would be applied against the $100,000.[74]

It was eventually revealed that in addition to the $35,000 advanced by the Snake River Land Company, the Teton Lodge Company spent $46,578 on buildings and equipment at Moran bringing the total cost of renovation to $81,578. Rayburn maintained that 85 percent of this amount was paid to Jackson Hole firms and individuals. He also pointed out that the 1930 taxes on the Moran property, assessed before the improvements, were $468. In 1932, Teton County received $1,401 in taxes from the lodge.[75]

One other situation arose whereby the Snake River Land Company and the Teton Investment Company came into contact. This situation also involved Jackson Lake Lodge, Inc. Jackson Lake

---

*One of the persistent rumors concerning Rockefeller's operations in the valley relates to the family association with Standard Oil. The rumor had Rockefeller requiring all gas stations within Grand Teton National Park to be Standard Oil affiliates. None of the agreements between the Park Service and Rockefeller, nor any of his corporations associated with Grand Teton National Park, nor any donations of land or money to the Park contains a requirement or suggestion of any specific brand of gasoline.

Lodge was owned by a group of Wyoming citizens who wished to sell their company to the Snake River Land Company. However, Jackson Lake Lodge, Inc. operated its facility on government land through a Forest Service lease. It owned only one acre of land. The Snake River Land Company did not want to buy the business, and since the government already controlled the commercial activity, it was decided that such a purchase would be an unnecessary expenditure.

With the refusal of the Snake River Land Company, Dr. L. C. Hunt, representing the stockholders of Jackson Lake Lodge, Inc., approached the directors of the Teton Investment Company with an offer to sell. The Teton Investment Company did not have the capital to accept the offer. However, they made a counter offer that involved the consolidation of the companies through a stock exchange. Dr. Hunt rejected the offer stating they were interested in getting their money out of the lodge, not expanding their operations.

R. S. Ellison of Casper, Wyoming, the president of Jackson Lake Lodge, Inc., then picked up the negotiations. Eventually, a satisfactory arrangement was concluded whereby all the stock of Jackson Lake Lodge, Inc. was transferred to the Teton Investment Company, and the stockholders of Jackson Lake Lodge, Inc. received stock in the Teton Investment Company valued at $40,000 and $35,000 in cash. The cash was advanced by the Snake River Land Company, which received title to the one acre of land. The Teton Investment Company agreed to repay half the $35,000 during the last three years of its lease on the Moran properties.[76]

By 1933, additional investors had been found, and the representation of states among the stockholders was as follows: one each from California, Colorado, Idaho, Kansas, New York, Ohio, Oklahoma, and Oregon; 16 from Utah and 13 from Wyoming. Because the criticism leveled at the Teton Companies was partly due to the Utah residency of a majority of the stockholders, those men agreed to sell their shares to any Wyoming men who would take them. None of the companies had ever paid a dividend, and the Utahans were willing to sell for what they had paid into the company. No one from Wyoming accepted their offer.[77]

The investigation into the history of the Teton Companies and their relationship to the Snake River Land Company failed to reveal any improper activities. It did, however, reveal that this was not the first investigation of the companies and their relationship with Rockefeller. On December 17, 1930, at Senator Carey's request, the Senate Special Committee on Wildlife Resources had reviewed the relationship in Senator Carey's presence, and in 1931, the Senator was informed of the willingness of the Utah stockholders to sell their shares to Wyoming citizens. The hearings did not reveal Senator Carey's motive for insisting that the companies be reinvestigated in 1933.

Jackson Hole Historical Society and Museum 2003.0078.029

The Moose fishing tackle and gas station on the west side of the Snake River.

The remainder of the hearing dealt with a variety of topics. The committee heard residents of Mormon Row complain that the Snake River Land Company had not purchased their lands. They wanted their lands reinstated in the Rockefeller project. This must have provided more embarrassment for Senator Carey as he was responsible for the elimination of the Mormon Row properties from the purchasing program. The Forest Service presented economic information on the Teton National Forest. This testimony was apparently presented to show that certain areas of the Forest Service domain in Jackson Hole contained resources too valuable to be included in a national park. Senator Carey also took the time to deny having ever stated that the Snake River Land Company had burned ranches to force people to sell. He assured the committee that the reporter, Miss Frances Wayne, had misquoted him.[78]

Of all the testimony received during the four days of hearings, perhaps no one expressed the deep general feelings of the valley's populous better than William Deloney when he urged the committee to act in a manner that would settle the issue permanently. He stated:

...regardless of where it goes; settle it, and it will result to our benefit. The increase in tourist traffic will more than compensate the businessman for the loss of business he has had through the moving out of these people. ... Whatever the conclusion of this committee, and whatever the resulting act of Congress is, it should by all means, in fairness to these people, bring this question to a definite conclusion and stop it, as near as it can be stopped in the future, so we will know what to do, know what to look forward to, what to work to, and what we can expect.[79]

If Senator Carey expected to receive political mileage from the investigation, he must have been disappointed. Senator Norbeck certainly was not impressed. He remarked, *"Then this country does not want to be rescued by this committee; ... it would appear from all that has occurred here that Mr. Rockefeller is having a mighty hard time of it trying to do nothing more than give away a couple of million dollars of his money."*[80]

Because the Jackson Hole hearings revealed little, if any, evidence of wrongdoing, the second subcommittee hearing attendant to Senate Res.

Courtesy Josephine Fabian

Harold Fabian, Leslie Miller (Governor of Wyoming), Dick Winger, and Dr. Charles Huff on Two Ocean Pass after the exoneration of the Snake River Land Company, September 1933.

226, scheduled to be held in Washington, D.C., was canceled.

The newspapers also seemed to be let down by the whole affair. The *Denver Post* said the "scandal" resembled *"...a back-fence spat between neighbors who have nothing better to do. The charges of coercion of settlers and destruction of property in Jackson Hole have not been supported by any evidence.... The whole thing is too small to be dignified by the usual 'tempest in a teapot' designation. It is a squall in a thimble and may now be forgotten."* [81]

The *Wyoming Tribune* said the hearings dispelled much of the smoke from the controversy but offered no solutions. *"Adjustment of the complexities of this problem remains to be accomplished and, as with the road to Tipperary, there is apparently a long, long way to go."* [82]

The *Salt Lake Tribune* was the most critical. It stated:

Nothing more than a political echo emerged from the four day's hearing of a senate subcommittee on park extension plans in the Jackson Hole country in Wyoming. As a result, Senator Carey of Wyoming, who had assayed the role of herald, promising scandal to rival Teapot Dome, assumes a ridiculous position before his people. The promised explosion of crookedness and graft fizzled out like a toy balloon.

...Meanwhile, the controversy, so far as the home folk are concerned, is just about where it started. They still are torn between the promised revelations of Senator Carey and a factual examination which failed to establish either scandal or sensation.

In political turmoil, this is the inevitable conclusion and the Jackson Hole probe is essentially the result of political plotting. Neither the fight nor the hearing have served any useful purpose for the residents of the Jackson Hole country, for the rest of Wyoming or for the federal government. Ill effects have been felt and will continue to be felt until the whole argument is dissipated, and helpful, cooperative policies supplant the selfish ambitions which now prevail.

The investigation already has cost the government in excess of $5000. It probably will run higher and, in the end, the argument will be just about where it is now and where it was before the government undertook the roving, probing expedition into the west. Senator Norbeck is not far wrong when he characterizes this excursion as a political football, costing the government an outrageous expenditure of public funds. [83]

~

During the remainder of 1933, only one event was as universally reported throughout the state

John Benjamin Kendrick

www.wyohistory.org

Left: The 15-year old orphan who broke horses for room and board.

www.wyohistory.org

Right: Cowboy who came to Wyoming on a cattle drive from Texas and built a 210,000-acre ranch in southern Montana and northern Wyoming before entering politics in 1910.

Hoff Collection, Trail End State Historic Site

Above: Kendrick gave the first outdoor Wyoming gubernatorial inaugural speech. He was one of Wyoming's most powerful national politicians.

211

as the Senate hearing in Jackson. That event was the death of Senator Kendrick on November 3, 1933. T. A. Larson, in his *History Of Wyoming,* described Kendrick as one of the three most popular politicians in the history of the state, and Jim Griffith, Sr., a Wyoming newspaper editor, described Kendrick as *"...the craftiest politician the state has ever produced."* [84] After considerable controversy, Governor Miller appointed Joseph C. O'Mahoney to complete the late Senator's term.

As for Jackson Hole, the year ended with a bright economic note. Grand Teton National Park, whose budget had been reduced because of the controversy, received $32,400 in NRA (National Recovery Administration) funds for trail and road improvement. This not only brought new money into the valley's economy, it also provided 75 new jobs. Additionally, work began on the fish hatchery, which provided another 100 jobs. And, despite the Depression, tourism in Yellowstone National Park and in Grand Teton National Park continued to increase. [85]

CHAPTER TWELVE

1934-1936

The old west of history and romance is dead. The hordes of civilization have trampled every part, the last frontier has gone. Within the memory of living men even Jackson Hole has passed from the primitive, has felt the touch of despoiling hands.

But in order that a portion of that last frontier might be revived and forever preserved, that the old west might be more than a cherished memory, philanthropic men have turned their eyes to Jackson Hole. Their dream and the desire of a large majority of local residents by the aid of Wyoming's senators in Congress may now soon be realized through the extension of Grand Teton National Park.

Jackson Hole Courier, 1934[1]

Jackson Hole Historical Society and Museum p1958.0518.001

As technological advances reached the valley, residents were quick to make improvisations to ease the hardships of life in Jackson Hole, especially in the winter. Jack Tevebaugh built a wooden snowplow that he attached to his Buick to try and keep the road open to the AMK Ranch.

At the beginning of 1934, the majority of the valley's residents' moods could only be described as optimistic. True, the Depression was still a national problem, but compared to the rest of Wyoming, the Depression had been kind to Jackson Hole. Originally, the state had taken great pride in her self-reliance. Wyoming was the only state to refuse federal loans from the Reconstruction Finance Corporation, but by 1934, the number of undernourished children and the high unemployment forced the state to accept federal aid.[2]

In Jackson Hole, Rockefeller had injected $1.5 million into the economy. Some of the people who sold to Rockefeller paid their debts and left the valley. Others moved into town and invested their money in local businesses. Additionally, Grand Teton National Park had been established, and the government had been spending appreciable amounts of money to develop and maintain the new reserve. The Teton Investment Company spent most of its money in Jackson Hole, and the county was receiving additional revenue from the Snake River Land Company in the form of taxes on land which had previously been in default. Also, tourism, though lessened in the rest of the state, remained strong in northwestern Wyoming.

The New Deal programs also helped Jackson Hole. As noted in the previous chapter, the NRA (National Recovery Administration) gave additional funds to Grand Teton National Park for trail construction. A fish hatchery was being built, roads were being oiled, and dikes were begun on the Snake River to protect the community of Wilson. Grand Teton National Park and Teton National Forest received funds to clean up debris within their domain. By the summer of 1934, more than 500 men would be employed at CCC camps within the valley.

As far as the *Jackson Hole Courier* was concerned, the only depressing note was that President Roosevelt predicted that the Depression would end. The *Courier* noted that many of the above-described projects were not new ideas. For years, Jackson residents had been working to have them accomplished, but they had never been able to get them funded during the "good times." The editor commented, *"And now, just when everything is going good, when men have work and things are being done, the administration announces that the 'depression,' a lasting local benefit, is about over. Can you beat that?"* [3]

The general economic condition of the valley was not the only reason for optimism. There were strong indications that the park extension issue would, at long last, be settled. In fact, by the end of January, a tentative agreement was reached.

The compromise plan was worked out during meetings in Washington, D.C. between Senators Carey and O'Mahoney, Jack Scott of the Wyoming Game and Fish Commission, Struthers Burt, Kenneth Chorley, Vanderbilt Webb and Harold Fabian. Senator Carey sent a copy of the plan to C. R. Van Vleck along with a letter asking him to discuss the plan with the Jackson Hole people and to let him know the prevailing attitude of the residents. In this letter Carey stated, *"The most difficult thing was the position taken by Mr. Rockefeller that his lands must be given to the Park Service and no other agency, his reason for this being that he felt the Park Service would*

Jackson Hole Historical Society and Museum

CCC Camp at Jenny Lake

During the duration of the Civilian Conservation Corps (1933-1942) more than 12,800 Wyoming men (about 5% of the state's population) were employed, and at least 36,100 men were employed on projects within the state. Expenditures by the CCC within Wyoming exceeded $38,500,000.[4]

protect the lands as to the scenery and would not allow buildings to be placed upon them. I felt that I would never get any agreement unless I would agree to this." [5] Since Van Vleck was an opponent of park extension and the Jackson Hole Plan, Senator Carey apparently felt the need to explain further his position on the compromise. He wrote,

Frankly, I have not changed my views regarding park extension, but I think that an intolerable situation has developed in Jackson's Hole which makes any further progress impossible until this matter is settled. I can prevent any legislation being enacted as long as I am here, but naturally my tenure of office is uncertain and there might come a time when the Wyoming delegation would agree to some plan far less satisfactory than this one. [6]

Carey then urged the plan be accepted because *"...it would mean that the balance of the Hole could go ahead and develop which is not possible under the present conditions."* [7]

The plan [See Appendix Two-D to read the full document] that Senator Carey enclosed with his letter included some of the more important aspects of the Jackson Hole Plan. In addition to specifying (by township and range) an extension area that closely resembled that area suggested in the Jackson Hole Plan, he proposed that the land east of the Snake River, south of the Buffalo Fork River, west of the Teton National Forest, and north of the Gros Ventre River be administered by the Biological Survey for elk refuge purposes. Additionally, that provisions be made for the movement of cattle across the extension area to and from their seasonal grazing allotments, that Teton County be compensated for lost taxes resulting from the transfer of private land to the government, and that all land previously withdrawn from settlement by Executive Orders and

not included in the area described be reinstated to their former status. [8]

This agreement prompted a short-lived flurry from the opposition through its newspaper, but even *The Grand Teton* could see it had lost the battle. While *The Grand Teton* condemned the agreement, William Deloney wired Senator Carey stating, *"Glad to read of agreement on Teton Park. Meets approval of majority of people. However, you make error in not making entrance at least at Gros Ventre River, preferably Flat Creek Bridge. Such entrance, with building of Snake River Canyon Road, will ensure permanent highway through Jackson."* [9]

While nearly everyone was glad to hear that a settlement was at hand, not everyone was entirely pleased with the compromise. A majority of the local merchants wanted the park extended south to the edge of town. They believed this would ensure more visitations by tourists to the town and thus provide a greater benefit to the local economy. There was also a concern that if the south

Karl C. Allen Papers, Box 7, Folder 25, American Heritage Center, University of Wyoming

C. R. Van Vleck and his daughter Jean, 1935

Van Vleck owned a hardware store in Jackson and was the valley's undertaker. He was considered an opponent to the establishment of Grand Teton National Park, its enlargement, and the Rockefeller project. Nevertheless, he was a strong supporter of the community, and his legacy is the establishment of the Van Vleck House. This facility provides youth and family services ranging from abuse prevention to residential care relating to behavioral, emotional, and mental health issues.

Grand Teton National Park

1933 Grand Teton National Park Staff

Front row: Sherman, Woodring, Mrs. Woodring, Hanks, Hayden. Back row: Munn, Ickes, Watson, Smith, Sprunt, Secrest, Fryxell.

boundary was established at the Gros Ventre River, another community or other commercial developments might be established between Jackson and the Park. This boundary adjustment issue seemed to be related more to a desire to prevent future business competition rather than concern for the potential scenic impairment of the area.

In support of this extension, an effort to convince the Wyoming Delegation to include the area immediately north of the town of Jackson within the Park was initiated. The Jackson Hole Commercial Club was formed to further this cause as well as economic growth in general. Jackson had not had an active commercial club since the Lions Club published its resolution opposing park extension. This new club began with 75 members, and its officers were elected from the ranks of the pro-park extension businessmen.[10] The club, in addition to pursuing the desired boundaries for the extended Grand Teton National Park, actively worked to obtain land for an airport which provided the basis for future controversy and animosities within the valley.

Eleven ranchers at Mormon Row also pursued a favorable and early settlement of the park extension issue. They signed a petition that they sent to President Roosevelt, Attorney General Cummings, the Wyoming Congressional Delegation and the members of the Senate Committee on Public Lands. This petition stated in part:

We want you to know that the local and state sentiment is preponderantly in favor of Mr. Rockefeller's beneficent plan for the protection of our wonderful scenic beauty and wildlife. We want to sell our ranches. We are praying for immediate action. We feel that posterity, the United States, Wyoming, Jackson Hole and Mormon Row will be greatly benefitted by a larger Grand Teton National Park along the lines offered by John D. Rockefeller, Jr. and his associates.[11]

John F. Woodman put forth this petition. When the *Courier* contacted Woodman about the petition, he stated, *"If Senator Carey or any other of those opposing park extension desire to keep these lands in private ownership, why don't they come out and buy the land for themselves? If they don't want to do that, we certainly challenge their dog in the manger attitude in preventing us from selling to whomsoever we can."* [12]

By the end of April 1934, it appeared even more likely that the park extension issue would soon be settled. Senator O'Mahoney predicted an early settlement and stated that he had received a great deal of mail favoring the extension.[13] Senator Nye, also of the Public Lands Committee, stated he expected a park extension bill to be ready shortly. He also stated, *"The bill is not expected to meet much, if any, opposition in Congress and should be approved without delay by the President, since it is entirely in accord with administration's policy in this respect."* [14]

Gradually Teton County began to unite and prepare itself for park extension. The county prepared a report on the projected loss of tax revenue due to the expected donation of Rockefeller's land to the Park Service. It was necessary to ascertain that figure in order to determine the amount of compensation needed from the federal government. The proposed legislation provided for compensation to the county for a period of 20 years. It was determined that $17,000 would be needed the first year, but the residents were unable to agree on whether that amount should be received every year for 20 years or if that amount should be reduced by 5 percent each year for 20 years. It was argued by some that the county would continue to grow, as would the value of taxable property within its boundaries; so the amount of reimbursement should be decreased each year. Some far-sighted residents believed the county could better handle the eventual cessation of federal funds at the end of the 20 year period if the reimbursements gradually tapered off.[15] They compromised and decided they would ask for the full amount for the first ten years with reduced payments during the final period.

In May 1934, the voice of the opposition, *The Grand Teton*, ceased to speak. The *Courier* purchased *The Grand Teton* and for five weeks both papers were printed as one; i.e., one paper carried both names with the management and

editorial stand of the *Courier* prevailing. Wilford Neilson had the dubious honor of being the only man to hold the title of editor for both the *Jackson Hole Courier* and *The Grand Teton*.

Neilson, who throughout the controversy had called for a united front by county residents, published an editorial on the efforts of Teton County to influence the proposed legislation. He admitted he originally opposed park extension but eventually saw it was inevitable. He noted that people failed in previous years to unite in order to obtain the best legislation possible for the community. Neilson called the newfound unity an "eleventh hour effort." He stated, *"But of course, last minute efforts are better than none at all, and it is hoped that when the bill is finally passed, it will contain every provision possible in the interest of our people."* [16]

Guy Bush Photo Jackson Historical Society and Museum p19580025001
Wilford Neilson, 1965
Neilson was an attorney who also owned and edited the *Jackson Hole Courier* during this period. He would eventually sell the paper and serve the community as County Attorney. During the latter part of the Jackson Hole Monument controversy, he would again work as editor of the newspaper. Under his supervision, the *Courier* originally opposed the expansion of Yellowstone National Park southward, but it later supported protection for the valley through proposals such as the Jackson Hole Plan. His editorials and articles were noted for their tongue-in-cheek commentary and frequent allusions to classical literature. He was sometimes blamed/credited for the eventual elimination of gambling in Teton County.

217

~

On May 2, 1934, Senator O'Mahoney, Wyoming Governor Miller, Arno B. Cammerer and Hillory Tolson (both representing the National Park Service), and Vanderbilt Webb of the Snake River Land Company met with Senator Carey in Washington to discuss the details of the proposed legislation.[17] The efforts of these people, combined with the efforts of Jackson Hole locals to communicate their desires to the Senator, resulted in a bill that truly reflected the desires of a majority of the people involved in the park extension issue. There would never be another Teton Park extension bill that would so completely accommodate the various local concerns.

Jackson Hole Historical Society and Museum 1958.2226.001n

Dr. Charles and Edna Huff

Dr. Huff was the only doctor in the valley for many years and a consistently re-elected mayor of the town of Jackson. He was a supporter of the Jackson Hole Plan that proposed an enlarged Grand Teton National Park if a tax compensation provision for the county could be attached.

On May 28, 1934, Senator Carey introduced, in the 73rd Congress, 2nd Session, S. 3705 to extend the boundaries of Grand Teton National Park. On June 6, 1934, the Senate Committee on Public Lands and Surveys reported favorably on the bill without amendments. The provisions of this legislation generally followed the Jackson Hole Plan and indicated the eleventh-hour efforts by the residents of Jackson Hole were successful.

Of special interest to the valley residents were (1) the establishment of the southern boundary of the park at the northern edge of the town of Jackson, (2) the right of ranchers to move their herds across park lands in the spring and fall, (3) the compensation of Teton County for the loss of taxes resulting from transfer of private property to the federal government, (4) authorization for the Secretary of the Interior to purchase additional private land within the boundary of the park (including Mormon Row), (5) the continuation of wildlife management by the state of Wyoming, and (6) restrictions on new commercial development within the extended area of the Park. Additionally, this bill attempted to correct the injustice endured by Albert Gabbey regarding his rejected homestead extension application by directing the

Secretary of the Interior to grant Gabbey a patent for his stock-raising homestead entry numbered 015468.[18]

One of the reasons the community received so much of what it wanted was that Senator Carey changed his attitude toward the park proposal after the 1933 hearings. While he may not have changed his personal opinion concerning the issue of park extension, he seemed more receptive to the desires of the majority of the valley populace. The *Jackson Hole Courier* noticed the change and remarked that Senator Carey, *"... since the time of the Senate investigation here last summer, has been very active in the interests of Teton County and the people directly affected by the extension."*[19] Also, Dr. C. W. Huff, who was just re-elected mayor, and Bruce Porter, a town councilman, went to Washington, D.C. to express the concerns and desires of the community. Huff and Porter worked closely with Senators O'Mahoney and Carey to ensure the interests of the

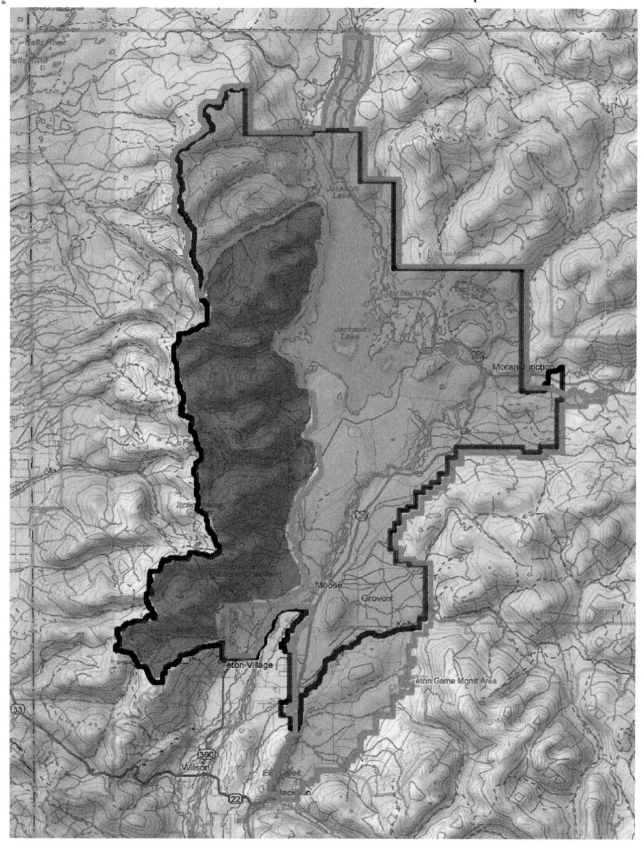

Proposed extension of Grand Teton National Park boundaries in S. 3705.

Current GTNP boundary
Original GTNP
Proposed GTNP Extension
S. 3701 (1934)

S. N. Leek Collection, American Heritage Center, University of Wyoming ah0318_1992

Viewing the Tetons from Oxbow Bend continues to be a favorite stopping point for Park visitors. The Oxbow Bend area was not added to Grand Teton National Park until 1950.

valley would not be neglected. They were successful in this endeavor.

As expected, the Senate passed the bill and it was sent to the House. The House Committee on Public Lands reported favorably on the bill with one amendment. The Bureau of the Budget requested that amendment which required that Teton County be compensated for the loss of taxes by some means other than federal funds. The same day the bill was reported out of committee, June 18, Congress adjourned, effectively killing the meticulously designed bill that would have satisfied the majority of the valley's residents while still accommodating the goals of the Snake River Land Company and the National Park Service.[20]

It has been speculated, in hindsight, that Rockefeller would have saved a considerable amount of money in the long run if he had agreed to pay Teton County the taxes on the land he anticipated donating to the Park Service according to the schedule specified in S. 3705. Ultimately, he paid taxes on the property for an additional 16 years, and he and the valley endured nearly two more decades of controversy and acrimony. It is unclear if he was given such an option. Since the

bill was not reported from the House Committee until the last day of the session, there was no time for a discussion on this issue. Even if Rockefeller was aware of the conditions required by the Bureau of Budget, and even if he had agreed to make available the funds to compensate Teton County, the bill would likely have failed to pass the 73rd Congress. Any change made in the bill by the House Committee, even if passed by the House, would have had to endure a reassessment by the Senate and perhaps a conference committee to secure ultimate approval. There was insufficient time for these negotiations.

Overlooked by those who suggested Rockefeller should have agreed to pay the taxes is the possibility that the taxes paid on the land in question may not have come from his pocket. Unknown is the amount of money from leases, rents, and other revenue received by the Snake River Land Company from its operations in the valley. Even if the tax returns for the company were readily available, it would be nearly impossible to determine if revenues matched, exceeded, or fell short of the associated tax obligation for the property purchased by Rockefeller. Some of the people who sold to the Snake River Land Company retained life tenure or specified term leases with the attendant obligation to pay the taxes. It is unknown if the operations of the Snake River Land Company, excluding the initial investment, provided a profit or a financial drain during the remaining years of the controversy.

The problem was the request by the Bureau of the Budget that another source of compensation for Teton County be found. Section 5 of S. 3705 provided for Teton County to be compensated in the following manner: for the first ten years, the county would receive an annual payment equal to the average tax levied on the land and improvements in question during the years 1929 through 1933– not to exceed $25,000 per year. The second ten-year period would have the same base level of compensation– reduced, however, by 10 percent for the 11th year, 20 percent for the next year, and so forth. Compensation payments were to be paid from revenue received from the operation of Grand Teton and Yellowstone National Parks.

The Bureau of the Budget reported that Section 5 of the bill would be in conflict with the financial program of the President. The bureau said it would approve the bill if compensation for Teton County could be made by any method *"...not involving any expenditure of Federal funds."*[21] Most of the people in Jackson Hole were not so much concerned where the funds originated as long as the compensation provision remained in the bill.

The remainder of 1934 was rather uneventful as far as the park extension issue was concerned. The bill that failed in 1934 provided all that could be hoped for by a majority of the valley's populace, but there was little that could be done until the next session of Congress. It was left to the Wyoming Congressional Delegation to find the solution.

Disappointment in the valley was great over the fate of S. 3705, but it was at least partially mediated by a 75 percent increase in tourist travel. In 1933, Grand Teton National Park recorded 42,500 visitors. Nineteen thirty-four brought 75,000 tourists heralding optimistic economic expectations within the valley.[22]

Shortly after Senator Carey's park extension bill failed to pass, Wilford Neilson retired as editor of the *Jackson Hole Courier*. Neilson remained active in the community serving as county attorney, but the *Courier* lost some of its character. The new editor, Maurice Konkel of Cheyenne, was not as emotionally involved with the local issues and his articles and editorials lacked the thought-provoking enthusiasm, wit, and fire for which the *Courier* was previously known.

As 1934 drew to a close, the valley lost one of its leading citizens. Robert E. Miller died at the age of 71. During his 50 years of residence in the valley he had been a fur trapper, homesteader, supervisor of the Teton National Forest, rancher, banker and purchasing agent for the Snake River Land Company. He was a powerful and influential man in the community and, while he was not universally liked throughout the valley, he was generally respected. Even today, he seems best remembered for his exorbitant (for the time) interest rates rather than his accomplishments.

Jackson Hole Historical Society and Museum p1958.2352.001
Grace and Robert Miller at their home on what is now part of the National Elk Refuge.

Although he opposed park extension efforts, he supported the concept of protecting for future generations a portion of the valley of Jackson Hole.

〜

Nineteen thirty-five, like the year before, began with the hopes that a solution to the park extension issue would be found. Senators Carey and O'Mahoney worked to produce a bill that would satisfy the Bureau of the Budget while including the provisions necessary to satisfy the residents of Jackson Hole. As far as the Senators knew, the only problem with S. 3705 had been the section concerning compensation of lost taxes to Teton County. Their "solution" really was not a solution at all, but in view of the stand taken by the Bureau of the Budget, it was probably the best they could do.

The new bill, S. 2972, which the Senators introduced jointly on June 3, 1935, was, with a few exceptions, the same as S. 3705. The new bill differed in that it provided, in addition to the extension of Grand Teton National Park's boundaries, for the establishment of Jackson's Hole National Game Refuge. The bill was, therefore, a combination of S. 3705 and H.R. 478– the old Winter Bill from 1928 (see Chapter Eight).

In S. 2972, Section 301 contained the tax compensation provisions keeping the same formula as Section 5 of S. 3705 but without specifying the source of funds. There was also a provision that the county could, at its option, accept a lump sum payment instead of the 20-year payoff. The compromise was that the extended boundary of the Park and the game refuge, as described in Section 1 of the bill, would not become effective until a source for the compensation could be found.*

wyomingtalesandtrails.com

The south entrance to Jackson Hole came through Hoback Canyon. Winter travel was challenging, but summer travelers through the canyon also found the route adventurous.

Jackson Hole Historical Society and Museum p1991.4055.001

If the bill passed, Congress would have approved an extension of Grand Teton National Park and the establishment of the Jackson's Hole National Game Refuge along specific boundaries. However, neither would become a reality until a solution to the compensation problem was found. Actually, the Bureau of the Budget had recommended this type of compromise in its amendment to S. 3705. Nevertheless, the Bureau wanted the bill to require compensation from a source other than the U.S. Treasury. While S. 2972 did not provide for compensation from federal funds,

---

*There is no specific evidence to speculate that the Senators had Mr. Rockefeller in mind when they wrote the tax compensation provision for this bill. However, the language of the provision seems particularly applicable to his situation. This bill would have provided for the legislative accomplishment of his goals regarding his purchases in Jackson Hole, requiring only an infusion of additional funds to consummate the project. The lump sum payment provision might have been an additional incentive for Rockefeller to provide the funds and thus attain his original goals.

neither did it specify compensation from private sources. Thus on July 3, 1935, the Bureau of the Budget advised the Department of the Interior *"...that S. 2972 would not be in conflict with the financial program of the President provided there is eliminated therefrom Section 301, which provides compensation in lieu of taxes to the County of Teton over a 20 year period."* [23]

While the Department of the Interior and the Senate Committee on Public Lands and Surveys worked to find a way to appease the Bureau of the Budget, opposition to other portions of the bill arose. This new opposition came from a most unexpected source– the National Parks Association. The association generally favored the bill to extend the boundaries of Grand Teton National Park, but it was opposed to the inclusion of Jackson Lake within the Park. Since 1919, the association opposed the inclusion of commercial waters within the national parks and, in this regard, had never lost a battle. It also opposed the extension of the southern boundary to the town of Jackson. The association did not think it advisable to provide a "front yard" park for the commercial interests in Jackson.[24]

Shortly thereafter, the Izaak Walton League expressed its opposition to the inclusion of lands east of the Snake River as well as Jackson Lake within the extended boundaries of the Park. The League, in previous years, purchased and donated land in Jackson Hole to the U.S. Government for elk refuge purposes. They felt the land east of the river should have been given to the Biological Survey. The League resolved:

WHEREAS, The Izaak Walton League of America believes in and has defended standards for our National Parks consistent with the outstanding character of established National Park areas and excluding commercial uses,

THEREFORE BE IT RESOLVED that the Izaak Walton League of America oppose the inclusion of Jackson Lake Reservoir Reclamation Project and other commercial reservoirs within the Teton National Park.

BE IT FURTHER RESOLVED that we oppose the inclusion within the Teton National Park of valley lands east of the Snake River valuable for the use by the Biological Survey in providing for the elk. [25]

S. N. Leek Collection, American Heritage Center, JHHS&M bc.0040

Izaak Walton League members observing the Jackson Hole elk feeding operation, 1927

The National Elk Refuge is another locally originated conservation effort for which the settlers are rarely given credit. Initially, the locals donated money to buy hay to feed the elk and convinced the state to provide additional funding. Five feeding stations were established, both north and south of town, with a rancher responsible for feeding the elk in each district. In 1911, Congress appropriated $20,000 for the feeding program and in 1912 established the National Elk Refuge with an appropriation of $45,000. Congress designated 1,000 acres of public land, and 1,760 acres of private land was purchased to create the refuge. In 1925, the Izaak Walton League spent $36,000 to purchase 1,760 acres which was accepted by Congress for elk refuge purposes in 1927. In the 1930s, President Roosevelt signed Executive Orders withdrawing 3,783 acres of public land from settlement to enlarge the refuge. Other acquisitions, including 3,000 acres from the Snake River Land Company, expanded the refuge to its current size of approximately 25,000 acres.

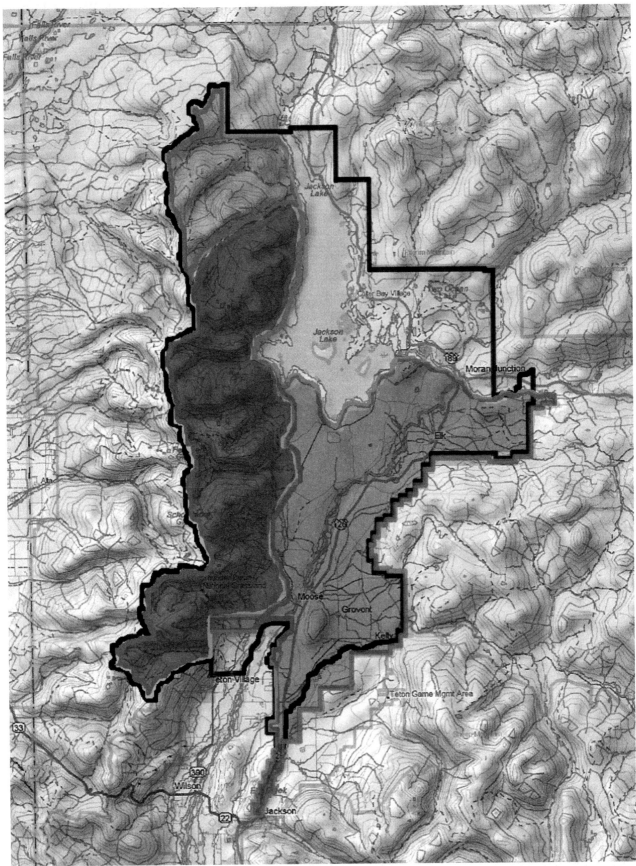

Extensions to Grand Teton National Park as proposed in
S. 2972 (1935)

Current GTNP boundary
Original GTNP 1929
Proposed GTNP Extension

The Izaak Walton League failed to appreciate the complexity of the issue which the bill's authors had so appropriately resolved. The bill provided that the lands east of the Snake River, although included in the Park, would have been administered by the Biological Survey. The bill also required the approval of the Secretary of the Interior for the design and location of any buildings, sheds or other structures which might be contemplated by the Biological Survey on the land in question.

The conditions that required the above provisions were actually set forth by John D. Rockefeller, Jr. He did not oppose the use of the land east of the Snake River for elk preservation purposes. In fact, it was his original intent that the land be utilized for the benefit of the Jackson Hole elk herd, but Rockefeller believed only the Park Service could be trusted to protect the land from unsightly structures. He set forth as a condition for his donation of land that all 33,000 acres be given to the Park Service.

The provision, as written by Senators O'Mahoney and Carey, allowed the Biological Survey to pursue the activities for which it was best equipped– providing for the elk while the Park Service was allowed to control the human impact on the land. As the Senate Committee on Public Lands and Surveys was unable to accommodate the demands of the Izaak Walton League in this regard without violating the conditions set forth by Rockefeller for the donation of his lands, that section of the bill was not changed.

The Jackson Hole Lions Club had remained quiet since the Senate hearings in 1933 but reassumed its former role when the National Parks Association and the Izaak Walton League expressed their opposition to S. 2972. This time, the Lions adopted the position of the National Parks Association. While the inclusion of Jackson Lake within the Park may not have been an important issue for most valley residents, the southern boundary of the Park was deemed critical by most of the town's businessmen, making the position taken by the Lions Club a surprise. Perhaps a few animosities still existed between the Lions Club and the Jackson Hole Commercial Club. The Commercial Club's officers were composed of businessmen who resigned from the Lions Club when

it passed its resolution opposing park extension and condemning William Deloney.

Whatever the reason for the re-emergence of a local opposition faction, a compromise was, at least, possible concerning the Jackson Lake issue. The Senate Committee on Public Lands and Surveys acquiesced to the National Parks Association concerning Jackson Lake, but it attempted a compromise on the southern boundary issue. The legislation, as proposed in 1934, transferred much of the land immediately north of the town of Jackson, which had been controlled by the Biological Survey, to the Park Service. The compromise established by the Public Lands Committee maintained the southern boundary of the Park at the Flat Creek Bridge at the north end of town. Flat Creek, from the bridge north, was established as the eastern boundary of the Park. This returned, at least, some of the land to the Biological Survey. The eastern boundary continued north along the west border of the Teton National Forest to the Buffalo Fork River. Then, instead of crossing the Buffalo, as in S. 3705, the boundary followed that river downstream to its confluence with the Snake River. The boundary continued westerly along the Snake River to the Jackson Lake Dam, and from that point, it followed the south and west shoreline of the lake to the point where the Snake River met the lake's high water line at the north end of Jackson Lake. Then the boundary ran west to the crest of the Teton Mountain Range.

One of the negative effects of this boundary change was that a sensitive corridor between Yellowstone National Park and the proposed boundary of Grand Teton National Park was lost. That corridor was desired by the Park Service to prevent roadside development between the two parks. The corridor, as originally proposed, would not have actually been transferred from the Forest Service to the Park Service. The Park Service would simply have had jurisdiction over lease applications for activities within a one-mile wide strip encompassing the highway. This protection was not possible under the provisions required by the National Parks Association.

In 1934, what had seemed to be a straightforward piece of legislation was, in 1935, becoming a confused mass of compromises. The Department of the Interior, because of the position of the Bureau of the Budget and the changes in the proposed boundaries, informed the Senate Committee on Public Lands and Surveys that additional time would be needed to study the proposed legislation before a final report could be made on the bill. What had only months before been an optimistic outlook for the settlement of the Park issue was now clouded with gloom. The Department of the Interior decided to delay its report to the Senate Committee on the bill, the Bureau of the Budget filed an adverse report on the bill because of the compensation provision, Teton County would not support legislation which failed to provide compensation, and the National Parks Association and the Izaak Walton League were dissatisfied with the compromise on the southern boundary of the

Park. Also, in 1934, Jackson Hole had given the impression it was essentially united in its support of the bill. In 1935, the stand taken by the Jackson Lions Club in support of the National Parks Association destroyed what was perhaps only an illusion of unity. Therefore, Senator Carey, whose heart probably was not in the bill anyway, reported he would *"...not push the bill because of the differences of opinions."* [26] The bill was not reported out the committee.

∽

In the history of human occupation of the valley of Jackson Hole, it is a rare thing when unity of thought prevails. Most of these events did not result in a true consensus; the minority of thought on an issue simply acquiesced for a brief time to the majority. If the desired action was not accomplished quickly, the cause was usually lost. The opposition did not remain quiet or weak for long. Nineteen thirty-four was one of these rare events when consensus seemed to reign. But, after the failure of park extension efforts in 1935, there appeared to be no great optimism that it would happen in 1936. As in 1919, when Idaho's Senator

Jackson Hole Historical Society and Museum hs.0438

Robert Bruce Porter
1891 - 1961

In the 1931 election, Bruce Porter won his Town Councilman seat by 111 votes as a pro-Jackson Hole Plan candidate. In 1935, he lost the seat by nine votes to Homer Richards. Born in Nebraska, Porter graduated from the College of Pharmacy, at Creighton University in Omaha. He moved to Jackson in 1914 and worked as a pharmacist at Jim Simpson's Jackson Drug Store. From 1917 to 1919 (World War I) he served in France with the U.S. Army's 116th Ammunition Train, Company G. After returning to Jackson, he bought the Jackson Drug Company and through astute entrepreneurial endeavors established himself as a prominent and successful businessman. He also maintained a large cattle ranch south of town– one of the few that remain in operation today. He had a reputation for altruism and community service. Among his many contributions was the initial financial donation that created the organization known today as the Grand Teton Natural History Association.

Jackson Hole Historical Society and Museum 1958.1196.001

J. Chester Simpson (right), Lew and Mable Eynon (left)

Chester Simpson, a supporter of the Jackson Hole Plan, lost his town councilman seat to J. S. Smith in the 1935 election by nine votes. After several election cycles where pro-plan candidates seemed unbeatable, the 1935 election returned supporters to office by narrow margins or rejected them by narrow margins.

226

Nugent, through his own misunderstanding of the proposed boundaries, killed H.R. 13350 which would have annexed the Tetons into Yellowstone National Park, the moment had passed. In 1935, even though the majority of thought was still strongly in favor of park extension, attitudes and values were changing.

～

The town elections in 1935 substantiated some of these changes. Since the publication of the Jackson Hole Plan in 1930, candidates favoring the plan won every local election– usually by a two to one margin. In the fall of 1935, the tradition was broken. Dr. C. W. Huff was re-elected Mayor over William L. Simpson, the former editor of *The Grand Teton*, but the vote was 220 to 160– Huff's lowest ever margin of victory. For the three councilman seats, only one supporter of the plan, George Poulson, was elected. Poulson defeated John Wort 210 to 161. Homer Richards unseated Bruce Porter by nine votes– 191 to 182, and J. S. Smith unseated J. C. Simpson by nine votes– 188 to 179.[27]

NPSHPC-George A. Grant photo-HFC#201-T

Guy D. Edwards, the second superintendent of Grand Teton National Park, held the position from September 1, 1934, to November 30, 1936.

Whatever changes may have been occurring within the valley politically, they did not keep the tourists away. Guy Edwards, the new superintendent of Grand Teton National Park, reported 100,000 tourists visited the Park in 32,000 automobiles during the 1935 season.[28] Tourism, by this time, was well recognized throughout the state as a beneficial industry. In the spring of 1935, the *Tribune-Leader* (Cheyenne) encouraged a publicity campaign to attract tourists to Wyoming. Fearing the publicity resulting from the 1934 Century of Progress Exposition in Chicago might entice people to the eastern states, that paper stated, *"If the tourist business, which those interested say adds considerable* [sic] *to Wyoming's wealth, is to be maintained or improved, concerted action must be taken. Otherwise the astute Yankees are likely to draw the tourist money away from us to their mountains the size of foothills."* [29]

Jackson Hole and Grand Teton National Park did receive some free publicity during 1935. The Union Pacific Railroad utilized the scenic attractions of both Yellowstone and Grand Teton National Parks in its advertisements encouraging western travel, and the state of Wyoming helped by decorating its highway maps with photographs of the Tetons. Also, the Jackson Hole Lions Club, under the direction of its new president, Clifford P. Hansen, erected signs at selected points in Wyoming and Idaho to direct tourist traffic to the valley.

While Jackson Hole accomplished a degree of success in obtaining favorable advertising in support of its growing tourist industry, the valley was also the recipient of some adverse publicity. An Associated Press photographer visited Jackson to photograph the famous elk herd. Most of the people who were aware of his presence apparently believed his photographs would provide more favorable publicity for the region and they made every effort to accommodate his project. The resulting articles that were distributed across the nation shocked the residents.

One of the photographs, published in the *St. Louis Post-Dispatch*, was an aerial view of the elk herd gathered on the government feed grounds. The caption read: "Legions of the hunted. A herd of elk fleeing in terror from an approaching plane bearing marksmen who were brought to the Teton

Mountains in Wyoming to shoot large numbers of them for food." [30] The *St. Louis Globe-Democrat* printed the same picture with the following caption: "Elk Herd Flees From Approaching Plane. Frightened by the strange noise from the sky heralding the approach of death, these elk are in full retreat across the snow expanses of the Teton Mountains in Wyoming. Flight is futile, however, for the marksmen in the plane will mow them down in great numbers to feed humans." [31] The same paper also printed a second photograph of elk being fed from a haystack. This caption read, "Elk Feast Before Meeting Death. Lured to their doom by hay spread by huntsmen, these elk are munching contentedly in the Teton Mountains, Wyoming, before guns are turned on them. The state slaughters the excess supply each year to feed the destitute." [32]

Since the activities described by the Associated Press did not exist, the locals were justifiably distressed. They assumed the photographer had confused the purpose of the elk refuge and the renegade elk-control program that was conducted by the state. Since the establishment of the government feeding grounds, most of the elk had learned to concentrate in the vicinity of the government hay sheds. A relatively few stubborn individuals declined the cafeteria atmosphere of the refuge in preference to the haystacks of local ranchers. Although their numbers were small, relative to the 20,000-member herd, they were capable of inflicting considerable damage and economic hardship upon the ranchers.

The Game and Fish authorities opposed a suggested policy allowing the ranchers simply to shoot the offending animals. It was feared such a policy would initiate an era of legalized poaching. Instead, they decided to reimburse the ranchers for the damages caused by the "renegade" elk. There were several problems with this solution. First, in order to receive compensation, a claim had to be filed, investigated, approved and then paid. Depending on the amount of damage and the severity of the winter, the bureaucratic delays could be as damaging as the elk. Second, the state of Wyoming, during the Depression, had pressing human needs for all its funds. It was decided to authorize Game and Fish personnel to shoot the

offending animals in areas such as Jackson Hole where the elk population was high. The carcasses of the animals were then distributed to destitute families within the state, saving the state money while fighting starvation from the doors of some of Wyoming's needy inhabitants.[33]

Since no elk had been hunted on the refuge, the residents of Jackson Hole could only imagine the photographer became confused, but they were, nevertheless, irritated that such misinformation was broadcast to the world. Before the year was over, the residents would find the Associated Press' articles to be a prediction of the future closer to the truth than most would care to admit.

In November 1935, Jackson Hole residents learned the state intended to slaughter 1,000 elk and sell the meat to large eastern packing companies. It is impossible to know whether the Associated Press learned of the planned slaughter and printed the story prematurely, was confused by other animal control programs, or if the state got the idea from the articles. A coincidence seems unlikely.

Jackson Hole Historical Society and Museum 1958.2221.001

Roads opened to automobile travel- Spring, 1936

In any case, the plan was not received well in Jackson Hole or the rest of the country. In the view of the local populace, as well as sportsmen's and conservation groups across the nation, it was one thing to kill a few problem animals and distribute the meat to undernourished families within the state, but altogether another issue to kill large numbers of animals within a refuge and sell the meat to big business in the East for resale at a profit. Thus the elk and Jackson Hole, once again, became the focal point of a controversy national in scope.

Despite the protests, the state erected holding pens and a slaughterhouse on the refuge. Contrary to the Associated Press articles, the elk were not gunned down from airplanes. They were slaughtered in the same manner as cattle. The Izaak Walton League was perhaps the most vocal of the protesting conservation groups, and it had the firmest foundation for opposing the state action. It had purchased and donated a considerable amount of land in Jackson Hole for the preservation of the herd, not for its slaughter. While the state maintained the herd was too large and needed to be reduced, sportsmen's organizations felt the herd should be reduced through hunting. The argument might easily have resulted in a debate of the biological merits of the various methods of controlling big game populations had not the interested parties kept it on a purely emotional level.

The Wyoming Game and Fish Commission, although embarrassed by the public condemnation of their action, could not back away from the project because a contract with the Bell Packing Company had already been signed. They did, however, proffer a compromise. The Commission proposed to allow residents the first choice of the carcasses with a condition providing for the slaughter of an unlimited number of elk by the state.[34] This was unacceptable to the residents of Jackson Hole and demonstrated the failure of the state to understand the real issue.

Perhaps every long time resident of the valley, at various times, had experienced a variety of emotions concerning the elk. Nearly everyone, at some time, had thrilled to the sound of an elk

bugling, been awed by their magnificence, sympathized with their struggle during hard winters, fought them to protect the food supplies of domestic livestock, loved, hated, hunted, respected, and protected the Jackson Hole elk herd. Additionally, the valley residents felt an uncommon degree of pride that the love/hate relationship between man and elk in Jackson Hole, unlike most areas of the nation, had not resulted in the elimination of either species.

In the local view, the elk were once again in need of protection– this time from the state of Wyoming. The Commission failed to understand that although the Supreme Court had ruled that elk and other wildlife belonged to the state within whose borders they lived, in the minds of the valley's residents the elk would always belong to Jackson Hole. In short, Jackson Hole's elk were not for sale. At least not so blatantly.

During the last week of November, the *Jackson Hole Courier* reflected the emotional tone of the valley by declaring, *"The largest natural resource of the state upon which millions of dollars have been spent for protection are to be cut down in a far from sportsmanlike manner."*[35] William Simpson wrote to the Game and Fish Commission informing them of his intent to file suit against them and file criminal charges against anyone attempting to carry out the slaughter. This turned out to be an idle threat when an examination of the legislation creating the Game and Fish Department affirmed the considerable latitude provided the commission in managing the state's wildlife.

By the second week in December, Game and Fish employees had slaughtered 246 elk. Since verbal protests had failed to protect the elk, an anonymous citizen or citizens elected to take matters into their own hands. By the dark of night, someone removed a portion of the fence holding the elk for imminent slaughter, releasing the doomed elk and delaying the program until the elk could be rounded up again. This action inspired the publication in several Wyoming newspapers of a cartoon in which armed Jackson residents stood guard over the elk herd.[36] The incident also prompted the renewal of the protests and adverse publicity for the state agency.

A week after the new year began, the Game and Fish employees collected a new batch of animals for slaughter. On the eve of the slaughter, the fences were again torn down and 300 elk were given a last minute reprieve. Finally, armed guards were posted at the holding pens to ensure the continuation of the program.[37]

With the situation rapidly approaching an armed conflict between state employees and Jackson residents, the Game and Fish Commission decided to terminate the slaughtering program. The decision to end the program was at least partially prompted by the packing company's desire to disassociate itself from the controversy. The elk meat was selling well in the east, but because of the adverse publicity the company agreed to cancel the contract after fulfilling the orders on hand. The slaughter was not terminated until an additional 225 elk were killed.[38]

In all, 545 elk lost their lives as a result of the program, but it may have been a small price to pay for the resulting benefits. The U.S. Congress, with the nation's attention focused upon the Jackson Hole elk herd, finally provided the Biological Survey with the necessary appropriations to accomplish the land purchases described in the old Winter Bill. The refuge was eventually enlarged so the elk could be cared for more adequately during the winter months.*

At the beginning of 1936, Jackson Hole lost another long-time resident, J. R. Jones. He was born in Nevada City, California, on May 10, 1873. His youth was probably quite wild, having prospected and gambled his way through the gold fields of Nevada, California, and Oregon. In 1899, he married Fidelia Humphrey and eight years later settled in Jackson Hole where they successfully homesteaded a site on the Gros Ventre River.

Among Jones' skills was a talent for writing. He wrote numerous articles on wildlife, history and nature, three of which gained him national exposure. The *Saturday Evening Post* published "My Bet With Uncle Sam" and "Playing The Gold Camps," and "Handlers of Sixes" was printed in *Sunset Magazine*.

Bruce Porter Collection, Courtesy Liz Lockhart

Hungry elk raiding a haystack on the National Elk Refuge

*The winter of 1936 was a tough one, and the elk were not the only wild animals in need of assistance. The U.S. Government, through the Forest Service, fed roughly 500 wild ducks in the Kelly area.

J. R. Jones was one of the valley's most ardent conservationists. He was one of the three men who conceived the National Recreation Area plan agreed to at Maud Noble's cabin in 1923. In August 1930, he sold his 293 acres to the Snake River Land Company and moved into town where he became a successful merchant. He died on January 10, 1936, at the age of 63.[39]

A little over a month after the death of J. R. Jones, another supporter of Grand Teton National Park and conservation, in general, was lost. Roger Toll, the superintendent of Yellowstone National Park, was killed in an automobile accident near Deming, New Mexico. At the time of his death, Toll was a member of a six-man commission investigating potential international parks and wildlife refuges along the Mexican-American border.[40]

~

Politically, 1936 was a relatively quiet year in Jackson Hole. No park extension legislation was introduced, but some strong feelings developed when Idaho began another attempt to obtain a formal treaty with Wyoming concerning the Snake River. Along with the Snake River Compact controversy, Idaho selected a site within

Wyoming for another dam on the Snake River. They proposed an $8,000,000 structure 350 feet high at The Narrows, just within the Wyoming border, storing 435,000-acre feet of water. In addition to their resentment of Idaho's appropriation

Jackson Hole Historical Society and Museum 1958.2442.001
Fidelia and J. R. Jones

Jones was a prospector, miner, gambler, homesteader, author, and supporter of several local initiatives to protect the scenic and recreational values of the valley.

Library of Congress 8c15786u

Forest Service road from the Jackson Lake Dam to Jenny Lake

of Wyoming's water, the people of Jackson had other reasons for opposing the dam. After years of urging the Wyoming Highway Department to construct a road through the Snake River Canyon, the CCC was in the process of constructing that highway. The Idaho proposal would inundate that new road under 350 feet of stored water. This controversy was destined to endure for another 13 years.

~

In the elections of 1936, a number of offices changed hands. Robert Carey lost his U.S. Senate seat to a Casper lawyer, Harry Schwartz. Also, William Deloney lost his State Senate seat to P. C. Hansen. It is impossible to determine the role the controversies in Jackson Hole played in Carey's defeat if any. His conduct and public statements regarding Rockefeller and the Jackson Hole Plan, in light of the testimony obtained during the 1933 investigative hearings, did not enhance his stature as a Senator, but his post-hearing conduct demonstrated his willingness to work in the best interest of his constituents. Deloney's defeat probably reflected a change in attitude by many locals concerning park extension. As had happened so many times in Jackson Hole, the pendulum of opinion was on the back swing as far as an enlarged Grand Teton National Park was concerned.

While attitudes may have been changing within the valley, the trend of economic growth was continuing. Travel in Grand Teton National Park increased by 25 percent. For the season ending September 30, 1936, an estimated 125,000 people visited the Tetons in 36,000 cars.[41] Also, Grand Teton National Park received a new superintendent. Thomas Whitcraft, the chief ranger at Glacier National Park, replaced Guy Edwards, who was transferred to Boulder Dam.

The valley of Jackson Hole seemed immune to the debilitating economic factors affecting most of Wyoming and the nation. Relative to the rest of the nation, Jackson had not suffered greatly from the Depression. Neither was it unduly

bioguide via Wikimedia Commons

Henry Herman "Harry" Schwartz (D)
1869-1955

Schwartz was born in Mercer County, Ohio. He attended public schools and began a career in the newspaper business from 1892 to 1896. He also studied law and was admitted to the bar in 1895. His political career began with a term in the South Dakota House of Representatives. He then worked for the General Land Office in Washington State, Montana, and Washington, D.C. until 1910. He moved to Casper, Wyoming in 1915. He was an unsuccessful candidate for the U.S. Senate in 1930 but unseated Robert Carey in 1936. He failed to retain the Senate seat in the 1942 elections and was appointed by Franklin Roosevelt to the National Mediation Board in 1943. He returned to Casper in 1947 and resumed his private law practice.

affected by the drought of 1936. Additional government funds allowed some of the CCC camps to continue operating during the winter providing jobs. Also, the continued popularity of Grand Teton National Park stimulated a 10 percent overall growth in local business.[44] Whatever the uncertainties concerning the future of the north end of the valley, the residents of Jackson Hole continued to prosper.

CHAPTER THIRTEEN

1937-1938

Jackson Hole is unique. Most of us here aren't happy unless we're miserable. We have our bitter feuds here, but we don't have any clan killings– we try to worry each other to death. Our idea of winning a battle is to put out as much propaganda as possible on one side and get the people with us, and then, when they lose interest, the other side puts out their propaganda and gets the people with them.

Richard Winger, 1938[1]

S. N. Leek Collection, American Heritage Center, University of Wyoming ah03138_1675

Fishing on Jackson Lake before the flooded trees were removed by the CCC

As 1937 began, the fervor for park extension was largely forgotten. Judging from past histories of Jackson Hole controversies, one might think the lack of active support for park extension was due simply to the fact that no one was actively fighting it. However valid such an observation might be, other factors were at work too. While the Depression still gripped the nation, economic conditions were improving, at least in Jackson Hole. Many people who supported the extension efforts in hopes of selling their property had, by necessity, endured the worst part of the Depression. While there were still people who wanted to sell their land to the government, others had decided to hold on to their property. With the resulting change in attitudes toward the future, the park extension movement seemed to have lost some of its support.

Also, there were a variety of other issues to be considered. Large among these issues was Idaho's continued attempts to obtain additional water rights within Wyoming and to formalize preemptive uses over existing sources. There was, of course, no division of thought in Jackson Hole over that issue. The Wyoming State Legislature passed H.B. 98 appropriating $2,500 to defend the interests of water users in Teton County.* As Mark Twain supposedly observed, *"Whiskey is for drinkin'; water is for fightin'."*

Other events also added to the general optimism in the valley. A new state Game and Fish Commission was established, and Jackson Hole was guaranteed a voice on that body when Governor Miller appointed Richard Winger to head the commission.[2] Improved communication with

University of Alaska Archives

Almer Acie "Ben" Bennett

Bennett with the Zenith Model 6A (N392V) he helped design and flew in Alaska, Montana, Wyoming, and Idaho. He would later establish the Flying B Ranch in Idaho. The Zenith 6A had an enclosed cabin for six people with the open pilot cockpit behind the cabin.

Jackson Hole Historical Society and Museum
bc0282

First airmail flight from Jackson

(L to R): Clara M. Murie- postal clerk, J. R. Riggan- carrier, R. B. Landfair- postmaster, A. A. Bennett, unnamed.

*The battle between Idaho and Wyoming concerning water allocation from the Snake River would continue until the signing of the Snake River Compact in 1949.

the outside world became more than just a dream with the introduction of regular (weather permitting) winter mail service. A. A. Bennett obtained a government contract to fly the mail during the winter between Jackson and Rock Springs, Wyoming. Of course, once the mail reached Jackson, it was still delivered by dog sled or on horse-drawn sleds, but to post and receive mail on anything approaching a regular basis during the winter was a new luxury for valley residents. Additionally, Western Union announced plans to extend its wire service to Jackson. It also appeared likely that the Wyoming Highway Department might attempt to keep the Hoback Canyon Road and Teton Pass open during the winter months. This would provide the single most important ingredient for the development of a winter economy based on tourism.

Some residents noticed the newfound confidence in the economy spawned a proliferation of roadside signs. Once again, the local dude ranchers led the way in an organized attempt to convince merchants to remove the unsightly advertising.[3] The *Jackson Hole Courier* noticed other undesirable business practices as well and stated, *"The day of 'sticking' the traveller* [sic] *because it's the last chance at him should be past. Improved roads and improved transportation make the 'extra charge for huge freight rates over the hill' sound ridiculous. Jackson's future lies with returning guests."* [4]

Although there were numerous reasons for optimism, Jackson Hole also joined the rest of the state in mourning the passing of former Governor and Senator Robert Carey. Additionally, in September 1937, Jackson Hole suffered one of its greatest tragedies. Dr. Charles W. Huff died. He was a staunch supporter of the Jackson Hole Plan and had recently been re-elected Mayor. Dr. Huff was born in Maryland on March 19, 1888, and moved to Jackson on June 1, 1914. It appeared he had ignored, for some time, his own illness to administer to several patients in remote portions of the valley. When he became incapacitated by his condition, he was flown by A. A. Bennett to the hospital in Idaho Falls, Idaho, where it was determined he had contracted a rare streptococcus infection. Even though a specialist was called

in from Salt Lake City, Utah, and phone consultation was conducted with doctors at the Mayo Clinic and other parts of the nation, no successful treatment was accomplished, although blood transfusions seemed to help. When locals learned that blood was needed, 20 people left Jackson immediately for Idaho Falls, while others organized into groups and prepared to make the trip so that various shifts would always be on hand at the hospital if more blood was needed. Their efforts were, nevertheless, in vain. Penicillin, which almost certainly would have saved him, was developed two years after his death.

Dr. Huff was the only doctor most Jackson Hole residents had ever known. In 1932, he received a Fellowship in the American College of

Jackson Hole Historical Society and Museum p1958.2470.001
Dr. Charles William Huff

Acroterion CC BY-SA 3.0 via Wikimedia Commons

Huff Memorial Library

Surgeons in recognition of his service to this remote Wyoming community. He was forty-nine at the time of his death.[5] The *Jackson Hole Courier* eulogized Dr. Huff by stating:

> *Columns could be written, great shafts of marble erected, songs composed, but none could give more than a slight indication of the esteem in which Dr. Huff was held by the residents, the dudes, and the visitors who sought his advice and services. Marble fountains, bronze plaques, granite obelisks, all have been suggested. But with so many of his accomplishments at hand to testify to his nobleness such things pale by comparison.[6]*

The local library became his memorial.

The absence of medical services in Jackson Hole did not endure. Within a month two doctors, D. G. MacLeod of Sheridan, Wyoming and L. B. Lawton* of Leslie, Michigan, announced they would move to Jackson. Dr. MacLeod would eventually earn the love, respect and degree of esteem approaching that bestowed upon Dr. Huff.

In November 1937, the Department of the Interior revived the legislation to accomplish an extension of Grand Teton National Park. In Washington, the major stumbling block continued to be the tax compensation provision. While the Bureau of the Budget feared the provision would set a dangerous precedent†, the Wyoming Congressional Delegation and Governor Miller would not support a bill which failed to provide compensation for Teton County.

These men in Washington were working under the assumption that a vast majority of Jackson residents still supported the park extension plan. While the assumption may have been valid, the real strength of each side of the controversy was unclear because the supporters had become conspicuously quiet. The news of another attempt to extend the Park boundaries stimulated a new round of publicity that, by its nature, indicated the growing strength of the opposition. The *Jackson Hole Courier*, under its new management,

reversed its former policy of supporting the plan and became the primary voice of the anti-extension movement. It appeared, on the surface, at least, a majority of the valley residents now stood in opposition to the new legislation.

A number of possibilities might explain this apparent change in the valley's attitude toward the Park. First, the opposition apparently found new strength from the "newcomers" who had recently moved into the valley. Many of these people had suffered hard times in other areas of the country because of the Depression and having found

NOAA, George C. Marsh Album, theb1365

Above: Dust storm approaching Stratford, Texas, 1935
Below: Dustbowl ravaged farm near Dallas, South Dakota, 1936

While the dust bowl ravaged the Midwest and the Depression put millions of people out of work in most of the nation, the economy in Jackson Hole seemed to hold its own. Cattle prices, of course, dropped, but the tourist industry appeared to expand gradually. The Depression had its adverse impacts on the valley, but, comparatively, Jackson Hole was an economic oasis.

Department of Agriculture, Image Number: 00di0971

---

*Dr. Lawton was the nephew of prominent Jackson businessman, C. R. Van Vleck.
†Sharing federal revenues with state and municipal governments was unheard of at the time.

a valley where, because of tourism, the economy remained relatively stable, they could not understand any action which would remove any private land from development. One such person, Dr. F. C. Naegeli, a dentist, wrote Wyoming's Congressional delegation stating the best thing for Jackson Hole would be the elimination of the presidential orders withdrawing land from development around the Park. Naegeli wanted the area reopened for summer home sites and, unlike the people who had initially attempted to farm the area, he believed the land to be prime farm and ranch country. He also declared:

Surely if you honorable gentlemen are loyal to the interests of the State of Wyoming, the County of Teton, and the people who live here, you will oppose any Park Extension bill that may be drafted and presented to the Congress; you will work for the cancellation of the Executive Withdrawal Orderes [sic] imposed on this region in 1927 and 1930 which withdrew our lands from development and prevented lands of the national forest from being utilized for any permanent purpose.

Why should you gentlemen even consider Park Extension when practically 100 per cent of the people living here are opposed to Park Extension? Why should you favor a few who would benefit by Park Extension through concessions and drive the remaining residents of Teton County from the country?

If you gentlemen are loyal to the State of Wyoming and the best interests of the people here, you will see to it that the Park Extension question is defeated for all time, and let the country go on and develop the way it should and the way it will if this threat is removed for good.[7]

While Dr. Naegeli's opinions were not universal in the valley, they were representative of those people who were not residents during the late 1920s and early 1930s. This portion of the opposition faction seemed to have no knowledge of the philosophical attitudes or practical justifications that had culminated in the pro-park legislation of 1934 and 1935. Also, to intimate a knowledge of

the attitudes of 100 percent of the valley's populace seemed naive in light of the historical perspective of this controversy.

Some long time residents did support development in the north end of the valley, but this was not a new idea. Throughout the years of park controversy, the type of economic progress was always the real issue. Valley residents, regardless of the position on the issue, never espoused a course that would blatantly destroy the scenic attractions of the area. The conflict arose from their divergent views of the most suitable industry to push. Each side believed their vision of future economic prosperity was most appropriate for the valley in the long run.

It is of interest to view the types of development the opposition felt should occur on the lands withdrawn by Presidential order in support of park legislation. They favored farming, ranching, and summer home construction, but they opposed the construction of hotels or any development that would provide services to the traveling public. This would expand the business base for merchants in the town of Jackson but would restrict competition. Any service activity within the National Park was disparagingly labeled a

Jackson Hole Historical Society and Museum p1999.0020.001
Floyd C. Naegeli was the valley's dentist and a vocal opponent of park extension and Rockefeller's project.

Harold C. Clissold

Harold Clissold homesteaded 160 acres north of Moose in 1916 and established the Trail Ranch. He sold the ranch in 1929 and moved to town.

monopoly, providing the basis for one of the arguments against park extension.

Some of the opposition's proposals seemed to border on the ridiculous. In this regard, Stephen Leek suggested all the land purchased by Rockefeller be reopened to homesteading.[8] Since Rockefeller's land was deeded property, Leek's scenario would require the government to condemn the land and pay for it so it could be offered free to someone else. It seems unlikely Rockefeller would donate the land to the government knowing it would be opened for homesteading again. Either action would, at least for a period of several years, remove the land from the tax rolls of the county and create the situation that the opposition had used to oppose the proposed park extension. Even the supporters of the park extension plan opposed a situation in which Rockefeller's land was transferred to the government without compensation to Teton County for lost taxes.

H. C. Clissold, who had become mayor after Dr. Huff's death, also believed the northern portion of the valley should be opened to farming. Additionally, he stated:

> *The only reason left for park extension is to permit Mr. Rockefeller to get out of the necessity of paying taxes and maintaining this large block of land and further to give the park service some excuse for making an admission charge. Even tho they now have the principal attractions within the park boundaries they can hardly make a charge for a park that only takes several minutes to drive thru. With the addition of this land the tourists would be in the park for a longer period of time thus justifying the admission charge even tho the points of interest are a long ways from the several proposed entrances.[9]*

A second possible explanation for the apparent strength of the opposition might be that the opposition was never really as weak as it appeared to be in 1933. There may have been a good number of people who opposed park extension and the Jackson Hole Plan in 1933 but did not wish to be associated with the unscrupulous methods employed by the Jackson Lions Club and the opposition newspaper, *The Grand Teton*. Considering the emotional nature of the controversy in the early thirties, it would have been difficult for anyone to express opposition to the Jackson Hole Plan and avoid the distasteful stigma of association with the highly visible and less honorable wing of the anti-extensionists. Their silence would have supported the assumption that all but a few of the residents favored park extension. This new opposition movement, having begun on a more reputable basis, may have permitted the formerly silent members of the community an opportunity to state their point of view honorably.

This same rationale might also explain the notable absence of support for the new legislation. Some of the provisions in the new bill may have been sufficiently unacceptable to silence the support it might otherwise have enjoyed. Additionally, several incidents that occurred within Grand Teton National Park may have denied social acceptability to any pro-park position– even among those who believed the new park extension bill to be desirable. One such incident might have been the dismissal of the first park superintendent, Sam Woodring, as a result of allegations of moral misconduct (mentioned in Chapter Eleven).

In support of the second theory, the names most frequently associated with this park opposition movement were either new or the same as those formerly opposed to the Jackson Hole Plan. As would be expected, the names of the more notable supporters of the Jackson Hole Plan did not appear in the opposition column, but it's interesting to note that the names of most of the Jackson Hole Plan supporters do not appear at all. The *Jackson Hole Courier* would later broach this subject by asking, *"Why is it that offers of this newspaper to publish letters or information on the subject have been accepted only by the opposition? Is it that no one wants Park Extension or are the Extensionists afraid to reveal their identity?"* [10]

In any case, the *Courier* recognized that more substantive information was needed concerning the proposed legislation before any solid arguments could be formulated against it. To get that information, the editor wired Wyoming Congressman Paul R. Greever stating:

No completed park extension bill available here stop Teton County citizens want full understanding of what is transpiring and opportunity to study provisions stop Can we be assured that bill will not be railroaded thru at this special session giving people here opportunity to study contents and contact our representatives stop Draft we have here is not protective of all interests stop Please send by air mail copy of present amended bill so we may publish it for benefit of our subscribers. [11]

Congressman Greever replied, *"Park extension bill has not yet been introduced and will not be introduced at this session and of course before action is taken on this bill citizens of Teton County will be given full opportunity to present their views regarding it."* [12]

Jackson Hole Historical Society and Museum p1958.1309.001
The Trail Ranch homestead

The Trail Ranch was originally homesteaded by Harold Clissold in 1916. The 160 acres were later merged with 100 acres homesteaded by Clifford Ward in 1922. Clissold sold the ranch to Steven Conover in 1929, who sold the property to the Snake River Land Company in 1939. The ranch was subsequently leased from the Snake River Land Company and the National Park Service, who eventually burned the buildings.

Such assurances did not calm the opposition, and the *Jackson Hole Courier* continued to publish articles and editorials condemning the park extension. Most of the anti-extension arguments were the same as those presented in 1919, 1928 and 1933.

Concerning the opposition to the granting of monopolies within the Park the *Courier* stated:

What was the use of Mr. John D. Rockefeller's philanthropic program– all the tearing down of displeasing signboards–fences– and the wrecking of buildings because they did not conform to nature's beauty? The new bill provides for their reconstruction under what amounts to government encouraged monopoly.... The only thing the business enterprises enjoying the park monopolies need worry about is proper assuagement of political office holders– a new set every four years and new regulations along with them.

In centuries to come when future historians write of the episode what will they be able to say about a procedure where intelligent humans work hard to provide a back-to-nature playground for their fellow men and others work just as hard to substitute an accumulation-of-dollars motive for the nature part of the picture? [13]

The last paragraph was obviously intended to disparage those businessmen who operated in the area proposed for inclusion within the Park's boundaries. Depending on the point of view, the editor's argument could just as easily have been applied to those members of the opposition who saw an opportunity for economic gain if the north end of the valley were developed rather than protected.

Another argument against park extension which resurfaced, and which has never died, was the allegation that Horace Albright, during the 1928 hearings, promised that if the people agreed to the creation of the national park in Jackson Hole, the Park Service would not attempt to expand the Park at a later date– it would be the end of park extension and creation in Wyoming.

Concerning that allegation, Albright wrote in 1933:

I do not recall making any such promise, and do not see how I could have made such a promise, nor why anyone should have sought to exact such a promise from me. I could not have bound my successors, nor could I have been so unfair to Mr. Rockefeller who had been induced to undertake his Jackson Hole project on my representations.

What doubtless happened was that I agreed that there should be no more Yellowstone Park extension agitation, if its boundaries could be adjusted along the north, east and south as proposed by the 1925 Commission. Even here, it seems that I would have felt disinclined to make any promises of this kind, because they would amount to nothing more than one man's opinion. Furthermore, I was a subordinate in the National Park Service, and could not even commit my Chief, Director Stephen T. Mather. There is nothing in the records to show that he expressed himself along these lines. [14]

Also, with regard to the alleged promise, two United States Senators who were members of the committee that conducted the 1928 hearings later testified that no such agreement was made. When the issue was raised during the 1933 hearings, Senator Peter Norbeck of South Dakota stated, *"I talked to the parties who were in disagreement over that question, and I have reached a conclusion that there was a misunderstanding."* [15] Senator Nye of North Dakota also remembered the 1928 hearings and stated he had *"...no recollection whatever of anything resembling an agreement or understanding reached at that time."* He further recalled, *"...there was sympathy expressed on every hand by members of the committee with the people of Jackson Hole respecting their own local problems, and the more general agreement, if agreement it can be called, was involved into the assurance, if it was an assurance, that the matter would have to be approved or understood by the Wyoming Representatives in Congress."* [16]

Disregarding the evidence, or rather the lack of evidence, and the statements of Senators Nye and Norbeck to the contrary, the *Jackson Hole Courier* rationalized, *"Where there is so much smoke there must be some fire, so the only conclusion is that no further park extension was to follow the creation of the present Grand Teton National Park boundaries."* [17]

Harris and Ewing Library of Congress [Public domain] via Wikimedia Commons

Paul Greever (D)
(1891-1943)
Paul Ranous Greever with Wyoming Governor Nellie Tayloe Ross.
Greever was a first lieutenant in World War I in the 314th Trench Mortar Battery, 89th Division. He was admitted to the bar in 1917, served as mayor of Cody, Wyoming, and a trustee of the University of Wyoming. He died in 1943 from an accidentally self-inflicted gunshot wound while cleaning a shotgun.

S. N. Leek Collection, American Heritage Center, University of Wyoming, ah03138_1986.

A. A. Bennett's Zenith 6A landing at the airstrip just south of the town of Jackson near the fairgrounds.

One of the few distinguishing aspects of this controversy was the attitude of many of the opposition members toward John D. Rockefeller, Jr. Rockefeller was no longer accused of unfair methods or of attempting to monopolize the services within and around the Park through a maze of subsidiary companies. Of course, some opposition members found other accusations to place at Rockefeller's door, but the *Courier* treated him as a truly benevolent person who had acted in good faith upon the unreliable and inaccurate information provided by Horace Albright.

The *Courier* stated that Mr. Rockefeller:

...who has perhaps done more for future generations than any man alive– was led to believe it was all necessary if the people of the nation were to be saved a museum specimen of the type of country that their forefathers thought common. Mr. Rockefeller thinks in terms of all the people– not the self-indulgent minority. According to the way he was allowed to see it here was an opportunity to protect and perpetuate to posterity one of the country's greatest scenic attractions– an attraction so noble it overshadowed anything Yellowstone Park with its man-despoiled nature was able to offer.

No! No one can criticize Mr. Rockefeller for trying to do something really magnificent for future generations. But for once

the astute Mr. Rockefeller reckoned without the mercenary impulses of mankind. With the money spending crowds that throng Yellowstone Park as an example and the policy of the National Park Service of granting exclusive franchises it was not hard for money-minded persons to visualize a commercial empire. Wherever there is an opportunity to make money you find men ready to take advantage of that opportunity.[18]

It is somewhat difficult to determine who, specifically, the *Courier* was criticizing. The anti-extension group opposed the legislation because they desired the profit attendant to the development of the north end of the valley. Yet the *Courier*, who was undoubtedly the voice of the opposition movement, seemed to condemn the profit motive when criticizing the park extension plan. Since the businesses within the area proposed for inclusion in the Park were owned mostly by valley residents, the *Courier's* logic seems somewhat convoluted. The language of the proposed legislation undoubtedly stimulated this fear of the newspaper's unspecified "despoilers."

The *Courier* was careful to avoid condemning two other groups who were obviously interested in the park problem. One group was composed of those residents who originated the idea of protecting the valley. Of this group the editor remarked:

241

Actuated by only the most noble motives– absolute protection for the exquisite natural beauties of the Teton Range and assured propagation of the wild game– these

men represented no class, but listed among their numbers old settlers, summer residents and local business people. It was the idea of this group to provide an area where nature would be allowed to proceed in her own way, so that their children and their children's children– future generations– would find the forest unaltered by mankind and presenting exactly the same scenes that led the first nature lovers– the mountain men– to return again and again to this region.[19]

CCC clean up of the Jackson Lake shore.

As the Depression progressed, programs such as the Civilian Conservation Corps were established to provide work for unemployed young men. The Bureau of Reclamation and Grand Teton National Park were provided $50,000 each to sponsor CCC projects specifically dedicated to clean up the shore of Jackson Lake.

Jackson Hole Historical Society and Museum bc.0199

Jackson Hole Historical Society and Museum hs.0605

The *Courier* also stated that this group had gradually begun to realize the federal government, through the granting of monopolies, would do more harm to the area than good. But, by the time they changed their minds, Rockefeller had already been induced to invest his money to protect the valley rendering them unable to halt their initiative. This representation by the *Courier* of the attitudes of the pro-park extension residents obviously ignored the testimony presented during the 1933 hearings and the efforts of the Jackson Hole Commercial Club in 1934 that occurred after Rockefeller purchased the majority of his land in the valley.

The other group with which the *Courier* dealt kindly was the Park Service employees who lived in the area. The editor classified this group as *"...the men in the field who not only live next to nature but with her. They take great but pardonable pride in their park areas, their mountains, streams and rivers, and in the fundamental traditions of the park service.... With these men Nature is truly a product of the creator and they abhor any intrusion of objects foreign to the scene."* [20]

Apparently the editor felt these men would not "abhor" the summer homes, farms and ranches proposed by the opposition movement or would not consider them "objects foreign to the scene." Also, the editor believed these men would oppose the effort to extend the Park's boundaries to include the reservoired lakes and land already under cultivation if, in order to protect their jobs, they did not have to parrot their superiors in Washington. The *Courier* article suggested the local park employees would perceive no advantage from park extension because their salaries were not tied to the acreage of the Park.

Since none of these people responded publicly to the article, their feelings toward the patronizing pen of the *Courier's* editor remains unknown. The *Courier* was not as solicitous with two other groups that it described as the franchise seekers and the park service bureaucrats.

Concerning the first of these groups, the *Courier* warned that despite the guarantees contained in the original Grand Teton Park legislation, this new legislation could *"...let the empire builders in at the back door."* [21] As for the second group, the editor assured his readers that this new effort to expand the Park was nothing more than an attempt on the part of the bureaucrats to enlarge the scope of their authority and thus their power. The editor even declared that the attempt to extend the Grand Teton National Park boundaries was merely a front for an eventual enlargement of Yellowstone National Park; the motive was to allow the Yellowstone Park concessionaires (monopolies) to extend their profits.

⁓

Interior Department personnel and the Wyoming Congressional Delegation were acting on the basis of the support demonstrated during the 1933 Senate hearings unaware of the strength of the opposition and lack of support for the extension proposal. They continued to work toward a compromise in an attempt to create an acceptable piece of legislation. The illusion of strong local support would not last long, but during this period, the activities in Washington gave the opposition a reason to exist and organize.

Horace Albright, who resigned his directorship of the National Park Service in 1933, exemplified the government's misconception regarding the local opposition. When questioned by the press about the latest Teton Park proposal, he indicated his support for the legislation and stated the *"...opposition in Wyoming to the project comes from the same sources as opposition in the past to all creation of all the national parks, namely by a few who might suffer temporary inconvenience or loss."* [22] Secretary of the Interior, Harold Ickes, also refused to take the opposition seriously. It was reported he suspected the Forest Service of stirring up the opposition and encouraging complaints.[23]

While it was true the Forest Service was less than enthusiastic about the proposal to turn over any more of its domain to the Park Service; it was also unlikely the Forest Service was the driving

Jackson Hole Historical Society and Museum
2005.0026.004

Dead trees and other vegetation were collected in piles and burned.

National Archives

Church service for the CCC crew at Jackson Lake

force behind the opposition. Local Forest Service managers did initiate economic studies and reports designed to substantiate their position that the land would be more valuable if it remained under the Forest Service dominion. A. C. McCain, a retired Teton Forest supervisor, was active in the opposition movement, but there was little, if any, evidence to prove that the agency actively sought to incite the populace against the Park Service. Besides, the Forest Service had its own popularity problems in the West. The agency was trying to institute more stringent regulations over livestock grazing activities in their domain and increase the use fee ranchers paid for grazing privileges. This caused many westerners to view the Forest Service with the same suspicious eye they focused upon the Park Service.

Nineteen thirty-eight held the promise of intense controversy for Jackson Hole. The opposition to an enlarged Grand Teton National Park was based not solely upon real or imagined threats resulting from the proposed legislation, or interagency jealousy, or greed but also upon a more general opinion which rejected a further expansion of government control and influence in the valley. Because 1938 was an election year, it was not likely or even reasonable to expect, the issue could be settled strictly on its merits. There was too much emotion.

Early in 1938, Wyoming's chief executive visited the Jackson Hole area. Governor Miller came to Jackson to visit the famous elk herd and agreed to attend a public meeting to listen to local problems. The Park extension opponents attended this meeting in force, and while a number of local problems were discussed, the primary attention was devoted to the park extension issue. A standing vote was taken at the meeting, and of the 165 people in attendance, 162 stood in opposition to the extension proposal. The entire audience, however, was in favor of a permanent resolution to the problem.[24]

Despite the strong showing of the opposition, Governor Miller was noncommittal on the issue.

Jackson Hole Historical Society and Museum 19990016001

A. C. "Mac" McCain
Supervisor of the Teton National Forest from 1918 to 1936

A rising star in the Forest Service bureaucracy, at his own request, McCain left the Forest Service Regional Office in Ogden, Utah where he was acting district forester to assume the supervisory position of the Teton National Forest and return to "the field." He understood the importance of the federal lands he administered to the Jackson Valley and the settlers who were trying to survive in this remote and harsh corner of Wyoming. He was sensitive to needs and desires of cattlemen, hunters, loggers, skiers, recreationists, and state and county officials; a challenging administrative balancing act beyond the abilities of many supervisors.

He stated, *"...I will do that thing which in my heart I feel is best for Teton County."* [25] Unsure the meeting was truly indicative of the majority of the valley's residents, he suggested a committee be established to evaluate the situation and suggest a solution to the problem that would be satisfactory to the residents of Jackson Hole.* Miller stated he wanted *"... to be sincere in the knowledge that the people were certain once and for all, that they knew what they really wanted, not today, not tomorrow, but for all time."* [26] This was, of course, unrealistic because in Jackson Hole only

---

*The committee was composed of Felix Buchenroth, Sr., president of the Jackson State Bank, chairman; Harry Barker, State Representative; P. C. Hansen, State Senator; M.R. Yokel, Chairman, Board of County Commissioners; J. Chester Simpson, businessman; Joe E. May, Grovont rancher; Dr. F. C. Naegeli, dentist; and A. C. McCain, retired Teton Forest Supervisor.[27]

the mountains last forever. Even unanimous opinions and decisions are like the seasons. They come and go.

The members of the committee were selected at that meeting and from its composition there could be little doubt as to the nature of its future recommendation. Although the report of the committee was predictable, the opposition failed to use this opportunity to present fairly and objectively its arguments to either the valley's populace or to Governor Miller. Rather than articulate their vision and desire for a prosperous economic future, they chose to present a grossly one-sided document in which the conclusions were based upon rather obvious omissions and misinterpretations of historical facts and events.

The greatest portion of the report was devoted to outlining the history of the park extension efforts in Jackson Hole as viewed by the opposition. It claimed the pro-park extension attitude had always rested with only a few individuals who saw an opportunity for personal gain. Horace Albright and Harold Ickes, in support of the park extension legislation, had made similar detracting statements regarding the opposition.

The report ignored the support demonstrated during the 1928 hearings that resulted in the establishment of Grand Teton National Park. It ignored the testimony of valley residents during the 1933 hearings and the widespread support for the Jackson Hole Plan, as well as the local encouragement of the legislation introduced in 1934 and 1935. The report brushed aside the repeated victories of pro-park extension political candidates over the opposition candidates during the period of 1928 to 1935. The document declared, *"A history of the Park extension movement is a surprising picture of the will of a Federal Bureau and a relative few private individuals, some of whom stand to gain personal advantages, to harass and coerce the residents of a progressive community to an extent which has seriously retarded normal development of the potentaially [sic] rich resources of this region over a period of forty years."* In another portion of the report, the authors stated, *"...the present chaotic and intolerable condition within Teton County is the result of many years of agitation, fostered by the National Park Service and a relatively few persons, most of whom are not residents of Teton County or the State of Wyoming...."* The committee stated that all park proposals since 1889, with the exception of one, failed to pass the United States Congress. Their declaration that this indicated Congress had never found merit with the proposals obviously was false.

Jackson Hole Historical Society and Museum bc0167

Mike Yokel on his way to compete in the world wrestling championship in Australia. He snowshoed over Teton Pass to the train station in Victor. Yokel was a member of the committee requested by Governor Miller to recommend solutions to the Grand Teton National Park extension controversy. He homesteaded the land that now accommodates the Stagecoach Bar in Wilson, Wyoming and was possibly the first realtor in the valley. Yokel won the World Champion Middleweight Wrestling title. He died at the age of 102.

Despite the length of the report, the committee's recommendations required only three paragraphs and were presented in the form of a resolution. It stated:

NOW, THEREFORE, BE IT RESOLVED that the National Park Service be required to cease lending its support and encouragement to the Park extension movement in Teton County, and

BE IT FURTHER RESOLVED that the President's Executive Order of July 8, 1918 and the interdepartmental agreement between the National Park Service and the National Forest Service which precludes formal administration of the National Forest lands within the Teton National Forest, also all other land withdrawals made in the interest of Park extension within Teton County, be immediately abrogated; and

BE IT FURTHER RESOLVED that the Governor of the State of Wyoming, also the Wyoming Congressional Delegation be hereby requested to immediately, without equivocation, begin aggressive action to effectively meet the requests in the two preceding resolutions.[28]

In accordance with Governor Miller's instructions, another meeting was held so that the report could be presented to the people. The *Jackson Hole Courier* reported the residents of Jackson Hole accepted the report and its recommendations unanimously, but the article did not indicate the number of people in attendance.[29]

Governor Miller had reason to equivocate regarding his support for the apparent strong showing of park opposition emotion demonstrated at this meeting. An examination of Senator O'Mahoney's official papers archived at the American Heritage Center includes correspondence from Miller regarding the Jackson Hole issue. Miller forwarded copies of letters received from valley residents supporting both viewpoints. In fact, Miller sent several copies of these letters to Senator O'Mahoney with a note expressing his opinion that unanimity of thought in Jackson was absent. Demonstrating a sense of humor he wrote:

I know of no reason why you shouldn't be spending half your time on this Jackson Hole matter so as I get these communications, I will pass them along. If and when you get fed up, let me know and I will send you some more.[30]

The opposition did not rely wholly on local support for the committee's report to influence the governor and the Congressional delegation. The Lions Club solicited petitions and resolutions from their brotherhood around the state as well as sportsmen's clubs and chambers of commerce. Newspapers throughout the state began to crowd the bandwagon once again and political candidates, such as Frank O. Horton, made states' rights and federal encroachment major issues in their campaigns.

The statewide outcry encouraged the Wyoming Senators to take a harder look at the Department of the Interior's park extension proposal. They introduced, in the 75th Congress, a resolution providing for another subcommittee hearing to be held in Jackson. Senate Resolution 250, "A Resolution To Investigate The Questions Of The

Jackson Hole Historical Society and Museum-1958.0312.001p

Felix Buchenroth, Sr.
President of the Jackson State Bank

Buchenroth was a German immigrant who graduated from the University of Heidelberg. He served in the U.S. Army and, for a time, was stationed with a military detachment at the south entrance to Yellowstone National Park. During World War I, he was stationed in New Jersey and was not sent overseas, possibly because of his German birth. After the war, he moved to Jackson and worked for the Forest Service and then at the bank for Robert Miller. He bought the Jackson State Bank from Miller in 1935, and would play an active role in local and state politics. He opposed, sometimes stridently, park expansion and increased federal control in the lives of valley residents.

Possibility Of Enlarging Grand Teton National Park In Wyoming," was passed by the Senate in May. It stated in part:

The Department of the Interior has recommended the enactment of legislation extending the boundaries of the Grand Teton National Park in order to include certain lands which John D. Rockefeller, Jr., has offered to donate to the Government of the United States and certain publicly owned lands. The proposal would operate to reduce materially the revenues of Teton County, Wyo., within which the park is situated.

Numerous factors enter into the problem and there appears to be a sharp division of opinion among the residents of Teton County as to whether or not the extension should be granted. In the opinion of the Committee on Public Lands and Surveys, it is desirable that an inquiry be made upon the ground.[31]

The senators received some praise from the local press which welcomed the investigation. The *Courier* stated the Senators *"...deserved recognition for the attitude they have taken in making arrangements for the residents of Teton County to voice their opinions in the matter."* The editor also reported the general feeling that *"...an inspection of the territory in dispute could not help but demonstrate to the Senators that Teton County has a just grievance in opposing the proposal."* [32]

Due to the action taken by the Wyoming Congressional Delegation, the Department of the Interior could no longer ignore the local opposition. They also were not willing to back away from the proposal and abandon the foreground of Grand Teton National Park to the type of development Mr. Rockefeller sought to eliminate. The Interior Department, in July, published a report of its own entitled "A Report By The National Park Service On The Proposal To Extend The Boundaries Of Grand Teton National Park, Wyoming." This

16-page report presented the National Park Service's point of view on the issue and provided an explanation of each section of the bill in laymen's language.

The Park Service also took advantage of this opportunity to justify some specific areas of the proposed boundary extensions. The area affected by the bill was much the same as that described in Senator Carey's 1934 bill (S. 3705). That is, Jackson Lake was once again designated for inclusion within Teton Park's boundaries. Perhaps prompted by renewed opposition from national conservation groups regarding that aspect of the boundary extension, the Park Service report stated, *"There is some difference of opinion among conservationists as to the wisdom of including Jackson Lake in the extension because it has been dammed and artificialized. Certainly everyone regrets that such an important feature in one of*

American Heritage Center, University of Wyoming ah03138_0782
Stephen N. Leek
1858-1943

Leek personifies the Jackson Hole settler who loved the natural beauty and wildlife of the area but stridently opposed its inclusion in a national park. He came to the valley in 1889 as a trapper and tried ranching on a homestead in the southern portion of the valley. He established a hunting and fishing lodge on the shore of Jackson Lake and worked as an outfitter and hunting guide. One of his clients, George Eastman, gave him a camera and launched a new career for Leek. His photographs and prose describing the plight of the starving elk during the winter of 1909 were published nationally and featured as an exhibit at the New York Museum of Natural History. His efforts were a major force in convincing Congress to establish the National Elk Refuge.

the finest scenic regions of America ever had to be violated by any change from its natural condition." Noting that the Park Service had taken the lead in the cleanup of the lake's shore line, the report continued, *"Since the essential land area for addition to the park entirely surrounds Jackson Lake, and because the National Park Service has already been authorized to extend some protection to the lake itself, it is impracticable, insofar as the National Park Service is concerned, to consider excluding the lake from the extension proposal."* [33]

The Park Service was convinced Jackson, Emma Matilda and Two Ocean Lakes, as well as their surrounding terrain were *"...naturally component parts of the area dominated by the Teton Mountains, and therefore logically belonged in the park area."* [34] The report maintained the inclusion of this area within the Park was justified, if for no other reason than to protect and provide a proper setting and approach to the mountain range itself. Other values were at stake, too. Despite the impact of man on these lakes, the lakes nevertheless provided a breeding habitat for a variety of indigenous and rare species of wildlife. The authors noted, *"The few remaining Trumpeter swans flock back and forth between these lakes of the Teton region and those of the Yellowstone. In recent years, breeding swans have been shot in this area, and even the most secluded swan nesting ground has been opened to fishing."* On this issue, the report concluded:

> *If the wildlife about these lakes and, in fact, the primitive grandeur of the whole area, are to be restored and preserved, the area must be made a national park. It should be made once more the teeming wilderness which the early trappers discovered over a hundred years ago. Historically, Jackson Hole is magnificent. Here is an opportunity to conserve that historic picture by setting aside the area involved as a part of the park for the benefit and enjoyment of all the people for all time.* [35]

The report's explanation of the proposed legislation revealed the bill was similar to the Jackson Hole Plan and the legislation introduced in 1934 and 1935, but some sections of the bill were not as advantageous to Teton County and some of its residents as the previous legislation. As alluded to earlier in this chapter, the bill itself may have acted to suppress local support for the extension proposal.

One such section was the tax compensation provision. Two aspects of the provision in Section V worked to decrease the amount of compensation Teton County could expect to receive. First, the formula for determining the amount of compensation was changed. The base period for

wyomingtalesandtrails.com
The main building at Ed Sheffield's Flagg Ranch
The Grand Teton National Park extension proposal included a corridor along the road between the north end of Jackson Lake and the south entrance of Yellowstone National Park. As the Flagg Ranch facility just south of Yellowstone developed, the Park Service feared the Forest Service might allow similar developments or advertising billboards to proliferate along this corridor.

Jackson Hole Historical Society and Museum 1991.3667.017

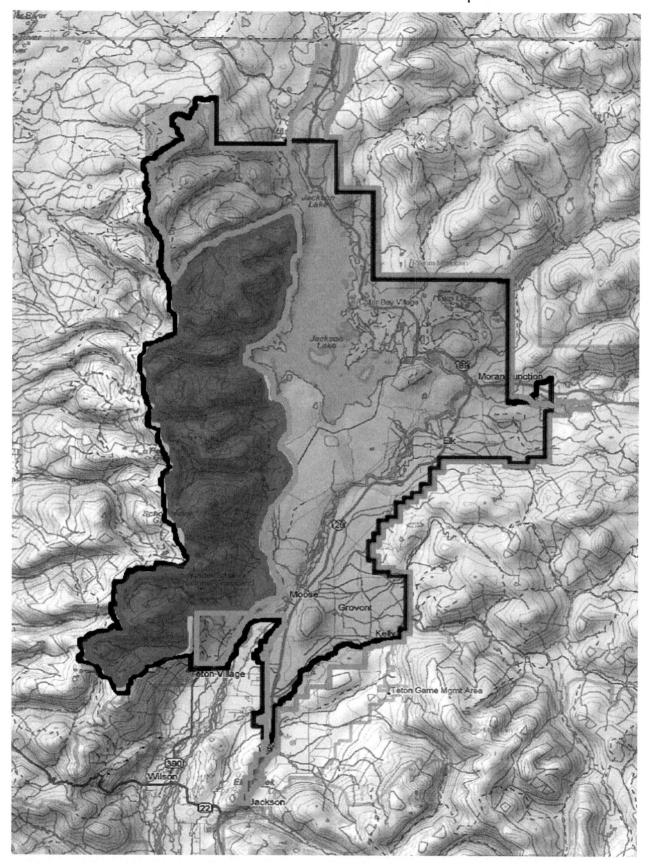

The National Park Service proposed extension of the boundaries of Grand Teton National Park, 1938.

Current GTNP boundary
Original GTNP (1929)
Proposed GTNP Extension 1938

determining the average annual tax levied on the land and improvements in question was changed to 1933 through 1937. By this time, Rockefeller had removed most of the improvements contained on the purchased land; thus, the base tax computation would be lower. A point could be argued that since the improvements were removed for the purpose of more closely matching the land with Park Service ideals, a base period during which the original improvements existed should have been specified.

Jackson Hole Historical Society and Museum p1958.1740.001

Harvesting Ice
It is virtually universally understood that settlers in remote locations like Jackson Hole had to work hard during the summer months to stockpile supplies such as food and firewood in order to survive the winters. It is less apparent that they also had to work during the winter to aid their survival during the summer. Ice was harvested from local lakes and stored in well-insulated cabins to "refrigerate" perishables during the warmer months.
Jackson Hole Historical Society and Museum 2005.0009.100

Richard Winger, during the 1938 Senate Hearings in Jackson, presented the other side of this argument. Winger pointed out that while a few of the improvements, due to their deteriorated condition, had been destroyed by the Snake River Land Company, most of the buildings were sold or given to people who moved the structures to their own property outside the purchase area. Thus, the county was still collecting taxes on the buildings from new owners. The improvements in question were simply located in a different section of the county. Arguments of this nature, supporting the legislation, were rare and not widely published.

The other aspect of the tax provision that was not popular concerned the limit of total compensation allowed by the bill. As in the previous legislation, a compensation period of 20 years was established, but the annual payment to Teton County could not exceed the revenues of Grand Teton National Park or $15,000, whichever was less. Also, payments to Teton County would cease after a total payment of $150,000, no matter how many years might remain in the compensation period. Under these provisions, the county might receive considerably more money than the government was offering, over the 20 year period, if, (1) Rockefeller's land remained on the tax roles and, (2) the public lands withdrawn from entry by the Executive Orders were reopened to development. With these tax revenue issues, it is possible that some residents who would normally have favored park extension could not, in good conscience, publicly support legislation which failed to compensate Teton County adequately for lost taxes.

Another section that may have cost the extension proposal some support dealt with the authorization for ranchers to move their cattle across the proposed park to and from summer rangelands. The language of the provision, rather than the intent, was the problem. The Department of the Interior recognized the need for rights-of-way across the proposed extension for the purpose of moving cattle, and that this would necessitate some grazing during the drives. However, the terminology used in the bill worried some of the ranchers. Specifically, the provision provided for the cattle to be "moved" through "rights-of-way." The ranchers referred to this activity as "drift."

Drifting implies a rather slow movement of the herds from one point to another. This leisurely pace is necessary for two reasons. First is the need to allow the cows and calves to travel as pairs within the herd. Cows and calves that become separated instinctively try to return to the last place the calf suckled. The faster the herd moves, the more likely that cows will become separated from their calves which result in large numbers of cattle attempting to return to the drive's point of origin. Second, the basic goal of the ranching industry is the production of meat. An excessive expenditure of energy during the drives results in lost weight and lower values when the cattle are sold.

Because the provision referred to the right to "move" cattle, the ranchers were not certain they would be assured the time to "drift" their herds across the land in question. Also, the term "rights-of-way" created another uncertainty as to the intent of the Department of the Interior. Drifting requires a certain amount of space and the term "rights-of-way" created a vision of narrow corridors that would be unacceptable to the ranchers. This may seem like a minor detail, but there is always reason for skepticism when a bureaucrat presumes to write regulations for an industry he or she does not understand. Even Richard Winger testified that this provision might not contain sufficient guarantees for the local cattle interests. The ranchers who would be most affected by the extension, regardless of their

Jackson Hole Historical Society and Museum hs.0449

Depending on weather and road conditions, the harvested ice was hauled on horse-drawn sleigh, wagon, or by truck to heavily insulated ice cabins.

Harrision Crandall Photo: Jackson Hole Historical Society and Museum 2005.0052.093

A partially buried ice cabin in the lower right-hand corner of the above photograph. Ice blocks sawed from the local lakes were stored in such cabins to provide refrigeration during the summer months. 1939

position on the park extension issue, had some reasonable justification for reservations about the bill.

Section I of the proposed bill contained, in addition to a legal description of the intended expansion, a provision which allowed the opposition to capitalize on the legendary fear that the Park Service would allow monopolies within the Park. While traditional supporters of the park extension may not have agreed that the provision was designed to introduce monopolistic commercialism into the valley, the tone of the provision concerning future commercial activities within the extended area was not the same as in the original Teton Park legislation. It stated:

Provide further; That for the purpose of providing accommodations for the visiting public the Secretary of the Interior may, in his discretion, permit guest ranches to

operate within the area hereby added to the park, subject to such rules and regulations as he may prescribe.[36]

Part of the justification for this provision was to permit the continued existence of some of the established guest ranches in the area. Some of these ranches were still privately owned while others had been purchased by the Snake River Land Company and leased back to the former owners. These leases, should they become part of the Park, would have to be recognized by the government. This provision, first of all, provided these people a guarantee, in the event of park extension, that their businesses could continue just as other provisions guaranteed cattle ranchers and others that they would not be summarily expelled from the area.

Secondly, the provision provided the authority to the Secretary of the Interior to renew these

Grand Teton National Park GRTE-00430_1118

Grand Teton National Park Staff, 1937
(left to right) Hanks, Stagner, Witness, Whitcraft, Rabb, Bressler, Routh

Thomas E. Whitcraft, the 3rd superintendent of Grand Teton National Park, met with a group of Jackson residents in 1936 to establish and promote educational and cultural resources for visitors to the Park. With a donation of $50 from Bruce Porter, the Jackson Hole Museum and Historical Association was established in 1937. The name was changed in 1956 to the Grand Teton Natural History Association. Superintendent Whitcraft's 1936 initiative has expanded beyond Grand Teton National Park to support education, art, and research in the National Elk Refuge, Bridger-Teton National Forest, and the Caribou-Targhee National Forest- an under-appreciated legacy to the valley and its visitors from the Park Superintendent.

Charlie Petersen, Sr. Collection
Thomas E. Whitcraft

leases, if the people desired renewal, and if the government found the service to be desirable. This, in reality, was not far from the intent of the plan agreed upon at Maud Noble's cabin in 1923 or from the Jackson Hole Plan.

The wording of the provision also provided the Secretary of the Interior, "at his discretion," the authority to allow the establishment of new guest ranches in the extended area. This, in the eyes of some extension supporters, may have reduced the degree of protection proposed for the extended area. Rockefeller's opinion of the proposal by the Park Service to allow the re-establishment of commercial development in the area he had purchased and cleared of buildings is unknown. During the 1938 hearings, the Director of the National Park Service, Arno B. Cammerer, would admit that the language of the provision was not an oversight. The intent was to provide for both the protection of existing guest ranches as well as the possible establishment of new guest ranches.[37]

This provision was, to some extent, in conflict with the preservation ethic supported by extension advocates as well as the original Teton Park legislation. The act that created Grand Teton National Park prohibited new commercial activities and the construction of new roads within the Park's boundaries without the expressed approval of the United States Congress. The proposed legislation would place the authority to determine future commercial activities in the extended area with a political appointee rather than with the people's elected representatives.

These examples of problem areas contained in the proposed legislation may seem minor. While these deviations from the principles of the Jackson Hole Plan may not have been sufficiently disagreeable to cause great numbers of extension supporters publicly to join the opposition, they may have spawned an atmosphere of benign neglect, creating the appearance that the proposal had only minimal local support.

～

The hearing on the proposed legislation was held in August and required three days– two days for the testimony and one for a tour of the 221,610 acres suggested for inclusion into the 96,000-acre

Grand Teton National Park GRTE-00430_1369
The north entry station for the original Grand Teton National Park
The station did not have a structural foundation. It was built on skids so it could be moved off the road during the winter to facilitate snow plowing operations.

Grand Teton National Park. The status of the land under consideration was as follows:

National Forest lands, exclusive of lakes	99,345
Surface of lakes	31,640
State school lands	1,400
Withdrawn public land	39,323
Land acquired by Snake River Land Company	32,117
Remaining private land	1 7,785
Total acreage	221,610[38]

Since the 1938 hearing was not an investigation of alleged wrongdoing, the subcommittee did not appoint a special counsel. It was the intention of the Committee on Public Lands and Surveys to allow the residents and other interested parties an opportunity to express themselves on the issues. The opposition, which now referred to themselves as the Jackson Hole Committee, was too well organized to permit a haphazard presentation of its views. Thus, Milward Simpson, the son of former *Grand Teton* editor, William Simpson, was selected to represent the opposition at the hearing. Milward was destined for political limelight, but at this point in his career, he was simply a lawyer from Cody, Wyoming, whose father was best known for his unscrupulous pen while editor of a discredited newspaper.

To his credit, the younger Simpson, while he did not abandon the emotional aspects of the controversy, collected, organized and presented evidence and testimony which adequately substantiated the valid concerns of much of the opposition. Although the testimony was largely opinion and many of the "facts" could easily have been challenged, the Senators were presented with an accurate picture of the economic conditions and tax problems facing Teton County. He successfully demonstrated the inequities of the tax compensation provision of the proposed bill by detailing the county's tax structure.

Simpson had attacked each provision of the bill in a manner designed not only to discredit the legislation but also to paint the Park Service as an insensitive bureaucratic agency. Thinking the Department of the Interior had authored the compensation section, he also attempted to disparage that agency. His attack on the tax provision caused him a moment's embarrassment, though. He began his attack on the provision by calling it a "joker." Senator O'Mahoney responded, *"I hope you won't call that a joker, because the Wyoming delegation put that in there."* [39] Simpson quickly softened his approach to the financial shortcomings of the provision.

Senator O'Mahoney interrupted Simpson's presentation briefly to explain that the Bureau of the Budget had previously objected to what it considered a direct contribution from the U.S. Treasury to Teton County because of the precedent it would set. The provision had to be worded so that the reimbursement did not appear to be an outright donation. By tying the compensation to the revenue received by the Park, the bureau had been appeased. After the explanation of the provision, O'Mahoney stated, *"...the committee, I am sure, will be glad to have any statement or evidence that you may care to submit as to what a proper reimbursement would be."* [40] That statement indicated the subcommittee did not view the amount of compensation as being critical to the legislation as a whole. They seemed perfectly willing to make adjustments in the amount of compensation so that Teton County would be fairly reimbursed for lost taxes as long as the wording that satisfied the Bureau of the Budget was retained.

Arno Cammerer
1883-1941

Cammerer received his law degree from Georgetown University in 1911. He served as Assistant Park Service Director under Stephen Mather after Horace Albright was named Yellowstone Park Superintendent and held the position when Albright was named Park Service Director in 1929. He became the third National Park Service Director in 1933. During his term as director, the nation's national parks tripled in area and annual visitation expanded from an estimated 2 million to 16 million persons. He resigned in 1940 and died on April 30, 1941, from a heart attack.

According to the data presented by Simpson, Teton County encompassed 1,733,120 acres, but most of that land was not taxable because it belonged to either the federal government or the state government. Only 113,769 acres were assessable land and of that amount 49,902 acres were located within the proposed park extension. The total assessed valuation of Snake River Land Company land and personal property was $442,891, and the valuation of other privately owned land in the proposed area was $333,811. If Rockefeller's land were donated to the federal government, and if the government purchased the other privately owned land within the extension area, Teton County would have its assessed valuation lowered by $776,702 or nearly one-third. [41]

In terms of the actual tax revenue affected by the proposed legislation, the data showed that the county could expect to receive tax revenue of $63,758. If the privately owned land and other personal property within the extension area were

The boat rental concession at Jenny Lake, like numerous other tourist activities within and around the Park, were leased to individuals by the Snake River Land Company.

for the lifetime of the lessee, and summer home leases would last for 25 years. All these buildings and other personal properties would remain on the tax roles, at least for a time. An adjustment of Simpson's figures reflecting the above considerations would still have presented an unacceptable financial situation for Teton County.

While the actual amount of revenue the county would receive under either of the options was important, the real fear of many of the opposition members was that the county would cease to exist. The creation of Teton County had required a special act by the Wyoming State Legislature because the valley lacked sufficient population and assessed valuation to qualify under the existing statutes. Teton County, with such a small tax base (7 percent of its total area) and a bonded indebtedness of $35,000 for schools, really could not afford to lose any revenue. The county was already charging the maximum mil levy allowed by state law, so a tax increase was not an option. With any appreciable decrease in revenues, the only option would be to dissolve the county government and merge with an adjacent county. The tax compensation provision of the proposed legislation might cost the people of Jackson Hole an appreciable degree of self-rule and self-determination.

removed from the tax roles, the county would receive only $42,877– a decrease of $20,881.[42] Since the proposed legislation provided for an annual compensation in the amount of $15,000 or less (depending on the revenues of Grand Teton National Park), the inadequacy of the tax compensation provision became a valid basis for opposition to the bill.

The bill limited the total compensation to $150,000 over a 20 year period. Without the park extension, the county could expect, if all things remained constant, revenues from the land in question to exceed $400,000 for the same period. Additionally, it was Forest Service policy to share a percentage of its revenues from the sale of timber and other lease operations with the county in which those activities occurred. Since the area of the extension would take in 99,345 acres of Forest Service land, the county would likely lose some additional revenue from the withdrawn timber and leasing resources.

The data presented by Simpson failed to consider that the commercial operations within the proposed area of the extension would remain, according to the bill, for at least ten years. Some of the guest ranches, although purchased by Rockefeller, were leased back to the sellers for various periods, some of short duration but others

Another understandable aspect of the opposition's argument dealt with the withdrawal of land from settlement by various Executive Orders. To many Jackson Hole residents the withdrawals, which began in 1918, had handicapped the economic development of the valley by closing the land to entry for any purpose. The 13 Executive Orders withdrawing land in Jackson Hole in support of possible legislation between July 8, 1918, and July 30, 1937, had removed 39,323 acres from potential settlement and taxation.[43]

This withdrawn land within Teton County existed in a kind of hiatus with no one knowing its future disposition or use. For 20 years the future status of the withdrawn public lands had retarded the planning and economic development in Jackson

Hole, and nearly everyone seemed to agree that this situation was not in the best interest of the valley. While the two sides of the park controversy might argue over the best utilization of land, nothing could be done about it until the extension issue was settled. For those members of the opposition who desired the reopening of the land to settlement and development, it was imperative that the park extension proposal be killed forever. Of course, Simpson supported this approach to the issue during the hearings. [See Appendix Two-F for a complete listing of the Executive Orders.]

Jackson Hole Historical Society and Museum 1958.3149.001
C. R. Van Vleck held two leases for private cabins on Forest Service land (Photos above and below). The Forest Service offered a renewable 15-year lease while the Park Service proposed a single 25-year term for pre-existing leases.

Others viewed the problem as a question of direction for the valley's economy. If the Park were extended, the cattle and agricultural interests would know where they stood with respect to markets, grazing rights and water rights. The rest of the valley could actively pursue the tourist dollar. If the park extension efforts were killed and the public land reopened, the summer home, cattle, and agricultural interests could expand, and businesses in Jackson could develop accordingly. Some of these residents no longer cared how the issue was settled as long as it was settled. They believed the valley would prosper either way if only the questions concerning the future of the land's use were removed.

While no organized presentation was made in support of the extension proposal, Park Service Director Cammerer, who represented his agency at the hearing, was permitted to ask questions of the witnesses called by Simpson. Cammerer used this privilege to correct misstatements of facts when they occurred and to present alternate viewpoints when misleading impressions were introduced by the opposition.

For instance, Simpson, at one point implied that a concession had been granted within Grand Teton National Park in violation of the commercial prohibition contained in the original bill creating the Park. Cammerer was able to explain that the activity, a boat rental on Jenny Lake, pre-dated the National Park and was operated from land owned by Rockefeller, not the National Park Service. Also, C. R. Van Vleck, a long time

Charlie Petersen Sr. Collection

opponent of park extension, complained that he could not justify the investment for improvements to a summer home lot on Jackson Lake, which he leased from the Forest Service. He stated the Forest Service would normally have allowed a 15-year lease on the land, but the interdepartmental agreement between the Park Service and the Forest Service limited the term to one year on land being considered for park status. Van Vleck wanted the extension proposal killed so he could obtain a 15-year lease and make the improvements he desired. Director Cammerer pointed out that the proposed legislation guaranteed lease-holders a 25-year term on their lease. It was possible that the Forest Service would be more likely to renew the lease at its expiration for another 15 years. However, a "guaranteed" 25-year lease seemed better than a "possible" 30-year lease.

Hannes and Margaret Harthoorn

Hannes Harthoron immigrated to the United States from the Netherlands and filed a homestead on land in the Mormon Row area. His Patent (0003141) was approved on May 29, 1918. Margaret was the spokesperson for a group of neighbors who supported the extension of Grand Teton National Park if their lands were purchased by the government prior to the extension.

Other testimony expressed concern about the granting of concessions within the extended boundary resulting in a loss of revenue to Jackson merchants. Cammerer responded that more commercial development of that type was likely to occur if the Park was not extended and the area opened to uncontrolled and unrestricted development. In addition to the testimony of 19 witnesses called by Simpson, 15 written statements were introduced opposing the park extension. Simpson also included in the hearing record 41 resolutions from organizations around the state opposing the legislation and several articles from the defunct *Grand Teton.*

While the opposition far out numbered the supporters of the plan at the hearing, Director Cammerer did not stand alone. Margaret Harthoorn informed the committee that she had been selected by her neighbors in the Mormon Row area to present a statement on their behalf. The statement was in the form of a resolution. [See Appendix Two-L to read the entire resolution.] This resolution revealed that 10 of the 12 property owners in that area favored park extension as long as their properties were purchased prior to being

included in the Park; however, all desired the controversy be settled as soon as possible. Their combined property totaled 2,920 acres.[44]

Another resident who spoke in support of the park extension was Mrs. C. Seelamire. She felt the proposed extension was deficient in that it failed to include a particular area of the valley. Mrs. Seelamire's testimony revealed that she owned a 907-acre ranch in the area in question and that she wished to sell the land then lease it back as had others who had dealt with the Snake River Land Company. While her testimony was straightforward and honest, she briefly hesitated to answer a question from Senator O'Mahoney. The Senator asked Mrs. Seelamire how long she had lived on the ranch. She responded, *"I hate to tell my age."* O'Mahoney stated, *"We wouldn't want to ask you that."* But Mrs. Seelamire acquiesced, *"Oh, I don't care. Forty-five years, practically."* [45] Later Senator O'Mahoney asked her why she desired the extension. She replied:

I may be a little altruistic, but I think Mr. Rockefeller's idea was a very good idea. I think it would be bringing revenue into the State to have the vast playground that is planned, and if the town of Jackson wants more tourists, they will probably get more, many more, if they have that sort of playground there. We all know that Mr. Rockefeller has built up many parks and

Mrs. Coulter D. Huyler

Mrs. Huyler and her husband owned and operated the Bear Paw Ranch.

has done a great deal along that line. If one could see the fine families in the city that live on a 50-foot lot and have very little chance for a summer vacation, but once they get out into a place like Yellowstone, one would know what this would mean. That is a big idea, of course; but I know that is what Mr. Rockefeller has in mind.[46]

Another member of the committee, Senator Reames, asked her if the principal motivation for supporting park extension was to sell her land. She responded, *"Partly, yes. You can call it what you please. It's not only that. I have been for park extension for 35 years."* [47] When Senator Hitchcock asked if she would have to move if she sold the land, she replied, *"No; I don't think so. The Snake River Land Co. is very generous about giving leases for enough to pay the taxes. If people will pay their taxes, they can have any kind of a lease they want from the Snake River Land Co., as I understand it; and, so far as I know, we could lease the land and stay there if we wanted to."* [48]

The only other woman who testified at the hearing, Mrs. Coulter D. Huyler, probably expressed the sentiments of quite a few residents when she declared, *"...I don't know at all whether I am for or against park extension. Sometimes I think I'm for it and sometimes I think I'm against it."* [49] Mrs. Huyler could not agree with Simpson's argument that if the Park was extended the landowners in the affected area would leave the valley, and, thus local businesses would be destroyed because of the lost trade. She stated:

...I would like to say ... that those of us who live in this valley, who have property that might be taken in up against the hills- in fact, that would be taken in- if this park extension went ahead, probably will stay right here. I don't know of any who would think of leaving the valley, because there are other properties that we could get. I think we would still want to retain some property in Jackson Hole, so that the small businesses

Jackson Hole Historical Society and Museum -1958.2746.001

Richard Winger
1888-1966

in Jackson would still have whatever trade comes from these people, for we probably would still be here. We love this valley too much to leave it.[50]

With no particular point in mind, it is interesting to note that, with one exception, the only Jackson Hole residents who testified in favor of park extension were women. The one exception was Richard Winger. Winger was, at the time of the hearing, the resident agent for the Snake River Land Company and the president of the Wyoming Game and Fish Commission. He never mentioned his position on the Game and Fish commission during his testimony, and he assured the Senators that his presence before their committee was as an individual, not as a representative of the Rockefeller interests. In fact, Winger stated that the Snake River Land Company, its agents, and employees had been instructed to stay out of the controversy.*

Mostly, Winger's testimony traced the history of the park extension movement in Jackson Hole and his role in its evolution. He also explained some of the company's actions that Simpson had cited in his allegations against the Rockefeller organization. For example, Simpson, through the

---

*Josephine Fabian confirmed this directive during an interview with the author.

testimony evoked from his witnesses and through written statements, implied that the Snake River Land Company, after removing fences and allowing cattlemen to drift their cattle across company property, reconstructed the fences when the cattlemen refused to support the park extension plan. Winger explained that the property had to be refenced because some of the cattlemen allowed their animals to overgraze the drift area. Winger maintained that after three years of overgrazing, the drift area was nearly devoid of vegetation and resembled a barnyard corral. The area was refenced and irrigated at great expense. When the land recovered, it was put up for lease. According to Winger, the grazing lease was offered to R. H Charter, but he declined because he was attempting to purchase grazing land south of Jackson. Charter had recently sold his ranch to the Biological Survey. A rancher, Gill Huff, who owned about a thousand head of cattle, eventually leased the land. After Huff's death, the land was leased to Misters Bean and Hein, who also owned the Jackson Market. Winger assured the Senators that the refencing of the land was not due to any vindictiveness but rather because some ranchers had shown they could not use the land responsibly without some degree of regulation.

Winger also addressed the issue of taxation denying Simpson's implication that the Snake River Land Company was trying to avoid taxes. Winger admitted that he had paid the previous year's taxes under protest but for different reasons than Simpson implied. Winger maintained that certain rocky and barren properties had been assessed at a rate usually assigned to meadowland. Winger requested and was denied permission to accompany the assessor during his evaluations, so the taxes were paid under protest.

While Simpson did not question the testimony of the female witnesses, he did attempt, with little success, to neutralize Winger's testimony. He was unsuccessful largely because Winger was an uncooperative witness. Winger would not be led into traps. He refused to answer Simpson's questions until the purpose of the question was revealed. Even then, if he did not wish to answer, Winger would verbally attack Simpson, accusing him of spreading propaganda by innuendo.

Several times the verbal fireworks and battles had to be stopped by the chairman of the subcommittee. Senator O'Mahoney would often determine the issues raised by Mr. Simpson were *"...not relevant to this proceeding"* or not *"...material to the inquiry...."*[51]

The only other park extension supporter to make a statement at the hearing was Director Cammerer. His statement closely followed the reasoning established in the Interior Department's previously discussed pamphlet. Unlike most of the witnesses, the committee members and Simpson questioned Cammerer rather closely.

The questioning by the committee members indicated that, in spite of the preponderance of opposition feelings demonstrated by the local populace, some Senators still believed a compromise was desirable. Much of the questioning centered around a possible guarantee by the director that no further agitation for additional park extensions or new parks within Wyoming would be made if an extended Grand Teton National Park was granted. Cammerer stated that he, personally, would have no problem with such a position, but he reminded the committee that he could not bind his superiors or his successors. The Senators, mindful that they likewise could not bind a future Congress, seemed to accept Cammerer's position on the issue as a stepping stone for a possible compromise.

Simpson tried to discredit Cammerer by introducing, out of context, several paragraphs from a report entitled Recreational Use Of Land In The United States Part XI Of The Report On Land Planning, November 1934, by The National Park Service. Simpson prefaced his attack by reminding the committee that Cammerer, during his questioning by the Senators, stated that he had no personal desire to see Yellowstone National Park extended or to have other national parks established in Wyoming. Simpson then established that the previously mentioned report had been submitted by Cammerer and that the report was a recent publication (1938). Simpson revealed that the report recommended the consideration for federal action by the Park Service, among others, the *"Wind River National Park, Wyo.; in the Washakie National Forest and the Wind River Indian Reservation"* and the *"Big Horn Canyon*

National Park, Mont.-Wyo.; spectacular canyon on the Big Horn River; mostly within the Crow Indian Reservation." Among additions suggested by the report for existing national parks, Simpson found *"Yellowstone National Park: Thorofare and upper Yellowstone country"* and *"Grand Teton National Park (legislation recently submitted to Congress.)"*[52]

Despite Simpson's attempt to establish that Cammerer's testimony concerning future parks in Wyoming did not coincide with his previously recorded position on the issue, Director Cammerer was able to show that the report, although published in 1938, was formulated four years earlier. Local interests in Montana and Wyoming originally suggested the two proposed parks to the Department of the Interior. The proposed areas were studied and found to be undeniably scenic, but in the view of the Park Service, they were insufficiently unique to qualify for national park status. Simpson failed to mention that the Park Service had already rejected the areas as future national parks and that Cammerer authored the adverse reports on the two areas.

As for the report's suggested extension of Yellowstone National Park, Cammerer explained that that project had been initiated before he became Park Service Director. Also, the section of the report dealing with the Yellowstone extension did not actually recommend an extension of that Park. A full reading of the section revealed that the list of possible park extensions was prefaced with the following statement, *"That in view of the proposed extension of federal activities in both national forests and national parks, the following areas which have previously been under consideration be again studied to determine how the public interests would be served best."*[53] Additionally, Cammerer stated that of the approximately 190 projects currently suggested for Park Service consideration, most had been stimulated by local agencies, and none were the result of his peronal initiative.

Cammerer also addressed another issue that was stressed by the opposition during the hearings. Simpson placed great emphasis on the differences in management policies between the Park Service and the Forest Service. The opposition repeatedly praised the Forest Service's multiple use ethic and criticized the Park Service's policy of "nonuse." Cammerer suggested that the comparison was misleading and inappropriate. He agreed that the policies of the two agencies were often in conflict, but he did not believe the nation's parks were not being used or were non-productive of revenue.

The director pointed out that 12,556 visitors entered Yellowstone National Park from Jackson Hole in 1927. By 1937, that number had increased to 64,773. Cammerer maintained that those visitors not only "used" the Park but also, during their travel to the Park, contributed to the revenue

Harris and Ewing Library of Congress [Public domain] via Wikimedia Commons

Nevada Senator Key Denson Pittman (D)
1872 - 1940

Pittman was born in Vicksburg, Mississippi and attended Southwestern Presbyterian College in Tennessee. He became a lawyer, but was distracted by the Klondike gold rush and worked as a miner until 1901. In 1902, he established himself as a lawyer in Nevada and was elected to the U.S. Senate in 1913. He held that office until his death in 1940. On the eve of the 1940 election, which Pittman was favored to win, he suffered a severe heart attack, and his aides were informed that death was imminent. Democratic party officials suppressed the Senator's actual condition, stating he had been hospitalized because of exhaustion, but his condition was not serious. Pittman won the election but died on November 10. His win allowed the Governor to appoint a Democrat to assume that seat in the Senate. Political shenanigans aside, Pittman was president pro tempore of the United States Senate from 1933 to 1940. He co-sponsored the Pittman-Robertson Wildlife Restoration Act of 1937, which provided funds from the federal ammunition tax to states for the purpose of establishing wildlife refuges.

of local businessmen, the town of Jackson and the state of Wyoming.[54] In Cammerer's view, national parks did generate revenue for the communities near their borders.

As a justification for the Park Service's refusal to lease home sites around the lakes within its domain, Cammerer stated that to do so would allow the lakeshore to be *"...literally dotted with summer homes for a favored few, to the exclusion of the rest of the people."* [55] In a final justification for the Park Service policy of conservation through preservation, the director of the Park Service avowed, *"...we believe there are certain areas in the United States which, because of their scenic beauty or other unusual characteristics, should be preserved for all time for all the people instead of the few in the immediate vicinity."* [56]

As far as the *Jackson Hole Courier* was concerned, Milward Simpson's performance at the Senate hearings had been a success. The editor believed the Senators, faced with an almost unanimous display of opposition, would have to reject the proposed legislation. Much of this belief was based upon the remarks of Nevada's Senator Key Pittman. Pittman, who was not particularly opposed to national parks, stated, *"...when large areas are to be taken out of the potential taxable property of the State, the wishes of the people should be considered, not so much as reflected by the opinions of their Senators and Representatives in Congress, because they come and go, but it must be the wishes of the people themselves."* [57] Another statement which the opposition particularly liked declared:

We have a case here where it has been very difficult, and continues to be very difficult, to raise sufficient revenue for them to conduct a county. They want a county government of their own or they wouldn't have had a county created in the first place. Now, when they testify, as they have in this record today, that it is very difficult to increase their returns from taxation, and unless they

Jackson Hole Historical Society and Museum p1958.0930.001
(L to R) Harry Clissold (Mayor), John Wort (hotel and "casino" owner), Ed Fuez (rancher- watching), and Mike Yokel (real estate agent) playing poker at the Wort Hotel. All of these men at various times opposed and supported plans to protect the northern portion of the valley. Gambling was illegal in Wyoming but openly tolerated in Jackson Hole.

can keep up their county revenue they are through, isn't it a question of balancing the advantages, on the one hand, of the recreational area, and, on the other hand, of the natural right of the people to stay on their lands? [58]

Pittman also remarked, *"When you have a condition such as this, with all this primitive area right adjoining, I should hesitate to stand against the wishes of the people who have settled the community.*[59]

Wyoming's Senator O'Mahoney continued to walk the middle ground hoping for a compromise. He believed that some extension of the Park could be made if the government would promise there would be no more extensions at a later time.[60] This position was not popular with many of the opposition members. On this issue, W. B. Sheppard stated, *"It is abject surrender and gross betrayal. For what? To enable Rockefeller to let go of his sack, without the slightest compensatory return to Wyoming or Teton County, but rather immense and irreparable loss."* [61]

Years later opponents to renewed park extension efforts would maintain the committee had issued an unfavorable report on the proposed legislation. In reality, no recorded recommendation or report was ever made by the committee members who conducted the hearing, and no statements of recommended action, either positive or negative, were preserved as a part of the hearing transcript. However in 1943, O'Mahoney would state as a part of his testimony attendant to consideration of H.R. 2241 (a bill to abolish the Jackson Hole National Monument, see Chapter Fifteen) that he had made a negative verbal recommendation to the full committee.

Since nothing could be accomplished regarding the proposed park extension until the next session of Congress, the fervor of the controversy should have subsided, but in September 1938, the Jackson Lions Club began a personal attack against Richard Winger that briefly extended the life of the controversy.

This attack took the form of a resolution addressed to Governor Miller requesting the removal of Winger from the Wyoming Game and Fish Commission, as well as the Commission's Executive Secretary, J. W. Scott. Like the Lions Club resolution of January 9, 1931, attacking William Deloney and the Jackson Hole Plan, this resolution contained mostly misleading and inaccurate information and accusations. Also like the

Wyoming Governor Leslie Miller (left) and Senator Joseph O'Mahoney (right) in 1935. Both men were Democrats and, for the most part, enjoyed political favor from the Wyoming electorate. Miller served two terms as governor and later in the Wyoming Legislature. Both men sought compromise on the Jackson Hole controversy. Their views diverged when President Roosevelt created the Jackson Hole National Monument in 1943.

earlier document, this resolution moved beyond expressing an opinion or support for a particular action. It might have presented a valid criticism and concern regarding the propriety of state officials testifying, even as private individuals, in a way that presents the appearance of a conflict of interest with the official position they hold. The Lions Club lost the opportunity to make that point by choosing to employ language best described as superlative inflammatory hyperbole. It was an outrageous document that most reasonable people found embarrassing. Many Jackson Hole residents were quick to distance themselves from this resolution and the Lions Club. It was, of course, written by William Simpson, the former editor of *The Grand Teton.* [See Appendix Two-G for the complete resolution.]

The resolution declared that testimony given to the Sub-Committee on Public Lands and Surveys proved the citizens of Teton County and the state of Wyoming were strongly averse to any national park extension and *"...unalterably opposed to any compromise with the Rockefeller interest."* It predicted the extension of the national parks would exclude the state of Wyoming from rightful management and control of the wildlife, and, because both Winger and Scott had supported the park extension legislation, they were acting in contradiction of their official duties as officials of the Wyoming Game and Fish Commission. The resolution further stated that by supporting the legislation the two men were *"...representing the Rockefeller plan of conquest..."* and were using *"...their official positions to destroy our local community...."* The Lions Club then resolved both Winger and Scott should be immediately removed from their official positions by the governor *"...for advocating, proposing, and attempting to destroy all the economic interests of Teton County, and within the State, and particularly the hunting and fishing privileges of the people, by methods such as are herein set forth."* [62]

The governor initially refused to take the petition seriously, believing it to be politically motivated. The Lions Club responded with a wire to the governor that stated, in part, *"The Lions Club positively denies any political action or intent to embarrass you or your administration, but do earnestly request that this matter have your immediate attention."* [63]

Miller appeared unwilling to dismiss the two men on the basis of one group's allegations and without the opportunity for a hearing. Another consideration that probably was not lost on the state's chief executive was that the gubernatorial election, in which he was running for an unprecedented third term, was only one month away. If Miller lost the election, as it appeared he might, a new Game and Fish Commission would likely be appointed. It would be more appropriate to deal with the allegations if and when he was reelected. The governor sent the following wire to William Simpson:

Accepting your assurances that Lions Club of Jackson Hole is not acting politically and in view of well known fact that any action in this or any other regard which I take at this particular time is construed by opposition as guided by partisan political motives, I am setting Saturday, November

Jackson Hole Historical Society and Museum p1958.0125.001

Jackson Mayor Harold Clissold and Wyoming Governor Nels H. Smith (1884 - 1976) at the Colter Monument. Smith moved to Wyoming from South Dakota in 1907. He served in the state legislature and was elected on the Republican ticket as Wyoming's 18th governor. He served one term.

Jackson Hole Historical Society and Museum 2005.0006.009

Town of Jackson, 1930s. Population approximately 900.

Twelfth, Ten A.M. as a consistent date for a hearing in the matter which you direct to my attention, and will at that time give full consideration to all facts and arguments which may be presented with respect to Mr. Winger and his official position.[64]

The Jackson Lions Club was unwilling to wait until after the November 8 election, and they did not like the idea that Governor Miller was willing to allow the right of due process by scheduling a hearing on the matter. They wanted Richard Winger fired based solely upon their allegations. They threatened the governor with an action they thought would embarrass him. Their response to the governor stated, in part:

The Lions Club of Jackson's Hole is disappointed and dissatisfied with your very obviously political and equivocal answer to the direct and straightforward request made of you in our recent telegram demanding the removal of Richard Winger....

Please be advised that you have now forced us in defense of our community stand to publish all of the resolutions and correspondence so that the people of Wyoming may know that we cannot expect action from you in this emergency. We now leave the issue to the people of our state.[65]

The Lions Club followed through with its threat, but the correspondence contained no damaging revelations. If the club thought it could force Miller into taking action, it evidently was unacquainted with the man's nature. Wyoming historian T. A. Larson described Miller as *"...frank, straightforward, outspoken, courageous, and stubborn."* [66] A Wyoming newspaper said of him, *"His judgement is not infallible, but if it's his considered judgement he stands by it. He does not maintain a closed mind, may be convinced by reason, facts and circumstances, but he is about as difficult to drive as a Brahma bull."* [67]

Governor Miller's correspondence from Jackson Hole was not limited to the Lions Club. M. R. Yokel of Wilson, who was not an advocate of park extension, wrote to the governor concerning the Winger controversy. His letter stated, *"I notice by the Jackson's Hole Courier that the local Lions Club is asking for the resignation of Richard Winger and can assure you that the local Lions Club are only a small minority of the people of Jackson Hole and in my estimation are using unfair methods in settling a personal grievance."* [68]

Governor Miller lost the election to Nels H. Smith, a rancher from Weston County. Since officials of the Game and Fish Commission are political appointees, the makeup of the Commission usually changes with new administrations. The

Jackson Hole Historical Society and Museum 1958.3007.001

Fishing continued to be a primary attraction for travelers to Jackson Hole. Depending on the season, snowshoes were often an essential part of an angler's gear.

Winger controversy was settled by the election rather than by personal vendetta.

It is unlikely that the Lions Club's "revelation" materially contributed to Miller's defeat. Although he was possibly one of the best governors ever to serve the state of Wyoming; his reelection bid was handicapped by a variety of obstacles. First among those problems was his being a Democrat in a normally Republican state. Second, Wyoming only infrequently returns a governor to office and, as previously noted, Miller was trying for a third term. Third, a state sales tax was implemented during his administration. Fourth, the state, generally, had become displeased with many aspects of the New Deal, which were associated with Miller's administration even though Miller, being a conservative, was not particularly enchanted with the New Deal programs. Additionally in 1938, the Wyoming Democratic Party suffered from infighting and could not present a strong united front. In 1934, Miller had been enthusiastically returned to office but carried only two counties in 1938.[69] With all these other factors, it was unlikely that any action taken by the Jackson Hole Lions Club, either for or against the governor, would have altered the outcome of the election.

Miller was not the only Democrat to suffer defeat in the 1938 election. Frank O. Horton, a dude rancher from the community of Saddlestring, replaced Wyoming's lone representative in Congress, Paul Greever. Horton's campaign carried the familiar "states' rights" issue to new heights, declaring, *"...the so called public lands lying within our borders are not public lands at all. They belong to Wyoming."* [70] He stated that federal control and regulation of the public lands amounted to an invasion of state lands. The Grand Teton National Park extension controversy was one of his prime examples. His platform called for the transfer of most of the public land in Wyoming to state ownership. Horton's campaign rhetoric has familiar echoes in the modern day orations in favor of the sagebrush rebellion.

~

With the Senate hearings a thing of the past and the election settled, the extension controversy took a back seat to other local issues. While tourist travel in Yellowstone National Park declined by 9 percent, Grand Teton National Park recorded 154,353 visitors– an increase of 14.3 percent.[71] The tourist industry had helped all of Wyoming. The Department of Commerce and Industry reported that during 1938 tourists spent $15,120,279 in the state.[72] Once again, neither the national Depression nor local feuding was able to dampen the economic outlook for Jackson Hole. In spite of the controversies, Jackson Hole continued to prosper.*

---

*The fears of Jackson Hole residents that Rockefeller's proposed donation of land to the government would create financial hardships for the county were valid. There was also the concern that the people who sold their land to the Snake River Land Company would move out of the valley causing an economic decline for local merchants. It follows that the activities of the Snake River Land Company should have caused a decrease in the population of Teton County. Some of the settlers indeed moved to more temperate areas of the nation, but many, it appears, moved to town to start businesses of their own. According to the U.S. Census Bureau, the county population grew by 27 percent during the decade of the 1930s. The population of the town of Jackson grew by 96.2 percent for this same period.

CHAPTER FOURTEEN

1939-1941

The original purpose and intent in creating Grand Teton National Park was to retain the wilderness character of the area. That part of the park which is not taken up by rugged mountains is restricted in extent and leaves little more than the actual shoreline of small lakes available for public purposes. In the beginning, it was used by only a small number of visitors. In recent years, however, the popularity of the park and growth of attendance figures have been rather phenomenal and the park is now threatened with serious damage due to its popularity.

Arno P. Cammerer
May 1940[1]

Jackson Hole Historical Society and Museum 1958.2375.001

The frozen surface of Jackson Lake in winter made good landing areas for airplanes with skis.

Nineteen thirty-nine was a relatively quiet year for Jackson Hole. Idaho was still trying to solidify its claims to water from the Snake River drainage, but generally, the populace remained rather calm. Even Congressman Horton with his grandiloquent speeches against the federal government could not inspire another controversy in the valley.

Horton was appointed to three House committees and was proud of his positions. He stated he was particularly pleased that he had been appointed to the Public Lands Committee because, as a member of that body, he would be able to *"...push his plans for the development of oil on public lands in Wyoming, and to develop his crusade for a return of vast areas of public lands in*

Wyomingtalesandtrails.com
Park Service snowplow at Jenny Lake gas station

Wyoming to the state." He declared, *"Wyoming has been deprived of 65 per cent of its own land. This tremendous percentage is under the control one way or another of the Federal Government. As Wyoming's Representative in Congress, and as a member of the Public Lands Committee, I am never going to let up on the fight to turn these millions of acres now on public domain back to the control of the State of Wyoming."*

As a member of the Irrigation and Reclamation Committee, Horton evidently forgot his stand on state sovereignty and pledged to *"... promote irrigation and reclamation projects in Wyoming...."*[2] He did not explain how he would promote federal reclamation projects on lands he was trying to remove from federal influence and control. He

was equally inconsistent concerning to his membership on the Roads Committee. He apparently was not opposed to the "invasion" of the state by the federal government if they built more roads during the raid.

~

Among the more encouraging aspects of the winter of 1939 was the increase in winter tourism that resulted from the state's attempt to keep both the Hoback Canyon road and Teton Pass open. Evidently, the elk herd and openly tolerated gambling were the main attractions for these tourists since the road to Teton and Yellowstone National Parks was not plowed. Such was the attraction of Jackson Hole in the winter that some tourists had to be taken into the homes of residents due to insufficient winter accommodations in the town.[3]

Because of the popularity of the winter season, Grand Teton National Park's chief ranger, Allyn Hanks, announced that the Park had ordered a snowplow so that roads into the Park could be opened for winter travel. This created the potential for a year-round tourist economy that seemed more likely in 1939 than it ever had before.

~

Several events occurred that year which might normally have created more controversy in the valley. Maybe the residents were too exhausted from the battles of 1938 to overreact. First among these events was the announcement by Interior Secretary Harold Ickes that, in an attempt to make the parks self-supporting, an admission charge would be instituted in both Grand Teton and Yellowstone National Parks. Grand Teton National Park would charge $1 per car, and Yellowstone National Park would charge $3 per car. This fee was good for the entire season, and the fee for entrance to Grand Teton was applicable to the Yellowstone fee. The expected objections by outraged residents who had always entered and enjoyed the parks without charge did not materialize. Perhaps the conservative nature of the valley's residents allowed an understanding and appreciation for any argument that proposed fiscal responsibility on the part of the federal government.

A second event stimulated a minor response from some of the valley's residents. This time, the incident was initiated by the Biological Survey. Adolph Hamm, the district agent in charge of predator control for the U.S. Biological Survey out of Cheyenne, wanted to begin a poisoning campaign against coyotes in Jackson Hole. Hamm worked closely with the Woolgrowers Association to eradicate the sly predator. He evidently enjoyed the reputation he had built with that association and, on several occasions had been an honored speaker at the association's meetings. There is no evidence that Hamm's proposal was made for any other reason than that the coyote existed in the valley and was generally unmolested. The coyote population in Jackson Hole existed at risk when in the proximity of local cattle herds, but no concentrated eradication program had been implemented within the valley. His only reason for the proposed campaign was the suggestion that Jackson Hole served as a breeding ground for predators.[4]

Since there were no sheep in Jackson Hole, the campaign seemed ludicrous to the *Jackson Hole Courier*, and the paper printed articles opposing the proposed activity. Jackson Hole was probably the only area of the state where the coyote was not universally disparaged. For those residents who understood that in an area where tourism was the major economic factor and every wild animal was an economic asset, Hamm's proposal was unacceptable. Because of the objections of the residents of Jackson Hole, an agreement was reached whereby no poisoning would be conducted north of the Hoback River.

~

In May 1939, the valley received some unexpected publicity at the New York World's Fair. The exhibit sponsored by Eastman Kodak presented scenes of the American West and among these were several photographs of the Tetons. Although the exhibit may have had little or no effect on the 1939 tourist season, in June, the *Courier* reported that the tourist business in Jackson was up 10 percent from the same period in 1938. Teton Park also reported a record number of visitors for its opening day of the season.[5]

While the scenic and recreational attractions of Grand Teton National Park continued to prove their worth as an economic benefit to the residents of the valley, Congressman Horton was introducing legislation to abolish the Park. His bill (H.R. 6959) would return the park area to the jurisdiction of the Forest Service. Congressman Horton's espoused reason for introducing the legislation seems a bit reactionary. He said his bill was prompted by another bill which, if passed, would permit water power and irrigation projects within Kings Canyon National Park. He claimed that, *"The California bill is but an entering wedge designed by the Interior Department to permit reclamation and irrigation projects in other National Parks."* Horton forgot, was unaware, or ignored the numerous battles that the National Park Service and Jackson Hole settlers had been required to fight periodically to save the valley's scenic lakes while the land was within the domain of the Forest Service. It was the multiple use policy of the latter agency that had placed the lakes in jeopardy. The Congressman seemed out of touch with the realities of the issue when he stated, *"If we*

Photo courtesy Richard Holm

John Krause with coyote pelts, 1940s.
As this photograph shows, there was a healthy population of coyotes in Jackson Hole. However, cattle, at most times of the year and except for unusual conditions, are less susceptible to coyote predation than sheep.

must permit reclamation projects in our national parks there is no need for the national park system. The only safe place for our beautiful Tetons seems to be in the Forestry Service." [6]

Horton's motives in this incident were unclear. He might have assumed that because of the apparent widespread opposition to the Teton Park extension, the people also objected to the existence of the national park as established in 1929. By attacking the Park, he might gain some political advantage. On the other hand, because of his position on the House Irrigation and Reclamation Committee, Horton may have wanted the lakes removed from the protection of the Park Service so that irrigation interests might develop them. Perhaps his bill was simply an attack against the Department of the Interior for the purpose of publicity.

In any case, his bill, which eventually failed, did not incite a controversy or create any significant publicity or local conflict. The *Jackson Hole Courier* noted the introduction of the bill, but it did not take a stand on the issue. The paper did ask a number of people to express their opinions concerning the legislation. The responses covered the spectrum ranging from rejection, to

Wyoming State Library

Frank Ogilvie Horton (R)
1882-1948

Horton attended Morgan Park Military Academy in Illinois and the University of Chicago. He began ranching in Wyoming in 1905. He served only one term in the U.S. House of Representatives failing to retain the office in the 1941 election. After leaving Congress, he returned to his ranch in Saddlestring.

support, to essential indifference. E. C. Benson, the owner of the Jackson Hole Light and Power Company stated, *"I think we all feel glad that we have active support in Washington and I believe we should all send our congratulations to Congressman Horton."* Mrs. M. E. Moulton, a Republican precinct committee-woman (Horton was also a Republican), responded, *"I don't think much of Mr. Horton and his plan of abolishing Teton National Park. I think it is absurd. I think it is just a blind for some other action and our interests are about to be sold out to another state by Mr. Horton. I certainly don't approve of our Congressional delegate carrying on in this manner."* David B. Anderson, an attorney, remarked, *"The park should stay as it now stands. Just because some crackpot in Washington wants some publicity, we have to contend with screwy ideas like this. Instead of abolishing the park, let's abolish Senator [sic] Horton the next time his name appears on the ballot."* Nephi Moulton stated, *"I haven't quite made up my mind one way or the other. I think there is something else connected with it. I don't know just what to think."* Finally, H. G. Weston responded, *"It's all right, I suppose."* Congressman Horton's bill was quickly forgotten. [7]

~

In the fall of 1939, it appeared briefly that Rockefeller had renewed his purchasing program within Jackson Hole. Three purchases were made which caused this speculation. Rockefeller bought 38.9 acres from Mr. and Mrs. J. D. Kimmel, 640 acres from Shad Hobbs and 622 acres from Lewis Fleming. All of these properties were near Phelps Lake, and some rumors suggested the Snake River Land Company was going to purchase the land west of the Snake River as far south as the community of Wilson. Richard Winger revealed that the purchases were of a personal nature and not a part of the Snake River Land Company operations. [8]

As 1939 drew to a close, two additional events occurred which were considered positive in nature by Jackson Hole residents. The first of these was an agreement among the state of Wyoming, the Park Service, and the Bureau of Reclamation concerning road development near Moran. The subject of this agreement concerned the need for a bridge across the Snake River. The flow of traffic in that area indicated a bridge was desirable near the dam. The state was not anxious to allocate the money for the structure. Instead, the state wanted the bureau to allow traffic to cross the dam, thus saving the state the cost of constructing the highway approaches as well as the cost of erecting a new bridge. The bureau was reluctant to allow the dam to be used as a highway, but they acquiesced during a conference held in Washington, D.C. between Wyoming's governor and the federal officials. This would provide an easier and more attractive access for tourists leaving Yellowstone National Park by the south entrance to Teton Park and the town of Jackson. It was hoped those tourists who might normally have exited the valley by the northeast route toward Dubois might be attracted toward the southern portion of the valley and to the merchants who desired their business.[9]

The other event was the announcement by park officials that the road through Grand Teton National Park would be kept open during the winter. This, of course, was viewed as another promising step toward the further development of a winter tourist industry. With a successful summer season behind them, many residents were optimistic about the coming winter season.

While the valley's residents reveled in the prospects of the improving winter economy, they were also mindful of the deteriorating state of world affairs. As if to share the valley's good fortune, the Finnish Relief Fund was established with Mrs. O. J. Murie as chairman.

Although the threat of world conflict was unable to dampen the spirits of local businessmen, the Wyoming Highway Department found a way to stir up the populace. The state ordered the snow plows off Teton Pass for the winter. This action was the result of budget constraints, but

Jackson Hole Historical Society and Museum 1991.3737.026

Dog team races were part of the winter carnival attractions.

Jackson residents were irate. Money had already been spent on advertising the winter attractions of Jackson Hole, the Park Service had purchased a snowplow so that the Park would be accessible, and the community had organized and planned races, sports events, and a winter carnival.

The residents were determined to have winter access to the valley from the west. Jackson Hole had always been big on committees, and whenever a crisis arose, somebody formed a committee from which resolutions and statements emanated. This time, a spontaneous committee of roughly 200 residents gathered, commandeered the snow plows and personally opened the Teton Pass road. This group called themselves the "Borrowing Committee." [10] The Highway Department was furious, but there was little they could do. The Committee returned the keys to the machinery when Governor Smith interceded in the issue and provided additional funds so that the pass could be maintained. While this might prove that some committees are capable of more than literary activity, the effect of this group's action was mitigated by the fact that Idaho plowed its approach to the pass irregularly.

～

Early in 1940, Grand Teton National Park received a new superintendent. Charles Smith,

271

Jackson Hole Historical Society and Museum 1958.0753.001p

The snow plows that were commandeered by the "Borrowing Committee" to open the Teton Pass road.

the Superintendent of Petrified Forest National Monument,* and Thomas Whitcraft, Superintendent of Grand Teton National Park, exchanged positions.[11] Smith was not a newcomer to the region, having been a ranger in Yellowstone National Park before automobiles were permitted in that reserve. Because of his background, he was generally considered by most people to be a traditional frontier man. He had been a guide in New Hampshire's White Mountains where he earned the nickname "White Mountain Smith." He was also a stagecoach driver on Florida's Ormond Beach before moving west. In Wyoming, Smith started as a stagecoach driver in Yellowstone National Park. He was the driver of the second coach in a line of 17 stages robbed in a single day by a lone highwayman in 1908. Smith was also one of the first civilian Yellowstone Park rangers. Even as a "government man," he was cordially received.[12]

≈

In April, as Milward Simpson announced his plans to run for O'Mahoney's U.S. Senate seat, Congressman Horton was warning that new efforts were afoot to extend Grand Teton National Park. Horton claimed to have learned from an "unrevealed source" that Secretary Ickes had initiated a new bill to add 220,000 acres to Teton Park.[13] Such a bill, if it actually existed, was never introduced in Congress. Congressman Horton, although he certainly tried, seemed unable to incite the residents of Jackson Hole. His continued exhortations regarding park extension proposals failed to inspire even one publicly recorded response within the valley by either the populace or the newspaper.†

It appeared the only controversy in which Horton could involve himself concerned a decision by the Park Service to eliminate powerboats on Leigh Lake and to close the road that provided automobile access to that lake. The *Jackson Hole Courier* reported that a petition protesting the closure and containing 400 signatures had been sent to Washington.[14] Congressman Horton also wrote to Director Cammerer in this regard and Cammerer's response was printed in the Courier. It stated in part:

The presence of the road, into the Leigh Lake section of the park brings thousands of people into a small, fine acreage so that its sylvan character is gradually being changed and the natural features being overrun by use. Each summer a larger number of

---

*Petrified Forest National Monument was established on December 8, 1906, by Presidential Proclamation. The monument was converted to a National Park in 1958.

†Horton may have erred in his statements regarding the proposed legislation, but his warning about pending efforts to extend the boundaries of Grand Teton National Park would be proven correct.

motor boats are brought to both Leigh Lake and Jenny Lake and the noise and activity which they create is far from what might be expected in a wilderness area. There is still time, however, to retain the original objectives, if proper steps are taken now. Accordingly, we have decided to eliminate the Leigh Lake road and the use of motor boats from the lake. Access will then be possible by means of a fine scenic trail to be built entirely around the lake.

Jackson Lake, which is a much larger body of water and which has good fishing, plenty of space for cruising, and, many other advantages for motor boating, is easily available to those in the Jackson Hole region interested in that type of sport, and is decidedly more suitable for it.

Compared with the few persons who may have a personal interest in the use of Leigh Lake for boating, thousands visit Grand Teton National Park to enjoy the quiet and inspiration of its wilderness character.[15]

In his book, *A Place Called Jackson Hole,* historian John Daugherty maintains the Leigh Lake road was removed because it was constructed in violation of the 1929 act creating Grand Teton National Park. That act prohibited the construction of new roads within the national park. Daugherty's cited source for this version was Superintendent Woodring's monthly report from 1930 and his annual report from 1932. It is odd, however, that this rather logical excuse was never mentioned by the Park

Grand Teton National Park GRTE-00430_1441
Scenic turnout on the Leigh Lake road

The road was eliminated by Grand Teton National Park. One recent Park historian stated that the road was removed because it was constructed in violation of the enabling legislation that created Grand Teton National Park in 1929. However, a 1927 U.S. Geological Survey map (Grand Teton Quadrangle) clearly shows the Leigh Lake road. The CCC did build the turnout pictured above and made improvements to the road after the Park was established. (Bottom photo) That legislation did not prohibit maintenance or improvements to the existing road.

Grand Teton National Park GRTE-00430_401

Service nor by the Secretary of Interior when locals and Wyoming's Congressional delegation complained about the road's elimination. The federal officials only stated they wanted to reduce automobile traffic in the area and eliminate motorboat access to the lake. It likewise seems improbable that the residents who so adamantly insisted on the restriction of new road construction within park boundaries in 1928 would have silently acquiesced to the construction of this road if it violated the compromise that allowed the Park to be established.   Horace Albright was

director of the National Park Service at the time Daugherty says the road was built. It is hard to imagine he would have approved a new road in violation of the prohibition provision he claimed to have authored during the Senate hearing in Jackson in 1928. (See Chapter Eight.) The CCC built vehicle turnouts along the road after the Park was established and they may have even extended the road. However, it is difficult to argue that the road was constructed after the Park was established.

Thus, the residents of Jackson Hole witnessed the first of what would become an appreciable list of closures and restrictions imposed on the Teton Park area. The Park's growing popularity necessitated most of these restrictions. It was also becoming apparent that the greatest threat to the nation's parks was the people who visited them. Concerning the inappropriate conduct of some visitors in the national parks, Harold Ickes, the Secretary of the Interior, in a speech seven years earlier to the American Civic Association, remarked, *"If I had my way about national parks I would create one without a road in it. I would have it impenetrable forever to automobiles, a place where man would not try to improve upon God. I sometimes think that people should be barred from the parks– so few know how to use them. Crowds and parks are incompatible ...."* [16]

S. N. Leek Collection, American Heritage Center, University of Wyoming
ah 03138_1015

Predating the creation of Grand Teton National Park, this map clearly shows the road to Leigh Lake (in the square) where a boat ramp allowed access for motorized craft. It is a mystery why the Park Service would feel the need to invent the "illegally constructed road" excuse for eliminating the Leigh Lake road. Numerous maps show the road existed prior to the restrictions enacted in the 1929 park legislation. This disingenuous action further justified the suspicious attitudes locals often held regarding the National Park Service. This map also predates the Forest Service road connecting the Jenny Lake road to the Jackson Lake Dam. Another map showing the road to Leigh Lake, dated 1929, is viewable online at the Library of Congress website. (Call number: G4262.Y4 1929.B6TIL; Catalog number: 97683583)

~

In May 1940, the *Jackson Hole Courier* learned that the Snake River Land Company transferred its holdings in Jackson Hole to a newly formed New York corporation. This new corporation, the Jackson Hole Preserve, Incorporated, was established as a member corporation of the University of New York under a provision of that state's Membership Corporation Law, Section II,

Article 2. This procedure facilitated the corporation's organization as a nonprofit charitable, educational and scientific entity– an eleemosynary trust. Section 2 of the Jackson Hole Preserve's Articles of Incorporation declared:

The purposes for which the corporation is formed are exclusively charitable, educational and scientific, and are to restore, protect and preserve, for the benefit of the public, the primitive grandeur and natural beauties of the landscape in areas notable for picturesque scenery, and particularly in the Jackson Hole area in the State of Wyoming, to provide for the protection, feeding and propagation of wild game in such areas, to maintain and develop historic landmarks and other features of historic or scientific interest in such areas, to provide facilities for the public use, understanding, appreciation and enjoyment of the scenic, biologic, scientific and historic features of such areas, and in general to promote, encourage and conduct such other activities as are germane to these general purposes.[17]

Some familiar names were among the list of officers and board members of the new corporation. The board of Trustees was composed of Horace M. Albright, Kenneth Chorley, Harold P. Fabian, Olaus J. Murie, Laurance S. Rockefeller and Vanderbilt Webb. Laurance Rockefeller and Harold Fabian served as president and vice president of the corporation.

The Snake River Land Company released a press statement concerning the transfer of its holdings to the Jackson Hole Preserve, Inc. The former company had spent in excess of $1,320,000 to purchase 33,000 acres of land. Another 2,000 acres had been turned over to the

U.S. Government through the purchase of relinquishments of pending homestead entries for $80,000. Additional expenses incurred in connection with the acquisition of the properties and the net carrying cost of the properties amounted to another $350,000. Thus, Rockefeller had spent approximately $1,750,000 in Jackson Hole as of 1940. Revenue from the operation of the Jackson Hole properties was not mentioned.

The original intent, with regard to the disposition of this land, was to donate the property to the U.S. Government. However, various circumstances and controversies had thus far obstructed the fulfillment of that objective. The release stated:

In view of this situation and the fact that it may continue to exist, it has now seemed desirable to provide a more appropriate organization for the continued administration of these properties in the public interest.

The Snake River Land Company was incorporated merely as a temporary medium for taking title to these lands and for their

Karl C. Allen Papers, Box 7, Folder 10 American Heritage Center, University of Wyoming

Grand Teton National Park Staff, c. early 1940s

In barely a decade, the Grand Teton National Park ranger force expanded from less than a dozen to 35 even though the Park had not been enlarged and the areas where visitors could easily travel had been reduced. A larger park staff was deemed necessary to deal with its increasing popularity.

anticipated conveyance to the United States. Jackson Hole Preserve, Inc. has been organized with broader and more permanent powers, which enable the Board of Trustees to develop and administer for the public benefit any of the properties which it may acquire and also to carry out Mr. Rockefeller's original intention of transferring the lands in question to the United States if and when the Board of Trustees find this can and should be done.[18]

While the *Jackson Hole Courier* failed to comment on the formation of the Jackson Hole Preserve, Inc., other than to report its creation, the *Cody Enterprise* condemned the action as "insulting charity." The *Enterprise* stated:

On the one hand we read about Eastern slums wherein conditions are so appalling as to be scarcely believable, about political scandals in comparison to which our little messes are indeed small potatoes, about un-American Nazi and Communist activities shocking to our people, about crimes scummy and beneath the honor of any good Western shooter-upper. On the other hand we find an Eastern group of meddling park-extensionists, backed by the well-intentioned Mr. Rockefeller, has formed a New York corporation with purposes, "exclusively charitable, educational and scientific and are to restore, protect and preserve ...the primitive grandeur and natural beauties of the landscape... particularly in the Jackson Hole area in the State of Wyoming."

How insulting! How insulting to the people of Wyoming and, indeed, to the people of the entire West! How insulting are those expressed purposes of that New York corporation to the people who not only make their livelihood in these mountains, but love them with a depth of feeling impossible in the summer visitor flitting through the country in an automobile with the visibility of a submarine, ohing and ahing and trying to see how many miles he can cover in a day.

For the benefit of Eastern industrialists and to garner Eastern votes they would

destroy our stock industries by admitting cheap South American meat. For the idle pleasure of Eastern trippers they would turn our country into a glorified city park and convert the inhabitants into museum specimens to decorate the scenery.

If meddling Easterners plan similarly to exercise their charity on us, let them have the consistency first to clean up their own mess. When they have, we might consider taking up our niches in the Great Western Museum, so carefully planned for us by those who sit in New York offices and, with especially God-given insight into what's good for the rest of the world, plan 'Jackson Hole Preserve, Inc.'[19]

Jackson Hole Historical Society and Museum
The Snow King chairlift provided locals a chance to recreate in the winter, but also helped to attract winter tourists. This lift replaced a rope tow and extended access to the top of the mountain.

The corner of Broadway and Cache Streets was the hub of commerce during the summer tourist season.

The attitude of the *Cody Enterprise* appeared to have been the exception rather than the rule. As far as most people could see, no real change had occurred as a result of the formation of the new corporation. Rockefeller's desire to give his land to the U.S. Government had been public knowledge since 1930. The benevolent objectives of his purchasing program were also common knowledge. The only real difference appeared to be the name on the deed to the land in question, and the fact that the Jackson Hole Preserve, Inc. was organized in New York while the Snake River Land Company was organized in Utah.

Although it was not obvious at the time, the creation of the Jackson Hole Preserve, Inc. was an auspicious event. With its extended scope, the corporation could channel additional funds toward the preservation of other unique and representative sections of the nation for the enjoyment of future generations. Jackson Hole Preserve, Inc. was, of course, only one of many Rockefeller philanthropic endeavors. The family had already contributed massive amounts of money for charity, the arts, education, health, research and scenic preservation. The formation of this particular organization confirmed the Rockefellers' continued interest, concern, and commitment to saving a portion of our nation's heritage. Much

of the National Park System as it exists today is the result of the activities of the Jackson Hole Preserve, Inc.

Laurance Rockefeller's position with the Jackson Hole Preserve was also significant. It was about this time that the Rockefeller brothers began to perceive and assume their future roles concerning the family's affairs. Laurance appeared to have a predisposition for the family's conservation activities and assumed responsibility for the Jackson Hole Preserve as well as a leadership role in other national conservation organizations. Although World War II interrupted the brothers' ascension to power, Laurance and the organizations he supported became an important and respected force in the nation's postwar conservation activities.

~

Nineteen forty was another good year for the tourist industry in Wyoming. Once again the travel figures verified the growing popularity of Grand Teton National Park and the Jackson Hole region. Yellowstone's travel figures showed that the Park had an increase in visitation of 8.1 percent more than 1939. The south entrance to the Park experienced a 16 percent increase in traffic.[20]

While the national parks continued to prove their economic value to adjacent communities

277

and the state, Milward Simpson began his campaign for O'Mahoney's U.S. Senate seat by attacking the incumbent's compromise stand on the park extension issue. In a speech delivered in September to Jackson residents, Simpson stated, *"If I am elected to the U.S. Senate I'm going to prove to the people of Jackson, Teton County and the whole State of Wyoming, that the threat to their homes and livelihood, everlastingly presented by the specter of National Park encroachment, can be removed once and for all time. Unless the present uncertainty is removed there can be no security, no chance for proper development of the region. It must be settled."* [21]

William Simpson in front of the
Colter Monument

William L. Simpson was born in Ft. Lyons, Colorado on January 26, 1868, and at age 15 moved to Wyoming Territory to find work as a ranch hand. He appears to have first visited Jackson Hole in 1883 as a member of a posse tracking horse thieves. Bill had little formal education, but he decided to become a lawyer and demonstrated considerable initiative to educate himself. He successfully passed the oral Wyoming Bar exam in 1892 and married his Latin tutor, Margaret Lou Burnett, in 1893.[24] Their son, Milward, was born in Jackson in 1897. William Simpson was one of the most avid and aggressive opponents of Grand Teton National Park and the various proposals for its extension. Two months before his death at age 72, he stood in line with a group of much younger men insisting he be allowed to register for the draft.

Simpson also took a page from Congressman Horton's book of rhetoric and claimed that impending legislation to extend the Park was likely because of O'Mahoney's failure to take a firm stand against any extension effort. O'Mahoney denied that any such bill was pending or that such a bill had any chance of being introduced. Additionally, it was illogical that the Park Service or the Department of the Interior would contemplate the introduction of a park extension bill during an election year.

Simpson also based his campaign upon anti-Communist hysteria claiming the New Deal programs were controlled by fifth columnists. He asserted that O'Mahoney was *"...a firm believer in the New Deal and therefore in national socialism."* O'Mahoney responded that Simpson's fifth column talk was *"...the purist kind of bunk."* [22]

While the campaign heated up, so did world affairs, and 384 Teton County residents registered with the Selective Service. The draft did not appear to be a significant campaign issue within the county, and the election drew a record number of voters. Within Teton County, Roosevelt defeated Willkie 728 to 628 and Horton beat McIntyre 681 to 540. O'Mahoney narrowly defeated Simpson 675 to 625, but outside Teton County O'Mahoney did much better. He was returned to the Senate by a 19,000-vote margin– a veritable landslide for such a sparsely populated state.[23] Statewide, Horton was defeated by McIntyre.

Barely a month after Milward Simpson's defeat, his father, William Simpson, died of a heart attack. Although he was somewhat more infamous than famous, he was nevertheless honored in death by the valley residents as one of Wyoming's pioneer attorneys.[25]

〜

Nineteen forty-one was also a rather quiet year for Jackson Hole as far as park extension was concerned, and the valley continued to reap the economic benefits of an expanding tourist industry. Many residents believed this trend would endure and expand, especially if an airport could be established within the valley. Previously, airplanes landed at a small strip near the high school just one block from the center of town during the summer. In winter, small planes used a portion of the elk refuge several blocks north of the center of town. Neither of these strips was considered adequate for the type of commercial service some residents believed necessary for the valley's progress. The age of aeronautics was developing rapidly, and the construction of an airport meant more than increased accessibility to the valley for tourists. It symbolized the inclusion of the valley into the civilized world– a world less remote and more mobile. The site selected by the leaders of the community for a "real" airport was nine miles north of the town, essentially at its present location. The spot they chose was on public land, and this led to a minor confrontation with the federal government. In almost any other section of the country, the proposed site probably would

bioguide.congress.gov [Public domain] via Wikimedia Commons
Milward Lee Simpson (R)
1897-1993

Milward, the son of William L. Simpson, was born in Jackson and attended public schools in several Wyoming communities. He graduated from the University of Wyoming, received his law degree from Harvard University Law School, and established himself in Cody, Wyoming. He served in the U.S. Army during World War I as a second lieutenant in the infantry. Narrowly elected governor in 1954, he was also narrowly defeated in the next election. In 1962, he was elected to the Senate and is sometimes remembered as one of six Republican senators who voted against the 1964 Civil Rights Act. However, it should be noted that as governor in 1957, he signed the law that forbade racial discrimination in Wyoming.

have been approved with little hesitation. The area, with the exception of its view of the Teton Mountain Range, was generally unexciting. It contained no trees, no known mineral wealth and, without irrigation, was of marginal grazing value. It was simply a sagebrush flat and its terrain was of a character that neither Jackson Hole nor the state of Wyoming was destitute.

The land for the proposed airport was under the jurisdiction of the General Land Office, an agency of the Department of the Interior. Because of the past park controversies and the possibility of future park extension proposals, the General Land Office was reluctant to permit such a development. Nevertheless, the requested lease for the purpose of constructing an airport seemed assured after Donald Connolly, the director of the Civil Aeronautics Administration, intervened on behalf of the community of Jackson.[26]

The construction of an airport was not the only indication that civilization and its attendant impositions upon individual rights had reached Jackson Hole. Societal laws began to take precedence over individual desires as Al Austin's friends learned. Mr. Austin had been a resident of the valley for 40 years and was known for his talent as a poet and photographer. Austin had spent considerable time in Jackson Hole's backcountry photographing wildlife. His collection of photographs, both stills and movies, were of professional quality and were contributed without fee to several eastern organizations for educational purposes. The natural environs of Jackson Hole had been a consistent theme in his verse and had provided countless happy moments for this unusually sensitive man. He stated to his friends that when his time was up, he hoped to die in the wilderness he cherished. He abhorred the idea that he might be buried in the local cemetery. Austin, who in 1941 was about 70 years old and of failing health, decided death was near and made his preparations. He drove his car to the north end of the valley and concealed the vehicle in the woods. He then hiked into the wilderness and constructed a teepee on Arizona Creek where two forest service employees, Bill Ferrin and Bud Thompson, later found his body. Considering the date of his disappearance and the date of the last entry in his diary, which simply stated "snow," it was estimated he might have survived 20 days, 18 of which were during a snowstorm.

There was a time in Jackson Hole when his selected burial site might have been considered as hallowed as any legally designated cemetery. That situation was as much frontier history as the trapper era, so Austin's remains were retrieved and interred in the Jackson Cemetery.[27] The following poem by Mr. Austin was published after his death and provides an insight into the nature of the man.

I'll Turn My Footsteps There

I love to eat and sleep near snow-capped peaks,
The Rocky Mountains grand.
I love the smell of stately pines
That tower on every hand.
The streams that leap through canyons deep,
The wind's low melody.

I hear their call and love them all,
The wilds is home to me.
I love the croon, the low sweet tune,
Of the night winds thru every tree.
I love to dream in the campfire's gleam,
Of days that used to be.

And the coyote cries to star-lit skies,
Echoing on the evening air.
I hear them all as the shadows fall,
And turn my footsteps there,
Into the hills like an old bull elk,
When e'er my time is nigh." [28]

For better or worse, the valley of Jackson Hole began to relax its embrace with its frontier heritage.

Karl C. Allan Papers Box 7, folder 25, American Heritage Center, University of Wyoming

Al Austin

Jackson Historical Society and Museum 1958.1762.001

Game warden Austin on winter patrol.

CHAPTER FIFTEEN

1942-1943

The establishment of the Jackson Hole National Monument in Wyoming, made possible by a proclamation signed by President Roosevelt today, preserves for the enjoyment of future generations a 221,610 acre area adjacent to the Grand Teton National Park which is rich in scenic beauty and in the tradition of American frontier history. I am glad that the President saw fit to authorize the establishment of this area as a new national monument. In one sense, it is a symbolic evidence of our intention to maintain intact our priceless heritages of natural resources for the people's enjoyment after the war is over.

Secretary of Interior
Harold L. Ickes[1]
March 1943

From every side comes assurance that the people of Teton County will have ample support in their efforts to fight this latest episode of the 25-year struggle against park extension. And if we lose the battle it will only be after we have lifted our bloody heads for the last feeble effort to raise anew our banner, which stands for justice and the democratic way of life.

Editor, *Jackson Hole Courier*
March 1943

S. N. Leek Collection, ah03138_1989, American Heritage Center, University of Wyoming

Uncertain highway conditions and the harsh winter climate made for a difficult winter economy in the town of Jackson. Accommodations for tourists during the summer were inadequate for the demand while only a few hotels and motels, like the Ideal Lodge, could afford to remain open during the winter season.

Like the rest of the nation, Jackson Hole began 1942 fully involved in the war effort. Feelings of outrage and patriotism were strong, and the community lost little time forming a rationing board for sugar, tires, gas and other items. The people of Jackson Hole believed they took a leadership role for the state in these efforts and were especially proud that Teton County led the state in the purchase of U.S. War Bonds exceeding its quota by 274.2 percent.[2]

While World War II may have been uppermost in the minds of Jackson's residents, they did not ignore their promotion of the local tourist industry. The community planned a mammoth winter sports program that lasted most of the winter, but the usual prizes were replaced with defense bonds. The elk herd remained the greatest attraction for winter visitors to Jackson. On one day 969 people viewed the herd on horse-drawn sleds.[3] Another segment of Jackson's economy, big game hunting, also remained strong. The federal government publicly encouraged this activity on the grounds that leather from the hides was needed for the war effort and that the activity would reduce grazing competition with domestic animals.[4]

During this time, thoughts and worries concerning the extension of Grand Teton National Park were forgotten. Even the campaigns for the November 1942 elections, which resulted in

Jackson Hole Historical Society and Museum 1999.0031.001
Rope tows at the Snow King Ski Area and winter-oriented activities were expanded in an attempt to attract more winter business to the valley.

changes in three of the state's four top political offices, ignored the issue of park extension. Lester Hunt, a Democrat, defeated Governor Smith; Frank Barrett assumed John McIntyre's seat in the House of Representatives, and E. V. Robertson replaced Harry Schwartz in the Senate. Senator O'Mahoney was not up for re-election.*

While Jackson Hole residents may have forgotten about park extension, or at least re-ordered the priority of their concerns, John D. Rockefeller, Jr. had not. On November 27, 1942, Rockefeller wrote a letter to Interior Secretary Harold Ickes briefly reviewing his operations in Jackson Hole and expressing his continued interest in national parks. [See Appendix Two-G for the complete letter.] He also stated:

In view of the uncertainty of the times, like everybody else, I am and have been for some time reducing my obligations and burdens insofar as I wisely can. In line with that policy I have definitely reached the conclusion, although most reluctantly, that I should make permanent disposition of the property before another year has passed. If the Federal Government is not interested in the acquisition, or being interested, is still unable to arrange to accept it on the general terms long discussed and with which you are familiar, it will be my thought to make some other disposition of it or, failing in that, to sell it in the market to any satisfactory buyers.[5]

It is perhaps impossible to be certain if Rockefeller was serious in his threat to sell his Jackson Hole properties on the open market. Josephine Fabian believed he would never have abandoned the project. She was sure the letter to Ickes was a bluff designed to stimulate action by the United States Government.[6] It is most likely the letter was merely the initiating move in a planned and previously agreed upon stratagem to accomplish the completion of his Jackson Hole project, although there is some evidence that Rockefeller was not as committed to the continuation of the

*Tim McCoy, the famous actor in Hollywood westerns, ran unsuccessfully for the Republican nomination for the U.S. Senate in this election. At the time, he was a rancher near Thermopolis, Wyoming.

Jackson Hole Historical Society and Museum 1958.2585.001

Cutter races on Broadway Street, through the town of Jackson, were part of the winter carnival the community promoted to encourage winter tourism. During World War II the usual prizes and trophies were replaced with defense bonds.

project as many people believed. After the failure of the Park Service initiative to extend the boundaries of Grand Teton National Park in 1938, Albright indicated to Harold Fabian that Rockefeller had asked him if he thought he (Rockefeller) could get 50 cents on the dollar if he sold the land. Albright wrote, *"If he ever loses interest in this project it is gone for good."* [7]

On December 4, 1942, Secretary Ickes responded to Rockefeller's letter expressing his understanding of Rockefeller's concerns and stated, *"...I will do everything within my power to bring about the acceptance of your gift as an addition to the national park system."* [8] [See Appendix Two-H to view the complete letter.]

Although Ickes promised to utilize his considerable power to accomplish the acceptance of Rockefeller's gift, there was no reason to believe that legislative approval for an extension of Grand Teton National Park would be more easily obtained in 1943 than it was during the late

1930s. Moreover, because of the war, it was unlikely that sufficient national interest in the project could have been generated to warrant another legislative effort. However, a method other than congressional legislation was available to the executive branch by which Rockefeller's land could be accepted and the project completed. This involved the establishment, by Presidential Proclamation, of a national monument. The authority for such an action was provided by Section 2 of the 1906 American Antiquities Act (34 Stat. L. 225), sometimes referred to as the Lacey Antiquities Act.

It is generally believed that Rockefeller's letter of November 27, 1942, forced the consideration and use of this Presidential power, but Robert Righter, in his book *Crucible for Conservation*, documents a much earlier consideration of the monument option. As with the inflammatory phrase "rim to rim," which Richard Winger claimed to have originated, and which was widely attributed to Rockefeller, the proclamation option for Jackson Hole has its first documentation within a letter from Winger to Albright dated January 7, 1932. He suggested, *"It would be nice if President Hoover would decide to make the territory embraced in the Jackson Hole Plan into a National Monument."* [9]

No action resulted from Winger's suggestion until the defeat of the legislative effort of the National Park Service to expand the boundaries of Grand Teton National Park in 1938. During the first month of 1939, Park Service Director Cammerer* directed his staff to consider the monument option. This action was taken as a result of meetings and correspondence between Park Service personnel and Rockefeller staff concerned with the Jackson Hole project. In June of that year, Acting Director Demaray sent the draft of the monument proposal to Rockefeller. Robert Righter revealed that Kenneth Chorley advised his employer to delay consideration of the proclamation route, and Chorley made a final attempt to negotiate an acceptable compromise with the opposition in Jackson Hole, but he was unable to overcome the now historic problem of compensation to Teton County for lost taxes.[10]

The National Park Service once again attempted to convince the Bureau of the Budget to modify its position on the taxation issue but failed. Consequently, on August 1, 1940, Acting Director Demaray reported to Interior Secretary Ickes that *"...establishment of the area as a national monument at the appropriate time appears to be the only course available."* [11]

For a time, the proposed monument was the subject of considerable discussion within the Park Service including field personnel. While the consideration of the monument option was not conducted publicly, neither was it treated as a secret issue. Perhaps more surprising than the fact that the national monument was considered long before it was actually approved is that the opposition did not learn of the proposal until it became a reality. It is possible these discussions sparked the rumors which led Congressman Horton to predict renewed park extension legislation as well as

Arthur E. Demaray
1887-1958

Demaray completed his high school education by taking night courses, having been forced to drop out of the regular curriculum to help support his family. He began his federal employment as a messenger boy for the Geological Survey and then he trained as a draftsman. He was a topographic draftsman when he transferred to the National Park Service in 1917. He served as an assistant director for most of his career and was the primary liaison person for dealing with Congress and the sometimes difficult Secretary of Interior Harold Ickes. Demaray was active in a number of conservation and civic planning organizations and was decorated by the King of Sweden with the Order of Knight Vasa. As a reward for his loyalty and work with the Park Service, Interior Secretary Oscar Chapman appointed Demaray to the directorship of the National Park Service in 1951 in which capacity he served for less than a year. Although Mather, Albright, and Drury received more press, Demaray may have exercised more influence in developing Park Service policies than any other person.

Milward Simpson's similar warnings during his unsuccessful campaign for O'Mahoney's Senate seat.

Robert Righter's documentation of the behind-the-scenes meetings between Rockefeller and Secretary Ickes shows that Ickes was encouraged to pursue the monument option. The secretary on two occasions lunched with President Roosevelt for the purpose of discussing the proposed monument. The president's positive attitude toward the proposal inspired Ickes to forward, on March 5, 1943, to the President a memorandum explaining Rockefeller's position concerning to the Jackson

*Arno Cammerer resigned from the Park Service in August 1940 for health reasons and was eventually succeeded by Newton B. Drury. Arthur Demaray served as acting director in the interim.

Hole properties. This memorandum also recommended the establishment of a national monument in the Jackson Hole area with boundaries similar to the proposed park extension of 1934 and 1938. The action proposed in this memorandum was bound to cause controversy and generate criticism for Rockefeller, Secretary Ickes, and President Roosevelt. The Secretary warned the President that the proclamation would give him problems in Congress. Rockefeller and Ickes discussed this subject during a meeting at Christmas time in 1942.[12] All three men chose to bear the expected negative publicity from their detractors in order to complete the Jackson Hole project.

It is not known if these men fully anticipated the intensity of the coming controversy, but Secretary Ickes may have been better prepared than the others. At the request of the Bureau of the Budget, the Secretary met with Wyoming Senator O'Mahoney and revealed the monument proposal. Ickes stated the action would be accomplished *"...in such a way that he, O'Mahoney, would be absolved from blame by any of his constituents."*[13] The fact that Ickes realized O'Mahoney would need to be protected from any perceived or actual association with the monument plan indicated the Secretary knew the action would be unpopular.* Secretary Ickes failed to obtain O'Mahoney's approval for the proclamation and shortly thereafter received a letter from the Senator expressing doubt as to the constitutionality of the action. O'Mahoney also suggested the proposed Presidential Proclamation would be inappropriate since Congress had already rejected a similar legislative measure.[14] Ickes was not deterred. Oddly, Senator O'Mahoney never informed his constituency in Wyoming of this meeting. He may have felt his response to the Secretary of Interior was sufficient to deter the monument idea, and the proposal was moot, although most politicians are quick to inform the voters of any action on their behalf. Certainly most other Wyoming legislators would have publicized the approach by the Secretary and his or her response.

Ickes' March 5, 1943, memorandum to the President, in an attempt to explain the reason for recommending a monument rather than an extension of the existing national park, failed to mention previous congressional and local opposition. The memorandum only stated that, *"Attempts to secure legislative authority to accept these lands for addition to Grand Teton National Park have failed principally because of threatened loss of taxes to Teton County, Wyoming."*[15]

Obviously, the establishment of a national monument would not solve the tax compensation problem and in this regard, Secretary Ickes seemed insensitive to the potential financial hardship his proposal would inflict on Teton County. On the other hand, the apparently irreconcilable problem of federal reimbursement to local governments had recently attracted the attention of the nation. Previously, Congress had honored the

Elias Goldensky [Public domain] via Wikimedia Commons
Franklin Delano Roosevelt (D)
1882-1945
Roosevelt signed the controversial Presidential Proclamation 2578 creating the Jackson Hole National Monument on March 15, 1943.

---

*It is uncertain why Ickes approached O'Mahoney at all, except that the Bureau of the Budget thought it prudent. O'Mahoney was the only Democrat in the Wyoming Congressional Delegation, and he wielded some power as a member of the Senate Finance Committee. The Bureau of the Budget may have foreseen future budgetary problems if the Senator from Wyoming was antagonized. The Bureau would be proved prescient.

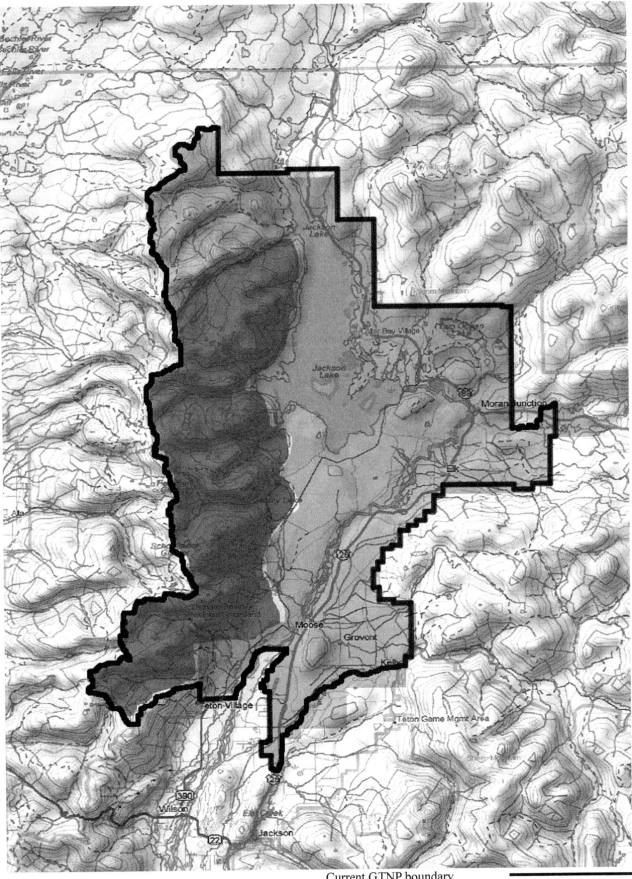

The Jackson Hole National Monument

Current GTNP boundary
Original GTNP (1929)
Jackson Hole National Monument

policy of the Bureau of the Budget against such reimbursements because Teton County was the only county affected and such revenue sharing was unprecedented. However, the war had stimulated increased acquisitions of land by the federal government for defense activities resulting in many counties throughout the nation experiencing the financial problems Teton County feared.* A sufficient number of legislators, mindful of their own constituency, now viewed the possibility of federal compensation favorably. Congress had approved funds for a special subcommittee to investigate the problem and it seemed likely that a method by which Teton County, as well as other counties throughout the nation, might receive compensation in lieu of taxes would soon be a reality.†

While Secretary Ickes did not mention the possible future solution to this problem to the President, both men were almost certainly aware of the activities of the subcommittee, and may have believed that a solution to the compensation problem was imminent. In any case, the Secretary, in addition to his memorandum, forwarded for the President's consideration, a form of proclamation and a letter briefly describing the scenic, historical, and scientific nature of the proposed monument.‡ He also stressed the urgency of the action stating, *"The area proposed to be established as a national monument now lacks unified protection and administration, and is in danger of over-development and commercial exploitation."*[16]

On March 15, 1943, Franklin D. Roosevelt signed Presidential Proclamation 2578 creating the Jackson Hole National Monument. This action also initiated the most bitter and emotional controversy in the history of Jackson Hole and created the basis for the state of Wyoming's most loudly contested states' rights battle; a battle fought not only in the press but also seeking legislative and judicial remedy.

When news of the President's action reached Jackson, the community was stunned. Unfortunately, the Interior Department's press releases on March 17 and 21 did not provide a clear picture of what had actually happened for Jackson Hole residents. The local populace did not know what portions of the valley were to be affected, if grazing rights had been lost, if the hunting of big game would be allowed to continue, if taxable property had been removed from the county rolls or if the state had lost control of the elk herd. This uncertainty resulted in unfounded speculation and rumors that added to the emotional distress of the valley.

Olaus Murie, a respected big game biologist, recalled the circumstances by which he learned of the Executive Order. He had spent the day counting winter-killed elk along the Gros Ventre River. Upon returning to town, he parked his car near the post office where he saw Felix Buchenroth, Sr., the owner of the Jackson State Bank. Olaus and Buck, as the banker was known to his friends, worked together with the local Boy Scout troop. Olaus approached the community leader to ask about an upcoming Court of Honor. The banker responded, *"Boy Scouts! How can we talk about Boy Scouts now? Haven't you heard what they have done? The President has put our whole valley in a park!"* [17]

The *Jackson Hole Courier* had no more factual information upon which to base its articles than did the public. The paper observed that *"From all present indications it was a secret political play."* The editor also stated, *"The matter has taken everybody, including the Governor of the State and the Wyoming Senators, by complete surprise. It*

---

*A form of revenue sharing did exist under certain circumstances. The Forest Service and Bureau of Land Management returned a percentage of revenues to adjacent counties received from grazing, mining, and timbering activities within those federal reserves. The legislation creating the National Park Service did not contain the authority for revenue sharing from receipts received as a result of their operations. This particular revenue sharing issue was nevertheless unique because it stemmed not from operations within the parks, but as a form of tax compensation, and the federal government is not taxable by the states.

†New military training areas, defense plants, storage facilities, and other war and defense related programs and activities were being located away from the nation's coastal regions to reduce the possibility of seaborne attack. The nationalization of land and facilities removed large amounts of taxable property from local tax rolls.

‡Use of the Antiquities Act for the establishment of a national monument requires the area in question contain historic sites or scientific phenomena.

may be that when the full text of the Presidential Proclamation becomes known, the project can be viewed in a more favorable light." [18] Felix Buchenroth, Sr., in an effort to obtain more information regarding the Monument called Senator E. V. Robertson, but the Senator was no better informed than anyone else in Wyoming. With some quick research, Senator Robertson was able to gather a few facts that he forwarded to Buchenroth by telegram. By this communication, the valley

Harris and Ewing, Library of Congress [Public domain] via Wikimedia Commons

Joseph Christopher O'Mahoney (D)
1884-1964

O'Mahoney came to Wyoming in 1916 as a newspaper reporter to work as the city editor for the *State Leader* (Cheyenne), a paper owned at the time by Governor John B. Kendrick. When Kendrick was elected to the U.S. Senate, he took O'Mahoney with him as his executive secretary. While working for the Senator, he obtained a law degree from Georgetown University Law School. Kendrick died in office and O'Mahoney was appointed by Wyoming Governor Miller to complete the term. O'Mahoney retained the seat in the next election and would become a powerful member of the Senate Appropriations Committee. Allen Drury, a reporter for United Press covering the Senate from 1943-1945 (and eventually a Pulitzer Prize-winning novelist), described O'Mahoney as, *"...the sharp-eyed and sharp-minded, soft-spoken, shrewd and hard-hitting Democrat from Wyoming."* [23]

learned that the new Monument began north of Jackson, excluded the National Elk Refuge, comprised approximately 220,000 acres, the boundaries of which encompassed 32,000 acres of Rockefeller land and 17,000 acres of other private land, and that this new area would be managed by the National Park Service. The Senator also stated, *"Am trying to obtain all information regarding this and will forward same to you. Please advise all interested parties and rest assured that I am here to help in every way possible the serious situation which has been brought about by this sudden action."* [19] Unfortunately for the people of Jackson Hole, the Senator's telegram did not include specific information concerning the rights of those who had an economic interest in the area in question, fueling even more concerns about the future. [See Appendix Two-M to read the Presidential Proclamation.]

While some officials were willing to wait for a full disclosure of the specifics of the proclamation, Governor Hunt was quick to condemn the President's action as an *"...invasion of state's rights."* Likewise, his public statement illustrated his failure to understand the motive behind the decree. He stated that the federal government had been attempting to force the state to reduce its game herds, and he believed *"...the State's actions in refusing to comply with these federal requests resulted in this action in Teton County."* [20]

On March 19, 1943, Congressman Barrett introduced, in the 78th Congress, 1st Session, H.R. 2241, to abolish the Jackson Hole National Monument. Also on that day, Congressman Barrett and Senator O'Mahoney made speeches in Congress condemning the establishment of the Monument by proclamation. Senator O'Mahoney did not believe the power existed for such an action and he stated, *"If this proclamation is a proper exercise of executive power, then every foot of United States territory may be set aside as a national monument, as this land within the boundaries of the State of Wyoming has been set aside, without regard to the opinions or the will of the sovereign people concerned."* [21]

So great was the immediate opposition by valley residents to the Monument that the *Jackson Hole Courier* could not wait another week to print an additional paper. On March 22, the *Courier* published an "extra" which dealt almost solely with the Monument issue. The articles, statements, speeches and letters printed in the special issue unanimously opposed the President's action. As could be predicted, another "official committee" was created to fight the proclamation and this committee declared, *"This act is particularly vicious in view of the fact that our young men are fighting to preserve those principles of Democracy our government has now renounced by this secret and un-American stab in the back."*[22]

A close inspection of the actual proclamation revealed the federal land affected was not substantially different from the area considered for park status during the previous decade. Also, the proclamation guaranteed that all valid existing rights on or to that land would be honored. On the surface, it appeared that nothing had changed in Jackson Hole except for administrative responsibilities over a portion of the federally owned land in the valley.

In an attempt to calm the growing storm of protest resulting from the proclamation, Secretary Ickes issued a policy statement concerning the administration of the new Monument. He promised, *"...all permits issued by the Forest Service or other federal agencies for use of lands now within the national monument will be honored by the National Park Service during the life-time of the present holders, and the members of their immediate family."* [24]*

For the cattlemen, he assured that *"Cattlemen desiring in the spring and fall to drive their cattle across the monument lands between their respective ranches and the summer ranges on National Forest or other lands will be permitted to do so."*[25]

The Secretary promised the cooperation of the National Park Service and the Fish and Wildlife Service with the Wyoming Game and Fish Commission in reaching solutions to any wildlife problems that might arise as a result of the proclamation. Likewise, Teton County was assured the right to continue to collect taxes on private property, unless acquired by the federal government, as well as state and local sales tax within the Monument and Park. Ickes gave his support to pending legislation that would allow for a sharing of revenue from the operation of parks and monuments with counties whose borders encompassed, in whole or in part, those federal reserves. Lastly, the secretary promised the people of Teton County ample opportunity to present their views before any changes in the above-stated policy would be adopted.

Since the federal government had just established the National Monument with a method preempting public comment or representation by their elected representatives, the Secretary's last assurance provided no comfort to those who were affected by the proclamation. Indeed, it probably served to diminish the Secretary's credibility concerning the preceding policy guarantees. Thus, Secretary

Biographical Directory of the United States Congress [Public domain] via Wikimedia Commons

Frank Aloysius Barrett (R)
1892-1962

Barrett served in the U.S. Army Balloon Corps during World War I. He moved to Wyoming in 1919 and practiced law in the community of Lusk. He was elected to the United States House of Representatives in 1942 and held that office until 1950. He also served as Wyoming's 21st governor and then unseated Senator O'Mahoney for a term in the Senate.

---

*Secretary Ickes would later release an additional policy statement providing greater flexibility regarding rights of landowners within the monument. Specifically, he extended recognition of rights and privileges beyond the lifetime of the lessee of record to heirs and assignees.

Ickes' statement accomplished little with regard to local opposition. The editor of the *Courier* attacked his statement and while the editor's rebuttal was not always logical, it reflected the emotional nature of the opposition in Wyoming. During this portion of the controversy, the paper's reporting mirrored a tone reminiscent of William Simpson's *The Grand Teton*. Character assassination and disregard for facts once again became acceptable journalism in 1943.

As an example, the *Courier* printed a telegram from Regional Park Service Director Lawrence Merriam to Teton Park Superintendent Smith in which Merriam directed Smith to *"Advise hold-*

Zion National Park, Neg.4287

Charles J. Smith served as superintendent of Grand Teton National Park from May 1, 1940, to June 30, 1943. He was initially named in the suit filed by the state of Wyoming to test the legality of the Executive Order establishing the Jackson Hole National Monument. After the suit had been filed, the Park Service transferred Smith to Zion National Park where he served until April 30, 1952.

ers that...permits and leases will continue in effect .... Grazing permits will not be changed during the lifetime of permittee, if they so desire, in accordance with procedure of Service when new areas established." [26]* Also, the *Courier* printed a letter to the editor from Superintendent Smith which stated:

> *Nothing will be done at the present time in the way of enforcing park regulations or establishing of procedures which would modify practices or disrupt methods of operation which have heretofore been in effect. Also nothing will be done on the issuance of permits or imposing of restrictions without full conference and written notification to cattlemen or other holders of current permits or leases.* [27]

On the same page with these assurances that grazing and drifting rights would continue, the editor of the *Courier* claimed that Jackson Hole's cattle industry was in a state of confusion because of the loss or uncertainty of the status of grazing permits. The editor declared that the industry would be ruined if the monument order was allowed to stand.

The controversy continued to grow. In Wyoming, John Charles Thompson, the editor of the *Cheyenne Tribune* likened the proclamation to the Japanese attack on Pearl Harbor. In fact, nearly every newspaper in the state joined the controversy and called for the abolishment of the Monument. The president of the Wyoming Stock Growers Association, Charles Myers, declared to that organization's convention, *"The cloven hoof of our most ruthless bureaucrat Secretary Ickes was never more plainly in evidence than in the proclamation.... This is the 'Boston Tea Party,' and we will never rest until we are in fact, as well as in name, Sovereign States. Not only will we retake the Monument, but the Taylor Grazing Lands with the mineral rights that should pass to our state with them...."* [28]

---

*Regional Director Merriam's telegram further confuses the issue. Conceivably as an oversight, he assured the continuance of grazing leases for the lifetime of the permit holder, but he did not extend the privilege to the permit holder's immediate family. Secretary Ickes previously included the immediate family. To the cattlemen in Jackson Hole, it appeared the Interior Department was withdrawing a portion of the Interior Secretary's assurances without consultation with those affected, as had been promised.

The *Casper Tribune-Herald* was not as vicious in its criticism as were most Wyoming newspapers. It allowed that the land in question was worthy of park extension or monument status, and supported the Snake River Land Company purchases which had halted development *"... that would mar the primitive beauty of the area."*[29] The same article condemned the creation of the Monument because of the method by which it was established. It called the proclamation an act of subterfuge and an abuse of executive authority.

On a national level, the initial reaction was much the same as in Wyoming. A nationally syndicated columnist and constant critic of President Roosevelt, Westbrook Pegler, compared the creation of the Jackson Hole National Monument to Hitler's annexation of Austria. A *Saturday Evening Post* editorial suggested *"...the motto of the U.S.A. has been changed from 'E Pluribus Unum' to 'Never Give a Sucker an Even Break.'"*[30]

Francis James Westbrook Pegler
(1894-1969)

The recipient of the first Pulitzer Prize awarded for reporting; Peglar was a critic of every president from Hoover to Kennedy. He was particularly tough on FDR, unions, New Deal programs, and the Communist Party. In 1941, he finished third after Franklin Roosevelt and Joseph Stalin for *Time Magazine's* "Man of the Year." At the time of the creation of the Jackson Hole National Monument, his syndicated columns were distributed six days a week to 174 newspapers with an estimated readership of 10 million.

Rapidly, various organizations joined the opposition. Among them was the Farm Bureau Federation, which passed a resolution opposing the creation, enlargement, or extension of parks, monuments, and recreation areas.[31] Additionally, at their annual conference, Wyoming's Governor Hunt convinced the western governors to oppose the President's proclamation unanimously.

Governor Hunt also wrote a letter to President Roosevelt protesting the creation of the Monument stating that the disruption of the cattle industry in that area would adversely affect the war effort, that the action would displace citizens who had settled in the area, and that, *"Businessmen in the town of Jackson and other parts of the area will also be seriously affected, if not completely ruined. In fact, a large community will be disrupted and many people compelled to start anew in some other place."* The governor was also miffed that he was not included in the decision-making process. He stated, *"In ignoring me in the matter, I believe he [Secretary Ickes] has departed from a precedent which has been long established and should not be passed over lightly."*[32]

Roosevelt responded that the matters raised in the governor's letter had been considered. The President wrote, *"The benefits to be derived by the Nation were the compelling reasons for the establishment of this national monument, but I believe that the step will prove equally beneficial to Teton County and the State of Wyoming. In issuing the proclamation, I was careful to protect all private interests now established in the monument area."* The President, likewise, affirmed that existing grazing rights would not be affected and rejected the governor's contention that the livestock industry would be disrupted. He maintained that the wording of the proclamation plus Secretary Ickes' statement of administrative policy for the Monument was sufficient to ensure there would be *"...no adverse affect upon the production of livestock, now so vital to the war program."*[33]

Concerning the impact of the proclamation upon the community of Jackson and Teton County, the President noted that while there might be a temporary loss of revenue to Teton County because of the transfer of Forest Service land to the Park Service because the Park Service was not authorized to share revenues from grazing and other leases, he would view favorably:

>...*some equitable means by which a portion of the revenues of Yellowstone, Grand Teton and Jackson Hole* [Monument] *could benefit Teton County. There is an indirect benefit, of course, in the resulting increase in local business and assessed valuations which experience has shown to follow the establishment of parks and monuments as tourist attractions. I am informed that in 1941 your own State of Wyoming collected more than $151,000 in taxes from Yellowstone National Park alone. This was due in no small measure to the Federal developments that made the area available and added to the possibilities for human enjoyment. I honestly believe that the resumption of tourist travel, which will undoubtedly follow the war, will result in a great deal more money flowing into Teton County and the State of Wyoming than if the Federal Government had not established the Jackson Hole National Monument.*[34]*

Governor Hunt was not appeased. In a speech delivered in Cheyenne, he announced his intention to fight the monument proclamation with all the power of his office. He directed the office of the state's Attorney General to investigate the legal options available to the state to fight the federal action. Hunt also stated he would utilize all the authority at his command *"...to evict from the area any Department of the Interior official who attempts to assume authority."*[35]

While such rhetoric from Wyoming's chief executive was well received in Jackson Hole, the local newspaper had to question the last statement. The *Courier* was not opposed to a show of force against the federal government but questioned whether the governor's actual police powers extended beyond the control of the state's few Highway Department patrolmen.

The Wyoming Attorney General's office took a "wait and see" position largely formulated from Senator O'Mahoney's speech before the Senate questioning the authority of the proclamation. Deputy Attorney General John McIntyre vowed

that the state was anxious to challenge that authority in the courts but would wait until the Park Service attempted to enforce any regulation over the new reserve. Local cattlemen were told to report any action on the part of the Park Service regarding leases or grazing rights in the Monument area. McIntyre called the reserve a "pretend monument." This remark became a popular catch phrase in Jackson Hole and the *Courier* and subsequent resolutions often referred to it as the "pretend monument" or the "so-called monument."

Meanwhile, the verbal fireworks continued. The *Jackson Hole Courier* forgot or ignored the history of local support for Rockefeller's purchases and called the project a "land grab."[36] Senator O'Mahoney introduced a resolution (S. Res. 134) providing for an investigation into the land acquisition policies of the Department of the Interior. The actual wording of the resolution was so general that it would have taken years to accomplish the demands of the document. It stated:

Wikimedia Commons

John Joseph McIntyre (D)
1904-1974

McIntyre served one term in the U.S. House of Representatives in the 77th Congress. At the time of the establishment of the Jackson Hole National Monument, he was deputy attorney general for Wyoming and commanded Troop K of the Wyoming National Guard. He served in the 660th Field Artillery in World War II and was decorated with the French Croix de Guerre. In 1960, he was elected to the Wyoming Supreme Court and would continue in that position until his death in 1974.

Resolved, that the committee on Public Lands and Surveys, or any duly authorized subcommittee thereof, is hereby authorized to make a full and complete study and investigation with respect to the methods and purposes of, and the administration of the laws relating to, the establishment and fixing of the boundaries of national monuments, national forests, Indian reservations, and national parks.[37]

In spite of the broad scope of the resolution, it was clear that the intent was to investigate the creation of the Jackson Hole National Monument.

As spring approached, the controversy intensified. This was the time when some cattlemen would need to drift their herds across Monument lands to grazing allotments both within and outside the Monument boundaries. Considering the repeated assurances by Grand Teton Park Superintendent Smith, Regional Park Service Director Merriam, National Park Service Director Drury, Secretary of the Interior Ickes, and President Roosevelt that grazing leases and drift rights would not be changed, the cattlemen's concern for the upcoming drive seemed unfounded. Perhaps the only explanation for the opposition's continued predictions of doom for the industry and a possibly dangerous confrontation lay in the emotion of

the situation. Indeed, the emotional level of the controversy in Jackson Hole had reached a point where logic and reason no longer could calm the opposition as they continued to demand privileges which were already guaranteed. To that group, nothing short of the abolishment of the Monument would have been satisfactory.

The moment of truth would arrive when the ranchers began their cattle drive. The focus of the opposition's attention was directed to that event, and the cattle drive of 1943 resulted in the state's top news story of the year. Wyoming historian T. A. Larson devoted a single paragraph to the affair in his book *Wyoming's War Years, 1941-1945*. According to Larson, *"...forty heavily armed men ... drove a herd of cattle across one corner of the newly created monument without asking for Park Service permission."*[38] The drive was not challenged.

Another author, Donald Hough, in his book *The Cocktail Hour In Jackson Hole,** gave greater attention to the drive and with considerably more humor. He even had the actor Wallace Beery encouraging the cowboys to "shoot to kill."[39] Undoubtedly, Hough's version makes the best story, but as a consummate storyteller, he might not have allowed the truth to stand in the way of a good tale. Hough's narrative presents a

Jackson Hole Historical Society and Museum 2004.0111.159

The 1943 cattle drive across the Jackson Hole National Monument
Clifford Hansen (left), actor Wallace Beery to his left on the white horse he borrowed from Clifford's sister, Parthenia Stinnett.

---

*The premise of this humorous book is that the cocktail hour in Jackson Hole begins on Labor Day when the tourist season ends and the "dudes" leave the valley, and lasts until Memorial Day when the tourist season starts and the "dudes" arrive back in the valley.

of hay per year. Virtually all of a rancher's deeded arable land was necessary to raise and store hay to feed the cattle during the six to seven winter months. The grazing leases for summer pasture were of considerable value to the rancher and the transferability of these permits a necessity if he decided to sell or needed to borrow money. A bank would not likely view the ranch as collateral if it did not have transferable grazing leases.

Jackson Hole Historical Society and Museum bc 0284

Feeding cattle in the winter.

Jackson Hole's long and often severe winters required ranchers raise sufficient hay to sustain the herd for six, and sometimes seven, months of the year. The short summer growing season combined with cool alpine temperatures limited hay production to one cutting per year. Every acre of private land was needed to produce the hay, so each summer the cattle were moved off the ranch to grazing allotments leased from the Forest Service.

scenario wherein a group of ranchers, emotionally opposed in principle to the federal action, ignored the fact that they actually had not been harmed by the proclamation.

In reality, the ranchers were adversely affected in both the short and in the long view by the creation of the Jackson Hole National Monument. A more detailed explanation of the impact to the ranchers is presented later in this chapter, but it may be appropriate to clarify here the importance of the federal grazing allotments to the cattlemen.

Few ranches in the West contained sufficient deeded land to graze enough cattle to be profitable. Leased grazing land was particularly important in Jackson Hole where the winters are long and the growing season is short (on average just 21 frost-free days per year).* A rancher in Jackson Hole would usually get only one cutting

Jackson Hole Historical Society and Museum bc 0032

Wallace Fitzgerald Beery
1885 -1949

Beery first came to Jackson Hole to make the location shots for one of his movies– *Bad Man of Wyoming*. Like others before him, he fell in love with the valley. His ranch, as the *Saturday Evening Post* called it, consisted of a half acre of leased Forest Service land, upon which he had constructed a summer home. His livestock comprised of one milk cow that died during the summer of 1943, and because he did not own a horse he borrowed one from Clifford Hansen's sister so he could participate in the cattle drive. The photo above is from the movie *Bad Bascomb*.

---

*Over the last 90 years the climate has gradually warmed and the average number of frost-free days has increased. Nevertheless, ranchers still expect just one crop of hay per summer.

The Monument controversy did not alienate the Park Service from its closest friends in the Jackson Hole area. Pictured above, a group enjoys an outing on Jackson Lake. (L to R) Struthers Burt, Grand Teton National Park Superintendent Charles J. Smith, Coulter Huyler, Harold Fabian. The people behind are Snake River Land Company employees.

Under the Forest Service, a rancher could anticipate that, in the absence of abuse of the privilege or violation of the regulations, his children's children could continue to operate the ranch and utilize federal grazing lands, if they so desired. The Park Service believed they had benevolently protected the rights of the ranchers (and other lease-holders) by allowing them to continue to operate as they had in the past but only for a limited time. Thus, the cattlemen had just had their ranches devalued as a business asset, the opportunity to expand their business (herd size) frozen at a time when, because of the war, cattle prices were strong and rising, and the family's future in the ranching business had been arbitrarily restricted.

At that point in time, no one would have guessed that land in Jackson Hole would appreciate to the degree it has. Even proponents of park extension who predicted economic prosperity for the valley due to increased tourist popularity could not have foreseen the present land values. Ranchers who saw only financial ruin from the establishment of the Monument now find their deeded land, no matter how small, to be considerably more valuable than their actual business opportunity as producers of cattle.

Regardless of all the claims of impending disaster precipitated by the proclamation, some of which were debatable, the underlying emotion and force behind the opposition was due to the proclamation itself. The principle upon which the opposition to the National Monument was based was the issue of representation. The Presidential Proclamation had denied the people of Jackson Hole the opportunity to express their views on the subject. Even their elected representatives in Congress had been bypassed, and many people believed a fundamental right had been subverted. The emotions were particularly bitter in light of the sacrifices being made by Jackson Hole residents on the battle fronts. Most of the ranchers whose grazing allotments had been encompassed by the Monument had sons and daughters in the military and these young people, if they survived the war, would return home and discover the government for which they had risked their lives had eliminated their futures in this valley. In that context, the actions and statements of the opposition are perhaps more understandable.

The *Jackson Hole Courier* treated the 1943 cattle drive over Monument lands somewhat more seriously than Mr. Hough. The editor awarded the armed locals the status of heroes even though their "act of defiance" had been given prior approval on numerous occasions. While no skirmish occurred, the paper believed the men had accomplished a considerable victory.

According to the *Courier*, Clifford Hansen and J. G. Imeson led the cattle drive, and while Mr. Beery was a part of the group, it remains hard to believe that these cattlemen could have been incited or controlled by his speeches as implied by Hough. Whatever Beery's role in the event, he found time to pose for photographs which later appeared in the *Salt Lake Tribune* accompanying an article on the cattle drive. The drive was also given national publicity, and at least one article described Beery as one of the ranchers.

The reports of "forty armed men" herding their cattle across the Monument in defiance of the federal government seems overly ominous. The "trespass" was a publicity stunt designed to attract the attention of the nation to the perceived injustices of the President's Proclamation. In reality, the cattle had to be moved, and this normal business operation was chosen as an event that would catch the eye of the national press. As with previous cattle drives, the group of "armed" cattlemen was not gender specific. A successful ranching operation was the result of a family effort and women contributed no less than men.

Participants of the cattle drive, when interviewed in later years, recalled the drive with good humor and readily affirm they knew the "trespass" would be unopposed. Some remembered having rifles primarily for the benefit of the press. Clifford Hansen recalled he took his favorite 30-30 rifle, but he was unsure if he bothered taking ammunition. They did not anticipate a confrontation with park rangers. One cowboy recalled with some chagrin that his horse impolitely unseated him, but fortunately, it was after the photographs had been taken and the media representatives had departed.[40]

Historian Robert Righter suggested the idea to publicize the drive was Stanley Resor's. Resor was an advertising executive and part-time resident and rancher in Jackson Hole. Clifford Hansen and others who participated in the drive could not remember if Resor played any part in the drive or its publicity. They felt if credit for the idea could be placed with one individual it would probably have been Charles Kratzer, the editor of the *Jackson Hole Courier*.[41]

Since the right to drift cattle across the Monument had been affirmed in the Presidential proclamation, and reaffirmed by the Secretary of Interior and the director of the National Park Service, it would appear that the "trespass" violated no laws or regulations. This was not totally true. Clifford Hansen, the president of the Jackson Hole Cattle and Horse Association, wrote the Association members stating:

> *Please disregard any application for grazing permits mailed to you by the Park Service. The conditions which you have to sign are such that no free American can sign and be a free American. Our cause is just and we will defend it.*[42]

Hansen assured the members the association would defend any cattleman named by the Park Service in a trespass suit as long as that member followed the usual use of his allotment as provided in previous permits.[43] The Park Service, realizing the attempt to issue grazing permits would only contribute to the unrest in Jackson Hole, requested the Forest Service issue the permits for the 1943 season for pertinent lands formerly supervised by the Forest Service but now included within the Monument. The Forest Service agreed to do so, but the ranchers, recognizing that that agency was acting as an agent for the Park Service, refused to sign the permits. Thus, the cattlemen did participate in a form of civil disobedience during the 1943 grazing season by grazing their cattle on public lands without fee and absent permit.[44]

Although the cattlemen involved in the drive later professed a non-violent intention, Grand Teton Park Superintendent Smith probably exercised good judgment when he directed his rangers to avoid the area. First of all, considering the emotional fervor of the opposition, a confrontation, no matter how small, would only have aggravated the situation. Second, Smith's superiors had already publicly approved the movement of cattle across the Monument, and there was no reason to interfere with the drive. While Superintendent Smith apparently wished to avoid any unnecessary confrontation, the official Washington reaction to the "trespass" and its attendant publicity served only to anger the cattlemen further. When questioned about the event, Secretary Ickes stated that *"...some ghost-hunting cowboys put on their best mail-order regalia, added single-barreled shotguns and rifles, and went out to defend their rights and liberties– they put on a bit of mock heroics."* [45]

The reaction to Secretary Ickes' remark was predictably strong. The *Jackson Hole Courier* quoted Clifford Hansen as stating, *"Every cowman in Jackson Hole knows that national parks and monuments aren't created to be grazed. Ickes' statement that no privileges or rights have been violated is a damn lie. Anytime he tries to keep us from using this area he better be sure his escorts aren't 90-day wonders packing shotguns."*[46]* Roy Van Vleck advised, *"Trust in God, keep your powder dry and watch Ickes and the national park service."* [47]

To the latter-day newcomer to the valley, the above statements may sound like an overreaction to a verbal slight, but it might be well to imagine the era in which this controversy occurred. Jackson Hole was still a remote western valley with many inhabitants who lived close to the land and whose values were steeped in self-reliance and independence. Horses were at least as common as automobiles and perhaps more reliable. Injustices, perceived or otherwise, were not tolerated. Any attempt to understand the perspective of the ranchers should include recognition that these people sincerely felt an injustice had been perpetrated against them, their families, and their future generations. It might also be helpful to understand some of the other personalities involved.

Harold LeClair Ickes enjoyed a relatively short tenure in Grand Teton National Park

history primarily associated with the Jackson Hole National Monument. Nationally his name was a household word, and he might be characterized as the Democrats' version of Interior Secretary James Watt. T. H. Watkins made this analogy in an article for *Audubon*. Watkins described him as *"A hard-nosed and often arrogant administrator, he bullied and intimidated those around him and shook his department from top to bottom. Fiercely ideological, politicized up to his earlobes, loudly opinionated, and eminently visible, he both antagonized and delighted the press and*

www.doi.gov [Public domain] via Wikimedia Commons
Harold LeClair Ickes (R)/(P)/(R)/(D)
1874-1952
32nd U.S. Secretary of Interior

Ickes, a Republican, who moved to Theodore Roosevelt's Bull Moose Party in 1912, was active in Chicago politics supporting primarily progressive Republican candidates. After the 1932 election, FDR was seeking a progressive Republican as a cabinet member, and Ickes was recommended. He served as Secretary of Interior from 1933 to 1946, the longest tenure of any Interior Secretary. A supporter of national parks and civil rights, he also supported legislation that would have opened Alaska for resettlement of European Jewish refugees. (Alaska was a U.S. Territory, not a state, and thus immigration quotas could be circumvented.) The legislation failed. Often arrogant and contentious, he was generally distrusted by residents and politicians of the Western states.

---

*Some 50 years after the event I asked Senator Hansen about his statement. He responded with a smile and said, "That's pretty strong stuff."

was a particular favorite of editorial cartoonists, who drew him with venom and relish." [48] Gifford Pinchot, an icon of American conservation, called him the "American Hitler." [49] Describing himself to a *Time* reporter, he said, *"I'm not a popular man, and I know it. I'm short tempered... I'm arbitrary—but I get things done."* [50] For the western working man of the 1940s who had little leisure time for ideological fanaticism, Ickes was an easy man to dislike and, even more intensely, distrust.

∿

www.pwrc.usgs.gov/resshow/perry/bios

Ira Gabrielson
1889-1977

Gabrielson began his professional career as a high school biology teacher in 1912. He began working for the Biological Survey three years later and in 1940 was appointed Director of the Fish and Wildlife Service. He retired from the Service in 1946, but he remained active in conservation endeavors throughout his life. In 1961, he helped organize the World Wildlife Fund (United States) and became its president and a trustee of the World Wildlife Fund (International). The author of numerous field guides to birds and books about conservation, he also edited *Fisherman's Encyclopedia* (1951) and *New Fish Encyclopedia* (1964). While his name may not be a household word with modern environmentalists, for those with sufficient tenure in the conservation movement, he is considered on a par with his friend Aldo Leopold in terms of his contributions to wildlife conservation.

The President's proclamation establishing the Jackson Hole National Monument created some interagency problems as well. In fact, the number and type of ancillary problems resulting from the creation of this Monument support the contention that it was a hastily conceived and minimally planned arbitrary action. Setting aside for the moment the fact that the area included within the Monument boundaries did not conform, either physically or in legislative intent, to the requirements specified in Section 2 of the Antiquities Act, the map of the Monument seemed irrational. The boundaries encompassed three impounded lakes, an airport, most of the National Elk Refuge, 17,000 acres of privately owned (non-Rockefeller) land, grazing allotments for 29 ranchers, numerous irrigation canals and ditches, and several mining leases. It seems obvious, at least in hindsight, that a sensible assessment of the area would have allowed a monument boundary that excluded a majority of the controversial pre-existing uses.

The new Monument completely enveloped the Jackson Lake Dam and Reclamation Project. Lands and lake areas had been withdrawn from entry and additional lands purchased for reclamation purposes under the authority of the act of June 17, 1902 (32 Stat. 388). The Park Service had to recognize these prior claims, and a memorandum of agreement was negotiated, but it was not formally completed until January 1946. (See Chapter Seventeen)

The Monument boundaries also included lands administered by the Fish and Wildlife Service, which were considered essential to the operation of the National Elk Refuge. The National Elk Refuge in Jackson Hole was established on August 10, 1912 (37 Stat. 293). At the time of the Monument's creation, it contained 24,000 acres composed of purchased lands, public lands specifically set aside for elk refuge purposes by Presidential Proclamations and Executive withdrawals, and lands leased from John D. Rockefeller, Jr. The inclusion of refuge lands in the Monument created overlapping jurisdictions with potentially conflicting management activities. Because an act of Congress established the refuge, it could not be deemed to have been abolished by the proclamation.* Dr. Ira Gabrielson, director of the Fish and Wildlife Service, identified three problems resulting from the creation of the National Monument:

> *1. The problem of administration with respect to the National Elk Refuge.*
> *2. The problem of future management with respect to the Jackson Hole elk herd.*
> *3. The legal question concerning the status of the lands purchased for Refuge purposes which have been included within the boundaries of the Jackson Hole National Monument.*[51]

In April 1943, a conference was convened in Gabrielson's office with Dr. Gabrielson, Mr. Drury, Mr. Demaray, Mr. Kavanagh, and Mr. Lee Muck in attendance. Cooperative agreements were reached for the first and third problems, but the second problem could not be conclusively resolved because the actual management of the elk involved the Wyoming Game and Fish Commission, and no one from Wyoming was invited to this meeting. Muck, in a memo to Secretary Ickes, stated, *"It should be pointed out ... that the prohibiting of hunting within the Monument raises a serious question with respect to the disposition of the surplus animals and the management of the elk herd in cooperation with the State of Wyoming."* [52]

This memorandum indicated that hunting rights had been lost on some of the land included in the Monument. It appears inconsistent that the indignation so verbalized in the *Jackson Hole Courier* over the disruption of the cattle industry, which in fact had not been immediately disrupted, was not matched by indignation over the loss of hunting opportunity, which had been abrogated. There is a reason for this. Hunting in portions of the north end of the valley had been prohibited or extremely limited since 1905 when the Wyoming Legislature established the Teton Game

Preserve,[53] and most residents avoided hunting on the open expanse of the valley floor because it was considered unsportsmanlike.

Although acreage included in the Monument actually available for hunting may have been small, hunting, in general, was important for at least five reasons. First, hunting was a source of food for valley residents. Second, hunting was an income producing industry employing locals to guide sportsmen in the fall. Third, hunting was the most effective tool for wildlife managers in controlling populations of big game species.† Fourth, the hides of the animals harvested were an important source of leather that was in great demand during the war years. And fifth, through the sale of licenses, hunting provided revenue for the state of Wyoming. Additionally, the right to hunt and the continued oversight by the state of Wyoming regarding wildlife was another principle of states' rights. It may also be remembered that nearly every previous proposal for an enlarged Yellowstone Park, a separate Teton Park, a recreation area, or extension of Grand Teton Park had included the right to hunt and the continued role of the state in matters of game management in the affected areas. The concern of the Fish and Wildlife Service was that hunting was the only tool available to keep the elk population within the limits which could be accommodated by the resources of the National Elk Refuge.

Regarding the overlapping jurisdictional problems with the Fish and Wildlife Service, the resolution to the first and third items was as follows:

> *1. The Fish and Wildlife Service will administer all lands included within the boundary described in Presidential Proclamation No. 2578, dated March 15, 1943, lying east of the Jackson-Moran Highway and south of the Gros Ventre River, for refuge purposes.*
> *2. The National Park Service will administer all lands included within the boundary*

---

*Although the issue was never raised in the lawsuit challenging the legality of the use of the Antiquities Act, or in numerous legislative hearings concerning the abolishment of the monument, an argument could have been made that the Antiquities Act cannot be used to change the status of federal land already designated by Congress.

†Many comprehensive studies of big game animals indicate large ungulates tend to cyclically over-populate even in the presence of abundant predators. Among the more detailed examples of such studies are Adolph Murie's *The Wolves of Mount McKinley* and L. David Mech's *The Wolves of Isle Royale* and *The Wolf*.

described in Executive Orders No. 7489, dated November 14, 1938, and No. 7680, dated July 30, 1937, lying west of the Jackson-Moran Highway and north of the Gros Ventre River, for monument purposes.[54]

~

In May 1943, the state of Wyoming filed a suit in Cheyenne challenging the legality of the creation of the Jackson Hole National Monument. The state delayed the filing primarily waiting for the Park Service to act in any way that would constitute an exercise of authority over the land in question. When the Forest Service, acting as an agent of the Park Service, mailed grazing permit applications to ranchers, the measure was considered an exercise of authority. The suit originally filed named Charles J. Smith, the Superintendent

Courtesy Mesa Verde National Park MEVE 1472_250.000 ITEM 00414a

Paul R. Franke

Paul Franke served as the fifth superintendent of Grand Teton National Park from July 1, 1943, to April 20, 1946. He was the first superintendent to bear the burden of administrative responsibility for the Jackson Hole National Monument with a congressional prohibition against the expenditure of any Interior Department funds for its management.

of Grand Teton National Park, as the defendant. Smith was almost immediately transferred to another park, and Paul R. Franke assumed the job of superintendent. The suit was refiled as *State of Wyoming v. Paul R. Franke*. The U.S. Government cannot be sued without its permission, so the state named the individual vested with the power to exercise authority. The trial and judgment attendant to this lawsuit occurred in 1944 and 1945, and the arguments and decision will be presented in subsequent chapters.

~

The *Jackson Hole Courier* continued to print articles relevant to monument issues that, at least for a while, supported the opposition's perspective, and also reprinted articles from other sources opposing the Presidential action. In fact, five months passed before any issue of that newspaper would be entirely bereft of monument discussion. There was plenty to report. The legal action initiated by the state of Wyoming, described above, was one event. Another was the House hearings on H.R. 2241, Congressman Barrett's bill to abolish the Jackson Hole National Monument, which began in Washington, D.C. before the House Public Lands Committee in May. During these hearings, the National Park Service faced a generally unsympathetic committee. Of the 18 members on this committee, 13 expressed support for Congressman Barrett's bill prior to the hearings.[55]

In addition to Congressman Barrett, the committee heard testimony supporting the legislation that opposed the creation of the Jackson Hole National Monument from Wyoming Senator E. V. Robertson, Wyoming Senator Joseph O'Mahoney Wyoming Deputy Attorney General John McIntyre, Milward Simpson of Wyoming, Stanley Resor of Jackson Hole and New York City, Clifford Hansen of Jackson Hole, Charles Kratzer, Editor of the *Jackson Hole Courier*, C. R. Van Vleck of Jackson Hole, U.S. Congressman Mike Mansfield (Montana), and Colorado Congressman Robert F. Rockwell. Testimony opposing the legislation and in support of the Monument was presented by Newton B. Drury, Director of the National Park Service, F. M Fryxell of the U.S. Geological Survey; former Wyoming Governor Leslie A. Miller; Secretary of Interior Harold Ickes, and Horace

Albright. Less declarative was testimony by L. P. Kneipp, assistant chief of the Forest Service.

Having introduced the proposed legislation that was the subject of the hearings, Congressman Barrett was allowed to make the first statement. His statement was lengthy, partly because of the volume of petitions, resolutions, letters, and published articles he produced opposing the Monument, and partly because of the questions asked by other members of the committee during his presentation. Most of the committee members were unfamiliar with the Jackson Hole area, and many of the questions posed were for clarification of the history of the settlement of the valley, the conditions in the valley and the attitudes of the residents of the valley.

Some questions were very relevant to the issue. As an example, Congressman O'Connor inquired, *"Has anybody, to your knowledge, gone into the question as to whether or not this act of Congress* [the Antiquities Act] *has ever been construed by the courts to include such a procedure as we are now confronted with?"* [56] Congressman Barrett said he had researched this and assured the committee the Antiquities Act had never been tested in the courts.* It was noted the state of Wyoming had recently initiated such an action, but the suit had not yet been heard. In concluding his statement, Congressman Barrett listed nine reasons the Jackson Hole National Monument should be abolished.

First, this use of the Antiquities Act was really an attempt to extend the boundaries of Grand Teton National Park, which Congress had declined to do on several occasions and was an action taken *"...contrary to the expressed will of Congress."* Second, the action would hamper the production of livestock in that area at a time when the government was encouraging the increased production of beef for the war effort, and the action was inappropriate while the nation was at war. Third, the Monument would interfere with the hunting of big game and the management of

wildlife by the Wyoming Game and Fish Commission. Fourth, the tax burden placed on the county by the formation of the Monument would make it *"...impossible to operate the county and carry on the normal functions of government."* Fifth, the area encompassed in the Monument was not of the character specified by the Antiquities Act, and the size of the Monument was far beyond the *"minimum acreage necessary"* specified by the

Bain News Service [Public domain] via Wikimedia Commons

Willis Van Devanter
1859-1941

Supreme Court Justice Willis Van Devanter received his law degree from Cincinnati Law School in 1881 and moved to Wyoming Territory in 1884. In 1896, he successfully represented the state of Wyoming before the Supreme Court in the case of *Ward v. Race Horse* (discussed in Chapter One and Chapter Ten). Van Devanter was nominated to the Eighth Circuit Court of Appeals by Theodore Roosevelt in 1903 and to the Supreme Court by Howard Taft in 1909. For a two-decade period he, along with Justices McReynolds, Butler, and Sutherland, dominated the Court. They were called The Four Horsemen. He wrote the majority opinion in the first judicial test of the Antiquities Act.

This was not correct. President Theodore Roosevelt created the 806,400 acre Grand Canyon National Monument in 1908. This action was challenged on the grounds that the area did not qualify for monument status under the Antiquities Act. In 1920, the Supreme Court ruled (252 U.S. 450) that the Grand Canyon did qualify as "... an object of unusual scientific interest." Justice Willis Van Devanter of Wyoming wrote the decision.

Antiquities Act. Sixth, the use of the Antiquities Act to extend Grand Teton National Park in contradiction of the will of Congress *"...tends to destroy confidence in representative government."* Seventh, *"The creation of this monument constitutes an invasion on the rights of the sovereign State of Wyoming. The people of Wyoming are entitled to work out their destiny without interference from, or domination of, outsiders."* Eighth, the creation of the Monument was accomplished secretly without notification to the people living in the area or their elected representatives and was *"...not in any sense representative of government by the people."* Ninth, it was unfair to military service personnel from Teton County who would *"...return to find their homes and their livelihood injured by the very Government they are fighting to maintain."* Barrett concluded, *"I know of no fair and proper solution of this intolerable situation except the outright abolishment of the monument by congressional action."* [57]

Arguments for and against the Monument were heard, and much of the testimony repeated previous debates now familiar and already documented regarding earlier legislative endeavors. However, several new justifications for the protection of the area now incorporated in the Monument were introduced in this hearing which were not stressed in previous hearings. These arguments resulted from the nature of the law authorizing the establishment of national monuments by executive action as opposed to parks and monuments created by legislative enactment. The Lacey Antiquities Act authorized the creation of a national monument by Executive Order to protect specifically *"...historic and prehistoric structures, and other objects of historic or scientific interest that are situated upon the lands owned or controlled by the Government of the United States..., the limits of which in all cases shall be confined to the smallest area compatible with the proper care and management of the objects to be protected...."* [58]

Accordingly, a presidentially designated monument should meet three criteria. It must contain an identified historic, prehistoric, or scientific site, structure or object, it cannot be use to appropriate or encumber lands not owned or controlled by the federal government, and its boundaries must constitute the smallest acreage necessary for the protection of the site, structure or object. Because of this requirement in the Act, and because Barrett's bill challenged the legal propriety of the new Monument, the Park Service was forced to describe the scientific and historical justifications for the action by the President as well as defend the size of the Monument.

The Park Service historical argument related to the use of the valley by trappers beginning shortly after the Lewis and Clark Expedition. That celebrated expedition did not see nor enter Jackson Hole, but it did create an interest in the West on the part of fur entrepreneurs and explorers. The Park Service presented a rich history of

S. N. Leek Collection, American Heritage Center, University of Wyoming ah03138_1112

Cunningham Cabin was one of several sites the Park Service previously considered an eyesore that needed to be removed. In 1943, they identified the same structure as a valuable historic site in need of protection, thus, justifying the use of the Antiquities Act to establish the Jackson Hole National Monument. It is currently listed on the National Register of Historic Places.

the area documenting the travels of John Colter, Wilson Price Hunt, John Jacob Astor, and the valley's namesake, David Jackson. Park Service Director Newton B. Drury cited the western historian, Frederic Paxson, and his book *History of the American Frontier* (for which he won a Pulitzer Prize):

> *Jackson Hole at the base of the Grand Tetons is not only a great scenic treasure, but also an important early center of mountain fur trade and exploration of the far West. It should be preserved as a national asset.*[59]

Jackson Hole Historical Society and Museum HS 0457

Drury also noted the existence of the Cunningham Cabin and the remains of the old Menor's Ferry, among other structures, which he indicated the Park Service intended to restore and maintain. He, disingenuously, assured the cowboy history of the area would be preserved because of its *"...historic interest to the thousands of tourists."*[62] Director Drury completed his testimony by stating, *"To perpetuate not only the scenic charm and wildlife species, but also the historic background of Jackson Hole, and make it live again in the minds of future visitors, will be one of the objects of the administration of this national monument."*[60]

It is interesting, from the present day perspective, that although the Park Service has maintained the Cunningham Cabin and constructed a replica of the Menor's Ferry, it has been reluctant to preserve some of the other historical sites and has totally eliminated some historic dude ranch structures, such as those which existed at the Half Moon Ranch. Additional testimony revealed that the intent of the management principles of the

Menor's Ferry (c. 1900s) has also been restored and maintained by the Park Service, but these historic sites obviously would not justify a 221,000-acre monument.

Jackson Hole Historical Society and Museum 2003.0122.040

The Half Moon Guest Ranch on Cottonwood Creek near the Taggart Lake parking lot.

Peter Karppi established the Half Moon Ranch in 1922 and resisted selling out to the Snake River Land Company much longer than most settlers with land near the base of the Tetons. When title issues eventually allowed, the Park Service removed rather quickly all evidence of the ranch structures. Ironically, the Grand Teton National Park website presents a photograph of the Half Moon Ranch on its historical photos page, even though they hastily destroyed all evidence of the "historic" structures.

303

Monument, in spite of the guarantees regarding the continuance of ranching activities such as grazing, would be to eliminate those "cowboy" activities eventually, which would, at least, obscure its history.

For the scientific arguments supporting the establishment of the Monument, the need to protect several endangered species was cited. Among these were the trumpeter swan and the sage grouse. One report from that time lists only three swans in the valley. A reporter in a *Los Angeles Times* article opined, *"...Mr. Ickes would have done better not to mention the birds. Setting aside 21,000 acres of water for three birds seems rather excessive."* [61] Director Drury testified the Park Service intended to restore bison, otter, and white-tail deer.* The elk herd was also cited, but counter arguments from Monument opponents regarding this species were equally valid. The elk herd under the existing management could not be said to be endangered. It was the largest elk herd in the world. In fact, one of the perennial problems relating to elk was that insufficient numbers were being harvested by hunters to keep the population within the resources available to the Fish and Wildlife Service for winter feeding. As noted earlier, the establishment of the Monument, with its prohibition of hunting, could exacerbate the elk population problem. In June 1943, Albert Day of the Fish and Wildlife Service substantiated this perception when he recommended 6,500 elk needed to be killed in order to have the refuge herd reduced to the carrying capacity of the winter range.[62]

Although the protection of endangered species may appear to be an important argument for protecting the area encompassed in the Monument, it should also be remembered that scenic and wildlife values of an area are not, according to the Antiquities Act, a justification for a

Nathaniel H. Darton - U.S. Geological Survey Photographic Library

Devil's Tower in Wyoming, 1900
Devil's Tower was the first national monument and was established by Executive Order in 1906 by Theodore Roosevelt. This Monument, encompassing only 1,347 acres, met the intent of Congress when it bestowed limited authority over U.S. territory to the Executive Branch.

Wayne Johnson photo

Fossil Butte National Monument near Kemmerer, Wyoming was created in 1972 by an act of Congress rather than by Executive Order. It encompasses 8,198 acres.

---

*Bison have been reintroduced to the valley and seem to be expanding at a rate constituting a problem for other wildlife. Otter may never have been extinct from the valley. They certainly exist today, but they were subject to trapping during that era. White-tail deer are another matter. Wyoming Game and Fish big game biologists with whom this author spoke felt the white-tail deer was simply unable to compete with the expanding populations of elk, mule deer, and moose; and thus, their diminishing numbers within Jackson Hole were probably a natural phenomenon.

presidentially proclaimed national monument. For wildlife to be considered appropriate for the establishment of a monument under the authority of the Antiquities Act, the species would have to be extinct. Examples would be Dinosaur National Monument in Utah-Colorado, and Fossil Butte National Monument in Wyoming.* The Antiquities Act does not authorize the creation of wildlife refuges by Executive Order.

When considering the size of the Monument and the Antiquities Act requirement of the minimal acreage necessary, the effort on the part of the Park Service to justify the Monument's creation for historic and wildlife preservation seemed extremely frail. Their strongest and perhaps most reasonable, argument for the scientific importance of the land within the new Monument was its geology. The opposition arguments, concerning the importance of the geological evidence contained in the Monument, centered around the fact that the mountains with their glaciers, granite peaks, hanging canyons, and moraines were already inside the boundaries of Grand Teton National Park. While it might be nice, and even proper, to protect the valley floor immediately in front of the Park from unsightly development, the real and obvious scientific attractions were already situated within the Park boundary.

The Park Service countered by citing books and articles written by noted geologists, including Fritiof Fryxell, which pointed out that the Teton Mountain Range tells only half the geologic story– the uplift half. The subsidence half is the valley floor. Additionally, the valley floor contained evidence of Piedmont glaciation that at times covered much of the valley floor north of the present town of Jackson. The area encompassed in the Monument contained evidence of three glacial periods not found, or at least so obvious, within Grand Teton National Park. Drury stated:

wyomingtailesandtrails.com

Above is a typical homestead the Park Service considered an eyesore and wanted to remove until required to justify the use of the Antiquities Act. When the use of the Antiquities Act was challenged by Congressman Barrett's bill and the state of Wyoming's lawsuit, such structures suddenly became valuable and unique historic buildings in need of federal protection. However, after the National Monument was abolished in favor of an enlarged Grand Teton National Park, most of those "historic" structures were destroyed.

Geologically, it is one of the most impressive areas in the United States. Nowhere in the National Park System is there an example of block faulting of the magnitude found along the bold front of the Teton Range.

The Jackson Hole and the Teton Range region are inseparable in the mind of the geologist. The upthrust mass of the range and the level floor of the basin complement each other, just as the cliffs and the valley of Yosemite are part of one great natural spectacle.[63]

Undoubtedly, the Park Service developed a newfound appreciation for the history and scientific phenomenon of Jackson Hole when required by the legal imperative of the Antiquities Act. They had never mentioned these attractions in prior legislative efforts to expand either Yellowstone National Park or Grand Teton National Park. The old homesteader's cabins which they now found

---

*Woodrow Wilson signed a Presidential Proclamation in 1915 creating Dinosaur National Monument. Fossil Butte National Monument would have qualified for executive action under the Antiquities Act except that, as a result of the creation of the Jackson Hole National Monument, Wyoming is now exempt from Section 2 of that Act. An act of Congress established Fossil Butte in 1972. Interestingly, in light of the controversy discussed in this chapter, Clifford Hansen deserves considerable credit for the establishment of Fossil Butte National Monument. He supported the legislation and "herded" its passage through Congress during his tenure in the U.S. Senate.**

so worthwhile, and in need of protection, were the same structures they previously testified needed to be removed to reestablish the scenic views.

Perhaps the most surprising testimony received by the House Public Lands Committee came from former Wyoming Governor Leslie Miller. His was perhaps the first public statement by a person not associated with the federal government in support of the Monument. He explained that he felt the opposition element might

Grand Teton National Park GRTE-00430_276

Leslie Andrew Miller (D)
1886-1970
Governor Miller (left) visiting a CCC camp in Jackson Hole

Miller was the 17th governor of Wyoming, serving from 1933 to 1939. His family moved from Kansas to Wyoming in 1892. His open support for the Jackson Hole National Monument and Rockefeller's Jackson Hole Project gained him a board of directors position with the Jackson Hole Preserve, Inc.

have placed in the minds of the committee members the impression that all of the people of Teton County and all of Wyoming opposed the Monument. He told the committee:

The truth is that a relatively small number of people of the state have been interested in the present controversy at all and many of these have been misled by the highly distorted picture which has been portrayed to them. Seldom, if ever, in the history of Wyoming has a project which should be entitled to sympathetic consideration been so grossly misrepresented. [64]

Governor Miller spoke favorably regarding the Monument and recounted the various periods when Jackson Hole residents had supported park expansion initiatives but failed to mention those times when park opposition attitudes seemed to prevail. (The opposition did the same thing in reverse, only identifying times when the opposition seemed strongest and ignoring periods of proponent preponderance.) Miller pointed out that during the past ten years, the population of Jackson had grown at a faster rate than any city in Wyoming. He suggested the prosperity driving this growth could not be attributed to the ranching industry because the number of cattle taxed in that county had remained nearly static.* The growth had to be from the expansion of the recreation and tourist industry. He also revealed, from the state Examiner's records, the Jackson State Bank resources had increased from $254,839 in 1936 to $962,537 in 1942. [65] In urging the committee members to reject Congressman Barrett's bill, he concluded:

So deeply do I feel that a great mistake may be made today if the opposition to this project succeeds in its will to defeat the purpose of Mr. Rockefeller, the President, and the National Park Service in the enlargement of Teton National Park,† ... I predict and utter the prediction in all sincerity that

---

*The population of Teton County increased by 560 people between 1930 and 1940. The number of cattle taxed in 1942 was 12,580.

†Miller's comment is further evidence that nearly everyone, at least tacitly, understood that the creation of the Monument was simply an expedient for extending the boundaries of Grand Teton National Park, which is not a Presidential power authorized by the Antiquities Act.

306

the day will come when Wyoming will hang her head in shame and regret the act as she will regret nothing else in her proud history.[66]

The committee members, to their credit, focused the majority of their attention and questions on several very basic issues and avoided the most emotional aspects of the testimony. One, did the Monument boundaries actually include any objects or structures appropriate for protection, as specified by the intent of the Antiquities Act? Two, was the acreage included within the boundaries in keeping with the minimum necessary specification of the Antiquities Act? Three, was the Monument consistent in character with monuments previously established under its authority? And four, was the Monument established to provide protection for objects as prescribed by that act or, rather, to enable the extension of the boundaries of Grand Teton National Park by a means other than legislative enactment? (The former being proper and the latter an abuse of executive power.)

Congressman Barrett allowed:

...Jackson Hole is rich in historical significance, at least to us in Wyoming. The valley is mentioned in the earliest history of the trappers and was settled in the early days, and to my way of thinking has retained more of the spirit of the Old West than any other community; however, I cannot say that it is one of outstanding historical interest, as there are many points in Wyoming that outrank it in that respect. I might add that certainly these 221,000 acres do not include anything of the character stipulated in the Antiquities Act. The most that could be said for this monument area is that it affords a view of the Tetons, and of course that will be there in any event.[67]

As to the consistency with previously established monuments, the committee members were uncertain. Congressman O'Connor indicated the Organ Pipe Cactus National Monument in his state (Arizona) had been established by Presidential proclamation. He said he was not consulted by the executive branch, but while not opposed to

the protection of the site, he believed they incorporated a much larger area (330,874 acres) than was necessary.

Most national monuments were considerably smaller than the Jackson Hole National Monument, but some very large national monuments had been created. Katmai in Alaska, created in 1918, covered 2,792,137 acres. Glacier Bay, created in 1925, encompassed 2,803,840 acres. Death Valley, created in 1933, included 1,907,760

Jackson Hole Historical Society and Museum p1958.0162.001
J. Pierce Cunningham and his wife Margaret, 1900

John Pierce Cunningham was one of the early settlers to enter Jackson Hole. He came to the valley in 1885 and by 1900 was working a homestead south of Spread Creek. With Margaret, his wife, they established a cattle ranch. The cabin that was the subject of historical debate in 1943 is all that remains of the ranch buildings.

Jackson Hole Historical Society and Museum 1958.0161n

J. Pierce Cunningham

acres. Nevertheless, most national monuments ranged from 1 to 50,000 acres. As an example, Devil's Tower in Wyoming, which was created in 1906 and was the first national monument, encompassed 1,347 acres.[68]

The Park Service and pro-monument advocates did not make a terribly strong argument for the historic and scientific "objects" within the Monument. Although the trappers entered Jackson Hole, it was too inaccessible to be a common haunt for these men. Other areas in Wyoming, Utah, Idaho, and Montana contained sites of greater historical significance to the trapper history. The annual gathering of trappers, called a rendezvous, for trading, re-supply, and frivolity never occurred in Jackson Hole. The Green River country near Pinedale, Wyoming has a more legitimate claim to historical trapper activity than does Jackson Hole. The fact that the fur-bearing animals in Jackson Hole were not trapped to the verge of extinction as they were in other parts of the mountain west is strong evidence of the lack of intense trapper activity in the valley.

The terrain of the Monument when viewed with the Tetons to one's back was much like any other section of country in the western states. And while it is obvious that one cannot easily envision the valley without the Tetons, that feature was already protected in a national park. The issue was the qualification of the Monument area as specified by the Antiquities Act.

At one point when Drury explained the desire of the Park Service to eliminate existing unsightly structures such as concession stands and gas stations along the highway, Congressman Peterson recalled that on several occasions while traveling through vast unpopulated sections of the West, he found the appearance of a long hoped for gas station to be a rather pleasant experience. Drury agreed he had experienced some of those moments, too. Peterson's point was, of course, that while gas stations and other concessionaires may not be deemed natural or beautiful, they were often considered appropriate and necessary by the traveling public.

~

Secretary of Interior Harold Ickes was known for his aggressive and sometimes witty repartee. Few men could hold their own in a verbal battle with the man. When asked by Congressman Barrett to *"...tell the committee the specific object or historic landmark or historic or prehistoric structure or object of historic or scientific interest in these 221,000 acres that you are seeking to protect...,* Mr. Ickes responded, *"To me, my personal observation would be the size of the mosquitoes."*[69] When asked if he did not feel that the people of Jackson Hole and Wyoming should have had a chance to express their opinions prior to establishing the Monument, he replied, *"No."* He believed since most of the acreage in the Monument was federal land, it was a national issue, not a local issue. Ickes' position was that people who lived adjacent to federal lands had no opinions worthy of consideration relative to the future use of those lands, and no rights unless previously

Jackson Hole Historical Society and Museum 1958.3395.001

Park Service Director Newton B. Drury testified to Congress that it was his ultimate goal to eliminate, eventually, "cowboy" activities from Jackson Hole National Monument.

Courtesy John Turner, Triangle X Ranch

registered with an appropriate federal agency, such as grazing leases. Since the land belonged to all the people and the Monument was created for all the people and would be managed for all the people, no rights had been abused, and no subterfuge was involved. If others disagreed with his perspective, then a difference of opinion existed, and that dispute in no way obligated him to accept the differing viewpoint or act in any way contrary to his perception. Ickes complained in his testimony that the committee was *"...placing the narrowest possible interpretation on the language of the American Antiquities Act under which national monuments are established."*[70]

In general, the pro-monument advocates stressed the need to protect the scenic values contained within the Monument boundaries. Although historic and scientific values had never been mentioned in previous efforts, the Park Service assured the committee such items did exist in this area and were unique. They maintained the boundaries were not excessive, and no rights had been in any way eliminated or lessened. Some of the Monument advocates stressed that the opposition was primarily composed of a few people motivated by self-interest.

The anti-monument speakers maintained the Monument lacked any significant objects of historic, prehistoric, or scientific interest sufficient to qualify for protection under the Antiquities Act, and the boundaries were far in excess of the acreage required to protect the few sites Park Service officials had described. Clifford Hansen noted the only item of interest concerning Cunningham's Cabin was that two horse thieves had been shot at that site. Whereupon, one committee member expressed the opinion that horse thieves should not be memorialized.[71] The anti-monument supporters believed the President's action was merely a means of extending the boundaries of Grand Teton National Park so that Rockefeller could donate his lands to the National Park Service. The Antiquities Act was just an expedient, illegally employed,

Jackson Hole Historical Society and Museum 2005.0020.023

Former Wyoming Governor Leslie Miller's testimony that tourism sparked growth in economic prosperity was certainly valid. However, efforts to enhance winter tourism relied more heavily on the elk herd, the town ski hill, and gambling rather than Grand Teton National Park. Tours through the elk herd on horse-drawn sleighs were the highlight for winter visitors to the valley. The Elk Refuge remains a popular attraction for large numbers of winter visitors.

to allow the extension of the Park boundaries without the approval of Congress or the people who lived in the area. The use of the Presidential proclamation was a method by which the Park Service and Rockefeller could avoid public comment and consideration by either the citizens of the nation or their elected representatives. They maintained that if there was any support locally for the Monument, it was by a few individuals motivated by self-interest. There was also a deep sense of betrayal that the government would misuse its power and establish the Monument in a thinly veiled maneuver to extend the boundaries of Grand Teton National Park and accommodate Rockefeller's desire to donate his land to the federal government.

Some of these issues are worthy of closer examination. Were any rights abrogated? Yes. The Park Service stated their policy that parks and monuments were created to protect the wildlife therein, in addition to scenic values. Accordingly, there would be a prohibition of hunting. Secretary Ickes indicated he was willing to allow another season of hunting within the Monument during the 1943 season because the elk herd had expanded to the point where the health of the herd was endangered from over population. But this raised the question of whether or not the no-hunting policy would in future years result, not in the protection of the herd, but rather in the endangerment of the herd. The example was given of a situation in Yellowstone National Park when rangers shot large numbers of elk to reduce the population and avoid an over-grazing condition which would have placed the entire herd in danger.* Ickes stated he hoped the Park Service, the Fish and Wildlife Service, and the Wyoming Game and Fish Commission could cooperate on the appropriate management principles for the elk.

The Secretary's talk of cooperation was perceived as a false promise by most valley residents. The Park Service had "cooperated" with locals regarding the boundaries of Grand Teton National Park, excluding privately owned land. Then, four months after the Park was created the Interior Department obtain authority and appropriations to condemn privately owned land adjacent to the Park. Because the Interior Department and the National Park Service made no effort to "cooperate" with the state of Wyoming when establishing the Jackson Hole National Monument, there was little reason for confidence in the Secretary's "hope" for cooperation concerning wildlife management issues. His testimony that hunting would be prohibited within the Monument did not indicate an attitude of cooperation to the committee or to Wyoming officials.

Were the cattle interests in Jackson Hole adversely affected? Yes and no. The policy as stated in the Presidential proclamation, reiterated and later expanded by the Secretary of the Interior, protected certain rights based on particular existing situations or "classes" of individuals. First, people who owned property (8 percent not counting Rockefeller's land) within the boundaries of the Monument could continue to lease from the Park Service the lands they had previously leased for grazing from the Forest Service, but which now were included in the Monument. As explained by Ickes, this right would continue for the life of the

lessee, his or her heirs, and assigns. This would imply that the rancher could sell the ranch to an individual, and the grazing rights would be transferable to the new owner. Ickes confirmed this interpretation in his testimony before the committee, but Director Drury testified he was unsure if this would actually be the case. He indicated Park Service legal staff had not been able to agree as to the meaning of "assigns."† If the more apparent interpretation was correct, those ranchers would not have been affected either in the short or long term except that the rancher would not be allowed to expand his herd size by leasing additional adjacent land within the new Monument.

Also, an issue not pursued during the hearing was the right of a person who might buy a ranch and grazing rights within the Monument. That is, assuming the existing landowner could sell his ranch and have the attendant leased lands transferred to the new owner, would the new owner be

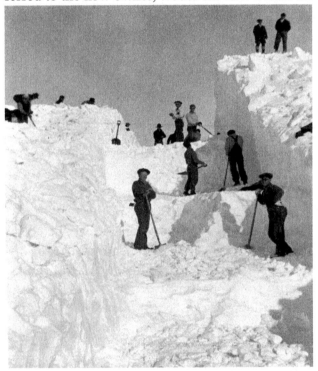

Jackson Hole Historical Society and Museum BC. 0073

Keeping roads open in and out of the valley during the winter often required community involvement. Here, citizens work to clear a snow slide that blocked the highway south of town.

---

*At the time, this action created a controversy between sportsmen and the National Park Service. In a battle of euphemisms, the sportsmen called the action a "government slaughter" while the Park Service said they were "pruning the herd."

†Interior Department lawyers also failed to reach a consensus on the number of generations included in the term "immediate family."

allowed to transfer the lease if and when he sold the ranch? Even if the current landowner could transfer grazing rights at the point of sale, it might be difficult to find a buyer if the new owner could not transfer the leased grazing opportunity in the future. The secretary's statement of policy only spoke to the current landowner and his or her assigns. Neither Director Drury nor Secretary Ickes thought the grazing lease issue for ranches encompassed by the Monument boundary was particularly important because it would be the goal of the Park Service to buy out these inholdings which would terminate the leases.

These statements by Drury and Ickes concerning the grazing lease issues further inflamed the ranchers. Clifford Hansen recalled that he believed the Secretary and the Director had just indicated that the specifics of the grazing rights were insignificant because the Interior Department intended to take these ranches, possibly by condemnation. To Hansen and other ranchers, this was further evidence that the assurances of the President, the Secretary of Interior, and the National Park Service Director that all rights of property owners encompassed by the Monument would be respected was a lie.

The second group of ranchers whose leases and rights the Park Service agreed to respect were those of the ranchers whose private land was outside the boundaries of the Monument, but who needed to cross the Monument to reach grazing leases also situated outside the Monument boundaries. The right to cross the Monument was recognized and could continue in perpetuity. Ranchers in this "class" had not been appreciably affected by the creation of the Monument.

The third group of individuals was ranchers whose private land was outside the Monument, but whose Forest Service grazing leases were now encompassed by Monument boundaries. These grazing leases were guaranteed for the life of the leaseholder and his immediate family but were not transferable. This seemed a very fair solution to Secretary Ickes as it would allow these ranches to continue to operate, possibly for

quite a few years but would eventually eliminate the presence of cattle in the Monument. It might appear that these ranchers were not affected, at least in the short run; but as was explained earlier in this chapter, the property and business of this group of ranchers was effectively devalued because without transferable grazing leases, a ranch would not be desirable to a potential buyer, an asset attractive to a potential lender if loans were needed, or a valuable business to succeeding generations.*

Several other items revealed during testimony were also interesting. One was the condition of the rangelands relating to the joint occupancy of cattle and wildlife. The cattlemen, while under the oversight of the Forest Service, had operated as good stewards of the land. Grazing of domestic cattle had not adversely affected the wildlife, its habitat, nor the scenic values of the valley. Park Service personnel confirmed there were no areas within the Monument which displayed any degradation to either wildlife habitat or scenery as a result of half a century of grazing. The Park Service aversion to cattle had virtually nothing to do with range management science, but rather with an ideological and philosophical concept that cattle were not "natural." Forest Service representatives testified that when wildlife values had been at issue, the cattlemen cooperated with the Forest Service by adjusting range, numbers of animals, and duration of grazing time so that both groups of animals prospered. Another interesting aspect of testimony at the hearing indicated the Forest Service felt cattle grazing had helped avoid some disastrous wildfires because grazing reduced fuel on the forest floor during dry seasons. Assistant Chief Forester L. P. Kneipp testified that without the cattle the grass would be stirrup high.

The *Jackson Hole Courier*, reporting on the testimony received by the House Public Lands Committee, stated the National Park Service had invented "Objects of Historical Significance." The *Courier* also reported that on June 14, a citizen's meeting was held at the Legion Hall to hear

---

*Try to forget present day property values and the developers standing in line to buy a ranch at almost any price. Rockefeller paid about $39 per acre for the land he bought, and that was nearly three times the assessed valuation.

reports from the locals who had attended the hearings in Washington on H.R. 2241. According to the paper, 125 people attended the meeting, and all voted to continue the effort to have the Monument abolished.[72]

~

The House hearing on Congressman Barrett's bill to abolish the Jackson Hole National Monument was not the only political maneuvering at work as a result of the proclamation. Senator O'Mahoney attached an amendment to the Interior Department's appropriation bill providing that none of the funds approved for that agency could be utilized for administration or any other activity associated with the Jackson Hole National Monument. The amendment was unanimously approved by the committee.[73] O'Mahoney's amendment forced the Park Service to ask the Forest Service to continue its management functions over land formerly in its domain, but which had been transferred to the Park Service by the monument proclamation.[74] Although considered in 1943, this appropriation bill was for the 1944 fiscal year. Effectively, the Park Service had a brand-new National Monument but was prohibited from managing it.

In June 1943, Senator O'Mahoney and Senator Pat McCarran of Nevada introduced legislation (S. 1046) to repeal Section 2 of the Antiquities Act[75] removing Presidential authority to establish national monuments by proclamation. The Senate Public Lands Committee reported the bill to the full Senate favorably with no amendments. Concerning this bill, Senator McCarran noted the recent creation of the Jackson Hole National Monument and stated the committee approved the bill to repeal Section 2 of the Antiquities Act *"...lest its authority be used in other public lands states to establish national parks contrary to the wishes of the people involved and contrary to the vote of Congress."* [76]

~

In mid-August, the residents of Jackson Hole were provided another opportunity to communicate directly with Congress. Senator O'Mahoney planned to hold his investigative hearing for S. Res. 134 concerning the boundaries and acquisition policies of the Interior Department,

Harris and Ewing [public domain] via Wikimedia Commons

Patrick Anthony McCarran (D)
1876-1954

Nevada Senator McCarran was born to Irish immigrant sheep ranching parents. He attended the University of Nevada, Reno, but he had to abandon his formal studies to run the family ranch when his father was severely injured. He continued to study law independently and passed the Nevada state bar exam in 1905. He was elected to the Senate in 1932 and was one of only a few Democrats who rejected Roosevelt's New Deal programs. He was best known for his legislative efforts regarding national security and as early as 1933 recommended the establishment of a separate military division that is today the U.S. Air Force. In 1943, he joined with Wyoming Senator O'Mahoney to introduce legislation to repeal Section 2 of the Antiquities Act.

and Congressman Peterson came to the valley on a tour investigating *"...the effect of the withdrawal of a great amount of public land by various Departments, Army and Navy included, and upon the tax problems of the counties involved."*[77] Another congressional committee wanted to investigate the effect the new Monument status might have on the accessibility of several mineral deposits. These were considered potentially important to the war effort but were now situated within the Monument's boundaries. Although the hearings on Congressman Barrett's bill to abolish the National Monument had closed, the Congressman wanted the valley residents to have an opportunity for further expression.

The Interior Department was asked to make the arrangements and coordinate the tours around

Jackson Hole for the various committees who would converge in the valley in August. Conrad Wirth was assigned the task, and he arrived in Jackson in late July. The planning for this congressional convergence would not be of particular interest except that it sparked the public re-emergence of the pro-park extension element within the valley and showed how divisive the monument issue had become among valley residents.

Accommodating the needs and wishes of three congressional committees, arranging for the tours and dealing with the opposing Monument factions was a major endeavor. Senator O'Mahoney and Congressman Barrett thought it appropriate for the hearing to include testimony relating to the monument abolishment issue. Congressman Peterson indicated that the hearing on that subject was closed, and the committee he was bringing to Jackson was funded to study the tax issue, not the monument issue.

Congressman Barrett was distressed that no hearing was being planned because he had already indicated to the people of Jackson that a hearing would occur. Barrett also questioned the authority of the Park Service involvement in the arrangements because O'Mahoney's amendment to the Interior Department's appropriations bill prohibited the expenditure of funds for the Monument. Wirth responded that the O'Mahoney budget amendment applied to the administration of the Monument. The current situation was the result of a request from the House Public Lands Committee to assist in the investigation of legislation specific to tax issues and O'Mahoney's Senate investigation of boundary and acquisition issues. Monument administration was not involved. Barrett then agreed to help organize a local group composed of both pro and anti-monument factions to plan a program to accommodate the needs of the visiting senators and congressmen.[78]

According to Wirth, this group met at 8:00 p.m. on August 11 at the Jackson State Bank. Chief of Lands Wirth, with Regional Park Service Director Merriam, met with Felix Buchenroth, C. R. VanVleck, Clifford Hansen and Milward Simpson for the opposition, and Struthers Burt,* Dick Winger, John Wort, and Walter Spicer

Rockefeller Archive Center, SRLC Series 1030, Box 11, Folder 110

The building that currently serves as the grocery store at Dornan's, just east of the bridge at Menor's Ferry, was under construction when the senators and congressmen toured the Monument in 1943. The smaller building in the distance was the gas station and displayed a white sign (enlarged below) expressing Jack Dornan's view regarding the Monument issue. Other buildings throughout the northern portion of the valley displayed similar signs opposing or supporting the Monument. The signs were placed with the knowledge that the Congressional committee members would be touring the area.

Rockefeller Archive Center, SRLC Series 1030, Box 11, Folder 110

---

*Barrett specifically asked Wirth to include Struthers Burt as a member of the pro-monument group. Although Burt and the Congressman viewed the monument and park extension issues differently, Barrett apparently held Burt in great esteem and believed the former dude rancher's contribution would be beneficial to the investigations of the various committees visiting Jackson Hole.

for the proponents. The meeting was often contentious especially regarding the desirability of a public hearing. Opponents of the Monument wanted a hearing while supporters did not. The group eventually decided on accommodation and transportation arrangements for the congressmen.

Distrust and suspicion were so apparent between the pro and anti-monument factions that it was decided a member of each faction would

Even with improved roads into the valley and the gallant efforts of the highway department to keep the roads open, it was not always easy for winter visitors to appreciate Grand Teton National Park. The snow banks often blocked the view of the mountains.

Attempting to view the Tetons in winter.

ride in each of the cars transporting congressional committee members. This increased the number of vehicles required for the tour because each car in which members of the various committees rode also had a representative of the Park Service, a local representative of the opposition, and a local representative of the park supporters. Since Wirth did not have enough vehicles to accommodate such a large group, half the cars were provided by the government and half by locals. During the two-day tour of the valley, several conferences were held between Congressman Peterson, Senator O'Mahoney, Senator Robertson, and Congressman Barrett. They eventually decided to have a hearing at the theater in Jackson on August 17. [79]

Most people assumed this hearing was related to Congressman Barrett's bill to abolish the Jackson Hole National Monument. The local opposition group, The Committee for the Survival of Teton County, once again assisted by Milward Simpson, made preparations to testify and present evidence on this issue. Because the actual authority and funding for this hearing did not relate directly to Barrett's bill, much of the testimony organized by Simpson was not presented. The senators and congressmen toured the valley on August 15 and 16 and held a hearing on the next day.

This was a rather unusual hearing in that it became an unofficial joint hearing of both the House and Senate Public Lands Committees.* Senator

---

*It is hard to imagine a more efficient congressional investigation, having gathered members of the Committees on Public Lands from both the House and the Senate, some of whom also served on the Appropriations Committee, and representatives from five federal agencies to consider four legislative issues at one sitting. Legislators in attendance were, Wyoming Senator Joseph O'Mahoney, Chairman; Wyoming Congressman Frank Barrett; Florida Congressman J. Hardin Peterson; Wyoming Senator E. V. Robertson; North Dakota Senator Gerald P. Nye; South Dakota Senator Chan Gurney; and Colorado Congressman J. Edgar Chenoweth. Governor Hunt represented the state of Wyoming. The Department of Interior was represented by Michael Straus, First Assistant Secretary; Newton Drury, Director of the National Park Service; Dick Rutledge, Director of the National Grazing Service; Conrad Wirth, Chief of the Lands Section of the National Park Service; J. David Wolfsohn, Assistant Commissioner of the General Land Office; and Lawrence Merriam, Regional Director of the National Park Service.

O'Mahoney explained the situation during his opening remarks. Although the primary focus of the hearing pertained to O'Mahoney's resolution, three other legislative issues were being investigated concurrently. Each of these three issues touched, in some manner, on various aspects of the newly established National Monument. O'Mahoney explained, first, that after Congressman J. Hardin Peterson had closed the hearings pertaining to Congressman Barrett's bill to abolish the National Monument, he received numerous requests from people and organizations who wanted to present testimony. He did not feel it appropriate to reopen the hearings and hoped the Jackson hearings might provide an opportunity for additional comment on the issue.

Second, Congressman Peterson had introduced legislation to provide federal compensation to counties whose lands had been appropriated by the federal government. As indicated previously, because of the war effort, considerable land had been procured by the government to the extent that tax revenue problems for local governmental entities throughout the nation had become a serious consideration. Rockefeller's stated intention to donate his property in Jackson Hole to the National Monument would create severe revenue problems for Teton County. Federal compensation in lieu of taxes had been a problem for this county since the establishment of the National Elk Refuge. Peterson and several members of the House Public Lands Committee were in Jackson Hole to investigate the local situation relative to his bill.

The third ancillary congressional investigation related to the development of the nation's mineral resources.* The new Monument included within its boundaries several withdrawals, by Executive Order, of mineral bearing lands considered vital to the war effort. Thus, several of the legislators were interested in the probable management policies of the Park Service relative to the mineral needs of the nation in a time of war.

The representatives from the Department of Interior were closely questioned regarding the rights of property owners within and outside the

Monument's boundaries. Drury's testimony essentially restated and affirmed Secretary Ickes' statements before the House Public Lands Committee in Washington attendant to Congressman Barrett's bill to abolish the Jackson Hole National Monument. A point of contention developed around Ickes' assurances of rights to property owners, specifically concerning the meaning of

Harris and Ewing Library of Congress.[Public domain] via Wikimedia Commons

J. Hardin Peterson (D)
1894-1978

Peterson was elected to the U.S. House of Representatives from Florida in 1932 and served consecutive terms until 1951. He was chairman of the Committee on Public Lands in the 78th, 79th, and 81st Congresses. (The Republicans regained control of the House for the 80th Congress.) Peterson was sympathetic to hardships and uncertainties faced by Jackson Hole residents resulting from the proclamation creating the National Monument. However, he voted against Barrett's bill to abolish the Monument and authored the Public Lands Committee's minority report on the bill. He was not a supporter of the Monument, but he encouraged Barrett to amend his bill to reflect the Clifford Hansen compromise and provide legislative protection for the ranchers and individual land owners affected, and provide tax compensation to Teton County. He argued that abolishing the monument might be a moral victory, but would not keep the President from creating another monument in the valley at a later date. Enlarging the Park on the west side of the Snake and designating land east of the Snake as Elk Refuge would remove the threat of a future monument proclamation.

---

*Information presented at the hearing indicated the withdrawal for coal was 53,774 acres, the withdrawal for phosphate was 18,907 acres, while acreage for the asbestos and vanadium withdrawals were not given possibly because of national security reasons.

"assigns" and "immediate family." Drury was unable to satisfy the committee explaining that the department's legal staff had been unable to agree on the definition of "assigns" or to agree on the number of generations included in the term "immediate family." [80] When asked by Senator Gurney if the Park Service might use condemnation to acquire some of the lands within the Monument boundaries, Drury allowed that the power existed, but that the procedure would require an act of Congress. Drury added, *"In fact everything we do is by an act of Congress."* To which O'Mahoney responded, *"Except, of course, creating National Monuments."* [81] Unclarified, by either the Washington hearings or the Jackson Hole hearings, was the apparent conflict of the Park Service's stated desire to preserve the historical aspects of ranching, which they cited as one justification for the Monument[82] with their stated policy that was designed to eliminate ranching activities.[83]

Concerning the mineral withdrawals within the Monument, it seemed the Park Service would most likely acquiesce if minerals deemed necessary for the war effort were, in fact, located on these lands, and there was no alternative reasonably available. The example was noted for tungsten mining in Yosemite National Park. Senator O'Mahoney indicated such a development would probably have to be a matter of critical necessity and conducted by a government corporation, rather than for the convenience of a private operation.[84]

Clifford Hansen testified for the Teton County Commissioners, and he presented an accurate picture of the tax revenue problems faced by the county due to the uncertainty of the ultimate disposition of Rockefeller's lands and other private lands, within the boundaries of the Jackson Hole National Monument. Hansen outlined the status of land within Teton County. Teton County encompassed 1,788,800 acres. Of that acreage, the Grand Teton National Park contained 95,600 acres, National Forest lands amounted to 1,511,223 acres, Elk Refuge lands included 21,499 acres, state-owned lands contained 4,884 acres, public domain lands occupied 42,720 acres, and privately owned lands constituted 112,874 acres. If the privately owned lands within the

Clifford Hansen
1919-2009

Hansen was chairman of the Teton County Commissioners and president of the Jackson Hole Cattle and Horse Association when the monument was established. He stridently opposed its creation, but he suggested a compromise that would eventually bring opposing sides to mediation and result in National Park status for much of the valley.

Monument boundary were acquired by the federal government, either by donation or purchase, the remaining taxable property would be only 61,928 acres. The Jackson Hole National Monument encompassed 221,000 acres, but these lands had been transferred from the National Forest Service and public domain. Hansen's figures represented ownership prior to the establishment of the Monument.

Purchases of private land by the Biological Survey for Elk Refuge purposes, which began in 1920, and the removal of improvements on land owned by the Snake River Land Company had the effect of reducing county revenues. Taxes had been raised on private property to meet the needs of local government. Teton County was currently taxing its residents at the maximum allowed by state law, 8.5 mils. Hansen testified that the county had been able to operate without deficit spending, and the only debt attributable to the county was the bonded indebtedness for schools totaling

Hansen Family Collection

$33,500.[85] If Rockefeller's lands were donated to the federal government and removed from the tax rolls, the county would be forced into deficit spending and thus bankruptcy.

As with previous considerations regarding extensions of the National Park System into the valley, the tax revenue problem remained the most valid argument for the opposition. The opposition did not abandon the arguments of principle or personal preference, but the revenue problem was real and quantifiable to essentially disinterested observers.

The committee asked Hansen if the county had not benefitted from increased development as a result of the creation of Grand Teton National Park. Hansen responded that, while the creation of the Park and the attendant publicity may have attracted people to the valley, the primary impetus for development within Jackson Hole had been from enhanced accessibility as a result of highway improvement and maintenance by the Wyoming Highway Department. He suggested that the creation of a national park, no matter how beautiful, could not appreciably help the economic development of adjacent communities if the park was inaccessible to the traveling public. He also indicated that Grand Teton National Park had not adversely affected the economy because its establishment did not include any private lands or grazing allotments.[86]

Another important aspect of Hansen's testimony related to the cattle grazing issue. Prior to his testimony, the livestock issue had been extensively discussed, but mostly in a philosophical or ideological context. It had been considered a pre-existing activity or right that the Park Service was willing to tolerate for an indefinite but ultimately limited amount of time. Hansen's testimony made the economic activity real. Using a map of the area, he described each grazing allotment (both within and outside the boundaries of the Monument), the numbers of animals allowed on each allotment, and the drift areas necessary

for the utilization of those allotments. Interior Department testimony had maintained there would be no immediate impact on the ranching community, and any effects of the Monument would be gradual and occur over a span of many years. Hansen's presentation clarified the potential impact on the future of the livestock industry in Jackson Hole due to the establishment of the Jackson Hole National Monument.

At the end of his testimony, Hansen made a personal statement which, considering his previously documented position regarding the Monument, was somewhat surprising. Couched in the lingo

Jackson Hole Historical Society and Museum 2005.0009.001

Keeping roads open during the winter was never easy and was sometimes dangerous. Avalanches in both canyon approaches and on both mountain pass approaches were a constant hazard. In the photo above, a highway department snowplow was swept into the Hoback River by an avalanche. In the bottom photo, the vehicle is being extracted from the river, and the damage is considerable. Today, the highway department uses sophisticated avalanche forecasting technology and explosive devices to mitigate avalanches in Hoback Canyon and on Teton Pass.

Jackson Hole Historical Society and Museum 2005.0009.004

of a rancher, he suggested a compromise, a "cutting out" of lands. In a ranching environment, this refers to a separating of assets by purpose, type, or value. For example, various types of animals may, on occasion, graze the same pasture simultaneously. Prior to shipping, calving, vaccination, or other typical ranching activities, the animals will be "cut" or separated into like groups so that the desired activity may be accomplished more efficiently. Hansen made it clear his suggestion was his own. He was not representing any group or faction concerned with the controversy.

He acknowledged the good work of the Park Service in protecting the nation's especially scenic areas and assured the committee the people of Jackson Hole recognized the scenic and recreational values associated with Grand Teton National Park. However, he believed the Park Service would have a difficult job administering their policies on the eastern side of the Monument because the boundary was an irregular survey line rather than a natural boundary. His presentation clearly showed the most important lands for livestock were east of the Snake River, and he did not believe ranching had to be eliminated in order to protect the scenic and recreational assets of the valley. He suggested the Monument lands west of the Snake River be included in Grand Teton National Park. Because the majority of economic utilization, mostly relating to livestock, occurred east of the Snake River, he suggested that area be

Amy Rabb Photo: Jackson Hole Historical Society and Museum
2003.0082.013

Calving time on the Lucas ranch

Snow drifts and standing water in irrigation ditches are inherent hazards to newborn calves. Calving time in Jackson Hole is a 24 hour, seven days a week job– usually in cold weather.

returned to the Forest Service.[87] His proposal would have also eliminated most of the mineral withdrawals from within the Monument boundaries.

Hansen's compromise proposal deserves some consideration. Despite the government's statements justifying the invocation of the Antiquities Act, it seems obvious the Monument was established to extend the boundaries of Grand Teton National Park so as to facilitate the donation of Rockefeller's land. Legislation to accomplish this extension failed, and Rockefeller was putting pressure on the federal government to accept his donation of property for National Park purposes. Arguments put forth by the Interior Department to make the valley floor fit the criteria of the Antiquities Act were, with the exception of the glacial features, weak. Monument status would require administrators protect "historic" structures they had previously testified were eyesores that should be eliminated. The policies of the Monument were in conflict, ideologically, with the preexisting and important

Floyd Naegeli photo, Jackson Hole Historical Society and Museum
p00hs.426903

Many of the valley's ranchers depended on land included in the Jackson Hole National Monument for summer grazing allotments or as drift areas through which they moved their cattle to and from summer grazing allotments on Forest Service land.

economic activity of ranching that was necessary to the community and the war effort. Hansen's suggestion would allow the Park boundaries to be extended so as to protect the foreground of the Teton Mountain Range, and thus, eliminate the need for a monument and its attendant conflicts associated with the Antiquities Act. The irregular eastern boundary of Grand Teton National Park would be replaced with a natural boundary, the Snake River. The eastern side of the Snake River would continue to provide the economic basis for the cattle industry, which was not a threat to the glacial features the Interior Department had suddenly found to be so significant.

Hansen's proposal did not address two issues: compensation in lieu of taxes and Rockefeller's lands east of the Snake River. Congressman Peterson's bill might solve the first item. The second item would obviously require Rockefeller's cooperation. However, his purchases east of the Snake River had always been of secondary importance in the larger scheme of his project. It is perhaps impossible to know how he might have reacted to the suggestion, but those lands east of the Snake River might have been donated to the Fish and Wildlife Service* to ensure elk migration corridors. This was one of the stated purposes identified when his project was revealed to the public (See Chapter Nine) and similar to the compromise he had accepted with Senator Carey's 1934 bill to extend the boundaries of Grand Teton National Park.

Committee members had previously indicated they might introduce legislation that would provide some form of perpetuity for grazing rights in the Monument. When asked his opinion of such legislation, Hansen indicated he did not think that was appropriate. He stated:

...I think that we would be toying with something which would be very dangerous

to our National Park System to try to permit all of the uses which now exist in this area to continue to exist while having it a National Monument. I think it would be much better to shrink the area to a size compatible with the administration of the Grand Teton National Park and then attempt to exclude the use and the private property interests, in so far as possible....[88][†]

Senator O'Mahoney asked, *"Do I understand you mean you see no objection to some extension of the boundaries of the Grand Teton National Park in order to make the administration and the protection of the Grand Tetons and that general area more easy, so to speak?"* To which Hansen responded, *"I think that is right."* [89]

Clifford Hansen's compromise proposal caught everyone off guard. Since the creation of the Monument six months earlier, there had been no public indication of support for an enlarged Grand Teton National Park. Hansen was the local leader of the opposition, had urged fellow cattlemen to reject federal grazing lease procedures, led an armed "trespass" over Monument land,

Jackson Hole Historical Society and Museum 1958.0211.001
Dog sleds were common even after the acceptance of automobiles in the valley. Travel to a local store for supplies was sometimes impossible for cars during the winter. Note the snow level relative to the roof eave and gas pump.

---

*The Fish and Wildlife Service and the Biological Survey may be considered interchangeable terms for the period of Teton Park history. The Biological Survey was established in 1905 within the Department of Agriculture. The Biological Survey and the Bureau of Fisheries were transferred to the Department of Interior in 1939, and the two agencies were merged in 1940 to form the Fish and Wildlife Service.

†It might be assumed that Clifford Hansen had made a self-serving compromise to protect his own vested interest. However, it should be noted his grazing allotment was in the Pot Holes area west of the Snake River. His suggestion would have benefitted most of the ranchers who were faced with National Park Service restrictions, but his ranch operation, along with those of two other ranchers, would have remained encumbered and in jeopardy from Park Service bureaucracy within the extended park.

testified in Washington in support of abolishing the National Monument, and had just presented a strong case for the problems facing Teton County and local ranchers as a result of the President's proclamation. Barrett's bill to abolish the National Monument appeared to have a good chance of passage, and the state of Wyoming had filed a lawsuit which might also reverse the President's action. The press and various organizations across the nation indicated support for abolishing the Monument. There seemed to be no imperative or advantage at that time to suggest a compromise. Hansen would later receive pressure from the opposition groups and individuals, including Governor Hunt and Milward Simpson, to reject compromise and "stay the course" for abolishment. His compromise suggestion may have been the first public indication of the kind of politician he would become. He was destined to be revered as one of the most beloved, respected, and trusted politicians in Wyoming history.

Hansen's testimony and subsequent questioning by committee members ended about four p.m. in the afternoon leaving only a few hours for additional testimony. Milward Simpson arranged for a considerable number of people to testify before the committee, but only a few were able to present their statements. Senator O'Mahoney allowed written statements from those who could not be heard to be submitted and included in the record. The committee heard testimony from Frederick Champ who was a national director of the United States Chamber of Commerce and a director of the National Forestry Association; Lester Bagley of the Wyoming Game and Fish Commission; Russell Thorpe of the Wyoming Stock Growers Association; J. Elmer Brock who was the past president of the National Livestock Association; and Milward Simpson. The above-listed peo-

ple testified in opposition to the Monument and indicated there should be no compromise regarding the abolishment of the Jackson Hole National Monument.

Lester Bagley's testimony dealt primarily with the elk herd and hunting issues. Bagley noted the Supreme Court ruled that game animals belong to the state within whose boundaries they reside.* He acknowledged the right of the Park Service to manage elk within Yellowstone National Park, but once those animals exited the Park, they became the property and responsibility of the state of Wyoming regardless of the establishment of the Monument. Park and Monument policy prohibited the hunting of wildlife, and hence the conflict between the state and the Monument. If the state was not allowed to authorize the reduction of the herd through hunting, the park rangers would eventually have to kill large numbers of elk in order to restrict their numbers to match the resources of the refuge. Bagley stated:

The policy of the Park Service relative to the outright slaughter of wild animals to control population can never be looked

Jackson Hole Historical Society and Museum bc.0340
Chester Simpson feeding elk on the refuge.
Insufficient harvesting of elk during the hunting season resulted in the herd population exceeding the capability of the refuge to provide winter feed. Note the dead elk in the foreground.

---

*As mentioned in previous chapters, the Supreme Court ruled in the case of *Ward v. Race Horse* that the wild animals within the boundary of a state belonged to that state. However, there are two exceptions. One relates to migratory birds, which remain federal. Duck hunters need to purchase a Federal Duck Stamp. The other exception is Yellowstone National Park. Yellowstone was exempted from the ruling because it was made a park before Wyoming was made a state, and thus, the state of Wyoming has never had jurisdiction in Yellowstone except as provided for by subsequent specific purpose legislation passed by Congress. An example would be the right to collect sales tax on commerce within the Park.

upon with favor by those who own, and value, the animals for game. It is impossible for people in the west to understand why it is necessary for an elk to be shot by a Park Ranger rather than by some deserving and interested sportsman.

We might be prepared to agree that the Park Service can enforce such restrictions in Yellowstone National Park. But we know it to be within the power of the Service to permit hunting on the monument area, if it so desires, and I am confident that if the Wyoming Game and Fish Commission continues to control and manage the elk herd as it has done during the past 25 or 30 years, these highly valued animals can be managed and maintained at the desired population. At the same time, the Commission can afford opportunities for deserving sportsmen to take from the area approximately 5,000 elk a year, and thus accomplish through hunter harvest what the National Park Service would achieve by planned campaigns of slaughter.[90]

Jackson Hole Historical Society and Museum bc.39

Elk starvation on the refuge.
Hunting was, and remains, the primary tool of big game managers to maintain a healthy population relative to resources. The Jackson Hole elk herd numbered around 20,000. An annual reduction of at least 5,000 elk was deemed necessary to maintain the herd within range carrying capacity and refuge resources.

Simpson's testimony was the most vitriolic. He restated the arguments and accusations previously offered by the anti-park faction for virtually every park extension or creation proposal since 1919. However, one new allegation stood out. Simpson told the committee that the Jackson Hole Plan was not a local initiative. This was surprising because the plan, which had the support of a majority of the valley's populace from 1930 to 1935, was penned and circulated by four long-time residents and homesteaders, one of whom was previously a vocal opponent of park extension. Simpson stated the Jackson Hole Plan *"...was never devised in this valley by Jackson Hole people, but it was the Rockefeller-Albright plan, if you please, to take this valley and make it over according to their own plans."* [91]

Simpson also raised the issue of forty-five miles of state highway included within the Monument boundaries. His concern was that the Monument might not allow commercial traffic or winter travel through its boundaries, as was the case with Yellowstone National Park. Such a policy would eliminate an important transportation link for the state's economic interests, and northern access and egress for residents of the valley. This seems an unlikely concern because Director Drury had previously testified on this issue assuring the committee that state roads fell under the protection of pre-existing rights specified in the Presidential proclamation.*

No testimony was received from supporters of the Monument other than by Interior Department representatives. Most of this testimony, as expected, supported the actions of the President, the Secretary of Interior, and Rockefeller. The comments of Dick Rutledge, director of the National Grazing Service, are worth noting. Over the preceding 23 years, Rutledge had accompanied every Congressional committee investigating land

---

*Mr. Simpson probably overstated the importance of winter travel by the northern highway to the residents of Jackson Hole. In July 1943, residents learned the state highway department lacked the funds and labor to keep all three approaches to the valley open during the winter. The department agreed to keep one highway open and allowed the residents of Teton County to vote as to which road was most desirable. A meeting was held in Jackson on July 19 and was attended by 175 people. They voted to keep the southern approach, the Hoback Canyon road, open that winter. Their second choice was Teton Pass to the west.[92]

issues in Jackson Hole and was very familiar with the country and the issues. He was a supporter of recreation on public lands, sympathetic to wildlife values as they related to habitat requirements, and had a professional background relative to the needs of grazing interests. When asked by the committee to provide his personal opinion on the issue at hand, he complied. He offered several suggestions for the resolution of the controversy that complimented the compromise proposal presented earlier by Clifford Hansen. He thought the north-south highway, currently located west of the Snake River, should be moved to the east side of the river. This would provide two benefits. First, it would provide a magnificent panoramic view of the Tetons, and second, it would move commercial traffic away from the mountains with less mileage between Togwotee Pass and the town of Jackson. He suggested that by confining park and monument lands primarily to the west side of the Snake River, some 6,000 acres of private land, not owned by Rockefeller would be excluded from within the Monument. This would lessen the conflict between nonconforming private landowner activities and Park Service policy. The primary grazing lands necessary to the stockmen would

Public Lands Foundation Archives,. Archive #1324.
Colorado Congressman Edward Taylor (left) and Richard H. Rutledge (right)

Taylor sponsored what is now called the Taylor Grazing Act, and Rutledge was the second director of the U.S. Grazing Service. The Grazing Service and the General Land Office were merged in 1946 to form the Bureau of Land Management. Rutledge broke ranks with other Interior Department staff to support Clifford Hansen's compromise proposal regarding the Jackson Hole National Monument.

no longer be a contentious issue for the Monument. He suggested several stock driveways or drift lanes, perhaps two miles wide, could be established for the cattlemen which would allow their movement of livestock to and from summer ranges while also ensuring migration routes and forage for the elk herd. For the relatively few stockmen who had grazing interests on the west side of the Snake River, he suggested a smaller drift lane paralleling the west side of the Snake to the Pot Holes area. Rutledge also recognized the difficulty faced by the Wyoming Game and Fish Department regarding the elk population if hunting were removed as a management tool in the area immediately north of the refuge. Placing the eastern boundary of the Park along the Snake River would resolve this issue.[93]

At the end of Rutledge's statement, the following conversation occurred:

> Senator O'Mahoney: *In other words, in your judgement, it is not necessary to liquidate the livestock interests in order to secure the objectives of preserving the scenic attractions of this area?*
>
> Mr. Rutledge: *Not at all. Not at all. It wouldn't be at all necessary if we get our heads together.*[94]

This hearing was probably less than satisfying for the Committee for the Survival of Teton County because it became apparent the joint subcommittee members were interested in a compromise. During questioning by the committee members about the Monument boundaries, Director Drury indicated he thought the boundaries were appropriate, but he was willing to meet with interested parties to determine if adjustments could or should be made. Clifford Hansen and Dick Rutledge had proposed ways whereby a compromise might be reached. After Rutledge's statement, Senator O'Mahoney asked Assistant Secretary Straus:

> *Do you think it would be possible for the Department of the Interior, the National Park Service, and the Grazing Service, to sit down with the County Commissioners, or representatives thereof, and representatives*

of the people of Teton County, and with the Governor of the State or his appointees, to consider a modification of the boundaries of this Monument and legislation which would make effective, in the interest of all, the various related matters which have been under discussion here today?

Straus replied in the affirmative and O'Mahoney then inquired if Governor Hunt had any questions. The governor replied:

> *I have nothing to say, Senator O'Mahoney, except that we appreciate your attitude, Mr. Secretary. We would have greatly appreciated that same attitude prior to the issuing of the Proclamation. Now we are confronted with a problem that looks as though we might be able to meet around the conference table and settle. I should be glad to go along with such a plan, providing it is thoroughly agreeable with Congressman Barrett and with Senator Robertson and with the county officials of Teton County.*[95]

Neither Senator Robertson nor Congressman Barrett objected to the meeting, but Barrett stated he agreed with Governor Hunt that a matter of principle was involved. Barrett felt the present controversy could have been avoided if the people of Wyoming and their representatives had been contacted prior to the proclamation. However, it seems unlikely such a compromise, as suggested by Hansen and Rutledge, could have been accomplished prior to the Presidential proclamation. Several legislative attempts to extend the boundaries of Grand Teton National Park during the previous decade failed, and the opposition faction would have perceived no imperative to compromise. Only the real and present threat occasioned by the actual creation of the Monument made a compromise seem desirable.

~

Prior to the tour of Jackson Hole by the Congressmen and Senators, there had been a noticeable lack of public comment by supporters of the Park or the new Monument. This ended with the hearings. On August 16 a group of eight Jackson businessmen sent a letter to Congressman Peterson opposing the abolishment of the Jackson Hole National Monument. The letter was signed by W. L. Spicer, Ben Goe, John and Jess Wort, H. C. Richards, R. T. Black, Jack Moore, and A. Martin. Later in August, Congressman Peterson received a petition from a group of Monument supporters

Jackson Hole Historical Society and Museum b29166
John and Jess Wort

John and Jess Wort continued in the service industry established by their father. The Wort Hotel provided the first complete service hotel in Jackson. In addition to guest rooms, it contained a restaurant, bar, and gambling facilities. Prior to the construction of the hotel, the family ran a livery (bottom photo) that stabled horses for visitors to the town of Jackson. Both brothers signed letters and petitions supporting the Jackson Hole National Monument if legislative guarantees could be passed protecting the cattlemen, private property owners, and providing tax compensation for Teton County. In the 1930s, John Wort ran unsuccessfully for local office opposing the Jackson Hole Plan.

Jackson Hole Historical Society and Museum 2012.0058.001

signed by 87 valley residents.[96] [See Appendix Two-J to read the full petition.]

This petition was more reasonable in tone and content than some earlier petitions emanating from the valley. The petition presented what the authors considered seven *"…simple facts…"* regarding the controversy. First, Jackson Hole was a special place and should be protected. Second, the cattle business was an essential industry of the valley that should and could continue to operate along with the recreation industry. Furthermore, the rights of the cattlemen to graze and drift their cattle to and from summer allotments *"…should*

Spicer Family Collection, Courtesy Geri Spicer Stone

Walter L. Spicer with first wife Ruby (Curtis)Spicer 1912
1887-1967

Walt Spicer was a prominent Jackson Hole businessman who joined other businessmen in supporting the National Monument if certain guarantees could be codified to protect cattlemen, private property owners and provide tax compensation for the county. Walt came to Wyoming from North Carolina in 1901. He cut railroad ties for the Union Pacific in Rock Springs then moved to Jackson Hole in 1904 buying a ranch in the upper Gros Ventre area. He married Ruby Curtis in 1912, and they eventually moved to Jackson. Over a span of years, Walt owned, in whole or in part, several mercantile stores, a saloon, a Ford dealership, a Chevrolet dealership, and a hotel.

be secured to them, their heirs and assigns, by national legislation and should not be left subject to change at the will of bureau chiefs." Third, the state of Wyoming should continue to manage the wildlife in the area with cooperation from the federal agencies. Fourth, Teton County could not continue to exist as a separate entity unless it could be compensated for lost tax revenue in the event private lands in the protected area should be acquired by the federal government. Fifth, federal legislation was needed to ensure the protection of the scenic views, lakes and watersheds of the valley. Sixth, while signers of the petition would have preferred an act of Congress to protect the north end of the valley and to specify the protections for cattlemen, property owners and other valid claimants, they thought the Monument should remain *"…unless and until more comprehensive legislation is enacted by the Congress of the United States."* Seventh, they believed the residents and the Congressional delegation should stop quarreling, reject the Barrett bill, and concentrate their efforts *"…for constructive legislation that will supplement the monument proclamation, by giving permanence and certainty to the foregoing rights which, although now guaranteed by statements of officials of the Interior Department, should be placed beyond any possibility of doubt by legislative action."* The authors of the petition were W. Spicer, R. T. Black, John Wort, W. J. Grant, Orin Seaton, Virgil Ward, and J. Wallace Moulton. The 87 signatures affixed to this petition represented residents and business people from throughout the valley.[97]

This petition was important for several reasons. It contradicted the opposition's contention that the people of Jackson Hole were unanimously opposed to the Monument. Conversely, by recognizing various uncertainties occasioned by the Presidential proclamation and requesting a legislative remedy of these issues, the petition made credible the opposition's arguments regarding tax revenues and the rights of cattlemen who depended on the northern portion of the valley for their existence. If supporters of the Monument were not reassured by the statements of policy by the Secretary of the Interior and the Park Service director, the cattlemen's concerns were more compelling. At issue here is the lack of perpetuity and perhaps confidence in any bureaucrat's promise or policy as compared to specific directions mandated by legislation formulated and passed by the elected representatives of the people. The Secretary's statement of policy would only last until he changed his mind, or a new Secretary of Interior decided on a different management policy.

The opposition was quick to respond to the petition. They agreed Jackson Hole was a great outdoor recreation area, but they did not believe the Monument enhanced those opportunities. In fact, they suggested recreational opportunities would be reduced because of the mandates of the Antiquities Act by which the Monument was created. The Act did not authorize, nor was it intended for the creation of monuments for recreational purposes. The Act provides for the creation of monuments for historic and scientific preservation and study. The establishment of the Jackson Hole National Monument neither protected nor assured the continuance of recreational activities. The opposition's response asserted that any lands in Jackson Hole set aside for park purposes should be accomplished by Congressional legislation. They maintained if the Monument were abolished, the county would not need a welfare check from the federal government in lieu of taxes or additional legislation to protect the rights of the cattlemen and other residents.[98]

For some opposition members, the prospect of specific legislation protecting their rights did not offer a secure resolution to their concerns. John D. Rockefeller, Jr., the National Park Service, the Department of the Interior, and the President of the United States had just ignored the restricting language and intent of the Antiquities Act to create the Jackson Hole National Monument. There was little confidence that the executive branch of the government or its agencies would abide by or be inhibited by future legislation they might find inconvenient.[99]

Department of the Interior photo [Public domain] via Wikimedia Commons

Newton B. Drury
1889-1978

Drury became National Park Service Director in 1940. He was the first to be appointed to that position from outside the Park Service ranks. He was an advertising executive with a strong interest in conservation having served as Executive Director of the Redwoods League. He resigned in 1951 after several conflicts with Interior Secretary Chapman because of the Secretary's support for dams on the Green River in Dinosaur National Monument.

As a result of the Jackson hearings, and after additional communication between Senator O'Mahoney and Governor Hunt, the date of September 4, 1943, was set for a meeting in Cheyenne to discuss a possible compromise regarding the monument issue.* The local opposition group agreed to send representatives to the meeting to discuss a possible compromise but indicated any compromise, including a future limited extension of Grand Teton National Park, would be predicated upon the abolishment of the Jackson Hole National Monument. No matter how the specific issues might be settled to their benefit and satisfaction, they would not agree to a compromise that did not include the abolishment of the Monument. This was a matter of principle that could not, in their minds, be arbitrated.

---

*Attending the meeting from Jackson were Clifford Hansen, Felix Buchenroth, Charles Kratzer, J. R. Riggan, Fernie Hubbard, J. G. Imeson, and A. W. Gabbey. C. R. Van Vleck also traveled to Cheyenne but became ill and did not attend the meeting. R. H. Rutledge, Newton Drury, and Lawrence Merriam represented the Department of the Interior. State officials present were Governor Hunt, Congressman Barrett, Senators O'Mahoney and Robertson, Lester Bagley of the Game and Fish Commission, Deputy Attorney General John McIntyre, and Laramie State Senator Pat Norris.[100]

Depending on the predisposition of the reporter, the results of the meeting were reported differently by several sources. The *Jackson Hole Courier* reported it was agreed the Jackson Hole National Monument would be abolished, and a joint bill would be introduced by the Wyoming delegation to provide a limited extension of the eastern boundary of Grand Teton National Park. According to the *Courier*, it was also agreed Teton County would need to be compensated for taxes lost by the intended donation of Rockefeller's lands to the federal government, and the rights of other property owners and cattlemen would be assured by congressional legislation.[101]

On September 7, Park Service Director Drury wrote a memorandum to Interior Secretary Ickes providing a summation of the meeting, but his report did not completely conform to the *Courier's* version of the agreement. Drury identified five primary issues considered by those who participated in the meeting. First, according to Drury, it was generally agreed the Barrett bill to abolish the Monument could not be enacted. (This certainly was not the opinion of the Jackson contingent and probably not the attitude of Congressman Barrett.) Drury believed Senator O'Mahoney wanted to amend the Barrett bill by abolishing the National Monument, but simultaneously adding lands to Grand Teton National Park, and limiting that extension to the west side of the Snake River (Hansen's compromise). Second, the secretary's statement of policy, previously confirmed in the House Public Lands Committee, would be enacted into law through the amended Barrett bill.

Third, an adjustment of the eastern boundary of the Monument would appease most of the local interests while simplifying Park Service management of the area. Fourth, Teton County should be compensated in some manner for the loss of tax revenue. Fifth, Drury believed neither the governor nor the Congressional delegation thought the state could win the lawsuit which had been filed regarding the establishment of the Monument, and hoped a compromise on the Barrett bill would save the state the cost of the court action. In his memorandum, Drury indicated participants representing the Park Service made no commitments regarding these issues, other than agreeing to study them. He concluded:

> *I believe that if Mr. Rockefeller is willing, some adjustment can be made along the south and east boundary. I have already discussed the general considerations with Mr. Chorley and Mr. Albright, and have asked them to apprize Mr. Rockefeller of the situation. You will undoubtedly want to discuss the specific proposals with him when they are formulated.*[102]

Perhaps the primary difference in the two reports on this compromise meeting is that the Jackson residents felt they had reached an agreement with the federal government, while the government representatives believed they had met to listen to compromise proposals. Drury denied having entered into an agreement of any kind.

Subsequent Interior Department memoranda provided more detail regarding this meeting. Conrad Wirth, the Chief of Lands for the Park Service, wrote a memorandum for the director on September 9. According to Wirth, Governor Hunt opened the meeting in his office urging those in attendance to try to work out their differences and settle the issue. He called on each participant to state his position. Wirth gave a synopsis of each individual's statement, and each of the statements can generally be categorized into several themes. All the federal employees agreed to consider and study any suggested compromises with Rutledge offering the only specific suggestions. He suggested, as a starting point for discussion, eliminating from the Monument most of the land east of the Snake River. The Fish and Wildlife Service could assume control of public lands south of the Gros Ventre River for elk refuge purposes, and the lands north of the Gros Ventre River could be developed as a grazing district. His proposal would have eliminated many of the administrative complexities for the Park Service created by the current Monument boundaries. Eliminated from Park Service consideration would be 1,280 acres of state school land, 7,660 acres of public domain, 7,460 acres of Rockefeller land, and 8,360 acres of other private land. His proposal would leave only 1,050 head of cattle grazing within Park Service jurisdiction and eliminate the hunting complication altogether. Director Drury indicated some support for Rutledge's proposal, but he stipulated the boundaries would need to be studied on the ground, and the other parties including the Fish and Wildlife Service and, of course, Rockefeller, would need to be consulted.

State and local representatives' statements generally expressed a desire to have the Monument abolished, on principle, with a willingness to consider a limited extension of the National Park by legislation that also provided protection for the rights of valley residents, and financial compensation for Teton County in lieu of lost tax revenue. A. W. Gabbey was the only participant who would not agree to an extension of Grand Teton National Park.

After a lunch break, a smaller committee was established to discuss specific details for a

Jackson Hole Historical Society and Museum 1993.4776.011
Albert Gabbey's gas station and store was on his Square G Ranch.

Gabbey had been unjustly denied title to a homestead extension, and the decade-long fight had recently (1940) been settled in his favor. It was believed that the National Park Service, and Horace Albright specifically, had inappropriately blocked his land patent. He harbored a healthy distrust of the Park Service, was unwilling to compromise on the extension of Grand Teton National Park, and adamantly opposed being included in the Jackson Hole National Monument.

recommended compromise.* This committee established ten items that all accepted as necessary for a compromise. In addition to the familiar points such as tax compensation, abolishment of the Monument, protection of grazing rights, and the extension of Grand Teton Park's boundaries eastward to the Snake River, the federal government would agree to no additional purchases of private land outside the Park boundaries as created by the compromise. It was also agreed that the north–south highway through the area would always allow commercial traffic; that the Jackson Hole Preserve, Inc., lands must be turned over to the government for park or monument purposes without any strings attached;† that the land south of the Gros Ventre River be put into the elk refuge under the Fish and Wildlife Service; and that the remaining public lands and Rockefeller lands, not previously described, be considered for placement in a grazing district under the Grazing Service.[103] Rutledge, on September 16 filed a memorandum for Secretary Ickes regarding the Cheyenne meeting that did not deviate from Wirth's memorandum.[104]

After the Cheyenne meeting, Director Drury met with First Assistant Secretary Michael Straus, Assistant Secretary Oscar Chapman, director of the Fish and Wildlife Service Ira Gabrielson, and Rockefeller representatives Chorley and Albright. These meetings resulted in another memorandum for Secretary Ickes dated September 17, 1943. The document assured the Secretary the proposal contained therein did not reflect any commitments but rather an exploration of feasible options. The proposal recommended the extension of Grand Teton National Park's boundaries to the east, incorporating a majority of the lands contained in the Monument, by legislation. Monument lands

*This committee included Hansen, Kratzer, Buchenroth, Drury, Rutledge, and McIntyre. Ex-officio members were Senators O'Mahoney and Robertson, Congressman Barrett, and Governor Hunt.

†This consideration resulted from a rumor that Rockefeller, in transferring his property to the government, intended to keep 2,700 acres near Moose, Wyoming for private purposes. The speculation suggested he would create a completely new town, which he could develop and control, in competition with the town of Jackson. It is possible the proponents of this rumor confused Rockefeller's private purchase of the JY Ranch, and other adjacent properties, for a residence with property purchased by the Snake River Land Company.

not included in the Park, approximately 20,000 to 30,000 acres would remain under Interior Department jurisdiction through administration by the Fish and Wildlife Service. It was also observed the Park Service had no reasonable prospect of being able to purchase private property in the foreseeable future and would thus have to accommodate a considerable amount of grazing activity for a long time. The proposal would remove from Park Service jurisdiction the principal source of the controversies attendant to the Monument.

The proposal did not eliminate from Park Service control as much acreage as Rutledge's plan or recommend the establishment of a grazing district. Chorley and Albright had indicated Rockefeller would be agreeable to the transfer of his land to the Park Service and the Fish and Wildlife Service but not for a grazing district. It was acknowledged a grazing district would find more appeal with the cattlemen, but since the Fish and Wildlife Service was legally permitted to issue and administer grazing leases and to allow hunting, this option would likely be acceptable to the cattlemen, sportsmen, and the state of Wyoming.

The memorandum further justified the proposal by stating:

The Monument would stand as it is until passage of the act adding the recreational area to the park and placing the refuge area under the jurisdiction of the Fish and Wildlife Service.

Our analysis of the situation is that the Department and you could probably stand pat on the monument as is with the overwhelming probability that the Barrett bill would be defeated. There would, however, be some risk to this and it would leave a record of local enmity and political disturbance that would be a handicap to the park and the Department. Another feasible alternative would be to retain the monument, and substitute the grazing and tax commitments that you have already made before the House Public Lands Committee for the Barrett bill, thereby taking a good deal of difficulty out of the situation, but still leaving a politically vulnerable record and also

adding to the administrative difficulties of the National Park Service because of constantly recurring pressure for hunting and grazing and the existence of the large body of private lands which the National Park Service has no prospect of acquiring.

The proposal herein made not only simplifies administration, but it also finally and completely eliminates the political and philosophical issue of the executive procedure in securing these lands for the Department of the Interior.[105]

The memorandum requested the Secretary's approval for proceeding with the proposal or providing a direction that would meet his approval. Secretary Ickes approved proceeding with the proposal on September 22, 1943.[106]

~

An observation relative to the memoranda presented above relates to the intent of the establishment of the Jackson Hole National Monument. The authority providing for the establishment of national monuments by Presidential proclamations limited those actions to the protection of historic or scientific sites. Secretary Ickes was prompted to request the establishment of the Jackson Hole National Monument by a letter from Rockefeller indicating he might sell his lands in Jackson Hole if the government could not accept his donation in a timely manner. That scenario alone would suggest the Monument was established primarily to accommodate Rockefeller's proposed gift rather than because of an eminent threat to historic or scientific structures or sites. This observation is further substantiated by Drury's memorandum indicating that some elements of the compromise proposals were worthy of consideration, but needed the approval of Rockefeller. Thus, the Department of the Interior was unable or unwilling to agree to a reasonable compromise because the modification in boundaries would exclude a portion of the land Rockefeller wished to transfer to the government, not because the boundary change would exclude elements protected by monument status as specified in the Antiquities Act. The Park Service needed Rockefeller's cooperation in order to adjust the boundaries of the Monument, without consideration for the historic and scientific values they claimed existed and justified the Presidential proclamation. If the Monument had been established solely for the purposes and within the intent of the Antiquities Act, Rockefeller's opinion would have mattered no more or no less than any other citizen of the nation.*

Additional evidence that the Interior Department did not feel bound to abide by the specific restricting language nor by the intent of the Antiquities Act is contained in the September 17 memorandum previously cited:

> *The establishment of an addition to the Grand Teton National Park was the original purpose on which the Department embarked. It was also the original purpose of the Rockefellers acquiring these lands. Your action to date has effectively saved these lands for recreational purposes† and was a logical step toward their final incorporation in the park. The historical precedent of establishing a monument by executive action as an intermediate step to establishing a national park is conclusive. This was the sequence and procedure used in establishing Grand Canyon, Carlsbad Caverns, Arcadia National Park and others.[107]*

Whether or not the above-cited areas began as monuments for the sole purpose of incubating national parks is not the subject of this book. However, Grand Canyon and Carlsbad Caverns were obvious extraordinary scientific sites. Prior to the creation of the Jackson Hole National Monument, the Park Service had never indicated an interest

Barnett M. Clinedinst [Public domain] via Wikimedia Commons

John Fletcher Lacey (R)
1841-1913

Lacey was born in Virginia, but he moved to Iowa in 1855 with his family. He joined the Union Army in the spring of 1861 with Company H, 3rd Iowa Volunteer Infantry Regiment. He was captured at the Battle of Blue Mills (also called the Battle of Liberty) and later released on parole. He then joined Company D, 33rd Iowa Volunteer Infantry Regiment as a Sargent major and was promoted to lieutenant and transferred to Company C of that regiment. By the end of the Civil War, he was assistant adjutant general on the staff of General Frederick Steele. After the war, he studied law and was admitted to the bar in 1865. He was first elected to the U.S. House of Representatives in 1890 and would eventually serve eight terms in the House. He was chairman of the Public Lands Committee for 12 years. He sponsored numerous conservation oriented bills and was responsible for much of the nation's early conservation law.

---

*It is solely a matter of speculation to consider where the eastern boundary of the monument might have been drawn if Robert Miller had followed the original land purchasing plan and bought only the properties west of the Snake River. It is clear that the monument was not created to protect antiquities or scientific phenomenon but rather to encompass the land owned by John D. Rockefeller, Jr. If the land Rockefeller wanted to donate had existed totally west of the Snake River, it is likely the eastern monument boundary might have been the Snake River. Therefore, blame for this contentious battle may have its origin in Miller's failure to follow the land purchasing directives originally described in his contract with the Snake River Land Company. On the other hand, and also speculative is the likelihood that had the monument been established with the Snake River as the eastern boundary, the area east of the river might now be crowded with commercial development and residential subdivisions. Thus, Miller can be blamed for creating this era of contentious controversy because he failed to focus his purchasing efforts to the west side of the Snake River, or conversely, credited with saving the eastern side of the valley from unsightly development by his unauthorized purchases east of the river.

* Regardless of its testimony to Congress and press releases, the Park Service, at least in their internal communications, thought of the monument as a recreational asset rather than an area of scientific and historic significance.

in the historic and scientific aspects of the valley. With the exception of testimony presented to justify the establishment of the Monument, Interior Department personnel seemed only to value scenic and recreational values. Likewise, the willingness on the part of the Park Service to abandon control of the lands on the eastern side of the Snake River lessens the validity of its previous statements which cited evidence of Piedmont glaciation sufficient to warrant protection in a national monument. It is rare, indeed, when the Park Service expressed concern regarding historic, prehistoric, or scientific values. Historical precedents accomplished illegally are nevertheless illegal. It is likely the legislators who enacted the Antiquities Act in 1906 would have deemed the creation of the Jackson Hole National Monument to be an abuse of executive authority.*

~

During the period of hearings and meetings relating to the monument issue in the fall of 1943,

other issues also relating to the Monument were being considered in Washington. On September 10, Secretary Ickes wrote Frank Yates, the acting comptroller general, for clarification of Section 8 of Public Law 133, the Interior Department Appropriations Act. Section 8 contained Senator O'Mahoney's amendment that prohibited use of the appropriations for the management of the Jackson Hole National Monument. O'Mahoney's amendment provided:

No part of any appropriations contained in this act shall be used directly or indirectly by way of wages, salaries, per diem or otherwise, for the performance of any new administrative function occasioned by the establishment of the Jackson Hole National Monument as described in Executive Proclamation No. 2578, dated March 15, 1943.[109]

At issue is the interpretation of the words *"any new administrative function."* The question

wyomingtalesandtrails.com

Town of Jackson in the early 1940s. Hitching rails for horses have been removed to provide parking for automobiles.

---

*When Congressman Lacey presented the bill on the floor of the House, Congressman Stephens of Texas questioned him about the intent of the bill. Stephens was concerned the bill might ultimately be used to withdraw large portions of the public domain from development. Lacey assured Stephens the bill was meant to cover cave and cliff dwellers. Stephens asked if the executive branch might use the legislation to set aside large tracts of land as was the case with the Forest Reserve Act. Lacey responded, *"Certainly not. The object is entirely different. It is to preserve these old objects of special interest and the Indian remains in the pueblos in the southwest, while the other reserves the forests and water courses."* [108]

is whether Section 8 was intended to *"...prohibit all functions not previously carried on by the National Park Service or only such functions as have not heretofore been carried on by any Federal agency."* [110] The Secretary's apparent concern related to the use of Interior Department appropriations for functions within the Jackson Hole National Monument by agencies of the Interior Department, whose lands, in whole or in part, had been included in the Monument. The agencies he had in mind were the Reclamation Service, who managed the dam on Jackson Lake, the Fish and Wildlife Service, who managed the elk refuge, and the General Land Office, who managed the public domain lands within Jackson Hole.

O'Mahoney explained his amendment did not seek to interfere with the normal functions of the Forest Service, the Fish and Wildlife Service, nor the Reclamation Service relative to their normal activities prior to the establishment of the Monument. He stated, *"There is no desire to interfere with any of those previous functions, but the purpose of the amendment, approved by the committee, is to prohibit the administration of the monument as a national monument."* [111]

Yates reviewed the relevant information and replied to Secretary Ickes on September 22, 1943. He stated there would be no objections to the continuance of the previous activities but would object to *"...expenditures by way of wages, salaries, per diem or otherwise for the performance of any administrative function or the enforcement or issuance of any rule or regulation which appears to have been undertaken only by reason of the status of the area as a "national monument."* [112]

The comptroller general's ruling did not greatly clear the fog of this issue. Yates seemed to be stating the Park Service could administer some of the new lands transferred to its jurisdiction, if the administrative action had been a prior normal activity of the previously controlling agency, did not require an expenditure of wages or salaries, and did not include the issuance or enforcement of new rules attendant to the creation of the National Monument. It is hard to imagine any administrative action, new or customary, that would not require the payment of wages for the person or people assigned the task. Additionally, the only authority for the Park Service to administer lands and activities in areas previously within the jurisdiction of, for example, the Fish and Wildlife Service, was due to the establishment of the Monument. It was unclear if the memorandum of understanding between the Park Service and the Fish and Wildlife Service, dated April 23, 1943, (previously discussed in this chapter) could be implemented because the agreement was occasioned by the Presidential Proclamation. Senator O'Mahoney obviously intended that the Fish and Wildlife Service, as well as other agencies, continue to manage the land under their jurisdiction prior to the establishment of the Monument, as long as that management did not occasion new rules or regulations pursuant to considerations of monument status of the land in question.

The grazing lease issue was also being debated in Washington, but this was not a discussion of grazing rights within the Monument. The Secretary's statement of policy was relatively clear, but the cattlemen had not signed their grazing leases or paid fees for 1943. In October, Director Drury sent a memorandum to Secretary Ickes reviewing the situation and suggesting a proposal. Director Drury wrote:

In view of the possibility that the legislation now being considered as a substitute for the Barrett bill will be enacted prior to the 1944 grazing season, it is proposed to leave the grazing situation in status quo. With the enactment of the substitute legislation, we will be in a position then to consider covering the 1943 season's grazing in any permits that may be issued for the area at that time. [113]

The proposal was approved by Secretary Ickes on November 8, 1943. [114]

∼

On December 23, the *Jackson Hole Courier* reported the approval of Congressman Barrett's bill by the House Public Lands Committee with a vote of 12 to 7 and the pretrial hearings on various motions connected with the state's suit challenging the Monument.* Many in Jackson Hole hoped the next year might bring a permanent solution to the controversy associated with the Monument, but the stirring obituaries of young men who had left their homes in the valley to join the armed forces were a constant reminder of more critical national concerns.†

Publicity both for and against the Monument proceeded unabated. Olaus Murie, Struthers Burt, Leslie Miller, and Fritiof Fryxell wrote some of the noteworthy articles favoring the Monument. These men wrote of the history of efforts to protect the scenic and recreational values of the valley. They felt the action of the President was justified to ensure the public interests in these values for future generations. With the exception of Fritiof Fryxell, they did not explore the more technical questions of the use of the Antiquities Act for the protection of the area. Fryxell, of course, presented the scientific importance of the glaciated valley floor but made a further point. He maintained the protection of an area for one asset did not depreciate its other values. He suggested one visitor to Yellowstone National Park might be more impressed by the scientific phenomenon while another might find the scenery or the wildlife most memorable. The establishment of the Jackson Hole National Monument for its scientific value to geologists in no way abrogated its value for scenery and wildlife

Jackson Hole Historical Society and Museum 1958.2389.001
Walter Spicer, Jr. at his father's gas station. Gas Light Alley now occupies the site.

virtues.[118] Articles opposing the Monument were more likely to concentrate on the misuse of the Antiquities Act by the President, and stressed the peril to other sections of the country and citizens if the abuse of power was allowed to endure.

The remainder of 1943 was relatively quiet for the residents of Jackson Hole. All that could be done to influence Congress and the Interior Department had essentially occurred. Legislation had been introduced, suits were filed, and compromises defined. Time would reveal the success or failure of each side's efforts.

---

*U.S. Judge T. Blake Kennedy denied the federal government's motion for a summary judgment and approved the state's motion to amend its complaint.[115]

†Two of the obituaries were particularly saddening. Lieutenant Walter Spicer, Jr., who had been married less than two months, was killed while trying to land his fighter, which he radioed had control problems and an overheating engine. He was authorized by radio to parachute from the aircraft, but he elected to try to save the plane. The aircraft exploded as he approached the runway.[116] Lieutenant Harvey Hagen had been married just two weeks when his medium bomber crashed on a training flight.[117] The bodies of both men were returned to Jackson for burial.

CHAPTER SIXTEEN

1944 - 1945

I know quite a little bit about that Jackson Hole project myself. After Mr. Rockefeller got through buying land in Jackson Hole, he still had some money left.

Will Rogers[1]

Jackson Hole Historical Society and Museum p1991.3962.001
Winter operation of the Snow King Ski Hill, 1940s

The community continued to strive to create a winter economy by expanding the ski area on Snow King Mountain and promoting winter recreational activities. All of their efforts were dependent on the state highway department's ability to keep roads open during the winter.

The beginning of 1944 provided little new impetus for the emotional and factual elements of the controversy surrounding the Jackson Hole National Monument, but a feeling of optimism was growing. Many believed the tide of the war had turned in favor of the Allies and people were looking to the future. Road projects, delayed because of the war, were discussed while Teton County continued to lead the state in war bond drives. A quota of $87,000 was set for the county in the latter part of 1943. By mid-February, Teton County was credited with bond sales of $112,000.[2] Teton County was also the first county in the state to meet and exceed its Red Cross drive quota of $2,100. The *Courier* reported in March that the county had raised $2,419.[3]

Grand Teton National Park (unnumbered)
Grand Teton National Park Headquarters

Minor confusion resulted at the end of March when the official report concerning the House Public Lands Committee's approval of Congressman Barrett's bill to abolish the Jackson Hole National Monument was made public. The *Courier* reported this event in December 1943 and was surprised with the new press release. The facts concerning the report by the committee were the same as those reported by the *Courier* in December, except for the date. The *Courier* contacted Congressman Barrett, who responded by wire, *"Statement incorrect. However, report filed and bill placed on consent calendar."*[4] As a matter of record, the Committee's report (Report No. 1303, 78th Congress, 2nd Session) approving the Barrett bill was in fact dated March 28, 1944. It is possible the vote was taken in the previous session, reported to the *Courier* by Congressman Barrett, and the official report filed at the later date.

As mentioned in both the December 1943 *Courier* article and the March 1944 press release, 7 of the 19 members of the House Public Lands Committee voted against the Barrett bill. Congressman Peterson wrote the minority report. After his visit to Jackson Hole in August 1943, Peterson apparently developed the opinion that the Barrett bill should be amended to reflect the compromises suggested during the Jackson Hole hearings and subsequently at the meeting in the Governor's office in Cheyenne. His report was short but made the following points: While of the opinion Congress, rather than the executive branch, should define boundaries of parks and monuments, he believed previous Presidents had established a precedent for the creation of monuments by proclamation. His primary problem with Congressman Barrett's bill was that, while it might provide a moral victory, it did not solve the problem for the people of Jackson Hole. He wrote:

The matter should be set at rest and the passage of this bill does not accomplish this purpose. It merely abolishes the Jackson Hole Monument as established by the Presidential Proclamation. The President could immediately enter another Executive Order providing for another monument with slightly different boundaries.

The Grand Teton Mountains and the adjacent scenery constitute one of the greatest scenic spots in the world. A great elk refuge is in this area also. A portion of the land in the monument should be placed within the boundary of the Grand Teton National Park so as to have proper approaches to the park, so as to enable the park area to give views of the mountains from different localities and to protect streams from pollution and to prevent unsightly buildings on the approaches to this beauty spot. The present boundaries of the Grand Teton National Park are inadequate to do this. A portion of the land should be placed in the elk refuge to assist in feeding the great elk herd, and a portion should be definitely by law set apart as a driveway to be allowed for the drifting and grazing of cattle from one range to another, and some portion of it should be taken out of the monument.[5]

In reporting the Barrett bill as written, Peterson thought an opportunity had been lost to accomplish the compromises for park extension, elk refuge development, acceptance of Rockefeller's gift of land, and the rights of cattlemen and other land owners. Moreover, a properly amended Barrett bill would have provided these compromises with the force of law rather than uncertain executive policy.

Closely following the House Public Lands Committee's favorable report on the Barrett bill, the American Planning and Civic Association, headed by Horace Albright, issued a press release warning that a number of legislative initiatives currently before Congress endangered the nation's parks and monuments.[6] The range of these bills, all directed at the Antiquities Act, indicated on one hand, congressional concern regarding the Presidential power contained in the act, and on the other hand, a difference of opinion as to how that power should be adjusted. The O'Mahoney-McCarran bill in the Senate, and its twin, the Diamond-Chenoweth bill in the House, would retain the protective provisions of the Antiquities Act regarding historic, prehistoric, and scientific sites. However, it would repeal Section 2 which provided the power for establishment of monuments by Executive Order. Congressman Barrett's bill proposed to abolish the Jackson Hole National Monument but leave the Antiquities Act intact. Senator Robertson's bill would amend the Antiquities Act preserving the Presidential authority, but requiring the approval of the state legislature of the state within whose boundaries the proposed monument rested. The last bill seemed least appropriate to the novice constitutional scholar. Robertson's bill would have given veto power to state legislatures over a Presidential action relating to federal domain.

⁓

A long time supporter of protection for Jackson Hole died in April 1944. J. D. 'Si' Ferrin was born in Eden, Utah on April 19, 1873. He married Emmaline Heninger in 1893 and moved to Jackson Hole in 1900. Settling initially on a desert claim near Twin Creek, north and east of the town of Jackson, he later homesteaded in the north end of the valley along the Buffalo Fork River. Emmaline died in April 1904, and Ferrin married Edith McInelty in November 1905. He was a successful rancher and, with the help of his sons, expanded the family's holdings which eventually included the Skinner property (Hatchet Ranch). At one time, the Ferrins operated one of the largest ranches in the valley.

During his early years in Jackson Hole, he worked as a game warden and was considered "aggressive" in his duties. He is credited with breaking up the Binkley and Purdy Gangs of elk tusk hunters and poachers. Ferrin was one of the men who met with Horace Albright at Maud Noble's cabin in 1923 to devise a way to create a recreation area and protect the Tetons and the lakes at their base (see Chapter Five). He was one of the men who circulated a petition in 1925 asking the government to set aside the northern portion of the valley as a recreation area (see Chapter Six), and he was one of the authors of the Jackson Hole Plan initiated in 1930 (see Chapter Nine). He was among the first to sell a portion of his property to the Snake River Land Company in 1928. His

Jackson Hole Historical Society and Museum p1958.3377,001
This photograph includes members of the posse that captured the elk poachers. (L to R), Charles Harvey, Rube Tuttle, and J. D. Ferrin. During a 1983 interview, Mel Innis was asked how Ferrin was able to capture the Purdy and Binkley gangs of elk poachers. Mel replied, *"J. D. was aggressive."*

testimony before the 1933 Senate Investigating Committee in Jackson helped vindicate the Park Service and the Rockefeller operations of the charges made by Senator Robert Carey (see Chapter Eleven). Before Horace Albright or John D. Rockefeller, Jr. set foot in Jackson Hole, J. D. Ferrin recognized the scenic and recreational values of the valley, and actively worked to ensure those values would be protected for future generations.

Ferrin was instrumental in creating some of those future generations. At the time of his death, he was survived by his second wife, seven sons, five daughters, 25 grandchildren, and three great grand-children. His first son was killed fighting in France during World War I.[7]

Jackson Hole Historical Society and Museum

William Binkley (left) and Charles Purdy shortly before their incarceration for poaching elk for their ivory tusks.

~

In April 1944, Congress considered the Interior Department's 1945 appropriations bill. In this regard, Park Service Director Drury testified before the House Appropriations Committee. The Park Service included in their request $7,275 for the Jackson Hole National Monument. That request resulted in the following dialogue:

Congressman Johnson: *Are you gentlemen of the Park Service laboring under any hallucination that the distinguished Senator for Wyoming, who is a powerful member of* *the Senate, would ever permit this appropriation to go in if this committee even considered it? Jackson Hole* [National Monument] *has never been created by law and no doubt never will be. Do you not think it is your duty to pay some attention to the wishes of cCngress and don't you agree that these two committees* [appropriations] *actually represent the wishes of the members of Congress, of both houses, on this matter?*

Secretary Drury: *We surely think it our duty, but in order to ascertain the wishes of Congress, we have to make a proposal.*

Congressman Johnson: *Well, let's move on. Let us not waste too much time on Jackson Hole.*[8]

When the Senate considered the appropriations, the same amendment Senator O'Mahoney had placed on interior appropriations the previous year was again approved. The Interior Department's appropriation for 1945 was passed on June 28, but the Park Service was prohibited from administering or maintaining the Jackson Hole National Monument.[9]

Although the Barrett bill had been reported favorably by the House Public Lands Committee, the House Rules Committee had not cleared the bill. Barrett organized a bi-partisan delegation of congressmen to approach the Rules Committee with the purpose of requesting the release of the bill. The delegation included four Democrats and nine Republicans and was successful in obtaining a favorable report and release of the Barrett bill by the Rules Committee clearing the way for a vote in the House.[10]*

~

Despite the Congressional prohibition mandated by Senator O'Mahoney's appropriations amendment relating to management activities in the Monument, the Park Service, on July 31 through August 2, held a meeting in Superintendent Franke's office which considered several issues relating to the monument. The purpose of

*The delegation consisted of, Frank Barrett, James O'Connor (D) of Montana, Mike Mansfield (D) of Montana, Compton White (D) of Idaho, Henry Dworshak (R) of Idaho, James Mott (R) of Oregon, Harris Ellsworth (R) of Oregon, Lowell Stockman (R) of Oregon, Hal Holmes (R) of Washington, Edgar Chenoweth (R) of Colorado, William Hill (R) of Colorado, Robert Rockwell (R) of Colorado, and Alfred Elliott (D) of California.

this meeting was to tour the monument and consider proposals for boundary adjustments, campsite development, and the proposed relocation of Highway 189 to the east side of the Snake River. Director Drury, Regional Director Merriam, Superintendent Franke, Chief of Lands Conrad Wirth, and Chief Landscape Architect Thomas C. Vint represented the Park Service at this meeting. Kenneth Chorley, Harold Fabian, and A. Edwind Kendrew represented the Rockefeller interests. Kendrew was the architect for Colonial Williamsburg. Horace Albright also attended this meeting, but the basis of his participation is unclear. He was no longer employed by the Park Service, but his long involvement in the Jackson Hole project may have warranted an invitation to participate. Or, he may have been one of the Rockefeller representatives even though he had previously testified before the House Public Lands Committee that he had no affiliation with the Rockefeller interests.[11]

The meeting provided extended tours of the Monument, and the men reached an easy agreement on several issues. It was agreed to construct a campground and cabins on the east shore of Jenny Lake. It was also agreed that the grazing and drift of cattle would not be a consideration in the discussion of possible boundary changes, indicating rejection of the compromise proposals made by Clifford Hansen and Dick Rutledge at the joint subcommittee hearings in Jackson the previous August, and the compromise elements identified at the meeting in Governor Hunt's office.* Chorley, Albright, and Fabian expressed the opinion that Secretary Ickes' policy statement regarding the rights of cattlemen needed further clarification. They also agreed *"...all of the lands, **whether public or private** [author's emphasis], within the present Monument boundary should be under the administration of the Park Service or the Fish and Wildlife Service."* [12]

This agreement reeks of arrogance as it further demonstrates that the Park Service, having used the Antiquities Act to obtain control of land for purposes outside the intent or authority of the act, did not feel compelled to abide by the

Grand Teton National Park (unnumbered)
Thomas C. Vint on left. (others unnamed)
1894-1967

Thomas C. Vint, National Park Service Chief Landscape Architect on an earlier visit to Grand Teton National Park. Vint was the architect for the Going-to-the-Sun Road in Glacier National Park. He also provided a strong influence on other projects such as Blue Ridge Parkway, Yosemite, Colonial National Historical Park, Oregon Caves National Monument, and Mission 66.

restricting language of the act. The Antiquities Act specifically limits federal authority to federal land and cannot be used to obtain or encumber privately owned property. It is likely the state of Wyoming might also have held a different opinion concerning the 1,280 acres it owned within the monument's boundaries. Additionally, the previously quoted statement seems to be in conflict with Secretary Ickes' policy statement, as well as the monument proclamation, which guaranteed the continued rights of property owners within the monument.

It was agreed that any lands transferred from the monument to the Fish and Wildlife Service, and any lands the Fish and Wildlife Service might acquire in the future, whether by purchase or donation, would be managed to preserve Park Service values. The improvement of any existing

---

*This indicates that Park Service officials had rejected the compromise elements discussed in Governor Hunt's office or never intended to compromise and had met with state and local representatives in bad faith.

structure or the construction of any new structure contemplated by the Fish and Wildlife Service would require the concurrence of the Park Service.[13]

Each of the men had minor differences regarding possible boundary adjustments, but none of their suggestions reflected a consideration of the compromises that had been suggested. They generally agreed to a transfer of lands south and east of the Gros Ventre River to the Fish and Wildlife Service, but Superintendent Franke, Regional Director Merriam, Chief Wirth, Kendrew, and Fabian suggested additional extensions of the monument boundary. Albright, Chorley, and Vint seemed to be comfortable with the current boundaries.

Two suggestions were made for relocating Highway 189 to the east side of the Snake River. Architect Vint suggested a road that would pass west of Blacktail Butte and along the bluff overlooking the Snake River. Kendrew thought the road should be east of Blacktail Butte and along the eastern boundary of the monument at the base of the foothills and presented a list of 12 arguments favoring his proposed route and opposing Vint's suggestion. Vint did not argue for his route except to say Kendrew had made some good points and that he (Vint) thought the tour of the routes the previous day spoke for itself.* The points were discussed, and Director Drury called for a vote. Merriam, Fabian, Wirth, Albright, and Franke favored the Vint proposal while Chorley voted for the Kendrew route.[14]

The issue of ranching was considered at the conclusion of the meeting. Director Drury indicated he felt, in keeping with Park Service philosophy, that when ranch lands purchased by Rockefeller were transferred to the Park Service, they should be allowed to revert to their natural condition. Albright, Chorley, and Fabian reminded the Director it had been part of the original concept for this area that historical activities such as ranching would be perpetuated. Director Drury did not acquiesce to this point but suggested

some type of museum might be established to memorialize the history of the activity he sought to eliminate.[15]

As arrogant as the recommendations of this group may seem, it might also be remembered the purpose of the meeting was not so much to create policy but rather to suggest policy to the Secretary of the Interior. Nevertheless, the recommendations are further evidence the Park Service did not feel bound by the powers or restrictions specified in the Antiquities Act to protect antiquities. They

Grand Teton National Park (unnumbered)
Fritiof Melvin Fryxell
1900-1986

Fryxell was the first naturalist ranger in Grand Teton National Park, mountain climber, author, senior geologist for the U.S. Geological Survey, and professor of geology at Augustana College. During World War II, he was involved in the crucial role of selecting landing sites in the South Pacific as well as Africa and Europe while in the service of the Military Geological Unit.

---

*At the time the main north-south highway crossed from the east side of the Snake River to the west side at Moose, Wyoming, and essentially followed the current inner park road to Jenny Lake and northward to the Jackson Lake Dam.

considered the act as a vehicle for incubating national parks and the Monument as an extension of Grand Teton National Park. Additionally, this meeting may have been illegal in light of O'Mahoney's appropriations rider. Almost certainly, expenses were incurred for wages, transportation, and per diem for some of the attendees, and most of the issues on the agenda were specific to the management and administration of the monument.

~

On August 2, 1944, a special hearing was held in Federal District Court in Cheyenne, Wyoming for the purpose of receiving testimony in the case of *State of Wyoming v. Paul R. Franke,* challenging the legality of the Monument. Dr. Fritiof Fryxell, senior geologist for the United States Geological Survey, and Dr. LeRoy R. Hafen, historian for the State Historical Society of Colorado and professor of history at the University of Denver, provided expert witness for the government.

Dr. Fryxell's research in the Jackson Hole area, which culminated in his doctoral dissertation, began in 1926. He was also the first naturalist ranger in Grand Teton National Park. There probably was no one who could testify more authoritatively on the geology of Jackson Hole at that time. His testimony identified the geologic features of the area encompassed by the Monument, and he stressed that while other areas of the nation also provided such evidence, there was no place in the country where all these features were contained in such a compact area. He noted many universities utilized Jackson Hole as a study area

for their geology students, including the University of Wyoming.[16]

Dr. Hafen, who was particularly conversant with the history of the western fur trade era, maintained Jackson Hole was an important site for the early trappers beginning in 1827. These early fur trappers initiated the nation's westward migration and settlement of the Rocky Mountain region. He also noted the American Pioneer Trails Association had selected Jackson Hole for an annual convention site.[17]

The trial was heard in Sheridan, Wyoming before Judge T. Blake Kennedy on August 21 through 24. The federal government was represented by Ralph Boyd of the Department of Justice; Carl Sackett, United States Attorney; and John Pickett,* Assistant United States Attorney. The state of Wyoming was represented by John McIntyre,† Ray Lee, and L. C. Sampson, all special assistants to the Wyoming Attorney General.

The state of Wyoming, being the plaintiff, presented its case first.‡ The state's case was based on three basic propositions. First, that the Monument was established to accomplish the extension of Grand Teton National Park– an action or purpose not authorized by the Antiquities Act. Second, the area encompassed by the boundaries of the monument contained no historical or scientific sites as contemplated by the Antiquities Act. And third, the establishment of the Monument and its administration by the defendant had caused, or would result in, financial harm to the state of Wyoming. The state had

---

*Pickett's position in this trial seemed ironic. At this point in his career, he was defending the federal government in a suit alleging an abuse of power for the purpose of extending the boundaries of Grand Teton National Park. In 1933, he was the special counsel nominated by Senators Kendrick and Carey for the Senate committee investigating the actions of the Park Service and the Rockefeller organization within Jackson Hole. In the role of special counsel, he attempted to prosecute the federal government (Park Service) and Rockefeller for abuses related to the attempt to extend the boundaries of Grand Teton National Park (see Chapter Eleven). President Truman nominated John C. Pickett for a U.S. Circuit Judgeship on September 23, 1949. Pickett was confirmed by Congress and received his commission on October 13, 1949, and he held that position until his death on September 1, 1983.[18]

†After this suit was filed in 1943, McIntyre joined the U.S. Army. The Army gave him a special leave for the purpose of returning to Wyoming to argue the state's case.

‡Jackson Hole residents who presented testimony for the state of Wyoming were Clifford Hansen, C.R. Van Vleck, Holly Leek, Felix Buchenroth, A. W. Gabbey, C. H. Brown, Frank Toppen, and Stanley Resor. Additional testimony for the state was presented by Lester Bagley of the Wyoming Game and Fish Commission; J. R. Bromley of the Wyoming Highway Department; Joseph Weppner and Warren Richardson of the Wyoming Historical Landmarks Commission; Dr. Horace Thomas, Wyoming State Geologist; and Dr. Samuel Knight, head of the Geology Department at the University of Wyoming.

T. Blake Kennedy (R)
1874-1956

Kennedy served as U.S. District Judge of Wyoming from 1922-1955. He was nominated by President Warren G. Harding on October 17, 1921, and was confirmed by the United States Senate on October 25, 1921. Kennedy was the presiding judge in the Teapot Dome Case (*United States vs. Mammoth Oil Company*) in 1925, and the case regarding Japanese-American draft resisters from the Heart Mountain Relocation Center during World War II (*United States vs. Kiyoshi Okamoto, et al.*).

to claim financial harm in excess of $3,000 in order to qualify for federal court jurisdiction.

Much of the testimony presented at this trial repeated familiar arguments previously described concerning earlier congressional hearings, but several items are important because they relate to evidence necessary to the state's case. Lester Bagley testified that Park Service management of the monument area, occasioned by Presidential Proclamation 2578, would adversely affect the ability of the state to manage the elk herd and cause a loss of revenue from the sale of hunting licenses. J. R. Bromley noted 43 miles of state highway constructed at a cost of $890,000 had been included within the Monument. This testimony was apparently intended to substantiate a financial loss to the state if toll booths and guard

stations were placed at the entrances to the Monument, limiting commerce and control by the highway department.* Joseph Weppner testified that although trappers certainly used the valley of Jackson Hole, the area was no more, and probably less, significant historically than many other areas of the West. Under cross-examination, he stated the Landmarks Commission placed a marker in Jackson Hole in honor of the trappers, but he maintained they had merely acquiesced to repeated requests by Stephen Leek for a marker. Drs. Thomas and Knight testified the area included in the Monument did not contain sites of unique and

Dr. Samuel K. Knight, 1916.
1892-1975

Knight earned his undergraduate degree from the University of Wyoming in 1913 and his doctorate from Columbia University in 1916. He returned to teach at the University of Wyoming, but beginning in 1917; he served as a 1st Lieutenant in Army Intelligence in World War I surveying battlefield terrain. During his 60 years at Wyoming, he expanded the geology department from one professor (himself) to a nationally recognized program and personally taught more than 10,000 students. From 1933 to 1940, he served as Wyoming State Geologist. Knight testified that the Jackson Hole National Monument did not contain evidence of geologic phenomena not found in other parts of the state and that the observable geologic phenomena situated within the Monument did not require 221,000 acres for its protection.

---

*Bromley failed to mention that the federal government provided $600,000 of the $890,000.[19] Another interesting aspect of this issue was that in 1930, Governor Emerson indicated to Senator Carey that he approved of a limited extension of Grand Teton National Park so as to include the highway, thus relieving the state of the attendant financial obligations for its maintenance (See Chapter Ten).

outstanding geologic interest not in evidence in other parts of the state. The state also introduced several documents as evidence of Interior Department intent concerning the Monument. Some of these documents specified the intent of the government to acquire private lands within the Jackson Hole National Monument by donation, purchase, or eminent domain, which would deprive the state of tax revenue. Objections by the U.S. Government to the introduction of these documents were overruled by Judge Kennedy.[20]

Jackson Hole Historical Society and Museum p1958.1833.001

Dedication of the Trapper Trail Monument in Jackson Hole by the Wyoming Landmarks Commission, 1931
S. N. Leek (2nd from left), Samuel Swanner (2nd from right), William Simpson (right).

The U.S. Government presented its case with the help of Dr. Olaus Murie of the Fish and Wildlife Service; Dr. Harold Anthony of the American Museum of Natural History; Merrill Mattes of the Scotts Bluff National Monument; Dr. Leland Horberg, Professor of Geology at University of Illinois; and Dr. Rudolph Edmund, a geologist with Shell Oil Company. Predictably, these witnesses supported the government's contention that the Jackson Hole National Monument contained elements appropriate for its establishment. The government presented no evidence to justify the size of the Monument. Counsel for the government maintained there had been no exercise of authority by Superintendent Franke over the Monument lands and no harm to the state of Wyoming. They also filed a brief maintaining the district court lacked jurisdiction to hear the case.

Judge Kennedy found that the state had presented sufficient evidence of the threat of financial damage to exceed the minimum amount required to plea for a declaratory judgement. He also ruled that the state provided evidence that Charles J. Smith, in whose name the suit was originally filed had, at the direction of his superiors, acted in a way to exercise administration of the monument. The transfer of personnel by the Park Service and the subsequent refiling of the suit naming the individual assuming the former superintendent's responsibilities, combined with the fact that the new superintendent, Paul R. Franke, had not exercised his authority only because Congress had withheld funds for the monument's management, did not

abrogate the state's allegation. Judge Kennedy ruled the district court did have limited jurisdiction in this case. At the conclusion of the trial, Judge Kennedy gave both sides until December 15, 1944, to present additional briefs. The court's decision was not expected until early 1945.[21]

≈

During the fall of 1944, amid the controversy of the monument trials and legislative action, the residents of Jackson Hole also continued to deal with local issues. Two cases of polio were diagnosed in the valley and the water supply for the town of Jackson was considered a possible source or medium for the spread of the disease. The effort to assure a safe water supply received an appreciable portion of the people's attention.[22] On a more positive and somewhat ironic note, Teton County received $130,000 in Civil Aeronautics Administration funds for development of the airport.[23] While one federal agency, the Park Service, was being denied funds for the protective management of the Monument, another federal agency, the CAA, was spending money to expand activities within the Monument's boundaries. Additionally, Mayor Clissold decided to delay awarding a contract for the operation of the airport until after the end of the war. A number of young men from Jackson had entered the air branches of the military, and the mayor thought it likely some of those men might wish to be considered for the franchise. He believed it would be unfair to offer a franchise for the operation of the airport until those men returned from the war.[24]

Nineteen forty-four was an election year, and there was an abundance of political activity. Congressman Barrett was up for re-election, and he found considerable support in Teton County. President Roosevelt, in his bid for an unprecedented fourth term, was running against Thomas E. Dewey. Dewey used the Jackson Hole National Monument to appeal to western voters. He said the Executive Order was characteristic of the New Deal and its lack of respect for the rights and opinions of the people it affected.[25] In the previous national election, Roosevelt had found more favor than Willkie with Teton County voters. In 1944, Dewey received 637 votes to Roosevelt's 499.[26]

Thomas Edmund Dewey (R)
1902-1971

Dewey was the 47th governor of New York and unsuccessful presidential candidate in 1944 and 1948. He was the leader of the moderate/liberal faction of the Republican party and was considered, especially in the Mid-West, "Eastern Establishment." Nelson Rockefeller would later be assumed Dewey's position as leader of the moderates in the Republican Party.

Greystone Studio, New York {public domain] via Wikimedia Commons

On November 16, 1944, Congressman J. Hardin Peterson introduced in the 78th Congress, 2nd Session a bill, H.R. 5469, *"Providing payments to the State of Wyoming and for rights-of-way, including stock driveways, over and across Federal lands within the exterior boundary of the Jackson Hole National Monument, Wyoming ...."* [27] Wyoming's Congressional Delegation introduced legislation directed at the Monument and the Antiquities Act, but none of their bills attempted to accomplish a compromise which would provide an end to the controversy. Peterson must have believed Congressman Barrett's bill would not be successful, or he would not have introduced this legislation which implied the continued existence of the Monument. His bill proposed to provide the force of law to Secretary Ickes' statement of policy concerning the rights of cattlemen and others who were affected by the President's proclamation. It also attempted to solve the long-standing problem of revenue compensation to Teton County created by the impending transfer of Rockefeller's land, or any other private land, to the Monument. The compensation provision provided payments to the state of Wyoming for distribution to Teton County over a span of 20 years. The amount of the first year's payment would be equal to the tax assessed on the private land for the year in which the government acquired it. The payments would be reduced by 5 percent each succeeding year thereafter. The source of the funds for such payments would be from the revenues collected by the Park Service from the national parks and monuments under its jurisdiction.[28]

On December 11, 1944, Congressman Barrett's bill to abolish the Jackson Hole National Monument passed the House of Representatives with 178 votes for, 107 votes against, and 142 congressmen not voting.[29] The bill was then forwarded to the Senate. The Senate Public Lands Committee held hearings on December 15 and received testimony not substantially different from the hearings cited previously regarding testimony in the House. The Senate committee gave a favorable report on the bill, voting nine to four for its passage. The Barrett bill passed the Senate with unanimous consent on December 19, 1944, and was sent to the President.[30]

342

It was not likely President Roosevelt would sign the Barrett bill and, as expected, he exercised a pocket veto.* On December 29, 1944, he issued a memorandum of disapproval explaining his reasons for the veto. He stated he established the Monument to protect the scientific and historic sites contained within its boundaries, and, in this memorandum, included the scenic values of the area. He said the Monument provided *"...the necessary foreground for the great mountain peaks in the adjoining Grand Teton National Park...."*[31] He noted every President before him, beginning with Theodore Roosevelt, had exercised the authority provided by the Antiquities Act establishing 82 monuments by proclamation. He believed, the wording of Proclamation 2578, he had protected the rights of individuals with interests in the Monument and indicated he would view favorably legislation to codify those rights. He also addressed the tax problem faced by Teton County and promised to view sympathetically legislation he might receive to remedy the situation. He concluded:

> *I believe that whatever reasonable objections may exist to the continuance of the monument can be overcome without depriving this area of the protection to which it is justly entitled under the Antiquities Act of June 8, 1906, and under the other laws relating to national monuments. Therefore, it would seem to me that the proper remedy in this situation is not the undoing of what has been done, but the making of such adjustments as may be appropriate to meet the local conditions.*[32]

~

By the start of 1945, local support for the Jackson Hole National Monument was becoming more outspoken, and the *Courier* reported a group of local citizens had requested the County Commission cease its official opposition to the monument. The group believed that since the County Commission was obligated to represent all of the county's taxpayers, and since there was a difference of opinion on the part of the taxpayers, the County should not choose to promote one point of view over another. Their written request stated:

> *We, the undersigned taxpayers of Teton County request the county commissioners to reimburse Teton County for the money they expended fighting the Jackson Hole Monument and not to use any more county funds either for or against same.*[33]

Harrison Crandall Photo: Jackson Hole Historical Society and Museum 2003.0117.250

Homer Richards at various times could be considered both an opponent of the Park or a proponent of the Park. Like other valley residents, park attitudes were sometimes dependent on the era, the specific proposal, or other issues. By the mid-1940s, Richards was a successful motel operator and could see the value of protecting a portion of the valley as a national park as well as the deleterious effects of the social turmoil resulting from the Jackson Hole National Monument. From this point forward, he can be considered a supporter of federal protection for the northern portion of the valley with certain conditions. Those conditions included compensation to Teton County in lieu of lost tax revenue and legal (rather than statements of policy) protection for the cattlemen and private landowners affected by the Monument proclamation.

---

*A pocket veto occurs when the President takes no action on a bill received from Congress within ten days of the legislature's adjournment. Had Roosevelt simply vetoed the bill, there might have been time for Congress to consider an override vote. A two-thirds majority in both houses is required to override a Presidential veto. This might have been possible in the Senate where the bill passed unanimously, but it was uncertain in the House. An override vote in the House would have required the support of all 142 congressmen who had not voted on the measure initially.

The signers of this request were William Wallace, Ben F. Goe, Cecil Jensen, H.C. Richards, and Jess Wort. Commissioner Clifford Hansen stated that *"...the board considered the wishes of the majority to be the greatest guide to their actions, and that the expression of seven hundred persons who last year voted to oppose the establishment of the monument would be given prior consideration."* [34]

Toward the end of January, Charles Kratzer sold the *Jackson Hole Courier* to James (Jimmy) Huidekoper. Kratzer had owned and edited the paper for nearly 10 years and maintained a general, and sometimes fiery, opposition to park extension proposals in the valley. Huidekoper made no public announcements regarding editorial policy but, at least for 1945, the newspaper was less strident in its coverage of the monument controversy.

Congressman Peterson's bill, H.R. 5469, which was introduced late in 1944, had met resistance from the Interior Department because of the tax compensation provision. The concept of revenue compensation was not the problem it had been previously, but the Park Service had reservations regarding the details of the provision that identified the source of funding. The bill specified that payments to the state of Wyoming would derive from revenues collected from all the parks and monuments administered by the Park Service. There were objections to the use of revenues collected within a state other than Wyoming for tax compensation to a Wyoming county. These delays resulted in a failure of Congress to consider the legislation and the bill died at the close of the session.

On January 9, 1945, Congressman Peterson introduced H.R. 1292 in the 79th Congress, 1st Session. The new bill was essentially the same as the former

bill except for a paragraph added concerning the payments to the state of Wyoming. The schedule of payments and the amount of payments stayed the same, but the source of funds would come from fees paid by tourists who visited the Jackson Hole National Monument, Grand Teton National Park, and Yellowstone National Park. Additionally, regardless of the amount due the state for a particular year as set forth in the schedule, the government would not pay Teton County more than 25 percent of the fees collected for that year.[35] This provision provided less assurance of full compensation to Teton County than the previous bill because the payments would be limited to a percentage of the fees collected from the tourists in just three park areas. It was assumed travel

Jackson Hole Historical Society and Museum p1958.1753.001

Because of deep snow near the base of the mountains and the difficulty in keeping roads open, there was little tourist activity in the Monument or Park areas in the winter. Above: Jenny Lake Inn with snow to the eaves. Below: Jenny Lake Inn (c. 1927) during the summer.

Jackson Hole Historical Society and Museum 1958.1748.001

to the parks would increase after the war and the Park Service was optimistic the revenues would be sufficient.

∽

Roughly two years had passed since Rockefeller wrote Secretary Ickes giving one year for the government to accept his donation of land in the Jackson Hole area. With Congressman Barrett's bill dead from a Presidential veto and Congressman Peterson's bill having been reintroduced, Secretary Ickes thought it an opportune time to initiate another action. On January 10, 1945, he wrote Rockefeller suggesting the time was right for the transfer of the land in Jackson Hole to the Park Service. In this letter, the Secretary reasoned that a delay in the transfer would provide the opposition time to introduce another bill to abolish the monument. He thought that if such a bill again passed both houses, it probably would not have the support necessary to override a Presidential veto. Nevertheless, another veto would not engender the friendly attitudes in Congress necessary for the compromises required to end the controversy in Jackson Hole. With the timely transfer of Rockefeller's lands to the

Jackson Hole Historical Society and Museum 2004.0113.112
The development of the rotary snowplow allowed the north-south highway to be reopened earlier in the season. Also, access roads into the valley were more easily maintained during the winter with this equipment.

government, Ickes believed that the tax problem in Teton County would become acute, and both sides of the controversy would be forced to rally support for Congressman Peterson's bill. *
He concluded:

It seems possible that, if your planned gift is completed before the extremist opposition gets into organized action again, there would not only be prompt and satisfactory tax relief for Teton County, but also conceivably the adoption of a systematic plan for sharing revenues covering the entire national park and monument system.[36]

Rockefeller responded on January 16, 1945. He stated his reluctance to transfer the land at this time because of the pending ruling by the court on the suit filed by the state of Wyoming, Senator O'Mahoney's rider to the Interior Department's appropriations bill prohibiting the management of the land in accordance with his original goals, and the likelihood of the reintroduction by Congressman Barrett of legislation to abolish the Jackson Hole National Monument. He reasoned, *"...if the Monument were for one reason or another eventually abolished and my property had then been already transferred to the Government, it would have passed out of my hands without accomplishing the purpose I had in mind in purchasing it."*[37] Rockefeller decided to keep his land in private ownership for the time being, but he suggested the time was appropriate for a meeting between the Secretary and the Wyoming Delegation to see if a program of compromise could be accomplished.

Secretary Ickes replied to Rockefeller on January 24 indicating that if the lawsuit resulted in a favorable ruling for the state of Wyoming, it would be appealed. A ruling for the state of Wyoming might encourage Senator O'Mahoney to attach his rider to the 1946 appropriations bill, but with a ruling for the government, he might not force its inclusion. He noted the introduction of Congressman Peterson's bill and stated:

---

*Secretary Ickes was not suggesting the time was judicious for the transfer of the Jackson Hole property in fulfillment of Rockefeller's goals, but rather for the intentional manipulation of Teton County to the brink of bankruptcy in order to gather support for Congressman Peterson's legislation. Ickes was ruthlessly indifferent to the fate of Teton County if Rockefeller's land was transferred to the Park Service and Peterson's bill failed to pass Congress.

Charles Wesley Andrews photo- wyomingtalesandtrails.com

Teton Pass road in the winter
While summer tourism continued to increase, attempts to create a winter tourist economy remained problematic. Winter access to the valley remained challenging and uncertain.

For these reasons, I have been somewhat reluctant to invite the Wyoming Delegation for a conference as it would appear that the only matters that could be compromised at this time would be the present boundaries of the monument. Unless you have some suggestions as to boundary changes I would be inclined to stand by the boundaries of the monument as now established.[38]

The President's veto also sparked activity within the Wyoming State Legislature. On February 8, 1945, Senate Joint Resolution No. 2 was presented to the Committee of the Whole urging the Wyoming Congressional Delegation and the Wyoming governor to continue the official opposition to the establishment of the Jackson Hole National Monument. Senator Grieve of Carbon County and Senator Buchenroth of Teton County sponsored the resolution. The measure was objected to by Senator Leslie Miller from Laramie County. Miller previously served as governor of Wyoming, had supported the Monument in the House Public Lands Committee hearings, and had written a nationally published article defending the President's proclamation. The resolution was passed with only Miller objecting.[39]

On February 10, 1945, the U.S. District Court released its ruling in the case of *State of Wyoming v. Paul R. Franke*. Judge T. Blake Kennedy seemed to agree with nearly every argument presented by the state and rejected most of the arguments presented by the defense, but he eventually dismissed the case.

Concerning to the state's claim that the Monument was established for the purpose of extending the boundaries of Grand Teton National Park, the judge wrote, *"For the judiciary to probe the reasoning which underlies this Proclamation would amount to a clear invasion of the legislative and executive domains."* And elsewhere in the decision, *"Neither can the court take any judicial interest in the motives which may have inspired the Proclamation described as an attempt to circumvent the Congressional intent and authority in connection with such lands."* [40]

The judge placed greater importance on the power bestowed to the President in Section 2 of the Antiquities Act than on the detail of the items or sites described for protection. His focus was on the following language of the Act, *"The President of the United States is authorized, **in his discretion** [author's emphasis], to declare by public proclamation historic landmarks, historic and prehistoric structures and other objects of historic or scientific interest that are situated upon lands owned or controlled by the Government of the United States."* In the court's view, Congress had given the President the power to exercise discretion in determining the significance of the objects or sites subsequently specified in the act.

The decision claimed the court had the jurisdiction to rule on the evidence presented by both sides but elected not to. Thus, the second of the state's three arguments that the Jackson Hole National Monument did not contain sites specified by the Antiquities Act was rendered moot by the failure of the court to rule on the evidence. The judge indicated that had the plaintiff presented evidence demonstrating none of the features identified in the act existed within the boundaries of the monument as established, without expert rebuttal testimony to the contrary, he could have ruled on the alleged abuse of executive authority. Because both sides presented conflicting expert testimony on this issue, the court was faced with an analysis of where the preponderance of evidence rested. Judge Kennedy wrote, *"This in substance, amounts to no more in the end than the Court's opinion of what the evidence in the case purports to show and itself implies an exercise of the Court's discretion."* [41]

The Park Service was disappointed the judge chose not to rule on the validity of the evidentiary testimony.[42] Had the court dismissed the case on the basis of the testimony presented by the defense witnesses to substantiate the presence and significance of the historic and scientific sites within the monument, the Park Service would have had a significant judicially approved precedent for justifying future monuments. In other words, they would have preferred a ruling stating that the evidence justified the establishment of the monument.

Eventually, Judge Kennedy wrote:

In short, this seems to be a controversy between the Legislative and Executive Branches of the Government in which, under the evidence presented here, the Court cannot interfere. Undoubtedly great hardship and a substantial amount of injustice will be done to the State and her citizens if the Executive Department carries out its threatened program, but if Congress presumes to delegate its inherent authority to Executive Departments which exercise acquisitive proclivities not actually intended, the burden is on Congress to pass such remedial legislation as may obviate any injustice brought about as the power and control over and disposition of government lands inherently rests in its Legislative branch. What has been said with reference to the objects of historic and scientific interest applies equally to the discretion of the Executive in defining the area compatible with the proper care and management of the objects to be protected.[43]

The judge also spoke to the evidence presented by both sides reflecting either support or opposition to the monument by citizens and organizations. He wrote:

The argument and propaganda which have been circulated in forums and through the press of the nation, and even volunteered for the use of the court, largely concern a policy of segregating the area for its natural scenery and inherent beauty as a national playground or in the alternative, a policy representing in effect an encroachment upon the State's sovereignty over lands within its boundaries by adding to the already large acreage of public lands over which the Federal Government exercises authority, more lands, and more restrictive measures, thereby retarding the State's growth and development. Such discussions are of public interest, but are only applicable as an appeal for Congressional action.[44]

Judge Kennedy's ruling was perhaps a greater victory for the Park Service and the executive branch than was immediately realized. At the time, both the state of Wyoming and the Park Service expressed disappointment with Kennedy's decision, but a legal precedent was established that essentially abrogated the intent of Congress relative to Section 2 of the act. In his ruling, Judge Kennedy interpreted the discretionary power bestowed on the President by Congress to include the determination of appropriate objects for protection and the size of the area necessary for protection. The intent of Congress, as judged by the hearing transcripts attendant to consideration of the bill and recorded speeches and debate on the floor of Congress, indicate that Section 2 of the act, while empowering the President to create a monument, was also intended to limit the actions of the President with regard to the objects of antiquity and the size of a monument. It was not intended that the President would exercise discretionary power for the analytical determination of appropriate objects of antiquity or the size of the area deemed necessary for the protection of the object. Those determinations were assumed

Jackson Hole Historical Society and Museum 20040028003a

A southeast view of the town of Jackson and part of the town square in the 1940s

to rest with archaeologists, geologists, and other scientists. Congress intended to bestow upon the President the discretion to act, not analyze.

As a result of Judge Kennedy's interpretation, combined with the failure of Congress to rectify the interpretation through subsequent legislative action, the precedent was established for future Presidents to establish monuments far in excess of the original expectations or intent of Congress. The state of Wyoming allowed the appeal period to pass (June 1945) without action, concluding this proceeding in the monument controversy.

⁓

Following the court's ruling, Congressman Barrett on February 12, introduced H.R. 2109 to abolish the Jackson Hole National Monument and return the lands within its boundaries to their status prior to the President's Proclamation. Additionally on March 20, Congressman Barrett introduced H.R. 2691 which provided for all the public lands within the monument to be administered by the National Forest Service. The public record does not provide a definitive motivation for the second bill, but it may have been the Congressman's intent to offer a form of compromise. While the preponderance of opinion in Jackson Hole was still anti-monument, there was demonstrative support for protection of the area. H.R. 2691 would provide some protection for the public domain lands contained in the Monument but by a federal agency more acceptable to the opposition.

Although legislation continued to be introduced by Wyoming's Congressional Delegation

that would lend uncertainty to the future of the Monument, the Park Service continued planning for the eventual administration of the area. On March 17 Director Drury submitted a memorandum to the Secretary of the Interior regarding the management plan for the Jackson Hole National Monument. Acknowledging the historical aspect of ranching activity in the valley, the Park Service sought the Secretary's approval of the following statement:

One of the purposes of the Jackson Hole Plan since the beginning has been the perpetuation of those aspects of the region that represent the 'Old West.' Administration and interpretation of the Monument will take this into account. Not only the earlier and nationally significant phases of the history, such as the fur-trade and pioneer-exploration periods, but also the more recent and local phases will be revealed to the public. Pioneer structures like Menor's Ferry and the Cunningham Cabin will be restored, protected, and displayed. The 'dude ranches' represent a colorful native institution and provide an informal and unique method of caring for visitors. They should be continued and fitted into the over-all program of accommodations. Cattle ranching is also an essential part of the Jackson Hole setting and of the tradition of Western America. The authorized seasonal drifting of stock, and the presence within or

A southwest view of the Jackson Town Square in the 1940s

adjacent to the area of holdings upon which cattle ranches are operated, are essential to the distinctive atmosphere of 'The Hole.' Assurances already given by the Department of the Interior as to the continuance of existing grazing privileges will mean the retention of this aspect of the scene.[45]

Secretary Ickes approved the statement on March 26, 1945.

At this point in the history of the controversy, the Park Service began to soften its policy statements regarding future management of the Monument. Director Drury's previous statements regarding ranching activities within the Monument accepted their continuance merely because they were pre-existing operations recognized by the proclamation. It was his stated goal to eliminate cattle from the Monument. This policy statement seemed to be a public relations move to acknowledge the ranching activities as a historic aspect of the Monument experience. A more cynical view was that several legislative proposals being considered by Congress at that time would have required the Park Service to accommodate grazing within the Monument in perpetuity. Congressman Peterson's bill was one of those proposals. A Park Service policy that expressed appreciation for historic ranching activities might negate the justification for such legislation and thus allow the elimination of cattle grazing at a future date.

≈

On April 12, 1945, President Franklin D. Roosevelt died. Harry S. Truman became the 33rd President of the United States. Truman was not expected to make drastic changes in programs established and supported by Roosevelt, so it was unlikely this transition would affect the Monument controversy. However, the personal relationship between Truman and Ickes was not as warm as the relationship between Roosevelt and Ickes. The Secretary's influence in the administration was expected to diminish. Shortly after President Roosevelt's death, the war in Europe officially ended and the focus of the nation's war effort was directed at Japan.

≈

As if to ensure the local controversy did not wane, a group of 36 monument supporters decided to organize a chapter of the Izaak Walton League. Membership was extended to anyone who would be willing to sign the group's statement of purpose. The stated general purpose of the local chapter was in keeping with the national organization's conservation ideals, but some of the specific local goals were inflammatory to the monument's opposition group. Potential

Jackson Hole Historical Society and Museum 1991.3978.001

Jim Van Nostrand in training at Camp Hale, Colorado wearing winter camouflage, backpack, and rifle. A total of 299 young men and women from Jackson Hole served in the military during that conflict, approximately 12 percent of the county's population. Nine Jackson Hole youths served with the 10th Mountain Division. Below, Van Nostrand carries the American flag in a Veterans Day parade in 2010.

Jackson Hole Historical Society and Museum 2011.0056.008

members had to pledge support for the Monument and oppose the restrictions placed by Congress on the administration of the Monument, *"...so that the inadvertent fostering of lawlessness by congressional action may be terminated...."* [46] They supported hunting and fishing but opposed fishing restrictions by landowners over streams on private land, and vowed to protect the wilderness character of public lands in Jackson Hole. They expressed support for the cattlemen as long as domestic sheep were not introduced.

The organization of the Jackson Hole Chapter of the Izaak Walton League might have occurred without much notice except that 80 members of the Monument opposition group requested membership applications and were refused. The rejected men decided to form their own chapter of the league and stated membership would be open to anyone *"...interested in the true principles of the League,"* and that *"...support of the Jackson Hole National Monument and criticism of the actions of Congress in regard to the Monument, will not be required of the members of the proposed chapter."* [47] The conflict was indeed minor and did not contribute in any meaningful way to the controversy except to indicate the continued difference of opinion within the valley. Nevertheless, several weeks of newspaper coverage of the incident almost certainly helped keep the *Courier's* readers entertained. More somber news regarding local men wounded in battle in the Pacific and just before the cessation of hostilities in Europe were probably strong reminders of the truly life and death events of the time. The *Courier* reported Harold Hagen and George Fleming, both with the 10th Mountain Division in Italy, were wounded, and that Martin Murie, a sniper also with the 10th Mountain Division, had received the Combat Infantry Badge.[48]

The war, with the attendant rationing of tires and fuel, resulted in a decline in travel to national parks and reduced tourism throughout the country. In May 1945, Yellowstone National Park announced it would open for the summer season but would offer no bus, hotel or lodging services.[49] However, at the close of the season, on September 6, the Park would report the number of tourists visiting Yellowstone doubled from 1944.[50] Another optimistic indicator was a report by the *Courier* that two airlines had been authorized to provide service to Jackson Hole in 1946. Western Airlines was approved for service from Logan, Utah, and Summit Airlines was authorized to operate between Evanston, Kemmerer, Afton, and Jackson.[51]

Without immediate controversy, the Park Service indicated it would issue grazing permits in July for the use of lands within the Monument boundaries to all cattlemen who could show permitted privileges during 1942.[52] Permits would normally have been issued earlier in the year, but the government's 1945 fiscal year, in which appropriations were denied, did not end until June 30. No permits were issued during the 1943 and 1944 grazing seasons because of Senator O'Mahoney's amendments to the Interior Department's appropriation bills. The Park Service assumed such an amendment would not be attached to the current appropriations bill before Congress. They were premature in their assumption. When passed on July 3, 1945, the appropriation bill (Public Law 122) contained an amendment prohibiting the use of Interior Department funds for the management of the Monument.[53]

With nearly every indicator pointing to reasons for optimism, the Reclamation Service found a way to threaten Jackson Hole. Late in July, they revealed plans for three dams on the Snake River, two of which would adversely affect the local economy. The Service wanted to construct the Palisades Dam near the Wyoming - Idaho border, the Canyon Dam near Blind Canyon, and the Hoback Dam two miles downstream from the confluence of the Snake and Hoback Rivers. The last two dams would flood the existing road constructed by the CCC through the Snake River Canyon, the highway through Hoback Canyon, and many of the ranches south of the town of Jackson. The Hoback Dam would have backed up water nearly to the community of Wilson and to within five miles of Jackson. B. W. Matteson, the division engineer for the Public Roads Administration, indicated that a new road through the Snake River Canyon, which had been planned for construction after the war, would be too expensive to construct if the canyon was flooded. Thus, funds were not being budgeted for that project and improvements

Jackson Hole Historical Society and Museum p1958.1062.001
The memorial to the Jackson Hole men and women who served in the armed services during the time of war. The memorial was commissioned and paid for by Homer Richards. It is located in the Jackson Town Square.

scheduled for the Hoback Canyon road were also in doubt.[54] The two upper dam proposals would eventually be defeated with considerable credit accruing to the efforts of the Teton National Forest.

~

On August 10, the Japanese agreed to surrender, and the people of Jackson Hole and the nation could direct their energies with more optimism toward the future. Rationing of critical items gradually abated, and the men and women who had served in the armed forces began to return home. The *Courier* published a full page "Honor Roll," listing all the Teton County residents who had served in the military. [55] Of the 299 men and women listed, 11 had been killed in action, 22 were wounded, and five survived prisoner of war camps. Nine men from Jackson Hole had served with the elite 10th Mountain Division.[56]

~

In November 1945, Governor Hunt announced a plan to create a wildlife display area in the north end of the valley. This plan, which was a cooperative effort between the state of Wyoming and the Jackson Hole Preserve, Inc., would establish on 1,280 acres of Rockefeller purchased land, an area where tourists could view wildlife indigenous to Wyoming. The area would be fenced to ensure the presence of the wildlife near the highway. The plan proposed three pastures—one for elk, deer, and moose; a second for bison; and a third for white-tailed deer and pronghorn. The Wyoming Game and Fish Department would manage the animals with the release of excess animals whenever their population reached or exceeded the carrying capacity of the range. Species such as bison, pronghorn, and white-tailed deer, which were not abundant or common to the valley, would be transported from other parts of the state. The animals would be fed during the winter when forage would be in short supply. A nonprofit corporation would administer the project, and the property would remain on the tax roles of Teton County.[57]

As might be expected, the residents of Jackson Hole had differing views regarding the project. The editor of the *Jackson Hole Courier* believed most people disapproved of the project because *"...it was not in keeping with Jackson Hole's natural environment for wildlife."* Felix Buchenroth, the state senator from Teton County, and Harold Clissold, the mayor of Jackson, approved of the plan. Buchenroth indicated he was *"...gratified to see the state at least making a move to do something about their wildlife instead of waiting for the federal government to do it."* Clissold liked the idea of a plan enabling the public to see wildlife in its natural habitat, but said he would be opposed *"...to any 'zoo' type of exhibit."*[58]

Most notably opposed was Olaus Murie. Today, Olaus and his wife Mardy are icons for modern conservationists, but in 1945, he was a big game biologist with the Fish and Wildlife Service in Jackson Hole and had authored a definitive study of elk in the valley. He resigned from the Service in October of that year to assume the leadership role of the Wilderness Society. Regarding this project he stated:

> *A menagerie is a wonderful service to the public in larger cities where the animal's environment is not available. It is a ludicrous intrusion in a place like Jackson Hole, where we have the real thing, and*

where the interested visitors can get their chief pleasure in discovering the animals for themselves.[59]

In December, the Jackson Hole Game Park was incorporated in the state of Wyoming and the location of the lands Rockefeller provided was revealed. The site was between Pacific Creek and Jackson Lake Junction and adjacent to the Oxbow of the Snake River downstream from the Jackson Lake Dam. The Jackson Hole Preserve maintained ultimate control of the land by leasing the property to the corporation rather than transferring a deed. An unnamed local was quoted as stating, *"It will sure make poaching easier."*[60]

~

The final political initiative of 1945, concerning the monument, was the formalization of a memorandum of agreement between the Park Service and the Bureau of Reclamation relating to their respective management roles regarding the Jackson Lake Dam, Jackson Lake, and other lands previously withdrawn and acquired for reclamation purposes. The Bureau of Reclamation retained exclusive jurisdiction of the dam, lands and the lake with the exception of regulations controlling hunting, fishing, and trapping. The dam managers retained the right to control river flow and change the level of Jackson Lake according to the needs of irrigation interests for whose benefit the dam had been constructed. The Park Service was given authority and control over the reclamation area regarding all matters relating to scenic, recreational, historic, and scientific values. The two agencies agreed to consult each other regarding their management plans and any contemplated changes or developments. Any conflicts that could not be mediated between the two agencies would be settled by the Secretary of the Interior.[61]

The Memorandum of Agreement was signed by Park Service Director Drury and Bureau of Reclamation Commissioner H. W. Bashore on December 7, 1945, and subsequently approved by Interior Secretary Ickes on January 4, 1946.[62]

CHAPTER SEVENTEEN

1946 - 1947

Federal protection is needed to protect the country from overzealous 'developments' that would ruin the natural qualities that make Jackson Hole the attractive place that it is. This beautiful valley needs no apologies, needs no window dressings. All it needs is protection from exploitation, and whatever reasonable accommodations are needed for visitors.

Olaus Murie[1] 1946

At a fairly early age I discovered that one of the most common and persistent habits of the human mind is to take sides and argue pro and con about any new project, suggestion, or discovery, long before most of the debaters have any clear information as to what is really going on. Furthermore, the passion and acrimony displayed is, as a rule, in direct proportion to the ignorance.

Struthers Burt[2] 1946

Jackson Hole Historical Society and Museum 2010.0079.028

Western Airlines provided the first commercial air service to Jackson.

In January 1946, the *Jackson Hole Courier* again changed editors. James Huidekoper relinquished the position to Wilford Neilson. Neilson previously edited the paper from 1932 to 1934 when the preponderance of local opinion favored an extension of Grand Teton National Park according to the Jackson Hole Plan. During his earlier tenure as editor, the *Courier* was distinguished by frequent tongue-in-cheek editorials and occasional allusions to classical literature. Under Neilson's supervision, the newspaper was considerably more entertaining.

Rockefeller Archive Center, Gabor Eder Photo, Box 8, Folder 156, 814142_me,

Laurance Spelman Rockefeller
1910-2004

Laurance would later become a prominent national figure in venture capital and philanthropic endeavors. At this point, the Rockefeller brothers were assuming roles and responsibilities based on their innate interest. Laurance seemed inclined toward the family's conservation and philanthropic activities for which he would eventually receive national acclaim. However, he was not a one-trick pony. He inherited his grandfather's seat on the New York Stock Exchange and in 1946, with his brothers and sister, formed a venture capital partnership that later became Venrock Associates. This venture capital organization provided the start-up financing for many technology companies including Apple Computer and Intel. Other technologies that benefitted from his investments are; lasers, aerospace, composite materials, electronics, high-temperature physics, data processing, thermionics, optics, instrumentation and nuclear power.

Little in the way of legislative activity concerning the Jackson Hole National Monument occurred during 1946. However, the valley has only rarely endured periods in which some issue was not contemplated that provoked contested opinions and 1946 was not without its controversies.

The year began with the public acknowledgment by Mr. Rockefeller of the transfer of most of the Snake River Land Company property to the Jackson Hole Preserve, Inc. The actual transfer occurred in October 1945, but the news release was not issued until January 1946. This nonprofit corporation was established in 1940 to facilitate the philanthropic endeavors of the Rockefeller family. At its inception, Laurance Rockefeller assumed a leadership role in the corporation, but he resigned at the beginning of World War II and joined the Navy. After the war, he resumed his position as president, and from that time forward would orchestrate much of the conservation activities of the family.

The controversy regarding the Jackson Hole Game Park, announced by Governor Hunt the previous year, became more vocal in 1946. Unlike the controversy surrounding the expansion of Grand Teton National Park, the statements of support or disapproval, and an occasional satirical article, did not engender obvious personal rancor. Possibly this is because the majority of Teton County residents in 1946 still maintained strong attitudes regarding the rights of private property owners. The Rockefellers owned the land, and the project had the support of the state of Wyoming, who by law owned the wildlife. While many residents may not have approved of the game park, considerable latitude was accorded the conduct of a property owner on his own land.

Olaus Murie, the big game biologist turned Wilderness Society executive, continued to be the most outspoken opponent of the project. He wrote articles and made speeches to various conservation groups condemning the Jackson Hole Game Park. The Park Service, along with many Jackson Hole residents, was not supportive of the project. The Park Service had anticipated the 1,280 acres strategically located at one of the most scenic sites in the valley would be transferred to their jurisdiction. Various conservation groups expressed disappointment with the plan, and Murie resigned from the Board of the Jackson Hole Preserve because of the project.[3] Opposition arguments to the game park reflected a philosophical distaste for the idea of confining wild animals in pens without regard to the size of the pens or that the fences containing the animals would be mostly out of sight of the tourists.

Struthers Burt articulated a different point of view. Burt's position stopped short of endorsing the project, but he suggested the Rockefellers had never proposed a project that had not aided humanity. He wrote:

Why not, therefore give him the benefit of the doubt, and at least five years or so in which to see whether, in this instance, he's making his first mistake or not?

Finally, it's his land isn't it? If he wanted to, he'd have every right to run an ostrich farm. I'm sure that isn't his intention. But whose business would it be but his own if it were? [4]

Laurance Rockefeller and a member of the Preserve's board of directors, Fairfield Osborn, conceived this project, which changed its name in 1946 to the Jackson Hole Wildlife Park.* Osborn was also chairman of the New York Zoological Society. Both men assumed that providing an opportunity for tourists to photograph wildlife at a specific location would lessen the probability of the wildlife being molested or harassed in other parts of the Grand Teton and Yellowstone National Parks. Additionally, they proposed to establish a facility from which wildlife research studies could be conducted.

The Park was created and formally dedicated on July 19, 1948.[7] In addition to the fenced compounds, several log buildings were constructed to provide a biological research station for scientists and students. The reality of the Park was that the animals did not fare well in the confined areas. Twelve bison had been trapped and transported to the Park. They contracted Bang's disease† and had to be destroyed. More bison were transplanted, but found the fences a minor deterrent to their

Jackson Historical Society and Museum 2005.0018.001
Bison released into the Jackson Hole Wildlife Park, 1947

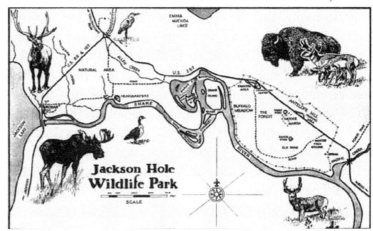

National Park Service
The Jackson Hole Wildlife Park
For more information about the Jackson Hole Wildlife Park see: www.nps.gov/history/history/online_books/npsg/research_station/sec4.htm

---

*Other than having purchased the acreage in question, John D. Rockefeller, Jr. had little involvement in this project. Correspondence between Rockefeller and Horace Albright refer to the plan as the Laurance/Osborn project.[5] Laurance and Fairfield had worked together on various projects beginning with the New York Zoological Society's exhibit at the 1939 World's Fair. The idea for the Jackson Hole Wildlife Park probably had its origin in that exhibit. The exhibit was designed to encourage a new type of zoo, one where wild animals would be exhibited in a natural habitat rather than cages or pens. Additionally, there was greater emphasis placed on education rather than recreation.[6]

†Bang's disease, also known as brucellosis, is an infectious disease among domestic cattle and other ungulates that result in spontaneous abortion and is transmittable to humans. It was named for Danish veterinarian Bernard L. T. Bang.

Jackson Hole Wildlife Park Dedication
(Seated L-R) Lester Bagley, Fairfield Osborn, Carl Jorgensen, Foster Scott, Governor Lester Hunt, James Simon (first director of the Wildlife Park). Laurance Rockefeller standing.

urge to roam, and they only occasionally cooperated with the goals of the project by remaining in their pasture. The moose became dependent upon the food supplied them and declined to forage on native vegetation.[8] Eventually, the Wildlife Park would be allowed to die a quiet death, and the corporation was dissolved in 1953. As well-intentioned as the motives were, and in spite of the support of the state of Wyoming, the project ultimately was unsuccessful. Its eventual abandonment was not a result of the opposition attitudes of locals or political maneuvering, but rather because it was just an ill-conceived idea. The National Park Service did make a valiant, if somewhat ineffectual, effort to contain the bison in fenced pastures into the 1970s, but the sand traps at the golf course near the south end of the Park were a strong attractant to these animals who enjoyed rolling and dusting themselves in fine-grained sediments.

Most histories of Grand Teton National Park give scant attention, if they mention it at all, to the Jackson Hole Wildlife Park. It is considered little more than a minor aberration amidst the considerable contributions of the Rockefellers to conservation throughout the world. Lost in the controversy surrounding the confinement of wild animals is the enduring contribution of the Biological Research Station to the education of young scientists and our understanding of our wild environment. The "exhibit" portion of the plan was abandoned, but the facilities constructed by the Wildlife Park for research remained under the joint management of the New York Zoological Society and the University of Wyoming for another 25 years. Beginning in 1978, the research station was relocated to a less visible location within the Park (the AMK Ranch), and it continues to be managed by the University of Wyoming in cooperation with the Park Service. Countless research projects have been accommodated within Grand Teton National Park because the facilities and the concept were established through the efforts of Laurance Rockefeller and his "mistake."

～

The Bureau of Reclamation proceeded with its plans for dams on the Snake River, and while there was little support for the projects within

Jackson Hole, the publicity surrounding the proposals kept the locals engaged regarding the potential impact on the valley. On January 24, 1946, the Bureau announced the Palisades Dam project would commence in the spring. This dam was sited in Idaho, but the reservoir would extend upstream into Wyoming. The town of Alpine would have to be relocated,* the shoreline prepared, and a new road surveyed. It was estimated the dam would impound 1,400,000-acre-feet of water, house a 30,000-kilowatt power plant, and provide irrigation for 650,000 acres of land in Idaho.[10] Because the project included the construction of new roads to replace any flooded highways, there appeared to be little potential negative impact on the valley of Jackson Hole.†

The two other proposed Snake River Canyon dams mentioned in the previous chapter were of greater interest to the valley. The proposed Grand Canyon Dam,‡ just upstream from the backwater of the Palisades Reservoir, would be 285 feet high, create a reservoir of 262,000-acre-feet of water, and house a 70,000-kilowatt power plant. The Hoback Dam would be 275 feet high, create a 1,223,000-acre foot-reservoir, and produce 40,000-kilowatts of power.[11]

The *Courier* noted the presence of a group of Bureau of Reclamation men conducting an economic survey in the valley to determine the damage to local industries resulting from the proposed impoundments. The editor allowed that an additional storage facility downstream would permit the Jackson Lake Dam to operate more

Bureau of Reclamation

Palisades Dam and Reservoir, constructed on the Snake River in Idaho, backs water into Wyoming. It is an earth-fill structure 270 feet high containing 13,571,000 cubic yards of material. At the time of construction, it was the largest earth-fill dam attempted by the Bureau of Reclamation. The dam was completed in 1957 and provides flood control, irrigation, and hydroelectric power. The power plant with upgrades added in 1994 provides a rated output of 176,600 kilowatts. The reservoir capacity is 1,401,000-acre-feet of water.

efficiently for flood control purposes, but he noted, *"...valuable and additional lands in the south part of Jackson Hole would be submerged if the program goes through."* Neither was he enamored with the idea of *"...putting another chunk of Jackson Hole under water for the benefit by irrigation and electric power, of lands and settlers in the State of Idaho."*[12]

The decade following World War II brought numerous reclamation and hydroelectric projects throughout the nation, but Wyoming had always looked with apprehension, or perhaps wariness, at

---

*While certainly inconvenient for the residents, the relocation of the town offered the opportunity to solve some local problems. In 1946, the main street of the town was also the Wyoming-Idaho state line. Over the years, as the job of postmaster changed hands, the mailing address for the residents would change, back and forth from Idaho to Wyoming, depending on which side of the main street the new postmaster resided. The town did not have a post office, and thus, the mail was delivered to, and distributed from, the home of the postmaster. Elections were also a problem. The postal address determined whether the residents could vote in Idaho or Wyoming elections.[9]

†Once constructed, this dam and hydro plant would eventually provide the region, including Jackson Hole, with reliable electrical power.

‡In Chapter Sixteen, this proposed dam was called the Blind Canyon Dam. In 1946, the Reclamation Service abandoned that project in favor of a dam site nearer the high water line of the proposed Palisades Reservoir at a point currently referred to as "The Narrows." The new dam site was also given a new name, the Grand Canyon Dam. Ferdinand Vandiveer Hayden named the Snake River Canyon between Hoback Junction and the community of Alpine the Grand Canyon of the Snake in the late 1860s.

proposals by neighboring states to appropriate water originating within her boundaries. Reclamation officials, of course, were focused on the benefit the impounded water would provide downstream users and argued that the portion of the Snake River they proposed to dam could not efficiently or practically be utilized by the state of Wyoming. Nevertheless, the Bureau of Reclamation faced an unsympathetic populace and Wyoming state government with its proposal to construct two dams within Wyoming boundaries for the sole benefit of Idaho irrigation interests. This was especially true if they intended to inundate productive land within the state. One economic aspect that may not have occurred to the Bureau was the Teton County tax problem that would result from the acquisition of the private lands they proposed to flood.

Although dam proposals for the Snake River Canyon would recur through the years, those impoundments were never constructed. Considerable effort by the Forest Service played a major role in protecting the river from the proposals long before the river's potential for recreation was recognized or even imagined.

∽

In February 1946, President Truman nominated Edwin Pauley for the position of Under Secretary of the Navy. At Pauley's confirmation hearings, Secretary of Interior Ickes testified negatively regarding this appointment, and Truman, who felt at least some of Ickes' negative allegations were intentionally untrue, held a press conference stating his support for Pauley *"...no matter what Mr. Ickes said."* [13] Secretary Ickes submitted his resignation, which Truman accepted. Those are the facts concerning the secretary's departure from government service, but there are more interesting details regarding the Truman-Ickes relationship.

In 1940, Truman sought Ickes' support during his campaign for a second term in the Senate. Ickes coolly informed Truman that he was endorsing Lloyd Stark, Missouri's governor, also a Democrat, who was running against Truman for the Senate seat. [14] Truman won that election. In 1944, President Roosevelt selected Truman as his vice-presidential running mate over Henry Wallace and Harold Ickes. Truman revealed to

Merle Miller, the author of *Plain Speaking, an oral biography of Harry S. Truman*, another incident that defined his relationship with the Interior Secretary. On the train returning from Hyde Park after Roosevelt's funeral, Truman overheard Ickes *"...carrying on about how the country would go to hell now that Roosevelt was gone. He said there wasn't any leadership anymore, something like that. He went on and on. He was a man who carried on a good deal."* Truman believed Ickes intended for him to hear the remarks about a lack of leadership. When asked why he didn't fire the Secretary, Truman responded, *"I didn't have to. I knew the kind of man he was. He was a resigner."* [15] Truman compared Ickes to Salmon P. Chase, the Secretary of the Treasury in Lincoln's Cabinet whose frequent resignations were ignored by Lincoln. Ickes had resigned on several occasions, but Roosevelt, like Lincoln with Chase, never accepted the resignations. Truman stated, *"I knew he'd turned in his resignation a few times while Roosevelt was President. So I knew I could wait."* [16]

When Secretary Ickes inevitably submitted his resignation, Truman told him he could leave immediately. Ickes' resignation stated he believed Truman's statements at the press conference publicly indicated a lack of confidence which was true. It apparently never occurred to Secretary Ickes that as a member of Truman's Cabinet, he owed a certain amount of loyalty to his boss. Truman recalled Ickes' letter of resignation was *"...the sort of resignation a man sent in, knowing it would not be accepted."* Ickes indicated he would like to stay on for six weeks, but President Truman gave him only one additional day to vacate his office. [17]

Ickes' passing from the political scene was viewed with relief by residents of the western "public lands" states. His stated disdain for the rights and opinions of the individual when confronted by what he viewed as the national good, combined with the power of his office, had created a general sense of distrust of bureaucrats and the federal government. Both Senator Robertson and Congressman Barrett released statements expressing the hope that Ickes' successor would be more familiar with the west and understanding of the needs of states with high percentages of public land. Senator Robertson stated he believed ex-Secretary Ickes had been *"...one of the most detrimental influences..."* to the development and prosperity of the western states.[18]

On February 26, President Truman nominated Julius A. Krug for the position of Secretary of Interior. Krug was a Wisconsin native and had previously served as chairman of the War Production Board from 1941 to 1945. In this post, he demonstrated exceptional organization and management skills. He was confirmed rather quickly on March 5, 1946.

～

In April, the superintendent of Grand Teton National Park, Paul R. Franke, was promoted and transferred to the National Park Service office in Chicago. Franke became the Assistant Supervisor for Concessions. Several of the memoranda quoted in previous chapters favorably mentioned his deportment concerning the lawsuit filed by the state of Wyoming. Undoubtedly, the suit enhanced rather than detracted from his career. John S. McLaughlin, the superintendent of Mesa Verde National Park, was named his successor at Grand Teton.[19]

Julius Albert Krug
1907-1970

Krug served as the 33rd U.S. Secretary of the Interior. He would eventually resign under allegations of fiscal misconduct.

Chief Ranger Allyn F. Hanks (left) and Superintendent Charles J. Smith

Smith was the fourth superintendent of Grand Teton National Park and the first to bear the responsibility for the Jackson Hole National Monument. When Paul R. Franke, the fifth superintendent, was transferred to the NPS office in Chicago, Hanks, the chief ranger, served as acting superintendent of the Park from April 1946 to May 1946. Although this was a temporary position for Hanks, National Park Service documents list Hanks as the sixth superintendent of Grand Teton National Park. John S. McLaughlin became the seventh superintendent in May of 1946.

As the summer season arrived, it became apparent that predictions of increased tourist travel after the end of the war would be realized. By June, local dude ranches were booked to capacity and Yellowstone Park's accommodations were full.[20] Along with the positive economic indicators, the Jackson airport inaugurated its first commercial flights between Jackson and Salt Lake City, Utah on July 5, 1946. The community celebration of this event probably startled the first passengers to fly into Jackson Hole. When the Western Airlines DC-3 stopped at the newly constructed log terminal, the plane was surrounded by mounted riders, a stage coach drawn by a four-horse team, and a crowd of approximately 500 locals dressed in western garb. The passengers were served a barbecue lunch, and actor Wallace Beery was one of the cooks.

Jackson Hole Historical Society and Museum bc0230

Commercial air service to Jackson Hole was initiated with a single daily flight by a Western Airlines DC-3.

An enhanced tourist economy was the obvious value of air transportation to the valley. Less obvious were equally important benefits to the community. On this first flight, a shipment of blood plasma arrived for the hospital, and a packet of mail was delivered. Outgoing letters were dispatched when the plane departed marking the beginning of regular airmail service for Jackson Hole.[21]

The airport, located within the boundaries of the Jackson Hole National Monument and eventually within Grand Teton National Park, would provide the catalyst for future controversy in the valley. The Park Service, some residents, and a number of environmental groups would attempt to abolish the airport as a non-conforming use within a national park. It is perhaps most surprising that the local populace, in their exuberance to procure air transportation to the valley, failed to recognize the threat created by the establishment of the Jackson Hole National Monument or the extension of Grand Teton National Park. The Presidential Proclamation recognized pre-existing rights within the Monument, but the lease from the federal government for the land on which the

airport was built was of limited duration. It would seem apparent that if the Park Service considered cattle, quietly grazing within their boundaries, to be non-conforming, albeit historical, their attitude toward an airport, which was neither conforming nor historical, would certainly be unsympathetic. At this point in the history of the Park, both the Park Service and the opposition ignored the future of the airport.

The initiation of air service to Jackson Hole had little to do with the record-setting travel figures reported by both Grand Teton and Yellowstone National Parks for 1946. One daily flight by a 20 passenger airplane was not likely to appreciably affect visitation to the parks. The end of the war and the discontinuation of rationing were the primary impetus for recreational travel. The 1946 travel season, which officially ended in September, provided both parks with the largest seasonal visitation experienced to that date. Grand Teton National Park recorded 133,612 visitors, which was 94,723 more visitors than in 1945, and 8,483 more than the previous high attendance year of 1941.[22]

The previous high visitation year for Yellowstone National Park was also 1941 when 587,761

Jackson Hole Historical Society and Museum, 1958.3111.001

The first commercial airline flight into Jackson was met by locals on horseback and in wagons. A Bar-B-Q was prepared to celebrate the occasion.

people visited the Park. In 1946, the number was 814,907.[23] Two other figures concerning travel to Yellowstone are also worth noting. There was an appreciable increase in what the Park Service called house trailers. Today we call them campers or travel trailers. In 1940, 1,711 of these trailers entered the Park. In 1941, the number dropped to 1,479. But in 1946, 4,022 trailers were hauled into the Park. The other 1946 figure of interest shows that a few people still maintained some attachment to their heritage. Tourists entering the Park on horseback numbered 298.[24]

~

During a visit to Jackson, Wyoming State Republican Chairman Ewing T. Kerr, predicted a predominance of Republican victories in November's off-year elections. He was partially right. Teton County voters favored Republican candidates on election day, but the rest of the state was not so partisan. Senator O'Mahoney, a Democrat, won his re-election bid against Harry B. Henderson. Governor Hunt, also a Democrat, defeated his Republican challenger Earl Wright. Republican Congressman Barrett, opposed by John J. McIntyre, was also returned to office.[25] Senator Robertson's term had not expired. Nineteen forty-six brought no change in the state's top four political offices.

Olie Riniker Photo Jackson Hole Historical Society and Museum
1958.2785.001

The first terminal building at the Jackson Hole Airport

~

Legislation introduced earlier, that is, Barrett's second bill to abolish the Jackson Hole National Monument, Barrett's bill to place all public lands in the Jackson Hole National Monument under the jurisdiction of the Forest Service, Robertson's bill to require state approval for monuments established under the Antiquities Act, and Peterson's second bill to provide payment to Teton County in lieu of taxes, all failed to pass during the 79th

Jackson Hole Historical Society and Museum- 20060283002

John McAteer, Clarence 'Curly' Harris, and Ralph Cole posed in front of the second airport terminal. All three were certified weathermen but often found their job required chasing cattle and horses off the runway.

Congress. Predictably, a new series of legislative initiatives was launched in 1947.

On January 8, 1947, Wyoming Senator Robertson introduced S. 91 in the 80th Congress, 1st Session, to amend the Antiquities Act. The bill required the President to notify the governor of the affected state, the senators of that state, the representative at large, and the representative of the affected congressional district, or districts six months prior to the issuance of a proclamation establishing a national monument. The proposal would also have to be published for four consecutive weeks in a general circulation newspaper in the county seat of the county or counties affected. Additionally, subsection (c) of the bill stated:

Effective as of December 7, 1941, no proclamation declaring a national monument shall be made unless such monument has the approval in writing of a majority of the persons to whom notice of intention to make proclamation is required to be sent under the provisions of subsection (b); and no monument shall be considered to have been lawfully established since that date and prior to the date of enactment of this Act.[26]

This bill would have the effect of abolishing the Jackson Hole National Monument and any other monument established by proclamation after December 7, 1941. The intended significance of the date specified in this legislation is uncertain although it is clear that it was not Robertson's intent to abolish other national monuments. In fact, only one other national monument had been created since 1941. Castle Clinton National Monument, in New York, encompassed just one acre and was created in 1946. Since it was established by an act of Congress rather than by proclamation, it would not have been affected by this

bill.[27] An obvious interpretation would be that Senator Robertson intended to make a comparison between Japan's sneak attack on the United States at Pearl Harbor and the view that an act of subterfuge had created the Jackson Hole National Monument– an act which accomplished an action previously rejected by Congress, and without regard to the opinions or concerns of the residents of Jackson Hole.

On January 27, Congressman Barrett introduced H.R. 1330 to abolish the Jackson Hole National Monument and return all public land within its boundaries to their status prior to Presidential Proclamation 2578. Hearings by the House Committee on Public Lands concerning this bill were scheduled for April of that year, and Secretary Krug submitted an unfavorable report from the Interior Department concerning H.R. 1330 on April 9, 1947.[28]

Congressman Peterson also submitted new legislation, H.R. 3035, on April 14 providing payments to Teton County in lieu of lost taxes resulting from the creation of the Monument. His bill also prosed to provide stock driveways across and within the Jackson Hole National Monument. This legislation contained the same schedule of payments proposed in his previous bill and

Charles Wesley Andrews photo, Jackson Hole Historical Society and Museum 2005.0138.016

Even with automobiles, snow plows, and airplanes a familiar sight in Jackson Hole by the mid-1940s, horse-drawn sleighs were sometimes required to haul freight over Teton Pass. This photo is dated 1946.

codified the grazing and property rights of individuals affected by the establishment of the Monument.[29]

The hearings held in Washington regarding H.R. 1330 began on April 14 and continued for four days. The testimony received was similar to that recorded in 1943 with a few notable differences. The election of 1946 had accorded Republicans control of the House, and Congressman Richard J. Welch had replaced J. Hardin Peterson as chairman of the House Public Lands Committee. While Peterson chaired the subcommittee that held hearings on Barrett's original bill, Barrett was given the chairmanship of the subcommittee conducting the hearings on H.R. 1330. There is evidence to suggest that when Peterson was chairman, he declined to hold hearings on Barrett's second attempt to abolish the Monument, and he would have blocked hearings on this bill if he had retained that position in the 80th Congress.[30]

Other differences marked the changing times. Several of the newer congressmen on the committee had never visited Jackson Hole and asked the Park Service to present color photographs of the area. Apparently, the Park Service did not have such images in its possession but provided the committee members with Greyhound Bus Company advertising literature that did have color photographs of Jackson Hole. Also, at least some of the witnesses traveling from Jackson Hole went to Washington by airplane rather than by train.

Perhaps the most important difference between the 1943 hearings and the 1947 hearings was that testimony revealed a strengthening of support for the Monument. It is likely an accurate assumption that in 1943 an overwhelming majority of people in Jackson Hole, and perhaps throughout the nation, opposed the Monument. That was certainly the impression established during the earlier hearings. That does not imply that a majority of the valley's residents opposed protection for the scenic, wildlife, and recreational values of the area. However, the establishment of the Monument by proclamation came suddenly and unexpectedly which created an atmosphere of uncertainty. The residents of Jackson Hole had been given no opportunity to consider the ramifications of the action prior to its execution.

While the proclamation recognized pre-existing rights, leases, and permits, Secretary Ickes and President Roosevelt had not fully considered the consequences of the proclamation. They did not anticipate the resulting conflicts regarding Park Service policy and its effect on the cattle industry and wildlife management activities in the area. It was hard for rational

Jackson Hole Historical Society and Museum 1958.2735.001

Mardy and Olaus Murie

Olaus Murie (1889-1963) was a noted big game biologist whose research ranged from Alaska to New Zealand and resulted in numerous publications. Perhaps his most important literary work was *The Elk of North America* based on his research with the Jackson Hole elk herd. He resigned from the Fish and Wildlife Service to assume the position of president of the Wilderness Society.

Mardy Murie (1903-2003) became a conservation icon in her own right, receiving the Audubon Medal (1980), the John Muir Award (1983), the Robert Marshall Conservation Award (1986), and the J.N. Ding Darling Conservationists of the Year Award (2002). She received the Presidential Medal of Freedom in 1998. Mardy was the first woman to graduate from what is now the University of Alaska and later received an Honorary Doctorate of Humane Letters from the same institution. Noted for her work with wilderness issues, she also authored numerous publications, including several books. *Two in the Far North* and *Wapiti Wilderness* (coauthored with Olaus) are among the most valued by collectors.

people to correlate the stated purpose of the Monument with the boundaries. If the Monument was established to protect scientific, historic, and scenic values, why did the southern boundary of the Monument extend down to the town of Jackson and include private property and even a gas station on the north edge of town? Why did it include lands already protected within the National Elk Refuge? Part of the confusion resulted from the fact that the stated justification for the proclamation was expressed in language necessitated by the Antiquities Act while the boundaries seemed to indicate a different purpose. The boundaries provided by the proclamation obviously had not received the analytical consideration specified by the Antiquities Act.

Unstated in the proclamation, but suspected by the residents of the valley, was the primary motivation of accommodating Rockefeller's desire to donate his lands in Jackson Hole to the Park Service. The boundaries reflected a defacto extension of Grand Teton National Park so as to include Rockefeller's holdings. It is hard to imagine Roosevelt's administration or Congress, would seriously have considered any park or monument suggestions for Jackson Hole during the war years had Rockefeller not sent his letter forcing the issue. No other parks or monuments were suggested during that time.

The timing of the action was also confusing to the residents of the valley. Olaus Murie, who eventually became an outspoken supporter of the Monument, recalled his wife's reaction when he told her about the proclamation. Mardy Murie's reaction was, *"But we're in the middle of a war! Why do it now?"* [31] In 1943, it was difficult for anyone to determine if President Roosevelt had imposed adversity or benefit upon the community. Uncertainty is not a state avidly embraced by human nature.

During the four-year interim between the congressional hearings, the residents of Jackson Hole had time to consider the Monument and its potential effect on the valley. Gradually, the Monument gained support. Most supporters, including Olaus Murie, recognized the imperfections of the Monument as it was established, but foresaw more positive impact than negative. Additionally, national publicity by proponents of

the Monument convinced conservation groups to support the proclamation.

Testimony from Wyoming residents opposing H.R. 1330 was presented by Leslie Miller, Olaus Murie, and Charles Moore. The Subcommittee also received testimony from Wyoming residents supporting the bill from Senator Robertson, J. Elmer Brock, Felix Buchenroth, Stanley Resor, J. B. Wilson, Clifford Hansen, and Dr. Floyd Naegeli. Although strident testimony from both sides of the monument issue was presented at the 1947 hearings, the Jackson Hole people were congenial with each other, demonstrating acknowledgment of different viewpoints and quick to agree on issues where attitudes converged.

Some of the most aggressive conduct was exemplified by several of the Subcommittee members. Congressman A. L. Miller confronted Fairfield Osborn, who appeared before the subcommittee representing two organizations, the New York Zoological Society and the Jackson Hole Wildlife Park. Miller was concerned because Osborn claimed he represented 2,900 members of the Zoological Society but revealed under questioning that the Society had not polled its membership to determine their attitudes concerning the issue. Miller stated:

Rockefeller Archive Center. Box 10, Folder 584, 814143_me

Henry Fairfield Osborn, Jr.
1887-1969

Born into the wealthy Osborn family, Fairfield was able to devote much of his adult life to environmental and conservation causes. He was secretary and a board member of the New York Zoological Society from 1923 to 1940 and then president until his death in 1969. He authored several celebrated environmental books including *Our Plundered Planet* (1948) and *The Limits of the Earth* (1953). His cousin, Aileen Osborn, married Vanderbilt Webb.

I think it is important, Mr. Chairman, that we should have the background of these witnesses, because, after all, if you are only representing 2,000 people in New York City that pay $10 to hire someone to sponsor something out in Wyoming, and then a paper organization which is incorporated, and the gentleman sets himself up as a director and the head of it, which has no membership to represent, the thinking of the people of the West is on rather thin ice.[32]

Congressman Miller maintained that because Osborn claimed to represent a corporation with no membership and an organization with membership which had not been polled, he really was representing a personal opinion and his testimony was *"...null and void...."*[33]

Testimony presented by some conservation groups indicated a lack of familiarity with the area and the actual issues attendant to the controversy. Their opposition to H.R. 1330 appeared to be philosophical and assumed the cattlemen were trying to gain control of the public domain at the expense of the general public. They seemed unaware of the tax problems faced by Teton County or the complexity of the game management issues.

Subcommittee members, particularly those representing western states, seemed impatient with such testimony. Ultimately, testimony of this type probably served to strengthen the congressmen's support of the Barrett bill.

Of notable interest was the testimony of two of the conservation groups that indicated a reversal of previously held philosophies at least regarding the Jackson Hole National Monument. Fred Packard, representing the National Parks Association, testified in support of the Monument. In 1935, the National Parks Association had been a major force in opposing Senator Carey's bill to extend the boundaries of Grand Teton National Park in accordance with the Jackson Hole Plan. In 1938, the Association again opposed a Park Service proposal to extend the boundaries of Grand Teton National Park. Their opposition to these initiatives related to the inclusion of the Jackson Lake Reservoir and because the southern boundary of the proposed park extensions abutted the town of Jackson. The Association had a long history of opposing the inclusion of "commercial waters" in national parks, but in 1947, it apparently found the Monument's inclusion of commercial waters an acceptable circumstance worthy of their support.[34] In 1935, the Izaak Walton League assumed

The Million Dollar Cowboy Bar was a favorite watering hole for tourists in the town of Jackson.

a stance similar to that of the National Parks Association regarding the inclusion of Jackson Lake in a national park, but in 1947, it supported the inclusion of the reservoir in the Monument.

As a matter of principle, the opposition testimony presented to Congress in 1947 still supported the abolishment of the Jackson Hole National Monument. Clifford Hansen again suggested a compromise that found favor with the Subcommittee and some of the witnesses on both sides of the issue. The compromise suggestion followed his previous proposal to include the portion of the Monument west of the Snake River into Grand Teton National Park with the remaining acreage to be administered by the Fish and Wildlife Service and the National Forest Service. Hansen's proposal would provide a managed "foreground" for the Park and an easily definable eastern boundary, the Snake River. The Fish and Wildlife Service would administer the land east of the Snake River having primary value to wildlife issues. The

Forest Service would manage all other public land east of the river. Thus, most of the 17,000 acres of private land not owned by Rockefeller would be excluded from the Park. Also eliminated from park jurisdiction were most of the non-conforming grazing activities, as well as the hunting issue and the airport. If Highway 189 was eventually relocated to the east side of the Snake River, the issue of commercial traffic within the Park would also be resolved. Hansen suggested no billboards nor other types of advertising or development would be allowed along any right-of-way on the land in question east of the Snake River, but summer home development could occur on Forest Service land along the eastern foothills.*

National Park Service Director Drury testified on behalf of the Park Service, but his testimony was contradictory. His testimony also served as an example of why the Park Service and their guarantees through policy statements were distrusted. He restated the intent of the Park Service to pro-

Jackson Hole Historical Society and Museum hs0021

Town of Jackson showing the developing ski area on Snow King Mountain, 1947. Population approximately 1,200.

*Summer home development would not be tolerated today, but in 1947, this was a common practice in many National Forests. The construction of summer homes provided economic benefits for local communities, tax revenue to the counties, and the Forest Service returned 25 percent of the lease revenue to the county in which the homes were constructed.

tect the rights of private property owners, but in the 1944 meeting, discussed in Chapter Sixteen, he supported a policy that mandated all lands within the Monument "whether public or private" should be subject to the administration of the Park Service. He restated the Park Service intent to protect the grazing interests, but in 1943 testified it was his intent to eliminate grazing within the Monument. During the above-mentioned meeting in 1944, he again indicated his goal of eliminating grazing in the Monument. Then, in 1945, he obtained approval of a policy statement from Secretary Ickes declaring ranching to be one of the historical elements of the Monument that would be perpetuated. Now, in 1947, he assured the House committee that the Park Service would protect the grazing interest, but indicated in a later part of his testimony that it was his ultimate intent to eliminate grazing in the Monument. Drury promised to cooperate with the state of Wyoming and the Fish and Wildlife Service on game management issues but indicated hunting would eventually be prohibited in the area. He also stated the intent of his agency would be to acquire the privately owned land within the Monument. He referred to Congressman Peterson's bill to provide tax compensation and grazing rights and indicated support for that legislation. Thus, there was little faith in the protection guarantees based on policy statements emanating from the Park Service.

Congressman Barrett asked Director Drury if the Park Service would be agreeable to a compromise whereby a portion of the Monument west of the Snake River would be included in Grand Teton National Park, and the portion east of the Snake River delegated to the Fish and Wildlife Service and the Forest Service. Drury responded, *"No. But everything we do stems from acts of Congress."* [35]

Of special interest was the map provided to the subcommittee depicting the Monument and the status of lands within its boundaries. The Jackson Lake Reservoir was disingenuously portrayed. The Park Service had drawn the lake in its natural shoreline before the dam was built, presenting the impression that the reclamation area included in the Monument was considerably smaller than actually existed. Felix Buchenroth noted the discrepancy in his testimony, and the Park Service admitted the inaccuracy. Conrad Wirth stated they had merely intended to show Jackson Lake had once been a natural feature. [36]

After the hearings in Washington, Congressman Barrett arranged a conference with Wyoming's senators in which it was decided to amend his bill to accomplish a compromise and resolve the controversy over the Monument. [37] Congressman Barrett's bill, with amendments, was reported favorably by the subcommittee to the full committee, and the House Public Lands Committee reported the amended bill favorably to the House with only one dissenting vote on July 15, 1947. [38] The amended bill abolished the Jackson Hole National Monument, but it provided elements of the Hansen compromise for the public lands within the Monument. Grand Teton National Park boundaries were extended from the northeast corner of

Two views of Jackson Lake

The map on the left shows Jackson Lake prior to its impoundment in 1908 (Lake level elevation 6,760). The map on the right shows Jackson Lake at its current high level (Elevation 6,800).

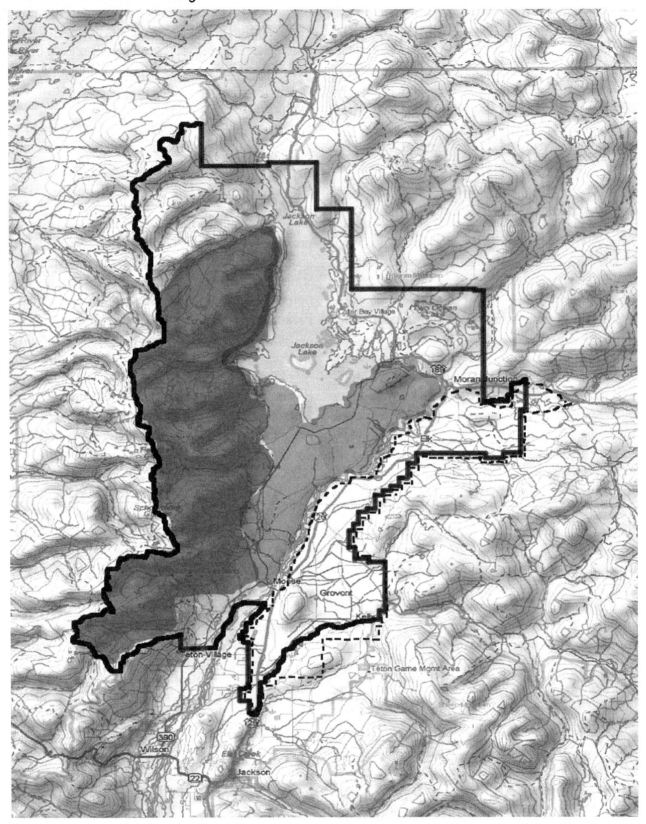

Congressman Barrett's compromise bill H.R. 1330 (as amended)

Current GTNP boundary
Original GTNP (1929)
Proposed GTNP Extension in
Elk Refuge

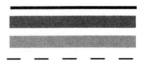

the existing Park to the west shore of Jackson Lake, then south and east along the lake shore to a point on the east side of the Snake River then south along the eastern shore of the river, plus 50 feet, to the point where the southeastern Park boundary intersected the Snake River near Moose, Wyoming. Teton National Forest would be administered public lands east of the Snake River. The Subcommittee report stated:

The committee feels that this is a fair, equitable and just solution of the problem arising out of the creation of the Jackson Hole National Monument by Executive Order. All of the witnesses appearing before the committee indicated that some changes should be made in the area included in the Jackson Hole National Monument, and the purpose of this bill is to terminate the controversy and to settle on a reasonable basis the extent of the area to be administered for park purposes. The committee is of the opinion that the Snake River represents a natural

boundary line and that the lands to the west of that river should properly become part of Grand Teton National Park and that the lands east of the Snake River, other than the 50-foot strip immediately joining said river, should be added to the Teton National Forest.

It was the considered judgement of the committee that the Forest Service of the Department of Agriculture could administer the public lands east of the Snake River in such a manner as would adequately protect that area in the national interest and would at the same time be able, under its accepted practice, to administer same on a multiple-purpose basis so as to permit the use of those lands for recreational, grazing, hunting, and other purposes consistent therewith. The committee was decidedly of the opinion that this was the only solution which would safeguard the interest of the people of Teton County and Wyoming and at the same time protect the national interest.[39]

Pauline Goe Jillson photo, Jackson Hole Historical Society and Museum 1958.2349.001

Gambling, although illegal, was openly tolerated in Jackson Hole until the 1950s. Scenery, wildlife, hunting, recreation, mountain climbing, and skiing were strong attractions for the tourist economy, but gambling and the nightlife in the town of Jackson contributed significantly to the appeal of the valley as a vacation destination.

Considering the nonconforming uses that the Park Service faced in administering the Jackson Hole National Monument, the amended Barrett bill was probably the best compromise possible at the time. Only Rockefeller's desire to donate his lands east of the Snake River to the National Park Service was neglected although not completely overlooked. Testimony before the House Public Lands Committee revealed the state of Wyoming was willing to purchase some of his property in the northeast corner of the valley for elk preservation purposes.[40] Additionally, the compromise did not prohibit Rockefeller from donating his land east of the Snake River to the Fish and Wildlife Service.

If the opposing sides of the controversy were not completely satisfied with Barrett's amended legislation, they could at least hope for a settlement of the issue. H.R. 1330 contained some elements that were certain to be objectionable to the Park Service and the Bureau of the Budget. An example was Section 6 of the bill, which provided for tax compensation to Teton County. One might assume that Congressman Barrett would have utilized the language contained in Congressman Peterson's bill regarding this issue since the Interior Department and the Bureau of the Budget had already provided favorable reports on that proposed legislation, but Barrett's bill omitted Yellowstone National Park from the revenue base, and required the payments in lieu of taxes to be paid only from the receipts of fees collected in Grand Teton National Park. There was no declining payment schedule or limiting period for the payments as described in Congressman Peterson's bill. With Barrett's bill, the Park Service would assume, in perpetuity, the tax obligations for private lands it acquired within Teton County, whether through donation or by purchase. When the bill came up for a vote on July 21, it was objected to and passed over.[41] The bill was not dead, but its prospects for passage were considerably dimmed.

∼

The legislative hearings and articles printed in national publications had repeatedly discussed most of the non-conforming activities associated with the Monument controversy. In the latter

part of 1947, another issue materialized which provided additional evidence that the Monument boundaries were poorly considered at the time of the proclamation. The boundaries included portions of several mineral leases which, after the war, attracted oil and other extractive mineral exploration companies. Because the proclamation established the Monument "...subject to all valid existing rights ...," the Park Service was forced to consider this additional non-conforming use. The prospect of a national monument with oil derricks certainly fell short of the Park Service ideal. In reality, only a very small portion of the Monument was affected by these claims. The geology of the Teton National Forest provided more promising possibilities for the discovery of petroleum deposits than the glaciated valley floor. However, the mineral claims existed, and since Forest Service lands largely circumscribed the Monument and Park boundaries, the possibility existed for oil exploration and other mining activities to occur adjacent to and possibly within the Monument. Thus, the inadequately considered decision to establish the Jackson Hole National Monument had committed the Park Service to operating and managing a national monument with mineral exploitation as a sanctioned activity.

On August 30, 1947, Interior Secretary Krug signed a memorandum clarifying the conditions for oil and gas exploration in the Jackson Hole area. Essentially, the memorandum required an approved unit plan prior to exploration and drilling– the 1947 equivalent of an environmental impact statement and operating plan. The approval of a unit plan required a report from the Geological Survey indicating that lands identified in the plan contained structural conditions that would warrant a belief that oil or gas might exist in that area. Additionally, leases and unit plans had to "...contain a provision vesting in the Secretary of the Interior, or his duly authorized representatives, control over the rate of prospecting and development, including, in particular, the spacing of wells and such other conditions as may be deemed necessary in any case for the protection of the wildlife or scenic values within the area."[42]

Unnecessarily confusing was a paragraph which stated:

Prospecting and development under an approved unit plan shall not be permitted until all lands within the area are made subject to the unit plan unless a determination shall be made by the Secretary or his representative that the unit operator has made every reasonable effort to utilize all lands and the uncommitted land is insufficient in amount or so located that the orderly development of the unit area will not be adversely affected. If any part of the geological structure is located on Federal lands which are within the Jackson Hole National Monument, the Teton Wilderness Area, or which are otherwise unavailable for leasing, a unit plan for the remaining available acreage on the structure will not be approved unless the Geological Survey reports that oil or gas development, limited to the available lands, is in the bests interests of the United States. [43]*

～

Tourism again showed its economic value to the valley of Jackson Hole. Western national parks continued to experience record-breaking visitation in 1947. Grand Teton National Park recorded 144,261 visitors– an 8 percent increase over 1946. There was a notable increase in campers and trailers, as well as participation in naturalist hikes and museum visitation. Four mountaineering organizations held their annual expeditions in the Tetons and approximately 500 successful ascents were made on peaks within Grand Teton National Park. [44]

As an indicator of economic growth, largely attributable to tourism, the Jackson State Bank (the only bank in Jackson Hole at the time) had about $500,000 in deposits in 1929 when Grand Teton National Park was created. In 1947, deposits exceeded $2,000,000. The bank had one of the highest deposits to capital ratios for any bank in the nation. [45] In 1931, according to the earliest records available, there were 108 consumers of electrical power. By 1947, there were 560. In 1935, there were fewer than 250 telephones compared to 600 in 1947. [46]

During this period of economic growth, the number of cattle in the valley fluctuated. A variety of factors makes it impractical to judge the

Jackson Hole Historical Society and Museum 1992.4377.015
Ed Benson with his water powered generators.

Jackson Hole Historical Society and Museum 1998.0023.022
Benson's water powered electric generating plant provided the first electricity to the town of Jackson. It went online in January of 1921. He built a dam on Flat Creek to hold the water and ran a penstock (pipe) to the generator located closer to town. Benson also owned a hardware store on the east side of the town square.

*The above paragraph was submitted to several geologists and one company conversant with federal mineral leasing procedures for interpretation. While no one professed to understand the paragraph, the suspected translation was that, where a unit plan covered a geologic structure situated on both Forest Service and Monument lands, the operator had to utilize the Forest Service lands first, and if it was necessary, for valid operational reasons, to extend the operation onto Monument lands, it would be necessary for the Geological Survey to file a report stating that such activity within the Jackson Hole National Monument was in the national interest.

growth or decline of the cattle industry in Jackson Hole based merely on the number of livestock in the valley on one date as compared to another date. In the mid-1920s, market prices were low and ranchers either sold off more cattle in order to meet obligations or to reduce production costs for the winter and the following year. The market had begun to rebound, and herd sizes were expanding when, in 1929, the Depression forced cattle prices below the 1900 levels. Year to year climate conditions could also affect the number of cattle in the valley. A drought year might reduce the amount of hay that could be raised for winter feeding and force a rancher to sell off more animals than normal. Another factor making analysis of the cattle economy difficult by merely assessing herd size is the fact that Rockefeller's purchasing program had eliminated several of the large and quite a few of the smaller ranches. World War II created a strong demand for beef and leather encouraging ranchers to again expand their herds, although labor was in short supply. Finally, perhaps one of the most important determinants of a rancher's herd size in Jackson Hole related less to the amount of land available for grazing leases and more to the amount of land he owned suitable for raising hay for winter feed.

In 1929, the year Grand Teton National Park was created, Teton County assessment rolls indicated less than 7,000 head of cattle.[47] In 1936, after the Rockefeller purchases, Teton County recorded 10,838 head of cattle even though there were fewer ranchers. Just prior to the establishment of the Jackson Hole National Monument in 1943, records indicated there were 12,580 cattle in the valley.[48] By 1947, there were approximately 13,000 cattle in the valley.[49]* Over the decade, the cattle industry had experienced a steady if modest growth.

Jackson Hole Historical Society and Museum hs4191006

Although tourism was growing, cattle remained the primary economic force in the valley and the Monument's potential adverse effect on this aspect of life in Jackson Hole was real. (Above) Cattle from the southern ranches were driven over Teton Pass to the railroad at Victor, Idaho. (Below) Paul Miller (Hansen Ranch), Maurice Horn (Powderhorn Ranch), and Lloyd Van DeBurg (Snake River Ranch) check cattle cars loaded and ready to leave for Omaha.

Union Pacific Railroad Photo Jackson Hole Historical Society and Museum 2002.0015.085

*The above figures do not count calves because calves were not taxed and, thus, were not included on the assessment rolls for that period. Teton County no longer taxes cattle.

Some proponents of the Monument used these figures to justify the need to provide protection for the area included in the reserve. Opponents of the Monument did not discount the figures or the value of the increasing tourist economy but pointed out that under Forest Service management, the area in question had not been despoiled or altered in a way that would endanger the attractions of the area to visitors. They argued that if the Forest Service had not provided the appropriate protection for the area, the Park Service would not have found the area desirable for inclusion in a national park. From the opposition perspective, the primary difference was that the Forest Service accomplished this protection without disrupting other uses, while the Park Service sought to eliminate, in favor of a single use philosophy, other valuable economic endeavors important to the community, even while acknowledging those activities had not adversely impacted the scenic and wildlife values of the area. It was difficult for the Monument opponents to understand why it was necessary to destroy a viable economic institution for the philosophical enhancement of another industry (tourism) when it was evident both could, and had been able to, exist simultaneously.

The Monument controversy did not prevent the park rangers and their families from enjoying themselves.

Dog sleds provided winter travel for visiting neighbors.

Park Superintendent McLaughlin with a dance partner at a costume party.

Karl C. Allen Collection, Box 7, American Heritage Center, University of Wyoming (All photos)

Left: a tea party for ranger wives in the Frances Judge home. (L to R) Frances Judge, Davenport Esther Jepson, Helen Smith, Esther Allen, and Mardy Murie (standing). Right: Superintendent McLaughlin dancing with Helen Smith at one of the dance halls Rockefeller found so offensive when he visited the valley in 1927.

~

The *Jackson Hole Courier*, during the time span of this chapter, chronicled the passing of a pioneer generation. Numerous editions of the paper contained obituaries of men and women who had homesteaded in the Jackson Hole area before, or soon after, the turn of the century. They had entered the valley on horseback, in horse drawn wagons, or on snowshoes or skis. They survived most of their lives without electricity or indoor plumbing. They witnessed the construction of the first roads, the arrival of the automobile, the telephone, the radio, and the airplane. They experienced hardship, disaster, joy and satisfaction that few modern residents of the valley could imagine. Their legacy remains not only in their descendants but in the names attached to creeks, hills, and streets in the town of Jackson.

Among those settlers whose deaths were recognized by the *Courier* (and the year they came to the valley) were: Martin Henrie, 1897; Ben Sheffield, 1888; George Wilson and his wife, 1889; F. H. Sensenbach and his wife Elizabeth, 1913; Mrs. T. A. Moulton, 1910; Mrs. Emily Nelson Coe, 1902; Louis H. Joy, 1904; Butch Robinson, 1900; Joseph B. Heninger, 1900; John A. Bircher, 1897; John L. Eynon, 1905; John Christian Anderson, 1896; Effie Blair Wilson, 1893; Jennie Groch, 1902; William Lafferty, 1904; and Herbert G. Whiteman, 1896.

In addition to recognizing the deaths of Jackson Hole pioneers, the *Courier* also noted the passing of Gifford Pinchot, one of America's earliest conservationists, and William O. Owen, the man "officially" credited with the first ascent of the Grand Teton.

CHAPTER EIGHTEEN
1948 - 1949

As long as I am Secretary of the Interior there will be no boundary changes or area reductions in national parks or monuments except where the evidence is so powerful that even a blind man could see the desirability- and that's putting it pretty strong.

Julias A. Krug[1]
Secretary of the Interior
December 4, 1947

Much as I love it, sometimes I feel as if the only way you'll ever get Jackson Hole to work together is to rope us, hog-tie us, and pile us all up together so that we can't get away from each other. We've got everything there is, and heaven too, save for just one absolutely necessary thing- cooperation.

Struthers Burt[2]
February 19, 1948

It is difficult to see how 531 members of Congress can agree on an issue pertaining to one state when citizens of that state themselves cannot agree on what they want or think best.

Wyoming Eagle editorial[3]
April 1, 1948

Grand Teton National Park GRTE-00430_51-16E

Trailer campers at Jenny Lake campground, 1940s

375

On January 7, 1948, Senator Robertson introduced in the 80th Congress, 2nd Session, S. 1951, a companion bill to Congressman Barrett's compromise legislation to abolish the Jackson Hole National Monument. Robertson's bill was nearly identical to H.R. 1330. Both bills abolished the Monument and added the federal land west of the Snake River into Grand Teton National Park and the federal land east of the river into the Teton National Forest. Each bill recognized and protected all valid claims, leases, permits, and ownership of lands previously included in the Monument, provided for periodic renewal to the permit holder, his heirs, and assigns, and required the establishment of open rights-of-way to assure the movement of livestock when needed. Grazing leases appurtenant to privately owned land within the Monument boundaries would remain with the land until title to that land was transferred to the federal government by donation or purchase.

Both bills assured the authority for the state of Wyoming to tax personal property and improvements under private ownership within Grand Teton National Park as extended. The bills contained identical provisions for tax compensation to Teton County from revenues received from tourists entering Grand Teton National Park. Each bill prohibited the President from exercising the power granted by the Antiquities Act to change the status of lands established by the enactment of the legislation.[4] The only difference between the two bills was that Senator Robertson's bill made the east bank of the Snake River the east boundary of Grand Teton National Park while Congressman Barrett's bill added a 50-foot strip of the eastern river bank to the park boundary.

A news release regarding this legislation was issued from Senator Robertson's office in Washington describing the bill as a compromise measure offering a solution to the controversy in Jackson Hole. After an explanation of the elements of the bill Senator Robertson stated:

> *This bill offers a solution to a problem of long standing, and represents a compromise agreed upon by all those having a major interest in the controversy. I believe it is to the advantage to every inhabitant of*

Teton County, and to Wyoming as a whole. It would remove all obstacles to the full development of this magnificent area as a scenic wonderland and recreational center.[5]

The release prompted an editorial by Wilford Neilson in the *Courier* on January 15 questioning the purported benefits of S. 1951. First, Neilson had little faith the compromise proposed in the bill would solve, once and for all time, the controversy within the valley. He reminded his readers that Grand Teton National Park was created in 1929 as a result of a compromise approved by a Presidential Coordinating Commission and meetings with local interested parties and members of the United States Senate. That compromise and legislation had not eliminated controversy in the valley. Second, the editor doubted all interested parties had been consulted because there were too many sides to the issue at this point. Some people simply wanted the Monument abolished, some wanted the Monument to remain, and some wanted the Monument divided. There were probably other preferences not widely circulated within the valley whose proponents likely would not

United States Senate Historical Office [Public domain] via Wikimedia Commons

Edward Vivian Robertson (R)
1881-1963
Robertson served in the Third Battalion of the Welsh Regiment during the Second Boer War (1899-1902), and studied mechanical and electrical engineering prior to immigrating to the United States and Wyoming in 1912. He was elected to the U.S. Senate in 1942 and served one term.

be mollified by Senator Robertson's bill. Third, he maintained no compromise was possible until the disposition of Rockefeller's land was finally determined.[6] Typical of Neilson's style was the inclusion of four lines of verse, this time by Samuel Butler:

He that complies against his will,
Is of his own opinion still,
Which he may adhere to, yet disown,
For reasons to himself best known. *

The Interior Department issued an unfavorable report on S. 1951 on April 5, 1948, signed by Acting Secretary Chapman.[7] The report justi-

Department of Interior Photo [Public domain] via Wikimedia Commons
Oscar Littleton Chapman
1886-1978
Chapman would serve as the 34th U.S. Secretary of the Interior from December 1, 1949, to January 20, 1953. As Assistant Secretary of the Interior, he supported Truman's decision to recognize the state of Israel over the objections of the State Department and campaigned for Truman in the 1948 Presidential election. Secretary Krug did not support Truman, and Chapman was moved to the Secretary position when Krug resigned after Truman won the election.

fied the perpetuation of the Monument as established, for historic, scientific, and scenic reasons, but some of the arguments contained in this report were misleading or obviously untrue. Blatantly untrue was the report's statement that none of the lands the bill proposed for addition to Grand Teton National Park included Rockefeller's contemplated gift to the nation. In fact, 25,540 acres of the 33,000 acres Rockefeller proposed to donate were situated west of the Snake River and, thus, were included within the proposed new boundaries of Grand Teton National Park. The report also complained that only a token portion of the Monument, less than a quarter of the acreage, would be added to Grand Teton National Park with the vast majority being given to the Forest Service. This was a bit disingenuous in that the territory excluded by the bill from national park status included 8,360 acres of privately owned land not counting Rockefeller's property (7,460 acres) which the Monument encompassed but did not own. Also excluded from the park was 31,650 acres of Reclamation Service land and impounded water over which the Park Service had already ceded operational control, (see Chapter Sixteen),† nearly 1,300 acres of state-owned land, and 7,660 acres of public domain. There was also considerable acreage in the southeast portion of the Monument that had previously existed under the Fish and Wildlife Service jurisdiction for elk refuge purposes. The Park Service had already signed a memorandum of understanding vesting management of the lands south of the Gros Ventre River (13,000 acres) to the Fish and Wildlife Service (see Chapter Fifteen). When all totaled up, a substantial portion of the land (69,430 acres) the report lamented losing did not belong to the Park Service, was encumbered with leases providing for non-conforming uses, or was land for which the Park Service had already ceded management authority. Additionally, a considerable portion of

---

*From *Hudibras*, pt. III, canto III, l. 547.

†There is a disparity in acreage attributable to the Reclamation Service managed area. The Park Service sometimes mentions 21,000 acres for the Jackson Lake Reservoir and withdrawals in aid of the reclamation project. The surface of Jackson Lake, when full, is 25,530 acres. The total area of Reclamation Service authority and responsibility was 31,650 acres. The Park Service may have utilized the original lake surface in an attempt to mask or minimize the perceived significance of the "commercial waters" within the Monument from Congress, or to appease conservation groups such as the National Parks Association.

the land the Forest Service would gain through this bill was acreage they had previously administered and which had come under Park Service jurisdiction only because of the Executive Order creating the National Monument. This report from the Interior Department, because of its obvious inaccuracies, infers either a deliberate intent to mislead the Senate Committee or a failure to comprehend the ramifications of the legislation.

∽

On January 19, 1948, Congressman Barrett's compromise bill, H.R. 1330, again came up for a vote on the floor of the House. It was objected to a second time and stricken from the calendar.[8] H.R. 1330 originally had been placed on the House Suspension Calendar during the 1st Session of the 80th Congress. In the Senate, this is called the Unanimous Consent Calendar. The purpose of these calendars is to facilitate a quick passage or consideration of legislation that is non-controversial or of little interest to most of the legislators. No debate occurs on the floor. The delegates simply vote yes or no, and a single nay vote is sufficient to defer the bill's passage at that time. After the first objection, two options were available to Congressman Barrett regarding the future of the bill. The bill could remain on the Suspension Calendar, awaiting another vote

or be moved to a calendar that would take it to the floor for consideration in a more time-consuming and deliberative manner. The latter option would have required a simple majority for approval rather than unanimous consent. Barrett had elected to leave the bill on the Suspension Calendar. When the bill was called and objected to a second time in January 1948, it was stricken from the calendar. Barrett was then forced to push for its favorable consideration through the more laborious procedure.

The diminishing prospects for H.R. 1330 may have been the motivation for an increase in articles, speeches, and organizational resolutions concerning the bill in early 1948. Publicity opposing and supporting the Monument occurred more frequently in newspapers and magazines. While the editor of the *Courier* appeared to have a preference for the pro-Monument arguments, he reprinted articles presenting both sides of the controversy. Some of the commentaries were well-reasoned presentations of the issues that resulted in the author choosing to support one side or the other. Expectedly, there also were articles for both sides that vastly overstated or callously dismissed the adverse effects of the Monument on the people and the economy of Jackson Hole.

The most vitriolic and strident of the Monument's detractors were Teton County's state senator; local banker, Felix Buchenroth, Sr.; and Dr. Floyd Naegeli, the community's dentist. Exaggerated claims by either side were understandable for a short period following the Monument's establishment because there was a scarcity of information about the provisions of the proclamation. Five years after the fact, after three Congressional hearings (one of which was held in Jackson), numerous articles, press releases, and speeches, it was unlikely the populace of Wyoming was unaware of the facts concerning the controversy. Who, except the uninformed, would likely be swayed by Buchenroth's claims that 200 families would be forced from their homes or

Jackson Hole Historical Society and Museum bc0130

Monument controversy and legislative activity in Washington did not lessen the necessity of winter survival in Jackson Hole. Highway access was important. When a snowplow alone was not sufficient to open the road over Teton Pass, a small Caterpillar would pull the snowplow over the pass.

378

that 18,000 cattle would be eliminated from their grazing ranges? [9]   Documents presented at the 1947 House Public Lands Committee hearings, in Buchenroth's presence, showed 13,000 head of cattle in Jackson Hole with less than 8,000 head of cattle grazing in the Monument under 27 grazing leases.   Former Governor Leslie Miller's articles supporting the Monument did not lessen the heat of the controversy when he claimed the opposition was composed of only a few individuals with selfish motivations.   Local supporters of the Monument, in their letters and resolutions, recognized the problems the Monument posed for the cattlemen, the management of the elk herd, and the county from a loss of tax revenue.   Buchenroth's and Miller's positions seemed unreasonable at this point in the controversy.

Locally, neither Congressman Barrett's bill (H.R. 1330) nor Senator Robertson's bill (S. 1951) generated sufficient unity of thought on the issue to create an atmosphere of widespread support or compromise.   In February of that year, the Jackson Hole Chamber of Commerce did endorse the passage of the Barrett bill but suggested an amendment.   The business association preferred the eastern boundary of Grand Teton National Park be established along the west bank of the Snake River rather than 50 feet east of the river's eastern shoreline.[10]   The chamber also appealed to other commercial organizations in Wyoming communities to pass resolutions supporting both the Senate and House versions of the bill. This appearance of unity was quickly discredited when 35 of the 100 members signed a statement indicating they did not agree with the chamber's resolution and had not been polled for their opinions.   The officers of the Chamber of Commerce responded that the topic had been under discussion for five months, and the consensus had been that some type of compromise was needed to settle the issue.   The Barrett and Robertson bills were the only compromise proposals currently being considered, and the board acted in a way to accomplish the stated desire of the majority of the membership.[11]

Once again emotions flared, and there were threats by each side to boycott the other side's businesses and services.   Through the *Courier*, Wilford Neilson discouraged such action stating, *"It is recognized that a man will naturally pursue the course that to him the best welfare of his business interests dictates and that because he doesn't think alike with you on a controversial issue is little ground to sever business relations."* [12]

The Wyoming Game and Fish Commission joined the new round of publicity by releasing a statement indicating its position.   The commission did not officially support the proposed legislation, but they restated their concern regarding the state's right to exercise management authority over its wildlife and the need to control the elk population in Jackson Hole.   They indicated that one of two changes in the current situation would have to occur if the elk population was to be maintained at a level equal to the winter forage and supplemental feeding supplies available on the refuge.

1. The Monument boundary should be so modified as to permit the commission to control and manage the elk AS GAME ANIMALS and prevent the increase of their population beyond the carrying capacity of the refuge; or

Jackson Hole Historical Society and Museum p1991.3981.001

Political issues did not dampen the efforts of the community to develop a winter tourist economy.   Neal Rafferty constructed a platform upon which a four-wheel drive war surplus truck was driven, then blocked up with wheels off the ramp.   Ropes secured on the drive wheels allowed the construction of a rope tow for skiers on Teton Pass.

2. The park service regulations should be so modified as to permit hunting on the monument area, under the commission's management for the purpose of holding elk numbers below the critical levels of over-population.[13]

The commission believed it impractical to put enough hunters in the areas outside the Monument boundaries to accomplish the necessary reduction in the numbers of elk. Additionally, most of the traditional migration routes for elk moving down from the high country to the refuge traversed Monument lands. If one of the two conditions stated above were not accomplished, the elk would have to be slaughtered on the refuge to reduce their numbers.

Jackson Hole Historical Society and Museum P1958.0344.001

Jim Simpson and Bill Gardner in a typical hunting camp. Jim came to Jackson in 1890 and homesteaded the Red Rock Ranch on Crystal Creek.

As necessary as hunting within the Monument boundaries may have been to control the elk population, one aspect of this activity was perceived as distasteful. With the exception of the area north of the Buffalo River and north and east of Jackson Lake, the terrain of the Monument lands where this activity occurred was mostly sagebrush flats. Hunting in this area was widely considered a type of slaughter as undesirable as the suggestion that elk be shot after they reached the refuge. This area was called "the firing line" because hunters gathered beside the roads and shot at the elk on the

open flats as they migrated to the refuge. While the actual discharge of firearms was probably not as indiscriminate as most people believed, there was the likelihood of more wounded and maimed animals from this type of hunting because of the distances involved and the actions of a few hunters who simply fired into a herd rather than selecting a particular animal as a target. It is unlikely most residents of the valley at that time would have been considered anti-hunting, but this type of hunting was not regarded as sportsmanlike. Stimulated by the mental image of artist with their easels lining the roads and painting scenes of the valley, the locals referred disparagingly to road hunters as "gut-shot artists." Roughly 50 percent of the elk taken in Jackson Hole were shot within the Monument boundaries in this fashion.[14]

The dilemma posed by this aspect of the Monument controversy was essentially a choice between reducing the elk herd at the firing-line or reducing the herd by intentional slaughter on the refuge. Neither option held appeal for anyone except perhaps the road hunter. On the pro-Monument side, Olaus Murie expressed his distaste for either option but, if forced to choose between the two actions, preferred the reduction on the refuge as being the most humane for reducing the number of maimed animals.[15] Lester Bagley of the Wyoming Game Commission also stated his aversion to the firing line type of hunting but, if forced to choose, preferred that all hunting remain under the control of the state of Wyoming. He found the shooting of animals on feed grounds within the refuge more offensive.[16] Blurring the lines between the two sides were those who opposed both the Monument and the firing-line while recognizing the hunting prohibition policy of the Park Service would provide protection for the elk as they followed their migration routes to the refuge.

The Wyoming Game and Fish Commission's statement prompted former Governor Leslie Miller to attempt to broker a compromise. Miller privately arranged several meetings with Interior Department personnel and with Wyoming game officials. In these individual meetings, each group assented to several basic concepts and agreed to a meeting for their consideration.[17]

The basic plan called for the lands adjacent to and south of the Gros Ventre River to be vested with the Fish and Wildlife Service. The Wyoming Game and Fish Commission also wanted some of the lands along the Buffalo Fork River in the northeast corner of the valley to be excluded from the Monument because it contained two of the major elk migration routes. The Park Service would permit hunting on the east side of the Monument through regulations established in cooperation with the Wyoming Game and Fish Commission and the Fish and Wildlife Service. Hunting camps would be allowed along the eastern boundary of the Monument and in the north near Emma Matilda and Two Ocean Lakes and east of the Yellowstone-Moran highway. This would facilitate easier access for hunters to the area and possibly encourage a greater use of Forest Service lands for hunting. The reason the Park Service, rather than the Forest Service, was being asked to allow these facilities was that all the roads offering access to Forest Service lands in these areas were within the Monument. If the north-south

highway eventually was relocated to the east side of the Snake River, the Park Service would not interfere with hunter access or the transportation of animals taken on either Monument or Forest Service land. Cattle grazing and drifting rights would be protected, and a provision for the reimbursement of Teton County for lost tax revenue would be included.[18]

Park Service officials agreed to meet in Washington with representatives of the Fish and Wildlife Service and the Wyoming Game and Fish Commission. Governor Hunt gave his approval for the meeting but suggested Clifford Hansen be included to ensure the representation of the Jackson Hole livestock interests. If an agreement was obtained, it was intended that the Wyoming Congressional Delegation would be approached to see if the Barrett and Robertson bills could be amended to reflect the compromise agreed upon by the interested parties. This was considered a likely prospect because Barrett's bill, in its present form, had thus far failed to pass in the House. The meeting was set for April with the Wyoming Game Commission, Clifford Hansen, Senator O'Mahoney, Congressman Barrett, Secretary of Interior Krug, Park Service Director Drury, and Albert Day of the Fish and Wildlife Service. Leslie Miller was already in Washington when

American Heritage Center, University of Wyoming ah03138_1998
Visiting Grand Teton National Park during the winter was challenging.

he received word that the Wyoming people would not be attending the meeting. The reason Wyoming's representatives decided to cancel is not well documented, but Miller, in a letter to Wilford Neilson, stated that Governor Hunt requested Carl Jorgensen, the president of the Game and Fish Commission, travel to Jackson for the purpose of consulting with Teton County Senator Felix Buchenroth. Miller wrote that Buchenroth *"...flatly refused to agree or even to consider the program or any other proposal that would in any way deviate from the provisions of the pending Barrett or Robertson bills...."* [19] Because of the position taken by Buchenroth, Governor Hunt decided to postpone Wyoming's involvement in the Washington meeting, and, thus, this attempt to reach a compromise failed. Miller blamed Buchenroth's personal prejudice and political interference for the lost opportunity, and concluded:

I am convinced that had the agreement been carried out and had the committee gone down there where all consistently interested agencies would sit down at the same table and compromise their views as sensible men will do when face to face, an acceptable program could have been worked out in all its details, the problems with respect to the elk herd would have been settled to the satisfaction of all concerned, the rights and privileges of the stockmen fully protected, Teton County reimbursed for possible tax losses, and the controversy over the Monument eliminated in a manner agreeable to the people of Wyoming. [20]

The Jackson Hole chapter of the Izaak Walton League also attempted to produce a compromise for the Monument controversy. This was largely an effort to support former Governor Miller's initiative described above. Olaus Murie was successful in convincing some national conservation groups to support some adjustments to the Monument

boundaries, and the continuation of grazing and hunting rights, *"...so long as they do not thwart the purpose of the Monument."* [21] Because the Washington meeting negotiated by Miller did not occur, the required critical resolution of differences between the Park Service and the Wyoming Game and Fish Commission was never reached. Murie's efforts to align conservation organizations behind a compromise proposal rather than simply stand in opposition to the Barrett bill was doomed.

One can only speculate as to the probable acceptance or success of the proposed compromise attempted by Miller and Murie. Both men made a sincere effort to forge a solution to the problems, real or imagined, attendant to the establishment of the Jackson Hole National Monument. However, the compromise they sought did not provide for abolishing the Monument. Although the Monument had gained support within the valley since 1943, the opposition was still strong. And while a compromise was more acceptable in 1948 than it was in 1943, the continued existence of the Monument, established for reasons largely contrary to the specifications of the Antiquities Act, was emotionally unacceptable. The opposition by this time was willing to accept Clifford Hansen's 1943 compromise allowing an extension of Grand Teton National Park's boundaries to include portions of the Monument, but their acquiescence was still dependent upon the abolishment of the

Grand Teton National Park (unnumbered)

The 1940's equivalent of a fast food establishment was Getting's hamburger stand and gas station near Moran, 1948.

Monument. For this, reason Miller's and Murie's initiatives may not have held the potential of conflict resolution they believed was possible.

~

For the third year in a row, visits to Grand Teton National Park surpassed previous records. Superintendent McLaughlin indicated 152,770 tourists visited the Park in 1948– a 6 percent increase over the 1947 season.[22] Yellowstone National Park reported 1,013,531 visitors.[23] This was the first time in its 76 year history Yellowstone recorded more than a million tourists in a single season.

Accommodations in both Grand Teton and Yellowstone Parks were insufficient to meet demand. The Jackson Hole Chamber of Commerce maintained a list of locals who were willing to provide overnight housing for tourists unable to find commercial lodging. Yellowstone Park had overnight accommodations for 7,700 people while an average of 11,000 persons entered the Park daily during July and August.[24] It was common, during these busier months of the season, for people to sleep in their cars at turnouts or alongside the Park roads. The Parks reported considerable criticism from visitors regarding the lack of accommodations.

~

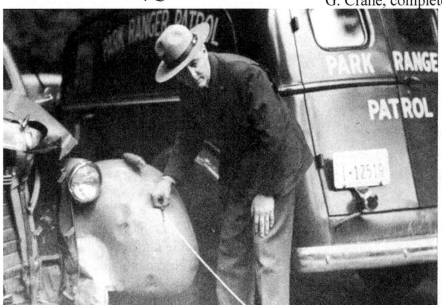

National Park Service, 20091209124952

The increase in park visits with its attendant increase in private automobile travel provided park rangers with an additional task. Accident investigation became another skill incumbent on the ranger force.

Although the Monument controversy was a campaign issue in the 1948 elections, Teton County tended to vote along party lines. The August 17 primary elections in Teton County demonstrated the relative strength of the opposition. Felix Buchenroth ran for re-election to the Wyoming Senate against two candidates who expressed their support for the Monument. He won the primary by a comfortable margin and stated, *"My actions in the last four years have been based on the expressed will of the people of Jackson's Hole, and the vote on August 17 assured me that the people approved of my actions."* [25]

At the November general elections, which had the largest voter turnout in the county's history, Buchenroth defeated his Democrat challenger, W. J. Wallace, 699 to 556. Wallace campaigned on a platform of maintaining the Monument as President Roosevelt established it. Within Teton County, Dewey was favored over Truman, Senator Robertson over his challenger Governor Hunt, and Congressman Barrett over L. G. Flannery. The Wyoming electorate returned Congressman Barrett to the U.S. House of Representatives and chose Lester Hunt over E. V. Robertson for the U.S. Senate. Wyoming state law provided that the Secretary of State, A. G. Crane, complete Hunt's term as governor.[26]

Nationally, the Democrats regained control of both the House and the Senate. Congressman Barrett, now a minority member of the House, lost some of his power to push his legislation. H.R. 1330 failed to pass the House and died at the close of the 2nd Session of the 80th Congress.

~

With the controversy still alive and all attempts at a compromise extinguished, the Dude Ranchers Association offered their initiative. At their annual gathering in November of that year, they suggested that the state of Wyoming and Congress jointly appoint a committee of all interested parties to work out a compromise to settle the controversy. It was their position that the lands encompassed in the Monument should be divided between Grand Teton National Park, the National Elk Refuge, and the Teton National Forest. While the group did not provide detailed proposals for boundaries, they did express the opinion that the Snake River should be protected from the possibility of summer home development which would limit previously available public access for fishing. If possible, they thought the divisions should be drawn in a way to exclude private property east of the Snake River from being encompassed by any one federal agency. These considerations, as well as other details relating to regulations and acknowledgment of rights, could be negotiated by the committee.[27]

This was not a dissimilar initiative from former Governor Miller's endeavor, except that Miller proposed to keep the Monument and achieve a regulatory compromise while the dude ranchers proposed a distribution of property to appropriate agencies eliminating the need for the Monument as a separate entity. At least one aspect of the Dude Ranchers' proposal seemed improbable. A boundary line for each agency excluding private property was probably impossible. The private lands not purchased by Rockefeller constituted a patchwork of inholdings. Even if those lands had existed with contiguous boundaries, the resulting federal parameters would have been extremely irregular and enforcement of the respective agency's policies difficult at best. Other concerns of the Dude Ranchers, such as a prohibition of summer home leases along the Snake River, could easily be accomplished with regulatory restrictions by whichever agency was ultimately assigned jurisdiction.

Realistically, the issue of the continued existence of the Monument as a separate entity should not have been a stumbling block for anyone concerned with a compromise as long as a considerable portion of the area was included in Grand Teton National Park. Numerous documents and testimony, previously quoted, indicated the Park Service viewed the Monument as an extension of the Park. There is no evidence the Park Service ever contemplated assigning a separate superintendent and staff to the Monument with responsibilities attendant to the management of the area in accordance with the intent of the Antiquities Act and discernable from Grand Teton National Park. Management of the area had been placed with the superintendent of the Park. With the exception of lip service to the historic and scientific aspects of the area, presented primarily to defend the use of the Antiquities Act, the Park Service had never demonstrated substantial interest in these assets in the Jackson Hole area. From the Monument's establishment, Congress prohibited the use of Interior Department funds for the management of the area, so there is no way to know what actions or activities the Park Service might have initiated in this regard.

Considering some of the proposed compromises contemplated for extending Grand Teton National Park's boundaries to include an appreciable portion of the Monument, while eliminating the majority of the non-conforming uses, the question arose as to why the Park Service refused to utilize these proposals as a basis for further discussions. Other than the consideration of accommodating Rockefeller's proposed gift, the Park Service defense

Jackson Hole Historical Society and Museum 1992.3136.041

Personal power boat cruising on Jenny Lake was a popular activity that is no longer tolerated by the National Park.

of the Monument as a separate entity may have had its strongest basis in the fear that the abolishment of the Monument would create an undesirable precedent regarding future monuments. If this was true, the position of the Park Service was not appreciably different from the opposition faction that required the Monument be abolished as a matter of principle.

～

The controversy in 1949 continued to focus more on the hunting issue rather than grazing. The Park Service had pursued no action to prohibit hunting because of their appropriation restrictions, but the state of Wyoming still feared the loss of control of the elk herd if some adjustment to the boundaries of the Monument or Park Service policy were not accomplished. The relationship between the two government entities deteriorated when the Park Service released a report indicating very few elk traversed the Monument during their biannual migration.[28] The report ignored research conducted by the state of Wyoming and the Fish and Wildlife Service and attempted to justify a position that hunting was not necessary on Monument lands.

Beginning with the 1942 season, the Game and Fish Commission had conducted extensive surveys of elk migration routes with game biologists camped day and night in the areas where elk traditionally crossed the Snake and Buffalo Fork Rivers. The state research indicated 68.6 percent of the elk wintering in Jackson Hole utilized the Monument during their migration to the Refuge. Additionally, the state game check stations recorded 23,540 elk killed in Jackson Hole over the subsequent seven-year period with 11,024 (47 percent) having been taken within the Monument's boundaries.[29] Obviously, not all elk entering the Monument were taken by hunters so the actual number of elk crossing into the Monument would be considerably greater than the number killed. Lester Bagley, of the Game Commission, indicated the Park Service had rejected both options for a solution suggested by the Commission and *"...continues to ignore a very real problem which must be faced and solved ...."* He also stated:

Jackson Hole Historical Society and Museum hs4269001
(L to R) Wyoming Governor Crane, Teton County Senator Felix Buchenroth, and Rep. John Wilson.

The problem certainly is brought no nearer to solution by surveys which find that few elk trail across the monument. Not when the record shows clearly that during the last seven years 47 per cent of the elk killed in Jackson Hole were taken on Monument territory.[30]

～

By the spring of 1949, the recurring restrictions on the Interior Department appropriations for the Jackson Hole National Monument had become so common the *Courier* no longer reported it. When the 1950 fiscal year Interior appropriations bill passed the House without the restrictive amendment, it was reported by a number of newspapers in the West. Congressman Barrett asked for the restriction, but the bill passed the House without its inclusion.[31] The *Denver Post* also noted the House version of the appropriations bill and counseled that previous restrictions on development of the Monument had obstructed the orderly advancement of the tourist industry in Jackson. The article suggested the absence of the amendment indicated *"...peace is in sight."*[32]

Optimism presumed by the House version of the appropriations bill was premature. Senator O'Mahoney again inserted his restrictive amendment in the Senate bill, and the Conference Committee consented. The Interior Department appropriations bill (Public Law 350) for the 1950 fiscal year (beginning July 1, 1949) again restricted the use of funds for the Jackson Hole National Monument.[33] Although Park Service Director Drury testified before the House Appropriations Committee in support of funding the Monument, there is evidence to indicate the Park Service subsequently requested Senator O'Mahoney attach his amendment to the Senate version of the appropriations bill. The reason for this reversal will be explained shortly.

∾

A meeting to negotiate a compromise regarding the Monument, such as that recommended by the Dude Ranchers Association and attempted by former Governor Leslie Miller the previous year,

was held in Washington on April 13-15, 1949. Senator O'Mahoney chaired the meeting with 22 people from various organizations and agencies assembled for the conference.*

At three p.m. on April 13, the group gathered in the Senate Appropriations Committee Room. Senator O'Mahoney called Clifford Hansen to present the position of the people of Wyoming. Hansen began by suggesting everyone try to forget past differences and start anew with the goal of reaching a compromise. He presented three issues most important to the people of Jackson Hole. First, the ownership and management of the Jackson Hole elk herd. Second, a guarantee

Parthenia Stinnett Collection, Jackson Hole Historical Society and Museum bc0103

Clifford Hansen and his mother Sylvia on a cattle drive in Jackson Hole, 1920s

---

*Among those attending were the three members of Wyoming's Congressional Delegation; Chiles Plummer, representing Governor Crane; John Loomis, Carl Jorgensen, T. S. Taliaferro, III, R. E. MacLoud, and Lester Bagley, all representing the Wyoming Game and Fish Commission; Felix Buchenroth, Clifford Hansen, Lloyd Van Deburg, and Nathan Resor, from Jackson; Oscar Chapman, Under Secretary of Interior; Arthur Demaray and Conrad Wirth of the Park Service; Albert Day of the Fish and Wildlife Service; Leslie Miller and Harold Fabian of the Jackson Hole Preserve, Incorporated; C. H. Gutterman representing the Wildlife Management Institute; and Carl Shoemaker of the National Wildlife Federation.[34]

of the rights of existing lease and permit holders on lands included in the Monument. Third, the tax problem. He then presented a nine-point plan agreed upon by the Teton County Commissioners, the Wyoming Game and Fish Commission, and the Wyoming Governor.

The points were:

1. Abolish the Jackson Hole National Monument.

2. Add to the Teton National Park that part of the Jackson Hole National Monument lying west of the west bank of the Snake River,* as outlined in Section 2 of H.R. 1330 of the 80th Congress.

3. Grant consent of the United States to Wyoming to tax improvements on private lands within the area described in Section 2 of H.R. 1330.

4. Incorporate balance of Monument lands into Teton National Forest, with following provisions:

(a) All Federal Lands in said area south of Grovont and east of present highway may be added to elk refuge.

(b) No mineral development in said area.

(c) Wyoming Game and Fish Commission shall have exclusive dominion and control over hunting wild game in said area.

(d) Provision shall be made to protect scenic value of said area not inconsistent with above provisions.

5. Adequate provision for continuance of present grazing rights on Jackson Hole National Monument, and right to trail across lands in Subdivision 4 during spring and fall of the year.

6. Provision for reimbursement for loss of taxes to Teton County from fees collected each year from visitors to Grand Teton National Park, if sufficient, and the balance, if any, from fees collected from visitors to Yellowstone National Park.

7. Provision that the President may not exercise authority under Antiquity Act to change status of lands as established by this act.

8. Cancellation of Executive Orders on lands described above to the extent of inconsistency of provisions hereof.

9. All provisions of law inconsistent with the provisions of the Act are hereby repealed to the extent of such inconsistency.[35]

biography.congress.gov [Public domain] via Wikimedia Commons

Senator Clifford P. Hansen (R)
1912 - 2009

Hansen was the most visible leader of the opposition to the Jackson Hole National Monument. However, it was Hansen's compromise proposal that moved the controversy to a successful mediation and settlement. Hansen would eventually earn acclaim as one of Wyoming's most popular political leaders, serving one term as Governor and two terms as a United States Senator. He resigned his position as Senator several days before his term expired allowing Governor Hershler, a Democrat, time to appoint Alan Simpson, a Republican, to complete the term. Simpson had won the Senate seat Hansen was vacating, and his 11th-hour appointment to the Senate moved him ahead of other freshman Senators in seniority. This was orchestrated to provide Wyoming with stronger representation in Congress.

---

*The "west bank of the Snake River" is inconsistent with Section 2 of H.R. 1330 which specified the east bank of the Snake River plus 50 feet. Either Hansen misstated the boundary, or this is a mistake in typing the Interior Department memorandum from which this information is cited.

Secretary Chapman indicated he could agree to the first item depending on the boundaries eventually agreed upon for the extension of Grand Teton National Park. He also thought all the other points could be agreed to without much trouble except items two and four. He stated he definitely would not agree to a transfer of land from the Monument to the Forest Service.[36]

After all the attendees had been provided an opportunity to present their views, a working committee was established to review the suggestions and draft a compromise proposal for presentation to the entire group. This group was composed of Clifford Hansen, Lester Bagley, Carl Jorgensen, Albert Day, Leslie Miller, and Conrad

National Park Service

Conrad L. Wirth
1899-1993

Wirth earned a degree in landscape gardening from Massachusetts Agricultural College (now the University of Massachusetts). He joined the Park Service as an assistant director for Land Planning in 1931. He is credited with the successful implementation of the Civilian Conservation Corps programs for federal, state and local parks during the Roosevelt administration. Wirth would become the sixth National Park Service Director in 1951. He may be best remembered for his "Mission 66" project, a ten year, one billion-dollar effort to revitalize the deteriorating infrastructure in the national parks in time for Service's 50th anniversary. He left the Park Service in 1964 when he lost favor with Secretary of Interior Stewart Udall.

Wirth. They met all day on the 14th and until mid afternoon of the 15th. Several drafts were generated, analyzed, and rewritten. Conrad Wirth noted there was considerable *"...bickering, talking, and compromising all the time."* He further stated, *"I will say, however, that it was conducted in a very pleasant manner, personalities were left entirely out of it, and very little of the back history of the controversy was brought out."* [37]

The special working committee had little trouble agreeing to a compromise position on most of the elements of the nine-point proposal presented by Clifford Hansen. The two difficult issues concerned boundary adjustments and game management issues. The committee dealt with easy compromises first.

Item number three, providing the right of the state of Wyoming to tax private property and improvements embraced within the current Monument boundaries, or Grand Teton Park boundaries as may be extended, was accepted. This right should never have been in doubt as the state had never been denied such authority within the Monument or in Grand Teton National Park. The issue may have loomed because of the special situation in Yellowstone National Park. The state collected sales tax in Yellowstone but not property tax, because the Park predated the inclusion of Wyoming into the Union.[38]

Item five, the grazing provision, was also agreed to easily. The right to graze and trail cattle as provided by President Roosevelt's proclamation and Secretary of Interior Ickes' policy statement was not necessarily the same thing as allowing grazing and drifting in a way beneficial to the herd. In other words, the Park Service believed they had accommodated the livestock interests by stating a willingness to allow grazing, but the ranchers needed to be assured the policies of the Park Service would sanction the activity in such a way as to avoid detriment to the herd. For instance, a single cow might be moved from its home ranch to a grazing allotment in seven days, where a herd of several hundred cows with calves might require 20 to 30 days. Within a herd, some animals will be stronger, younger, older, or healthier than others. Members of a herd move at different speeds. A number of such details specifically relating to cattle operations were discussed by the committee. The compromise on this issue agreed not just to a guarantee of a right or privilege but rather to the clarification of the intent of the policy.

An additional aspect of item five concerned the grazing rights of ranchers who owned property within the Monument. Again this involved a clarification of intent. Where previous Park Service policy had assured these rights to the owner and his or her "immediate family, heirs and assigns," the committee agreed these leases should be guaranteed as long as the property remained in private ownership. This eliminated any legal wrangling over the meaning of the term "assigns" or confusion as to who constituted "immediate family."

Another private land/grazing issue concerned ranchers who owned land both within and outside the boundaries of the Monument. The problem revolved around the Park Service policy of associating cattle that grazed in their domain with specific privately owned land also within their boundaries. That is, a rancher whose land was within the boundary of the Monument would be allowed to continue to utilize his grazing permits within the Monument in perpetuity, but, a rancher with land, both inside and outside the Monument, and with grazing permits in the Monument was not provided perpetuity of those rights. Ranchers in this situation did not necessarily associate a particular cow with a particular piece of land. It was of no great concern to the cattleman if a particular cow wintered on the upper ranch in 1947 and on the lower ranch in 1948. The current wording of the statements of policy regarding grazing in the Monument did not accord ranchers with multiple properties the same consideration as other landowners within the Monument. The committee agreed the Park Service should treat ranchers in this circumstance the same as those whose sole property was situated within the Monument, as long as the number of cattle grazed on that specific permit did not increase.[39]

Item six related to the compensation of Teton County for the lost revenue that would

Grand Teton National Park GRTE-00430_1364
Park Ranger Elt Davis stocking fish in String Lake

For much of the history of the Park Service, it was common practice to stock lakes and streams with fish as an additional attraction for visitors. Such activities are no longer considered appropriate by the National Park Service.

result from Park Service acquisition, by whatever means, of taxable property and improvements within the Monument area. The Park Service had indicated its approval of a solution to this problem as expressed in Congressman Peterson's bill, H.R. 3035. However, most of the committee members preferred the language contained in Congressman Barrett's bill, H.R. 1330. The difference between the two legislative provisions was discussed previously, but briefly, the Barrett language required the Park Service to pay, in perpetuity, the full amount of taxes assessed on the property for the year in which it was acquired rather than for a limited number of years on a declining scale.[40]

Item seven prohibiting the president from exercising the authority of the Antiquities Act to change the status of lands established by legislation consummating the compromise yielded little debate. Conrad Wirth noted that once an area is established by an act of Congress only Congress could change its status.* Nevertheless, the committee agreed legislation implementing

*This condition may seem to be a frivolous concern on the part of the Jackson Hole residents, but their concern was reasonable. The proclamation creating the Jackson Hole National Monument included land previously described, designated, and established as part of the National Elk Refuge by an act of Congress in 1912. If Wirth's opinion was true, then an argument could be made that the proclamation was illegal on the grounds that it incorporated into the Monument lands previously designated and established by an act of Congress.

the compromise should contain language prohibiting any additional extensions of national park or monument areas in Teton County, except as expressed by the U.S. Congress.[41]

Item eight pertained to the cancellation of the previous Executive Orders affecting the area. A discussion of this issue resulted in agreement but limited the intent to those withdrawals made in support of proposed national park, monument, or other recreational area legislation.

The last item which stated *"All provisions of law inconsistent with the provisions of this Act are hereby repealed to the extent of such inconsistency,"* was just boilerplate language often attached to proposed bills to avoid conflict adjudication with previously enacted legislation. The committee accepted this element without discussion.

The working committee agreed rather easily to exclude the lands in the southeast section of the Monument and transfer that acreage to the Fish and Wildlife Service for elk refuge purposes. Leslie Miller recommended the area east of the Snake River and south of an east-west line just north of Blacktail Butte as the northern boundary of this exclusion. Both Clifford Hansen and Albert Day agreed that the inclusion of the Mormon Row area of private land was not appropriate for the Elk Refuge. The compromise provided for the land east of the Snake River and south of the Gros Ventre River or south of an east-west line south of Blacktail Butte be transferred to the Fish and Wildlife Service.[42] A small area in the northeast section of the Monument along the Buffalo Fork River was designated to be excluded and returned to the Forest Service. It is a little surprising that a strident debate regarding the Snake River as the eastern boundary line for the park was not recorded. Wirth's memorandum to the director indicates the working committee accepted the boundaries of the Monument as established, with the exception of the two exclusions described above. In addition to the boundary changes, the working committee decided the name of the park would be changed to Jackson Hole - Teton National Park.

The game management issue was not as easily resolved. The compromise, as eventually accepted, provided in some respects very specific directions while some of the wording left the intent open to possible interpretation by both sides. The agreement advanced a possible resolution to the problem couched in face-saving language. The state of Wyoming refused to relinquish its authority over the elk, and the Park Service would not abdicate its policy regarding protection of wildlife or any other values attendant to national parks. The eventual agreement provided for the creation of a five-member advisory committee to

Jackson Hole Historical Society and Museum 2005.0023.016

Jackson Hole Historical Society and Museum p1992.4200.001

Jackson Hole Historical Society and Museum 1993.4821.001

As new technologies reached the valley, Verba Lawrence, the postmistress at Moran, traded her dog team for a home-made snowmobile and then eventually for an automobile to travel from her home at the AMK Ranch to the post office.

determine when, if, and how many elk should be eliminated from the herd as they traversed Park Service land. The committee would be composed of the Wyoming Game and Fish commissioner, the director of the National Park Service, the director of the Fish and Wildlife Service, the chief of the U.S. Forest Service, and a fifth person, who would serve as chairman, appointed by the President and agreeable to the governor of Wyoming. Each of the involved agencies would present their data to the advisory committee and that committee, having convened between February 1 and April 1, would make recommendations back to the agencies specifying the appropriate action for the coming year. The state of Wyoming preferred the area east of the Snake River be opened for public hunting whenever a reduction program was authorized, but the Park Service wanted hunting to be limited to the goal of reducing the herd by just the number of animals specified by the advisory committee. The Park Service did not want the word "hunting" used in the language of the agreement, and proposed the word "reduction." In the interest of reaching a compromise, both words were included, and hunting would be limited to a predetermined number of individuals. If the Advisory Committee recommended a herd reduction, the Wyoming Game and Fish Commission and the Secretary of the Interior would issue joint regulations providing for the *"...controlled and managed reduction hunting."* The state of Wyoming could authorize controlled and managed hunting while the Park Service could sanction a controlled and managed reduction program. The advisory committee would arbitrate any conflict arising from the joint regulations.[43]

This compromise allowed the Wyoming Game and Fish Commission to maintain it had not relinquished management authority for the Jackson Hole elk herd to the federal government. Neither had they abdicated the state's responsibilities to its wildlife. Rather, they were acting upon reasoned recommendations received from a knowledgeable advisory committee. The Park Service was not conceding its responsibilities concerning wildlife protection to the state of Wyoming. Neither had they abandoned their "no hunting" policy. Instead, they were cooperating

in a management program recommended by a multi-agency advisory committee. Additionally, the Park Service decided to require another procedural hoop. Individuals receiving a hunting license from the state of Wyoming for Park Service land would become temporary unpaid park employees, charged with the specific duty of reducing the elk herd by one animal while

Jackson Hole Historical Society and Museum bc 0254
From the earliest tourists in the 1800s to the newest visitor, fishing has been one of the premier attractions of Jackson Hole.

Jackson Hole Historical Society and Museum 2010.0079.047

adhering to whatever rules and regulations were specified by the Secretary of the Interior pursuant to the accomplishment of that job.* In other words, hunters authorized to pursue game within the park became unpaid rangers with an extremely restrictive job description.

At four p.m. on April 15 the group that gathered in Washington reconvened in the Senate Interior and Insular Affairs Committee Room to review the working committee's compromise document. While some of the group still maintained concerns on some of the issues, a consensus was obtained, and the Wyoming Congressional Delegation agreed to construct legislation which would incorporate the compromises negotiated by the committee. Congressman Barrett was not enthusiastic about the document preferring the provisions of his bill (H.R. 1330), but he did agree to support the new legislation if all parties agreed this compromise was best.

It was at this point that the Park Service decided it might be appropriate to have Senator O'Mahoney attach his restrictive amendment on the 1950 appropriations bill. They reasoned that should funding be permitted for the Monument prior to the enactment of this compromise legislation; they would be impelled by policy to enforce their prohibition on hunting in the area. Such an action would engender harsh feelings in Wyoming and possibly cause the disintegration of the compromise just mediated. With a resolution of the controversy so close at hand, it seemed advisable to maintain the status quo regarding the Jackson Hole National Monument.[44]

❧

Although funds for the Monument continued to be withheld, the Wyoming Congressional Delegation actively pursued funding for other projects in the Jackson Hole area. The Jackson airport received $160,000 for improvements to the terminal building and to pave the runway and apron.[45] Senator Hunt worked to increase the Interior Department's appropriations for highway maintenance in Jackson Hole. Considering his history of opposing Park Service activities in the valley, his efforts in this regard appeared to be contradictory initially. Hunt was primarily concerned with the deterioration of the Yellowstone-Moran highway. This road had received little attention and was a deterrent to travel between Yellowstone National Park and Jackson Hole. Testifying before the House Appropriations Committee, Hunt quoted a letter he had received while governor of Wyoming from a U.S. Senator who had visited both parks. The letter stated in part:

I traveled this road last summer and can testify that it is in miserable condition. In fact, it is hardly a road at all. It could barely be entitled to the name of a trail. I hope something can be done to improve the entrance to the Park from Moran. It will increase tremendously the travel between the two parks. It results in many Yellowstone Park visitors entering and leaving by another route than through the southern gateway.[46]

Jackson Hole Historical Society and Museum 2003.0073.049

Harold Fabian addressed the group gathered for the dedication of the restored Menor's Ferry. The Jackson Hole Preserve, Inc. paid for the construction of the replica ferry.

---

*Currently, Park policy prohibits the discharge of a firearm within the boundaries of a national park by anyone except a federal officer. The Park Service now cites this rule to justify this procedural requirement. However, at the time of the compromise, this was not an issue. The Park Service never mentioned this consideration and seemed more concerned with the appearance of having maintained the purity of their ideology than with the actual solutions to problems of species overpopulation. Another example of this attitude was the hundred-year policy of fire suppression that ignored the natural role of fire in the forests culminating in the massive and expensive Yellowstone fires of 1988.

Although both Grand Teton and Yellowstone Parks had registered record-breaking visitation during the previous three years, the south approach, with its spectacular views of Jackson Lake and the Teton Mountains, was the third most utilized of Yellowstone's entrances. Regardless of the Monument controversy, Senator Hunt recognized the value of the tourist industry, and he was endeavoring to remove, or remedy, an obstacle to travel between the two areas.

~

While the National Park Service was unable to allocate funds for activities within the Monument area, the Jackson Hole Preserve was not similarly restricted. Under the direction of Harold Fabian, a replica of the original Menor's Ferry was constructed and dedicated in August of 1949, and a museum established in the log structure that had been Menor's store. This effort evolved into a community affair. The dedication ceremony was the major social event of the year. Jackson Hole residents, regardless of their position on the Monument, contributed to the museum's collection. Among the interesting donated items was a buggy from Clifford Hansen, a Deadwood stage and white top (Conestoga wagon) by John Abbink of the 3–H Ranch, and an original Yellowstone Park stage by Irving Corse of the Bar BC Ranch. The event was covered by radio, film, and print news media.[47]

~

The trend for increased visitation to the northwest Wyoming national parks continued in 1949. Yellowstone National Park recorded 1,135,516 visitors reflecting an 11.8 percent increase over 1948.[48] Grand Teton Park travel increased by 9 percent with 166,613 visitations. Senator Hunt's effort to provide funds for the improvement of the Yellowstone-Moran highway was successful, but as the appropriations would not be available until July of 1950, travel through the south entrance remained the third most utilized by the public. The 1949 season marked Grand Teton National Park's 20th anniversary, and its popularity was rapidly exceeding the capacity of both its facilities and staff. The Park had only two campgrounds and,

Jackson Hole Historical Society and Museum 2003.0073.051

Above: John Abbink's Conestoga wagon crossing on the restored Menor's Ferry at the 1949 ferry dedication ceremony.
Below: Menor's general store on the west side of the Snake River before the Snake River Land Company restoration. The restored building is in the background in the top photograph.

Rockefeller Archive Center H.P Fabian photo, Series 1030, SRLC scrapbook.

Grand Teton National Park GRTE-00430_49-86A
Valley residents donated examples of transportation common to Jackson Hole during its early settlement for the Menor's Ferry Museum.

according to Superintendent McLaughlin, those were filled beyond their designed capacity with people turned away every night from June 20 through Labor Day weekend. The Grand Teton was climbed by 291 people that year and on occasion, a single ranger might have as many as 100 people show up for a naturalist hike.[49] The popularity of the Park was creating problems not foreseen by even the most farsighted of the early pro-park supporters. The valley simply did not contain adequate accommodations for the numbers of people who wanted to visit the area, and this situation was not likely to abate. Additional lodging facilities were constructed each year after the war, but the demand continued to exceed supply. One of the problems with lodge and motel

Carl Blaurock Photo: Jackson Hole Historical Society and Museum
p1958.0347.001

Albert Ellingwood on the NE Ridge of Mt. Moran, 1924.

Early supporters of protection for Jackson Hole and the Tetons undoubtedly recognized the economic attraction of recreational endeavors such as camping, hiking, fishing, hunting, skiing, and guest ranches. They probably did not anticipate the attraction of the mountains to climbers. In 1949, the Grand Teton was climbed by 291 people. During the 1955 season, there were 1,727 recorded ascents. Today, the activity is so popular a reservation is required to ascend that peak. In the photo above, the climber is alternately identified by some sources as Fritiof Fryxell.

development was that the facilities would most likely be utilized for only a few months each year. Jackson Hole was still a single season attraction. The investment required to construct a facility that might be filled for only two or three months was not easily justifiable. Thus, the tourist accommodation problem was difficult to solve. Superintendent McLaughlin predicted, *"The traveling public is just beginning to discover the Tetons, and every indication points to even greater future visitation and public use of the Park."* [50]

~

October 1949 witnessed the resolution of another Jackson Hole controversy. The negotiations between Wyoming and Idaho regarding water allocation from the Snake River reached a settlement. In June 1948, Congress passed an act (62 Stat. 294) permitting a treaty between the two states on this issue. In October 1949, the Snake River Compact was signed by representatives from Idaho, Wyoming, and R. J. Newell, a U.S. Government representative, and it was subsequently ratified by Congress. The Compact was an amply complicated document, but in essence, it provided Wyoming with 4 percent of the Snake River flow as measured at a point near the Wyoming-Idaho border. Domestic and agricultural use of the water was given precedent over all other potential uses, such as power generation and recreation. The Jackson representatives on the commission who negotiated the compromise were J. G. Imeson, Clifford Hansen, and Lloyd Van Deburg.[51]

~

In November 1949, Julius Krug resigned as Secretary of the Interior, and Oscar Chapman replaced him. Chapman was appointed assistant secretary in the Interior Department by President Roosevelt in 1933. He joined the Navy at the beginning of the war and returned to the Interior Department in 1946 as undersecretary. Senator O'Mahoney, upon hearing of the new appointment, remarked, *"A marvelous bit of news ..."* and stated:

> *Chapman probably understands the problems of the West better than any other man in the Department of Interior. He received a*

deserved promotion. I have the utmost confidence in him and know that other western senators share my feeling towards him.[52]

At the time, Krug's resignation was considered to be sudden and unexplained. Chapman, in a press interview in November 1949, stated he did not know why Secretary Krug resigned.[53] However, in an oral history interview conducted by Jerry N. Hess in September 1972, Chapman provided insight into this event. According to Chapman, the problem resulted from Krug's unwillingness to aid or participate in Truman's 1948 re-election campaign. Chapman stated Krug had been unavailable to the administration and the Interior Department office through much of the campaign choosing that time to make a tour of wildlife refuges. Krug believed Truman could not be re-elected and hoped to retain his position, or receive a more prestigious position, in Dewey's administration.[54]

The question remains as to why Truman waited a year to request Krug's resignation. Chapman believed Truman wanted to replace the secretary at the end of 1948, but he delayed for a reason not known to the public. Chapman explained that Krug was under investigation because of a lawsuit seeking repayment of a loan obtained during the time he had served as chairman of the War Production Board. The loan was made by a textile mill owner who allegedly received "favors" in the form of priority position for obtaining materials for his plant from the War Production Board. The fact that Krug had paid back $750,000 of the loan provided the appearance of him having used his position to obtain the loan and raised questions regarding the propriety of the "favors" the mill owner may have received. According to Chapman, Truman decided to wait for the results of the investigation and use it as justification for requesting Krug's resignation.[55]

In mid-December 1949, the lands purchased by John D. Rockefeller, Jr. in Jackson Hole were transferred from the Jackson Hole Preserve, Inc. to the United States Government. The deeds to 33,562 acres of land were presented to Oscar Chapman in a ceremony in Washington. Chapman stated:

It is a matter of great good fortune to present and future generations that Mr. Rockefeller's interest was enlisted during the middle 20's in the preservation of these lands for public use, and that he was willing to devote his funds so generously to their acquisition.

The lands were acquired with the sole purpose of turning them over to the Federal Government for national park purposes. Transfer of the lands is taking place at this time because it is felt that the project now has reached the point where it should be taken over by the Park Service and administered as part of the National Park System.[56]

It had been expected the transfer of these lands would continue to await the resolution of the Monument controversy by legislation due

Jackson Hole Historical Society and Museum 2003.0117.201

Although gambling was illegal in Wyoming, most of the Jackson saloons openly operated gaming facilities. Underlying the obvious scenic and recreational attractions of the valley of Jackson Hole, gambling was a strong enticement for visiation, expecially during the winter when below zero temperatures discouraged outdoor recreation.

to be introduced by Wyoming's Congressional Delegation in the next Congressional session. Rockefeller had earlier declined Secretary Ickes' offer to accept the lands because of the uncertainty attendant to the Monument. Although the situation concerning the Monument had undeniably progressed toward a compromise, there was still a degree of uncertainty relating to the provisions of the bill and its approval by both houses of Congress. The Jackson Hole Preserve apparently recognized this uncertainty and included a reversion clause in the document transferring the land to the federal government. The clause provided that *"...the lands so transferred shall be used for no other than public park purposes; and they will automatically revert to Jackson Hole Preserve, Incorporated, should the Government for any reason find it necessary to divert their resources to other purposes."*[57] Because of Rockefeller's donation of land to the federal government, Teton County was at risk financially and as a legal entity.

Optimism regarding a settlement of the Monument controversy may not have been the sole stimulus for the transfer of the deeds at that particular time. In the summer of 1949, the Teton County Board of Equalization made a decision to apply a special classification tax assessment to lands located within Jackson Hole National Monument. The Board's decision stated, *"...all lands within the exterior boundaries of Jackson Hole National Monument and Grand Teton National Park except irrigated cultivated first class lands and dry farm lands should be assessed as summer home, lodge or resort lands and should be valued at $30 per acre...."*[58] The effect of this decision increased the valuation of Rockefeller's personal property within the Monument from $37,436 to $125,820. The property held by the Jackson Hole Preserve increased from $358,050 to $1,064,808.[59]

Both Rockefeller and the Jackson Hole Preserve filed appeals with the Wyoming State Board of Equalization claiming Teton County had established a dual system of land classification for similar lands based solely on the boundary of the Monument. Their petitions alleged such a discriminatory dual system was *"...incorrect, arbitrary, confiscatory, and contrary to* *the proper classification and valuation of lands, and the same is in violation of the rights of complainant and others similarly situated under the Constitution of the United States and the Constitution and laws of the State of Wyoming."*[60] Subsequently, four other property owners joined the appeal. They were P. W. Spaulding, the administrator of Grace Miller's estate, Gerrit Hardeman of Kelly, Wendell Wilson of Kelly, and the Stockgrowers National Bank of Cheyenne.[61]

The appeal hearing was held on September 8 and an interim established for the filing of additional briefs. The ruling by the Wyoming Board of Equalization was still pending at the time the Jackson Hole Preserve transferred the deeds to the federal government. The board's secretary, Dwight Dahlman, issued a statement indicating the Rockefeller gift would not affect the board's ruling as the dispute was attendant to taxes assessed for 1949.[62] Whatever the outcome of the appeal, the Jackson Hole Preserve would not have to pay the taxes on the land in question in 1950.

Another possible consideration on this taxation issue would be from the county's point of view. A

Jackson Hole Historical Society and Museum p1958.0217.001

Gerrit Hardeman, a rancher in the Kelly area, joined the appeal initially filed by John D. Rockefeller, Jr. and the Jackson Hole Preserve, Inc. to overturn a tax assessment system implemented by Teton County for private lands within the boundaries of the Jackson Hole National Monument. The Wyoming State Board of Equalization eventually ruled that the county's assessment was illegal.

compromise on the Monument controversy was considered by most people to be close at hand. All suggested provisions for compensation to Teton County provided for reimbursement to be tied to the amount of tax assessed on the land in the year it was acquired by the federal government. Therefore, an increased valuation prior to federal acquisition would result in increased compensation to Teton County in future years.

The State Board of Equalization eventually ruled the county's action illegal and ordered the 1949 assessment of lands within Jackson Hole National Monument be set aside and reassessed using all land classification approved by the state board. The ruling found that Teton County had arbitrarily decided to utilize just three of the 11 authorized land classifications for property within the Monument and that assessing similar land with similar uses differently constituted an unconstitutional dual tax system.[63]

≈

In December 1949, Congressman Barrett issued a press release stating his intention to run for governor of Wyoming in 1950 rather than seek a fifth term in the U.S. House of Representatives. He explained he was making the statement *"...so there will be ample time for people to give due consideration to candidates for representative in Congress."*[64] Senator O'Mahoney was sufficiently optimistic for a settlement of the controversy in Jackson Hole to write President Truman suggesting a summer White House be established in the park.[65] As had occurred on previous occasions, there was a feeling among valley residents that a long and bitter controversy was about to be resolved. Sensing a victory William Voigt, Jr., Executive Director of the Izaak Walton League noted, *"There will be skirmishes and diversions for a while until things settle down, but the hard core conflict in this western sector is over. It is a genuine victory for the forces of recreational resource conservation."* [66]

Karl C. Allen Papers, Box11, American Heritage Center, University of Wyoming

Grand Teton National Park Chief Ranger Allyn Hanks and Superintendent John McLaughlin in a winter patrol cabin.

CHAPTER NINETEEN
1950

I have today approved S. 3409, which establishes a new Grand Teton National Park in the State of Wyoming. This legislation is a significant achievement in assuring the continued use and enjoyment by the public in one of the most majestic and colorful areas of our country.

President Harry S. Truman[1]
September 14, 1950

Jackson Hole Historical Society and Museum 2006.0271.001

While the impact of interspecies relationship between domestic livestock and wild animals was small or nonexistent, the negative effects of humans on wildlife behavior would create problems for the Park Service regarding management of species for safety and liability issues.

The Wyoming Congressional Delegation continued to work on the creation of a bill that would provide all the assurances and provisions for a successful compromise. In April 1950, Senator O'Mahoney and Senator Hunt introduced S. 3409. This bill would eventually be amended in several respects both in the Senate and the House, but it formed the working basis for legislation resolving much of the Jackson Hole National Monument controversy.

It provided for the consolidation of Grand Teton National Park and most of the Jackson Hole National Monument and changed the name to "Wyoming Jackson Hole National Park." Additionally, Section 1 provided, *"...no further extension or establishment of national parks or monuments in Wyoming may be undertaken except by express authorization of Congress."* [2] Repeal of the Antiquities Act would have been too controversial for the passage of this bill, but the above clause exempted Wyoming from Section 2 of its authority. This provision did not prohibit the establishment of new parks or monuments within the state, or require the approval of Wyoming's Congressional Delegation, or of a majority of Wyoming's residents. Instead, it provided that the creation of any new park or monument area within Wyoming would require the consent of the elected representatives of the people of the United States and presumably allow an opportunity for the people most affected by a proposed action to have their opinions considered.

Section 2 provided for the exclusion of 6,675 acres of Monument land from the new national park and placed that area in the National Elk Refuge under the jurisdiction of the Fish and Wildlife Service. Section 3 returned 2,806 acres to the Forest Service at the northeast corner of the Monument. The remaining portion of the Monument was incorporated into the new park. Section 4 provided for the protection of permit and leaseholders and establishing rights-of-way and livestock driveways across former Monument property. Specifically, grazing leases attendant to privately owned land within the new park would be renewable until the federal government acquired such property. Grazing leases held by other ranchers would be renewable for

Harry S. Truman (D)
1884-1972
33rd President of the United States

Truman signed the bill abolishing the Jackson Hole National Monument and Grand Teton National Park and creating the new Grand Teton National Park in 1950.

their lifetime and the lifetime of family members alive as of the passage of the bill. Ranchers with private land outside the Park and grazing leases outside the Park, but needing to cross Park Service lands, could continue to do so in perpetuity. Leaseholders of summer homes could have their leases renewed at expiration for an additional 25 years.

Section 5 was the tax compensation provision which provided payment to the state of Wyoming for the amount levied on the property for the year in which the federal government acquired it and for as long as the property remained a federal possession. The compensation would be paid from revenues collected from visitors to the Park and supplemented with similar revenue from Yellowstone National Park, if necessary.

Section 6 acknowledged the joint jurisdiction of the Jackson Hole elk herd by the state of Wyoming and the Park Service within the new Park. While this section did not create an advisory committee, it mandated an annual plan developed by the Park and the Game and Fish Commission with recommendations presented to the Governor of Wyoming and the Secretary of Interior providing, if necessary, *"...for controlled and managed reduction by qualified experienced hunters licensed by the State of Wyoming and deputized as rangers...."* The hunter/ranger would be allowed to kill one elk and remove the carcass.

Section 7 provided the authority for the Park Service to construct and maintain a building suitable as a summer residence for the President of the United States. Sections 8 and 9 were the boilerplate clauses revoking previous withdrawals and repealing any previously passed legislation to the extent of inconsistency with this bill. Additionally, Section 9 allowed any unexpended funds allocated to Grand Teton National Park to be used for management of lands formerly contained in the Jackson Hole National Monument.[3] Upon this bill's introduction, it was read twice and referred to the Senate Interior and Insular Affairs Committee.

On June 9, Secretary Chapman submitted the Interior Department's report on S. 3409. Chapman gave his approval of the bill if it could be amended in certain respects. He then suggested 20 amendments, most of which dealt with wording for clarification purposes. One of the major changes he recommended pertained to the name of the new park. He thought "Wyoming" should be removed from the name because it was not descriptive of the park's features. He also recommended the inclusion of the word "Teton" because it identified the mountain range that offered the primary attraction of the area. He suggested the name be changed to "Jackson Hole Teton National Park," a contraction of the names of the federal reserves being merged.[4]

Chapman indicated neither the Interior Department nor the Bureau of the Budget found appeal in the tax compensation provision as written. He suggested an amendment to Section 5 that would substitute the old Peterson bill language. That is, payments limited to 20 years with the amount declining each year by 5 percent. He also thought the legislation should include recognition of the reclamation withdrawals and the acknowledgment of the rights of the Reclamation Service to manage the Jackson Lake Dam facility.

The last significant recommended change concerned Section 6. As written, the section excluded the Forest Service and the Fish and Wildlife Service concerning elk management issues within the new park, and Chapman believed they should be included in such deliberations. Other language changes were suggested for this section to clarify that the state of Wyoming was not relinquishing, and the Park Service was not usurping management authority for the Jackson Hole elk herd beyond the boundaries of the new park. The Secretary restated Park Service opposition to hunting on lands in their jurisdiction, but he concluded, *"Section 6 of the bill represents what may prove to be the best solution that can be reached concerning the necessary control of the Jackson Hole elk herd."*

In approving passage of S. 3409, Chapman wrote Senator O'Mahoney:

> *This proposed legislation is a significant development which is the result of a great deal of study in recent years concerning the ultimate public use of the lands that were*

National Records Administration [Public domain] via Wikimedia Commons

President Truman and Frederick J. Lawton
Frederick J. Lawton
1900-1975

Lawton, the ninth director of the Bureau of the Budget, gave conditional approval to the tax compensation provision in the Hunt-O'Mahoney Bill. This was one of the critical compromises necessary for the resolution of the Jackson Hole National Monument controversy.

included in 1943 within the Jackson Hole National Monument. I know that you and your Committee are well aware of the many difficult problems concerning this area that have arisen. This bill represents, it seems to me, the most satisfactory and equitable solution yet proposed, so far as National and local interests are concerned.[5]

Additional discussions with interested agencies and individuals resulted in other suggestions for minor amendments to the bill. Through an article in the *Courier*, the people of Jackson Hole were offered an opportunity to suggest a name for the new park. The bill, as amended, was republished for additional consideration and received favorable coverage in the western press. The *Denver Post* noted the possibility of settlement of the Jackson Hole controversy and indicated the bill was *"...something of a precedent if it becomes law."* [6] The *Casper Tribune-Herald* called the proposed legislation *"...as fair an agreement as possible for the administration of the area."* [7] The *Salt Lake Tribune* praised the bill and stated, *"Settlement of this controversy is important to the entire intermountain west, the economy of which depends so much on tourists dollars."* [8]

As it was favorably reported from the Senate Interior and Insular Affairs Committee by Report No. 1938, the bill included most of the technical and language changes recommended by Secretary Chapman. Additionally, the bill provided for the merger of the two Park Service areas within a new "Grand Teton National Park." The primary difference in this section of the bill, other than the name change, was the repeal of the Act of February 26, 1929 (45 Stat. 1314) which created the original Grand Teton National Park. In a letter to Lester Bagley of the Wyoming Game and Fish Commission, Senator O'Mahoney explained that *"...Government attorneys and legislative counsel considered this change to be necessary."* [9] With this change both the original Grand Teton National Park and the Jackson Hole National Monument were abolished by this bill.

The tax compensation section was changed to limit the financial obligation of the federal government to 25 years. The payment schedule

President Truman, Assistant Secretary of the Interior C. Girard Davidson (center), and Secretary of Interior Oscar Chapman (right) in the Oval Office, 1950

suggested by Congressman Peterson in his earlier legislative attempts, and recommended by Secretary Chapman, was modified to require full payment of taxes levied in the year the land was acquired for the first five years. Subsequent payments would be reduced by 5 percent per annum for each succeeding year. A minor boundary adjustment reduced the amount of land transferred to the elk refuge from 6, 675 acres to 6,376 acres, and the construction of a "summer White House" was deleted.

The Senate Committee report also included a letter from F. J. Lawton, the director of the Bureau of the Budget conferring, approval of the bill with its tax compensation amendment reflecting Secretary Chapman's changes. The letter stated in part:

The Bureau would have no objection, in consideration of the special circumstances attendant upon the acquisition of some of the area of Jackson Hole Monument, to the adoption of the amendment proposed by the Department of the Interior. We would not, however, wish our position in this instance to be construed as a precedent for the approval of similar provisions in future legislation.[10]

On the floor of the Senate, Senator Schoeppel from Kansas objected to the 25-year payment schedule of the tax compensation amendment. He proposed the amendment be amended to limit federal compensation to 20 years. O'Mahoney accepted the change and the bill was passed on July 26, 1950.[11]

S. 3409 was sent to the House where Congressman Barrett requested and received committee approval for two amendments relating to the tax compensation section. The first amendment removed Senator Schoeppel's amendment and changed the five-year full payment provision to 10 years with declining compensation for 20 years thereafter. The second amendment added a few words that probably did not affect the intent of the tax compensation section but provided additional assurances to Teton County concerning the amount of compensation actually received. The bill, as it passed the Senate, provided compensation based on taxes *"...last assessed and levied on the land by public taxing units in such county...."*[12] Barrett's amendment changed the phrase to read *"...last assessed and levied on the land **together with any improvements thereon....**"* [13] (author's emphasis.) The Senate version could be interpreted as requiring compensation for taxes previously levied on only the land even though the county derived a considerable portion of its revenue from taxes levied on improvements associated with the land. Clifford Hansen explained the difference from Teton County's perspective.

> *...in school district two 38% of the revenue received in taxes came from improvements and personal property; school district three received 42% from those sources and on Mormon Row itself fifteen ranches paid 57% of their taxes on things other than the land itself.* [14]

While the first amendment might be viewed as a negotiating tactic to force a more lucrative settlement for the county, the second amendment sought to assure a proper compensation to Teton County. Both were financially significant for the county. The Snake River Land Company and the Jackson Hole Preserve had already removed most of the improvements on lands already transferred to the Park Service. The "improvements" amendment would relate more to the remaining 17,000

biguide.congress.gov [Public domain] via Wikimedia Commons
Lester Calloway Hunt (D)
1892-1954

Lester Hunt was the 19th governor of Wyoming and commissioned the design of the bucking horse and rider that has appeared on Wyoming's vehicle license plates since that time. He was elected to the U.S. Senate in 1948 and served in that position until his suicide in 1954. In 1953, his 20-year-old son was arrested for soliciting prostitution from a male undercover policeman. Typically, at that time, a first offense was not prosecuted by the Washington D.C. police. However, according to prominent syndicated columnist Drew Pearson, Republican Senators Joseph McCarthy of Wisconsin, Styles Bridges of New Hampshire, and Herman Welker of Idaho threatened the son's prosecution if Hunt did not retire immediately. Hunt refused to be blackmailed, and the D.C. police were pressured to prosecute Hunt, Jr. Senator Hunt publically attended his son's trial which resulted in a fine. If Hunt had resigned, Wyoming's Republican Governor could have appointed a Republican to complete the term which would have given Republicans a one-seat majority in the U.S. Senate. Hunt announced his intention to run for re-election in April 1954. Senator Bridges renewed his threat to publicize Senator Hunt's son's morals conviction in the coming election. After a visit to Bethesda Naval Hospital, Hunt notified the Wyoming Democratic Party that because of health concerns he would not run for a second Senate term, but he still refused to resign. He shot himself in his Senate office on June 19, 1954. Although he may have had some health problems, Pearson said Hunt had expressed concerns about having his son's misfortunes used as a campaign issue. Edward D. Crippa, a Republican from Rock Springs, was appointed by Governor Barrett to complete the last six months of Hunt's term.

acres of privately owned land within the boundaries of the new park.

The House Public Lands Committee submitted its favorable report on S. 3409 with the Barrett amendments on August 11, 1950.[15] The bill passed the House of Representatives and the amended version returned to the Senate. On August 28, the Senate reconsidered the bill, and Senator O'Mahoney moved that the Senate disagree with the House amendments and requested the establishment of a conference committee.[16] The committee* recommended, *"That the Senate recede from its disagreement to the amend-*

ments of the House numbered 1 and 2 and agree to same."[17] The Bureau of the Budget gave its approval to the bill on August 30, and the Senate approved the Conference Committee report the following day.[18] On September 1, 1950, Senator O'Mahoney wrote Wilford Neilson:

I was happy to be able today to wire Cliff Hansen that the conference report on the Jackson Hole bill with the maximum repayment period has been approved by both houses of Congress. As I write, the bill is being prepared for transmission to the

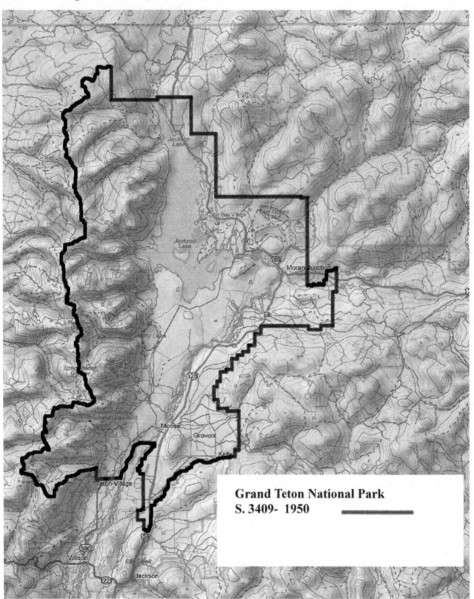

**Grand Teton National Park
S. 3409- 1950**

Grand Teton National Park as established in 1950 by Public Law 787 in the 81st Congress.

---

*The Conference Committee was composed of Senators O'Mahoney, Murray, Butler, Millikin, and Congressmen Peterson, Murdock, Morris, Crawford, and D'Ewart.

White House and I have had assurance that the President will approve the bill.

As you may imagine, there have been many conferences involved in this matter. The Interior Department has been cooperative since the bill was introduced by Senator Hunt and myself, but it has been essential to secure the acquiescence of the Bureau of the Budget which, as you know, is charged with the responsibility of keeping government expenditures down. Only day before yesterday, I was able to convince the Bureau of the Budget that approval should be granted and this morning I received assurance of White House approval.[19]

On September 14, President Truman signed S. 3409 which then became Public Law 787 of the 81st Congress. In the President's statement affirming his approval, he noted the several special provisions of the bill that constituted the compromises required to resolve the controversy. He stated:

These special provisions are, of course, intended to take care of particular circumstances in the Grand Teton area. Naturally, this does not mean that such provisions ought necessarily to be approved for other national parks or monuments.

The development of this legislation has required very careful study by the Congressional Committees and the Federal and State agencies concerned. The legislation provides a practical and equitable solution of the controversial issues which, in the past, have impeded effective use of the lands incorporated in the new Grand Teton National Park. S. 3409 offers a promising basis for effective administration of these lands in the public interest.[20]

～

Not all controversy ended with President Truman's signature. At least one issue was exacerbated by the creation of the new Grand Teton National Park. This was a temporary situation resulting from the hunting provision of the bill. In keeping with the compromise document issued by the committee that met in Washington in April 1949, Section 6 of the bill called for a meeting of the concerned agencies each year between February 1 and April 1 to recommend hunting/reduction regulations for lands within the Park. Since the bill enabling the meeting was not passed until September 1950, no such meeting occurred authorizing a reduction of elk traversing the Park. Passage of the bill had repealed management restrictions regarding appropriations, and the Park Service felt they were required by policy to prohibit hunting for the 1950 season. However, the bill became law after the hunting season began, and the state of Wyoming had already issued hunting orders and sold licenses to hunters for the area in question.

This procedural problem would, of course, be rectified in 1951, but in the fall of 1950, an impasse existed between the state of Wyoming and the National Park Service. Although not unreasonable on this issue, but in the absence of a duly derived recommendation from the agencies specified in Section 6 of S. 3409, Chapman felt compelled by policy to object to hunting within Grand Teton National Park. The state of Wyoming was unwilling to revoke hunting licenses it had already sold.[21]

As a result of conferences with the Secretary and the Governor, Senator O'Mahoney suggested a solution. Chapman wrote to Governor Crane objecting to the hunting of elk in the Park, acknowledging the state's position, and inviting the Governor to make suggestions as to how the dilemma might be resolved. Governor Crane responded, acknowledging the secretary's position, and recommended the elk reduction be allowed during the 1950 season by hunters who were legally licensed by the state of Wyoming prior to the effective date of the act creating the new Park. Secretary Chapman accepted the Governor's compromise.[22] With this compromise, Secretary Chapman could claim he had upheld established Park Service policy by objecting to hunting within Grand Teton National Park. The hunting that occurred in the Park in 1950 was the result of a compromise necessitated by a unique and temporary situation resulting from conditions pre-dating the establishment of the Park. Governor Crane could claim to have remained firm concerning state sovereignty of its rights to manage the elk herd. This procedural dance did not eliminate all criticism, but it allowed both sides to save face on this temporary unanticipated consequence of the passage of S. 3409.

Another issue that developed after the passage of the bill revolved more blatantly around party politics than the legislation. Since 1950 was an election year, this was not unusual. Although Wyoming is generally considered Republican, most state newspapers tend to reflect a Democratic sympathy and these editors applauded the efforts of Democrats O'Mahoney and Hunt while ignoring Republican Congressman Barrett's contribution to the successful legislation. Actually, Barrett may have had little involvement with the initial writing and introduction of the bill, but he had obtained amendments in the House which were particularly beneficial to Teton County. Even if he had been intimately involved in every aspect of the bill's development, it would seem reasonable to have Senators O'Mahoney and Hunt introduce the legislation. Democrats controlled both houses of Congress; the President was a Democrat, and likewise the Secretary of the Interior. Additionally, O'Mahoney held powerful positions on the Senate Appropriations and Interior Committees.* Legislation proposed by a Democrat was likely to receive a better reception throughout the process than a bill introduced by a Republican.

This was not a pro-Park or anti-Park issue. All three men stridently aligned themselves with the anti-Monument faction. Nevertheless, Barrett had won the Republican nomination for Wyoming Governor in the August primary, and some Republican editors were distressed that Congressman Barrett had been denied appropriate commendations in the coverage of the legislation.[25] Barrett won the Governor's race in November.

∽

At the end of the 1950 tourist season, John McLaughlin, the superintendent of Grand Teton National Park, became the Assistant Regional Park Service Director in the Omaha office. Edward Dixon Freeland, the superintendent of Shenando-

ah National Park in Virginia, replaced McLaughlin in the Tetons. Freeland had previously worked in several western national parks, including Yosemite, Grand Canyon, and Wind Cave.[26]

National Park Service

John S. McLaughlin (center) served as the seventh Grand Teton National Park Superintendent from May 18, 1946, to October 7, 1950. Also pictured are, (left) NPS Region III Director, Minor Tillotson and (right) NPS Region V Director, Daniel J. Tobin.

National Park Service, Shenandoah National Park

Edward D. Freeland
Eighth superintendent of Grand Teton National Park from 1950 to 1953.

---

*O'Mahoney had been one of five men considered probable for appointment to the position of Secretary of Interior when Julius Krug resigned. O'Mahoney's power in the Senate was considered more important for the President's agenda, and Chapman was nominated.[24]

Travel to Yellowstone National Park declined slightly in 1950. Entrance records indicated 1,109,926 tourists visited the Park, which reflected a 2.1 percent decrease from 1949. Prior to 1950, the Park counted each person passing through the entrance gates. Beginning with this season, the Park counted the cars and multiplied that number by 3.28. The multiplier was considered to be the average number of passengers per automobile derived from previous years' travel statistics. Travel via the south entrance remained steady with a slight decrease. The Yellowstone Park report suggested the decrease in visitation may have been at least partially a result of the Korean War, which began in June 1950.[27] America's involvement in Korea did not adversely affect travel to Grand Teton National Park. Visitation increased by 13 percent with 189,128 people entering the Park. Accommodations of all types were again insufficient to meet demand, and record numbers of tourists participated in naturalist hikes.[28]

~

On November 21, the worst air tragedy in the region* occurred in Grand Teton National Park. Around 6:30 p.m. residents of Moran heard an airplane and shortly thereafter saw a fire burning below the summit of Mount Moran. Highway Patrolman, Woody Womald, reported the fire to Jackson and the local Civil Air Patrol, headed by Mann McCain, contacted CAP headquarters in Cheyenne. It was determined that a DC-3 carrying 20 to 24 people, all members of the New Tribes Mission, an evangelical Christian organization, was overdue at Billings, Montana.

Efforts were organized to search for the plane, but weather prohibited

an aerial search. Paul Petzoldt, Blake Vande-Water, Jim Huidekoper, Dick Lange and Merle Stilt began an ascent of the peak, on skis and in bad weather, to determine if there were any survivors.[27] Petzoldt and VandeWater reached the crash site on the third day and radioed their base team that much of the plane had burned. There

Jackson Hole Historical Society and Museum 2005.0027.013
Memorial service at the crash site.

The New Tribes Mission's DC3, N74586, crashed on Mount Moran near the 12,000-foot level on November 21, 1950. All 21 members of the religious group on board perished. Relatives agreed to leave the bodies on the mountain to avoid risking more lives in an attempt to remove them. A funeral service was held at the crash site in August. The Park Service closed the mountain to climbing for several years.

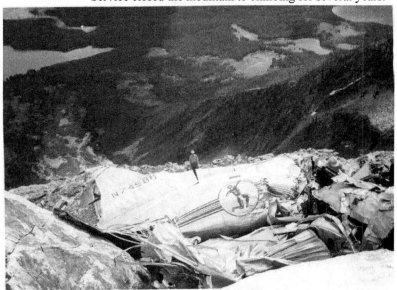

Jackson Hole Historical Society and Museum 2005.0027.014 (George Atteberry Photos)

---

*In October of 1955, United Airlines Flight 409, a DC-4 Propliner, crashed into Medicine Bow Peak in southeastern Wyoming. Sixty-three passengers and three crew perished. At the time, this was considered the deadliest commercial aviation accident in U.S. history.

were no survivors. They recommended to the Park that no further attempt be made to visit or investigate the crash during the winter because of the risks to additional lives. The mountain was placed off limits to climbing pending an investigation in the summer.[28] During the summer of 1951 Civil Aeronautics Administration (CAA) investigators and members of the religious group were instructed in mountain climbing techniques by Glenn Exum and Paul Petzoldt, who operated the School of American Mountaineering in Grand Teton National Park. In early August, it was determined that sufficient snow had melted to allow a proper investigation of the crash sight and to perform funeral services for the victims. Relatives of the victims had agreed to leave the bodies on the mountain rather than risk more lives attempting their removal. The Park Service placed Mount Moran off limits to climbing for an indefinite period.[29]

The last controversy of 1950 concerned the national census, or more specifically, the Wyoming census. The official count of Teton County residents indicated a population of 2,533, a decline of five people since 1940. No one believed this to be true, especially when eligible voters nearly matched the total population of the County as determined by the census. The *Courier* noted this inconsistency and postulated the residents must have voted *"... early and often ..."* in the November general elections.[30]

From trapper to tourist, the settlement of the valley known as Jackson Hole was arduous and often risky. Relatively few of the legendary trappers elected to make the difficult entry into the valley. Native Americans certainly passed through and hunted in the valley but usually wintered in more accommodating sections of the region. Even the Shoshones, who were perhaps the most genetically prepared humans to survive in

National Park Service

The five men who served as National Park Service Directors during the Grand Teton National Park controversy Front (L to R) Arno B. Cammerer, Stephen Mather, Horace Albright. Back (L to R), Arthur Demaray, Newton B. Drury.

Jackson Hole, preferred to visit the valley rather than live there. When Chief Washakie signed the 1863 peace treaty and committed the Shoshones to reside in the Wind River area of Wyoming, he stated, *"You have heard what I want. The Wind River Country is the one for me."*[31]

Military expeditions comprising soldiers, battle-hardened from the Indian wars, avoided the valley during the winter. The Doane Expedition barely survived a north–south traverse of the valley during the winter of 1876. The state of Wyoming acquiesced and allowed Idaho to appropriate one of the West's most valuable resources, the waters of the Snake River, because, in 1903, no one could imagine anyone would want to settle and live year-round in Jackson Hole. Even the offer of free land under the various homestead acts could not engender a rush to occupy the valley. Only after most of the available free land was taken in more temperate climates did Jackson Hole find favor with settlers.

Fortunately, the settlers who were attracted to Jackson Hole were drawn by more than just the lure of free land. The beauty and even the remoteness of the area attracted not just the hardy, but also the people who found value in the spiritual attributes of an area whose scenic wonders evoked awe of nature's mysteries. The men and women who literally fought to survive the valley's harsh environment led the effort to preserve the scenic assets for future generations. It was not just John D. Rockefeller, Jr. or Horace Albright who saved the valley, although their efforts, energy, wealth, altruism, and persistence were vital to the creation of Grand Teton National Park. The Park owes its origin to the foresight of the settlers who preceded those men in recognizing that the highest and best use of the land and the economic future of the valley rested with protection rather than development. The legacy preserved by those settlers resulted in a national park that does not dwell in the shadow of any other federal or state park. Grand Teton National Park is its own beacon of nature's majesty and inspiration and does not shine in the reflected glory of any other national park.

AFTERWORD

Thousands of children and even more adults in our larger cities have never known the thrill of a mountain stream cascading its white waters over the polished rocks. They have never pitched a tent in primitive surroundings where it seems that no white man has ever stood before. They have never been chilled by the piercing cry of the wolf or lulled to sleep by the yapping of distant coyotes. It has never befallen their lot to be wrapped in the solitude of towering mountains in a 'silence you most can hear.'* But they have thought of it, have dreamed of it, and in their hearts have yearned for it with a longing that only full realization of the experience can ever dispel. Many of them do not know that all these things are a part of their own homestead– that great estate that they have never even seen. Some day, if not they, at least their children's children may behold and enjoy these raptures of nature but only if the areas are properly conserved. How their dreams through the many years would be shattered if its realization found only a dustbowl, a forest of stumps, dry creekbeds and the bones of wild animals bleaching in the sun.

Wilford Neilson,
Jackson Hole Courier
March 30, 1950

Howard Sheffield Collection: Jackson Hole Historical Society and Museum 1991.4028.001

The photograph above has become the iconic symbol of the Jackson Hole Historical Society and Museum. The organization has amassed an appreciable collection of images, artifacts, and documents relating to Jackson Hole. Its research center and educational programs provide an invaluable service to the community.

---

*From *The Shooting of Dan Mcgrew* by Robert Service.

The magnitude of the national park controversy, which accompanied life in Jackson Hole since the late 1800s, abated with the passage of the Hunt-O'Mahoney bill. In 1950 Wyoming had been a state for 60 years.* Some form of park extension controversy raged for 52 of those years. With the creation of the new Grand Teton National Park, one might presume harmony had descended upon the valley, but long-held animosities did not dissipate quickly. The verbal slights and innuendos remained ingrained for decades. Contention and dissension within the valley were not abolished along with the Jackson Hole National Monument and the original Grand Teton National Park. Conduct is more easily legislated than attitudes. Only the passage of time would heal the social wounds the half-century of conflict had inflicted upon the residents of the valley. Even during interviews conducted 30 years after the events, there was sometimes a detectable anger on the part of participants in this controversy.

A fair portion of that residual anger was directed at the federal government in the form of the National Park Service and its use (abuse was often the word used) of the Antiquities Act to extend the boundaries of Grand Teton National Park. Nowhere in that act can be found the power or authority for a federal agency or the President of the United States to do what was done in Jackson Hole in 1943. [See Appendix Two- K to read the Antiquities Act.] There lingered the sense of betrayal because of the misuse of federal statutes by the President and the Park Service. Even today, though animosity is not particularly evident, there remains a degree of suspicion regarding that agency.

Nevertheless, with the passage of S. 3409 and its legislatively mandated compromises, the residents of Jackson Hole could look to a future

Jackson Hole Historical Society and Museum 2005.0162.019
Snowplanes and airplanes are no longer permitted on Jackson Lake.

with less uncertainty. The disputed potential use of unappropriated public land in the north end of the valley was settled. There would be no more homesteading or summer home development on federal lands. The natural lakes and free flowing streams were secure from the periodic threats of impoundment from Idaho irrigation interests. Teton County was no longer threatened with bankruptcy by Rockefeller's intended gift to the Park Service, and future expansions of the Park were prohibited unless authorized by the peoples' elected representatives in Congress. Only the ranchers faced a pessimistic future. The legislation ordained Director Drury's stated goal of eliminating the ranching industry.

From a purely economic point of view, the valley would have prospered under either a utilization or preservation initiative. It would be unrealistic to assume people would avoid the Jackson Hole area just because the foreground contained hotels, restaurants, and condominiums. Under either option, the valley would likely be as busy during the summer today even if the Park had not been extended across the valley floor. The only real, albeit important, difference is what the public sees and experiences while traveling through the valley. Both options had their supporters, and both options offered economic prosperity, but neither

---

*Wyoming became the 44th state on July 10, 1890.

vision could be advanced in an orderly manner because of the uncertainty associated with the possible future use of the public lands which constituted a large portion of Jackson Hole. Perhaps the greatest deterrent to orderly progress and improvement in the quality of life was the uncertainty, not so much in the direction, but rather regarding what was possible for the north end of the valley. The passage of S. 3409 eliminated some options for development in the valley while other opportunities were enhanced.

With the transfer of Rocke-feller's lands and the establishment of the new Grand Teton National Park, Horace Albright's dream was realized. However, the Park Service, in assuming control of the area, also acquired responsibility for a hodgepodge of leases, concessions, and permits. The Snake River Land Company negotiated purchase agreements which contained continuing, if limited, utilization rights by the seller, so the land transferred was not totally devoid of people, structures, and business-es. Some of the people who sold their land to Rockefeller retained lifetime tenure on the property, and some for less-er durations. Leases had been negotiated for boat tours on the lakes, horseback operations, and other businesses. The Snake River Land Company issued these leases to generate revenue to pay the taxes on the land acquired. When the property was eventually transferred, the Park Service had to honor these obligations. Park admin-istrators acknowledged the encumbrances knowing they were of limited duration, and similar situations were not unusual in newly established national parks. From the Park Service's perspective, they at least

Jackson Hole Historical Society & Museum 1991.3944.001

Skiers' clothing, equipment, and technique have evolved over the 50 years of park controversy. With reliable highway access and the busiest airport in the state, Jackson Hole has developed a winter economy based on recreation. Ironically, Grand Teton National Park contributes relatively little to the winter recreational economy. Jackson Hole, because of the airport, is a portal to Yellowstone National Park during the winter, but Grand Teton National Park continues to restrict and eliminate even traditional recreational activities during the winter.

Ray Atkeson Photo: Jackson Hole Historical Society & Museum
p1958.1444.001

had oversight control of the area, and the leases could be terminated or renewed upon expiration.

Management of Grand Teton National Park was and is a complicated endeavor. Since 1950, additional legislation and memoranda of understandings between the Park Service and various federal, state, and county agencies have added to the complexity of this job. The Act of August 9, 1955, authorized the relocation of U.S. Highway 187* (also numbered U.S. 89 and U.S. 26) from the west side of the Snake River to the east side of the river. This necessitated additional negotiations with the state of Wyoming. A Memorandum of Agreement dated May 5, 1955, provided that upon completion of the new highway, the Park Service would convey all rights and title to the land composing the right-of-way to the state of Wyoming, and the state would transfer its rights to the west side highway to the Park Service. An additional agreement dated January 1, 1970, placed the responsibility for administration and maintenance of this new highway with the Park Service. This agreement also prohibited the Park Service from restricting the use of the highway or collecting a toll for its utilization. In return, the

Park Service received title to all other state and county roads within the Park.

On March 31, 1959, the Park Service, Wyoming Game and Fish Commission, U.S. Forest Service, and the Bureau of Sport Fisheries and Wildlife (formerly the Fish and Wildlife Service) agreed to the establishment of an Advisory Council and Technical Committee to coordinate responsibilities concerning elk management and to conduct research. Later, on July 3, 1973, another agreement between the Park Service and the Game and Fish Commission would provide for the joint enforcement of fishing and boating regulations within the Park.

Because the Teton Mountain Range is so spectacular, one element of the five decades of controversy is usually overlooked. That element is the role of the elk in preserving the scenery millions of people enjoy every year. Wildlife preservation was the initial motivation for the U.S. Army to seek protection for Jackson Hole by annexing it to Yellowstone National Park. From that time, wildlife issues were a part of every piece of proposed legislation for the establishment of a park, the creation of a national recreation area or the extension of an existing national park. The requirements attendant to maintaining a sustainable elk herd, usually under state management, were the common threads connecting every initiative for preservation of the valley. Protection of the Jackson Hole elk herd initiated the effort for protection in 1898 and the management of the elk was the last element of the compromise reached by the group that met in Washington, D.C. in 1949 to forge an agreement for legislation enlarging Grand Teton National Park.

The previously signed Memorandum of Understanding between the Bureau of Reclamation and the Jackson Hole National Monument was updated on November 29, 1959. The specifications of the new agreement were not appreciably disparate from the original document.

S. N. Leek photo, ah03138_0273 American Heritage Center, University of Wyoming

The elk herd in the National Elk Refuge continues to be a popular attraction for people visiting the valley during the winter. Sleigh rides through the herd offer close proximity photo opportunities, and the chance to view other wildlife species such as bison, coyotes, eagles, swans, and wolves.

* **U.S. Highway 187 has been renumbered 191.**

414

The two agencies agreed to consult each other if changes in policy or operations were contemplated. The Park Service continued to exercise jurisdiction over scenic and recreational values, and the Bureau maintained the right to regulate discharge and storage activities in accordance with its obligations to Idaho irrigation interests.

Water rights within most of the state of Wyoming are the exclusive province of the state. At the time of the 1950 legislation creating the new Grand Teton National Park, there were 68 privately held water rights with points of diversion or conveyance developments (irrigation ditches) within the Park, and these rights had to be recognized and accommodated. On June 4, 1973, the Park signed an agreement with the Teton County Conservation District reaffirming both the right and the responsibility of the holders to construct and maintain these structures but with consultation between the two agencies.

Other administrative commitments were negotiated providing a special use permit for the airport on 760 acres of land now within the Park on a 20 year renewal basis, public utility rights of way, the Biological Research Station, Teton School District No. 3 for a school at Moran, the U.S. Geological Survey for river gauging stations, and other activities, both conforming and non-conforming, from the Park Service perspective: a veritable nightmare of bureaucratic paperwork, regulations, oversight, and exclusions. It is not surprising that superintendents of this Park, if they do not blatantly incite revolt or precipitate an inordinate number of lawsuits, often receive promotions when transferred after having survived several years of this bureaucratic minefield. More than one Park administrator indicated a private fondness for Clifford Hansen's boundary compromise proposal placing the land east of the Snake River (and its management problems) with the Forest Service.

New conflicts have emerged over the years concerning the Park and are likely to continue in the future. This unrest should perhaps be expected because of the non-conforming uses that were necessarily sanctioned as a part of the compromise required to establish the Park as we know it today. Many of the modern problems result not so much from the non-conforming uses, but rather from the public's ignorance of the reasons for those activities. The "institutional memory" of the history of the Park has been largely forgotten, or is just simply unknown, by the modern tourist, environmentalist, resident, and ranger.

As an example, in 1973, the director of the National Park Service received a letter from a Teton Park visitor, Mrs. Kent Leslie regarding the grazing of domestic cattle within the Park. Specifically, Mrs. Leslie seemed concerned that the cattle were owned by Clifford Hansen, who was a United States Senator at the time. She apparently presumed the Senator had used his political power to obtain grazing privileges in the National Park and, thus derived a subsidy at taxpayer expense. Like the majority of park visitors, she was unaware that Hansen's grazing permit for the area pre-dated park status, that his rights had been prescribed by Congress prior to his election to the Senate, and that although initially opposed to the Park, it was Hansen's compromise proposal that moved the controversy from a standoff to the

Fred Topping Photo: Jackson Hole Historical Society and Museum
2005.0018.092

A moose joins horses for a winter meal at the Moose-head Ranch, c. 1940s. Because the moose has a short neck and long legs, they must kneel to feed close to the ground prompting the adage that elk, deer, and antelope were made by God, while the moose was made by a committee. There is still relatively little conflict between domestic and wild animals in Jackson Hole, with the exception of predators. Ranchers throughout Wyoming conscientiously vaccinate their livestock against diseases spread by wildlife, such as brucellosis.

eventual creation of the Park. To Mrs. Leslie's credit, rather than simply complaining about the presumed abuse of political power, she wrote to inquire about the grazing situation in the Park. Grand Teton Park Superintendent Gary Everhardt answered her letter.* In addition to providing specific answers to her questions and clarifying the history of cattle operations on land currently encompassed by the Park's boundaries, he also noted that more revenue was received from the grazing fees than the costs of administering the activity, making the grazing operation, from the viewpoint of the U.S. Treasury, one of the few profit-making activities existing within Grand Teton National Park.†

We have not too many monuments of the past; let us keep every little bit of association with that which is highest and best of the past as a reminder to us, equally of what we owe to those who have gone before and how we should show our appreciation.

Theodore Roosevelt
November 16, 1903

Another example involved a park ranger and a spring cattle drive. Mary Mead, the daughter of Clifford Hansen, while moving cattle to their summer grazing allotment in the Park, was given a citation for having an unleashed dog within park boundaries. The canine was a herd dog assisting in the cattle drive. While not specifically provided for in the statute creating Grand Teton National Park, trained herd dogs, have been considered a normal part of the cattle drive operations

sanctioned in that legislation.‡ Mary accepted the citation without argument and later delivered it to the park superintendent who laughed and tore it up. Leashing a herd dog trained to work in concert with a mounted cowboy would be unproductive at best.

Rather than celebrate the democratic process which created the Park, modern activists sometimes instigate or lend their voices and financial resources to initiatives hopeful of abrogating the compromises so agonizingly accomplished over 50 years ago. It is unlikely the settlers and other early residents of the valley who worked so diligently to achieve protection for the northern half of the valley would countenance these modern initiatives. Men such as Struthers Burt, Olaus Murie, Fritiof Fryxell, and Horace Albright left written documentation of their vision for the valley, which included the continuation of ranching and hunting.

Struthers Burt, the dude rancher and ardent supporter of protection for the scenic and recreational values of the valley, considered Peter Hansen (Clifford Hansen's father), the cattle rancher and park opponent, his friend. Burt wrote fondly of times when the Hansens would stay a night at his dude ranch during spring and fall cattle drives. He believed cattle ranching was an important element of the history of the valley and found no conflict with his protective vision of the future and the presence of cattle.

Olaus Murie, the game biologist and wilderness advocate, counted among his treasured friends outfitters and guides and wrote about their trips in the back county. His articles and testimony before Congressional committees affirmed the need for hunting as perhaps the most effective tool of game managers to control elk populations within healthy parameters. He also supported a continuation of cattle grazing on Monument

---

*Gary Everhardt would move directly from Grand Teton National Park to become the ninth Director of the National Park Service.

†Technically, Senator Hansen did not hold a permit to graze cattle within the Park at that time. Upon election to the U.S. Senate, he transferred his grazing permit to his wife, Martha. The permit would eventually be transferred to their daughter, Mary Mead– all in accordance with Public Law 787.

‡Ironically, the Hansens and the Meads, as a general ranching practice, rely less on dogs than most of the valley's ranchers. They prefer competent cowboys on well-trained horses and often "work" the cattle on foot. Because of this practice, their cattle are less stressed and exhibit fewer nervous symptoms, such as scour, when in proximity to humans. However, when hiring ranch hands, finding a cowboy without a dog is problematic.

416

lands. As the author of a landmark study of the elk in Jackson Hole, he could not have taken such a position if he believed domestic grazing threatened the health and future survivability of the elk herd.

Fritiof Fryxell, the geologist who provided perhaps the most incontrovertible evidence in support of the Monument, testified that cattle grazing had not, and was not likely to, adversely affect the scientific phenomena unique to Jackson Hole. On several occasions, Horace Albright, sometimes considered the Father of the National Park Service, and who worked for nearly 35 years to obtain park status for the valley, found it necessary to remind Park Service Director Drury that the continuation of cattle ranching was an essential part of the plan for this National Park.

The park those men envisioned and successfully secured so that future generations could see and appreciate the valley's scenic beauty and human

William C. Muller Photo: Jackson Hole Historical Society and Museum 2003.0078.021

A few cattle ranches still operate in Jackson Hole, and there are still cattle drives within and across the Park.

Union Pacific Railroad photo, Jackson Hole Historical Society and Museum 2005.0015.088

Cattlemen and Jackson Hole cattle at the Omaha stockyards. 1954

(L to R) Maurice Horn (Powderhorn Ranch), Paul von Gontard (Melody Ranch), Paul Miller (Hansen Ranch), Lloyd Van Deburg (Snake River Ranch). The cattle from the four ranches were trailed over Teton Pass to the railroad station in Victor, Idaho. The arrival of the cattle in Omaha marked the payday for a year's work.

enterprise, should not be modified by the people for whom it was preserved. It is a matter of honor that one generation may protect representative examples of our nation's scenery, environment, and economic institutions for the enjoyment and edification of their descendants. It is the responsibility of those future generations to respect and remember what was so arduously won and preserved for them, and ensure the original intent is preserved for their heirs.

The cattle industry has nearly passed from the scene in Jackson Hole. In 1950, the Park recognized 29 grazing leases. In 2010, there were only two. The Moose Head and Pinto Ranches, hold these leases. Horses from the Moose Head and cattle from the Pinto graze on Park Service lands in accordance with the specifications of S. 3409. Their leases will not terminate until the federal government acquires the land. Of the other 27 grazing leases, some were terminated by federal acquisition of private property within the Park. Other ranches outside the Park have ceased business, and their leases were terminated. A few ranches utilized their park grazing privileges until the generational limitations established in S. 3409 expired. The last two of this type to graze in the Park ceased with the deaths of Jeannine Gill (Porter Estate- OVO brand) and Mary Mead (Hansen-Mead- X Diamond and Double T brands).

417

In 1950, cattle grazed 67,640 acres of park land. As of 1973 only 10,638 acres were available for grazing. By 1959, the number of grazing permits had decreased, and the Park believed it desirable to adjust some of the permits to enhance scenic and recreational values on the west side of the Snake River. The Park asked the three remaining permit holders operating west of the river if they would move from the open range Potholes-Moran grazing allotment to the fenced Elk Ranch allotment. A possible problem with this move related to the fact that part of the Potholes-Moran allotment was still on Forest Service land and a move to the east side of the river would make it difficult for the ranchers to move their cattle to that portion still in the National Forest. To make the request more attractive, the Park offered to increase the number of cattle each rancher could graze in the Park by the number of cattle permitted on the Forest Service portion of the allotment. This allowed the number of cattle permitted to graze within the Park to be increased although the rancher's actual herd size remained the same. The ranchers, Clifford Hansen, Arthur Brown, and Bruce Porter agreed to the proposal, and no cattle have grazed west of the Snake River since 1959.

It would be unfair to imply that the Park Service destroyed the cattle industry in Jackson Hole, although it was one of their stated objectives. The tourist industry probably contributed to the decline to a greater degree than any other reason. The popularity of the valley as a residence, combined with a mere 3 percent of the county in private ownership, caused property values to expand to a point where ranch lands became more profitable for residential development than for the raising of cattle. Ranching probably would have declined even if the Park had not been extended. The Internal Revenue Service also contributed to the demise of this industry. A cattle ranch simply could not generate the income to pay the "death tax" on land values in Jackson Hole.

Judging by the number of vehicles stopped beside the roads to photograph the spring and fall

Floyd Naegeli photo, Jackson Hole Historical Society and Museum
hs.4269.007

The vanishing heritage of Jackson Hole.

The valley still hosts dog sled races, cutter races, hunters, fishermen, mountain climbers, skiers, hikers, and campers, but few of the activities that relate to ranching. There is a rodeo each week during the summer where tourists can view exhibitions of cowboy skill, but the lifestyle of the cowboy is fading.

cattle drives, it can be assumed most visitors to the Park are not offended by the sight of cattle in the National Park. The enthusiasm of tourists who witness the cattle drives affirms the vision of the early proponents of the Park that this would be an activity worth perpetuating. This historic activity which played such a prominent role in the settlement of the valley and the controversy and compromise regarding the Park's establishment may be, one day, just a memory. Some of us will mourn the passing.

Perhaps most distressing is that it does not have to happen. Sun Valley, Idaho, a resort community sociologically and economically similar in many ways to Jackson, has elected to honor and encourage their heritage by celebrating the sheep raising industry that pioneered the settlement of that region. Each summer they hold a week-long celebration with a sheep drive through the town, scheduled events demonstrating skills specific to the industry, and cookouts featuring Basque cuisine and Dutch oven cooking. The event has become a popular tourist attraction combined with a local commemoration of the area's heritage. In Jackson, local environmental groups and alliances have actively worked to discourage the cattle industry on the assumption that cattle damage the Jackson Hole area, regardless of evidence to the contrary, and just because they are perceived as "unnatural." This is a breach of faith with the early settlers who labored so long to preserve not only the scenic splendor of the valley but also its historic social and economic institutions. Our ranching heritage may have to disappear before it will be appreciated.

While the attitudes of many modern residents of Jackson Hole have changed the essential character of the community, the Park Service experienced a notable change in attitude also. At least some of the newer rangers appear to perceive that their mission is to protect the Park from the visitors. Thirty years ago, most rangers gave the impression they were there to help the visitor enjoy the Park responsibly. It is a subtle but discernable difference to those members of the public old enough to have experienced the Park both ways. It may even be justifiable considering Teton Park is relatively small and now records in excess of four million visitors annually. In most years nearly a million more people will visit Grand Teton National Park than will tour Yellowstone. It is, nevertheless, a lamentable mutation of the role of the park ranger even though the potential adverse impacts on the Park from its popularity are very real. Fortunately, the pristine areas have been largely spared simply because most tourists do not venture far from their vehicles.

The Park still has not achieved its potential for the historical and geologic interpretation it promised in 1943. The Cunningham Cabin still exists and is on the National Register of Historic Places, and a replica of Menor's Ferry still operates, but little else has been accomplished to share with visitors the history and geologic phenomena which complete the landscape of the Park. For a time, the Park maintained a trappers museum at the Park headquarters in Moose, but it was eliminated to make room for a gift shop. There is a small geology "display" at Jenny Lake. These were/are meager manifestations of the promised commitment the Park Service made to Congress while attempting to justify the national monument. The Park Service apparently believes S. 3409 abolished the historical and geologic significance of the valley along with the original Grand Teton National Park and the Jackson Hole National Monument. Certainly the efforts thus far demonstrated by the Park Service to help the visitor identify and appreciate the historic and geologic significance of the valley would not suggest justification for the establishment of the Jackson Hole National Monument. Some years ago, the North District ranger was asked what plans the Park might implement to preserve Struthers Burt's homestead cabin at the Bar BC Ranch when the life tenure expired. He replied, *"We're the Park Service. We don't do history."* Almost certainly

---

Conservation is no more partisan than religion, and anyone who tries to make it so, does a dire thing.
Struthers Burt
Outdoor America November-December 1944

---

some rangers are energetic about historical and geologic interpretation, and they are undoubtedly enthusiastic in their efforts to share their knowledge with visitors. Those efforts, when they exist, do so despite benign neglect from the administrative powers. But this may be changing as several of the more recent superintendents have supported restoration efforts at the JY, Whitegrass, and the Bar BC ranches, and are more sensitive to the cultural aspects of the Park.

Still, almost in denial of its own history, the current Grand Teton National Park does not acknowledge the original Park when celebrating anniversaries. In the summer of 2000, the park celebrated a 50th anniversary rather than its 71st. The justification for this was that the original Park was abolished in 1950. Ignoring the original Park devalues, in a historical sense, the contributions of the settlers who spawned the concept and worked to procure protection for the area prior to and concurrent with the efforts of Horace Albright and John D. Rockefeller, Jr. In fact, it was those pioneer settlers who fought to keep the newly established Park Service from building highways through the valley's wilderness areas and up the canyons of the Teton Mountain Range. Left to their original intentions, the Park Service of the early 1900s would have created a much more developed national park than we see today. In fairness, not all Park Service personnel neglect the earlier Park. William Everhart's book, *The National Park Service*, which is an agency publication summarizing its history, identifies 1929 as the birth date of Grand Teton National Park.* If an official publication of the Park Service can pay homage to the origins of the Park, it would seem appropriate for the Park's administrators to acknowledge more fully the reserve's heritage.

If the park opposition element had prevailed, the foreground of Grand Teton National Park would undoubtedly appear differently than it does today. The privately owned lands composing the foreground of the 1929 Park would conceivably, by this time, contain hotels, fast food providers, subdivisions, and gas stations. Viewed in its most

benevolent and optimistic light, this imagined development might even have been constructed tastefully with an absence of gaudy signs and lights. Although many people are pessimistic toward man's ability to touch the land softly, humans are not necessarily incapable of intelligent and temperate use of the land. Nevertheless, it would be hard to argue that even the most unobtrusive developments would not affect the scenery now preserved within the Park.

Among the first to recognize this probability are prominent former members of the park opposition group. Milward Simpson, the opposition advocate who later became Governor and a U.S. Senator, remarked to his son, former Senator Alan Simpson, that had their opinion prevailed, the view along the outer park highway would be less attractive than it is today. The younger Simpson remembered his father stating, *"We were wrong ... but we gave them a hell of a fight."* Clifford Hansen, who also served Wyoming as Governor and U.S. Senator, agreed that park designation

MLewis 2005 (own work) [public domain] via Wikimedia Commons

Town of Jackson from Snow King Mountain Ski Area, 2007. The population of the town in 2010 was 9,577. The county population according to the 2010 census was 21,294.

---

* Dayton Duncan, Ken Burns' partner in producing the documentary, *The National Parks: America's Best Idea*, told the author that Park Service approval of their script concerning the history of Grand Teton National Park required they concentrate on the Rockefeller and Albright era rather than the pioneer effort to protect the valley.

has proven to be more beneficial to the valley than opponents ever imagined. Honorable men seem to have little reservation in acknowledging the validity of an opponent's argument when the facts are evident.

Ironically, it may be the early supporters of the park who, if still alive, would be most dissatisfied with the result of their labors. They were successful in halting, and even reversing, the unsightly development they believed threatened the scenic and recreational values they found paramount. For that, if nothing else, they deserve our gratitude. But there is little of the individual freedom they treasured to enjoy those activities. At least not as they experienced them. There is some bureaucratic hoop, limitation, regulatory restriction, required reservation, and probably a fee, for nearly every activity they found enticing or rewarding. With the increased popularity of the Park, these constraints are necessary to protect the range of values for which the Park Service was established. Nevertheless, the present Park does not quite provide the experience the proponents thought they were bequeathing to future generations. Fritiof Fryxell attended the dedication of the new Grand Teton National Park in 1950 and never returned. He preferred to remember the Park as it was rather than experience it as it had become.*

While the Park may not be all that its supporters envisioned, there is still an opportunity to discover something close to the experience those pioneers hoped to preserve. It requires that you visit the area during the shoulder seasons and that you leave your car. The crowds are much diminished in September and October, the elk are migrating and bugling, the leaves are turning, and the air is crisp. The locals call it Indian Summer. Portions of the past are still alive in Jackson Hole, but, perhaps appropriately, one must search a little harder and exert a greater effort to glimpse the scene and feel the pulse of the experience those pioneers believed worthy of perpetuating.

John Walter Collection, Jackson Hole Historical Society and Museum 2005.0051.038
The view across Leigh Lake toward Leigh Canyon, Mount Moran, and Falling Ice Glacier.

---

* Although Fryxell testified in support of the Jackson Hole National Monument, he was apparently more comfortable with the original Grand Teton National Park. He often disagreed with Superintendent Woodring's programs to improve trails and campsites within the more remote sections of the Teton Range. Fryxell believed the park experience was enhanced by the undeveloped character of the Park and the primitive hiking and camping skills required for its exploration and enjoyment. If Fryxell was distressed by the 189,000 visitors to the Park in 1950, he would certainly have been shocked to see 4,000,000 visitors in 2010.

CHRONOLOGY OF IMPORTANT EVENTS AND LEGISLATION ASSOCIATED WITH GRAND TETON NATIONAL PARK

March 30, 1891: Presidential proclamation by President Benjamin Harrison created the Yellowstone Park Timber Land Reserve comprising 1,239,040 acres east and south of Yellowstone National Park.

September 10, 1891: Presidential proclamation by President Harrison revised the Yellowstone Park Timber Land Reserve but did not change the acreage.

1895: Army Captain Hiram Martin Chittenden wrote *The Yellowstone National Park* in which he suggested the inclusion of the Teton region into Yellowstone National Park.

February 22, 1897: Presidential proclamation created the 829,440-acre Teton Forest Reserve from the southern portion of the Yellowstone Park Timber Land Reserve.

January 12, 1898: Colonel S.M.B. Young, acting superintendent of Yellowstone National Park, submitted to Interior Secretary Bliss a draft bill to extend the boundaries of Yellowstone National Park to include a portion of the Jackson Hole area.

February 1, 1898: Secretary of the Interior Bliss sent Colonel Young's bill to John F. Lacey, Chairman of the House Public Lands Committee. Lacey would author the Antiquities Act.

December 6, 1898: The 55th Congress, 3rd Session, passed a resolution, Senate Document 39, which requested additional information from the Department of Interior regarding the region south of Yellowstone National Park, and recommended protecting the region and the wild game therein.

December 16, 1898: In accordance with Senate Document 39, information was forwarded to the Senate including a report by Charles D. Walcott, Director of the Geological Survey, regarding the Jackson Hole area. Walcott's report was the first suggestion that the area south of Yellowstone should be made a separate park called Teton National Park.

March 18, 1902: Colonel Young's draft bill was again introduced in the 57th Congress, 1st Session.

May 22, 1902: Presidential proclamation changed the name of Yellowstone Park Timber Land Reserve to Yellowstone Forest Reserve, added lands to both the Teton Forest Reserve and the Yellowstone Forest Reserve and transferred some land from the Yellowstone Forest Reserve to the Teton Forest Reserve. The Yellowstone Forest Reserve now contained 1,809,280 acres and the Teton Forest Reserve encompassed 4,127,360 acres.

1903: President Theodore Roosevelt visited the Jackson Hole area.

January 29, 1903: Presidential proclamation included the Absaroka and Teton Forest Reserves into the Yellowstone Forest Reserve, which now comprised 8,329,200 acres, the largest forest reserve in the nation.

June 8, 1906: Public Law 209, the Antiquities Act enacted.

July 1, 1908: Executive order established a 1,991,200 acre Teton National Forest.

1910: Reclamation Service took steps to block park extension efforts which would limit enlargement of the Jackson Lake Dam.

1915: Stephen T. Mather and his assistant, Horace Albright, visited the Teton area on a tour of western parks. Mather was tasked with developing the National Park Service.

1916: National Park Service established.

1917: Secretary of Interior Franklin Lane appointed Stephen Mather Director of the National Park Service.

April 24, 1918: Wyoming Congressman Frank Mondell introduced H.R. 11661 in the 65th Congress, 2nd Session to include portions of the Jackson Hole area into Yellowstone National Park.

July 8, 1918: Executive Order 2905 by President Wilson withdrew certain public lands in Jackson Hole from entry in support of H.R. 11661.

December 7, 1918: Secretary Lane wrote Congressman Mondell requesting a delay of consideration of H.R. 11661 pending additional study of the boundaries. Accordingly H.R. 11661 was not reported from the House Public Lands Committee.

December 12, 1918: Congressman Mondell introduced H.R. 13350 in the 65th Congress, 3rd Session to extend the boundaries of Yellowstone National Park. This bill was essentially the same as H.R. 11661 but with different boundaries.

February 17, 1919: H.R. 13350 passed the House unanimously and was reported favorably by the Senate Public Lands Committee. However, a legislative jam near the end of the session threatened its passage unless it could be advanced on the Senate calendar. Advancement on the calendar required unanimous consent and Senator Nugent of Idaho refused consent. He mistakenly thought the western boundary would include grazing lands important to his constituents in Idaho. Thus, the bill failed by one vote.

May 21, 1919: Congressman Mondell introduced H.R. 1412 in the 66th Congress, 1st Session to extend the boundaries of Yellowstone National Park. This bill was similar to his two previous bills with minor boundary adjustments. However, local opposition to the expansion of Yellowstone Park was apparent, and the bill was not reported from the House Committee on Public Lands.

June 28, 1919: Horace Albright was appointed superintendent of Yellowstone National Park.

January 28, 1921: Executive Order 3394 by President Wilson withdrew from entry certain public lands in the Jackson Hole area for their evaluation and possible disposition relating to pending legislation.

July 26, 1923: Superintendent Albright was invited to a local citizens meeting at Maud Noble's cabin to discuss a means of protecting lands in the northern portion of Jackson Hole.

1924: The President's Committee on Outdoor Recreation established.

1925: A petition was signed by 99 Jackson Hole residents asking that the northern portion of Jackson Hole be protected as a recreation area.

July 1925: A coordinating committee was appointed by the President's Committee on Outdoor Recreation to arbitrate boundary conflicts between the National Park Service and the National Forest Service.

1926: John D. Rockefeller, Jr. visited Jackson Hole and became interested in a plan to preserve the area.

July 29, 1926: Executive Order 4486 by President Coolidge withdrawing certain public lands in Jackson Hole in support of pending legislation H.R. 9640.

August 18, 1926: Pursuant to Senate Resolution 237, 69th Congress, 1st Session, a hearing was held in St. Anthony, Idaho before a Senate subcommittee of the Committee on Public Lands and Surveys to consider S. 3427 with amendments. S.3427 incorporated the boundary recommendations set forth by the President's Coordinating Committee on National Parks and Forests. During this hearing, Wyoming Senator Kendrick suggested that rather than extend Yellowstone National Park to include the Tetons, he would prefer the creation of a new park called Grand Teton National Park of Wyoming.

February 25, 1927: The 69th Congress approved Public Resolution 56 authorizing the acceptance of certain lands owned by the Izaak Walton League for elk refuge purposes.

February 28, 1927: First meeting of the Commission on the Conservation of the Jackson Hole Elk was held in Washington, DC.

April 15, 1927: Executive Order 4631 by President Coolidge withdrawing certain lands for classification and possible use for elk refuge purposes.

April 25, 1927: Executive Order 4637 by President Coolidge revoked Executive Orders 2905 (July 8, 1918) and 3394 (January 28, 1921).

April 25, 1927: Senator Norbeck of South Dakota asked the Park Service to prepare a bill for the creation of a national park in Jackson Hole to be called Kendrick National Park.

July 7, 1927: Executive Order 4685 by President Coolidge withdrew certain lands in aid of proposed legislation.

July 15, 1927: President Coolidge, by Executive Order 4692, withdrew additional lands in Jackson Hole in support of the National Elk Refuge as requested by the Commission on the Conservation of the Jackson Hole Elk.

1927 - 1928: Rockefeller's representatives met with state and federal officials to explain his plan for land purchases in Jackson Hole.

1928: Snake River Land Company formed to accomplish Rockefeller's purchase of private land in Jackson Hole.

April 16, 1928: Supplemental Executive Order 4857 by President Coolidge modified Executive Order 4685 (July 7, 1927).

July 19-23, 1928: Pursuant to Senate Resolution 237, 70th Congress, 2nd Session, hearings were held in Cody, Jackson, and Wilson, Wyoming concerning the enlargement of Yellowstone National Park and the creation of Grand Teton National Park.

February 4, 1929: Supplemental Executive Order 5040 by President Coolidge withdrew additional lands for elk refuge purposes which were omitted in Executive Orders 4631 (April 15, 1927), 4685 (July 7, 1927), and 4857 (April 16, 1928).

February 26, 1929: Grand Teton National Park established by S. 5543, 70th Congress and signed by President Coolidge.

1929: Secretary of Interior Ray Lyman Wilbur toured Jackson Hole and filed a favorable report on the Rockefeller purchasing program to President Hoover.

December 4, 1929: The Commission on the Conservation of the Elk of Jackson Hole held its second meeting and approved the acceptance of lands that might be donated by Rockefeller.

1930: Rockefeller revealed his association with the Snake River Land Company and explained his intentions.

1930: The Jackson Hole Plan, a local initiative, was presented to the Senate Special Committee on Wildlife Resources during its visit to Jackson.

March 8, 1930: Executive Order 5296 by President Hoover withdrew certain lands in aid of legislation to extend the boundaries of Yellowstone National Park.

September 2, 1930: Executive Order 5436 by President Hoover withdrew certain lands within Jackson Hole from entry in aid of legislation.

November 13, 1930: Executive Order 5480 by President Hoover withdrew certain lands from entry in aid of pending legislation.

1931: A House Appropriations Subcommittee visited Jackson Hole, toured the Rockefeller purchasing project, and filed a favorable report but noted the local opposition to expanding the national park.

December 16, 1932: Executive Order 5649 by President Hoover withdrew certain lands from entry in aid of pending legislation.

August 7-10, 1933: Pursuant to Senate Resolution 226, 72nd Congress, hearings were held in Jackson by a Public Lands Subcommittee of the 73rd Congress to investigate the activities of the National Park Service, the Snake River Land Company, the Teton Transportation Company, the Teton Investment Company, the Teton Hotel Company, and the Jackson Lake Lodge Company. All parties were vindicated.

August 1933: A pamphlet, *Mr. John D. Rockefeller, Jr.'s Proposed Gift of Land for the National Park System in Wyoming* was published.

1934: The Jackson Hole Commercial Club passed a resolution calling for the Wyoming Congressional Delegation to attempt to obtain a park extension whereby the southern entrance to Grand Teton National Park would be located at or in the town of Jackson.

June 1934: A bill to extend the boundaries of Grand Teton National Park (the Carey bill, S. 3705, 73rd Congress, 2nd Session) was passed by the Senate and reported favorably from the House Public Lands Committee with one amendment. The amendment was requested by the Bureau of Budget requiring Teton County be compensated for lost tax revenue by a means other than the Federal Treasury. The bill was reported on the last day of the session, and Congress adjourned without acting on the bill.

June 3, 1935: Wyoming Senators Carey and O'Mahoney introduced S. 2972, 74th Congress, 1st Session, to extend the boundaries of Grand Teton National Park. The Bureau of the Budget did not favor the tax compensation provision, and the bill was not reported out of committee.

July 30, 1937: Executive Order 7680 by President Roosevelt Amended: EO 2177, April 21, 1915; EO 4631, April 15, 1927; EO 4685, July 7, 1927; EO 4857, April 16, 1928; Revoked: EO 3741, September 29, 1922, Superseded by

Proclamation 2578, March 15, 1943 (in part).

July 1938: The Park Service initiated a proposed extension to Grand Teton National Park through the publication of a pamphlet, *The Proposal to Extend the Boundaries of Grand Teton National Park.*

August 8-10, 1938: Hearings were held in Jackson to consider extending the boundaries of Grand Teton National Park as proposed by the Park Service initiative, pursuant to Senate Resolution 250, 75th Congress. The Park Service contended no report either positive nor negative, was made by the subcommittee. Senator O'Mahoney claimed to have made a verbal negative report to the full committee.

June 22, 1939: Wyoming Congressman Horton introduced H.R. 6959 to abolish Grand Teton National Park. The bill was not reported from committee.

November 27, 1942: Rockefeller wrote Interior Secretary Ickes suggesting he might sell his lands in Jackson Hole if the government could not accept his donation of those lands within a year's time.

December 4, 1942: Secretary Ickes wrote Rockefeller stating he would attempt to bring about the acceptance of the offered donation.

March 5, 1943: Secretary Ickes sent a memorandum and monument proclamation to President Roosevelt to establish the Jackson Hole National Monument by executive order under the authority of the Antiquities Act.

March 15, 1943: President Roosevelt signed Presidential Proclamation 2578 creating the Jackson Hole National Monument.

March 19, 1943: Wyoming Congressman Barrett introduced H.R. 2241, 78th Congress, 1st Session, a bill to abolish the Jackson Hole National Monument.

March 19, 1943: Wyoming Senator O'Mahoney and Congressman Barrett made speeches condemning the establishment of the Monument by proclamation.

March 1943: Senator O'Mahoney attached an amendment to the Interior Department's appropriation bill prohibiting any expenditure by the department for administering the Jackson Hole National Monument.

April 1, 1943: Wyoming Governor Lester C. Hunt wrote President Roosevelt protesting the establishment of the Monument.

April 8, 1943: Secretary Ickes issued a statement of policy regarding the rights of property owners and leaseholders attendant to lands now encompassed by the Monument.

April 23, 1943: The Park Service and the Fish and Wildlife Service issued an inter-bureau agreement concerning administrative responsibilities relating to lands encompassed by the Jackson Hole National Monument.

April 29, 1943: President Roosevelt replied to Governor Hunt's letter sustaining the national Monument proclamation.

May 3, 1943: Jackson cattlemen drove their cattle onto Monument lands without permits to publicize their protestation of the Monument.

May 13, 1943: A suit, *State of Wyoming v. Paul R. Franke,* was filed in federal court challenging the validity of the Presidential Proclamation establishing the Jackson Hole National Monument.

May 14-28, 1943: The House Public Lands Committee held hearings in Washington regarding Congressman Barrett's bill to abolish the Monument.

May 25, 1943: The Interior Department's unfavorable report regarding H.R. 2241 was sent to the House Committee on Public Lands.

August 15-17, 1943: Members of both the House and Senate Public Lands Committees toured Jackson Hole and held hearings relative to several issues affecting Jackson Hole.

September 4, 1943: A meeting to reach a compromise on the monument issue took place in Governor Hunt's office in Cheyenne, Wyoming.

March 28, 1944: The House Committee on Public Lands reported favorably on Congressman Barrett's bill to abolish the Jackson Hole National Monument.

May 29, 1944: The House Rules Committee reported favorably on a resolution to consider H.R. 2241 immediately, but the measure was not adopted.

June 28, 1944: The 1945 Interior Department's appropriation bill was approved, again containing Senator O'Mahoney's prohibition for funds for the Jackson Hole National Monument.

August 2, 1944: A special hearing in the case of

State of Wyoming v. Paul R. Franke was held in Cheyenne for the purpose of taking testimony.

August 21-24, 1944: The trial in the case of *State of Wyoming v. Paul R. Franke* was heard in Sheridan, Wyoming. The court took the case under advisement.

September 5, 1944: Chairman Peterson of the House Public Lands Committee and Congressman Barrett agreed not to call H.R. 2241 for a vote until after the November elections.

November 16, 1944: Congressman Peterson introduced H.R. 5469, 78th Congress, 2nd Session, to provide compensation to Wyoming for lost tax revenue resulting from the establishment of the Jackson Hole National Monument.

December 11, 1944: The House passed H.R. 2241 to abolish the Jackson Hole National Monument. The bill was then forwarded to the Senate.

December 15, 1944: The Senate Public Lands Committee held hearings on H.R. 2241. The committee voted nine to four in favor of the bill.

December 19, 1944: The Senate passed Congressman Barrett's bill to abolish the Jackson Hole National Monument by unanimous consent. There was no objection and no roll call.

December 29, 1944: President Roosevelt issued a memorandum of disapproval concerning H.R. 2241 and killed it with a pocket veto.

January 9, 1945: Congressman Peterson introduced H.R. 1292 in the 79th Congress to provide legislative protection of rights to individuals affected by the establishment of the Jackson Hole National Monument. It was similar to his previous bill, H.R. 5469, but it limited compensation for taxes to Wyoming to 25 percent of revenues received by the Park Service from lands administered in Wyoming.

January 10, 1945: Secretary Ickes wrote Rockefeller suggesting the transfer of his land in Jackson Hole to the Monument.

January 16, 1945: Rockefeller wrote Secretary Ickes stating that because of the pending ruling by the court regarding Wyoming's challenge to the Monument and other pending legislation, he thought it best to delay the transfer.

February 10, 1945: Judge T. Blake Kennedy dismissed Wyoming's suit challenging the validity of the establishment of the Jackson Hole National Monument.

February 12, 1945: Congressman Barrett introduced H.R. 2109 to abolish the Jackson Hole National Monument.

March 20, 1945: Congressman Barrett introduced H.R. 2691 providing for the administration of all public lands within Jackson Hole by the Forest Service.

June 1945: The appeal period passed in the case of *State of Wyoming v. Paul R. Franke* without further action by the state.

July 11, 1945: Acting Secretary of Interior Abraham "Abe" Fortas sent the House Public Lands Committee an unfavorable report on H.R. 2691.

January 4, 1946: A memorandum of agreement between the Park Service and the Bureau of Reclamation was reached regarding the administration of lands within the Jackson Hole National Monument.

January 8, 1947: Wyoming Senator Robertson introduced S. 91 in the 80th Congress to amend the Antiquities Act. The bill would have modified presidential proclamation authority retroactive to December 7, 1941, thus abolishing the Jackson Hole National Monument.

January 27, 1947: Congressman Barrett introduced in the 80th Congress H.R. 1330 to abolish the Jackson Hole National Monument and return the federal lands therein to their status prior to the establishment of the Monument.

April 9, 1947: Secretary of Interior Krug sent an unfavorable report to the House Public lands Committee on H.R. 1330.

April 14, 1947: Congressman Peterson introduced H.R. 3035 to provide compensation to Wyoming in lieu of taxes and to assure rights within the Monument.

April 14-18, 1947: Hearings were held by the House Public Lands Committee concerning H.R. 1330.

May 20, 1947: In the 80th Congress, Congressman Peterson introduced H.R. 3537 to provide revenue sharing from national parks, monuments, and other lands within their jurisdiction.

July 15, 1947: The House Committee on Public Lands reported favorably on H.R. 1330 with amendments.

July 21, 1947: H.R. 1330 was objected to and passed over in the House.

January 7, 1948: Senator Robertson introduced S. 1951 in the 80th Congress. This bill to abolish the Jackson Hole National Monument was very similar to Barrett's H.R. 1330.

January 19, 1948: Congressman Barrett's bill, H.R. 1330, was again objected to and was stricken from the calendar.

April 5, 1948: Acting Secretary of Interior Chapman submitted an unfavorable report on S. 1951.

April 13-15, 1949: A meeting was held in Washington with the Wyoming delegation and Wyoming citizens to discuss the monument issue.

December 16, 1949: Deeds to Rockefeller's land in Jackson Hole were presented to the federal government.

April 12, 1950: Senator O'Mahoney, for himself and Senator Hunt, introduced S. 3409 to establish the Wyoming Jackson Hole National Park.

September 14, 1950: President Truman approved S. 3409 abolishing the Jackson Hole National Monument and Grand Teton National Park while creating a new Grand Teton National Park. It became Public Law 787, 81st Congress.

Appendix Two Document A

Citizens' Petition Requesting the Northern Portion of the Valley Be Set Aside as a Recreation Area
December 1925

We, citizens of Wyoming and residents of Jackson's Hole, believe that the propaganda tending to discourage extension of Yellowstone National Park is largely based on deliberate misrepresentation. We are alarmed at the obvious misunderstanding of facts as disclosed by newspaper editorials over the State. It is evident, that the papers, perhaps acting in good faith, have drawn, for their information, on sources which either deliberately or through ignorance have misrepresented, not only the issue itself, but also the wishes of these residents of Jackson's Hole who will be most directly affected by the extension.

A survey of the actual situation, including statements of policy by both the Park Service and the Forest Service, discloses that the press of the State is not conversant with the matter under discussion. The result of this is to place the people of Jackson's Hole, whose opinion the papers profess to quote, in an embarrassing position.

The proposed extension of Yellowstone Park is drawn along definite lines. It is, in fact, little more than a transfer of Government lands from one Government department to the other. We believe that the press, and certain individuals who may be honest in their views, are unwittingly combating a plan which is necessary to preserve the scenic attractions and wildlife of this greatest of Western playgrounds.

We earnestly urge that before any action is taken on a proposition so vital to us and to the State as a whole, as complete and unbiased an investigation as possible be made. It is well to point out that the Park Service and the Forest Service both have public documents and public information which completely and entirely explain the issues as they actually exist. It does not seem probable that the business people of Wyoming should attempt a decision without such knowledge, but we wish to simply remind them of the availability of all information.

In fact, we believe that the entire Jackson's Hole should be set aside as a recreational area, or should be administered as a recreational area, through whatever agency, State or national, is considered best fitted to do it.

In this connection, we wish to point out that under the present administration of the public domain here, which is by the Forest Service, we are confronted by a policy which works to the detriment of stock raising without definitely turning over the country to wildlife and recreation. By trying to do two things at once, with the same area, thereby trying to please those interested in stock and those interested in recreation, the Forest Service has succeeded only in making life miserable for all concerned.

We have tried ranching, stock raising, and from our experience have become of the firm belief that this region will find its highest use as a playground. That in this way it will become the greatest wealth-producing region of the State.

The destiny of Jackson's Hole is as a playground, typical of the West, for the education and enjoyment of the Nation as a whole. It is inevitable that it shall someday become such a region, and we favor a definite setting aside of the country at one time, instead of piecemeal, to its recreational purpose. Small extensions of recreational values and range restrictions only cause confusion and tend to squeeze us out, little by little, from our business.

It is suggested that this matter be given serious consideration, to the end that such a move can be made, we do not care through what agency. We will be willing to not only cooperate in every way toward the realization of this big step, but we will at any time, in furtherance of it, sell our ranches at what we consider a fair price.

Signed by 99 Jackson Hole residents

The Jackson Hole Plan, 1930

Jackson, Wyoming
September 24, 1930
United States Senate
Special Committee on Wildlife Resources
Hon. F. C. Walcott, Chairman

Gentlemen:

We, the undersigned, appreciating the very diligent efforts which you are making in your investigation of our country, and feeling that you will welcome any ideas looking toward the completion of a constructive program, beg leave to submit to you the following for your consideration.

In formulating this plan we have given consideration to various factors which are sometimes overlooked when plans for the future of our country are under consideration and which we feel may well be considered by you in your investigation of wildlife resources.

The settlement of Jackson's Hole was begun in the early 80's by a class of pioneers who were attracted to the country by the abundance of free timber and free grass. Some of these early settlers and many of their descendants are carrying on the ranch and cattle business which was started here so many years ago and any plan for this area which does not give consideration to the cattle interests must be stamped unfair. The cattle ranches are a part of the charm of this area and have their definite place in a broad gauge plan for the enjoyment of the primitive west.

Our scenery and our wildlife is becoming one of the State's greatest assets. American citizens in countless thousands are turning to our country for their recreation. Our businessmen have built their businesses with this in view and due consideration must be given to their interests.

The game is the property of the State of Wyoming. We hold that it is essential that the proper winter feeding grounds with ample hay be provided; that lower winter range lands be set aside and that permanent protection be given the game in its natural crossings between the summer and winter ranges. Hunting is an important and essential part of recreation and the State of Wyoming, through its State Game and Fish Commission, is entitled to full control and regulation of its hunting areas.

The Forest Service, some time ago, set aside certain sections of our country to be maintained as a wilderness area. We are heartily in accord with this, and ask that they be allowed to carry out their program, reserving to the State, of course, the control and regulation of the game in these areas.

As a recreation area, we believe the destiny of this country is great. We have fought for years to see this end attained. The idea has been recognized, but definite action has never been taken. Investigators and commissions have visited us year after year; returned to Washington; and passed into oblivion. This is the first time that a committee from the Senate, with power and authority to act independent of bureaucratic jealousies, has come to us, and your assurances have encouraged us to think that we are at the successful end of a long trail.

We have no doubt that the problem here is simple of solution in a way that will adequately protect all interest entitled to protection and, at the same time, insure the conservation of this wilderness country and its game herd, and provide for its future administration in such a way as to insure its perpetuity.

We recommend the following:

(1) That the boundaries of the present Grand Teton National Park be extended.... This will insure the protection of the scenic side of the valley and a game sanctuary for the elk drift as they are driven

430

from the mountains by the winter storms and as they follow the receding snow in the spring- and for their winter range and feeding grounds. This area should never be open to hunting; but kept inviolate as a game sanctuary.

(2) That the upper Gros Ventre should be kept open to summer ranging of cattle, without the harassing restrictions now imposed.

(3) That, where and when necessary, suitable crossings and thoroughfares be provided through Park areas for cattle going to and from summer ranges.

(4) That, as a part of the legislation effectuating this plan, Congress appropriate $7,500 a year for five years and $5,000 a year for the next five years to be paid to Teton County to compensate for the withdrawal of its taxable lands.

(5) That there be appropriated the sum of $500,000 to purchase the privately owned lands outside of and in addition to the area in which the Snake River Land Company is making its purchases.

The predominant thought in our minds is that this region be kept in its primitive state as nearly as possible with no more improved roads than are required to provide trunk highways through the area, and with only such accommodations for the traveling public as are necessary to meet that demand and as are in keeping, in location and design, with the general character of this country.

We believe that this plan will meet with the approval of a majority of the Jackson Hole people and we will undertake to secure that approval, provided that we first have your approval of it and your assurance that you will do your part in having it enacted into Federal Legislation.

We are not concerned with the internal problems of administration which usually lead to petty differences of opinion. Our experience in the past has been that such discussions soon become magnified and the larger objective is lost sight of. Such matters must and should be left to your determination. But we are deeply concerned to have the general legislation passed which will assure the perpetuation of this country as a great outdoor recreation area for the people of America.

Yours very respectfully,

[Signed]
W. C. DeLoney
J. L. Eynon
J. D. Ferrin
Richard Winger

Lions Club Resolution- 1931

Whereas, Further National Park Extension, in North West Wyoming, vitally affects the future of our Community, as well as the entire Citizenship of Wyoming, and the future progress of Jackson Hole, as a factor of the State, and

Whereas, We believe it's for the best interest of the Community and the entire State, in view of certain well defined interests and propagandists who becloud the issues, thus submerging the view-point of the Citizens of this Territory, that the Jackson Lions Club, as successor to the Jackson Commercial Club, express by Resolution its attitude on 'Future National Park Extension,' the methods of men and Government Officials, Park Bureau Officials and paid individuals who by acts, words, propaganda and practice, are befuddling the issues as regards the position of the greater part of the people of the State of Wyoming, as residing in the Northwest part of the State.

Therefore, we do now present to, and hereby adopt as the act of the Lions Club of Jackson, the following and specific objections by way of this Resolution, that is to say

I

We are unalterably opposed to any further extension of the Yellowstone National Park south of the present lines, or the creation or extension of any other National Park in Northwest Wyoming, as inimical to the best interests of the people of the State and its future progress.

II

We are unalterably opposed to the purchase of lands by private subscription, for further National Park Extension, in whatever guise, or philanthropic ingenuity the method was or is conceived, the purpose being to wipe out the Citizenship of this Community, and destroy the taxable values necessary for a proper maintenance of Government in Teton County, Wyoming.

III

We oppose the secret methods used by the Snake River Land Company, with its vast Appropriations of Eastern money, now the owner of large areas of land in Teton County, Wyoming, dealing with, or conveying these lands to the Government of the United States for any purpose whatsoever, unless these lands be conveyed to the Forest Service Bureau of the Government, for use for livestock grazing, for game preservation or propagation or control, under the authority of the State to whom the Game of the State belongs.

IV

We call attention to the Legislature of the State of Wyoming, and to our Senators and Representatives in Congress, of the actual fact of the Snake River Land Company, a Utah Corporation, representing the interest before mentioned, its agents, stockholders, Directors and local paid employees in organizing and creating corporations, within the area of its present operations, for the express purpose of obtaining all of the valuable concessions within the proposed National Park Extension, the lakes, rivers, streams, camping places, roads, transportation, boating, hotels and permanent camps, all with the knowledge and consent of the National Park Service authorities, the National Park Service and the chief officers thereof who now control all privileges within the Forest Service over its domain, and over which it has heretofore had jurisdiction and control.

V

We particularly call attention to the Citizens of the State of Wyoming, Governor and all State Officials and County Officials, as to any further Park Extension as it affects our great recreational and hunting ranges of the State. For in Park Extension, the wild game of the State immediately reverts to Federal and Bureaucratic control, eventually, extinction. We maintain the present care and control of the wild life of the State is sane, reasonable and right, is for the benefit of the entire people of the United States under proper restrictions as to hunting within our game ranges.

VI

We oppose Federal or National Park Service control of the wild game of the State! We oppose the National Park authorities having any control of the wild life of the State, (outside of the present boundaries of the National Parks now created) and call attention to the fact, that the urgent necessity of, and the acts of the National Park Officials, in attempting to create by extension the Yellowstone National Park, was, and is conceived for the express purpose of the absolute control of the wildlife of the State, to the exclusion of the people of the State therein.

VII

We respectfully suggest to the State Legislature of the State of Wyoming, that the present member of the House of Representatives from Teton County, in no way represents this community in its view point on Park Extension; that his past record as opposed to Park Extension, not only in person, but as a sole representative of the Hon. Governor of the State on the important 'Elk Commission,' justified the voters of Teton County, in returning him to the House of Representatives of this State, his present position as this club is advised, and believes, is diametrically opposed to his former strong position and argument against future Park Extension he so logically presented at all meetings of the Elk Commission and in the Halls of our own State Legislature. It's not that we fear for ourselves, our community, our county or our State, but for the fullness of the change of heart of our heretofore valiant and able supporter, now enrolled under a banner of private interests to denude the State of its last remaining play ground for its people.

I hereby certify the above and foregoing was passed and approved by the Lions Club of Jackson, Wyoming, and I, as Secretary thereof, was instructed to furnish copies to all Lions Clubs in the State, to ask their influence and immediate support to prevent the further encroachment of the Federal Government and its National Park Service upon the Public Domain in the State, and the control of the wild game of the State, when its ultimate object is achieved, that this Resolution and proceedings be printed and copies forwarded to members of the United States Senate and the House of Representatives and all State Officials be furnished a copy hereof.

I hereby certify the above and foregoing resolution was duly passed and approved by the Lions Club of Jackson, Wyoming at its regular meeting on the ninth day of January 1931, and by the unanimous vote of said Club, except one.

Ben F. Gillette,
Secretary

Wyoming Congressional Delegation Compromise- 1933

1. The following territory to be added to and to become a part of the Teton National Park:
Starting at a point on the east boundary of the Teton National Park where the boundary line of the Teton National Forest intersects the east boundary of the Park (the same being just south of Jackson's lake): thence east along this boundary line to the Snake River: thence southwesterly along the Snake River to the point where that river intersects the east boundary of the Grand Teton National Park.

2. That the provisions of the Act of Congress prohibiting hotels and other concessions in the Grand Teton National Park apply to this additional area.

3. That the area east of the Snake River, south of the Buffalo Fork and north of the Grovont River and west of the boundary line of the Teton National Forest shall be set aside for a winter refuge for the elk and other game, the hay ranches within this area to be maintained as such to produce feed for the elk herd.

4. This area (described in paragraph 3) to be administered by a commission of five, said commission to be composed of a representative of the Bureau of Forestry, a representative of the Biological Survey, and two members to be designated by the Governor of Wyoming, preferably the State Game and Fish Commissioner and the President of the State Game and Fish Commission. These four to select the fifth member who would be the administrative officer in charge.

5. That within the area described in paragraph 3, permits or leases may be granted by the commission for the building of summer homes, hotels, resorts and other concessions. However, in granting such concessions consideration must be given to the protection of game and to preserving the scenic beauties of the area.

6. The owners of livestock in Jackson's Hole shall have the right to use this area (described in paragraph 3) for the grazing of their livestock from that time of the spring when they turn out of their meadows until such time as they move to the higher ranges for summer grazing and they shall have the same privilege when returning in the fall from summer pastures to winter feed grounds. Such grazing to be under the rules and regulations to be prescribed by the commission.

7. That all lands included in the proposal of the National Park Service to be added to the Teton National Park other than those above described be either restored to the public domain or to the Teton National Forest.

Appendix Two Document E

Senator Carey's 1934 Grand Teton National Park
Extension Proposal

1. The boundary of the present Grand Teton National Park to be extended from its present northeast corner east to the west shore of Jackson Lake; thence southerly along the shore of Jackson Lake to the intersection of the north line of Section 30, Twp. 46 North, Range 115 West; thence east to the west boundary line of Twp. 46 N., R. 113 West; thence south across the Buffalo River to approximately the 11th Standard Parallel; thence east to the Forest boundary; thence west and south along the Forest boundary to the Gros Ventre; thence southwesterly down the course of the Gros Ventre River to the west line of Section 35, Twp. 42 North, Range 116 West; thence north to the Snake River following the west boundary of the Snake River Land Company holdings; thence west to the present boundary of the Grand Teton National Park. Also include substantially that portion of the JY Ranch shown in yellow on the map of October 28, 1933. That portion of the above described area involving the property lying south of the Buffalo River and southeast of Elk is subject to variation to accommodate itself to the natural topography and the holdings of the Snake River Land Company there. Protection of the road approach from Boucher Hill northerly to the Gros Ventre should also in some way be provided.

2. That part of the above extension of the Grand Teton National Park lying north of the Gros Ventre River, east of the Snake River and south of the Buffalo River to be administered by the Biological Survey.

3. Provision to be made for cattle and horse drift over the southerly portion of the above area between cattle ranches in Jackson Hole and the summer ranges on the Forest Reserve lying to the east.

4. Provision to be made for compensating Teton County for the loss of taxable revenues resulting from the withdrawal from the assessment roles of the lands in the above area.

5. Present withdrawals of land outside of the above area to be terminated.

Appendix Two Document F

Executive Orders withdrawing public land from
settlement in Jackson Hole

No. 2905	July 8, 1918
No. 3394	January 28, 1921
No. 4486	July 29, 1926
No. 4631	April 15, 1927
No. 4637	April 25, 1927
No. 4685	July 7, 1927
No. 4692	July 15, 1927
No. 4857	April 16, 1928
No. 5040	February 4, 1929
No. 5296	March 8, 1930
No. 5436	September 2, 1930
No. 5480	November 13, 1930
No. 5649	November 16, 1932
No. 7680	July 30, 1937

Lions Club Resolution, 1938

A RESOLUTION, requesting the Governor of the State of Wyoming to remove Richard Winger, the Chairman, and John W. Scott, the Executive Secretary of the State Game and Fish Commission from office.

WHEREAS, it was apparent at the hearing before the Sub-Committee of Public Lands and Surveys that the citizenship of Teton County and of the State of Wyoming were strongly adverse and opposed to any National Park Extension of the present Grand Teton National Park, and were unalterably opposed to any compromise with the Rockefeller interests, that would in any wise, extend the present boundary thereof, and,

WHEREAS, it was testified by representatives of the National Park Service that the National Park, if extended, would control the wildlife within the areas of proposed Park Extensions to the exclusion of the State, the Forest; Service, and the Biological Survey, and

WHEREAS, Richard Winger, present Chairman of the State Game and Fish Commission, in his testimony before said Sub-Committee, strongly urged upon the Committee the proposed extension of the Teton National Park, regardless of the rights of citizens of Teton County or the State of Wyoming; thus excluding the State from the ownership, management and control of the wild life therein, and

WHEREAS, John W. Scott, present Executive Secretary of the State Game and Fish Commission, is, as we believe and so state, not only an advocate of the extension of the Grand Teton National Park, but also the extension of the Yellowstone Park over the Thorofare and upper Yellowstone countries; thus each are in accord, and are for positive National Park control of wild life within these areas, to the exclusion of the ownership, management, and control of the wild life therein, by the State of Wyoming, and

WHEREAS, the official attitude of the Chairman and Executive Secretary is absolutely contrary to the economic interests of all people of the State of Wyoming; is inimical to, and will destroy all the hunting and fishing privileges now enjoyed freely at a nominal cost by all people, both residents and non-residents; that the said Winger, and the said Scott, under their official positions, are acting in an incompatible and dual capacity, as Public Officials of the State and as private individuals, (representing the Rockefeller plan of conquest) in seeking to destroy all the economic values of the community and of the State; particularly the hunting and fishing privileges therein reserved to the people, of the State, under Statutory law; and in such incompatible and dual capacity, do not and cannot honestly and fairly exercise the official positions they now hold, in the interests of the people of Wyoming, but do, and have exercised their official positions to destroy our local community, by attempting to subtract therefrom 221,610 acres of public lands, containing large and essential economic values; thus eradicating Teton County and the residents thereof, as an integral part of the great State of Wyoming.

THEREFORE, BE IT RESOLVED, that the Governor of the State of Wyoming is respectfully requested to immediately remove from public office, Richard Winger, the present Chairman, and John W. Scott, Executive Secretary, of the State Game and Fish Commission, for advocating, proposing, and attempting to destroy all the economic interests of Teton County, and within the State, and particularly the hunting and fishing privileges of the people, by methods such as are herein set forth.

BE IT FURTHER RESOLVED, that certified copies of this resolution be sent to the Governor of the State of Wyoming, to our representatives in Congress, to all newspapers in the State of Wyoming; and that such other and suitable publicity should be given it as may be authorized by the Club.

Referred to the Board of Directors,
September 22, 1938, by William L. Simpson

Referred to the Lions Club, September 27, 1938, by the Board of Directors for action.

Passed and approved September 27, 1938, in Open Meeting

Appendix Two Document H

John D. Rockefeller's letter to Secretary of Interior Harold Ickes
November 27, 1942

My Dear Mr. Secretary:

Nearly 15 years ago I purchased some 30,000 acres in the Jackson Hole country on the earnest recommendation of the then Director of National Parks. This I did for two reasons: First, having in mind the winter feeding of great quantities of game which was being gradually exterminated by starvation; and, secondly, never for a moment doubting that the Federal Government would gladly accept the land as a gift for addition to its national park system and would forthwith take whatever steps were necessary to that end. During the years that have intervened there have been, as you know, numerous negotiations with Government representatives in regard to the matter. As you also know, all these negotiations have come to naught. Over this period I have expended in connection with the property, which cost me $1,000,000, half as much again for taxes, maintenance, handling, and so forth. Today it stands me in at a total cost of, roughly, $1,500,000.

In view of the uncertainty of the times, like everybody else, I am and have been for some time reducing my obligations and burdens insofar as I wisely can. In line with that policy I have definitely reached the conclusion, although most reluctantly, that I should make permanent disposition of the property before another year has passed. If the Federal Government is not interested in the acquisition, or being interested, is still unable to arrange to accept it on the general terms long discussed and with which you are familiar, it will be my thought to make some other disposition of it or, failing in that, to sell it in the market to any satisfactory buyers.

Because you have been desirous of having this property added to the National Park system and have given so generously of your time and thought in an effort to bring that result about, I would not for a moment think of proceeding to carry out the program above outlined without having first advised you of my decision. Having done that, I am confident that, being so familiar with the situation as you are, you will be the first to say that I have shown every consideration in the matter. Moreover, because you know so well how eager I have been to have this great area preserved for the benefit and enjoyment of the people of the Nation under the wise control and operation of the National Park Service, with which it has been my pleasure to cooperate so closely in many of its National Parks and for which I have long had such high admiration, you will realize better than most people with what regret I now face the possible abandonment of that dream.

(signed) John D. Rockefeller, Jr.

Secretary of Interior Ickes' letter to John D. Rockefeller, Jr.
December 4, 1942

My Dear Mr. Rockefeller:

I have received your letter of November 27 concerning your Jackson Hole investment and I understand exactly how you feel about this matter. This great conservation project which you have made possible would have been accepted long ago if it had been within my power to do so. You know the selfish local interests that have prevented the final consummation of your praiseworthy plan.

I have marveled at your patience in this matter and I understand and sympathize with your desire to put your affairs in the best shape possible, in view of what may be ahead of us in the near future. There is not even the slightest obligation upon you to continue to offer what has so far failed of acceptance. I suspect that I would have withdrawn the offer a long time ago if it had been mine. Notwithstanding, as a public official intimately concerned, I appreciate your further general attitude and within the year which you have allowed, I will do everything within my power to bring about the acceptance of your gift as an addition to the national park system.

Sincerely yours,

(signed) Harold L. Ickes
Secretary of the Interior

Appendix Two Document J

Pro-Monument Petition to House Committee on Public Lands Regarding HR 2241

Jackson, Wyo., August 1943
To the House of Representatives, Committee on the Public Lands,
 Hon. J. Hardin Peterson, Chairman:

INVESTIGATIONS IN CONNECTION WITH H.R. 2241

Gentlemen:

We, the undersigned, are long-time residents of Jackson Hole, Wyo., and are actively engaged in business here. For the past 25 years or more there have been arguments and disputes about the future of this valley that have at times become so bitter as to wreck old friendships and entirely to lose sight of the actualities and facts. The establishment of the Jackson Hole National Monument has caused these old feuds to flare up again, and we feel that so much misinformation is being given out in the heat of passion that we have concluded that some of us who have not been involved in these controversies should take it upon ourselves to bring before your committee the simple facts of the case as we see them. We have tried to separate the wheat from the chaff and these are our conclusions.

1. We believe that Jackson Hole is one of the finest outdoor recreational areas in the world and that it should be protected and developed as such.

2. We believe that the cattle business is an essential part of the industry of the valley and that it can and should continue along with the recreational activities. The cattle business is by the very nature of the country limited in its operations and the rights which the cattlemen have always had, to drive their cattle in the spring and fall across what is now a part of the National Monument, should be secured to them, their heirs and assigns, by national legislation and should not be left subject to change at the will of bureau chiefs. As private lands in the Monument pass to Government ownership, and the fences are taken down and the available area is thus enlarged, this right can, without detriment to other considerations, and should, become the right to drift and graze across the Monument to and from the summer range.

3. The wild game for which this region is famous, is the property of the State of Wyoming. There are many problems of management which should be left to the trained men of the State game department with whom the Wildlife Service of the Department of the Interior has always cooperated. We believe the State of Wyoming should continue in the management of its game herds and in the control of its big-game hunting.

4. We all know that if Teton County is to continue its existence as a county (and we believe it should because of its geographical location) it must be provided with funds to compensate for the loss of taxes on privately owned lands taken over by the Government within the Monument area. Both the President of the United States and the Secretary of the Interior have stated they would give their support to legislation to accomplish this.

5. The Jackson Hole Country, its beautiful lakes and watersheds, have been in constant danger of exploitation in the past. The Presidential proclamation of 1918 and subsequent proclamations and the vigilance and cooperation of our State officials have so far prevented such exploitation, but Federal legislation has long been needed to make permanent that protection.

6. While we would have preferred an act of Congress, setting aside the north end of Jackson Hole as a recreation area and incorporating in the act guarantees of protection for our country, the grazing

rights of the cattlemen and other existing valid claims, and private ownerships remaining in that area, nevertheless the Presidential proclamation of March 15, 1943, setting aside this section as the Jackson Hole National Monument, has provided the much needed permanent protection so long required and should be allowed to stand unless and until more comprehensive legislation is enacted by the Congress of the United States.

7. It is our final conclusion that it is time for us to work constructively together and put an end to quarreling, and we urge upon our congressional delegation that they transfer their efforts from the present Barrett bill to efforts for constructive legislation that will supplement the monument proclamation, by giving permanence and certainty to the foregoing rights which, although now guaranteed by statements of officials of the Interior Department, should be placed beyond any possibility of doubt by legislative action.

We have asked those of our fellow citizens who agree with us in our conclusions to indicate their approval by signing this letter with us, and so that may more readily be done we have signed this letter in six originals.

(Signed)
W.Z. Spicer
R.T. Black
John Wort
W.J. Grant
Orin H. Seaton
Virgil W. Ward
J. Wallace Moulton

Appendix Two Document K

American Antiquities Act of 1906
16 USC 431-433

Be it enacted by the Senate and House of Representatives of the United States of America in Congress assembled, That any person who shall appropriate, excavate, injure, or destroy any historic or prehistoric ruin or monument, or any object of antiquity, situated on lands owned or controlled by the Government of the United States, without the permission of the Secretary of the Department of the Government having jurisdiction over the lands on which said antiquities are situated, shall, upon conviction, be fined in a sum of not more than five hundred dollars or be imprisoned for a period of not more than ninety days, or shall suffer both fine and imprisonment, in the discretion of the court.

Sec. 2. That the President of the United States is hereby authorized, in his discretion, to declare by public proclamation historic landmarks, historic and prehistoric structures, and other objects of historic or scientific interest that are situated upon the lands owned or controlled by the Government of the United States to be national monuments, and may reserve as a part thereof parcels of land, the limits of which in all cases shall be confined to the smallest area compatible with proper care and management of the objects to be protected: Provided, That when such objects are situated upon a tract covered by a bona fide unperfected claim or held in private ownership, the tract, or so much thereof as may be necessary for the proper care and management of the object, may be relinquished to the Government, and the Secretary of the Interior is hereby authorized to accept the relinquishment of such tracts in behalf of the Government of the United States.

Sec. 3. That permits for the examination of ruins, the excavation of archaeological sites, and the gathering of objects of antiquity upon the lands under their respective jurisdictions may be granted by the Secretaries of the Interior, Agriculture, and War to institutions which they may deem properly qualified to conduct such examination, excavation, or gathering, subject to such rules and regulation as they may prescribe: Provided, That the examinations, excavations, and gatherings are undertaken for the benefit of reputable museums, universities, colleges, or other recognized scientific or educational institutions, with a view to increasing the knowledge of such objects, and that the gatherings shall be made for permanent preservation in public museums.

Sec. 4. That the Secretaries of the Departments aforesaid shall make and publish from time to time uniform rules and regulations for the purpose of carrying out the provisions of this Act.

Approved, June 8, 1906

Citizens' Petition to Congressional Committee- 1943

To The Park Investigating Committee:

We the undersigned land owners on Mormon Row, passed the following resolutions:

1. Since this controversy has lasted over 10 years we desire a settlement as soon as possible.
2. We are not against park extension providing our land is bought before it becomes part of the park.
3. Of the 12 property owners on Mormon Row 10 are willing for park extension.
4. Since every ranch left borders on Snake River land or vacant Government land there is very little chance for community development.
5. Due to the ranches being surrounded by vacant land we find it hard to cope with weeds, rodents, etc.
6. Since such a few of us are left we are at great expense to keep up schools for a very few pupils.
7. Since so much land was bought in the north end of the valley we haven't sufficient outlet for our produce.

Acreage of land owners:	Acres
Joe Pfeifer	160
Mrs. Geck	160
Joe Heninger	160
John Moulton	160
T A. Moulton	160
Andy Chambers	320
Wallace Moulton	320
H. Harthoorn	320
Mae Kafferlin	160
Henry May	560
James Budge	280
Joe May	160

(Signed) J. W. Moulton, Mae O. Kafferlin, Mrs. J. W. Moulton, James Budge, Joe Pfeifer, J. B. Heninger, Mrs. J. B. Heninger, John A. Moulton, H. Harthoorn, Margaret C. Harthoorn, Mary A. Budge, Ida B. Chambers, A. D. Chambers, T. A. Moulton, Mrs. T.A. Moulton.

Appendix Two Document M

ESTABLISHING THE JACKSON HOLE NATIONAL MONUMENT – WYOMING

BY THE PRESIDENT OF THE UNITED STATE OF AMERICA

A PROCLAMATION

WHEREAS the area in the State of Wyoming known as the Jackson Hole Country, including that portion thereof which is located in the Teton National Forest, contains historic landmarks and other objects of historic and scientific interest that are situated upon lands owned or controlled by the United States; and

WHEREAS it appears that the public interest would be promoted by establishing the aforesaid area as a national monument to be known as the Jackson Hole National Monument:

NOW, THEREFORE, I, FRANKLIN D. ROOSEVELT, President of the United States of America, under and by virtue of the authority vested in me by the act of June 4, 1897 (30 Stat. 11, 36; U.S.C., title 16, sec. 473), and the act of June 8, 1906 (34 Stat. 225; U.S.C., title 16, sec. 431), do proclaim that the Teton National Forest lands within the aforesaid area are hereby excluded from the said national forest together with all other lands within the following-described area are reserved from all forms of appropriation under the public land laws and set apart as a national monument, which shall hereafter be known as the Jackson Hole National Monument:

beginning on the present western boundary line of the Grand Teton National Park at a point where the hydrographic divide between Web Canyon and Snowshoe Canyon intersects the hydrographic divide or the Teton Mountains (within what will probably be when surveyed section 1, township 45 north, range 117 west, sixth principal meridian); thence northerly and northeasterly along the divide formed by the crest of the Teton Range to the projected position of what will be when surveyed the line between sections 4 and 5, township 47 north, range 116 west; thence south along the section line between sections 4 and 5, 8 and 9, to the point for the corner of sections 8, 9, 16, and 17; thence east along the line between sections 9 and 16, 10 and 15, 11 and 14, 12 and 13, township 47 north, range 116 west, sections 7 and 18, 8 and 17, 9 and 16, to the point for the corner of sections 9, 10, 15, and 16, township 47 north, range 115 west; thence south along the line between sections 15 and 16, 21 and 22, 27 and 28, to the point for the corner of sections 27, 28, 33, and 34; thence east along the line between sections 27 and 34, 26 and 35, to the point for the corner of sections 25, 26, 35, and 36; thence south along the line between sections 35 and 36, township 47 north, range 115 west, sections 1 and 2, 11 and 12, 13 and 14, 23 and 24, to the section corner common to sections 23, 24, 25, and 26; thence east along a line between sections 24 and 25, township 46 north, range 115 west, sections 19 and 30, 20 and 29, 21 and 28, 22 and 27, 23 and 26, 24 and 25, township 46 north, range 114 west, sections 19 and 30, township 46 north, range 113 west, to a point for the quarter section corner of sections 19 and 30; thence south along the meridional quarter section line of unsurveyed sections 30 and 31, township 46 north, range 113 west, and surveyed sections 6, 7, 18, 19 and 30, township 45 north, range 113 west, to the present boundary of the Teton National Forest; thence easterly, southerly, southwesterly along the Teton National Forest boundary to the corner of sections 25 and 36 on the east boundary of township 44 north, range 115 west; thence west three-fourths mile to the west one-sixteenth section corner of sections 25 and 36; thence south one-half mile to the west center one-sixteenth section corner of section 36; thence east one-fourth mile to the present boundary of the Teton National Forest; thence southerly along the Teton National Forest boundary to the south bank of the Gros Ventre River; thence westerly along the south bank of the Gros Ventre River to the line between sections 10 and 11, township 42 north, range 115 west; thence south to the section corner common to sections 10, 11, 14 and 15; thence west to the section corner common sections 8, 9, 16 and 17; thence south to the section corner common to sections 20, 21, 28, and 29, thence west one-half mile to the quarter section corner common to sections 20 and 29; thence south one-half mile to the center quarter section corner of section 29, township 42 north, range 115 west; thence west to the quarter section corner of sections 25 and 30 on the line between township 42 north, range 115 west, and township 42 north, range 116 west; thence south to the corner of sections 25, 30, 31 and 36; thence west to the corner of sections 25, 26, 35, and 36; thence south along the line between sections 35 and 36, township 42 north, range 116 west, sections 1 and 2, township 41 north, range 116 west, to the south and east bank of Flat Creek; thence southerly and westerly along the south and east bank of Flat Creek to the line between sections 27 and 28, township 41 north, range 116 west; thence along the section line between sections 27 and 28 to the quarter section corner between sections 27 and 28; thence west one-fourth mile; thence north one-half mile to the east sixteenth section corner between sections 21 and 28; thence north three-fourths mile; thence east one-fourth mile to the north sixteenth section corner between sections 21 and 22; thence north on the line between section 21 and 22, 15 and 16 to the section corner common to sections 9, 10, 15 and 16; thence east between sections 10 and 15 to the quarter section corner between sections 10 and 15; thence north one-fourth mile; thence east one-fourth mile; thence north one-half mile; thence east one-fourth mile to the north sixteenth section corner between sections 10 and 11; thence north on the line between sections 10 and 11, 2 and 3, to the corner common to sections 34 and 35, township 42 north, range 116 west, and sections 2 and 3, township 41north, range 116 west; thence west along the township line between townships 41 and 42 north to the quarter section corner between section 3, township 41 north, range 116 west, and section 34, township 42 north, range 116 west; thence northerly on the meridional quarter section line of section 34 to the north bank of the Gros Ventre River ; thence northeasterly along the north bank of the Gros Ventre River to the line between sections 34 and 35; thence north on the line between sections 34 and 35, 26 and 27, 22 and 23, 14 and 15 to the quarter section corner between said sections 14 and 15; thence west one-fourth mile; thence north one-fourth mile; thence west one-fourth mile; thence north one-fourth mile to the quarter section corner between sections 10 and 15; thence east one-fourth mile; thence north one-fourth mile; thence east one-fourth mile to the south sixteenth section corner between sections 10 and 11; thence northerly on the line between said sections 10 and 11 to the north sixteenth section corner between said sections 10 and 11; thence east one-fourth mile; thence north one fourth mile to the west sixteenth section corner of sections 2 and 11; thence in a straight line to the northwest corner of section 1, township 42 north range 116 west; thence west on the line between townships 42 and 43 north to the present boundary of the Grand Teton National Park; thence northerly along the east boundary and southwesterly along the north boundary of Grand Teton National Park to the place of the beginning; also a tract embracing the following lands: sections 5, 6, 7, 8, and 18 and those parts of sections 3, 4, 9, 10, 16, and 17, township 42 north, range 116 west; sixth principal meridian, lying west of the center line of the main channel of Snake River.

The reservation made by this proclamation supersedes, as to any of the above-described lands affected thereby, the withdrawals made for classification and other purposes by Executive Orders No.

3394 of January 28, 1921; No. 4685 of July 7, 1927; No. 4857 of April 16, 1928; No. 5040 of February 4, 1929; No. 5436 of September 2, 1930; No. 5480 of November 13, 1930; and No. 7680 of July 30, 1937.

Warning is hereby given to all unauthorized persons not appropriate, injure, destroy, or remove any feature of this monument and not to locate or settle upon any of the land thereof.

The Director of the National Park Service, under the direction of the Secretary of the Interior, shall have the supervision, management, and control of the monument as provided in the act of Congress entitled "An Act to establish a National Park Service, and for other purposes," approved August 25, 1916 (39 Stat. 535, U.S.C., title 16, secs. 1 and 2), and acts supplementary thereto or amendatory thereof, except that the administration of the monument shall be subject to the reclamation withdrawal heretofore made under the authority of the act of June 17, 1902, 32 Stat. 383.

IN WITNESS WHEREOF, I have hereunto set my hand and caused the seal of the United States to be affixed.

DONE at the City of Washington this 15th day of March in the year of our Lord nineteen hundred and forty-three, and of the Independence of the United States of America the one hundred and sixty-seventh.

BIBLIOGRAPHY

Allen, Esther, *A History of Teton National Forest* (unpublished), Forest Service Files, Jackson, Wyoming.

Baldwin, Kenneth H., *Enchanted Enclosure, The Army Engineers and Yellowstone National Park*, (Washington: Office of the Chief of Engineers United States Army, 1976).

Bartlett, Richard A., *Great Surveys of the American West*, (Norman: University of Oklahoma Press, 1966).

Betts, Robert B., *Along the Ramparts of the Tetons*, (Boulder: Colorado Associated University Press, 1978).

Blair, Bob, *William Henry Jackson "The Pioneer Photographer"*, (Museum of New Mexico Press, 2008).

Bonney, Orrin H. and Lorraine, *Battle Drums and Geysers: the Life and Journals of Lt. Gustavus Cheyney Doane, soldier and explorer of the Yellowstone and Snake River Regions* (Chicago: Sage Books, 1970).

Bonney, Orrin H. and Lorraine, *Guide to the Wyoming Mountains and Wilderness Areas,* (Chicago: Sage Books, 1965).

Bonney, Orrin H. and Lorraine, *The Grand Controversy*, (New York: The AAC Press, 1992).

Burt, Nathaniel, *Jackson Hole Journal*, (Norman: University of Oklahoma Press, 1983).

Burt, Struthers, *The Diary of A Dude-Wrangler*, (New York: Charles Scribner's Sons, 1924).

Calkins, Frank, *Jackson Hole*, (Alfred K. Knopf, 1973).

Chief of Engineers, U.S. Army Corp of Engineers, Annual Report of the War Department, Part 8, (Government Printing Office, 1900).

Chittenden, Hiram Martin, *The Yellowstone National Park*, (Cincinnati: The Robert Clarke Company, 1895).

Cohen, Stan, *The Tree Army*, (Missoula: Pictorial Histories Publishing Company, 1980).

Collier, Peter and David Horowitz, *The Rockefellers, An American Dynasty*, (New York: Holt, Rinehart, and Winston, 1976).

Coston, Charles T., Forest Supervisor, *Land Use Planning,* (Forest Service Files, Jackson, Wyoming).

Coutant, C.G., *History of Wyoming*, Vol. 1 & 2, (Argonaut Press, 1966).

Daugherty, John, *A Place Called Jackson Hole*, (Grand Teton Natural History Association, 1999).

Davis, Lynn and Meade, *Jackson Hole from A to Z*, (Cheyenne: Pioneer Printing, 1979).

Diederich, Leo J., et al., *Compendium of Important Papers Covering Negotiations in the Establishment and Administration of the Jackson Hole National Monument*, Wyoming, Grand Teton National Park Library.

Diem, Kenneth L. and Lenore L., *A Community of Scalawags, Renegades, Discharged Soldiers and Predestined Stinkers*, (Grand Teton Natural History Association, 1998).

Diem, Kenneth L. and Lenore L., and William C. Lawrence, *A Tale of Dough Gods Bear Grease Cantaloupe and Sucker Oil*, (University of Wyoming, 1986).

Drury, Allen, *A Senate Journal, 1943-1946*, (McGraw-Hill, 1963).

Ernst, Joseph W., ed., *Worthwhile Places: Correspondence of John D. Rockefeller, Jr. and Horace M. Albright*, (Fordham University Press,1991)

Erwin, Marie H., *Wyoming Historical Blue Book, 1886-1943*, (Bradford Robinson Printing, 1946).

Everhart, William C., *The National Park Service*, (New York: Prager Publishers, 1972).

Farabee, Charles R., *Death, Daring, & Disaster*, (Lamham: Taylor Trade Publishing, 2005).

Ferris, Warren A., *Life in the Rocky Mountains: A Diary of Wanderings on the Sources of the Rivers Missouri, Columbia and Colorado from February, 1830, to November, 1835*, Paul C. Phillips, ed., (Denver: Old West Publishing Co., 1940).

Final Report of the Yellowstone National Park Boundary Commission, 71st Congress, 3rd Session, House Document 710, Washington, D.C. (Government Printing Office, 1931.)

Frome, Michael, *Whose Woods These Are,* (Garden City: Doubleday & Company, Inc., 1962).

Fryxell, Fritiof, "The Geology of Jackson Hole",

National Parks Magazine, January-March, 1944.

Fryxell, Fritiof, *The Teton Peaks and Their Ascents,* (The Crandall Studios, 1932).

Fryxell, Fritiof, *The Tetons*, (University of California Press, 1966).

Gillette, Bertha Chambers, *Homesteading With the Elk*, (Salt Lake City: Utah Printing Company, 1967).

Gould, Lewis L., *Wyoming From Territory to Statehood*, (High Plains Publishing, 1989).

Haines, Aubrey L., *The Yellowstone Story, Vol I & II*, (Denver: Colorado Associated University Press, 1977).

Hampton, H. Duane, *How the U.S. Cavalry Saved Our National Parks*, (Bloomington: Indiana University Press, 1971).

Hardy, Ronald Loren, *Shooting From The Lip, The Life Of Senator Al Simpson*, (Norman: University of Oklahoma Press, 2011).

Hebard, Grace Raymond, *The Pathbreakers from River to Ocean*, (Lincoln: The University Publishing Company, 1911).

Hough, Donald, *The Cocktail Hour in Jackson Hole*, (New York: W.W. Norton, 1951).

Huidekoper, Virginia, *Wyoming In The Eye of Man*, (Cody: Sage Publishing Company, Inc., 1979).

Huidekoper, Virginia, *The Early Days in Jackson Hole*, (Boulder: Colorado Associated University Press, 1978).

Hunsaker, Joyce Badgley, *Sacagawea Speaks*, (Guilford: The Global Pequote Press, 2001).

Huyler, Jack, *and That's the Way It Was*, (Jackson Hole Historical Society, 2000).

Investigation of Proposed Enlargement of the Yellowstone and Grand Teton National Parks, 1933, Hearings before a Subcommittee of the Committee on Public Lands and Surveys, United States Senate, Seventy-third Congress pursuant to Senate Resolution 227 (72nd Congress), August, 1933.

Irving, Washington, *Astoria*, ed. Edgeley W. Todd, (Norman: University of Oklahoma Press, 1964).

Irving, Washington, *The Adventures of Captain Bonneville, U.S.A. in the Rocky Mountains and the Far West*, ed. Edgeley W. Todd, (Nor-

man: University of Oklahoma Press, 1961).

Larson, T.A., *History of Wyoming*, (Lincoln: University of Nebraska Press, 1955).

Larson, T.A., *Wyoming's War Years 1941-1945*, (Laramie: University of Wyoming, 1954).

Layser, Earle F., *The Jackson Hole Settlement Chronicles, The Lives and Times of the First Settlers*, (Alta: Dancing Pine Publishing, 2012).

Layser, Earle F., *I Always Did Like Horses & Women*, (Booksurge Publishing, 2008).

Lee, Ronald F., *Family Tree of the National Park System*, (Philadelphia: Eastern National Park and Monument Association, 1972).

Madsen, Brigham D., *The Northern Shoshoni*, (Caldwell: Caxton Printers, 1980).

Markham, John, *The Temporary Jackson Lake Dam, 1906-1910*, (unpublished), Forest Service files, Jackson, Wyoming.

Markham, John, *The Ashton, Idaho Moran, Wyoming Horse and Wagon Freight Line: Mid July of 1910 to October 15, 1927*, (Thurlock Printing, 1972).

Mattes, Merrill J., "Jackson Hole. Crossroads of the Western Fur Trade, 1807-1829", *Pacific Northwest Quarterly*, Vol. 37, No. 2, April 1946.

McKinney, Mary, *The View That Inspired A Vision*, (Mixed Sources 2010).

Miller, Merle, *Plain Speaking, an oral biography of Harry S. Truman*, (New York: Berkley Publishing Corporation, 1974).

Moore, Leanne Staley, *Jackson Hole's Birthday Club*, (Boise: Towanda, Inc., 2003).

Moulton, Candy Vyvey, *Legacy of the Tetons*, (La Frontera Publishing, 2007).

Murie, Margaret and Olaus, *Wapiti Wilderness*, (New York: Alfred A. Knopf, 1966).

Murie, Olaus, *Journeys to the Far North*, (Palo Alto: The Wilderness Society and American West Publishing Company, 1973).

Nelson, Fern K., *Soda for the Sourdoughs, Homesteading Jackson Hole*, (Teton Printing and Publishing, 1973).

Nelson, Fern K., *This Was Jackson's Hole*, (Glendo, Wyoming: High Plains Press, 1994).

Ortenburger, Leigh, *A Climber's Guide to the Teton Range*, (San Francisco: Sierra Club, 1965).

Orth, Donald J. and Roger L. Payne, *Principles, Polices, and Procedures: Domestic Geographic Names*, 1987, Online Edition, Geographic Names Information System, http://geonames.usgs.gov/pppdgn.html. 2003.

Paul, Elliot, *Desperate Scenery*, (New York: Random House, 1954).

Paullin, Charles O., *Atlas of the Historical Geography of the United States*, (Baltimore: American Geographic Society of New York Carnegie Institute, 1932).

Potts, Merlin K., *Campfire Tales of Jackson Hole* (Moose: Grand Teton Natural History Association, 1960).

Recreational Use Of Land In The United States Part XI Of The Report On Land Planning, November 1934, By The National Park Service, Submitted by Arno E. Cammerer, Director of National Parks, 1938.

Righter, Robert W., *Crucible for Conservation*, (Denver: Colorado Associated University Press, 1982).

Roberts, Phil, David L. Roberts, and Steven L. Roberts, *Wyoming Almanac*, (Laramie: Skyline West Press, 1994).

Sanborn, Margaret, *The Grand Tetons*, (Putnam, 1978).

Saylor, David J., *Jackson Hole, Wyoming: In the Shadow of the Tetons*, (Norman: University of Oklahoma Press, 1970).

Smith, Bruce L., *Where Elk Roam*, (Guilford: Lyons Press, 2012).

Spring, Agnes W., *William Chapin Demming*, (Arthur H. Clark, 1944).

Stone, Elizabeth Arnold, *Uinta County: Its Place in History*, (Laramie Printing Company, 1924).

Tilden, Freeman, *The National Parks*, (New York: Alfred A. Knopf, 1970).

Trenholm, Virginia Cole and Maurine Carley, *The Shoshonis Sentinels of the Rockies*, (Norman: University of Oklahoma Press, 1964).

Truman, Margaret, *Harry S. Truman*, (New York: William Morrow & Company, Inc., 1972.)

Wasden, David J., *From Beaver to Oil*, (Cheyenne: Pioneer Printing and Stationery Co., 1973).

Wernert, Susan J., Ed., *Our National Parks*, (Pleasantville: Reader's Digest, 1985).

Wild, Peter, *Pioneer Conservationists of Western America*, (Missoula: Mountain Press Publishing Co., 1979).

Winks, Robin W., *Laurance S. Rockefeller, Catalyst for Conservation*, (Washington: Island Press, 1997).

Wirth, Conrad L., *Parks, Politics, and the People*, (Norman: University of Oklahoma Press, 1980).

Wister, Owen, "Old Yellowstone Days," *Harper's Monthly Magazine* (March, 1936).

ENDNOTES

INTRODUCTION

1. Orrin H. and Lorraine Bonney, *Battle Drums and Geysers: the Life and Journals of Lt. Gustavus Cheney Doane, soldier and explorer of the Yellowstone and Snake River Regions*, (Chicago: Sage Books, 1970) p. 524.

2. Warren A. Ferris, *Life in the Rocky Mountains: A Diary of Wanderings on the Sources of the Rivers Missouri, Columbia and Colorado from February, 1830, to November, 1835*, Paul C. Phillips, ed., (Denver: Old West Publishing Co., 1940).

3. Donald J. Orth and Roger L. Payne, *Principles, Policies, and Procedures: Domestic Geographic Names, 1987*, Online Edition, Geographic Names Information System, http://geonames.usgs.gov/pppdgn.html, 2003.

4. Joyce Badgley Hunsaker, *Sacagawea Speaks*, (Guilford: The Global Pequote Press, 2001).

5. Washington Irving, *Astoria*, ed. Edgeley W. Todd, (Norman: University of Oklahoma Press, 1964) p. 257.

6. Merril J. Mattes, "Jackson Hole. Crossroads of the Western Fur Trade, 1807-1829," *Pacific Northwest Quarterly*, Vol. 37, No. 2, April 1946, p. 90.

7. Mattes, Ibid.

8. Charles O. Paullin, *Atlas of the Historical Geography of the United States*, (Baltimore: American Geographic Society of New York Carnegie Institute, 1932) Plate 31A.

9. Richard A. Bartlett, *Great Surveys of the American West*, (Norman: University of Oklahoma Press, 1966) p. 64.

10. Hiram Martin Chittenden, *The Yellowstone National Park*, (Cincinnati: The Robert Clarke Company, 1895) p. 357.

11. Chittenden, p. 358.

12. F.A. Boutelle, to Secretary of the Interior, August 18, 1889, Yellowstone National Park Archives, Vol. II, Letters Sent, p. 491.

13. Congressional Record, 49th Congress, 1st Session, XVII, Part 8, pp. 7866-7867.

14. Congressional Record, XCII, Part 7, p. 7841.

15. *22 U.S. Statutes at Large*, p. 627.

16. H. Duane Hampton, *How the U.S. Cavalry Saved Our National Parks*, (Bloomington: Indiana University Press, 1971) p. 82.

17. Hampton, p. 97.

18. Chittenden, p. 139.

19. Hampton, p. 101.

20. Michael Frome, *Whose Woods These Are*, (Garden City: Doubleday & Company, Inc., 1962) p. 48.

21. Frome, p. 50.

22. Leo J. Diederich, et al., *Compendium of Important Papers Covering Negotiations in the Establishment and Administration of the Jackson Hole National Monument, Wyoming*, Grand Teton National Park Library, Vol. I, p. 1. [Hereafter referred to as *Compendium*.]

23. *Compendium*.

24. Chittenden, p. 222.

CHAPTER ONE

1. Aubrey L. Haines, *The Yellowstone Story, Vol II*, (Denver: Colorado Associated University Press, 1977) p. 455.

2. http://www.autographsofamerica.com/d-govt360-BlissSig.html.

3. C.N. Bliss, Secretary of Interior, to John F. Lacey, Chairman, Committee on Public Lands, House of Representatives, February 1, 1898: House Document 500, 56th Congress, 1st Session, pp. 2-3.

4. Senate Resolution of December 6, 1898: Senate Document No. 39, 55th Congress, 3rd Session, p. 1.

5. The Constitution of the United States, Article IV, Section 3.

6. Thomas Ryan, Acting Secretary of the Interior, to President of the Senate, December 16, 1898: Senate Document No. 39, 55th Congress, 3rd Session, p. 2.

7. Charles D. Walcott, Report on the Region South of and Adjoining the Yellowstone National Park, with Especial Reference to the Preservation and Protection of the Forests and the Game Therein: 1898, Senate Document No. 39, 55th Congress, 3rd Session, p. 6.

8. Walcott, p. 5.
9. Walcott, p. 6.
10. Matt C. Bristol, Second Lieutenant, Thirteenth Cavalry, Report to John Pitcher, Captain, First Cavalry, Acting Superintendent, Yellowstone National Park, July 22, 1901: House Document No. 500, 57th Congress, 1st Session, p. 9.
11. John Pitcher, Captain, First Cavalry, Acting Superintendent, Yellowstone National Park, to Secretary of the Interior, August 26, 1901: House Document No. 500, 57th Congress, 1st Session, p. 8.
12. Ibid.
13. I.A. Macrum, Forest Inspector, Report to the Commissioner of the General Land Office, July 24, 1901: House Document No. 500, 57th Congress, 1st Session, p. 12.
14. Macrum., pp. 12-13.
15. Macrum, p. 12.
16. William M. Findly, Letter to E.A. Hitchcock, Secretary of the Interior, July 6, 1901: House Document No. 500, 57th Congress, 1st Session, p. 14.
17. F.E. Wyatt, Letter to President Theodore Roosevelt, November 2, 1901: House Document No. 500, 57th Congress, 1st Session, pp. 14-15.
18. Macrum, p. 11.
19. Ibid.
20. Macrum, p. 14.
21. Macrum, p. 11.
22. *Jackson Hole Courier*, September 24, 1924, p. 1.
23. Judge J.L. Smith, "Peril of the Wapiti Starvation from the Lack of Winter Pasture- Sheep Men Threaten to Appropriate Land Upon which the Deer Feed- An Armed Conflict is Feared," (excerpt from *The Kansas City Journal*), March 4, 1900: House Document No. 500, 57th Congress, 1st Session, p. 21.
24. John Pitcher, Major, Sixth Cavalry, Acting Superintendent, Yellowstone National Park, to Secretary of the Interior, February 5, 1902: House Document No. 500, 57th Congress, 1st Session, p. 26.
25. Struthers Burt, *The Diary of a Dude-Wrangler*, (New York: Charles Scribner's Sons, 1924), p. 259.

CHAPTER TWO

1. Burt, p. 120.
2. *Compendium*, Vol. I, p. 1.
3. *Progressive Men of Wyoming,* A.W Bowen & Co. 1908, p. 206 (Familysearch.org)
4. Charles T. Coston, *Land Use Planning*, Forest Service Files, Jackson, Wyoming, p. 1.
5. Esther Allen, *A History of Teton National Forest* (unpublished), Forest Service Files, Jackson, Wyoming.
6. "Forest Service Marks Fiftieth Anniversary This Month," *Jackson Hole Guide*, February 3, 1955, p. 4.
7. T.A. Larson, *History of Wyoming*, (Lincoln: University of Nebraska Press, 1955), p. 4.
8. Esther Allen, *A History of Teton National Forest* (unpublished), Forest Service Files, Jackson, Wyoming.
9. "Highlights in the History of Forest Conservation," *U.S.F.S., Bulletin No. 83*, p. 8.
10. P.M. Fogg, *A History of the Minidoka Project, Idaho to 1912*, Bureau of Reclamation Files, Burley, Idaho.
11. Ibid., p. 40.
12. John Markham, *The Temporary Jackson Lake Dam, 1906-1910*, (unpublished), Forest Service files, Jackson, Wyoming.
13. Ibid.
14. Ibid.
15. Fogg, p. 40.
16. Ibid., p. 41.
17. Ibid.
18. Ibid.
19. Ibid., p. 42
20. Ibid.
21. Ibid.
22. Ibid.
23. Ibid.
24. Elliot Paul, *Desperate Scenery*, (New York: Random House, 1954), p. 265.
25. Ibid.
26. F.A. Banks, "Annual Project History No. One, Jackson Lake Enlargement Project, Wyoming," Bureau of Reclamation Files, Burley, Idaho, p. 10.
27. Paul, p. 219-220.

28. Ibid., p. 258.

29. K. C. Allan, Interview, Forest Service Files, Jackson, Wyoming.

30. Ibid.

31. Ibid.

32. Paul, p. 265.

33. Fogg, p. 42.

34. F.A. Banks, "Annual Project History No. One, Jackson Lake Enlargement Project Wyoming, 1913," Bureau of Reclamation Files, Burley, Idaho. p. 10

35. Ibid., p. 11.

36. Ibid.

37. Ibid., p. 41.

38. Ibid., p. 13.

39. Ibid., p. 3.

40. F.A. Banks, "Annual Project History No. Two, Jackson Lake Enlargement Project, Wyoming - 1914," Bureau of Reclamation Files, Burley, Idaho, p. 65.

41. Ibid.

42. Ibid., p. 17.

43. F.A. Banks, "Annual Project History No. Three, Jackson Lake Enlargement Project, Wyoming- 1915," Bureau of Reclamation Files, Burley, Idaho, pp. 46-47.

44. Banks, "Project History No. Two," p. 41.

45. Banks, "Project History No. Three," p. 48.

46. Owen Wister, "Old Yellowstone Days," *Harper's Monthly Magazine* (March, 1936), p. 473.

47. Larson, p. 304.

48. Ibid.

49. Esther Allen.

50. Burt, p. 119.

51. Allen.

52. Burt, p. 121.

CHAPTER THREE

1. Horace Albright to Wilford Neilson, 1933, Grand Teton National Park Files, Grand Teton National Park, Wyoming.

2. Acting Superintendent to Stephen Mather, Assistant to the Secretary of the Interior, November 26, 1915, "Memorandum of Troop Withdrawal," NA, RG 79, Records of the National Park Service, File 12-12-24.

3. Hampton, p. 178.

4. Hampton, p. 181.

5. Ibid.

6. Letter published in the *New York Times*, October 14, 1917, from "A Sergeant, Ft. Yellowstone," NA, RG 79, Records of the National Park Service, File 12-12-24.

7. Albright to Neilson, 1933.

8. Ibid.

9. Horace M. Albright, Interview, by Haraden and Dilley, 1967, Grand Teton National Park Files, Grand Teton National Park, Wyoming.

10. Albright to Neilson, 1933.

11. *Jackson Hole Courier,* 1916.

12. Albright to Neilson, 1933.

13. Albright, Interview, 1967.

14. Ibid.

15. Ibid.

16. *Compendium*, Vol. II, Part 1, Exhibit 2.

17. House Committee on Public Lands, Report No. 938, 65th Congress, 3rd Session.

18. *Compendium*, Vol. I, p. 5.

19. Albright, Interview, 1967.

20. *Compendium*, Vol. II, Part 1 Exhibit 4.

21. "To Abolish the Jackson Hole National Monument, Wyoming," 1943, Committee Hearings, House of Representatives, 78th Congress, 1st Session, p. 279.

22. "Many Outsiders Interested in Park Extension," *Jackson Hole Courier*, April 24, 1918, p. 1.

23. "Here in Interest of Park Extension," *Jackson Hole Courier*, August 1, 1918, p. 1.

24. "Park Extension Discussed," *Jackson Hole Courier*, May 23, 1918, p. 1.

25. "Stock Association Holds Special Meeting," *Jackson Hole Courier*, July 18, 1918, p. 1.

26. H.R. 11661, 65th Congress, 2nd Session, House of Representatives.

27. "Letter From Congressman Mondell to Stockmen," *Jackson Hole Courier*, August 1, 1918, p. 1.

28. Albright to Neilson, 1933.

29. *Compendium*. Vol. II, Part 1, Exhibit 3.

30. Franklin K. Lane, Secretary of the Interior, "Addition of Lands to Yellowstone National Park," 1918, Report from Department of the Interior to House Committee on Public Lands concerning H.R. 13350.

31. "Jackson Hole Stockmen Hold Annual Meeting," *Jackson Hole Courier*, May 1, 1919, p. 1.
32. Ibid.
33. Letter from Struthers Burt to Frank Mondell, published in the *Jackson Hole Courier*, October 9, 1919, p. 3.
34. Ibid.
35. H.R. 11661, 65th Congress, 2nd Session, House of Representatives.
36. "Wyoming Stock Growers Oppose Enlargement," *Jackson Hole Courier*, April 24, 1919, p. 1.

CHAPTER FOUR

1. "Albright Still Working For Extension of Park," *Jackson Hole Courier*, August 5, 1920, p. 6.
2. Albright to Neilson, 1933.
3. Albright, Interview, 1967.
4. Ibid.
5. Ibid.
6. Albright to Neilson, 1933.
7. Ibid.
8. Ibid.
9. Ibid.
10. Ibid.
11. Ibid.
12. "To Abolish The Jackson Hole National Monument, Wyoming," 1943, Committee Hearings, House of Representatives, 78th Congress, 1st Session, p. 280.
13. Albright, Interview, 1967.
14. Albright to Neilson, 1933.
15. "More Roads: More Tourist," *Jackson Hole Courier*, April 15, 1920, p. 1.
16. Editorial, *Jackson Hole Courier*, April 29, 1920, p. 1.
17. "Stranger Within Thy Gates," *Jackson Hole Courier*, July 8, 1920, p. 1.
18. Albright to Neilson, 1933.
19. Albright, Interview, 1967.
20. "Albright Still Working for Extension of Park," *Jackson Hole Courier*, August 5, 1920, p. 1.
21. Albright, Interview, 1967.
22. "Jackson's Hole Labors Under Big Handicap," *Jackson Hole Courier*, September 16, 1920, p.1.

23. "Is Park Extension Question Really a Dead Issue?," *Jackson Hole Courier*, October 7, 1920, p. 1.
24. Albright to Neilson, 1933.
25. Annual Report of the Chief of Engineers, 1900, Part 8, p. 5453.
26. Albright, Interview, 1967.
27. Albright to Neilson, 1933.
28. Ibid.
29. Ibid.
30. Ibid.
31. Ibid.
32. Haines, p. 479.
33. Albright to Neilson, 1933.

CHAPTER FIVE

1. "Park Extension or Ruined Lakes - Which?" *Jackson Hole Courier*, January 18, 1923, p. 1.
2. "Park Needs More Roads Not Extended Boundaries," *Jackson Hole Courier*, November 30, 1922, p. 1.
3. *Jackson Hole Courier*, July 13, 1922, p. 1.
4. Larson, p. 319.
5. "Mondell's Stand On Park Extension," *Jackson Hole Courier*, July 27, 1922, p. 1.
6. Investigation of Proposed Enlargement of the Yellowstone and Grand Teton National Parks, 1933, Hearings before a Subcommittee of the Committee on Public Lands and Surveys, United States Senate, 73rd Congress pursuant to Senate Resolution 227 (72nd Congress), August 1933, pp. 151 & 152. Hereafter referred to as Hearings, S. Res. 226, 1933.
7. Albright, Interview, 1967.
8. "Jackson's Hole Menaced by Wooly Scourge," by J.R. Jones, *Jackson Hole Courier*, December 21, 1922, p. 5.
9. "Land Thrown Open," *Jackson Hole Courier*, January 26, 1922, p. 1.
10. "19,000 Acres Land Opened Entry Here," *Jackson Hole Courier*, March 9, 1922, p. 1.
11. "Park Extension or Ruined Lakes Which?" *Jackson Hole Courier*, January 18, 1923, p. 3.
12. Ibid.
13. "Renewal of Effort to Incorporate Tetons in Y.N. Park Albright Forecast," *Jackson Hole Courier*, December 21, 1922, p. 3.

14. Ibid.
15. Ibid.
16. "Park Extension - D.B. Sheffield Submits His View," *Jackson Hole Courier*, February 1, 1923, p. 1.
17. "Park Extension - For and Against," *Jackson Hole Courier*, February 8, 1923, p. 1.
18. Ibid.
19. "Grimmesey Against Park Extension," *Jackson Hole Courier*, February 8, 1923, p. 1.
20. "E.H. Johnson Against Park Extension," *Jackson Hole Courier*, February 22, 1923, p. 1.
21. "Park Extension," (Letter to the Editor) *Jackson Hole Courier*, July 5, 1923, p. 1.
22. Ibid.
23. Ibid.
24. Ibid.
25. Albright, Interview, 1967.
26. Albright to Neilson, 1933: also, Horace Albright, Interview, 1967.
27. Albright, Interview, 1967.
28. Hearings, S. Res. 226, 1933, p. 157.
29. Ibid.
30. Ibid.
31. Ibid.
32. Albright to Neilson, 1933.
33. Burt, p. 258.
34. Albright to Neilson, 1933.
35. Ibid.
36. Albright, Interview, 1967.
37. Albright to Neilson, 1933.
38. Albright, Interview, 1967.

CHAPTER SIX

1. Albright, Interview, 1967.
2. Peter Collier and David Horowitz, *The Rockefellers, An American Dynasty*, (New York: Holt, Rinehart, and Winston, 1976), p. 148.
3. Albright, Interview, 1967.
4. Joseph W. Ernst, ed., *Worthwhile Places: Correspondence of John D. Rockefeller, Jr. and Horace M. Albright*, (Fordham University Press, 1991), Rockefeller to Albright, August 15, 1924, pp. 24-25.
5. Albright, Interview, 1967.
6. *Jackson Hole Courier*, September 4. 1924, p. 2.
7. Ibid.

8. Ibid.
9. Ibid.
10. Albright to Neilson, 1933.
11. Ibid.
12. Albright, Interview, 1967.
13. Albright to Neilson, 1933.
14. Albright, Interview, 1967.
15. Albright to Neilson, 1933.
16. *Jackson Hole Courier*, August 6, 1925. p. 1.
17. Ibid.
18. *Jackson Hole Courier*, August 27, 1925, p. 1.
19. Ibid.
20. Ibid.
21. *Jackson Hole Courier*, September 3, 1925, p. 1.
22. *Jackson Hole Courier*, September 10, 1925, p. 1.
23. Ibid.
24. Ibid.
25. Hearings, S. Res. 226, 1933, pp. 293-294.
26. Ibid., 294.
27. Albright to Neilson, 1933.
28. *Jackson Hole Courier*, October 1, 1925, p. 1.
29. Hearings, S. Res. 226, 1933, p. 271.
30. Ibid., p. 270.
31. Ibid., pp. 266-267.

CHAPTER SEVEN

1. *Jackson Hole Courier*, March 11, 1926, p. 1.
2. *Jackson Hole Courier*, April 1, 1926, p. 1.
3. *Jackson Hole Courier*, April 15. 1926. p. 1.
4. Ibid.
5. Ibid.
6. S. 3427, 69th Congress, 1st Session.
7. Hearings Pursuant to S. Res. 237, 69th Congress, 1st Session, p. 1.
8. Ibid., pp. 34-35.
9. Ibid., pp. 51-52.
10. Ibid., p. 53.
11. Ibid., p. 67.
12. Ibid.
13. Ibid., pp. 67-68.
14. *Jackson Hole Courier*, March 3, 1927, p. 1.
15. Albright Interview, 1967.
16. Ibid.
17. Ibid.
18. Ernst, Albright to Rockefeller, September 29, 1926.

19. Ibid., pp. 62-63.
20. Ibid., Rockefeller to Albright, November 9, 1926, p. 69.
21. Ibid., Albright to Rockefeller, November 27, 1926, p. 69.
22. Ibid., Albright to Rockefeller, February 16, 1927, p. 75.
23. Ibid.
24. Ibid., p. 76.
25. Albright to Neilson, 1933.
26. Ibid.
27. Ernst, Albright to Rockefeller, February 16, 1927, p. 74.
28. Ibid.
29. Ibid., p. 73.
30. Ibid., p. 76.
31. Ibid., Rockefeller to Woods, February 28, 1927, p. 76.
32. Ibid., p. 78.
33. Hearings, S. Res. 226, p. 69.
34. Letter From Harold P. Fabian to Wilford Neilson, 1933, GTNP Files, Moose, Wyoming.
35. Ibid.
36. Ibid.
37. Ibid.
38. Senate Hearings, 1933, p. 195.
39. Ibid., p. 199.
40. Ibid., p. 201.
41. *Compendium*, Vol. I, p. 8.
42. *Jackson Hole Courier,* September 15. 1927. p. 1.
43. Fabian to Neilson, 1933.
44. Ibid.
45. Ibid.

CHAPTER EIGHT

1. *Jackson Hole Courier*, May 3, 1928, p. 1.
2. "Utah Company Buying Jackson Hole Ranches," *Jackson Hole Courier*, April 12, 1928, p. 1.
3. Ibid.
4. Ibid.
5. Fabian to Neilson, 1933.
6. "Park Extension Meeting Scheduled For July 22," *Jackson Hole Courier*, July 12, 1928, p. 1.
7. Albright, Interview, 1967.
8. Hearings, S. Res. 237, p. 21.
9. Hearings, S. Res. 226, p. 202.
10. Ibid., 204.
11. Albright, Interview, 1967.
12. Political Advertisement, *Jackson Hole Courier*, November 1, 1928. p. 4.
13. Larson, p. 451.
14. "Nye Introduces New Park Bill," *Jackson Hole Courier*, December 13, 1928, p. 1.
15. "Senate Action Favors Teton National Park," *Jackson Hole Courier*, January 31, 1929, p. 1.
16. *Public, No. 817*, 70th Congress, (S. 5543).
17. Everett Sanders, Presidential Secretary, to Horace Albright, February 26, 1929, as presented in Haines, *The Yellowstone Story*, Vol. II.
18. Ronald F. Lee, *Family Tree of the National Park System*, (Philadelphia: Eastern National Park and Monument Association, 1972), pp. 18-19.
19. "Coolidge Signs GTNP Bill Feb. 26," *Jackson Hole Courier*, March 14, 1929, p. 1.
20. Lee, p. 19.
21. Final Report of the Yellowstone National Park Boundary Commission, 71st Congress, 3rd Session, House Document 710, Washington, D.C., Government Printing Office, 1931.
22. Haines, p. 331.
23. "An Idea Crystallizes," *Jackson Hole Courier*, March 7, 1929, p. 1.
24. "Teton Park Is New Attraction," *Missoula Sentinel*, March 16, 1929.
25. "Grand Teton National Park Bill Signed," *Jackson Hole Courier*, March 7, 1929, p. 1.
26. "Congratulations Sam," *Livingston Enterprise*, April 5, 1929.
27. "Men Who Know In Charge," *Billings Gazette*, May 24, 1929.
28. Albright to Neilson, 1933.
29. "Nearer Park Grows Fast," *Jackson Hole Courier,* November 21, 1929.
30. "Chamber of Commerce Will Entertain Nation's Editors," *Jackson Hole Courier*, June 27, 1929, p. 1.
31. "Editors Join In Park Dedication Ceremonies," *Casper Tribune*, July 29, 1929.
32. "The Dedication Of Teton Nat. Park." *Salt Lake Tribune*, August 1, 1929.
33. Ibid.
34. "Editors Join In Park Dedication Ceremonies." *Casper Tribune*, July 29, 1929.

35. Ibid.

36. *Jackson Hole Courier*, May 23, 1929, p. 1.

37. Book Two, Deeds, 456638; Book Three, Deeds, 461561; Book Four, Deeds, 24, Teton County Clerks Office, Jackson, Wyoming.

38. Fabian to Neilson, 1933.

39. Ibid.

40. Hearings, S. Res. 226, p. 95.

41. Ibid., Also Fabian to Neilson, 1933.

42. Hearings, S. Res. 226, p. 166.

43. Larson, p. 421.

44. Hearings, S. Res. 226, p. 167.

45. Ibid p. 167.

46. Ibid., p. 168.

47. Editorial, *Jackson Hole Courier*, August 15, 1929, p. 1.

48. Albright to Neilson, 1933.

49. Fabian to Albright, August 26, 1929, printed in Senate Hearings Pursuant to Senate Resolution 226, p. 103.

50. Albright to Neilson, 1933.

51. Larson, p. 448.

52. From the mimeographed Proceedings of the Second Meeting of the Commission on the Conservation of the Elk of Jackson Hole, held in Washington, D.C., December 4-5, 1929, as cited in *Compendium*, Vol. I, p. 9.

53. Albright to Neilson, 1933.

54. Book Three, Deeds, pp. 563-597; Book Four, Deeds, pp. 293-295, Teton County Clerks Office, Jackson, Wyoming.

55. Hearings, S. Res. 226, p. 95.

56. Ibid., p. 60.

57. Albright, Interview, 1967.

58. Josephine Fabian, Personal Interview, Summer, 1975.

59. Hearings, S. Res. 226, p. 50.

60. Vanderbilt Webb to Robert Miller, December 5, 1927, Rockefeller Archive Center, SNLC, Box 84, Folder 780.

61. Allen, pp. 131-132.

62. Ernst, Albright to Rockefeller, January 4, 1927, p. 71.

63. Ibid., Albright to Rockefeller, January 15, 1929, p. 91.

64. "Yellowstone National Park," *Jackson Hole Courier*, September 19, 1929, p. 4.

CHAPTER NINE

1. "Courier Comments," *Jackson Hole Courier*, October 30, 1930, p. 1.

2. "Teton Asks Protection," *Casper Tribune*, as reprinted in the *Jackson Hole Courier*, January 16, 1930, p. 1.

3. Ibid.

4. "Bill Introduced In Congress Would Tax Yellowstone," *Jackson Hole Courier*, January 23, 1930, p. 1.

5. Ibid.

6. Fabian to Neilson, 1933.

7. Ibid.

8. Ibid.

9. "Governor Emerson Will Oppose Park Extension," *Jackson Hole Courier*, January 30, 1930, p. 1.

10. Fabian to Neilson, 1933.

11. Ibid.

12. Ibid.

13. Ibid.

14. Hearings, S. Res. 226, p. 85.

15. Ibid.

16. "Compromise Park Extension Plan Opposed Here," *Jackson Hole Courier*, February 13, 1930. p. 1.

17. "Governor Hopes For Favorable Park Boundary Report," *Jackson Hole Courier*, February 20, 1930, p. 1, (Reprinted from *Wyoming State Tribune*).

18. "No Addition To Elk Refuge At Present" *Jackson Hole Courier*, March 13, 1930, p. 1.

19. Fabian to Neilson, 1933.

20. Ibid.

21. "Snake River Land Company Officials Break Secrecy," *Jackson Hole Courier*, April 10, 1930, p. 4.

22. Ibid.

23. Ibid.

24. Ibid.

25. "Struthers Burt Writes Of Snake River Land Company," *Jackson Hole Courier*, June 5, 1930, p. 8.

26. Ibid., p. 1.

27. Ibid.

28. Ibid., p. 8.

29. "John L. Dodge Comments On Burt's Letter," *Jackson Hole Courier*, July 17, 1930, p. 1.

30. Letter from Hunter Lockwood Scott to Carl Pence, U.S. Forest Service, August 14, 1977, *Snake River- Wyoming, A Potential Wild and Scenic River, Draft Statement and Report,* USDA-FS-DES(LEG)79-02, L-11.
31. Ibid.
32. Albright to Neilson, 1933.
33. "Trail Work On Grand Teton Park Will Start Monday," *Jackson Hole Courier,* May 29, 1930, p. 1.
34. "Teton Park Gets Fire Protection," *Salt Lake Tribune,* July 25, 1930.
35. "Grand Teton National Park Growing In Popularity," *Jackson Hole Courier,* July 31, 1930, p. 1.
36. "Teton Park Travel Gains," *Jackson Hole Courier,* October 23, 1930, p. 1.
37. "Grand Teton Park Travel Shows Gain," *Salt Lake Tribune,* July 24, 1930.
38. "Assistant Secretary Of Interior Visits Teton Park," *Jackson Hole Courier,* July 24, 1930, p. 1. "Doctor Adds To Pictures In Grand Teton Park," *Salt Lake Tribune,* July 25, 1930. "Scion Mark Twain Visits Teton Park," *Salt Lake Tribune,* August 15, 1930. "Famous Author Visits Grand Teton National Park," *Jackson Hole Courier,* August 21, 1930, p. 1.
39. Hearings, S. Res. 226, pp. 85 & 86.
40. "Courier Comment," *Jackson Hole Courier,* October 30, 1930, p. 1.
41. Hearings, S. Res. 226, p. 86.
42. Ibid., pp. 155-156.
43. "Senatorial Game Committee In Jackson Hole," *Jackson Hole Courier,* September 25, 1930, p. 1; Also, Albright to Neilson, 1933.
44. Fabian to Neilson, 1933.
45. Hearings, S. Res. 226, p. 208.
46. Ibid.
47. Fabian to Neilson, 1933.
48. Hearings, S. Res. 226, p. 218.
49. "Buyers Will Offer This Land To The Government For Additional Park Lands," *Jackson Hole Courier,* November 6, 1930, p. 4.
50. "Over $200,000 Set Aside For 1931 Teton County Road Building," *Jackson Hole Courier,* November 6, 1930, p. 1.
51. "Jackson Lake Appropriation Meets Its Waterloo," *Jackson Hole Courier,* December 25, 1930, p. 8.
52. "Building Activities In County Over $200,000," *Jackson Hole Courier,* December 11, 1930, p. 1.

CHAPTER TEN

1. Editorial, *Jackson Hole Courier,* January 8, 1931, p. 4.
2. "Game Commission Head States Position Regarding Proposed Park Extension," *Jackson Hole Courier,* January 1, 1931, p. 1. Reprinted from *Dubois Frontier.*
3. Ibid.
4. "Courier Editor Comments On Jack Scott's Letter To The *Dubois Frontier,*" *Jackson Hole Courier,* January 1, 1931, p. 1.
5. Ibid.
6. Ibid.
7. Ibid., pp. 1 & 4.
8. Ibid., p. 4.
9. Editorial, *Jackson Hole Courier,* January 8, 1931, p. 4.
10. "Several Citizens Voice Opposition To Lions Club Resolution," *Jackson Hole Courier,* January 22, 1931, p. 4.
11. "Lions Club Resolution," *Jackson Hole Courier,* January 22, 1931, p. 1.
12. "Several Citizens Voice Opposition To Lions Club Resolution," *Jackson Hole Courier,* January 22, 1931, p. 5.
13. Ibid., p. 4.
14. Ibid., p. 5.
15. Ibid.
16. Ibid.
17. "Pioneer Resident Recounts Reasons Why He Opposes Further Park Extensions," By S. N. Leek, *Jackson Hole Courier,* January 15, 1931, pp. 1 & 8.
18. "Several Citizens Voice Opposition," Ibid.
19. "Public Statement," (Letter from George T. Lamb to Jackson Hole Courier), *Jackson Hole Courier,* January 22, 1931, p. 1.
20. Ibib., (Letter from Dr. C. W. Huff to *Jackson Hole Courier*), p. 1.

21. Ibid., (Letter from Carl Bark to *Jackson Hole Courier*) p. 5.
22. "Grovont And Kelly People Favor Jackson Hole Plan," *Jackson Hole Courier*, February 5, 1931, p. 5.
23. Ibid.
24. "Grovont Residents Express Views On Lions Resolution," *Jackson Hole Courier*, January 29, 1931, p. 4.
25. "Thompson Favors Park Extension," *Jackson Hole Courier*, January 29, 1931, p. 4.
26. "E. G. VanLeeuwen Comments On Jackson Hole Plan," *Jackson Hole Courier*, February 5, 1931, p. 5.
27. "No, We'll Have No Extension," *Jackson Hole Courier*, February 19, 1931, p. 1. Reprinted from *Salt Lake Tribune*.
28. Governor Frank C. Emerson to Senator Robert D. Carey, December 5, 1930, Printed in Senate Hearings pursuant to S. Res. 226, 1933, p. 219.
29. Ibid., p. 220.
30. "An Embarrassing Document," *Jackson Hole Courier*, February 12, 1931, p. 4. Reprinted from *Casper Star*.
31. "A Declaration Of Independence," *Jackson Hole Courier*, April 30, 1931, p. 1.
32. Ibid.
33. "Huff Again Elected Mayor," *Jackson Hole Courier*, May 14, 1931, p. 1.
34. "Home At Jackson Burned- Indignation Meeting Called," *Jackson Hole Courier*, July 16, 1931, p. 4. Reprinted from *Casper Tribune-Herald*.
35. Editorial, *Jackson Hole Courier*, July 23, 1931, p. 4.
36. "Kemmerer Gazette Again Embarrasses Wyoming," *Jackson Hole Courier*, August 13, 1931, p. 1.
37. Ibid.
38. Ibid.
39. Ibid.
40. "The Facts In The Matter," *Jackson Hole Courier*, August 13, 1931, p. 1.
41. "Jackson's Plight," *Jackson Hole Courier*, August 13, 1931, p. 1.
42. Fabian to Neilson, 1933.
43. Ibid.
44. Ibid.
45. Ibid.
46. Ibid.
47. Ibid.
48. Ibid.
49. Ibid.
50. "Courier Comment," *Jackson Hole Courier*, August 20, 1931, p. 4.
51. Fabian to Neilson, 1933.
52. Ibid.
53. Ibid.
54. "The Straight Facts," *Jackson Hole Courier*, October 8, 1931, p. 1. Reprinted from the *Sheridan Press*.
55. Editorial, *Jackson Hole Courier*, November 12, 1931, p. 4.
56. "The Retort, Courteous," *Jackson Hole Courier*, November 12, 1931, p. 4.
57. "Rockefeller Is Right," *Jackson Hole Courier*, December 24, 1931, p. 4. Reprinted from the *Wyoming Eagle*.
58. Ibid.
59. Albright, Interview, 1967.
60. "Keeping Jackson Hole Natural," *Jackson Hole Courier*, January 21, 1932, p. 1. Reprinted from *Idaho Falls Post-Register*.
61. Ibid.
62. "The Ghost Walks," *Jackson Hole Courier*, May 19. 1932, p. 1.
63. "Feudal Laws Now In Force In Jackson Hole: Rockefeller, Jr. Requires Rendition Of Feudal Service Before Giving Grants And Privileges," *Jackson Hole Courier*, May 26, 1932, p. 1. Reprinted from *The Grand Teton*.
64. "Cattle And Horse Association Held Annual Meeting Wednesday," *Jackson Hole Courier*, May 12, 1932, p. 1.
65. "Jackson Hole Cattle And Horse Assn. Hold Meeting," *Jackson Hole Courier*, June 2, 1932, p. 1.
66. "The Courier Pleads Not Guilty," *Jackson Hole Courier*, June 23, 1932, p. 1. Reprinted from *Inland Oil Index*.
67. Hearings, S. Res. 226.
68. Ibid.
69. "Yellowstone National Park Inquiry," *Jackson Hole Courier*, July 7, 1932, p. 4. Reprinted from *Inland Oil Index*.

70. "Jackson's Hole," *Jackson Hole Courier*, June 23, 1932, p. 4. Reprinted from *Sheridan Press*.

71. Editorial, *Jackson Hole Courier*, August 25, 1932, p. 4. Reprinted from *Sheridan Press*.

72. "Election Day Passes Quietly Despite Record Breaking Vote," *Jackson Hole Courier,* November 17, 1932, p. 1.

73. "Seventy-six Local Men Employed By Park Last Season," *Jackson Hole Courier*, November 24, 1932, p. 1.

74. Larson, p. 445.

75. "Editor Deming Of Tribune Visits Jackson's Hole: Land Of Scenic Wonders," *Jackson Hole Courier,* September 24, 1931, p. 1.

76. Ibid., p. 4.

77. Ibid.

CHAPTER ELEVEN

1. "Editorial," *Jackson Hole Courier*, April 13, 1933, p. 1.

2. "Carey, Kendrick, Carter Submit New Plan," *Jackson Hole Courier*, January 5, 1933, p. 1.

3. "The Turning Worm," by Julian Snow, *Wyoming Eagle*, as reprinted in the *Jackson Hole Courier*, December 29, 1932, p. 4.

4. "Carey, Kendrick, Carter Submit New Plan," *Jackson Hole Courier*, January 5, 1933, p. 1.

5. Fabian to Neilson, 1933.

6. "Take Up Your Bed And Walk," *Jackson Hole Courier*, January 5, 1933, p. 4.

7. "Lack of Leadership May Prove Expensive," *Jackson Hole Courier*, April 20, 1933, p. 4.

8. Fabian to Neilson, 1933.

9. Wire from Senator John B. Kendrick to Dr. R. A. Docker, Chairman, Wyoming Game and Fish Commission, "Wyoming Senators Oppose Game And Fish Activities," *Jackson Hole Courier*, January 26, 1933, p. 1.

10. House Bill 26, Wyoming House of Representatives, 1933, as printed in "Teton Land Act Passes House With 33-24 vote," *Jackson Hole Courier*, February 2, 1933, p. 1.

11. Ibid.

12. "Senate Unanimously Defeats Bill Aimed At Park Extension," *Jackson Hole Courier*, February 16, 1933, p. 1.

13. "Town Records Largest Vote In History," *Jackson Hole Courier*, May 11, 1933, p. 1.

14. "The Senate Investigation," *Jackson Hole Courier*, July 6, 1933, p. 4.

15. "Nation-Wide Scandal Predicted In Jackson Hole Land Hearing," *Denver Post* Reprinted in *Jackson Hole Courier*, "The Kingfish Spouts," July 20, 1933, p. 4.

16. Ibid.

17. "The Carey Interview," *Jackson Hole Courier*, July 27, 1933, p. 4.

18. "Pickett To Help In Park Plan Quiz," *Jackson Hole Courier*, June 8, 1933, p. 1.

19. "The Kingfish Spouts," *Jackson Hole Courier*, July 20, 1933, p. 4.

20. Hearings. S. Res. 226.

21. "Justice Blindfold?," *Jackson Hole Courier*, August 3, 1933, p. 4.

22. Fabian, Interview, 1975.

23. Albright, Interview, 1967.

24. Margaretta Corse Interview, 1970.

25. Testimony of Struthers Burt, Hearings, S. Res. 226, 72nd Congress, pp. 15 & 16.

26. Ibid., p. 16.

27. Ibid., Testimony of J. L. Eynon, p. 33.

28. Ibid., p. 27.

29. Kenneth Chorley to Horace Albright, March 18, 1929, S. Res. 226, 72nd Congress, Exhibit 33, pp. 223-224.

30. Ibid., and Kenneth Chorley to Horace Albright, April 16, 1929, Hearings, S. Res. 226, Exhibit 39, p. 225.

31. Ibid., Exhibit p. 39.

32. Fabian to Neilson, 1933.

33 John Daugherty, *A Place Called Jackson Hole*, (Grand Teton Natural History Association, 1999), p. 341.

34 Testimony of Albert W. Gabby, Hearings, S. Res. 226, pp. 300-331.

35. Testimony of Sam T. Woodring, Hearings, S. Res. 226, p. 428.

36. Harold Fabian to Kenneth Chorley, August 10, 1929, Exhibit 15, NPS File 610-01, part 4, Hearings, S. Res. 226, p. 104.

37. Ibid.

38. Ibid.

39. Testimony of Harold Fabian, Hearings, S. Res. 226, p. 109.

40. Kenneth Chorley to Harold Fabian, August 13, 1929, NPS File 610-01, part 5, Exhibit 10, Hearings, S. Res. 226, p. 101.
41. Arno B. Cammerer, Acting Director, NPS, to Kenneth Chorley, August 27, 1929, NPS File 610-01, part 5, Exhibit 13, Hearings, S. Res. 226, p. 103.
42. Horace M. Albright, Director, NPS, to Harold Fabian, January 14, 1930, NPS File 610-01, part 7, Exhibit 14, Hearings, S. Res. 226, p. 103.
43. Hearings, S. Res. 226, Exhibit 11, 102, Ibid.; Testimony of Harold Fabian, pp. 125-128; Ibid., Exhibit 19, p. 128.
44. Harold Fabian to Horace Albright, June 6, 1930, NPS File 610-01, part 9, Exhibit 20, Hearings, S. Res. 226, pp. 129-130.
45. Horace Albright, Director, NPS, to Major R. Y. Stuart, Chief Forester, U.S. Forest Service, June 18, 1930, NPS File 510-01, part 10, Exhibit 21, Hearings, S. Res. 226, p. 133.
46. Testimony of Harold Fabian, Hearings, S. Res. 226, p. 132.
47. Horace Albright to Harold Fabian, February 17, 1931, NPS File 610-01, part 15, Exhibit 22, Hearings, S. Res. 226, p. 135.
48. Larson, pp. 420-423.
49. Hearings, S. Res. 226, p. 136.
50. Ibid.
51. Fabian to Neilson, 1933.
52. Ibid.
53. "There Are No Yesterdays," *Jackson Hole Courier*, January 5, 1933, p. 4.
54. Testimony of Richard Winger, Hearings, S. Res. 226, p. 349.
55. Testimony of William L. Stilson, Hearings, S. Res. 226, pp. 239-240.
56. Testimony of Richard Winger, Hearings, S. Res. 226, p. 344.
57. Testimony of Jesse P. Chambers, Ibid., p. 246.
58. Testimony of Richard Winger, Ibid., p. 347.
59. Testimony of Fred J. Topping, Ibid., pp. 248-252.
60. Testimony of Richard Winger, Ibid., p. 345.
61. Daugherty, pp. 243-244, 252.
62. Testimony of Ed K. Smith, Ibid., p. 271.
63. Ibid., p. 272.
64. Harold P. Fabian to Richard Winger, November 27, 1929, Exhibit 52, Hearings, S. Res. 226, p. 346.
65. Testimony of Richard Winger, Ibid., p. 347.
66. Testimony of J.D. Ferrin, Ibid., p. 226.
67. Ibid., p. 269.
68. Ibid., p. 270.
69. Ibid.
70. J. H. Rayburn to Wilford Neilson, April 21, 1933, Grand Teton National Park Files.
71. Ibid.
72. Ibid.
73. Ibid.
74. Ibid.
75. Ibid.
76. Ibid.
77. Ibid.
78. Hearings, S. Res. 226, p. 150.
79. Testimony of William C. Deloney, Ibid., p. 212.
80. Hearings, S. Res. 226, p. 150.
81. "Editorial Comment," *Denver Post*, Reprinted in *Jackson Hole Courier*, August 17, 1933, p. 4.
82. "Editorial," *Wyoming Tribune*, Reprinted in *Jackson Hole Courier*, August 17, 1933, p. 4.
83. "Editorial," *Salt Lake Tribune*, Reprinted in *Jackson Hole Courier*, August 17, 1933, p. 4.
84. Larson, pp. 448-449.
85. "Work For Seventy-five Men Will Be Available At Park," *Jackson Hole Courier*, August 24, 1933, p. 1; "Yellowstone Park Travel Shows Increase For Year," *Jackson Hole Courier*, October 5, 1933, p. 1; "Work Starting On Hatchery," *Jackson Hole Courier*, December 7, 1933, p. 1.

CHAPTER TWELVE

1. "Jackson's Hole, The Last Frontier," *Jackson Hole Courier*, February 8, 1934, p. 4.
2. Larson, p. 443.
3. "Depression is Kind To Jackson Hole," *Jackson Hole Courier*, January 11, 1934, p. 4.
4. Stan Cohen, *The Tree Army*, (Missoula: Pictorial Histories Publishing Company, 1980), p. 155.
5. "Park Extension May Shortly Be Settled," *Jackson Hole Courier*, February 1, 1934, p. 4.
6. Ibid., p. 1.
7. Ibid.
8. Ibid., p. 4.
9. "Betrayed," *Jackson Hole Courier*, February 15, 1934, p. 4.

10. "Commercial Club Holds First Meeting Thursday Nite," *Jackson Hole Courier*, January 25, 1934, p. 1.

11. "Jackson Hole Again Center Of Attention At Nation's Capital," *Jackson Hole Courier*, March 22, 1934, p. 1.

12. Ibid.

13. "Sen. O'Mahoney Forecasts Park Agreement Soon," *Jackson Hole Courier*, March 29, 1934, p. 1.

14. "Park Addition Bill To Be Introduced At This Session Of Congress," *Jackson Hole Courier*, April 26, 1934, p. 1.

15. "Report on Probable Tax Losses Heard At Meeting Wednesday," *Jackson Hole Courier*, May 10, 1934, p. 1.

16. "The Eleventh Hour," *Jackson Hole Courier*, May 3, 1934, p. 4.

17. Hillory Tolson to Horace Albright, June 2, 1934, File 610-01, pt. 30, Box 1057, GT, NPS, RG 79, NA. Also see Righter, Robert G., 1982, *Crucible for Conservation*, (Denver: Colorado Associated University Press, 1982), p. 86.

18. "Park Extension To Follow 'The Jackson Hole Plan,'" *Jackson Hole Courier*, May 31, 1934, p. 1.

19. Ibid.

20. *Compendium*, Vol. I, p. 11.

21. Report on HR. 2065, House of Representatives, pp. 1-2.

22. "Travel In Teton Much Larger In Season Of '34," *Jackson Hole Courier*, October 25, 1934, p. 1.

23. Summary Of Tax Provisions Contained In Proposed Legislation Relating To Jackson Hole, *Compendium*, Vol. II, Part I, Exhibit 9, p. 2. Hereafter referred to as Summary of Tax Provisions.

24. "National Parks Association Favors Carey Bill For Park Extension But Opposes Two Portions Of Measure," *Jackson Hole Courier*, January 17, 1935, p. 1.

25. "Local Lions Club Endorses Park Association Program," *Jackson Hole Courier*, May 2, 1935, Vol. 27, No. 39, p. 1.

26. "Extension Of Park Not To Come Up In Congress In 1935," *Jackson Hole Courier*, July 25, 1935, p. 1.

27. "Dr. Huff Is Again Elected Mayor Of Jackson; 384 Votes Cast," *Jackson Hole Courier*, May 16, 1935, p. 1.

28. "Teton Park Has Largest Tourist Year In History," *Jackson Hole Courier*, October 10, 1935, p. 1.

29. "We Need Publicity," *Tribune-Leader*, as reprinted in *Jackson Hole Courier*, March 21, 1935, p. 4.

30. "Many Protests Expected To Follow Printing Of Elk Herd Photographs," *Jackson Hole Courier*, March 28, 1935, p. 1.

31. Ibid.

32. Ibid.

33. "Correct The Mis-Statements," *Jackson Hole Courier*, March 28, 1935, Vp. 4.

34. "New Solution Of Surplus Elk Problem Offered By Game Dept. After Protests," *Jackson Hole Courier*, November 28, 1935, p. 1.

35. Ibid.

36. "Who Let The Fence Down For The Elk," *Jackson Hole Courier*, December 19, 1935, p. 1.

37. "Fences Of Elk Pens Are Let Down; Second Time Within 30 Days," *Jackson Hole Courier*, January 9, 1936, p. 1.

38. "Elk Slaughtering Program To Cease," *Jackson Hole Courier*, January 16, 1936, p. 1.

39. "J.R. Jones Passed Away At Age Of 63," *Jackson Hole Courier*, January 16, 1936, p. 1.

40. Haines, p. 460; Also, "Supt. Roger Toll Killed In New Mexico," *Jackson Hole Courier*, February 26, 1936, p. 1.

41. "Travel In Teton Park Shows Over 25 Per Cent Increase," *Jackson Hole Courier*, October 22, 1936, p. 1.

42. "Business Shows 10 Per Cent Gain In Jackson Over 1935," *Jackson Hole Courier*, January 14, 1937, p. 1.

CHAPTER THIRTEEN

1. Hearings before a Subcommittee of the Committee on Public Lands and Surveys, United States Senate, 75th Congress, Third Session, Pursuant to Senate Resolution 250;

August 8 and 10, 1938, pp 215, 216. Hereafter referred to as Hearings, S. Res. 250.

2. "Dick Winger Will Head New State Game Commission," *Jackson Hole Courier*, February 25, 1937, p. 1.

3. "Objections to Roadside Signs Heard at Annual Dude Ranchers' Meet," *Jackson Hole Courier*, September 16, 1937, p. 1.

4. "Jackson- A Convention City," *Jackson Hole Courier*, June 10, 1937, p. 4.

5. "Jackson Hole Suffers Great Loss By Death of Dr. Charles W. Huff," *Jackson Hole Courier*, September 23, 1937, p. 1.

6. "If You Seek His Monument, Look Around," *Jackson Hole Courier*, September 30, 1937, p. 4.

7. "An Open Letter To The Wyoming Congressional Delegation," *Jackson Hole Courier*, January 6, 1938, p. 1.

8. "S. N. Leek Expresses Self on Teton Park Extension," *Jackson Hole Courier*, December 16, 1937, p. 5.

9. "Suggests That Land Be Opened For Farming," *Jackson Hole Courier*, December 23, 1937, p. 1.

10. "Just A Few Questions," *Jackson Hole Courier*, January 6, 1938, p. 4.

11. "Wire To Congressman Paul Greever," *Jackson Hole Courier*, December 16, 1937, p. 1.

12. "Park Extension Bill Will Not Be Introduced Before New Years, Says Congressman Paul Greever," *Jackson Hole Courier,* December 16, 1937, p. 1.

13. "The Nature Part Of The Picture," Jackson Hole Courier, December 9, 1937, p. 4.

14. Albright to Neilson, 1933.

15. Hearings, S. Res. 226, p. 204.

16. Ibid.

17. "Nothing New About Extension," *Jackson Hole Courier*, December 16, 1937, p. 4.

18. "Many Interests In Park Problem," *Jackson Hole Courier*, December 23, 1937, p. 4.

19. Ibid.

20. Ibid.

21. Ibid.

22. "Albright In Favor Of Teton Park Proposal," *Jackson Hole Courier*, January 27, 1938, p. 1.

23. "Opposition To Teton Park Expansion Irks Secretary H. Ickes," *Jackson Hole Courier*, March 31, 1938, p. 1.

24. "Jackson Hole Residents Express Opposition To Teton Park Extension In Meeting With Governor Miller," *Jackson Hole Courier*, January 13, 1938, p. 1.

25. Ibid.

26. Ibid.

27. Ibid.

28. "Report of Committee On Grand Teton National Park Extension Plan," as printed in *Jackson Hole Courier*, February 3, 1938, p. 5.

29. "Committee Report Advocating That All Park Extension Efforts Cease Adopted By Citizens At Meeting," *Jackson Hole Courier*, February 3, 1938, p. 1.

30. Governor Miller to Senator O'Mahoney, Joseph C. O'Mahoney Collection, Box 257, Teton Park Correspondence.

31. Senate Report No. 1571, 75th Congress, 3rd Session. Also Hearings, S. Res. 250, p. 2.

32. "Senate Committee Will Be Welcome To Local Residents," *Jackson Hole Courier,* March 10, 1938, p. 1.

33. "A Report By The National Park Service On The Proposal To Extend The Boundaries Of Grand Teton National Park, Wyoming," July 1938, Contained in *Compendium*, Vol. II, Part I, Exhibit 11, p. 4. Hereafter referred to as Report To Extend Teton Park. 1938.

34. Ibid., p. 2.

35. Ibid., p. 4.

36. Ibid., p. 7.

37. Hearings, S. Res. 250, p. 44.

38. Report To Extend Teton Park, 1938, p. 10.

39. Hearings, S. Res. 250, p. 62.

40. Ibid.

41. Ibid., pp. 178-179.

42. Ibid.

43. *Compendium*, Vol. I, p. 1.

44. Hearings, S. Res. 250, p. 199.

45. Ibid., p. 200.

46. Ibid.

47. Ibid.

48. Ibid., p. 201.

49. Ibid.

50. Ibid., pp. 201-202.

51. Ibid., p. 221.

52. Recreational Use Of Land In The United States Part XI Of The Report On Land Planning, November 1934, By The National Park Service, Submitted by Arno E. Cammerer, Director of National Parks, 1938, pp 25,27. Also see Hearings, S. Res. 250, p. 73.

53. Ibid., p. 202.

54. Hearings, S. Res. 250, p. 205.

55. Ibid., p. 204.

56. Ibid.

57. Ibid., p. 207.

58. Ibid., p. 208.

59. Ibid., p. 209.

60. "Park Extension Compromise?" *Jackson Hole Courier*, September 1, 1938, p. 1.

61. "Park Extension Compromise?" *Jackson Hole Courier*, September 8, 1938, p. 1.

62. "Resolution," *Jackson Hole Courier*, October 6, 1938, p. 5.

63. "Communications To And From Governor Miller," Ibid., Telegram of September 28, 1938, to Leslie Miller from Lions Club Of Jackson Hole.

64. Ibid., Telegram of October 1, 1938, to William L. Simpson from Leslie A. Miller.

65. Ibid., Telegram of October 3, 1938, to Leslie A. Miller from Lions Club of Jackson Hole.

66. Larson, p. 466

67. *Wyoming State Tribune*, August 1937, as quoted in Larson, pp. 466 & 467.

68. "Gov. Miller Receives Letter From M.R. Yokel On Winger Resignation," *Jackson Hole Courier*, October 13, 1938, p. 1.

69. Larson, p. 467.

70. "Horton Hits At Park Extension," *Jackson Hole Courier*, October 13, 1938, p. 4.

71. "Nearly Half Million Visit Yellowstone PK," and "Grand Teton Park Shows Tourist Increase Over 1937," *Jackson Hole Courier*, October 30, 1938, pp. 1 & 8.

72. "Fifteen Million Dollars Spent In Wyoming By Tourists Report Reveals," *Jackson Hole Courier*, January 26, 1939, p. 1.

CHAPTER FOURTEEN

1. Letter from Arno B. Cammerer, Director, National Park Service to Congressman Frank O. Horton, Printed in "National Park Director Refuses Petition on Leigh Lake Road and Boating," *Jackson Hole Courier*, May 2, 1940, p. 1.

2. "Horton Opposes Federal Invasion On State Lands," *Jackson Hole Courier*, January 26, 1939, p. 1 & 3.

3. "All Rooms Taken," *Jackson Hole Courier*, March 16, 1939, p. 4.

4. "Hamm Wants The Coyotes," *Jackson Hole Courier*, March 30, 1939, p. 4.

5. "Grand Teton Scenery Given Publicity At New York World Fair," *Jackson Hole Courier*, May 25, 1939, p. 1; "Tourist Business Up 10 Per Cent Over 1938," *Jackson Hole Courier*, June 1, 1939, p. 1; "Teton Park Opens With New Record Number Visitors," *Jackson Hole Courier*, June 8, 1939, p. 1.

6. "Wyoming's Congressman Frank O. Horton Introduces Bill At Washington For Abolishment Of Grand Teton National Park," *Jackson Hole Courier*, June 22, 1939, p. 1.

7. "A Few Comments On Bill Of Congressman Horton To Abolish Grand Teton Park," *Jackson Hole Courier*, June 29, 1939, p. 1.

8. "John D. Rockefeller, Jr. Purchases Property Near Phelps Lake," *Jackson Hole Courier*, November 23, 1939, p. 1.

9. "Washington Officials Agree To Use Of Jackson Dam As Bridge After Governor's Trip To Capital City," *Jackson Hole Courier*, October 12, 1939, p. 1.

10. "Gov. Smith Intercedes In Teton Pass Opening," *Jackson Hole Courier*, January 11, 1940, p. 1.

11. "Sup't. Whitcraft Transferred To Petrified Forest," *Jackson Hole Courier*, February 1, 1940, p. 1.

12. "White Mountain Smith, Teton Park Superintendent, Fulfills Traditions of Life In The Early Western Day," by C. Watt Brandon of *Kemmerer Gazette*, reprinted in *Jackson Hole Courier*, July 18, 1940, 1. Also see Haines, *The Yellowstone Story, Volume II*, pp. 149-153.

13. "Horton Reports New Try To Enlarge Park," *Jackson Hole Courier*, April 18, 1940, p. 1.

14. "National Park Director Refuses Petition On Leigh Lake Road and Boating," *Jackson Hole Courier*, May 2, 1940, p. 1.

15. Ibid.

16. "Ickes States Views On National Parks," *Jackson Hole Courier*, May 4, 1933, p. 4.

17. "Certificate Of Incorporation Of Jackson Hole Preserve, Inc.," *Jackson Hole Courier*, May 30, 1940, p. 4.

18. "Snake River Land Company Turns Holdings Over To Newly Formed Corporation," *Jackson Hole Courier*, May 16, 1940, p. 1.

19. "Insulting Charity," *Cody Enterprise*, July 3, 1940. As printed in *Jackson Hole Courier*, July 11, 1940, p. 4.

20. "South Entrance Shows Largest Travel Increase, Yellowstone Statistics Show," *Jackson Hole Courier*, October 17, 1940, p. 1.

21. "Milward Simpson Lashes Out At The Bureaucratic Oppression of Teton County At Open Meeting," *Jackson Hole Courier*, September 19, 1940, p. 1.

22. Larson, p. 451.

23. "Teton County Vote Hits 10 Per Cent Over Previous High," *Jackson Hole Courier*, November 7, 1940, p. 1.

24. Larson, p. 451.

25. "Services Held Here Tuesday, Dec. 17 For Wm. L. Simpson, Pioneer Attorney," *Jackson Hole Courier*, December 19, 1940, p. 1.

26. "Civil Aeronautics Administration Intercedes With General Land Office For Jackson Hole Airport," *Jackson Hole Courier*, November 6, 1941, p. 1.

27. "Heretofore Unpublished Poem By Al Austin Reveals Character," *Jackson Hole Courier*, July 3, 1941, p. 1.

28. Ibid.

CHAPTER FIFTEEN

1. *Compendium*, Vol. II, Part 2, Exhibit 32, Press Release by Department of Interior.

2. "Teton County Leads State In Bond Drive," *Jackson Hole Courier*, March 4, 1943, p. 1.

3. "Almer Nelson Speaks On Elk Herd Management Problems At Rotary Meet," *Jackson Hole Courier*, January 22, 1942, p. 1.

4. "Game Hunting Sanctioned By Federal Government," *Jackson Hole Courier*, July 16, 1942, p. 1.

5. *Compendium*, Volume II, Part 2, Exhibit 13. Also see Hearings on HR 2241 before Senate Subcommittee on Public Lands and Surveys, 1943, 78th Congress, p. 80.

6. Josephine Fabian, Interview, 1975.

7. Daugherty, p. 315.

8. *Compendium*, Volume II, Part 2, Exhibit 13.

9. Richard Winger to Horace M. Albright, January 7, 1932, "Grand Teton" Folder, Box 289, GT, NPS, RG 79, NA.

10. Righter, pp 104-105.

11. Memorandum from Arthur E. Demarey to Harold Ickes, August 1, 1940, in File 610-01, Part 36, Box 1059, GT, NPS, RG 79, NA.

12. Righter, p. 109.

13. Harold Ickes to John D. Rockefeller, Jr., February 19, 1943, NPS- National Monuments, Jackson Hole, Part 1, File 12-46, Department of Interior, RG 48, NA.

14. Joseph O'Mahoney to Harold Ickes, February 23, 1943, Ibid.

15. Memorandum For the President, March 5, 1943, Enclosure 310, from Secretary of Interior Harold Ickes, *Compendium*, Volume II, Part 2, Exhibit 14.

16. Letter to the President from Secretary of Interior Harold L. Ickes, March 5, 1943, Enclosure 2437843, *Compendium*, Volume II, Part 2, Exhibit 14.

17. Margaret and Olaus Murie, *Wapiti Wilderness*, (New York: Alfred A. Knopf, 1966), p. 122.

18. "President Signs Proclamation Establishing The Upper Jackson Hole Country As A National Monument," *Jackson Hole Courier*, March 18, 1943, p. 1.

19. Telegram from Senator E.V. Robertson to Felix Buchenroth, Sr. Printed in "Copy Of Telegram," *Jackson Hole Courier*, March 18, 1943, p. 1.

20. "Governor Hunt Issues Statement Criticizing Federal Government," *Jackson Hole Courier*, March 18, 1943, p. 1.

21. "Sen. O'Mahoney Hits Nat'l Monument Act," *Jackson Hole Courier*, March 22, 1943, EXTRA, p. 1. Also see Congressional Record, March 19, 1943, pp. 2269-2272 and 2277.

22. "Citizens' Meeting Sees Hope Monument Proclamation To Be Declared Invalid; Protest Committee Formed," *Jackson Hole Courier*, March 22, 1943, EXTRA, p. 1.

23. Allen Drury, *A Senate Journal 1943-1945*, (New York: McGraw-Hill, p.12.

24. Statement of Policy Concerning Administration of Jackson Hole National Monument, Wyoming, Harold L. Ickes, Secretary of Interior, April 8, 1943, *Compendium*, Volume II, Part 2, Exhibit 18. Also see House Hearings on HR 2241, pp. 85&397.

25. Ibid.

26. Telegram, Lawrence C. Merriam, Regional Park Service, Director to Charles J. Smith, Superintendent, Grand Teton National Park, printed in *Jackson Hole Courier,* March 25, 1943, p. 1.

27. "No Action To Be Taken Within Monument Area Without Written Notice To All Parties- Park Supt.," *Jackson Hole Courier*, April 8, 1943, p. 1.

28. Larson, *Wyoming's War Years 1941-1945*, (Laramie: University of Wyoming, 1954), p. 99. (Hereafter referred to as Larson, War Years.)

29. Ibid., p. 197.

30. "221,610- Acre Monument," *Saturday Evening Post*, August 28, 1943.

31. "Farm Bureau Federation Voices Opposition To Mon't In Resolution," *Jackson Hole Courier*, April 1, 1943, p. 1.

32. Letter to President Roosevelt from Wyoming Governor Lester Hunt, April 1, 1943. *Compendium,* Volume II, Part 2, Exhibit 17.

33. Letter to Wyoming Governor Lester Hunt from President Franklin Roosevelt, April 29, 1943. *Compendium*, Volume II, Part 2, Exhibit 17.

34. Ibid.

35. "Governor Hunt Says Action Violates Fundamental Principle of Democracy," *Jackson Hole Courier*, April 8, 1943, p. 1.

36. "Senator O'Mahoney Introduces Bill To Investigate Land Grabbing Activities of The Department of Interior," *Jackson Hole Courier*, April 22, 1943, p. 1.

37. Larson, War Years, p. 198.

38. Ibid.

39. Donald Hough, *The Cocktail Hour in Jackson Hole*, (New York: W.W. Norton, 1951), p. 241.

40. Clifford Hansen interview and conversations, 1981-1993.

41. Ibid.

42. "Stockmen Hurl Challenge At Park Service; Spurn Permits," *Jackson Hole Courier*, May 13, 1943, p. 1.

43. Ibid.

44. Memorandum for the Secretary, from Director Drury, October 26, 1943, *Compendium*, Volume II, Part 2, Exhibit 31.

45. Larson, War Years, p. 198.

46. "Jackson Hole Delegation To Go To Washington To Testify Before Public Lands Committee," *Jackson Hole Courier*, May 20, 1943, p. 1.

47. Ibid.

48. T. H. Watkins, "The Terrible-Tempered Mr. Ickes," *Audubon*, March 1984, 93.

49. Ibid., p. 97.

50. Ibid., p. 104.

51. *Compendium*, Vol. II, Part 2, Exhibit 19.

52. Ibid.

53. Robert B. Betts, *Along the Ramparts of the Tetons*, (Boulder: Colorado Associated University Press, 1978), p. 182.

54. *Compendium*, Vol. II, Part 2, Exhibit 20.

55. "Majority of House Committee Favors Barrett's Bill," *Jackson Hole Courier*, June 3, 1943, p. 1.

56. Hearings pursuant to H.R 2241, To Abolish the Jackson Hole National Monument, p. 50.

57. Ibid., pp. 61-62.

58. *Public-No. 209*, (34 Stat. L. 225), Section 2.

59. Statement of Newton B. Drury, Director, National Park Service, Pursuant to Hearings in the House of Representatives Regarding H.R. 2241, May 26, 1943. *Compendium*, Vol. II, Part 2, Exhibit 21, p. 7.

60. Ibid.

61. "Mr. Ickes and His Birds," *Jackson Hole Courier*, May 20, 1943, p. 1.

62. "Extensive Elk Hunting Season is Indicated By Need For Huge Kill," *Jackson Hole Courier*, June 17, 1943, p. 1.

63. Statement of Newton B. Drury, *Compendium.*, Vol. II, Part 2, Exhibit, 21, p. 2.

64. Statement of Leslie A. Miller before the House Public Lands Committee regarding H.R.2241, June 18, 1943, *Compendium*, Vol. II, Part 2, Exhibit 23. p. 1.

65. Ibid., p. 9.

66. Ibid., pp. 12-13.

67. Hearings pursuant to H.R. 2241, p. 51.

68. William C. Everhart, *The National Park Service*, (New York: Prager Publishers), Appendix II, pp. 253-254.

69. Hearings pursuant to H.R. 2241, pp. 271-273.

70. Ibid., p. 252.

71. Ibid., p. 186.

72. "Citizens Vote To Continue To Oppose Ickes' Land Grab," *Jackson Hole Courier*, June 24, 1943, p. 1.

73. "Wyoming Draws First Blood In Fight with Ickes Over Monum't," *Jackson Hole Courier*, June 17, 1943, p. 1.

74. Ibid.

75. "Jackson Hole Cited as Example In Bill To Repeal Act of 1906," *Jackson Hole Courier*, June 17, 1943, p. 3.

76. Ibid.

77. Hearings pursuant to S.Res.134, *Compendium*, Vol. II, Part 2, Exhibit 24, p. 20.

78. Conrad L. Wirth, Memorandum for the Files, September 6th, 1943, *Compendium*, Vol. II, Part 2, Exhibit 25, p. 2.

79. Ibid., pp. 3-5.

80. Testimony of Newton B. Drury before the House Public Lands Committee regarding H.R.2241, June 18, 1943, *Compendium*, Vol. III, Part 2, Exhibit 7, p. 70.

81. Ibid., p. 19.

82. Testimony of Harold Ickes before the House Public Lands Committee pursuant to H.R. 2241, *Compendium*, Vol. III, Part 2, Exhibit 7.

83. Hearings pursuant to S. Res.134, *Compendium*, Vol. II, Part 2, Exhibit 24, p. 9.

84. Hearings pursuant to S.Res.134, *Compendium*, Vol. II, Part 2, Exhibit 24.

85. Testimony of Clifford Hansen pursuant to S. Res. 134, *Compendium*, Vol. II, Part 2, Exhibit 24, p. 40.

86. Ibid., pp. 43 & 44.

87. Ibid., p. 56.

88. Ibid.

89. Ibid.

90. Testimony of Lester Bagley pursuant to S. Res. 134, *Compendium*, Vol. II, Part 2, Exhibit 24, p. 70.

91. Testimony of Millward Simpson pursuant to S. Res. 134, *Compendium*, Vol. II, Part 2, Exhibit 24, p. 109.

92. "Road Meeting Votes For Hoback Canyon," *Jackson Hole Courier*, July 22, 1943, p. 1.

93. Testimony of Dick Rutledge pursuant to S. Res. 134, *Compendium*, Vol. II, Part 2, Exhibit 24, pp. 84-87.

94. Ibid., pp. 87 & 88.

95. Hearings pursuant to S. Res. 134, *Compendium*, Vol. II, Part 2, Exhibit 24, pp. 89-90.

96. Speech of Hon. J. Hardin Peterson, Congressional Record, 78th Congress, Second Session, Wednesday, June 7, 1944. Also see *Compendium*, Vol. II, Part 2, Exhibit 32.

97. Ibid.

98. "Don't Be Fooled!," *Jackson Hole Courier*, August 12, 1943, p. 1.

99. Clifford Hansen interview and conversations, 1981-1993.

100. "Cheyenne Meet Agrees Monument To Be Abolished," *Jackson Hole Courier*, September 9, 1943, Vol. 26, No. 11, p. 1.

101. Ibid.

102. Memorandum for the Secretary by Newton B. Drury, September 7, 1943, *Compendium*, Vol. II, Part 2, Exhibit 26.

103. Memorandum for the Director by Conrad L. Wirth, September 9, 1943, *Compendium*, Vol. II, Part 2, Exhibit 27.

104. Memorandum for the Secretary by R.H. Rutledge, September 16, 1943, *Compendium*, Vol. II, Part 2, Exhibit 28.

105. Memorandum for the Secretary, September 17, 1943, *Compendium*, Vol. II, Part 2, Exhibit 29.

106. Ibid.

107. Ibid.

108. Congressional Record, Proceedings and Debates of the 59th Congress, First Session, Vol. XL, p. 7888.

109. *Public Law 133*, Section 8, July 12, 1943.

110. Frank L. Yates to Interior Secretary Ickes, September 22, 1943, *Compendium*, Vol. II, Part 2, Exhibit 30, p. 11.

111. Speech of Senator Joseph O'Mahoney, Congressional Record, Vol. 89, p. 6168.

112. Frank L. Yates to Interior Secretary Ickes, September 22, 1943, *Compendium*, Vol. II, Part 2, Exhibit 30, p. 12.

113. Memorandum for the Secretary from Park Service Director Drury, October 26, 1943, *Compendium*, Vol. II, Part 2, Exhibit 31.

114. Ibid.

115. "U.S. Judge Denies Federal Motion in Monument Suit," *Jackson Hole Courier*, December 2, 1943, p. 1.

116. Lieut. Walter L. Spicer, Jr. Killed in Aeorplane Crash," *Jackson Hole Courier*, September 9, 1943, p. 1.

117. "Lieut. Harvey Hagen Loses Life In Plane Crash in Florida," *Jackson Hole Courier*, September 30, 1943, p. 1.

118. Fritiof Fryxell, "The Geology of Jackson Hole," *National Parks Magazine*, January-March, 1944.

CHAPTER SIXTEEN

1. Will Rogers quoted by Horace Albright before the House Public Lands Committee, 1943, Statement by Horace Albright pursuant to H.R. 2241, *Compendium*, Vol. III, Exhibit 8, p. 480.

2. "War Bond Sales Total 112,000," *Jackson Hole Courier*, February 10, 1944, p. 1.

3. "Teton County First in State To Go Over the Top in Red Cross Drive," *Jackson Hole Courier*, March 9, 1944, p. 1.

4. Editorial, *Jackson Hole Courier*, March 29, 1944, p.1

5. Minority Report of House Public Lands Committee on H.R. 2241, J. Hardin Peterson, Report No. 1303, House of Representatives, 78th Congress, 2nd Session, *Compendium*, Vol. II, Part 3, Exhibit 36.

6. "Association Propounds Further Fallacy in Defense of Monument," *Jackson Hole Courier,* March 30, 1944, p. 1.

7. "Funeral Services Held Tuesday for J.D. 'Cy' Ferrin," *Jackson Hole Courier*, April 13, 1943, p. 1.

8. "Park Service May Ask in Vain For Monument Funds," *Jackson Hole Courier*, April 27, 1943, p. 1.

9. *Compendium*, Vol. I, p. 17.

10. "Barrett Bill Passes House Rules Committee," *Jackson Hole Courier*, May 5, 1943, p. 1.

11. Testimony of Horace Albright before the House Public Lands Committee pursuant to H.R. 2241, *Compendium*, Vol. III, Exhibit 8.

12. Memorandum for the Files by Conrad L. Wirth, August 28, 1944, *Compendium*, Vol. II, Part 3, Exhibit 33.

13. Ibid.

14. Ibid.

15. Ibid.

16. Memorandum for the Director, August 30, 1944, by Jackson E. Price, Chief Counsel, Supplement to Jackson Hole National Monument trial report of August 30, *Compendium*, Vol. II, Part 3, Exhibit 34.

17. Ibid.

18. Judges of the United States Courts, John C. Pickett, http://fjc.gov/history/home.nsf.

19. Memorandum for the Director, August 30, 1944, by Jackson E. Price, Chief Counsel, Supplement to Jackson Hole National Monument trial report of August 30, *Compendium*, Vol. II, Part 3, Exhibit 34.

20. Ibid.

21. Ibid.

22. "Two Cases Polio Reported Here," *Jackson Hole Courier*, August 3, 1944, p. 1.

23. "Jackson Airport Project Will Get $130,000 of CAA Program," *Jackson Hole Courier*, November 30, 1944, p. 1.

24. "Mayor Says No Air Port Franchise 'Til Boys Return Home," *Jackson Hole Courier*, August 10, 1944, p. 1.

25. "Dewey Objects to Jackson Hole Monument Deal," *Jackson Hole Courier*, September 21, 1944, p. 1.

26. Editorial, *Jackson Hole Courier*, November 9, 1944, p. 1.

27. H.R. 5469, 78th Congress, 2nd Session, November 16, 1945, *Compendium*, Vol. II, Part 3, Exhibit 35.

28. Ibid.

29. Congressional Record, Vol. 90, No. 173, December 11, 1944.

30. *Compendium*, Vol. I, p. 18.

31. Memorandum of Disapproval, Franklin D. Roosevelt, December 29, 1944, *Compendium*, Vol. II, Part 3, Exhibit 39, p. 1.

32. Ibid., p. 2.

33. "Local Group Asks Commissioners Cease Official Opposition," *Jackson Hole Courier*, January 4, 1945, p. 1.

34. Ibid.

35. H.R. 1292, 79th Congress, 1st Session, January 9, 1945, *Compendium*, Vol. II, Part 3, Exhibit 40, p. 4.

36. Secretary Harold L. Ickes to John D. Rockefeller, Jr., January 10, 1945, *Compendium*, Vol. II, Part 3, Exhibit 41.

37. John D. Rockefeller, Jr. to Secretary Harold L. Ickes, January 16, 1945, *Compendium*, Vol. II, Part 3, Exhibit 41.

38. Secretary Harold L. Ickes to John D. Rockefeller, Jr., January 24, 1945, *Compendium*, Vol. II, Part 3, Exhibit 41.

39. "Monument Deal Up in State Senate," *Jackson Hole Courier*, February 8, 1945, p. 1.

40. *State of Wyoming v. Paul R. Franke*, District Court, D Wyoming, Civil Action No. 2875, February 10, 1945, 58 F. Supp.890.

41. Ibid.

42. "Park Supt. Issues Statement Following Kennedy's Dismissal Of National Monument Suit," *Jackson Hole Courier*, February 22, 1945, p. 1.

43. *State of Wyoming v. Paul R. Franke*, District Court, D Wyoming, Civil Action No. 2875, February 10, 1945, 58 F. Supp.890, p. 8.

44. Ibid.

45. Memorandum to Secretary Ickes from Directory Drury, March 17, 1945, *Compendium*, Vol. 1, p. 21.

46. "Izaak Walton League Chapter Organized," *Jackson Hole Courier*, March 8, 1945, p. 1.

47. "Local Group to Apply for new Charter In Izaak Walton League," *Jackson Hole Courier*, March 29, 1945, p. 1.

48. "Two Jackson Boys Wounded in Italy," *Jackson Hole Courier*, May 3, 1945, p. 1.

49. "Yellowstone To Open May 26," *Jackson Hole Courier*, May 24, 1945, p. 1.

50. "Yellowstone Travel Double During Season," *Jackson Hole Courier*, p. 1.

51. "Air Routes Include Jackson; Two Lines Authorized To Service," *Jackson Hole Courier*, May 31, 1945, p. 1.

52. "To Grant Grazing Permits on Mon'm't," *Jackson Hole Courier*, July 5, 1945, p. 1.

53. *Public Laws-CH. 262*-July 3, 1945, p. 360.

54. "Reclamation Service Proposes Three Dams for Snake River," *Jackson Hole Courier*, July 26, 1945, p. 1.

55. "Honor Role," *Jackson Hole Courier*, August 16, 1945, p. 1.

56. "Jackson Men Fight In Famed Mountain Division In Italy," *Jackson Hole Courier*, March 1, 1945, p. 1.

57. "Hunt Discloses Further Details On Proposed Wildlife Exhibit," *Jackson Hole Courier*, November 8, 1945, p. 1.

58. "Local Interviews Indicate Disapproval of Project," *Jackson Hole Courier*, November 8, 1945, p. 1.

59. Ibid., p. 3.

60. "Quote Of The Week," *Jackson Hole Courier*, November 22, 1945, p. 1.

61. Memorandum of Agreement Between The National Park Service And The Bureau Of Reclamation Governing The Administration And Development Of Reclamation Lands In Jackson Hole National Monument, *Compendium*, Vol. II, Part 3, Exhibit 45.

62. Ibid.

CHAPTER SEVENTEEN

1. "Local Interviews Indicate Disapproval of Project," *Jackson Hole Courier*, November 5, 1945, p. 3.

2. "Struthers Burt Writes Views On Proposed Game Park For Pacific Creek Area," *Jackson Hole Courier*, May 2, 1946, p. 1.

3. Robin W. Winks, *Laurance S. Rockefeller, Catalyst for Conservation*, (Washington: Island Press, 1997), p. 61.

4. "Struthers Burt Writes Views On Proposed Game Park For Pacific Creek Area," *Jackson Hole Courier*, May 2, 1946, p. 1.

5. Ernst, pp. 225-226.

6. Winks, p. 43.

7. "The Jackson Hole Wildlife Park," *Appalachia,* Vol. 27, No. 3, June 1949, p. 376.

8. Winks, pp. 61-62.

9. "Palisades Dam on South Fork of Snake River Appears Slated for Early Construction,"

Jackson Hole Courier, January 24, 1946, p. 1.

10. Ibid., p. 5.

11. "Two reservoirs Are Planned For Grand Canyon of Snake River," *Jackson Hole Courier*, March 13, 1947, p. 1.

12. "Reclamation Party Making Snake River Survey," *Jackson Hole Courier*, March 7, 1946, p. 1.

13. Margaret Truman, *Harry S. Truman*, (New York: William Morrow & Company, Inc., 1972), p. 291.

14. Ibid., p. 125.

15. Merle Miller, *Plain Speaking; an oral biography of Harry S. Truman*, (New York: Berkley Publishing Corporation, 1974), p. 209.

16. Ibid., p. 210.

17. Ibid., p. 291.

18. "Senator Robertson Takes Final Kick At Ickes," *Jackson Hole Courier*, February 28, 1946, p. 1.

19. "Paul R. Franke Transfers to Duty In Office Of Director Of National Park Service In Chicago," *Jackson Hole Courier*, April 18, 1946, p. 1.

20. "Heavy Yellowstone Park Travel Finds Increasing Shortage in Hotel and Camp Accommodations," *Jackson Hole Courier*, July 4, 1946, p. 1.

21. "Regular Daily Air Service Inaugurated At New Town Airport North of Jackson Last Friday," *Jackson Hole Courier*, July 11, 1946, p. 1.

22. "Record Crowds At Grand Teton Park," *Jackson Hole Courier*, October 10, 1946, p. 7.

23. "Yellowstone Travel Hits Record In 1946," *Jackson Hole Courier*, October 10, 1946. p. 1.

24. "Yellowstone Park Reports Largest Travel Year in Its Entire History," *Jackson Hole Courier*, September 5, 1946, p. 1.

25. "Unofficial Returns Indicate Strong Republican Trend in Entire State," *Jackson Hole Courier*, November 7, 1946, p. 1.

26. S. 91, 80th Congress, 1st Session, January 8, 1947, *Compendium*, Vol. II, Part 3, Exhibit 46.

27. Freeman Tilden, *The National Parks,* (New York: Alfred A. Knopf, 1970), p. 536. Also see Everhart, p. 253.

28. H.R. 1330, 80th Congress, 1st Session, April 14, 1947, *Compendium*, Vol. II, Part 3,

29. H.R. 3035, 80th Congress, 1st Session, April 14, 1947, *Compendium*, Vol. II, Part 3, Exhibit 50.

30. Statement of Director Drury pursuant to H.R. 1330, 80th Congress, 1st Session, April 17, 1947, *Compendium*, Vol. II, Part 3, Exhibit 49, pp. 15-16.

31. Margaret and Olaus Murie, *Wapiti Wilderness*, (New York: Alfred A. Knopf, 1966). p. 122.

32. Testimony of Fairfield Osborn pursuant to H.R. 1330, 80th Congress, 1st Session, April 14-18, 1947, p. 62.

33. Ibid.

34. Testimony of Fred M. Packard pursuant to H.R. 1330, Ibid., pp. 89-98.

35. Testimony of Newton B. Drury pursuant to H.R. 1330, Ibid., p. 214.

36. Testimony of Felix Buchenroth pursuant to H.R. 1330, Ibid., p. 225.

37. "Jackson Hole Compromise Held Possible," *Jackson Hole Courier*, May 1, 1947, p. 1.

38. Report No. 914, 80th Congress, 1st Session, House Public Lands Committee, July 15, 1947.

39. Ibid., p. 9.

40. Testimony of Felix Buchenroth pursuant to H.R. 1330, 80th Congress, 1st Session, April 14-18, 1947, p. 234.

41. Compendium, Vol. I, p. 25.

42. Memorandum regarding gas and oil leases, August 30, 1947, Federal Register, p. 5859. Also see *Compendium*, Vol. II, Part 3, Exhibit 53.

43. Ibid.

44. "Teton Park Travel Breaks Record for 2nd Straight Year," *Jackson Hole Courier*, October 9, 1947, p. 1.

45. Testimony of Felix Buchenroth pursuant to H.R. 1330, 80th Congress, 1st Session, April 14-18, 1947, pp. 236 & 237.

46. Testimony of Leslie Miller pursuant to H.R. 1330, Ibid., p. 105.

47. Ibid., p. 103.

48. Testimony of Leslie Miller pursuant to H.R. 2241. 78th Congress, 1st Session, June 9, 1943, p. 383.

49. Testimony of Leslie Miller pursuant to H.R.

Exhibit 47.

1330, Ibid., p. 103.

CHAPTER EIGHTEEN

1. "Interior Sec'y Defends Jackson Hole Monument," *Jackson Hole Courier*, December 4, 1947, p. 5.
2. "Prominent Writer Makes Brief For Cooperation," *Jackson Hole Courier*, February 19, 1948, p. 6.
3. "Guest Editorial," *Jackson Hole Courier*, April 1, 1948, p. 4.
4. S. 1951, 80th Congress, 2nd Session, January 7, 1948.
5. "Editorial," *Jackson Hole Courier,* January 15, 1948, p. 1.
6. Ibid.
7. *Compendium*, Vol. II, Part 3, Exhibit 55.
8. *Compendium*, Vol. I, p. 23.
9. "No Precedent Established by Creating the Jackson Hole National Monument States Former Governor," *Jackson Hole Courier*, February 5, 1948, p. 1.
10. "Jackson Hole Chamber of Commerce Takes Action In Support of Barrett Bill To Divide Monument," *Jackson Hole Courier*, February 5, 1948, p. 1.
11. "Mon'm't Controversy Causes Rift in C of C," *Jackson Hole Courier*, March 4, 1948, p. 1.
12. Ibid.
13. "Sportsmen Clubs Take Monument Stand; Bagley Defines Game Commission Attitude," *Jackson Hole Courier*, March 18, 1948, p. 1.
14. "Present Monument Bounds Threaten State Control of Elk Herd, States Bagley," *Jackson Hole Courier*, February 19, 1948, p. 6.
15. Testimony of Olaus Murie pursuant to H.R. 1330, 80th Congress, 1st Session, April 14-18, 1947, p. 187.
16. Testimony of Lester Bagley pursuant to H.R. 2241, 78th Congress, 1st Session, August 17, 1943, p. 69.
17. "Letters," Leslie Miller to Wilford Neilson, *Jackson Hole Courier*, May 20, 1948, p. 5.
18. Ibid.
19. Ibid.
20. Ibid.
21. "Effort of Waltonians To Settle Monument Issue Fail," *Jackson Hole Courier,* May 20, 1948. p. 1.
22. "Teton Park Travel Again Breaks Record," *Jackson Hole Courier*, October 28, 1948, p. 1.
23. "Over A Million Tourists Visit Yellowstone Park," *Jackson Hole Courier*, October 28, 1948, p. 1.
24. Ibid.
25. "Foes Of Jackson Hole National Monument Hail Results Of Primary As A Victory," *Jackson Hole Courier*, August 19, 1948, p. 1.
26. "Record Numbers Vote in Tuesday Election," *Jackson Hole Courier*, November 4, 1948, p. 1.
27. "Dude Ranchers propose New Monument Division," *Jackson Hole Courier*, November 4, 1948, p. 1.
28. "Report Made on Jackson Hole Elk Herd Migration," *Jackson Hole Courier*, March 24, 1949, p. 7.
29. "Bagley Takes Issue With Interior Department Report on Monument," *Jackson Hole Courier,* April 7, 1949, p. 6.
30. Ibid.
31. "Interior Dept. Money Bill leaves House Committee Without J.H. Monument Ban," *Jackson Hole Courier*, March 31, 1949, p. 1.
32. "A New Hope Of Peace For Jackson Hole," *Denver Post*, March 31, 1949. Reprinted in *Jackson Hole Courier*, April 7, 1949, p. 7.
33. *Public Law-CH. 680,* October 12, 1949, p. 801.
34. Memorandum for the Director, by Conrad Wirth, April 21, 1949, *Compendium*, Vol. II, Part 4, Exhibit 56.
35. Ibid., pp. 2-3.
36. Ibid., p. 3.
37. Ibid., p. 5.
38. Ibid., p. 3.
39. Ibid., pp. 3-6.
40. Ibid., p. 6.
41. Ibid., p. 7.
42. Ibid., p. 7.
43. Ibid., pp. 8-10.
44. Ibid., p. 11.
45. "Funds Approved For Two Wyo. Airports," *Jackson Hole Courier*, April 14, 1949, p. 1.
46. "Senator Hunt Asks For Increased Funds For Park and Park Approach Highways," *Jackson*

Hole Courier, June 23, 1949, p. 1.

47. "Dedication of Reconstructed Menor's Ferry To Be Held Saturday Afternoon at Moose," *Jackson Hole Courier*, August 18, 1949, p, 1. Also, "Menor Ferry Dedication Draws nation-Wide Interest," *Jackson Hole Courier*, August 25, 1949, p. 1.

48. "All Time Record Set In Yellowstone Park," *Jackson Hole Courier*, October 13, 1949, p. 1.

49. "Grand Teton National Park Travel Tops Record for 4th Straight Year," *Jackson Hole Courier*, October 13, 1949, p. 1.

50. Ibid.

51. http://legisweb.state.wy.us/statutes/title/titles 41/ c12a05.htm

52. "Colorado Man Named Interior Secretary Following Abrupt Resignation of Krug," *Jackson Hole Courier*, November 17, 1949, p. 1.

53. Ibid.

54. Oral history interview with Oscar L. Chapman by Jerry N. Hess, Washington, DC, September 1, 1972, Truman Presidential Library, www.trumanlibrary.org/oralhistory/chapman.9htm.

55. Ibid.

56. National Park Service Information Release, December 16, 1949, Story-Int. 4482, *Compendium*, Vol. II, Part 4, Exhibit 56A.

57. Ibid.

58. "Tax Assessment Appeal Hearing Date Set For Lands of Jackson Hole Preserve, Inc.," *Jackson Hole Courier*, July 28, 1949, p. 1.

59. Ibid.

60. Ibid.

61. "Four More Join Tax Protest On Jackson Lands," *Jackson Hole Courier*, August 11, 1949, p. 1.

62. "Rockefeller Gift Will Not Affect Tax Case Ruling," *Jackson Hole Courier*, December 29, 1949, p. 8.

63. "State Equalization Board Orders Reassessment Here," *Jackson Hole Courier*, February 23, 1950, p. 1.

64. "Frank A. Barrett To Run For Governor," *Jackson Hole Courier*, December 22, 1949, p. 1.

65. "Summer White House In Tetons, Says O'Mahoney," *Jackson Hole Courier*, December 22, 1949, p. 1.

66. "Izaak Walton League Comments On Monument," *Jackson Hole Courier*, December 22, 1949, p. 1.

CHAPTER NINETEEN

1. Statement by President Truman pursuant to enactment of S. 3409, September 14, 1950, *Compendium*, Vol. II, Part 4, Exhibit 62.

2. S. 3409, 81st Congress, 2nd Session, April 12, 1950.

3. Ibid.

4. Interior Department report on S. 3409, 81st Congress, 2nd Session, June 9, 1950.

5. Ibid.

6. "Jackson Hole Plan May Solve Revenue Problems," Morris Cleavenger, *Denver Post*, July 10, 1950. Reprinted in *Jackson Hole Courier*, July 13, 1950, p. 1.

7. "A Fair Settlement" *Casper Tribune-Herald*, July 16, 1950. Reprinted in *Jackson Hole Courier*, July 27, 1950, p. 7.

8. "Plan To Merge Teton Park, J. H. Monument Would End Damaging Deadlock," *Salt Lake Tribune*, July 18, 1950. Reprinted in *Jackson Hole Courier*, July 27, 1950, p. 7.

9. Joseph O'Mahoney to Lester Bagley, June 25, 1950, *Compendium*, Vol. II, Part 4, Exhibit 59.

10. F.J. Lawton to Joseph O'Mahoney, June 8, 1950, Senate Committee on Interior and Insular Affairs Report No. 1938, 81st Congress, 2nd Session, July 1, 1950.

11. Congressional Record-Senate, 81st Congress, 2nd Session, Vol. 96-Part 8, p. 11045.

12. S. 3409, 81st Congress, 2nd Session, July 27, 1950, *Compendium*, Vol. II, Part 4, Exhibit 60.

13. "Revision To Park Bill Sought By Barrett," *Jackson Hole Courier*, August 10, 1950, p. 1.

14. Ibid.

15. House Public Lands Committee, Report No. 2910, 81st Congress, 2nd Session, August 11, 1950.

16. Congressional Record-Senate, 81st Congress, 2nd Session, Vol. 96-B Part 10, p. 13607.

17. Conference Report No. 3032, House of

Representatives, 81st Congress, 2nd Session, August 31, 1950.

18. "Persistence Wins," *Wyoming Eagle* as reprinted in *Jackson Hole Courier*, September 14, 1950, p. 1.

19. Joseph O'Mahoney to Wilford Neilson, September 1, 1950. Printed in *Jackson Hole Courier*, September 7, 1950, p. 4.

20. Statement by President Truman pursuant to enactment of S. 3409, September 14, 1950, *Compendium*, Vol. II, Part 4, Exhibit 62.

21. "Public Misled About Teton Park Measure," *Jackson Hole Courier*, October 19, 1950, p. 7.

22. Oral history interview with Oscar L. Chapman by Jerry N. Hess, Washington, DC, Truman Presidential Library, September 1, 1972, www.trumanlibrary.org/oralhistory/chapman.9htm.

23. "Factual Reporting Extends Credit To Mr. Barrett, Too," *Wyoming Tribune*. Reprinted in *Jackson Hole Courier*, September 14, 1950, p. 1.

24. "Park Superintendent Transferred To Omaha," *Jackson Hole Courier*, October 5, 1950, p. 1.

25. "Over 1,000,000 Visitors See Yellowstone Park," *Jackson Hole Courier*, October 19, 1950, p. 1.

26. "Grand Teton Park Travel Shows Steady Increase," *Jackson Hole Courier*, October 19, 1950, p. 4.

27. "California Airplane Believed Crashed Atop Mt. Moran," *Jackson Hole Courier*, November 23, 1950, p. 1.

28. "Petzoldt and VandeWater Issue Statement After Reaching, Exploring Plane Wreckage," *Jackson Hole Courier*, November 30, 1950, p. 1.

29. "LAST RITES HELD FOR MORAN CRASH VICTIMS," Jackson Hole Courier, August 9, 1951, p. 1.

30. "Riding the Range," *Jackson Hole Courier*, November 16, 1950, p. 7.

31. Virginia Cole Trenholm and Maurine Carley, *The Shoshonis: Sentinels of the Rockies*, (Norman: University of Oklahoma Press. 1964), p. 222.

Index

Symbols

A

H

K

N

X

Y

Z

CPSIA information can be obtained
at www.ICGtesting.com
Printed in the USA
LVOW02*2034220916

505676LV00001B/1/P